D1213880

ARLAND J. HULTGREN is professor of New
Testament at Luther Seminary, St. Paul,
Minnesota. He is also the author of *The Rise of
Normative Christianity* and *Christ and His Benefits:
Christology and Redemption in the New Testament.*

The Bible in Its World

David Noel Freedman, *General Editor*

Astrid B. Beck, *Associate Editor*

The Bible in Its World series offers an in-depth view of significant aspects of the biblical world. Individual studies apply up-to-date historical, literary, cultural, and theological methods and techniques to enhance understanding of the biblical texts and their context. Among the topics addressed are archaeology, geography, anthropology, history, linguistics, and religion as they apply to the Hebrew Bible/Old Testament, Apocrypha/Deuterocanonicals, and New Testament.

Contributors to The Bible in Its World are among the foremost authorities in their respective fields worldwide and represent a broad range of religious and institutional affiliations. Authors are charged to offer fresh interpretations that are scholarly, responsible, and engaging. Accessible to serious general readers and scholars alike, The Bible in Its World series will interest anyone who seeks a deeper understanding of the Bible and its world.

The Parables of Jesus

A Commentary

Arland J. Hultgren

WILLIAM B. EERDMANS PUBLISHING COMPANY

GRAND RAPIDS, MICHIGAN / CAMBRIDGE, U.K.

© 2000 Wm. B. Eerdmans Publishing Co.

255 Jefferson Ave. S.E., Grand Rapids, Michigan 49503 /

P.O. Box 163, Cambridge CB3 9PU U.K.

Printed in the United States of America

05 04 03 02 01 00   7 6 5 4 3 2 1

Library of Congress Cataloging-in-Publication Data

Hultgren, Arland J.

The parables of Jesus: a commentary / Arland J. Hultgren.

p.   cm.   (The Bible in its world)

Includes bibliographical references and indexes.

ISBN 0-8028-4475-8 (cloth: alk. paper)

1. Jesus Christ — Parables.

2. Bible, N.T. Gospels — Commentaries.

I. Title.   II. Series.

BT375.2.H78 2000

226.8'07 — dc21

00-037140

To
Those Whose Lives Have Been
Parables of the Kingdom

Arnold and Ina Hultgren
Ed and Ruby Strom
Rudolph and Ruth Benander
Carole Hultgren
Peter and Heather Hultgren
Stephen Hultgren
Kris and Kristina Fredrick

Contents

Preface

The parables of Jesus continue to intrigue, instruct, inspire, puzzle, and amuse. They are the basis for sermons in Christian churches around the world. They are the first stories of Jesus that are taught to children.

It is not surprising that many books have been written on the parables. Some of them deal primarily with the parables in the ancient world; others investigate the parables for their literary qualities; others make use of the parables within larger hermeneutical projects; and others provide popular, homiletical treatments.

What seems to be missing within the spectrum is a study of the parables that is comprehensive, drawing upon the wealth of parable research, and that is at the same time exegetical and theological. The purpose of the present work is to fill that void.

The research for this book stretches over several years. I have taught a course on the parables of Jesus to seminary students many times over, and the needs of that course have required careful attention to the parables of Jesus through extensive research, critical reflection, lectures, and conversation. In addition, a sabbatical leave for the academic year 1997-98 allowed time to follow up, expand, and enrich what was at hand, and to do most of the actual writing of the book.

It is my pleasure to extend sincere thanks to various persons. My heartfelt thanks go to Barbara A. Gaiser and Neal J. Anthony for assisting with the bibliographies. David Noel Freedman performed superb editorial work, giving attention to matters of content and composition alike. The book is considerably better in light of his skills, and I gladly acknowledge my gratitude to him. Finally, I am indebted to the persons who make institutional decisions and provide for support in carrying out research, teaching, and learning at Luther Seminary. These include members of the Board of Directors, administration, and faculty, who in one way or another make sabbaticals possible and provide encouragement to carry on one's work, and members of the library staff, who provide ready access to scholarly resources in skillful and pleasant ways.

ARLAND J. HULTGREN
Luther Seminary
St. Paul, Minnesota

General Abbreviations

Ancient Sources

Old Testament Pseudepigrapha

Jos. Asen.	*Joseph and Aseneth*
Jub.	*Jubilees*
Pss. Sol.	*Psalms of Solomon*
T. Ben.	*Testament of Benjamin*
T. Gad	*Testament of Gad*
T. Iss.	*Testament of Issachar*
T. Jac.	*Testament of Jacob*
T. Jos.	*Testament of Joseph*
T. Judah	*Testament of Judah*
T. Zeb.	*Testament of Zebulun*

Philo

Abr.	*De Abrahamo*
Leg. All.	*Legum Allegoriae*
Op.	*De Opificio Mundi*
Vit. Mos.	*De Vita Mosis*

Josephus

Ant.	*Jewish Antiquities*
J.W.	*The Jewish War*

Dead Sea Scrolls

1QM	*War Scroll*
1QpHab	*Pesher on Habakkuk*
1QS	*Manual of Discipline*
1QSa	*Rule of the Congregation*

Rabbinic Works

Abod. Zar.	*Abodah Zarah*
Abot.	*Pirke Aboth*
Abot R. Nat.	*'Aboth de Rabbi Nathan*
b.	*Babylonian Talmud*
B. Bat.	*Baba Batra*
B. Mes.	*Baba Mesia*
B. Qam.	*Baba Qamma*
Bek.	*Bekorot*
Ber.	*Berakhot*
Cant. Rab.	*Canticles Rabbah*
Der. Er. Rab.	*Derekh Eres Rabbah*
Eccl. Rab.	*Ecclesiastes Rabbah*
Erub.	*Erubin*
Esth. Rab.	*Esther Rabbah*
Exod. Rab.	*Exodus Rabbah*
Gen. Rab.	*Genesis Rabbah*
Git.	*Gittin*
Hor.	*Horayot*
Ketub.	*Ketubot*
Kil.	*Kilayim*
Lam. Rab.	*Lamentations Rabbah*
Lev. Rab.	*Leviticus Rabbah*
m.	*The Mishnah*
Meg.	*Megillah*
Mek.	*Mekhilta*
Midr.	*Midrash*
Midr. Cant.	*Midrash Canticles*
Midr. Tann.	*Midrash Tannaim*
Ned.	*Nedarim*
Nid.	*Niddah*
Pesiq. Rab Kah.	*Pesiqta de-Rab Kahana*
Pesah.	*Pesahim*
Qidd.	*Qiddushin*
Sanh.	*Sanhedrin*

Shab.	*Shabbath*
Sot.	*Sotah*
Sukk.	*Sukkah*
Taan.	*Taanit*
y.	*The Jerusalem Talmud*
Yebam.	*Yebamot*

Early Christian Literature

2 Bar.	*2 Baruch*
3 Bar.	*3 Baruch*
1 Clem.	*1 Clement*
Const. Ap.	*Apostolic Constitutions*
Eusebius, *Hist. eccl.*	Eusebius, *Ecclesiastical History*
Herm. Man.	*Hermas, Mandates*
Hippolytus, *Ref.*	*Refutationis Omnium Haeresium*
Ignatius, *Pol.*	*Epistle to Polycarp*
Ignatius, *Smyrn.*	*Epistle to the Smyrnaeans*
Ignatius, *Trall.*	*Epistle to the Trallians*
Jub.	*Jubilees*
Pol. *Phil.*	Polycarp, *Letter to the Philippians*
Ps. Clem. H.	*Pseudo-Clementine Homilies*

Nag Hammadi Tractates

Apoc. Jas.	*Apocryphon of James*
Gos. Thom.	*The Gospel of Thomas*
Gos. Truth	*The Gospel of Truth*

Other Greco-Roman Works

Appian, *Bell. Civ.*	Appian, *Bella Civilia*
Epictetus, *Dis.*	Epictetus, *Discourses*
Herodotus, *Hist.*	Herodotus, *History*
POxy	*Oxyrhynchus Papyri*

Journals, Reference Works, and Serials

AB	Anchor Bible
ABD	*The Anchor Bible Dictionary,* ed. David N. Freedman, 6 vols., ABRL (New York: Doubleday, 1992)
ABRL	Anchor Bible Reference Library

ABW	*Archaeology in the Biblical World*
ACJD	Abhandlungen zum christlich-jüdischen Dialog
ACNT	Augsburg Commentary on the New Testament
ACS	*African Christian Studies*
ACW	Ancient Christian Writers
AGSJU	Arbeiten zur Geschichte des späteren Judentums und des Urchristentums
AJBI	*Annual of the Japanese Biblical Institute*
AJP	*American Journal of Philology*
AJT	*American Journal of Theology*
AnBib	Analecta biblica
ANET	*Ancient Near Eastern Texts Relating to the Old Testament*, ed. James B. Pritchard, 2d ed. (Princeton: Princeton University Press, 1955)
ANF	*Ante-Nicene Fathers*, ed. Alexander Roberts and James Donaldson, 10 vols. (Buffalo: The Christian Literature Company, 1885-97; reprinted, Peabody, Mass.: Hendrickson Publishers, 1994)
ANTC	Abingdon New Testament Commentaries
APAW	Abhandlungen der kaiserlichen preussichen Akademie der Wissenschaften
ASeign	*Assemblées du Seigneur*
ASTI	*Annual of the Swedish Theological Institute*
ATANT	Abhhandlungen zur Theologie des Alten und Neuen Testaments
ATLABS	American Theological Library Association Bibliography Series
ATR	*Anglican Theological Review*
ATRSS	Anglican Theological Review Supplementary Series
AusBR	*Australian Biblical Review*
AUSS	*Andrews University Seminary Studies*
BA	*Biblical Archaeologist*
BabT	*The Babylonian Talmud*, ed. Isidore Epstein, 18 vols. (London: Soncino Press, 1961)
BAGD	Walter Bauer, W. F. Arndt, and F. W. Gingrich, *A Greek-English Lexicon of the New Testament and Other Early Christian Literature*, 2d ed., rev. F. W. Gingrich and F. W. Danker (Chicago: University of Chicago Press, 1979)
BBB	Bonner biblische Beiträge
BBib	*Bulletin of Bibliography*
BBR	*Bulletin of Biblical Research*
BDB	Francis Brown, S. R. Driver, and Charles A. Briggs, *A Hebrew and English Lexicon of the Old Testament* (Oxford: Clarendon Press, 1907)

BDF	Friedrich Blass, Albert Debrunner, and Robert W. Funk. *A Greek Grammar of the New Testament and Other Early Christian Literature* (Chicago: University of Chicago Press, 1961)
BETL	Bibliotheca Ephemeridum Theologicarum Lovaniensium
BEvT	Beiträge zur evangelischen Theologie
BGBE	Beiträge zur Geschichte der biblischen Exegese
BHH	*Biblisch-Historisches Handwörterbuch,* ed. Bo Reicke and Leonhard Rost, 4 vols. (Göttingen: Vandenhoeck & Ruprecht, 1962-79)
Bib	*Biblica*
BiH	Biblische Handbibliothek
BibInt	*Biblical Interpretation*
BibLeb	*Bibel und Leben*
BiblSac	*Bibliotheca Sacra*
BibNot	*Biblische Notizen*
BiKi	*Bibel und Kirche*
BiLi	*Bibel und Liturgie*
BiRe	*Bible Review*
BiTod	*The Bible Today*
BJRL	*Bulletin of the John Rylands Library*
BJS	Brown Judaic Studies
BNTC	Black's New Testament Commentaries
BR	*Biblical Research*
BT	*The Bible Translator*
BTB	*Biblical Theology Bulletin*
BTZ	*Berliner theologische Zeitschrift*
BZ	*Biblische Zeitscrift*
BZNW	Beihefte zur Zeitschrift für die neutestamentliche Wissenschaft
CBFV	*Cahiers bibliques de Foi et vie*
CBFVSup	Cahiers bibliques de Foi et vie Supplements
CBG	*Collationes Brugenses et Gandavenses*
CBQ	*Catholic Biblical Quarterly*
CBQMS	Catholic Biblical Quarterly Monograph Series
CChr.SL	Corpus Christianorum Series Latina
CJ	*Concordia Journal*
CJRT	*Canadian Journal of Religious Thought*
CleM	*Clergy Monthly*
ClW	*Classical Weekly*
ConBNT	Coniectanea Biblica, New Testament
ConJ	*Concordia Journal*
CSR	*Christian Scholar's Review*
CThM	Calwer theologische Monographien

CTM	Concordia Theological Monthly
CTR	Criswell Theological Review
CurTM	Currents in Theology and Mission
CV	Communio viatorum
DDSR	Duke Divinity School Review
DSD	Dead Sea Discoveries
EAPR	East Asian Pastoral Review
EDNT	Exegetical Dictionary of the New Testament, ed. Horst Balz and Gerhard Schneider, 3 vols. (Grand Rapids: Wm. B. Eerdmans, 1990-93)
EeV	Esprit et vie
EKKNT	Evangelisch-katholischer Kommentar zum Neuen Testament
EncJud	Encyclopedia Judaica, ed. Cecil Roth, 16 vols. (New York: Macmillan, 1971-72)
EstBib	Estudios bíblicos
EThS	Erfurter theologische Schriften
ETL	Ephemerides Theologicae Lovanienses
ETR	Études théologiques et religieuses
EvErz	Der evangelische Erzieher
EvQ	Evangelical Quarterly
EvT	Evangelische Theologie
ExpTim	Expository Times
FaM	Faith and Mission
FBBS	Facet Books, Biblical Series
FFF	Foundations and Facets Forum
FRLANT	Forschungen zur Religion und Literatur des Alten und Neuen Testaments
FV	Foi et Vie
GTJ	Grace Theological Journal
HBT	Horizons in Biblical Theology
HeTr	Helps for Translators
HeyJ	Heythrop Journal
HibJ	Hibbert Journal
HMPEC	Historical Magazine of the Protestant Episcopal Church
HNT	Handbuch zum Neuen Testament
HNTC	Harper's New Testament Commentary
HR	History of Religions
HSCP	Harvard Studies in Classical Philology
HTR	Harvard Theological Review
HTKNT	Herders theologischer Kommentar zum Neuen Testament
HUCA	Hebrew Union College Annual
HUTh	Hermeneutische Untersuchungen zur Theologie

IBC	Interpretation: A Bible Commentary for Teaching and Preaching
IBS	*Irish Biblical Studies*
ICC	International Critical Commentary
IDB	*The Interpreter's Dictionary of the Bible*, ed. George A. Buttrick, 4 vols. (Nashville: Abingdon Press, 1962)
IDBSup	*The Interpreter's Dictionary of the Bible: Supplementary Volume*, ed. Keith Crim (Nashville: Abingdon Press, 1976)
IJT	*Indian Journal of Theology*
IKaZ	*Internationale katholische Zeitschrift/Communio*
Imm	*Immanuel*
Int	*Interpretation*
IRM	*International Review of Missions*
IRT	Issues in Religion and Theology
ISBE	*International Standard Bible Encyclopedia*, ed. Geoffrey W. Bromiley, 4 vols. (Grand Rapids: Wm. B. Eerdmans, 1979-88).
ITQ	*Irish Theological Quarterly*
ITS	*Indian Theological Studies*
JAAR	*Journal of the American Academy of Religion*
JAC	*Jahrbuch für Antike und Christentum*
JBR	*Journal of Bible and Religion*
JC	Judaica et Christiana
JSOTSup	Journal for the Study of the Old Testament Supplement Series
JB	Jerusalem Bible
JBL	*Journal of Biblical Literature*
JES	*Journal of Ecumenical Studies*
JETS	*Journal of the Evangelical Theological Society*
JHC	*Journal of Higher Criticism*
JJS	*Journal of Jewish Studies*
JR	*Journal of Religion*
JSJ	*Journal for the Study of Judaism*
JSNT	*Journal for the Study of the New Testament*
JSNTSup	Journal for the Study of the New Testament — Supplement Series
JSOTSup	Journal for the Study of the Old Testament — Supplement Series
JSP	*Journal for the Study of Pseudepigrapha*
JST	*Journal for the Study of Judaism*
JTS	*Journal of Theological Studies*
JTSA	*Journal of Theology for Southern Africa*
KJV	King James Version
KuD	*Kerygma und Dogma*

LCC	Library of Christian Classics
LCL	Loeb Classical Library
LeDiv	Lectio divina
LingBibl	*Linguistica biblica*
LQ	*Lutheran Quarterly*
LQHR	*London Quarterly and Holborn Review*
LS	*Louvain Studies*
LSJ	Henry G. Liddell and Robert Scott, *A Greek-English Lexicon*, rev. by Henry S. Jones (Oxford: Clarendon Press, 1968)
LTJ	*Lutheran Theological Journal*
LTP	*Laval théologique et philosophique*
LUÅ	Lunds Universitets Årsskrift
LV	*Lumen vitae*
LXX	The Septuagint
MeyerK	Meyer, Kritische-evangelischer Kommentar über das Neue Testament
MGT	Marburger theologische Studien
MidR	*Midrash Rabbah*, trans. H. Freedman and Maurice Simon, 10 vols. (London: Soncino Press, 1939)
MM	James H. Moulton and George Milligan, *The Vocabulary of the Greek Testament* (Grand Rapids: Wm. B. Eerdmans, 1930)
MT	Masoretic Text
MTZ	*Münchener theologische Zeitschrift*
NAB	New American Bible
NAC	The New American Commentary
NBl	*New Blackfriars*
NCB	New Century Bible
NEB	New English Bible
Neot	*Neotestamentica*
NHLE	*The Nag Hammadi Library in English*, ed. James M. Robinson, 3d ed. (San Francisco: Harper & Row, 1988)
NHMS	Nag Hammadi and Manichaean Studies
NHS	Nag Hammadi Studies
NIB	*The New Interpreter's Bible*, ed. Leander E. Keck et al., 12 vols. (Nashville: Abingdon Press, 1994–)
NIBC	New International Biblical Commentary
NIV	New International Version
NKZ	*Neue kirchliche Zeitschrift*
NovT	*Novum Testamentum*
NovTSup	Novum Testamentum, Supplements
NPNF	*A Select Library of the Nicene and Post-Nicene Fathers*, ed. Philip Schaff, 14 vols. (New York: Christian Literature Company, 1888-90)

NRSV	New Revised Standard Version
NRT	*Nouvelle revue théologique*
NT	New Testament
NTAbh	Neutestamentliche Abhandlungen
NTF	Neutestamentliche Forschung
NTMes	New Testament Message
NTOA	Novum Testamentum et Orbis Antiquus
NTS	*New Testament Studies*
NTT	*Norsk teologisk tidsskrift*
NTTS	New Testament Tools and Studies
OBO	Orbis Biblicus et Orientalis
OCD	*Oxford Classical Dictionary*, 3d ed., ed. Simon Hornblower and Anthony Spawforth (New York: Oxford University Press, 1996).
OCP	*Orientalia Christiana Periodica*
OEANE	*Oxford Encyclopedia of Archaeology in the Near East*, ed. Eric M. Meyers, 5 vols. (New York: Oxford University Press, 1997)
OT	Old Testament
OTL	Old Testament Library
OTP	*The Old Testament Pseudepigrapha*, ed. James H. Charlesworth, 2 vols. (Garden City: Doubleday and Company, 1983-85)
PG	*Patrologia graeca*, ed. Jacques-Paul Migne, 161 vols. (Turnhout, Belgium: Brepols [and other imprints], 1857-66)
PGL	G. W. H. Lampe, *A Patristic Greek Lexicon* (Oxford: Clarendon Press, 1961)
PJ	*Palästinajahrbuch*
ProtoBib	*Protokolle zur Bibel*
PRS	*Perspectives in Religious Studies*
PSB	*Princeton Seminary Bulletin*
PTMS	Pittsburgh Theological Monograph Series
QR	*Quarterly Review*
RAC	*Reallexikon für Antike und Christentum*, ed. Theodor Klausner et al. (Stuttgart: Anton Hiersemann, 1950–)
RB	*Revue biblique*
RCT	*Revista de cultura teologica*
REA	*Revue des Études Augustiniennes*
RefRev	*Reformed Review*
RelArts	*Religion and the Arts*
RelLife	*Religion in Life*
ReMo	Recherches morales
ResQ	*Restoration Quarterly*
RevExp	*Review and Expositor*

RevQ	*Revue de Qumran*
RHPR	*Revue d'histoire et de philosophie religieuses*
RIDA	*Revue internationale des droits de l'antiquité*
RivB	*Rivista biblica*
RSR	*Recherches de science religieuse*
RSV	Revised Standard Version
RThom	*Revue thomiste*
RTL	*Revue théologique de Louvain*
RTP	*Revue de théologie et de philosophie*
SANT	Studien zum Alten und Neuen Testament
SBEC	Studies in the Bible and Early Christianity
SBF	*Studium biblicum Franciscanum*
SBLDS	Society of Biblical Literature Dissertation Series
SBLMS	Society of Biblical Literature Monograph Series
SBLSBS	Society of Biblical Literature Sources for Biblical Study
SBLSP	Society of Biblical Literature Seminar Papers
SBLSS	Society of Biblical Literature Symposium Series
SBS	Stuttgarter Bibelstudien
SBT	Studies in Biblical Theology
SBU	Svenskt bibliskt uppslagsverk
SC	*The Second Century*
ScEc	*Sciences ecclésiastiques*
SCM	Studies in Christian Mission
SE	*Studia Evangelica*
SEÅ	*Svensk Exegetisk Årsbok*
SémBib	*Sémiotique et bible*
SemSup	Semeia Supplements
SFEG	Schriften der Finnischen Exegetischen Gesellschaft
SHR	Studies in the History of Religion
SIG	*Sylloge Inscriptionum Graecarum*, ed. Wilhelm Dittenberger, 3rd ed., 4 vols. (Leipzig: S. Hirzelium, 1915-24).
SJT	*Scottish Journal of Theology*
SNTSMS	Society for New Testament Studies Monograph Series
SO	*Symbolae Osloenses*
SPB	Studia Post-Biblica
SPS	Sacra Pagina Series
SSRH	Sociological Studies in Roman History
ST	*Studia Theologica*
STK	*Svensk teologisk kvartalskrift*
StPat	*Studia Patristica*
Str-B	Hermann L. Strack and Paul Billerbeck, *Kommentar zum Neuen Testament aus Talmud und Midrasch,* 6 vols. (Munich: C. H. Beck'sche, 1922-61)

SUNT	Studien zur Umwelt des Neuen Testaments
SVTQ	*St. Vladimir's Theological Quarterly*
TalB	*The Talmud of Babylonia: An American Translation*, trans. Jacob Neusner et al. Atlanta: Scholars Press, 1984–.
TBei	*Theologische Beiträge*
TBT	Theologische Bibliothek Töpelmann
TD	*Theology Digest*
TDNT	*Theological Dictionary of the New Testament*, ed. Gerhard Kittel and Gerhard Friedrich, 10 vols. (Grand Rapids: Wm. B. Eerdmans, 1964-76)
TDOT	*Theological Dictionary of the Old Testament*, ed. G. Johannes Botterweck, Helmer Ringgren, et al., 10 vols. to date (Grand Rapids: Wm. B. Eerdmans, 1974–)
TEV	Today's English Version
TFTS	Theologische Faculteit Tilburg Studies
TGl	*Theologie und Glaube*
ThEd	*Theological Educator*
THNT	Theologischer Handkommentar zum Neuen Testament
ThR	*Theologische Rundschau*
ThRev	*Theological Review*
ThViat	*Theologia viatorum*
TJ	*Trinity Journal*
TJT	*Toronto Journal of Theology*
TLG	*Thesaurus Linguae Graecae*
TLZ	*Theologische Literaturzeitung*
TQ	*Theologische Quartalschrift*
TS	*Theological Studies*
TST	Toronto Studies in Theology
TTod	*Theology Today*
TU	Texte und Untersuchungen
TWAT	*Theologische Wörterbuch zum Alten Testament*, ed. G. Johannes Botterweck and Helmer Ringgren et al., 10 vols. projected (Stuttgart: Verlag W. Kohlhammer, 1973–).
TynB	*Tyndale Bulletin*
TZ	*Theologische Zeitschrift*
UBS	United Bible Societies
UCB	Die urchristliche Botschaft
USQR	*Union Seminary Quarterly Review*
VC	*Vigiliae Christianae*
VCh	*Vie chrétienne*
VR	*Vox reformata*
VS	*Vie spirituelle*
WBC	Word Biblical Commentary

WTJ	*Westminster Theological Journal*
WuD	*Wort und Dienst*
WUNT	Wissenschaftliche Untersuchungen zum Neuen Testament
WW	*Word & World*
ZDPV	*Zeitschrift des deutschen Palästina-Vereins*
ZNW	*Zeitschrift für die neutestamentliche Wissenschaft*
ZST	*Zeitschrift für systematische Theologie*
ZTK	*Zeitschrift für Theologie und Kirche*

Abbreviations for Frequently Cited Commentaries and Studies

W. Allen, *Matthew*   Willoughby C. Allen, *A Critical and Exegetical Commentary on the Gospel according to S. Matthew,* 3d ed., ICC (Edinburgh: T. & T. Clark, 1912)

K. Bailey, *Peasant Eyes*   Kenneth E. Bailey, *Through Peasant Eyes: More Lucan Parables, Their Culture and Style* (Grand Rapids: Wm. B. Eerdmans, 1980)

K. Bailey, *Poet*   Kenneth E. Bailey, *Poet and Peasant: A Literary-Cultural Approach to the Parables in Luke* (Grand Rapids: Wm. B. Eerdmans, 1976)

F. Beare, *Matthew*   Francis W. Beare, *The Gospel according to Matthew* (San Francisco: Harper & Row, 1981)

M. E. Boring, *NIB* (*Matthew*)   M. Eugene Boring, *Matthew* in *The New Interpreters Bible,* ed. Leander E. Keck, 12 vols. (Nashville: Abingdon Press, 1994-), 8:87-505.

M. Boucher, *Parables*   Madeleine I. Boucher, *The Parables,* NTMes (Wilmington: Michael Glazier, 1981)

R. Brown, *Introduction NT*   Raymond E. Brown, *An Introduction to the New Testament,* ABRL (New York: Doubleday, 1997)

R. Bultmann, *HST*   Rudolf Bultmann, *History of the Synoptic Tradition,* rev. ed. (New York: Harper & Row, 1968)

A. Cadoux, *Parables*   A. T. Cadoux, *The Parables of Jesus: Their Art and Use* (New York: Macmillan, 1931)

C. Carlston, *Parables*   Charles E. Carlston, *The Parables of the Triple Tradition* (Philadelphia: Fortress Press, 1975)

J. Creed, *Luke*	John M. Creed, *The Gospel according to St. Luke* (London: Macmillan, 1930)
J. Crossan, *Parables*	John Dominic Crossan, *In Parables: The Challenge of the Historical Jesus,* 2d ed. (Sonoma: Polebridge Press, 1992)
R. A. Culpepper, *NIB (Luke)*	R. Alan Culpepper, *Luke* in *The New Interpreter's Bible,* ed. Leander E. Keck, 12 vols. (Nashville: Abingdon Press, 1994–), 9:1-490.
W. D. Davies and D. C. Allison, *Matthew*	W. D. Davies and Dale C. Allison, *A Critical and Exegetical Commentary on the Gospel according to Saint Matthew,* ICC, 3 vols. (Edinburgh: T. & T. Clark, 1988-97)
C. H. Dodd, *Parables*	C. H. Dodd, *The Parables of the Kingdom,* rev. ed. (New York: Charles Scribner's Sons, 1961)
J. Donahue, *Parable*	John R. Donahue, *The Gospel in Parable: Metaphor, Narrative, and Theology in the Synoptic Gospels* (Philadelphia: Fortress Press, 1988)
B. Easton, *Luke*	Burton S. Easton, *The Gospel according to St. Luke* (New York: Charles Scribner's Sons, 1926)
J. Fitzmyer, *Luke*	Joseph A. Fitzmyer, *The Gospel according to Luke,* AB 28-28A, 2 vols. (Garden City, N.Y.: Doubleday and Company, 1981-85)
R. Funk, *Five Gospels*	Robert W. Funk et al., *The Five Gospels: The Search for the Authentic Words of Jesus* (New York: Macmillan, 1993)
J. Gnilka, *Markus*	Joachim Gnilka, *Das Evangelium nach Markus,* EKKNT 2, 2 vols. (Zurich: Benziger Verlag, 1978-79)
J. Gnilka, *Matthäus*	Joachim Gnilka, *Das Matthäusevangelium,* 3d ed., HTKNT 1, 2 vols. (Freiburg: Herder, 1993)
R. Gundry, *Mark*	Robert H. Gundry, *Mark: A Commentary on His Apology for the Cross* (Grand Rapids: Wm. B. Eerdmans, 1993)
R. Gundry, *Matthew*	Robert H. Gundry, *Matthew: A Commentary on His Handbook for a Mixed Church under Persecution,* 2d ed. (Grand Rapids: Wm. B. Eerdmans, 1994)
D. Hagner, *Matthew*	Donald A. Hagner, *Matthew,* WBC, 2 vols. (Dallas: Word Books, 1993-95)
D. Hare, *Matthew*	Douglas R. A. Hare, *Matthew,* IBC (Louisville: John Knox Press, 1993)
H. Hendrickx, *Parables*	Herman Hendrickx, *The Parables of Jesus* (San Francisco: Harper & Row, 1986)

W. Herzog, *Parables*	William R. Herzog, *Parables as Subversive Speech: Jesus as Pedagogue of the Oppressed* (Louisville: Westminster/John Knox Press, 1994)
A. Hunter, *Parables*	Archibald M. Hunter, *Interpreting the Parables* (Philadelphia: Westminster Press, 1960)
J. Jeremias, *Parables*	Joachim Jeremias, *The Parables of Jesus*, 2d rev. ed. (Upper Saddle River, N.J.: Prentice Hall, 1972)
L. Johnson, *Luke*	Luke Timothy Johnson, *The Gospel of Luke*, SPS 3 (Collegeville, Minn.: Liturgical Press, 1991)
A. Jülicher, *Gleichnisreden*	Adolf Jülicher, *Die Gleichnisreden Jesu*, 2d ed., 2 vols. (Tübingen: J. C. B. Mohr [Paul Siebeck], 1899)
J. Kingsbury, *Matthew 13*	Jack D. Kingsbury, *The Parables of Jesus in Matthew 13: A Study in Redaction-Criticism* (Richmond: John Knox Press, 1969)
S. Lachs, *Rabbinic Commentary*	Samuel T. Lachs, *A Rabbinic Commentary on the New Testament: The Gospels of Matthew, Mark, and Luke* (Hoboken: Ktav Publishing House, 1987)
J. Lambrecht, *Astonished*	Jan Lambrecht, *Once More Astonished: The Parables of Jesus* (New York: Crossroad, 1981)
J. Lambrecht, *Treasure*	Jan Lambrecht, *Out of the Treasure: The Parables in the Gospel of Matthew* (Grand Rapids: Wm. B. Eerdmans, 1992)
E. Linnemann, *Parables*	Eta Linnemann, *Parables of Jesus: Introduction and Exposition* (London: SPCK, 1966)
U. Luz, *Matthäus*	Ulrich Luz, *Das Evangelium nach Matthäus*, EKKNT 1, 4 vols. (Zurich: Benziger Verlag, 1985–)
T. W. Manson, *Sayings*	T. W. Manson, *The Sayings of Jesus* (London: SCM Press, 1949)
I. Marshall, *Luke*	I. Howard Marshall, *The Gospel of Luke*, NIGTC (Grand Rapids: Wm. B. Eerdmans, 1978)
A. McNeile, *Matthew*	Alan H. McNeile, *The Gospel according to St. Matthew* (London: Macmillan, 1915)
J. Meier, *Matthew*	John P. Meier, *Matthew*, NTMes (Wilmington: Michael Glazier, 1980)
J. Meier, *Vision*	John P. Meier, *The Vision of Matthew: Christ, Church and Morality in the First Gospel* (New York: Paulist Press, 1979)
B. Metzger, *TCGNT*	Bruce M. Metzger, *A Textual Commentary on the Greek New Testament* (New York: United Bible Societies, 1971)

C. Montefiore, *Synoptic Gospels*	Claude G. Montefiore, *The Synoptic Gospels*, 2 vols. (London: Macmillan, 1909)
G. F. Moore, *Judaism*	George Foot Moore, *Judaism in the First Centuries of the Christian Era: The Age of the Tannaim*, 3 vols. (Cambridge: Harvard University Press, 1927-30)
W. O. E. Oesterley, *Parables*	W. O. E. Oesterley, *The Gospel Parables in Light of Their Jewish Background* (London: SPCK 1936)
P. Perkins, *NIB (Mark)*	Pheme Perkins, *Mark* in *The New Interpreter's Bible*, ed. Leander E. Keck, 12 vols. (Nashville: Abingdon Press, 1994–), 8:507-733.
P. Perkins, *Parables*	Pheme Perkins, *Hearing the Parables of Jesus* (New York: Paulist Press, 1981)
N. Perrin, *Teaching*	Norman Perrin, *Rediscovering the Teaching of Jesus* (New York: Harper & Row, 1967)
R. Pesch, *Markus*	Rudolf Pesch, *Das Markusevangelium*, 2d ed., HTKNT 2, 2 vols. (Freiburg: Herder, 1977)
A. Plummer, *Luke*	Alfred Plummer, *A Critical and Exegetical Commentary on the Gospel according to S. Luke*, 5th ed., ICC (Edinburgh: T. & T. Clark, 1922)
A. Plummer, *Matthew*	Alfred Plummer, *An Exegetical Commentary on the Gospel according to St. Matthew* (New York: Charles Scribner's Sons, 1909)
A. Polag, *Fragmenta Q*	Athanasius Polag, *Fragmenta Q: Textheft zur Logienquelle* (Neukirchen: Neukirchener Verlag, 1979)
E. Schweizer, *Luke*	Eduard Schweizer, *The Good News according to Luke* (Atlanta: John Knox Press, 1984)
E. Schweizer, *Mark*	Eduard Schweizer, *The Good News according to Mark* (Richmond: John Knox Press, 1970)
E. Schweizer, *Matthew*	Eduard Schweizer, *The Good News according to Matthew* (Atlanta: John Knox Press, 1975)
B. Scott, *Parable*	Bernard B. Scott, *Hear Then the Parable: A Commentary on the Parables of Jesus* (Minneapolis: Fortress Press, 1989)
D. Senior, *Matthew*	Donald Senior, *Matthew*, ANTC (Nashville: Abingdon Press, 1998)
B. Smith, *Parables*	B. T. D. Smith, *The Parables of the Synoptic Gospels: A Critical Study* (Cambridge: Cambridge University Press, 1937)
R. Smith, *Matthew*	Robert H. Smith, *Matthew*, ACNT (Minneapolis: Augsburg Publishing House, 1989)

R. Stein, *Parables*	Robert H. Stein, *An Introduction to the Parables of Jesus* (Philadelphia: Westminster Press, 1981)
V. Taylor, *Mark*	Vincent Taylor, *The Gospel according to St. Mark* (New York: St. Martin's Press, 1952)
D. Tiede, *Luke*	David L. Tiede, *Luke*, ACNT (Minneapolis: Augsburg Publishing House, 1988)
D. Via, *Parables*	Dan O. Via, *The Parables: Their Literary and Existential Dimensions* (Philadelphia: Fortress Press, 1967)
H. Weder, *Gleichnisse*	Hans Weder, *Die Gleichnisse Jesu als Metaphern: Traditions- und redaktionsgeschichtliche Analysen und Interpretationen*, FRLANT 120 (Göttingen: Vandenhoeck & Ruprecht, 1978)
A. Weiser, *Knechtsgleichnisse*	Alfons Weiser, *Die Knechtsgleichnisse der synoptischen Evangelien*, SANT 29 (Munich: Kösel-Verlag, 1971)
D. Wenham, *Parables*	David Wenham, *The Parables of Jesus* (Downers Grove, Ill.: InterVarsity Press, 1989)

CHAPTER 1

The Parables of Jesus: An Introduction

Two things are generally known about Jesus of Nazareth that are beyond historical doubt, and they are known around the world by Christians and non-Christians alike. The one is that Jesus was crucified in the first century of the Common Era. The other is that he taught in parables. Other items are associated with him (his resurrection, his miracles, the Sermon on the Mount as an oration on a single occasion, and that the Christian church proceeds from his ministry in some way), but they are matters of dispute or affirmations of faith. But there can be no doubt that Jesus was crucified and that he spoke parables.

For Christian theology and experience, these two items of historical certainty are central. From the standpoint of faith, Jesus as the Christ is the Revealer of God and the Redeemer of humanity. His parables are the primary medium of revelation, and the cross is the primary means of redemption.

There may well be a connection between the parables of Jesus and his crucifixion. By means of his parables Jesus frequently referred to the kingdom of God and at times focused on it explicitly. Speaking in the historic Aramaic language of the Jewish people about a divinely established kingdom and thereby raising up and celebrating an ancient symbol associated with Jewish sovereignty in their own land, Jesus could well have been understood by officials of Roman-dominated Palestine as a would-be messianic pretender. From that understanding — or misunderstanding, as the case may be — it is not surprising at all that Roman officials would have moved to have him crucified.

Whatever the connections may be between the parables of Jesus and other aspects of his ministry and death, the parables are commonly considered the primary means of Jesus' teaching, and that is an accurate judgment, according to the sources available. But what is a parable? How many are there? What are they like? How might one interpret them? It is the purpose of this chapter to take up these and other issues, and to make some initial remarks about parables in general.

1

A. IDENTIFYING AND CLASSIFYING
THE PARABLES OF JESUS

The English word "parable" is a loanword from the Greek word *parabolē* (παραβολή in Greek lettering), and like its Greek antecedent its basic and primary meaning is a "comparison."[1] By means of parables Jesus — and others before and after him — carried on instruction by making comparisons between eternal, transcendental realities and that which was familiar to the common human experience of his day.

The parables of Jesus appear in the Synoptic Gospels (Matthew, Mark, and Luke) alone among the canonical Gospels; none appears in the Gospel of John.[2] Outside the canonical Gospels there are fourteen parables in the apocryphal *Gospel of Thomas,* of which ten are versions of parables known to us from the Synoptic Gospels. The other four are distinctive to that document. (For more information, see Chapter 10, "Parables in the *Gospel of Thomas.*")

To speak of the parables of Jesus as a discrete body of material for study is not as easy as it may sound. One of the major problems is that persons will disagree concerning what among the sayings of Jesus fits under the form-critical category of "parable" and what does not. In this regard the evangelists themselves are not much help. At times, to be sure, they write of speech material of Jesus as "parables," and the designation seems to fit. But they also call some materials "parables" that virtually no one would classify as such today.[3] And usually parables appear without being introduced as "parables" by editorial remarks by the evangelists.

Interpreters have provided various definitions of parables,[4] and they have accordingly differed on the answer to the question regarding how many parables there are in the Gospels, and on whether a unit is to be classified as a parable or not. Some estimates run as high as sixty or more,[5] although most books

---

1. *The Oxford English Dictionary,* 2d ed., ed. J. A. Simpson and E. S. C. Weiner, 20 vols. (Oxford: Clarendon Press, 1989), 11:177.

2. The English word "parable" appears at John 10:6 in the KJV. The Greek term there is παροιμία, which is translated "figure" in the RSV and "figure of speech" in the NRSV.

3. Günter Haufe, "παραβολή," *EDNT* 3:15: "In the Synoptics, παραβολή is used to identify *proverbs* (Luke 4:23; 6:39), *maxims* (Mark 7:17; Matt 15:15), *metaphorical sayings* (Mark 3:23; Luke 5:36), *enigmatic sayings* (Mark 4:11; Matt 13:10; Luke 8:10), *general rules* (Luke 14:7), *parables* (depicting a common occurrence: Mark 4:13, 30; 13:28; Matt 13:18, 31, 33, 36; 24:32; Luke 8:4, 9, 11; 12:41; 13:6; 15:3; 21:29), *parabolic stories* (depicting remarkable singular occurrences: Mark 12:12; Matt 13:24; 21:33; Luke 18:1; 19:11; 20:9, 19), and *paradigmatic illustrative stories* (Luke 12:16; 18:9).

4. Various definitions are provided by C. H. Dodd, *Parables,* 5; A. M. Hunter, *Parables,* 8; T. W. Manson, *The Teaching of Jesus: Studies of Its Form and Content,* 2d ed. (Cambridge: Cambridge University Press, 1935), 65; R. Stein, *Parables,* 22; B. Scott, *Parable,* 8.

5. A. Hunter, *Parables,* 11 ("about 60"); T. W. Manson, *Teaching of Jesus,* 69 (including doublets there are 65).

on the parables deal with fewer than that number, roughly three or four dozen.[6] An answer to the question of how many parables there are from Jesus is not easy to come by. For example, are the sayings of Jesus about not placing a patch of new cloth on old clothes and not putting new wine in old wineskins (Mark 2:21-22//Matt 9:16-17//Luke 5:36-38) to be classified as parables? Neither Mark nor Matthew calls them such, but Luke does (5:36). Some interpreters include them in their lists of parables, since these figures of speech make a comparison between the ministry of Jesus and the tearing of cloth and the bursting of wineskins.[7] Other interpreters do not.[8] Even though these sayings are to a certain degree parabolic (making comparisons), it is an open question whether they should be considered parables. They do not correspond fully with what are clearly the shortest of parables (the similitudes), in which an explicit comparison is made, such as "the kingdom of God is like . . . ," nor do they correspond to the longer parables that contain narratives.

The present study has been carried on with a working definition of a parable that can be stated in this way:

> *A parable is a figure of speech in which a comparison is made between God's kingdom, actions, or expectations and something in this world, real or imagined.*

There are two types of parables:

1. Narrative parables: the comparisons made include narration; these parables typically have a "once upon a time" quality about them and the particularity of stories set in the past.
2. Similitudes: the comparisons are made without stories but by means of the words "is like" or "is as if";[9] analogies are made between their subjects and general and timeless observations.

Under this definition there are at least thirty-eight units within the Synoptic Gospels that can be designated as parables. Admittedly this count may be

---

6. A. Jülicher, *Gleichnisreden,* covers 53 parables; C. H. Dodd, *Parables,* discusses 32; J. Jeremias, *Parables,* discusses 41; and B. Scott, *Parable,* discusses 29 (plus one appearing only in the *Gospel of Thomas*). According to J. Lambrecht, *Astonished,* 18, there are 42 parables; R. A. Culpepper, *NIB (Luke),* 9:297, provides a list of 49 parables.

7. A. Jülicher, *Gleichnisreden,* 2:188-202; C. H. Dodd, *Parables,* 6, 90; C. Carlston, *Parables,* 14-15, 62-66, 125-29.

8. R. Stein, *Parables,* 25, calls the sayings "possible examples of parables." J. Jeremias, *Parables,* 247-48, does not include them in his "Index of Synoptic Parables," but on p. 90 he mentions them while discussing "paired parables and similes," and on p. 117 refers to them as "sayings." W. O. E. Oesterley, *Parables,* does not include them.

9. Some examples: Matt 13:31, 33, 44, 45; Mark 4:26, 31; 13:34.

too high by one, since it contains one unit whose credentials as a parable are highly questionable, namely, the "Parable" of the Final Judgment (Matt 25:31-46). The passage consists of an eschatological discourse and can qualify as a parable only because of its beginning, in which the last judgment is compared to a shepherd's separating sheep from goats, but after that it no longer has the character of a parable as otherwise known. Yet the passage is routinely referred to as a parable and is often included within major studies of the parables of Jesus. The other units among the thirty-eight selected are generally considered parables in both common parlance and the scholarly literature. It is possible that additional units should be admitted for discussion as parables. In any case, it is not likely that those units chosen here would be contested; any others added most likely could be.

The five parables of the kingdom discussed in Chapter 8 can, as a group, be classified as "similitudes." Two others can be added. These are the Wise and Foolish Builders (Matt 7:24-27//Luke 6:47-49) in Chapter 4 and the Father's Good Gifts (Matt 7:9-11//Luke 11:11-13) in Chapter 5. That leaves thirty-one others as "narrative parables."

Some major interpreters maintain that there is a third type of parable besides the two indicated here, and that is the Exemplary Narrative (German: *Beispielerzählung*), and they place four parables (all in Luke) under that heading: the Parables of the Good Samaritan (Luke 10:25-37), the Rich Fool (12:16-21), the Rich Man and Lazarus (16:19-31), and the Pharisee and the Publican (18:10-14).[10] In a sense these are different from others in that they provide examples of human conduct to follow — and examples to avoid. Furthermore, as Adolf Jülicher put it, they actually need no interpretation, for "they are as clear and transparent as possible" and merely call for practical application.[11] Yet in form they are simply a subset of the larger category of Narrative Parables,[12] and other parables are not devoid of portraying their protagonists as examples.[13] In any case, the four sometimes placed in a separate category are treated as one type of Narrative Parable in Chapter 3.

In any discussion of the parables of Jesus the question arises whether one can classify them into subgroupings beyond the formal categories already indicated. Joachim Jeremias, for example, classifies the forty-one parables he treats into ten groups that "present a comprehensive conception of the message of Jesus."[14] Bernard Scott, on the other hand, classifies the twenty-nine parables of

10. A. Jülicher, *Gleichnisreden*, 1:114; 2:585-641; R. Bultmann, *HST* 177-79; B. Smith, *Parables*, 18.

11. A. Jülicher, *Gleichnisreden*, 1:114.

12. A point made also by Jeffrey T. Tucker, *Example Stories: Perspectives on Four Parables in the Gospel of Luke*, JSNTSup 162 (Sheffield: Sheffield Academic Press, 1998) 396-418.

13. For example, the six "Parables and Similitudes of Wisdom" (Chapter 4).

14. J. Jeremias, *Parables*, 115. Actually there are nine groups of *spoken* parables; the

his work under three major headings drawn from the "elementary aspects of Mediterranean social life and culture."[15]

Within the present work the thirty-eight parables discussed are placed under seven headings. The classification is primarily for the purpose of presenting the parables in an ordered and coherent way. The parables discussed seem to fall generally into the suggested categories, but the categories should not be used in a rigid way, and the parables should not be pressed into them at all costs to fit a scheme. The categories are: "Parables of the Revelation of God," "Parables of Exemplary Behavior," "Parables and Similitudes of Wisdom," "Parables and Similitudes of Life before God," "Parables of Final Judgment," "Allegorical Parables," and "Parables of the Kingdom." These categories are introduced at the outset of each chapter.

B. DISTINCTIVE ELEMENTS IN THE PARABLES OF JESUS

The parables of Jesus are rooted in form and imagery in Jewish culture from pre-Christian times. It has been said that "story parables only appear in Jewish literature and in the gospels."[16] Within the OT there is at least one passage that is customarily called a parable — that in which Nathan the prophet addresses King David after David's arranging for the death of Uriah and taking Bathsheba as his wife (2 Sam 12:1-4). The passage is not, however, called a "parable" within the OT itself, nor are any others that employ narration and partially resemble parables in content and function (e.g., 1 Kings 20:39-40; Isa 5:1-7; 28:23-29).

The term παραβολή is used frequently in the Septuagint, and in twenty-two cases it is the translation used for the Hebrew noun מָשָׁל (transliterated as *mashal*, plural מְשָׁלִים], *meshalim*).[17] But simply to translate that word as "parable" and understand it in light of the parables of Jesus would be a mistake. The term has a broad meaning and can signify a saying, mocking byword, similitude, riddle, allegory, oracle, fable, or proverb.[18] The Hebrew title of the book of Proverbs of Solomon (מִשְׁלֵי שְׁלֹמֹה), for example, could be rendered "The

---

tenth group consists of what Jeremias calls "parabolic actions." The nine themes are: Now Is the Day of Salvation, God's Mercy for Sinners, The Great Assurance, The Imminence of Catastrophe, It May Be Too Late, The Challenge of the Hour, Realized Discipleship, The Via Dolorosa and Exaltation of the Son of Man, and The Consummation.

15. B. Scott, *Parable*, 73. These are: "Family, Village, City, and Beyond," "Masters and Servants," and "Home and Farm."

16. Brad H. Young, *Jesus and His Jewish Parables: Rediscovering the Roots of Jesus' Teaching* (New York: Paulist Press, 1989), 1.

17. Elmar C. dos Santos, *An Expanded Hebrew Index for the Hatch Redpath Concordance to the Septuagint* (Jerusalem: Dugith Publishers, 1973), 124.

18. Friedrich Hauck, "παραβολή," *TDNT* 5:747-51.

Mishalim of Solomon."[19] There are no instances in the OT where the noun *mashal* is applied to a figure of speech in narrative form that moderns would call a parable.[20]

The parables of Jesus fit more precisely in form and content within the context of the various *meshalim* known from rabbinic sources. According to Harvey McArthur and Robert Johnston, some 325 known rabbinic parables exist from the Tannaitic period (roughly the beginning of the Christian era to A.D. 220),[21] and these can be examined for comparative purposes with the parables of Jesus. The main and most obvious similarity is that in both cases a narrative is told in order that the unknown can be illumined by the known. In addition, there are similarities that can be considered extraneous to the narrative itself but are frequent in connection with parables in the Gospels and almost always present in connection with the rabbinic parables. These include an introductory formula — either a question ("to what shall we compare" a thing? in Hebrew, מָשָׁל לְמָה הַדָּבָר דּוֹמֶה [*mashal lemah hadvar domeh*])[22] or simply a statement ("it [the matter at hand] is like" something; in Hebrew, מָשָׁל לְ [*mashal le*], or a variant) — and an application at the end (in Hebrew the נִמְשַׁל [*nimshal*], introduced by כָּךְ [*kakh*], meaning "similarly," "even so," "likewise").[23] These, in turn, may be bracketed by the narration of an occasion for the parable at the outset, and a scriptural quotation at the conclusion.[24] When all these elements are present, there are five items: narrated occasion, introductory formula, the *mashal* proper, the *nimshal,* and a scriptural quotation.

The question of the distinctiveness of Jesus' parables is difficult to assess. At one time it could be maintained with rather easy confidence that Jesus' parables are unique (i.e., one of a kind) in either form or content.[25] Early in the twentieth century, for example, Paul Fiebig claimed that the parables of Jesus show such originality and vividness that no one but Jesus could have created

---

19. According to tradition, Solomon spoke 3,000 proverbs (1 Kgs 4:32; MT, 1 Kgs 5:12 [מָשָׁל]; LXX, 3 Kgdms 5:12 [παραβολαί]). According to Josephus, *Ant.* 8.44, Solomon "composed . . . three thousand books of parables (παραβολῶν . . . βίβλους)"; quoted from *Josephus,* trans. Henry St. J. Thackeray et al., LCL, 10 vols. (Cambridge: Harvard University Press, 1961-81), 5:594-95.

20. David Stern, *Parables in Midrash: Narrative and Exegesis in Rabbinic Literature* (Cambridge: Harvard University Press, 1991), 9.

21. Harvey K. McArthur and Robert M. Johnston, *They Also Taught in Parables: Rabbinic Parables from the First Centuries of the Christian Era* (Grand Rapids: Zondervan, 1990), 9.

22. Wilhelm Bacher, *Die exegetische Terminologie der jüdischen Traditionsliteratur,* 2 vols. (Darmstadt: Wissenschaftliche Buchgesellschaft, 1965 [reprinted from the Leizpig ed., 1899-1905]), 121.

23. H. McArthur and R. Johnston, *They Also Spoke in Parables,* 99, 111, 112; D. Stern, *Parables in Midrash,* 8, 16, 21-22.

24. H. McArthur and R. Johnston, *They Also Spoke in Parables,* 99.

25. J. Jeremias, *Parables,* 12.

them.[26] But such claims have been met with the suspicion (spoken or not) that they have been made too often in the interests of asserting the superiority of Jesus over his contemporaries — or of Christianity over Judaism. The problem that one runs into is that there are so few extant parables from his contemporaries, such as Hillel (ca. 60 B.C.–A.D. 20), Shammai (ca. 50 B.C.–A.D. 30), and the first generation of the Tannaim (A.D. 10-80). The McArthur-Johnston volume contains only one parabolic unit that is attributed to Hillel, but its authenticity is contested,[27] and one each to the schools of Hillel and Shammai.[28] Rabbinic parables become more common after A.D. 70. In the same volume a half-dozen are attributed to Rabbi Johanan ben Zakkai (ca. A.D. 1-80)[29] and four to Rabban Gamaliel of the second generation (ca. 80-120).[30] In light of the paucity of the evidence, several interpreters have concluded that Jesus was the first Jewish teacher to make use of narrative parables in instruction; the rabbinic parables are of later origin.[31] At the conclusion of an eight-year study of all extant stories of late Western antiquity from the death of Alexander the Great (ca. 323 B.C.) to the accession of Constantine (early fourth century A.D.), James Breech has concluded that "Jesus' parables were dissimilar from all extant contemporary stories."[32] He goes on to contend that "Jesus' parables are utterly dissimilar from any other stories known in Hellenistic and Greco-Roman antiquity, including Rabbinic parables."[33] On the other hand, David Flusser has asserted that the parables of Jesus are similar to others; that the form was created by the sages of Israel prior to Jesus' time; and that he developed the form further.[34] That discussion will no doubt continue among specialists in the study of midrash and comparative literature. It would be too early to consider it closed. Nevertheless, in the course of writing this book, it has become apparent

26. Paul W. J. Fiebig, *Altjüdische Gleichnisse und die Gleichnisse Jesu* (Tübingen: J. C. B. Mohr [Paul Siebeck], 1904), 163.

27. H. McArthur and R. Johnston, *They Also Taught in Parables,* 90 (text), 107 (comment). The text is from *Abot R. Nat.* 15:3.

28. Ibid., 80. Text from *Gen. Rab.* 1:15.

29. Ibid., 23 (two), 27, 80, 90. Texts from *t. B. Qam.* 7:3; 7:4; *b. Shab.* 153a; *Gen. Rab.* 19:6; and *Abot R. Nat.* 22:1.

30. Ibid., 22-23. Texts from *t. Qidd.* 1:11 (three parables); and *t. B. Qam.* 7:2.

31. J. Jeremias, *Parables,* 12; Jacob Neusner, "Types and Forms in Ancient Jewish Literature: Some Comparisons," *HR* 11 (1972): 376; David Stern, "Jesus' Parables from the Perspective of Rabbinic Literature: The Example of the Wicked Husbandmen," in *Parable and Story in Judaism and Christianity,* ed. Clemens Thoma and Michael Wyschogrod (New York: Paulist Press, 1989), 43; idem, *Parables in Midrash,* 5; and H. McArthur and R. Johnston, *They Also Taught in Parables,* 106-7.

32. James Breech, *Jesus and Postmodernism* (Minneapolis: Fortress Press, 1989), 24-25.

33. Ibid., 64.

34. David Flusser, *Jewish Sources in Early Christianity* (Tel Aviv: MOD Books, 1989), 66.

that some things about the parables of Jesus are distinctive and characteristic, and these should be noted. When the six items that follow are combined, the parables of Jesus emerge as distinctive, even original and unique.

1. One of the most striking things about the parables of Jesus is their directness of address to the audience — a feature that is attested in various traditions and thus has the ring of authenticity. While this feature is present in all of the parables of Jesus, it is particularly evident (and confirmed) in those in which he begins to speak to his hearers with such penetrating questions as "Which one of you?" (Luke 11:5; 14:28; 17:7; 15:4//Matt 12:11),[35] "What woman?" (Luke 15:8), "What father among you?" (Matt 7:9//Luke 11:11), "What king?" (Luke 14:31), "Will any one of you?" (Luke 17:7), "Who then is the faithful and wise one?" (Matt 24:45//Luke 12:42), and "What do you think?" (Matt 18:12; 21:28); or there is the simple indicative: "everyone who hears . . ." (Matt 5:24). Such opening phrases engage the hearers immediately, putting them on the spot and eliciting a response.

2. The parables of Jesus are not simply building blocks within a larger, longer argument that is to be concluded outside of the parable itself. The parables are themselves front and center bearers of the message of Jesus; very little more needs to be said. At most there will be a single sentence or two of application (corresponding to the *nimshal* of the rabbinic parables), whether authentic or not in a particular case. Thereafter the parables of Jesus leave room for interpretation.

This point is important when comparing the parables of Jesus to known rabbinic parables. Interpreters have often made the point that the latter are primarily exegetical; their purpose is to interpret, clarify, and apply the scriptural tradition of Israel.[36] Typically the rabbinic parable interprets a biblical text, and its meaning is controlled by the text being cited. There is hardly any room for interpretation. It can thus be called a "closed text, not an open one."[37] However characteristic it may be of rabbinic parables to be exegetical, that is not typical of the parables of Jesus. There is only one parable that is elicited from Jesus on the basis of reference to a biblical text. That is the Parable of the Good Samaritan, which Jesus tells in response to the lawyer who asks "And who is my neighbor?" in connection with Leviticus 19:18.[38] Aside from that one instance, normally Jesus utters parables with an apparent sense of sovereign freedom. His

35. This formulation does not seem to have any contemporary parallels, according to J. Jeremias, *Parables*, 103.

36. Günther Bornkamm, *Jesus of Nazareth* (New York: Harper & Brothers, 196), 69; H. McArthur and R. Johnston, *They Also Taught in Parables*, 172; D. Stern, "Jesus' Parables from the Perspective of Rabbinic Literature," 58; and Daniel Boyarin, *Intertextuality and the Reading of Midrash* (Bloomington: Indiana University Press, 1990), 80-83.

37. D. Boyarin, *Intertextuality*, 82.

38. That is not to overlook the fact that scriptural allusions abound in the parables of Jesus. The most obvious are in the Sower and the Wicked Tenants (Mark 4:3-8; 12:1-12 and parallels).

manner of teaching by parables without recourse to biblical texts may be the basis for the claim that he taught "as one having authority, and not as the scribes" (Mark 1:22).

The feature just described sets the parables of Jesus off as distinctive not only from rabbinic parables but also from those from other, non-Jewish teachers within the Greco-Roman world. The term "parable" is used by Aristotle in his *Rhetoric*. He speaks of it there as an illustration that a person such as Socrates might use to confirm a proposition.[39] Plato used myths, allegories, and illustrations to further arguments, of which his "Allegory of the Cave" is perhaps best known.[40] He also employed figures of speech that he called "parables" to further his ideas within discourses.[41] Various Stoics and Cynics made use of figures of speech that can broadly be classified as parables as well.[42] But as in the case of Plato, their parables are used to confirm principles, and they appear within larger complexes of argumentation; they do not appear as independent units of teaching.[43]

3. The fact that the parables of Jesus are not used for argumentation in the sense of the "parables" of ancient philosophers, popular rhetoricians, or rabbinic masters is significant for the content of Jesus' parables. There is very little previous learning that Jesus' hearers need to bring to the occasion beyond what is gained through life experience. The subject of the parables is typically the familiar of everyday life: men and women working, losing, and finding; fathers and sons in strained and joyous relationships; kings, rich men, and slaves in stereotypical roles; domestic animals, seeds, plants, vineyards, leaven, and the like. These become symbols, to be sure, resonating with Jewish symbols of previous generations. Yet they would have been familiar to anyone who had even a rudimentary acquaintance with the Jewish heritage, an acquaintance that anyone of that time and place would gain from life experience.

---

39. Aristotle, *Rhetoric* 2.20 (1393). For further discussion of Aristotle's use of "parable," cf. George A. Kennedy, *Aristotle on Rhetoric: A Theory of Civic Discourse* (New York: Oxford University Press, 1991), 180 (n. 130).

40. Plato, *Republic* 7.514-17.

41. Plato, *Gorgias* 493d-94a; *Republic* 6.487e-89a; 7.532a-d. Other examples of stories, myths, and parable-like compositions of Plato employed to further his ideas can be found in his *Republic* 3.414c-e; 6.484; *Phaedrus* 246a-57a; 274c-75c; and *Philebus* 33b-c.

42. Examples can be found, for example, in Epictetus, *Dis.* 1.14.15; 1.24.19; 2.14.21-22; 2.16.9; 3.25.6-10; 4.1.105-10; 4.7.22-23; and 4.13.11-12. These are cited by F. Hauck, "παραβολή," *TDNT* 5:746 (n. 8).

43. The discussion of the use of παραβολή and *parabola* in Greek and Latin writers (Aristotle, Plato, Demetrius, Isocrates, Plutarch, Quintilian, Seneca, and still others) is reviewed by Marsh H. McCall, *Ancient Rhetorical Theories of Simile and Comparison* (Cambridge: Harvard University Press, 1969). In no case is their designated use comparable to that in the Gospels. In the *Rhetoric* of Aristotle, for example, a parable is useful as a proof in an argument, while in the *On Style* of Demetrius (first century A.D.), a parable — used sparingly — is said to be useful for the sake of style in prose composition (cf. pp. 147-55).

4. Perhaps most striking about the parables of Jesus is their ways of portraying God. The parables are thoroughly theological. But they do not get involved in descriptions of God's attributes or in theoretical discussions about God. What is characteristic rather is the sense of God's intimacy and familiarity through the use of striking but common metaphors — father, king, a shepherd, the owner of a vineyard, or a woman who sweeps her house. The concreteness of the metaphors keeps the discussion from abstractions. The verbal images and the behavior of the metaphorical figures described are more powerful than propositional language about God could convey.

5. Characteristic of many of the parables of Jesus, not all, is the element of surprise in the way they end. Over against common assumptions, the parables of Jesus do not always portray typical human behavior as illustrative of God. Time and again the behavior described is not typical, and that is decisive for the teaching at hand about God. Within the Parable of the Workers in the Vineyard (Matt 20:1-16), for example, in which the "eleventh-hour workers" receive pay equal to that of those who worked all day, "Jesus deliberately and cleverly led the listeners along by degrees until they understood that if God's generosity was to be represented by a man, such a man would be different from any man ever encountered."[44] Other major examples of atypical behavior of protagonists in parables as metaphors for God include the father in the Prodigal Son (Luke 15:11-32), the shepherd in the Lost Sheep (15:4-7), the king in the Marriage Feast (Matt 22:1-10), and more.

6. Finally, the parables of Jesus capture, combine, and make use of two major Jewish traditions: wisdom and eschatology. Often, in spite of contrary evidence, the two are thought to appear in separate spheres of thought and teaching. The wisdom tradition takes for granted that wisdom is timeless, consisting of truisms that are valid for all times and places. The eschatological tradition, on the other hand, makes assertions related to temporality. But the two traditions converge in the parables of Jesus, and this gives them a distinctive character. Some of the parables that are classified as "parables of wisdom" (Chapter 4) exhibit this feature most vividly. The ten maidens (Matt 25:1-13) can be divided into wise and foolish, but it is only the wise who in the end are admitted to the wedding feast. The hearer knows then that a certain kind of wisdom is needed to enter the kingdom, and that is made clear by the words: "Keep awake, therefore, for you know neither the day nor the hour" (25:13). The faithful and wise servant (Matt 24:45-51//Luke 12:42-46) considers his duty with care and performs it; if he does not, he is punished. The hearer is to be wise and apply the parable in such a way that he or she remains faithful, lest in the judgment he or she be cast out. Not all of the parables combine both the wisdom and eschatological traditions of the Jewish heritage, but the two tradi-

44. Norman Huffman, "Atypical Features in the Parables of Jesus," *JBL* 97 (1978): 209.

tions are so interwoven among so many of the parables that such an interweaving can be considered characteristic of the parables of Jesus.

C. THE UNIVERSAL AND THE PARTICULAR
IN THE PARABLES OF JESUS

One can generally agree with a statement by Amos Wilder concerning the parables of Jesus:

> We have here a Jewish mind and heart at that precise point of the heritage where the particular religious tradition becomes indistinguishable from a universal humanity.[45]

The parables of Jesus do in fact have universal appeal. Simply as stories they connect with the human condition very well. The Parables of the Prodigal Son and the Good Samaritan are prime examples.

Nevertheless, it should be abundantly clear that the parables of Jesus have been preserved, taught, and interpreted in the preaching of the church precisely because they are parables *of Jesus*, regarded as the crucified and resurrected Redeemer. There is truth in the adage of the radical nineteenth-century critic David Friedrich Strauss that, had it not been for belief in the resurrection of Jesus, his teachings (or at least many of them) would probably have perished:

> Jesus might still have taught and embodied in his life all that is true and good, as well as what is one-sided and harsh. . . . Nevertheless, his teachings would have been blown away and scattered like solitary leaves by the wind, had these leaves not been held together and thus preserved, as if with a stout tangible binding, by an illusory belief in his resurrection.[46]

Whether the teachings of Jesus in his parables are better than those of other great figures in the history of the religions of the world, so that they deserved preservation on the grounds of their intrinsic worth, can be debated. But the most obvious reason for their preservation is that they are parables of Jesus. They are valued in light of christological claims about him. How many other great teachers there have been whose teachings "true and good" have been "scattered like solitary leaves by the wind" we shall never know.

The parables of Jesus cannot therefore be treated purely as timeless, literary gems from a teacher of wisdom, regardless of how much Jesus was such.

---

45. Amos N. Wilder, *The Language of the Gospel: Early Christian Rhetoric* (New York: Harper & Row, 1964), 95.

46. David Friedrich Strauss, *The Old Faith and the New: A Confession*, 2 vols. (New York: Henry Holt & Company, 1873), 1:83.

They must be dealt with precisely as parables of Jesus. Further, they are related metaphorically not only to the larger drama of Jesus' "literary world," the OT, as with so many rabbinic parables of his day, but also to his distinctive proclamation of the kingdom of God. In a word, they presuppose and express Jesus' own theology. There is indeed truth to the statement of Eduard Schweizer, while commenting on the Parable of the Prodigal Son, that "without [Jesus' own] ministry the parable would not be true."[47]

D. INTERPRETING THE PARABLES OF JESUS

Although the history of the interpretation of the parables of Jesus is important, interesting, and instructive for the present, I have not taken up the topic here. It has been told many times, and very well, by various interpreters. The person interested in that history can consult those works.[48]

Three major questions have dominated the larger question of parable interpretation: (1) Does allegorization ever have a role? (2) What is to be interpreted: the "original" parable of Jesus or the parable as it is in the Gospels? (3) What method is most necessary and fruitful? We shall take up each of these in turn.

1. Parable and Allegory

The English word "allegory," like "parable," is a loanword from Greek. The word in Greek (ἀλληγορία) is a compound from ἄλλος ("other") and ἀγορία ("speaking"), and thus means "speaking otherwise than one seems to speak"; in common usage it is defined as "an extended or continued metaphor."[49] Allegorical interpretation of the parables of Jesus rests on the assumption that they are allegories to be interpreted, and the interpretation proceeds with assigning meaning to virtually every detail narrated in a parable. In the history of allegor-

---

47. E. Schweizer, *Luke*, 252.

48. The most extensive account is by Warren S. Kissinger, *The Parables of Jesus: A History of Interpretation and Bibliography*, ATLABS 4 (Metuchen, N.J.: Scarecrow Press, 1979), 1-239. Shorter treatments are those of A. Hunter, *Parables*, 21-41; R. Stein, *Parables*, 42-81; and Klyne R. Snodgrass, "From Allegorizing to Allegorizing: A History of the Interpretation of the Parables," in *The Challenge of Jesus' Parables*, ed. Richard N. Longenecker (Grand Rapids: Wm. B. Eerdmans, 2000), 3-29. A review of works from the time of Kissinger's work until his own essay has been provided by Craig L. Blomberg, "The Parables of Jesus: Current Trends and Needs in Research," in *Studying the Historical Jesus: Evaluations of the State of Current Research*, ed. Bruce Chilton and Craig A. Evans, NTTS 19 (Leiden: E. J. Brill, 1994), 231-54.

49. *The Oxford English Dictionary*, 1:333.

ical interpretation within the church the details have regularly been considered to refer symbolically to classic Christian doctrines. Such a way of interpreting the parables has persisted in popular Christian exposition well into modern times, as illustrated in a meditation on the Parable of the Talents (Matt 25:14-30) from a parish paper of the 1920s:

> The man who for an unknown period of time went into a far country is Jesus Christ. After He had completed the work of redemption, He returned to heaven. In an invisible manner He follows closely His work: when the time comes He will return, require a reckoning from us and pass a just and unchangeable judgment.
>
> The good and faithful servants are all who believe in Christ and especially the Christian pastors. The talents are the means of grace, the word and sacraments. Other blessings, such as bodily and spiritual gifts, education, wealth and other privileges are also included.[50]

Adolf Jülicher (1857-1938) is credited with making the break from allegorical interpretation of the parables, which had been dominant for all previous centuries of the Christian era. In his two-volume work, *Die Gleichnisreden Jesu* (= *The Parable Discourses of Jesus;* but the work was never translated into English; vol. 1 appeared in German in 1886 [2d ed., 1899]; vol. 2 appeared in 1899), he declared that the parables of Jesus are not allegories.[51] On the contrary, "the parable is there only to illuminate . . . one point, a rule, an idea, an experience that is valid on the spiritual as on the secular level."[52] Again, he says, the interpreter "must draw from the parable only one thought."[53]

Since the work of Jülicher, one cannot go back to the allegorical method of interpretation. Nevertheless, it is important to emphasize that parable and allegory were not sharply differentiated in the world of Jesus and his contemporaries; the term *mashal* covers both.[54] Terms like "father" and "servant" have metaphorical meanings in the parables of Jesus that are to be noticed by the interpreter, and as soon as that is done, a given parable may well be seen to have some allegorical elements within it.[55] The figure of a king in a parable of Jesus can surely be a pictorial representation for God, as in various OT texts (Exod 15:18; 1 Chron 16:31; Ps 93:1; Isa 24:23) and in many rabbinic parables.[56]

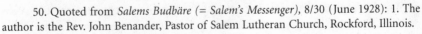

50. Quoted from *Salems Budbäre* (= *Salem's Messenger*), 8/30 (June 1928): 1. The author is the Rev. John Benander, Pastor of Salem Lutheran Church, Rockford, Illinois.

51. A. Jülicher, *Gleichnisreden*, 1:61.

52. Ibid., 1:317.

53. Ibid., 1:74.

54. Raymond E. Brown, "Parable and Allegory Reconsidered," in *New Testament Essays* (Milwaukee: Bruce Publishing Company, 1965), 324.

55. Ibid.

56. For illustrations, cf. Louis I. Rabinowitz, "Parable: In the Talmud and Midrash," *EncJud* 13:74; D. Stern, *Parables in Midrash*, 2, 19.

It is also fit and necessary to observe that some parables are allegorical through and through. These include the Wicked Tenants (Mark 12:1-12 and parallels), the Wedding Feast (Matt 22:1-14), and the Great Banquet (Luke 14:16-24). Still others have recognizable allegorical elements within them, such as the city that is destroyed in the Parable of the Marriage Feast (Matt 22:1-14), the bridegroom in the Parable of the Ten Maidens (25:1-13), and the shepherd in the Parable of the Final Judgment (25:31-46). Finally, some parables have allegorical interpretations appended to them, such as those units appended to the Parable of the Sower (Mark 4:13-20 and parallels), the Weeds among the Wheat (Matt 13:36-43), and the Dragnet (13:49-50). In these latter cases the appended interpretations may or may not be attributable to Jesus (a question to be taken up case by case in subsequent chapters), but they illustrate how fluid the dynamics were between parable and allegory in the first century.

It has often been maintained that the earthly Jesus would not have taught allegorical parables; therefore, any such parables do not come from him.[57] Yet that view (or assumption) needs to be challenged. For the most allegorical parable of all in both the Synoptic Gospels and the *Gospel of Thomas,* the Parable of the Wicked Tenants (Mark 12:1-12//Matt 21:33-46//Luke 20:9-19, and *Gos. Thom.* 65–66), may well have been uttered by Jesus of Nazareth in a more primitive form. That view is held by a wide range of scholars whose perspectives and methodologies differ from one another greatly (see the discussion of that parable).[58]

The result of this discussion is that the interpreter should recognize allegorical elements wherever they exist and respect them. Moreover, more than one symbol can appear in a given parable. But in the final analysis the interpreter should not work under the assumption that there are hidden meanings within the text that can be brought out by allegorizing.

2. What Is to Be Interpreted?

Jülicher can also be credited with pressing this question. He maintained that "one cannot identify the voice of Jesus with the voices of the evangelists."[59] The implication is that one must go back behind the Gospels to discern "the voice of Jesus." And it is simply assumed that that is what one must get at, and then

57. A. Jülicher, *Gleichnisreden,* 1:63-68; R. Bultmann, *HST* 197-99; B. Smith, *Parables,* 23-24; C. H. Dodd, *Parables,* 2-5, 8-11; and J. Jeremias, *Parables,* 18.

58. A major study that contends that allegorical elements are found in authentic parables of Jesus, and that recognizing allegory within texts must be distinguished from allegorizing them, is that of Hans-Josef Klauck, *Allegorie und Allegorese in synoptischen Gleichnistexten,* NTAbh 13 (Münster: Aschendorff, 1978).

59. A. Jülicher, *Gleichnisreden,* 1:11.

interpret what Jesus actually said. That way of thinking has been continued by others and has had a dominant place in the interpretation of the parables of Jesus. So, for example, A. T. Cadoux sought to discern the original setting and meaning of each parable within the context of Jesus' ministry;[60] C. H. Dodd set out to answer the question, "What was the original intention of this or that parable, in its historical setting?";[61] and Joachim Jeremias looked upon the task of studying the parables of Jesus as that of "recovering their original meaning."[62] As he puts it succinctly:

> Each of [Jesus'] parables has a definite historical setting. Hence to recover this is the task before us. What did Jesus intend to say at this or that particular moment? What must have been the effect of his word upon his hearers? These are the questions we must ask in order, so far as may be possible, to recover the original meaning of the parables of Jesus, to hear again his authentic voice.[63]

The problems that arise in trying to discern the historical setting of the parables are immense. The historical and cultural distances between the original setting and the present are obvious. But equally difficult is the question of the function of the parables in their original settings.[64] Cadoux claimed that the parables were weapons of controversy used by Jesus against his opponents;[65] similarly, Jeremias went so far as to assert that "all the Gospel parables are a defence of the Good News" addressed to critics.[66] But such sweeping generalizations, if applied rigorously to the interpretation of the parables, preclude the possibility that a given parable was uttered for a didactic purpose to the disciples or to the crowds. As one probes the possible setting of a parable, one should leave options open and entertain and even expect a variety of functions.[67] Even if some polemical parables have been transformed into didactic parables within the process of transmission and reapplication — a genuine possibility, to be sure — there is no need to conclude a priori that some parables could not have been didactic from the moment of their utterance. The view of Jülicher is worth considering. According to him, Jesus used the parables for a

---

60. A. Cadoux, *Parables*, 16, 23, 41-42, 136, 227, etc.

61. C. H. Dodd, *Parables*, vii-viii. Cf. also pp. 14, 18-19.

62. J. Jeremias, *Parables*, 13.

63. Ibid., 22.

64. Cf. the following comments: Martin Dibelius, *From Tradition to Gospel* (New York: Charles Scribner's Sons, 1935), 254: ". . . we do not know to what situation these parables were originally fitted"; and R. Bultmann, *HST* 199: "*The original meaning of many similitudes has become irrecoverable* in the course of the tradition" (italics in the original).

65. A. Cadoux, *Parables*, 13.

66. J. Jeremias, *Parables*, 145; cf. pp. 33-38.

67. The point has been made particularly by Claus Westermann, *The Parables of Jesus in the Light of the Old Testament* (Minneapolis: Fortress Press, 1990), 193-202.

wide range of objectives, to various audiences, and at various points in his ministry.[68]

The parable interpretation of the second half of the twentieth century showed that the historical approach is not the only possibility. Other interpreters, such as Robert Funk, Dan Via, John Dominic Crossan, and too many others to mention, have taken a literary approach to the parables.[69] The term "literary," however, has a broad meaning. It has come to include a number of methodologies that go by other names as well: rhetorical criticism, structural analysis, reader response criticism, and more.[70] Here the assumption is often that the original setting and the exact words of Jesus cannot be retrieved, and the parables can (and do) communicate to moderns; one does not first of all have to locate the original historical setting for them to do so.

Still other interpreters, such as Jack Kingsbury, John Drury, and John Donahue, have maintained that the parables of Jesus should be interpreted within the contexts of the books in which they appear, the canonical texts.[71] To go back behind the books is always speculative. To recreate an original setting within the ministry of Jesus and an original form of a parable is always hypothetical. What we do have is parables within texts at hand, and the analysis of them in their canonical texts is more surefooted than alternatives.

Giving attention to the literary settings and features of the parables, however, does not for a moment diminish the importance of historical work. The parables appear in texts that have historical settings within the ancient world. As in the case of any literary product of an era long gone, the interpreter must understand the parables as foreign to the present. They contain imagery and terminology that are not ready at hand for current speech or storytelling. What does it mean to speak of a son asking his father for his inheritance (Luke 15:12)? Why is the Samaritan a shocking figure in the parable that speaks of him as the one who helps the man in need — so shocking that the lawyer will not mention him as the hero of the story (Luke 10:37)? What does it mean for a master to forgive his slave ten thousand talents (Matt 18:24-27)? For what purpose would ten maidens go out to meet a bridegroom (Matt 25:1)? The questions keep coming. Whoever makes use of a Greek-English lexicon, a grammar of ancient Greek, or a Bible dic-

---

68. A. Jülicher, *Gleichnisreden,* 1:146.

69. Some of the works of those mentioned include: Robert Funk, *Language, Hermeneutic, and the Word of God* (New York: Harper & Row, 1966); idem, *Parables and Presence: Forms of the New Testament Tradition* (Philadelphia: Fortress Press, 1982); idem, *A Structuralist Approach to the Parables,* ed. R. Funk, Semeia 1 (Missoula, Mont.: Scholars Press, 1974); D. Via, *Parables;* and J. Crossan, *Parables.*

70. The methods in reference to parable study are surveyed by William A. Beardslee, "Recent Literary Criticism," in *The New Testament and Its Modern Interpreters,* ed. Eldon J. Epp and George W. MacRae (Philadelphia: Fortress Press, 1989), 177-83.

71. Jack D. Kingsbury, *Matthew 13;* John Drury, *The Parables in the Gospels: History and Allegory* (New York: Crossroad, 1985); and J. Donahue, *Parable.*

tionary or wordbook is doing historical-critical work, since that person is seeking to understand a word, phrase, or image in its ancient context.

It is incumbent upon the interpreter to seek the meaning of the parables from various vantage points, raising both historical and literary questions. Two difficulties are most obvious in the task, the one historical and the other literary. The one is the problem of "translation" from one culture to another. The "translation" is not just from ancient Greek to modern English; it is also from the worldview of the ancient Gospels to that of moderns. The other is the problem of "translation" from one mode of expression (the parable) to another (descriptive discourse). In both cases of "translation" there will be a loss. What may have been fully meaningful at one time can only be sought after in the time and place of the interpreter. That is why the art and science of interpretation is ongoing and is ever fruitful for those who are willing to expend the work and imagination that it requires.

3. What Method Is Most Necessary and Fruitful?

The question assumes that there is a correct way, and that other ways are wrong. But interpretation itself always has a context and goal. One must ask, Interpretation for what? What is one looking for? Here there are endless possibilities. The method should fit the goal, and since there are many goals, there are many methods.

The present study is carried on primarily for the sake of interpreting the parables of Jesus within the Christian church. Other interpreters may study the parables for other reasons. But interpreting the parables of Jesus for proclamation in the church is of major importance. After all, the parables exist in the Gospels, and the Gospels have been preserved essentially for that purpose.

That means that the parables need to be studied within their contexts, the canonical Gospels. We do not have Jesus at hand as a conversation partner, allowing us to ask him what he meant in the various parables. What we do have at hand are the Gospels, which are the basis for proclamation in the church. The church regards the canonical texts of Scripture as authoritative, not the Jesus of one's own reconstruction. When the parables are taken out of their contexts within the Gospels, there always lurks the danger of making of them what one will in the way of hermeneutical experiments,[72] finding in them an "inexhaustible hermeneutic potential" comparable to that of the patristic writers in their use of allegory.[73] Or

---

72. Cf. a similar concern of Birger Gerhardsson, "If We Do Not Cut the Parables out of Their Frames," *NTS* 37 (1991): 325: "Modern expositors can increase their hermeneutic freedom immensely, if they may cut the narrative meshalim out of their frames."

73. The imagery is that of Frank Kermode, *The Genesis of Secrecy: On the Interpretation of Narrative* (Cambridge: Harvard University Press, 1979), 44.

the interpreter will tend to place them within a preconceived notion of what their function "really was" in the ministry of Jesus. Both A. T. Cadoux and Joachim Jeremias, for example, thought of the parables of Jesus as "weapons of controversy."[74] These interpreters seem unable to think of the parables of Jesus as having didactic as well as polemical purposes.[75] Bernard Scott has written that the parables of Jesus "subvert" (a key word in his discussion of various parables) "the myths that sustain our world," and they force us to see "a world with which God is in solidarity."[76] And William Herzog has declared:

> Jesus used parables to present situations familiar to the rural poor, to encode the systems of oppression that controlled their lives and held them in bondage. . . . The parable, then, was not primarily a vehicle to communicate theology or ethics but a codification designed to stimulate social analysis and to expose the contradictions between the actual situation of its hearers and the Torah of God's justice.[77]

If that is so, the sharp critical comment of Hayden White applies, which he wrote about certain postmodern examples of literary criticism in general. One can say that the interpretation of the parables consists of "the unmasking of the ideological understructure of the text," since the parables (like other literary pieces from the past) are simply "an epiphenomenon of more basic human or social drives and needs."[78]

The choice of approach taken in this volume does not mean that there is no other way of interpreting the parables. It certainly does not mean that Christian faith is a presupposition for an adequate understanding of the parables of Jesus.[79] Nor does it mean that the works of other interpreters, following different methodologies, are to be ignored. On the contrary, there have been important results from literary and historical approaches that have enriched our understanding of both Jesus and the process of transmission of his teaching.

74. A. Cadoux, *Parables*, 13; cf. also pp. 12, 14, 59, 116; and J. Jeremias, *Parables*, 21.

75. Cf. A. Wilder, *The Language of the Gospel*, 80-81.

76. B. Scott, *Parable*, 424. The terms "subvert" and "subversion" appear frequently in the interpretation of parables (pp. 97, 125, 424, etc.).

77. W. Herzog, *Parables*, 27-28. Cf. also p. 87: "Jesus' parables codify systems of oppression in order to unveil them and make them visible to those victimized by them." In order for his view of the parables to work, the author has to limit himself to only nine parables. He admits that "some parables simply will not fit the framework proposed here" (p. 4).

78. Hayden V. White, *Topics of Discourse: Essays in Cultural Criticism* (Baltimore: Johns Hopkins University Press, 1978), 271.

79. D. Stern, "Jesus' Parables from the Perspective of Rabbinic Literature," 58, asks the related question: "Can Jesus' parables be understood unchristologically?" The answer has to be yes, but one needs to be aware that the Gospels themselves are colored by christological claims of the early church.

Questions of authenticity, for example, can rightly be raised for the sake of public responsibility concerning what can be considered to have come from Jesus. It is also appropriate to ask what a parable might have meant in its original setting, as long as the interpreter is aware of how speculative any proposal may be. The plain fact is that proposals continue to be made concerning "what the earthly Jesus really meant" in his parables, and a contemporary study of the parables must engage proposals and venture some possibilities.

Nevertheless, a text remains to be interpreted, and the texts at hand are texts produced by Christian writers within and for Christian communities. With that in mind, the primary interest within this volume is exegesis and theological reflection on the parables of Jesus as transmitted within the Synoptic Gospels. That calls for the use of a wide variety of tools, including textual criticism, philological work, the search for the meaning of words, phrases, and imageries in the Greco-Roman world (including ancient Palestine), following the flow of discourse in a parable, wide use of the work of others who have gone before, and theological engagement. And while there needs then to be a process of discerning and summing up the thrust, direction, and even "point" of a parable within such a project of interpretation, it is necessary to recognize that parables contain various interesting and suggestive facets that have theological significance.[80] While parables cannot mean just anything, they continue to provoke interpretations that, while similar, are certainly not all identical, nor should they be. The interpretations that follow are therefore hardly exhaustive, and definitely not final.

---

80. On the "point" that parables are "plurisignificant or polyvalent," cf. Mary A. Tolbert, *Perspectives on the Parables: An Approach to Multiple Interpretations* (Philadelphia: Fortress Press, 1979). The terms are defined on p. 35.

CHAPTER 2

Parables of the Revelation of God

Five parables are predominantly theological. That is, their central referent is God. That is not to say that they lack other meanings. In fact, one finds in them quite vivid implications for human conduct and, in one case at least, a call for pastoral care within the church.

Three of the parables are in the Gospel of Matthew alone; two are in the Gospel of Luke alone; and another is in both, presumably based on the source commonly designated Q.

Each of the parables contains delightful surprises and striking uses of hyperbole. That is so because their primary subject is God, as portrayed by Jesus. The first is about God's extraordinary capacity to forgive (the Unforgiving Slave), a story in which God is compared to a king who forgave a slave's debt that is worth an unimaginable amount. The second is about the immensity of God's grace (the Workers in the Vineyard), which, when expressed, can surprise both those who might claim it as due them and those who would not expect it for themselves.

The other three parables, all in Luke and one in Matthew as well, portray God's extraordinary love for the lost. These are the Parables of the Lost Sheep, the Lost Coin, and the Prodigal Son. The rich use of hyperbole in these parables is impressive. The ways in which God is portrayed by Jesus make God greater in love and in his tenacity for redeeming love than one would expect.

It would be a mistake for the interpreter to understand these parables as simply setting forth human behaviors that would have been typical in antiquity. An aspect of their being so very memorable is precisely their use of surprises and hyperbole. Such use must be considered integral to Jesus' own theological perspective about God and to his manner of doing theology. From the standpoint of later Christian theology, these parables can be considered media of revelation concerning God.

20

A. PARABLES OF GOD'S EXTRAORDINARY FORGIVENESS AND GRACE

2.1. The Unforgiving Slave, Matthew 18:23-35

23 *[Jesus said,] "Therefore the kingdom of heaven has become like a king who wished to settle accounts with his slaves.* 24 *When he began the reckoning, one was brought to him who owed him ten thousand talents;* 25 *and as he could not pay, his lord ordered him to be sold, with his wife and children and all that he had, and payment to be made.* 26 *So the slave fell down, did obeisance, and said, 'Have patience with me, and I will pay you everything.'* 27 *And being moved by compassion, the lord of that slave released him and forgave him the debt.*

28 *"But that same slave, as he went out, came upon one of his fellow slaves who owed him a hundred denarii; and seizing him by the throat he said, 'Pay what you owe.'* 29 *So his fellow slave fell down and implored him, 'Have patience with me, and I will pay you.'* 30 *He refused and went and put him in prison till he should pay the debt.* 31 *When his fellow slaves saw what had taken place, they were extremely upset, and they went and reported to their lord all that had taken place.*

32 *"Then his lord summoned him and said to him, 'You wicked slave! I forgave you all that debt because you besought me;* 33 *and should not you have had mercy on your fellow slave, as I had mercy on you?'* 34 *And his lord was angry and delivered him to be tortured, till he should pay all his debt.*

35 *So also my heavenly Father will do to every one of you, if you do not forgive your brother from your heart."*

Notes on the Text and Translation

18:23. The Greek term δοῦλος is translated here and subsequently as "slave" (as in the NRSV). It is translated as "servant" in several commonly used English versions (KJV, RSV, JB, TEV, and NIV; the NEB has "the men who served him" at 18:23, and "servant[s]" thereafter). On the meaning of the term, see Appendix 3.

18:24. Instead of προσηνέχθη (aorist passive of προσφέρω, so "was brought"), some important texts (B and D included) have the virtual synonym προσήχθη (aorist passive of προσάγω, so "was brought" as well). The latter is printed in Westcott-Hort and the 25th edition of Nestle-Aland; the former in the 26th and 27th editions of the Nestle-Aland Greek text, as well as the UBS text. It is slightly better attested in witnesses at this place, and various forms of the verb appear fifteen times in the Gospel of Matthew, whereas there are no instances of the variant (unless here). It does have a nuance that the variant lacks. That is that the person was not only brought, but carried into the presence of the king.

18:25. Instead of the present tense ἔχει ("he has"), some very important witnesses have the imperfect εἶχεν ("he had"). Both verbs are well attested. The former is the more difficult reading. The present tense is sometimes used to express relative time after verbs expressing speech.[1]

18:26. Some ancient witnesses (including ℵ) include κύριε ("Lord") as a polite form of address in the second half of this verse (so, "Lord, have patience . . ."), and its translation is reflected in the KJV and RSV. But a number of other important ancient witnesses (including B, D, Θ, and Old Latin and Syriac texts) omit it. It may be present due to allegorical interpretation; in any case, the shorter reading is to be preferred.[2] It is omitted in the Westcott-Hort Greek text and in the 27th edition of the Nestle-Aland Greek text. The term "Lord" is not included in major recent translations (NEB, JB, TEV, NIV, and NRSV).

18:29. Several Greek witnesses include εἰς τοὺς πόδας αὐτοῦ ("at his feet"), and that is reflected in the KJV ("[fell down] at his feet") and NEB ("[fell] at his [fellow-servant's] feet"). The phrase is not attested in more important witnesses, however, nor in the 27th edition of the Nestle-Aland Greek text. The shorter reading is to be preferred in this case.[3] Other versions (RSV, NIV, NRSV) do not have the phrase.

Exegetical Commentary

The parable appears only in the Gospel of Matthew. It is located at the close of a chapter (18:1-35) that is usually classified as one of the discourse sections of the Gospel of Matthew (along with chaps. 5–7, 10, 13, and 24–25), even though it is not entirely one discourse. There are bits of narrative (18:1-2, 21) and questions from the disciples (18:1, 21). In any case, the chapter consists primarily of teachings of Jesus concerning the relationship of Jesus' disciples to one another. At the level of the Gospel, it is devoted for the most part to ecclesiastical discipline. Just prior to the parable Peter asks the question how often he should forgive his brother or sister, suggesting that seven times might suffice. Jesus replies that one should be willing to forgive "seventy-seven times" (as in the NIV and NRSV; cf. the identical Greek expression in the LXX version of Gen 4:24, which militates against the larger figure of "seventy times seven" in the KJV, RSV, and NEB).

The parable consists of three main parts, plus an application at the end, divided as the paragraphs are above. The first part concerns the king's dealing with his slave (18:23-27); the second concerns that slave's dealing with his fellow slaves (18:28-31); the third concerns the king's dealing with his slave once

---

1. BDF 168 (#324). W. D. Davies and D. C. Allison, *Matthew*, 2:798, adopt the imperfect.
2. B. Metzger, *TCGNT* 46.
3. Ibid.

more in light of what has happened (18:32-34). The final verse (18:35) is an application.

18:23. The introduction begins with "therefore" (διὰ τοῦτο), which is normally used in the Gospel of Matthew to introduce a dominical pronouncement within a discourse in order to elaborate a point (6:25; 12:31; 13:52; 21:43; 23:34; 24:44) rather than to serve as a link between units. The parable that follows is most likely then to be considered a further elaboration on the theme of forgiveness.

The verb ὡμοιώθη (aorist passive of ὁμοιόω) appears also at 13:24 and 22:2, introducing the Parables of the Weeds among the Wheat and the Wedding Feast. It is found only in Matthean introductions and can be translated along with its subject as above, "the kingdom of heaven has become like," followed by the parable proper.[4] The kingdom is thus not "like a king," but rather it has already dawned in the ministry of Jesus and has become like the following case,[5] in which forgiveness received is the basis for forgiveness given. All who claim to be members of the kingdom are expected to heed the story that follows.

18:24. That the slave was "brought" before the king does not mean that he was brought out of prison.[6] He was "brought" because the king wanted to settle accounts with (all) his servants (18:23), and he begins with this one.

The man owes the king 10,000 talents, a truly astronomical figure. The term τάλαντον ("talent") originally specified a weight that varied in differing parts of the Middle East (ca. 42.5 kilograms in Greco-Roman times [ca. 93.7 pounds]). By means of its weight, a talent could designate value; a talent of gold or silver, for example, could be weighed out. By the first century A.D., however, the term commonly referred to a monetary unit equivalent to 6,000 denarii.[7] Since a denarius was a day's wages for a common laborer (see comment on 18:28), and he might work some 300 days per year, a talent would be worth nearly twenty years' wages. Multiplied by 10,000, the amount owed by the slave would be equivalent to nearly 200,000 years' wages for one man, or a year's wages for 200,000 persons.[8]

---

4. D. A. Carson, "The ΟΜΟΙΟΣ Word-Group as Introduction to Some Matthean Parables," *NTS* 31 (1985): 278.

5. On the use of the introductory formula using words of likeness, cf. J. Jeremias, *Parables*, 101.

6. Contra J. Jeremias, *Parables*, 211; E. Schweizer, *Matthew*, 377.

7. Marvin A. Powell, "Weights and Measures," *ABD* 6:907-8; K. Harl, *Coinage*, 482. [Note: Full bibliographical information for citations not found in the Abbreviations lists can be found in the Select Bibliographies to each section.]

8. The figures can be only approximate. The textual notes for the RSV and NRSV say that a talent was "more than fifteen years' wages of a laborer." That appears somewhat conservative. The textual note in the NIV reads, "That is, several million dollars," which is surprisingly meager. R. Funk, *Five Gospels*, 217, has "ten million dollars," which is small in the extreme.

The amount owed is ridiculously high. What slave could ever accumulate such a debt owed to a king? It is doubtful that even Herod the Great — certainly one of the richest persons of his day — could have paid such a debt. His will, prepared near the end of his life, provided for the distribution of his territories, residences, and some unspecified sums of money to his children and his sister Salome, and then some 1500 talents to various persons.[9] Not surprising, then, some interpreters have suggested that the evangelist has inflated the figure, and that in the original parable Jesus would have had a lower, more reasonable figure, such as ten talents or 10,000 denarii.[10] Or it is suggested that the person is actually a satrap (or governor) who owes taxes to the king from the province he controls.[11]

But the parables of Jesus do not always reflect what is reasonable, true to life, or typical.[12] Frequently they contain hyperbole and humor, displaying actions that are surprising and outlandish — as this one does here, and as it will again when the king forgives such a debt. Both the terms 10,000 and "talent" are "the highest magnitudes in use (10,000 is the highest number used in reckoning, and the talent is the largest currency unit in the whole of the Near East)."[13] The figure, however large, is actually mentioned elsewhere in Jewish sources. According to Josephus, the Romans exacted 10,000 talents from the Jews after Pompey's conquest of Palestine (63 B.C.).[14] There is no reason to reduce the size of the debt owed. It is precisely its fantastic size that makes the parable so memorable.

Furthermore, nothing is gained by saying that the debtor must be the governor of a province. The sum is still stupendous. According to Josephus, the taxes for the whole of Judea, Idumea, and Samaria for an entire year at the time of the death of Herod the Great (4 B.C.) amounted to 600 talents, and those for Galilee and Perea combined amounted to 200 talents.[15]

18:25. In this verse, and in following verses (18:26, 27, 31, 32, 34), the

---

9. Josephus, *Ant.* 17.146-47; cf. 17.321-23.

10. T. W. Manson, *Sayings,* 213, suggests ten talents; Martinus C. de Boer, "Ten Thousand Talents?" 278, suggests 10,000 denarii; J. Lambrecht, *Treasure,* 59-61, agrees. W. Herzog, *Parables,* 144, suggests 100 talents. B. Smith, *Parables,* 218, and W. D. Davies and D. C. Allison, *Matthew,* 2:795, 798, agree that some lower figure must have been original, but do not specify what that might have been.

11. A. Plummer, *Matthew,* 256; J. Jeremias, *Parables,* 210; C. Montefiore, *Synoptic Gospels,* 2:685; Günther Bornkamm, *Jesus of Nazareth* (New York: Harper, 1960), 86; J. Derrett, "Parable of the Unmerciful Servant," 33; D. Via, *Parables,* 138; J. Gnilka, *Matthäus,* 2:145; S. Lachs, *Rabbinic Commentary,* 272-73. W. Herzog, *Parables,* 137, considers the person coming before the king "a highly placed bureaucrat in the hierarchy of the court."

12. Cf. Norman A. Huffman, "Atypical Features in the Parables of Jesus," *JBL* 97 (1978): 207-20.

13. J. Jeremias, *Parables,* 210.

14. Josephus, *Ant.* 14.78.

15. Josephus, *Ant.* 17.319-20.

one who summons his slave is no longer called a "king" but the "lord" (or "master," κύριος) of that slave. Various interpreters suggest that the parable in the pre-Matthean tradition would have been about a wealthy master and his slave, and that Matthew has turned him into a king at 18:23.[16] That is possible, but not necessarily the case: (1) a king would be a slave's "lord" or "master" in the first place, and (2) typically the counterpart of a "slave" is a "lord" or "master." To speak of him as a king at the outset is sufficient to set the hearers' or readers' imaginations in motion to envisage the lord as a king in the scenes that follow.[17]

The legality of what the king orders is contested. Could a man, his wife, and children actually be sold for a debt he owes? According to the Torah, a man can be sold as a slave if he cannot make restitution for theft (Exod 22:1), and there are OT passages referring to the sale of children as slaves for the debt of their deceased father (2 Kings 4:1) or to pay off debts during a time of famine (Neh 5:5). But there are no legal grounds in Jewish law for the sale of a man in debt.[18] Nevertheless, Palestine was under Roman rule, and kings known to the hearers and readers of the parable were not observant Jews. Parables that have kings as major figures within them — whether they be parables of Jesus or of the rabbis (and there are plenty in both cases)[19] — can be expected to portray them in ways that the popular imagination supposed that they would act. As stock characters, they are typically wealthy, powerful, and ruthless. That is what kings are supposed to be, and if that were not the image desired, the storyteller should use a figure other than a king.

In addition to the question of the legality of the king's action, other questions are often raised by the modern reader: How would the sale of the slave and his family into the hands of another master lead to the repayment of the debt? Or why could not the debtor pay at least part of his debt and be on good terms? At this point it has to be said that some questions are out of order in listening to a parable; by asking them, one ruins a good story.

18:26. The slave "fell down" (πεσών, an aorist participle, "after he had fallen down") and "did obeisance" (προσεκύνει). The first of these verbs is

16. M. de Boer, "Ten Thousand Talents?" 226-27; J. Lambrecht, *Treasure*, 60-61; W. D. Davies and D. C. Allison, *Matthew*, 2:796-97. A. McNeile, *Matthew*, 269; and J. Jeremias, *Parables*, 28 (n. 17), consider it a possibility.

17. E. Linnemann, *Parables*, 175 (n. 8).

18. S. Lachs, *Rabbinic Commentary*, 273. Lachs points out that the passages in Jewish literature cited in Str-B 1:797 have to do with imprisonment for theft, not debt.

19. In the case of Jesus, cf. Matt 22:2-14; 25:31-46; Luke 14:31-33. According to H. McArthur and R. Johnston, *They Also Taught in Parables: Rabbinic Parables from the First Centuries of the Christian Era* (Grand Rapids: Zondervan, 1990), 174, kings are prominent in approximately half of the rabbinic parables. Twenty-four king parables are dealt with by David Stern, *Parables in Midrash: Narrative and Exegesis in Rabbinic Literature* (Cambridge: Harvard University Press, 1991).

regularly associated with the second to express devotion to a high-ranking person, especially when making a petition.[20] The second is used either with the first or independently to designate the custom of prostrating oneself before a king.[21] The slave asks that the king be patient with him. And then he says that he will pay "everything" (πάντα) that he owes. The promise is brash, to say the least. It would be impossible for anyone to pay such a debt, even if more time were allowed. There would not be enough years in the lifetime of the slave to pay it off.

18:27. The term for having compassion (σπλαγχνίζομαι) occurs a dozen times in the NT (in the Gospels only).[22] Apart from its use here and in two other parables in Luke's Gospel — the Good Samaritan (10:33) and the Prodigal Son (15:20) — the term is not used in reference to the emotions of persons. It is used in reference to God, expressing the divine compassion that is revealed in Jesus.[23] In this parable (as well as in the other two) the term is used in reference to persons who reflect divine compassion. The contrasting term (that the king "was angry") appears in 18:34.

The king cancels the debt. The term used here for "debt" is δάνειον — appearing only here in the NT — which normally means a "loan."[24] Some interpreters have made note of the noun and have considered it as decisive in some way for interpreting the parable,[25] or else have concluded that it is an ill-chosen word to translate a word from an Aramaic version of the parable.[26] But actually the word need not have such a narrow meaning. It is used (as here) with the verb ἀπολύω ("to release") in reference to the Jubilee in the writings of Josephus, in which he says that all "debtors are freed from their debts."[27] So here the king "freed" the slave (from his debt),[28] and "forgave him the debt." The second clause appears to be redundant, but the use of the verb "forgive"

20. BAGD 659 (πίπτω, 1, b, ב), citing Dan 3:5; Matt 2:11; 4:9; Rev 5:14; 19:4; 22:8; Josephus, *Ant.* 10.213.

21. Cf. 2 Sam 18:28; 24:20; 1 Kings 1:16, 53 (προσεκύνησεν τῷ βασιλεῖ (LXX, 2 Kgdms 18:28; 24:20; 3 Kgdms 1:16, 53).

22. Mark 1:41; 6:34//Matt 14:14; Mark 8:2//Matt 15:32; Mark 9:22; Matt 9:36; 18:27; 20:34; Luke 7:13; 10:33; 15:20.

23. Cf. Helmut Koester, "σπλάγχνον," *TDNT* 7:553-55.

24. LSJ 369; BAGD 170.

25. T. W. Manson, *Sayings,* 213: "the debtor had been working with capital lent for that purpose. . . . His deficiency could then be regarded as embezzlement." Cf. also J. Derrett, "Parable of the Unmerciful Servant," 39-40.

26. J. Jeremias, *Parables,* 211.

27. Josephus, *Ant.* 3.282: οἵ τε χρεῶσται τῶν δανείων ἀπολύονται; quoted from *Josephus,* trans. Henry St. J. Thackeray et al., LCL, 10 vols. (Cambridge: Harvard University Press, 1961-81), 4:454.

28. Contra the view that the king "freed" him from the hands of the officers who were about to take (or return) him to prison, as in J. Derrett, "Parable of the Unmerciful Servant," 33.

(ἀφίημι) is significant metaphorically, for it is the usual word used for the act of forgiving sins (e.g., Matt 6:14-15; Mark 2:5-10; Luke 7:47-49; 11:4) and the forgiving of others (Matt 18:21, 35).

The slave is not simply given an extension, which is all he had asked for, but he is forgiven the entire debt.

The king is a metaphor for God as elsewhere in parables of Jesus (Matt 22:2-14; 25:31-46) and often in rabbinic parables.[29]

18:28. The debt of the fellow slave is 100 denarii. A denarius was a silver coin worth one day's wages for a common laborer.[30] One hundred denarii would equal about four months' wages (figuring 24 workdays per month). The ratio of the two debts would therefore have been immense (about 600,000 to 1).[31]

The imagery of seizing a debtor by the throat is found also in the *Mishnah*.[32] The Greek construction εἴ τι ὀφείλεις (literally, "if you owe anything," which is unfitting, since it is known that the second slave does owe the first) would be expressed in classical Greek as ὅ τι ἂν ὀφείλῃς ("whatever you owe").[33]

18:29. The petition of the slave in 18:29 is virtually identical to that of 18:26, but it is actually a bit more modest. It is not as grandiloquent as that of the first slave, who confidently says that he can and will pay "everything" that he owes (18:29).

18:30-31. The refusal is quick, and retaliation is decisive. Putting his fellow slave in prison for debt was an act forbidden by Jewish law from biblical to talmudic times.[34] But various sources indicate that it was a widespread custom allowed by Greco-Roman law in the first century (and reflected in the Q saying, Matt 5:25-26//Luke 12:57-59).[35] The slave's act toward his fellow slave is swift indeed; one should normally expect a court procedure prior to imprisonment (cf. Matt 5:25-26//Luke 12:58-59), which is not mentioned here. But such details need not impede the progress of a parable.

The reaction of additional fellow slaves is to be "extremely upset" (ἐλυπήθησαν σφόδρα; RSV, NRSV, and NIV have "greatly distressed"). The ex-

---

29. Cf. n. 17 above. Contra R. Gundry, *Matthew*, 373, who claims that "lord" is a designation for Jesus as Lord.

30. John W. Betlyon, "Coinage," *ABD* 1:1086; a denarius was the usual daily wage for soldiers and farm workers in the first century A.D., according to K. Harl, *Coinage*, 278-79.

31. The first slave's debt of 10,000 talents would equal 60,000,000 denarii (one talent = 6,000 denarii), which is 600,000 times more than his fellow slave's debt of 100 denarii.

32. *M. B. Bat.* 10:8.

33. Cf. BDF 191 (#376).

34. Menachem Elon, "Imprisonment for Debt," *EncJud* 8:1304.

35. Adolf Deissmann, *Light from the Ancient East*, rev. ed. (New York: George H. Doran Company, 1972), 270, illustrates this from the Florentine Papyrus (ca. A.D. 85) and others; various sources are cited by S. Arbandt and W. Macheiner, "Gefangenschaft," *RAC* 9:327-28.

pression is used twice more in this Gospel (17:23; 26:22) to express feelings of dread.

18:32-33. The term "wicked slave" as a form of address appears also at 25:26//Luke 19:22 (Q, Greek words reversed). The first act of forgiveness was a response to a simple petition (18:32, referring back to 18:26) and based on "mercy" (18:33, referring back to 18:27, where the basis is actually the synonym "compassion"). Since he had been the recipient of mercy, he should have had extended mercy to his fellow servant.

18:34. More evident in Greek than in English, the phrase "And [his] lord was angry" (καὶ ὀργισθεὶς ὁ κύριος) stands in stark contrast to "And being moved by compassion, [his] lord . . ." (σπλαγχνισθεὶς δὲ ὁ κύριος) in 18:27.

The Greek expression τοῖς βασανισταῖς can mean "to the torturers, jailers."[36] The noun is found only here in the NT. Modern translations use such expressions as "to the tormenters" (KJV), "to the jailers" (RSV), "to torture" (NEB), "to be tortured" (NRSV), "to the jailers to be tortured" (NIV), or the like. The appropriate translation in this case should be related to realities of the time.

Jewish law provided for various forms of punishment, such as fines, imprisonment, flogging, and capital punishment. Flogging would be closest to torture, but it was allowed by Jewish law only as a corrective discipline, not for retribution.[37] On the other hand, stories of torture were plentiful in Jewish literature concerning non-Jewish despots, as in tales of the torture of Jews by Antiochus IV Epiphanes, Herod the Great, and the Romans.[38]

In 18:34 the king hands the slave over to be dealt with severely. It is not likely that he hands him over for incarceration. The use of the Greek term always has the nuance of torture, and kings in parables can do as they please. Therefore "to the torturers" (as in NRSV) seems to be the best translation.

The wording of the final clause ("until he should pay all the debt") is almost identical to that of 18:30, except that the word "all" appears here.

The slave has lost not only the forgiveness that he had received; his debt is back on his shoulders, and he must now face torture, which will no doubt lead to premature death. In any case, since there is no possibility of paying his debt of 10,000 talents, he will be among the torturers as long as he lives.

18:35. The verse makes an application, and the point of comparison is made as explicit as possible. Since God has forgiven the disciples so lavishly, they ought to forgive others in the same way. Theologically the verse recalls 6:15, a comment following the Lord's Prayer. Other passages that combine di-

36. BAGD 134.
37. Haim H. Cohn, "Flogging," *EncJud* 6:1348-51. The main Torah passage cited is Deut 25:1-3.
38. Regarding Antiochus, cf. 2 Macc 7:13, 17; 9:6; 4 Macc 6:10-11; 16:3, 5; regarding Herod, cf. Josephus, *J.W.* 1.548 (//*Ant.* 16.388); *Ant.* 16.245-52, 315, 320; 17.56-57; regarding the Romans, cf. *J.W.* 5.435-37; *Ant.* 19.34-35.

vine and human forgiveness — making the first a basis for the latter — are Sirach 28:1-7; Mark 11:25; and Matthew 6:12. To forgive the other "from the heart" means to forgive genuinely, not hypocritically (cf. *T. Gad* 6.3, in which "from the heart" is in contrast to deceit; Matt 15:19).

The teaching here is hortatory by intent, not a dogmatic statement for all time. Surely the parable does not teach that forgiving others is a prerequisite or means for gaining God's forgiveness. If human forgiveness is a precondition for divine forgiveness, no one can ever be forgiven by God. Human forgiveness is never perfect. One must rely on the mercy of God even when one's own best efforts to forgive have been made. The parable and its application seek to move the disciple to forgive: Since you have been forgiven so much, how can you not forgive the other person?

Critical questions are raised concerning the authenticity of the parable, its application, and its setting in Matthew's Gospel. Concerning the question of its authenticity, some interpreters claim that it was composed by the evangelist himself, basing their view on the fact that the passage contains an uncommonly high proportion of Matthean words and phrases.[39] Yet, in spite of that, others have concluded that it is an authentic parable of Jesus.[40] The Matthean words and phrases can be accounted for on the grounds that the evangelist was the first to place the parable in written form. Its use of hyperbole, its imagery of a king as symbolic of God, and its radical emphasis on the need to forgive are characteristic of the proclamation of Jesus.

Having said that, it is clear that the introduction (18:23a) has been recast into a familiar Matthean phrase; it is identical to what one finds at 13:24 and 22:2 except for the additional "therefore" (διὰ τοῦτο), which is also Matthean (used ten times in the Gospel, often to introduce dominical sayings; see comment on 18:23). The final verse (18:35) is also, in its present form, cast into Matthean terminology by its use of "heavenly Father" (cf. 5:48; 6:14, 26, 32; 15:13; 23:9) and "brother" for another member of the Christian community (cf. 5:22-24, 47; 7:3-5; 10:21; 18:15, 21; 23:8).

---

39. A list is provided by R. Gundry, *Matthew*, 371-72. According to Michael D. Goulder, *Midrash and Lection in Matthew* (London: SPCK, 1974), 402-4, the imagery is typically Matthean, and some 79 of the 214 words in the parable can be considered Matthean. Cf. also John Drury, *The Parables in the Gospels: History and Allegory* (New York: Crossroad, 1985), 92. The parable is an end-product of various stages of tradition, but composed at a pre-Matthean stage, according to Ivor H. Jones, *The Matthean Parables: A Literary and Historical Commentary*, NovTSup 80 (Leiden: E. J. Brill, 1995), 211-26.

40. A. Jülicher, *Gleichnisreden*, 2:305, 314; C. Montefiore, *Synoptic Gospels*, 2:685; J. Jeremias, *Parables*, 213; A. Weiser, *Knechtsgleichnisse*, 94-98; C. Dietzfelbinger, "Der Gleichnis von der erlassenen Schuld," 448-51; J. Gnilka, *Matthäus*, 2:148; J. Lambrecht, *Treasure*, 62-63; U. Luz, *Matthäus*, 3:66-68; W. D. Davies and D. C. Allison, *Matthew*, 2:794. The text (18:23-34 only) is printed in pink (= Jesus uttered something like this) in R. Funk, *Five Gospels*, 217-18.

Matthew has set the parable within a longer section on forgiveness within the community. The setting can be considered Matthew's own, but the question to be faced is whether that setting has distorted the meaning of the parable. Moreover, has the application (18:35) done so as well? The charge has been made that, since the parable has nothing to do with repeated forgiveness, it does not fit the Matthean context of 18:21-22.[41] Furthermore, the king (= God) does not live up to the saying about repeated forgiveness at all!

Some interpreters have tried to rescue the situation by saying that 18:21-22 deals with the quantity of forgiveness, and that 18:23-34 deals with its quality.[42] It seems sufficient to say that there is no need for the parable to be an amplification of the saying of Jesus in 18:22. The subject is forgiveness within the community. The point is made as strongly as possible that one is obligated to forgive on the basis of having been forgiven; that is stated most explicitly at 18:33.[43] That also means that the setting and the application (18:35), though Matthean by design in both cases, actually interpret the parable rather than distort it.

Yet there is more to this parable than exhortation and warning. The hearer and reader are reminded again and again that God deals with his children by grace (= favor) in a way that surpasses all human calculations of benevolence. The first slave petitions the king to be benevolent toward him and his family; he asks for more time. The king is not obliged in any way even to be benevolent. But he is more than benevolent; he cancels the slave's entire debt (18:27). Compassion (18:27) and mercy (18:33) are extended beyond what anyone could expect.

In this regard, the parable is a parable of hyperbole and surprise concerning God. No actual king would act in that way; no king would cancel such a huge debt. But God's actions surpass all human ways of acting by far. And because God is so hyperbolically portrayed in the proclamation of Jesus, the hearer and reader are faced with the question of their relationships, particularly their own manner of forgiveness (or lack thereof).

Exposition

The parable has to do with the Forgiver and the forgiven. In commenting on this text, Anders Nygren once wrote:

> The feature of the Divine Agape that is most prominent here is its boundless and its unconditional character. But if God's love and His will to forgive is

---

41. A. Jülicher, *Gleichnisreden*, 2:313; J. Jeremias, *Parables*, 97; N. Perrin, *Teaching*, 125; E. Linnemann, *Parables*, 107.

42. J. Gnilka, *Matthäus*, 2:143; J. Donahue, *Parable*, 73; J. Lambrecht, *Treasure*, 56.

43. Thus, with minor variations, E. Linnemann, *Parables*, 110; J. Donahue, *Parable*, 77; A. Weiser, *Knechtsgleichnisse*, 97-98; J. Lambrecht, *Treasure*, 63; B. Scott, *Parable*, 269; D. Hagner, *Matthew*, 540-41.

boundless and unconditional, it demands of those who receive its forgiveness that their love and forgiveness shall likewise be boundless and unconditional.[44]

The immediate problem of dealing with the parable may be how to "translate" the meaning of 10,000 talents. It would consist of billions of dollars, to be sure. It is an amount that equals the annual wage of up to 200,000 persons. One might be able to compare the number of persons to the population of a city. Or one can compare the value of the money involved to the annual payroll of some large multinational corporation.[45]

The humor of the parable should not be lost. Needless to say, no one could ever acquire such a debt. And what follows is just as astounding. The slave pleads for more time to pay the debt. He actually has the gall to say that he will pay everything he owes, if he can only have more time. The idea that he could pay it off is as fantastic as the debt itself.

But what does the king do when the man pleads for more time? He says in effect, "Ah, forget it. You don't have to pay me back anything at all. Go on home."

The slave who gets off lightly is a scoundrel. He will not forgive his fellow slave who owes him approximately four months' wages.

The slave who will not forgive represents potentially the hearer and reader of the parable. As one who has been forgiven so much by God, a disciple of Jesus cannot be stingy in forgiving others. Unless one is as ready to forgive others as God forgives, that person is like the slave who refuses to forgive his fellow slave.

The story is told that in a certain village in Africa there was a medicine man (not to be confused with a witch doctor). When people came to him due to illness, he did not ask, "Where is your pain?" The question he would ask is, "With whom have you had a dispute? If you want to get well, first you must take care of your relationship with that other person. You must forgive. You must be reconciled."[46]

Perhaps there is something etched in the physical and mental makeup of people that says that forgiving others is good for their health.

44. Anders Nygren, *Agape and Eros* (Philadelphia: Westminster Press, 1953), 91.

45. For example, at the time of writing, according to figures given by General Motors on the Internet, GM had some 647,000 employees in 190 countries. That number is too large. But — to approach a more fitting figure — GM North America (United States, Canada, and Mexico) had a workforce of 170,478. The annual payroll of GM North America is therefore somewhat smaller than, but comparable to, the value of 10,000 talents — not in real dollars, but in purchasing power in the first century A.D.

46. According to traditional thinking in parts of Africa, "many of the causes [of illness] can be traced back to jealousy, hatred or relationships which have gone sour." Quoted from Gerhardus C. Oosthuizen, *The Healer-Prophet in Afro-Christian Churches*, SCM 3 (Leiden: E. J. Brill, 1992), 54; cf. also p. 75. The importance of reconciliation in healing is discussed on pp. 120-22.

In any case, forgiveness is expected of the disciple of Jesus. The message of the parable is clear. To live well means to live with a generous and forgiving heart. The presupposition of it all, however, is the extraordinary gospel of God's compassion and mercy. Gospel, exhortation, and warning are woven together in this text — but in that order.

Select Bibliography

Boer, Martinus C. de. "Ten Thousand Talents? Matthew's Interpretation and Redaction of the Parable of the Unforgiving Servant (Matt. 18:23-35)." *CBQ* 50 (1988): 214-32.

Buckley, Thomas W. *Seventy Times Seven: Sin, Judgment, and Forgiveness in Matthew.* Collegeville, Minn.: Liturgical Press, 1991.

Cranfield, C. E. B. "The Parable of the Unmerciful Servant." *ExpTim* 104 (1993): 339-41.

Deidun, Thomas. "The Parable of the Unmerciful Servant (Mt 18:23-35)." *BTB* 6 (1976): 203-24.

Deiss, Lucien. "La Parabole du debiteur impitoyable." *ASeign* 76 (1964): 29-47.

Derrett, J. Duncan M. "Law in the New Testament: The Parable of the Unmerciful Servant." *RIDA* 12 (1965): 3-19. Reprinted as "The Parable of the Unmerciful Servant," in his *Law in the New Testament*, 32-47. London: Darton, Longman & Todd, 1970.

Dietzfelbinger, Christian. "Das Gleichnis von der erlassenen Schuld: Eine theologische Untersuchung von Matthäus 18,23-35." *EvT* 32 (1972): 437-51.

Fuchs, Ernst. "The Parable of the Unmerciful Servant." *SE* 1 [= TU 73] (1959): 487-94.

Güttgemanns, Erhardt. "Narrative Analyse synoptischer Texte." *LingBibl* 25 (1973): 50-73.

Harl, Kenneth W. *Coinage in the Roman Economy, 300 B.C. to A.D. 700.* Baltimore: Johns Hopkins University Press, 1996.

Keesmaat, Sylvia C. "Strange Neighbors and Risky Care (Matt 18:21-35; Luke 14:7-14; Luke 10:25-37)." In *The Challenge of Jesus' Parables*, 263-85. Ed. Richard N. Longenecker. Grand Rapids: Wm. B. Eerdmans, 2000.

Kelly, Louis G. "Cultural Consistency in Translation." *BT* 21 (1970): 170-75.

Patte, Daniel. "Bringing Out of the Gospel-Treasure What Is New and What Is Old: Two Parables in Matthew 18–23." *QR* 10 (1990): 79-108.

Scott, Bernard B. "The King's Accounting: Matthew 18:23-34." *JBL* 104 (1985): 429-42.

Scott, R. B. Y. "Weights and Measures of the Bible." *BA* 22 (1959): 22-40.

Senior, Donald. "Matthew 18:21-35." *Int* 41 (1987): 403-7.

Weber, Beat. "Alltagswelt und Gottesreich: Überlegungen zum Verstehenshintergrund des Gleichnisses vom 'Schalksknecht' (Matthäus 18,23-34)." *BZ* 37 (1993): 161-82.

———. "Vergeltung oder Vergebung!? Matthäus 18,21-35 auf den Hintergrund des 'Erlassjahres.'" *TZ* 50 (1994): 124-51.

2.2. The Workers in the Vineyard, Matthew 20:1-16

[Jesus said,] 1*"For the kingdom of heaven is like a landowner who went out early in the morning to hire workers for his vineyard.* 2*After agreeing with the workers for the usual daily wage, he sent them into his vineyard.*

3*"And going out about the third hour he saw others standing idle in the marketplace;* 4*and to them he said, 'You go into the vineyard too, and whatever is right I will give you.' So they went.*

5*"Going out again about the sixth hour and the ninth hour, he did the same.* 6*And about the eleventh hour he went out and found others standing; and he said to them, 'Why do you stand here idle all day?'* 7*They said to him, 'Because no one has hired us.' He said to them, 'You go into the vineyard too.'*

8*"And when evening came, the owner of the vineyard said to his manager, 'Call the workers and pay them their wages, beginning with the last, up to the first.'*

9*"And when those hired about the eleventh hour came, each of them received the usual daily wage.*

10*"Now when the first came, they thought they would receive more; but each of them also received the usual daily wage.* 11*And on receiving it they grumbled at the landowner,* 12*saying, 'These last worked only one hour, and you have made them equal to us who have borne the burden of the day and the scorching heat.'*

13*"But he replied to one of them, 'Friend, I am doing you no wrong; did you not agree with me for the usual daily wage?* 14*Take what belongs to you, and go; I choose to give to this last as I give to you.* 15*Or am I not allowed to do what I choose with what belongs to me? Or is your eye evil because I am good?'*

16*"So the last will be first, and the first last."*

Notes on the Text and Translation

20:1, 11. The Greek term οἰκοδεσπότης (literally, "master of a house") is translated variously as "householder" (KJV, RSV) or "landowner" (NEB, NIV, NRSV). The man actually runs the whole estate and pays out of his own pocket (20:15), so "landowner" is suitable. At 20:8 he is called "owner [Greek: κύριος] of the vineyard" in most of the translations mentioned (RSV, NEB, NIV, NRSV); KJV has "lord of the vineyard."

20:8. The Greek term ἐπίτροπος is translated as "steward" (KJV, RSV, NEB), "manager" (NRSV), or "foreman" (NIV). The term "steward" is rather archaic in modern English; a "foreman" is often part of a labor force itself, serving as its leader; a "manager" is decidedly a part of management and is to be preferred in this instance.

20:2, 9, 10, 13. The Greek term δηνάριος can be transliterated as "denarius" (RSV, NIV) or translated as "usual daily wage" (NRSV; NEB has "usual day's wage" [20:2], "the full day's wage" [20:9], and "the usual wage for the day" [20:13]). The denarius was a silver coin that had the value of one day's wages for a common laborer.[1] Although a bit cumbersome, "usual daily wage" communicates better than the transliterated term.

20:15. The verse begins with ἤ ("or") in the 26th and 27th editions of the Nestle-Aland Greek text. The conjunction is not printed in earlier editions nor in the Westcott-Hort edition. Nor is it represented in modern English versions (KJV, RSV, NEB, NIV, NRSV). The weight of evidence is slightly in favor of inclusion,[2] however, and is reflected in the translation above.

20:16. Some ancient witnesses (Greek uncials C, D, W, Θ, and others [the Majority text], plus Latin, Syriac, and Coptic texts) have an additional clause to what is already there, which can be translated: "for many are called but few chosen." That is reflected in the KJV. But the shorter reading is supported by major Alexandrian texts (the Greek uncials ℵ, B, and other ancient versions). It has probably been interpolated from 22:14.[3] It is not included in the Westcott-Hort and Nestle-Aland editions of the Greek text, nor is it represented in more recent English versions (RSV, NEB, NIV, NRSV).

Other textual critical issues exist, but they often have to do with word order and other minor variations that do not affect the meaning of the text.

Exegetical Commentary

The parable is found only in the Gospel of Matthew among the canonical Gospels, and it has no parallels in noncanonical Gospels. There are, however, rabbinic tales of later dates that have some similarities.[4] The closest in content is one concerning a certain Rabbi Zeira (ca. A.D. 325), who gave a funeral oration upon the death of Rabbi Bun, son of Rabbi Hiyya, who had died very young. In that parable Rabbi Zeira tells of a king who hired many workers, and he noticed that one was especially skillful. He asked the man to accompany him as he walked about. At the end of the day he paid him the same amount as he paid the other workers. The workmen grumbled, and the story continues:

1. John W. Betlyon, "Coinage," *ABD* 1:1086.
2. B. Metzger, *TCGNT* 50-51.
3. Ibid., 51.
4. Relevant rabbinic parallels are presented in S. Lachs, *Rabbinic Commentary,* 333-34, and C. Hezser, *Lohnmetaphorik,* 301-10; one is printed in Harvey K. McArthur and Robert M. Johnston, *They Also Taught in Parables: Rabbinic Parables from the First Centuries of the Christian Era* (Grand Rapids: Zondervan Publishing House, 1990), 58; summaries of others are on p. 190. The texts are *y. Ber.* 2:3c; *Eccl. Rab.* 5:11; *Cant. Rab.* 6:2.

"We have been working hard all the day, and this one who only laboured two hours receives as much salary as we do." "It is," answered the king, "because he has done more in two hours than you in the entire day. In the same manner [Rabbi Bun], although he had only studied the Law up to the age of twenty-eight, knew it better than a learned man or a pious man who would have studied it up to the age of a hundred years."[5]

Like the Parable of the Workers in the Vineyard, this one speaks of equal pay for all, regardless of the hours worked. But there is a major difference between them. In this story the one who receives pay equal to all the rest is given such because he has "done more in two hours" than those who worked "the entire day." In the parable of Jesus, however, those who receive pay equal to the all the rest are recipients of the extreme generosity of a very unusual employer; there is no hint that they performed as much work as or more work than the others.

The parable appears relatively late in Matthew's narration of the ministry of Jesus. It is set within the Judean ministry (19:1–20:34) prior to Jesus' entry into Jerusalem (21:1). It is addressed to the disciples (cf. 19:23).

The parable is a parable of the kingdom of heaven (or reign of God, 20:1). By means of it Jesus illustrates God's way of reigning in grace. It contains a surprise ending, in which there is equal pay for all of the workers, which is undeserved by those who had been hired later in the day than those who had worked all day. The parable surely does not make an economic prescription; its outcome is untypical of ordinary life, and that is what makes it so memorable.[6]

The parable can be divided into two chief parts: (1) the recruiting of the laborers for the vineyard in the morning and throughout the day (20:1-7); and (2) the settling up in the evening (20:8-15). The final saying (20:16) does not belong to the parable proper.

20:1-2. The expression "the kingdom of heaven is like" is a typical introductory phrase that introduces other Matthean parables (13:31, 33, 44, 45, 47).[7] It has been formulated by the evangelist, but signifying that the parable is a parable concerning the kingdom could be traditional. The comparison is not between the kingdom and a landowner, but between the kingdom and what follows in the parable as a whole. It is the case with the kingdom as with what follows.[8]

The time of the landowner's going out is not specified except that it was early in the morning. The hearer or reader is to imagine that it would be early

<hr/>

5. *Y. Ber.* 2:3c; quoted from *The Jerusalem Talmud: Berakhoth,* trans. Moses Schwab (New York: Hermon Press, 1969), 51. The rabbi's name is given as R. Aboon in the text, rather than the more usual R. Bun (used above).

6. Cf. J. Donahue, *Parable,* 81.

7. But the phrase could be traditional. The related expression "the kingdom of God is like" (with ὁμοία plus dative) appears at Luke 13:18.

8. Cf. J. Jeremias, *Parables,* 101.

enough to enlist workers who would begin their work at sunrise (cf. Ps 104:22-23), typically about 6:00 a.m.[9] That time is implied also by what follows. The next three times of recruitment are in segments of three hours each (20:3-5). Since the next time of hiring is at 9:00 a.m., the time of hiring the first group of workers would be 6:00 a.m. They are supposed to work for the entire day, as the promise of a day's wage implies. A denarius was considered adequate pay for a day's work,[10] neither generous nor miserly.[11]

The manner of recruiting workers is a familiar sight even today. The traveler to the Middle East can observe day laborers who wait beside streets or at street corners early in the morning to be hired by landowners or others who have work for them. One finds the same scene played out in various parts of the world (including the United States) wherever there are fruit and vegetable crops that need planting, weeding, or harvesting by migrant and other temporary workers. Those looking for work stand at a place where landowners can come in trucks and hire as many as they need.

The laborers portrayed in the parable have no permanent employment, no ongoing economic relationship with an employer. In this respect they differ from "slaves" who have permanent work on an estate. Their lives and livelihoods are less secure than those of slaves, since their employment is seasonal.[12]

The landowner who goes out to hire laborers is surely a metaphor for God[13] (cf. the designation of him as ὁ κύριος ["the lord/Lord"] at 20:8). Jesus' parables typically speak of kings, fathers, and masters as the major figures, and in each case the hearer or reader makes the metaphorical connection. To do so is not to allegorize.[14] To fail to do so, or to refuse to do so, is to tear the parables from their symbolic universe. That the landowner is a metaphor for God is confirmed by the use of the figure of a vineyard, which is a traditional symbol for Israel (Isa 5:1-7; Jer 12:10; Mark 12:1-12//Matt 21:33-46//Luke 20:9-19). The parable itself may not have to do with Israel specifically, but since the lord of the vineyard in Jewish tradition is God, so too in this case. Furthermore, "the

9. The usual working day for a laborer was from sunrise to sunset (twelve hours), according to Gustaf Dalman, *Arbeit und Sitte in Palästina*, 7 vols. (Gütersloh: Verlag C. Bertelsmann et al., 1928-41), 1:43-44. For other references, cf. Str-B 1:830.

10. Cf. Tob 5:15; other references in Jewish literature are given by J. Heinemann, "Status of the Labourer," 275 (n. 21). Cf. also J. Betlyon, "Coinage," *ABD* 1:1086. A denarius was the usual daily wage for a soldier or farm laborer in the first century A.D., according to K. Harl, *Coinage in the Roman Economy*, 278-79.

11. W. D. Davies and D. C. Allison, *Matthew*, 3:72.

12. On the seasonal employment and nonemployment of agricultural employees, cf. J. Heinemann, "Status of the Labourer," 272-73, 277.

13. Contra W. Herzog, *Parables*, 82, 84, 96, who disparages the "assumption" (his term on p. 84). B. Scott, *Parable*, 284, seems to dismiss the view that the landowner is a metaphor for God, but then on p. 297 he seems to take it for granted.

14. Contra V. Shillington, "Saving Life and Keeping Sabbath," 90-91.

metaphorical representation of God as an employer is quite popular in Judaism, and this is not the only Jewish parable to explain God's dealings with the human race in terms of the behavior of an employer."[15]

20:3-5. The landowner went out to hire more workers as the day wore on. These were at the third hour (20:3, 9:00 a.m.), the sixth hour (20:5, noon), and the ninth hour (20:5, 3:00 p.m.). That he would pay each "whatever is right" (20:4) implies that the pay would be proportionate, that is, less than a day's wages in each case. Whatever that will be, the actual amount to be paid remains suspended until the end of the story, adding suspense to it.

Interpreters raise the question why the landowner has to go out more than once to hire workers. Why did he not hire a sufficient number when he went out early in the morning? Scholars have speculated as to the reason. One proposal is that the work was particularly urgent; it had to be done prior to the onset of the rainy season.[16] A second proposal is that it was late August or early September; the grapes must be picked; it is probably a Friday; and the work has to be finished by sundown, the onset of the sabbath.[17] But neither of these proposals is sound. For one thing, they turn the parable into an account of an actual event. Moreover, if an actual event is being referred to, the landowner would surely have been aware of either of those conditions at the beginning of the day and would have hired all he needed.

Another proposal is that the landowner was out to exploit the workers. He had to bargain with those hired at the beginning of the day, but after that he did not have to. He could take advantage of their lack of employment.[18] In that way he could get very cheap labor. But that explanation is insufficient too, for in the end he pays those hired from mid-morning to late afternoon a full day's wage.

Still another proposal made is that it was only later in the day that some of the workers would show up.[19] But that view is contradicted by what is said in 20:6: the workers have been standing idle "all day." The only sufficient reply to the question of why the landowner hired workers at different times is that it makes a grand story consisting of a crescendo of events that leads up to the end that has been planned all along, when payments are made. The story has been composed with its end in view. It has not been composed as the narration of events in real life, starting from the beginning and ending in due course.

20:6-7. The first part of the parable comes to an end with the hiring of the "eleventh hour workers" about 5:00 p.m. The ending to this part is important,

---

15. L. Schottroff, "Human Solidarity and the Goodness of God," 135-36; she cites parables illustrated in Str-B 4:492-93.

16. J. Jeremias, *Parables*, 136; E. Schweizer, *Matthew*, 392.

17. J. Derrett, "Workers in the Vineyard," 72.

18. F. Herzog, *Parables*, 85-86.

19. F. Beare, *Matthew*, 402.

for even though five groups of workers are hired, the essential contrast in the parable is between those hired early and who work all day and those hired later who work for only one hour; only those two groups are mentioned when payments are made (20:8-10).[20] The landowner asks why they are "idle" (RSV, NRSV). The Greek term is ἀργός (literally "without work" or "unemployed"). There is no negative judgment placed upon them, as though they are lazy.[21] Their response that no one has hired them bears that out.

20:8-11. The second major part of the parable begins at 20:8. With the coming of the evening, it is necessary to pay the workers, as the law prescribed (Lev 19:13; Deut 24:14-15).[22] The landowner, now called "owner of the vineyard" (RSV, NEB, NIV, NRSV), orders the payments to be made, and they are made by the manager of the vineyard (and therefore of the workforce as well) on behalf of the owner.

Payments are made, beginning with the last hired. The sequence is surprising. One would expect that those hired earliest would come first, followed by the others, concluding with those hired last. Those who had been hired first and paid first would then be on their way and not observe what the others received.[23] But the parable contains a dramatic touch at this point. When a full day's wage is paid to those who worked for only one hour, there is suspense in the minds of all those who worked longer, particularly those who worked all day. The imagination of the hearer or reader of the parable goes to work. Those who worked longer will inevitably think that they will receive more. The thought is expressed in 20:10.

In the end, however, all the workers receive equal pay — one denarius (20:9, 10), the amount promised to those hired at the beginning of the day (20:2). Those hired early in the morning receive no more than those hired in the eleventh hour.

20:12. Those hired at daybreak object to the transaction. They charge the landowner with two injustices; he failed to take into account (1) the amount of time that they had spent on the job in contrast to the others; and (2) the fact that they had borne the heat of the day, while the others had not.[24] "For them (as for us!) this equal treatment is in fact unequal treatment."[25]

---

20. Cf. R. Bultmann, *HST* 190; Craig L. Blomberg, *Interpreting the Parables* (Downers Grove, Ill.: InterVarsity Press, 1990), 221; J. Lambrecht, *Treasure*, 73-74; W. D. Davies and D. C. Allison, *Matthew*, 3:72.

21. Contra J. Jeremias, *Parables*, 136-37, who says the question is a reproach, and that the workers' response "conceals their characteristic oriental indifference"!

22. That the law would have been effective in the first century is attested by its currency even in the second (*m. B. Mes.* 9:12).

23. D. Via, *Parables*, 148; E. Schweizer, *Matthew*, 392; R. Gundry, *Matthew*, 397; cf. J. Donahue, *Parable*, 80.

24. J. Jeremias, *Parables*, 137; R. Gundry, *Matthew*, 298.

25. J. Lambrecht, *Treasure*, 76.

20:13-15. The landowner retorts with a twofold response: (1) he had paid them what he owed (20:13), so he did not commit an injustice; and (2) his generosity to the others is not an injustice to them.[26] He also implies with his question at 20:15b that those who complain are envious.

The landowner addresses one of the workers with the term "friend" (20:13), a vocative in Greek (ἑταῖρε). The term is used in the same form in this Gospel also at 22:12 (where the king addresses the man without a wedding garment) and 26:50 (where Jesus addresses Judas in Gethsemane). The term is therefore not a positive one. It is used in cases where the person being addressed is insolent or deceitful and is being confronted and exposed.[27]

The response of the landowner is what has been called an instance of "reframing." The workers complain about unfairness, but the landowner does not give a direct response to their charge. He does not respond on their terms. Instead he comes up with a new frame of reference altogether, and that is the perspective of generosity.[28] The concepts of fairness and generosity are related sufficiently to make the transition possible from one to the other. But the shift calls for a whole new way of thinking, a new frame of reference for any future relationships.

At 20:15 both the NIV and the NRSV read: "Or are you envious because I am generous?" A literal translation of the Greek would be: "Or is your eye evil because I am good?" The "evil eye" is the eye of envy (cf. Sir 14:9-10: "the eye of the greedy person is not satisfied with his share. . . . An evil eye [ὀφθαλμὸς πονηρός] is envious over bread, and it is lacking on his table"). The term appears also at Sirach 31:13; Matthew 6:23; and Mark 7:22.[29]

20:16. This verse does not belong to the parable proper.[30] It is a floating

---

26. According to J. Crossan, *Parables*, 112-13, the parable ended at 20:13. Although he provides four reasons for his view, the result is unpersuasive. The assertion of the sovereign freedom of the landowner in 20:15 is crucial to the story, bringing the transactions of 20:8-9 (starting with the last, paying them more than expected) to a conclusion. Further, the expression of the contrast between the landowner's generosity and the envy of the workers in 20:15 coheres with the narrative.

27. Contra W. R. Herzog, *Parables*, 92, who says that the term is condescending and feigns courtesy.

28. Donald Capps, *Reframing: A New Method in Pastoral Care* (Minneapolis: Fortress Press, 1990), 60; cited by Robert G. Hughes, "Preaching the Parables," *The Promise and Practice of Biblical Theology*, ed. John Reumann (Minneapolis: Fortress Press, 1991), 167-68.

29. The metaphor is rooted in the saying of Deut 15:9 where one is warned lest "your eye act wickedly (πονηρεύσηται ὁ ὀφθαλμός σου) against your brother." A contrast between the "good eye" and the "evil eye" is attributed to Rabbi Eliezer (2d century A.D.) in *m. Abot* 2:9.

30. A. Jülicher, *Gleichnisreden*, 2:470-71; R. Bultmann, *HST* 177; T. W. Manson, *Sayings*, 220; C. H. Dodd, *Parables*, 94; B. Smith, *Parables*, 187; J. Jeremias, *Parables*, 36-37; E. Linnemann, *Parables*, 85-86; J. Lambrecht, *Treasure*, 71; D. Hagner, *Matthew*, 569; W. D. Davies and D. C. Allison, *Matthew*, 3:67.

saying that shows up elsewhere as well, including the verse just prior to the parable (19:30), so the parable is framed by the saying (cf. also Luke 13:30). To be sure, the saying is related to a portion of the parable itself (20:8), and that may well be the occasion for using it here.

Is the employer a good man or a bad one? The usual view is that he is good because of his grand generosity at the end. In fact, some interpreters prefer to give to the parable the title the Parable of the Good Employer, the Parable of the Generous Employer, or even the Parable of the Eccentric Employer.[31] C. H. Dodd has written:

> The point of the story is that the employer, out of sheer generosity and compassion for the unemployed, pays as large a wage to those who have worked for one hour as to those who have worked all day. It is a striking picture of the divine generosity which gives without regard to the measures of strict justice.[32]

On the other hand, it has been suggested that the landowner was a wealthy man who exploited those whom he hired. In this perspective he was hardly good, generous, or eccentric.[33] He seems to bargain with the first group early in the morning, but in fact he extends to them a "take it or leave it" proposition. In regard to those hired later, he does not bargain at all. He "takes advantage of an unemployed workforce to meet his harvesting needs by offering them work without a wage agreement."[34] But all this is to ruin a good story. It is difficult to deny that the employer is portrayed as unusually generous. (Those interpreters are correct who say that a denarius was not a generous wage.[35] Nevertheless, it was considered adequate.[36] But all that aside, the point of the man's generosity is not the payment of a denarius, but that he paid it to those who were hired later as well as those who worked all day.) From the outset he is portrayed as a fair man, promising the customary wage with the first group hired (20:2), and then promising to pay the next group "whatever is right" (or "just," δίκαιον, 20:4). Presumably he made the same promise to those hired at noon, and at 3:00 p.m. as well ("he did the same," 20:5). And then in the end he

---

31. J. Jeremias, *Parables*, 136, calls it "the parable of the Good Employer"; R. Fortna, "'You have made them equal to us,'" 72: Parable of the "Good (or Generous) Employer"; W. D. Davies and D. C. Allison, *Matthew*, 3:66: the "Generous Employer"; F. Beare, *Matthew*, 401: the "Parable of the Eccentric Employer"; R. Stein, *Parables*, 124: the "Gracious Employer."

32. C. H. Dodd, *Parables*, 94-95.

33. F. Herzog, *Parables*, 85-86.

34. Ibid., 86.

35. B. Scott, *Parable*, 283, 290-91; W. Herzog, *Parables*, 89-90.

36. Cf. K. Harl, *Coinage in the Roman Economy*, 278-80. Harl cites an example of a family of four living on 200 denarii per year in Italy (food and wine alone being calculated) and a family of four in Egypt on 125 tetradrachmae for a year (the latter equal to 125 denarii; cf. pp. 98 and 482 for the equivalency).

is more than just. He is extremely generous, as the words attest at the close of 20:15 ("because I am good"). Furthermore, if a "wage agreement" were worked out at each of the five stages of hiring, the effectiveness of the story at the end, when payments are made, would be undercut. As the parable stands, the hearer or reader is caught by surprise in the end, since the silence of the landowner leads one to expect that he will pay only "whatever is right," that is, a portion of a day's wage.

Discerning the point of comparison of the parable at the Matthean level must take into account certain redactional features. The use of γάρ ("for") at 20:1 indicates that the parable provides an elaboration on teaching that comes just prior to it in 19:30 and, perhaps more, concerning persons who will be first and last. Jesus has just declared to his disciples that they will have a role in carrying out the final judgment, and that all who have left earthly ties for his sake will receive a great reward ("a hundredfold," 19:29) and eternal life. Moreover, the parable is framed by passages concerning Peter (19:27), on the one hand, and concerning James and John (20:20-21), on the other. These three disciples had been called early on in the ministry of Jesus (4:18-22), and in the frame passages they either want to know about their reward for service (in the case of Peter, 19:27) or seek favors in the future kingdom (in the case of James and John by way of their mother's request, 20:21). These three were, in short, among the "first" of Jesus' disciples and the most worthy of rewards.[37] But what about others? For Matthew and his community the parable indicates that those who were called first will have no advantage in regard to salvation over those who are among the "last." The latter will also receive "a hundredfold," "eternal life," the same wages as those who had been disciples from the beginning. That is the way of God's ruling in grace. Neither time nor efforts in discipleship are decisive. What is decisive is that God's grace is beyond normal human expectations.

The parable is often considered by interpreters to have been spoken by Jesus.[38] If so, the question that arises is whether it would have been spoken to the disciples, as Matthew has it (cf. 19:23). It has been suggested and maintained

37. So also, with various nuances, T. W. Manson, *Sayings*, 218; J. Derrett, "Workers in the Vineyard," 90; J. Meier, *Vision*, 141; J. Donahue, *Parable*, 83-84; R. Smith, *Matthew*, 235-36; U. Luz, *Matthäus*, 3:153-55. Contra B. Scott, *Parable*, 285, who contends that, for Matthew, the "first" would have been the Pharisees and the "last" the disciples; contra also the view that the first are Jewish Christians and the last are Gentile Christians, as in R. Gundry, *Matthew*, 399; F. Beare, *Matthew*, 404; and D. Hagner, *Matthew*, 573. Other views are summarized in W. D. Davies and D. C. Allison, *Matthew*, 3.61.

38. C. H. Dodd, *Parables*, 95; C. Hezser, *Lohnmetaphorik*, 246-50; J. Derrett, "Workers in the Vineyard," 88-90; J. Lambrecht, *Treasure*, 74; H. Weder, *Gleichnisse*, 220 (n. 46); W. D. Davies and D. C. Allison, *Matthew*, 3:68-69; U. Luz, *Matthäus*, 3:141. R. Funk, *Five Gospels*, 224-25, prints Matt 20:1-15 in red font (= from Jesus), but 20:16 in pink (= Jesus probably said something like this).

widely that Jesus would have spoken the parable to his critics, such as certain Pharisees, who opposed his message and conduct, by which he proclaimed good news to those considered unworthy of it.[39] If such were the case, the parable has a double-edged meaning: God is gracious beyond normal human expectations, even to those who are considered unworthy, and it is a shame that some find fault with that.

It is difficult to discern the original occasion on which the parable would have been spoken. It is surely possible that the parable related to Peter, James, and John. Perhaps these original and notable apostles were upset that Jesus welcomed others into his fellowship, such as tax collectors and sinners. Jesus had to teach them about God's wider embrace (similar to the lesson that Jonah had to learn the hard way). Yet one can hardly refrain from the suspicion that originally the parable would have had a more general audience and application in the ministry of the earthly Jesus. If it were not for Matthew's framing it, one would expect it to have had a more public setting. It speaks of the mercy of God extended to all persons, regardless of their prior commitment to God — or lack of it; it portrays a graciousness on the part of God that exceeds any *quid pro quo* way of thinking. And so Adolf Jülicher could speak of this parable as "evangelium in nuce" ("the gospel in a nutshell").[40]

Exposition

It is important to recognize that parables do not always speak of what is typical in normal life (contrary to a lot of popular thinking about the parables). They are memorable precisely because they are shocking. This one is an example. The Parable of the Prodigal Son is another. In normal life the father should put his younger son on probation, but instead he honors him. In the Parable of the Laborers in the Vineyard there is a sense of outrage on the part of those workers who thought that they should receive more. Oftentimes the parables simply do not reflect what is typical. Jesus could be an outlandish storyteller and use the unusual to get his point across. The main figures are therefore not typical in their behavior, because they represent God.

The parable drives a wedge between two ways of thinking about the Christian life and one's relationship to God. The first way is centered on human effort, goodness, and working for the kingdom of God. That way of thinking affected even the great apostles — Peter, James, and John. And it has affected Christians

---

39. With various nuances, included here are A. Jülicher, *Gleichnisreden*, 2:466; C. H. Dodd, *Parables*, 95; J. Jeremias, *Parables*, 36; E. Linnemann, *Parables*, 86; D. Via, *Parables*, 149; J. Dupont, "Les ouvriers," 16-27; N. Perrin, *Teaching*, 118; R. Stein, *Parables*, 127-28; H. Weder, *Gleichnisse*, 227-29; L. Schottroff, "Human Solidarity and the Goodness of God," 145-46; B. Scott, *Parable*, 297; U. Luz, *Matthäus*, 3:141, 150-53.

40. A. Jülicher, *Gleichnisreden*, 2:471.

ever since. Everyone knows how important it is to do the long, hard work of God's kingdom in the world, and especially within the church. Furthermore, there is a genuine goodness to that. One cannot deny it. It is worthy of honor.

But there is a problem. That is that distinctions are easily and often made between those whose length of service and fervor for the kingdom are exemplary and those who have less to show. The simple standards of justice and the computations of time and effort determine degrees of worth.

The other way of thinking goes deeper into the gospel of God, a religious perspective that looks beyond the immediacy of human life to a larger picture revealed to us by Jesus. We cannot reason our way into it. It had to be revealed by Jesus in an outlandish parable. God's way with us is to make no distinctions. We are accepted and loved by God, and saved by God, not because of our efforts but purely by God's own grace. God saves us not because we are lovable, but because God is loving in a radical way.[41] That is the gospel. It is not from human wisdom. It has been revealed by Jesus as something very unusual and full of good news.

We either "take what belongs to us and go" — a way of living that cuts us off from true fellowship with God and others — or we receive from God what he has so graciously chosen to give.

While interpreting and applying this parable, the question inevitably arises: Who are the eleventh-hour workers in our day? We might want to name them, such as deathbed converts or persons who are typically despised by those who are longtime veterans and more fervent in their religious commitment. But it is best not to narrow the field too quickly. At a deeper level, we are all the eleventh-hour workers; to change the metaphor, we are all honored guests of God in the kingdom. It is not really necessary to decide who the eleventh-hour workers are. The point of the parable — both at the level of Jesus and the level of Matthew's Gospel — is that God saves by grace, not by our worthiness. That applies to all of us.

The church at worship does not first of all celebrate what its people do for God, but celebrates God and what God has done for them.

Select Bibliography

Amjad-Ali, Christine. "Whose Justice: The Parable of the Laborers in the Vineyard." *Al-Mushir* 30 (1988): 136-40.

Barré, Michael L. "The Workers in the Vineyard." *BiTod* 24 (1986): 173-80.

Bauer, Johannes B. "Gnadelohn oder Tageslohn?" *Bib* 42 (1961): 224-28.

Broer, Ingo. "Die Gleichnisexegese und die neuere Literaturwissenschaft: Ein Diskussionsbeitrag zur Exegese von Mt 20,1-16." *BibNot* 5 (1978): 13-27.

41. Anders Nygren, *Agape and Eros* (Philadelphia: Westminster Press, 1953), 81-91, uses this as one of three to speak of the love of God in the teachings of Jesus. The other two are the Parables of the Prodigal Son and the Unforgiving Slave. These are the clearest examples of the love and grace of God.

Bultmann, Rudolf. "Matthäus 20,1-15." In his *Marburger Predigten,* 159-68. Tübingen: J. C. B. Mohr (Paul Siebeck), 1956.

Busse, Ulrich. "In Souveränität — anders. Verarbeitete Gotteserfahrung in Mt 20,1-16." *BZ* 40 (1996): 61-72.

Cadbury, Henry J. "The Single Eye." *HTR* 47 (1954): 69-74.

Culbertson, Philip. "Reclaiming the Matthean Vineyard Parables." *Encounter* 49 (1988): 257-83.

Curtis, W. A. "The Parable of the Laborers (Matt. xx.1-16)." *ExpTim* 38 (1926-27): 6-10.

Derrett, J. Duncan M. "Workers in the Vineyard: A Parable of Jesus." *JJS* 25 (1974): 64-91.

Dietzfelbinger, Christian. "Das Gleichnis von den Arbeitern im Weinberg als Jesuswort." *EvT* 43 (1983): 126-37.

Doyle, B. Rod. "The Place of the Parable of the Labourers in the Vineyard in Matthew 20:1-16." *AusBR* 42 (1994): 39-58.

Dupont, Jacques. "Les ouvriers de la onzième heure. Mt 20,1-16." *ASeign* 56 (1974): 16-27.

———. "La Parabole des ouvriers de la vigne (Matthieu XX,1-16)." *NRT* 79 (1957): 785-97.

Elliott, John H. "Matthew 20:1-15: A Parable of Invidious Comparison and Evil Eye Accusation." *BTB* 22 (1992): 52-65.

Feuillet, André. "Les ouvriers de la vigne et la théologie de l'alliance." *RSR* 34 (1947): 303-27.

———. "Les ouvriers envoyés à la vigne (Mt XX,1-16)." *RThom* 79 (1979): 5-24.

Fortna, Robert T. " 'You have made them equal to us!' (Mt 20.1-16)." *JTSA* 72 (1990): 66-72.

Fuchs, Ernst. "Das Wunder der Güte: Predigt über Matth 20,1-16." In his *Glaube und Erfahrung: Zur christologischen Problem im Neuen Testament,* 471-79. Tübingen: J. C. B. Mohr (Paul Siebeck), 1965.

Glasswell, M. E. "Parable of the Labourers in the Vineyard (Matthew 20,1-16)." *CV* 19 (1976): 61-64.

Glover, F. C. "Workers for the Vineyard." *ExpTim* 86 (1975): 310-11.

Gryglewicz, Felix. "The Gospel of the Overworked Workers." *CBQ* 19 (1957): 190-98.

Harl, Kenneth W. *Coinage in the Roman Economy, 300 B.C. to A.D. 700.* Baltimore: Johns Hopkins University Press, 1996.

Harnisch, Wolfgang. "Metaphorical Process in Matthew 20:1-15." In *Society of Biblical Literature 1977 Seminar Papers,* 231-50. Ed. Paul J. Achtemeier. SBLSP 11. Missoula: Scholars Press, 1977.

Hatch, William H. P. "A Note on Matthew 20:15." *ATR* 26 (1944): 250-53.

Haubeck, Wilfrid. "Zum Verständnis der Parabel von den Arbeitern im Weinberg (Mt 20, 1-15)." In *Wort in der Zeit: Neutestamentliche Studien.*

Festgabe für Karl Heinrich Rengstorf zum 75. Geburtstag, 95-107. Ed. W. Haubeck and Michael Bachmann. Leiden: E. J. Brill, 1980.

Heinemann, H. "The Conception of Reward in Mat. XX,1-16." *JJS* 1 (1948-49): 85-89.

Heinemann, Joseph H. "The Status of the Labourer in Jewish law and Society in the Tannaitic Period." *HUCA* 25 (1954): 263-325.

Hezser, Catherine. *Lohnmetaphorik und Arbeiterswelt im Mt 20,1-16: Das Gleichnis von den Arbeitern im Weinberg im Rahmen rabbinischer Lohngleichnisse.* NTOA 15. Göttingen: Vandenhoeck & Ruprecht, 1990.

Hoppe, Rudolf. "Gleichnis und Situation: Zu den Gleichnissen vom guten Vater (Lk 15:11-32) und gütigen Hausherrn (Matt 20:1-15)." *BZ* 1 (1984): 1-21.

Knowles, Michael P. "'Everyone Who Hears These Words of Mine': Parables on Discipleship (Matt 7:24-27//Luke 6:47-49; Luke 14:28-33; Luke 17:7-10; Matt 20:1-16)." In *The Challenge of Jesus' Parables,* 286-305. Ed. Richard N. Longenecker. Grand Rapids: Wm. B. Eerdmans, 2000.

Lebacqz, Karen. "Justice, Economics, and the Uncomfortable Kingdom: Reflections on Matthew 20:1-16." In *The Annual of the Society of Christian Ethics,* 27-53. Ed. Larry L. Rasmussen. Dallas: Society of Christian Ethics, 1983.

Lowe, Malcolm. "A Hebraic Approach to the Parable of the Laborers in the Vineyard." *Imm* 24/25 (1990): 109-17.

Menahem, R. "*Epitropos/Paqid* in the Parable of the Laborers in the Vineyard." *Imm* 24/25 (1990): 118-31.

Meurer, Sigfried. "Zur Beziehung der Gerechtigkeit Gottes zum Recht: Dazu Auslegung von Mt 20,1-16." In *Das Recht in Dienst der Versöhnung und des Friedens: Studien zur Frage des Rechts nach dem Neuen Testament,* 29-44. ATANT 63. Zurich: Theologischer Verlag, 1972.

Mitton, Charles L. "Expounding the Parables: The Workers in the Vineyard (Matthew 20.1-16)." *ExpTim* 77 (1965-66): 307-11.

Nelson, Diedrick A. "Matthew 20:1-16." *Int* 29 (1975): 288-92.

Pak, C. H. "Die Arbeiter im Weinberg (Mt 20,1-16)." *BiKi* 52 (1997): 136-37.

Patte, Daniel. "Bringing out of the Gospel-Treasure What Is New and What Is Old: Two Parables in Matthew 18–23." *QR* 10 (1990): 79-108.

Rodríguez, Jose D. "The Parable of the Affirmative Action Employer." *CurTM* 15 (1988): 418-24.

Roloff, Jürgen. "Das Kirchenverständnis des Matthäus im Spiegel seiner Gleichnisse." *NTS* 38 (1992): 337-56.

Ru, G. de. "The Conception of Reward in the Teaching of Jesus." *NovT* 8 (1966): 202-22.

Schenke, Ludger. "Die Interpretation der Parabel von den 'Arbeitern im Weinberg' (Mt 20,1-15) durch Matthäus." In *Studien zum Matthäusevangelium: Festschrift für Wilhelm Pesch,* 245-68. Ed. L. Schenke. SBS. Stuttgart: Katholisches Bibelwerk, 1988.

Shillington, V. George. "Saving Life and Keeping Sabbath (Matt. 20:1b-15)." In

Jesus and His Parables: Interpreting the Parables of Jesus Today, 87-101. Ed. V. G. Shillington. Edinburgh: T. & T. Clark, 1997.

Schnider, Franz. "Von der Gerechtigkeit Gottes: Beobachtungen zum Gleichnis von den Arbeitern im Weinberg (Mt 20,1-16)." *Kairos* 23 (1981): 88-95.

Schottroff, Luise. "Human Solidarity and the Goodness of God: The Parable of the Workers in the Vineyard." In *God of the Lowly: Socio-Historical Interpretations of the Bible,* 129-47. Ed. Willy Schottroff and Wolfgang Stegemann. Maryknoll, N.Y.: Orbis Books, 1984.

Spies, Otto. "Die Arbeiter im Weinberg (Mt. 20:1-15) in islamischer Überlieferung." *ZNW* 66 (1975): 279-83.

Sutcliffe, Edmund F. "Many Are Called but Few Are Chosen." *ITQ* 28 (1961): 126-31.

Tevel, J. M. "The Labourers in the Vineyard: The Exegesis of Matthew 20,1-7 in the Early Church." *VC* 46 (1992): 356-80.

Weiss, Karl. *Die Frohbotschaft Jesu über Lohn und Vollkommenheit: Zur evangelischen Parabel von den Arbeitern im Weinberg, Mt 20,1-16.* Münster: Aschendorffsche Verlagsbuchhandlung, 1927.

Williams, W. T. "The Parable of the Labourers in the Vineyard (Matthew xx.1-16)." *ExpTim* 50 (1938-39): 526.

Wolf, Erik. "Gottesrecht und Nächstenrecht: Rechtstheologische Exegese des Gleichnisses von den Arbeitern im Weinberg (Mt 20,1-16)." In *Gott in Welt: Festgabe für Karl Rahner,* 2:640-62. Ed. Johannes Baptist Metz et al. 2 vols. Freiburg: Herder, 1964.

Zimmermann, Heinrich. "Die Gottesoffenbarung der Gleichnisse Jesu: Das Gleichnis von den Arbeitern im Weinberg: Mt 20,1-16." *BibLeb* 2 (1961): 100-104.

B. PARABLES OF GOD'S EXTRAORDINARY LOVE FOR THE LOST

2.3. The Lost Sheep, Matthew 18:12-14//Luke 15:4-7; *Thomas 107; Gospel of Truth 31–32*

Matthew 18:12-14

[Jesus said,] 12 *"What do you think? If a man has a hundred sheep, and one of them goes astray, will he not leave the ninety-nine behind on the mountains and go and search for the one that went astray?* 13*And if he finds it, truly I say to you, he rejoices over it more than over the ninety-nine that have not gone astray.*

14 *"So it is not the will of your Father who is in heaven that one of these little ones should perish."*

Notes on the Text and Translation

18:12. RSV and NRSV read: ". . . and one of them *has gone* astray," as though the aorist passive πλανηθῇ is indicative. But in this clause it is a subjunctive, and the clause sets up a present general condition.

The KJV reads, "doth he [= the shepherd] not leave the ninety and nine, and goeth into the mountains," thus depicting the shepherd as the one who goes into the mountains. The location of the phrase "on the mountains" prior to "and" (καί), followed by the Greek participle (πορευθείς) and main verb (ζητεῖ), however, makes this reading virtually impossible.

18:14. Literally the Greek reads: "So it is not the will *before* (ἔμπροσθεν) your Father." The preposition is reverential, but superfluous.[1] In the LXX it alternates with ἐν ὀφθαλμοῖς ("in [the] eyes"), thus meaning "in the eyes of someone," "pleasing in the eyes of someone," or simply "to someone."[2] Here, then, the clause can mean, "so it is not the will to [= for, of] your Father." Not surprisingly, the preposition is missing in some ancient Greek witnesses.

Some major texts (including B) read "my [μου] Father" rather than "your [ὑμῶν] Father" (א and others). The choice is difficult. "My father" may reflect the wording of 18:10.[3] The editors of the Nestle-Aland text (27th ed.) have printed ὑμῶν, which is followed here. Cf. also the NRSV against the RSV.

Luke 15:4-7

3 And [Jesus] spoke this parable to them: 4 "What man of you, having a hundred sheep, and having lost one of them, does not leave the ninety-nine behind in the wilderness, and go after the one that is lost until he finds it? 5 And when he has found it, he lays it on his shoulders, rejoicing. 6 And when he comes home, he calls together his friends and the people from the neighborhood, saying to them, 'Rejoice with me, for I have found my sheep that was lost.'

7 "Just so, I tell you, there will be more joy in heaven over one sinner who repents than over ninety-nine righteous persons who need no repentance."

Notes on the Text and Translation

15:6. Several witnesses, including D, have the more intensive middle voice, συγκαλεῖται [= "to call to oneself"], but the active συγκαλεῖ [= "to call together"] is better attested.

The term τοὺς φίλους, a masculine plural, is to be understood as inclusive of men and women; contrast the feminine at 15:9.

1. BAGD 257.
2. BDF 115 (#214, 6).
3. Cf. B. Metzger, *TCGNT* 45.

The term τοὺς γείτονας (a masculine plural) is translated "people from the neighborhood." See comment below.

Gospel of Thomas 107

Jesus said, "The kingdom is like a shepherd who had a hundred sheep. One of them, the largest, went astray. He left the ninety-nine and looked for that one until he found it. When he had gone to such trouble, he said to the sheep, 'I care for you more than the ninety-nine.'"[4]

Gospel of Truth 31–32

He [= Christ] is the shepherd who left behind the ninety-nine sheep that were not lost. He went searching for the one that had gone astray. He rejoiced when he found it, for ninety-nine is a number that is in the left hand that holds it. But when the one is found, the entire number passes to the right (hand). As that which lacks the one — that is, the entire right (hand) — draws what was deficient and takes it from the left-hand side and brings (it) to the right, so too the number becomes one hundred. It is the sign of the one who is in their sound; it is the Father.[5]

General Comments on the Texts

The parable appears in the Gospels of Matthew and Luke. The two versions are different enough to question whether the two evangelists took them from Q. There are those who think that they are so different that they should be assigned to M and L, respectively.[6] But the tendency is to assign them both to Q, allowing for the redactional work of the two evangelists to account for the differences.[7] Interpreters have not agreed as to which is more original; each ver-

---

4. Quoted from *NHLE* 137.

5. Quoted from ibid., 46.

6. Burnett H. Streeter, *The Four Gospels: A Study of Origins,* rev. ed. (New York: St. Martin's Press, 1930), 265; T. W. Manson, *The Teaching of Jesus: Studies of Its Form and Content,* 2d ed. (Cambridge: Cambridge University Press, 1935), 68; U. Luz, *Matthäus,* 3:25-26; and apparently I. H. Marshall, *Luke,* 601.

7. B. H. Streeter, *Four Gospels,* 291; C. Montefiore, *Synoptic Gospels,* 2:984; Gerhard Schneider, *Das Evangelium nach Lukas* (Gütersloh: Gütersloher Verlagshaus Gerd Mohn, 1977), 324-25; J. Lambrecht, *Astonished,* 37-42; idem, *Treasure,* 39-44; A. Polag, *Fragmenta Q,* 26, 72; J. A. Fitzmyer, *Luke,* 1073; J. Donahue, *Parable,* 147; P. Perkins, *Parables,* 29; B. Scott, *Parable,* 406, 410, 412; W. D. Davies and D. C. Allison, *Matthew,* 2:768; L. Johnson, *Luke,* 239-40; D. Hagner, *Matthew,* 525; R. E. Brown, *Introduction NT,* 119; S. Barton, "Parables on God's Love," 207. According to Michael D. Goulder, *Luke: A New Paradigm,* 2 vols. (Sheffield: JSOT Press, 1989), 2:604-6, Luke took the parable from Matthew and revised it.

sion has its defenders.[8] The attempt to establish which is the more original will not occupy our attention here. One must entertain the possibility that Jesus himself told the parable on more than one occasion and to different audiences — and therefore for different purposes — but he may have told it only once, and the Q tradition preserved it. Both evangelists have redacted the parable in their respective ways, as shown in the Exegetical Commentary on each below. That the parable can be attributed to Jesus of Nazareth is widely accepted,[9] and there are no serious grounds for rejecting that judgment.

In addition to the versions in Matthew and Luke, the parable appears also in the *Gospel of Thomas* 107 and the *Gospel of Truth* 31–32. Whether the version in the *Gospel of Thomas* has been derived from either of the Synoptic Gospels, or both, is in dispute.[10] The version in the *Gospel of Truth* may well be derived from Matthew's.[11]

There are major similarities among the four versions, and there are some important differences as well. In regard to the *similarities*, the following can be listed.

1. The story begins with a shepherd who has a hundred sheep, but has lost one of them.
2. The shepherd leaves the ninety-nine and goes searching for the one that had been lost.
3. The shepherd finds the one that had been lost.
4. The story ends with a comment on the shepherd's reaction to having found the one that had been lost.

8. That Matthew's is more likely original is defended by R. Bultmann, *HST* 171; B. Smith, *Parables*, 189; E. Linnemann, *Parables*, 67; and J. A. Fitzmyer, *Luke*, 1074. That Luke's is more original is held by C. Montefiore, *Synoptic Gospels*, 2:987; J. Jeremias, *Parables*, 40; K. Bailey, *Poet*, 153; F. Schnider, "Das Gleichnis vom verlorenen Schaf," 147; E. Schweizer, *Matthew*, 366; and B. Scott, *Parable*, 406.

9. T. W. Manson, *Sayings*, 282; C. H. Dodd, *Parables*, 92; J. Jeremias, *Parables*, 39, 132-36; N. Perrin, *Teaching*, 100-101; R. Gundry, *Matthew*, 365; J. Lambrecht, *Treasure*, 48-49; H. Weder, *Gleichnisse*, 173-75; W. D. Davies and D. C. Allison, *Matthew*, 2:768-69; U. Luz, *Matthäus*, 3:27. The parable (Matt 18:12-13//Luke 15:4-6, but not the application in Matt 18:14//Luke 15:7) is provided in pink font (= Jesus probably said something like this) in R. Funk, *Five Gospels*, 214, 355.

10. That *Gospel of Thomas* 107 is based on independent tradition is maintained by J. Jeremias, *Parables*, 24; W. L. Peterson, "The Parable of the Lost Sheep," 128-47; and Stephen J. Patterson, *The Gospel of Thomas and Jesus* (Sonoma, Calif.: Polebridge Press, 1993), 71. Dependence upon the Synoptics is affirmed by Bruce Chilton, "The Gospel according to Thomas as a Source of Jesus' Teaching," in *The Jesus Tradition outside the Gospels*, ed. David Wenham (Sheffield: JSOT Press, 1980-86), 158.

11. Cf. Christopher M. Tuckett, "Synoptic Tradition in the Gospel of Truth and the Testimony of Truth," *JTS* 35 (1984): 133-34. On this Gospel in general, cf. S. Kent Brown, "Truth, Gospel of," *ABD* 6:668.

These four elements belong to the story, and without any one of them the story would not be complete.

There are, on the other hand, major *differences* among the four versions.

1. The settings differ. Matthew's version is set within a context in which Jesus speaks to his disciples (18:1) concerning care for God's "little ones" (18:6, 10, 14). Luke's is set within a context in which Jesus makes response to the criticism of the Pharisees and scribes that he receives sinners and eats with them (15:1-2). The text in the *Gospel of Thomas* begins without a context. The version in the *Gospel of Truth* is set within a context in which Christ is spoken of as the one who "became a way for those who were gone astray"; he leads persons to true "knowledge" *(gnosis)* of the Father.[12]

2. In the versions of Matthew and Luke the parable begins with a question (Matt 18:12; Luke 15:4), but not in the *Gospel of Thomas* and the *Gospel of Truth*. For a parable to begin with a question is not unusual, for others do too that are derived from Q (the Faithful and Wise Servant, Matt 24:45//Luke 12:42), Luke's own special source (Friend at Midnight, 11:5; Building a Tower, 14:28; King Going to War, 14:31; Lost Coin, 15:8), and Matthew (Two Sons, 21:28).

3. The verb concerning the loss of the sheep differs. In Matthew's version the sheep has "gone astray" (πλανηθῇ, 18:12). In Luke's version the shepherd "has lost" (ἀπολέσας) his sheep (15:4). These two verbs, which appear again in the respective texts (Matt 18:12, 13; Luke 15:4, 6), are exegetically decisive in interpreting the two accounts (see below). The *Gospel of Thomas* and the *Gospel of Truth* have verbs similar to those of Matthew ("gone astray").

4. The sheep that is lost is simply one in the flock for Luke and the *Gospel of Truth*. In Matthew's version the lost sheep is also any one of the flock, but the closing application (18:14) implies that it is one of the little ones of the flock (see below). In the *Gospel of Thomas,* on the other hand, the one lost is "the largest" and valued more highly than the others.

5. The place where the shepherd leaves the ninety-nine differs in the two accounts; in Matthew they are left "on the mountains," in Luke "in the wilderness." There have been attempts to claim that the Semitic and Greek terminologies are not different. It has been suggested that the Aramaic term used in the speech of Jesus *(tura)* can mean both "mountain" and "open country."[13] And it has been suggested that the Greek term (standing in the source) for mountain (ὄρος) can signify both "mountain" and "desert," as illustrated by Greek papyri.[14] Such attempts are not particularly helpful. Matthew's expression is probably due to his use of a term from the LXX. See comment below on Matt 18:12.

6. In Luke's version, when the shepherd finds the lost sheep, he lays it

---

12. *Gospel of Truth* 31; quoted from *NHLE* 46.

13. Matthew Black, *An Aramaic Approach to the Gospels and Acts,* 3d ed. (Oxford: Clarendon Press, 1967), 133, n. 4. Cf. also J. Jeremias, *Parables,* 133.

14. MM 459.

upon his shoulders and presumably brings it back to the flock, which is a detail not found in the other three versions.

7. In the versions of Matthew and the *Gospel of Truth* the shepherd (alone) rejoices over the discovery of the one that had been lost. In Luke's the shepherd calls upon his friends and neighbors to join in his rejoicing. There is no rejoicing registered in the *Gospel of Thomas* version, but rather words of endearment by the shepherd to his sheep.

8. The emphasis in the versions of Matthew and the two apocryphal Gospels is on recovering the one lost or led astray. In Luke it is upon the joy of discovery.

9. The application differs in each case. For Matthew the point made is that God does not will the loss of a little one (18:14). For Luke it is that God rejoices over the repentance of a sinner who needs it (15:7). In the *Gospel of Truth* the restoration of the lost one brings the flock to completeness. The *Gospel of Thomas* has no application appended.

10. Metaphorically the lost sheep differs. For Matthew the lost sheep becomes a metaphor for the weak Christian who is lost but then restored to the flock. For Luke it becomes a metaphor for a sinner who repents. In the *Gospel of Thomas* and the *Gospel of Truth* the one found becomes a metaphor for the one most beloved by Jesus and the one who gains knowledge, respectively.

11. In both the *Gospel of Thomas* and the *Gospel of Truth* the person who does the seeking is identified forthrightly as a "shepherd," while in the canonical versions the person is simply a "man" who turns out to be a shepherd as the story is told, even though the term "shepherd" is not used.

The significance of the versions in the *Gospel of Thomas* and the *Gospel of Truth* has been assessed in different ways. In the former, as indicated, the one lost is the largest and the most valued of the flock. Therefore it is no surprise that the shepherd goes looking for it. As many interpreters have claimed, the largest sheep probably symbolizes the gnostic Christian, who is valued more highly than ordinary Christians.[15] It has been argued that the *Gospel of Thomas* version is not gnostic on the grounds that the lost sheep signifies Israel, not the gnostic Christian,[16] but the thesis is hardly convincing, since there is no evi-

---

15. Bertil Gärtner, *Theology of the Gospel according to Thomas* (New York: Harper & Brothers, 1961), 235; Hugh Montefiore and H. E. W. Turner, *Thomas and the Evangelists*, SBT 35 (Naperville: Alec R. Allenson, 1962), 56; Wolfgang Schrage, *Das Verhältnis des Thomas-Evangelium zur synoptischen Tradition und zu den doptischen Evangelienübersetzungen*, BZNW 29 (Berlin: Alfred Töpelmann, 1964), 193-96; N. Perrin, *Teaching*, 98-99; William R. Schoedel, "Parables in the Gospel of Thomas: Oral Tradition or Gnostic Exegesis?" *CTM* 43 (1972): 555-57; F. Schnider, "Das Gleichnis vom verloren Schaf," 146-54; Andreas Lindemann, "Zur Gleichnisinterpretation im Thomas-Evangelium," *ZNW* 71 (1980): 219; Michael Fieger, *Das Thomasevangelium: Einleitung Kommentar und Systematik*, NTAbh 22 (Münster: Aschendorff, 1991), 267.

16. W. L. Peterson, "The Parable of the Lost Sheep," 128-35. The author also claims

dence that this gospel otherwise speaks of a special concern for the covenant people Israel as a whole.[17] In any case, the versions in Matthew and Luke stand in stark contrast to it: the sheep that is lost is sought purely because it is lost, and none should perish. And it is actually quite surprising that the shepherd should leave the ninety-nine and go looking for it.

The *Gospel of Truth*, discovered at Nag Hammadi in 1945, is widely considered to have been composed in the middle of the second century as a Christian gnostic text with Valentinian affinities.[18] The parable is attributed to Jesus, and there is a play on numbers having to do with the perfection of those who belong to the Father.[19] The number one hundred is perfect; ninety-nine is not. So the shepherd really has to go out and complete the perfect number. This means that, as in the *Gospel of Thomas*, there is no surprise in the behavior of the shepherd.

The imagery of the shepherd and his sheep, used in a metaphorical sense, is common in the literatures of antiquity. The image of the shepherd to designate gods, kings, and other officers appears in writings from Mesopotamia, Egypt, Greece, and Rome.[20] In the writings of Homer, for example, the king is the "shepherd of the people" (ποιμὴν λαῶν) some fifty-six times.[21]

In the OT the imagery of the shepherd and his sheep, used in a metaphorical sense, is quite common. At Psalm 77:20 (Ps 77:21 in Hebrew), looking to the past, the psalmist declares that God led his people like a flock by the hand of Moses and Aaron. At Isaiah 40:11 the prophet looks to the future when God will feed his flock like a shepherd. But more distinctive are those passages that speak of the people of Israel — or the individual — as sheep lost or gone astray, and in need of God as a shepherd for their rescue. At Isaiah 53:6 the prophet says, "All we like sheep have gone astray" (πάντες ὡς πρόβατα ἐπλανήθημεν), and at 1 Kings 22:17 the people of Israel are spoken of as sheep scattered on the mountains. At Psalm 119:176 the writer speaks of himself as gone astray like a lost sheep (ἐπλανήθην ὡς πρόβατον ἀπολωλός, LXX 118:176) in need of God's

that the *Thomas* version is more primitive than those in the canonical Gospels. H. Hendrickx, *Parables*, 144, adopts both points. B. Scott, *Parable*, 407, accepts Peterson's view that the parable is not gnostic, but rejects his claim for its being more primitive.

17. It has also been argued that the *Thomas* version is more primitive than those in the Synoptics because, contrary to the latter, it contains no allegorizing. Cf. S. Patterson, *The Gospel of Thomas and Jesus*, 71. Yet there is certainly allegorizing in that version, too, in regard to the sheep that is the largest and most valued, whatever it represents.

18. Cf. Harold W. Attridge and George W. MacRae, "[Introduction to the Gospel of Truth,]" *NHLE* 36.

19. In addition, the "gnostic reader would recognize 'left' and 'right' as references to the left and right of the Demiurge or of the enthroned Jesus," according to Pheme Perkins, *Gnosticism and the New Testament* (Minneapolis: Fortress Press, 1993), 57.

20. J. Engemann, "Hirt," *RAC* 15:578-79.

21. Ibid., 15:579.

help. The prophets Jeremiah and Ezekiel go a step further. They speak against the leaders of Israel as shepherds who have not cared for the flock. Jeremiah says that the shepherds have led the people astray, and that the people are lost sheep (50:6; cf. 23:1-4). Ezekiel says that the shepherds have not cared for the sheep. Among other things, he declares: "the strayed you have not brought back, and the lost you have not sought" (34:4, LXX: τὸ πλανώμενον οὐκ ἐπεστρέψατε καὶ τὸ ἀπολωλὸς οὐκ ἐζητήσατε). Therefore the Lord himself will search (ἐκζητήσω, future tense!) for his sheep (34:11). There can be no doubt but what the passage from Ezekiel provided imagery for the Parable of the Lost Sheep and the discourse at John 10:11-18 where Jesus himself is the Good Shepherd who seeks his sheep.

In all four versions the shepherd is portrayed as having a hundred sheep. Is this a small, average, or large number? When one sees a Bedouin shepherd tending sheep today in the Middle East, and if that shepherd is alone, the flock is considerably less.[22] At Genesis 32:14, when Jacob presents a very generous gift to Esau, the flock amounts to 220 sheep. Even one hundred sheep is therefore a large flock indeed. The figure is a good round number by which Jesus paints a picture on a grand scale (as elsewhere in his parables). And the matter is important exegetically. To lose one sheep out of a hundred is a loss, but it is hardly devastating. The nuance to be observed is that the shepherd cares about the one that is lost, even if he could in fact get along without it.

Interpreters have been divided on how typical the action of the shepherd would have been in the world of the first century. Would a shepherd leave the ninety-nine in the wilderness or on the mountains in order to seek the one that had been lost? Some interpreters have suggested that the shepherd should be understood as a typical figure, the Palestinian shepherd ancient or modern. On his departure he would surely have placed the ninety-nine in the care of another — or in a sheepfold or cave — for protection, rather than leaving them vulnerable.[23] An alternative view is that the hearers/readers are to sense that the action was not typical, and that the nontypical behavior of the shepherd is important to the story. The shepherd is portrayed as having taken great risk in leaving the ninety-nine behind due to his extravagant care for the one that was lost.[24] There is merit

22. K. Bailey, *Poet*, 148, says that the average family may have five to fifteen animals. Even if we double the figures, the flock would consist of much fewer than a hundred sheep. J. Jeremias, *Parables*, 133, says that a hundred sheep would constitute "a medium-sized flock," but it seems that (1) that is not so, and that (2) he misses the grandiose way of parable telling at this point.

23. So E. F. F. Bishop, "The Parable of the Lost or Wandering Sheep," 45, 54; F. Bussby, "Did a Shepherd Leave Sheep upon the Mountains or in the Desert?" 93; B. Smith, *Parables*, 188, n. 2; J. Jeremias, *Parables*, 133; D. Wenham, *Parables*, 100; and K. Bailey, *Poet*, 149-50; idem, *Finding the Lost*, 72-73.

24. Norman Huffman, "Atypical Features in the Parables of Jesus," *JBL* 97 (1978): 211; N. Perrin, *Teaching*, 48; and B. Scott, *Parable*, 415.

to the latter viewpoint. The verb used by Matthew at 18:12 (ἀφήσει ["he will leave"]) — used in an interrogative clause ("Will he not leave?") — appears elsewhere in his Gospel to portray scenes in which the subject leaves behind, even abandons, another person or thing (4:11, 20, 22; 8:15; 19:27; 22:22; 26:56). The compound verb used by Luke at 15:4 (καταλείπει) is emphatic; it means "to leave behind" (cf. 5:28; 10:40).[25] The shepherd is portrayed — in a grand story — as one who acts in a nontypical fashion; he literally leaves his remaining flock behind, since he is so earnestly concerned about the one that has been lost. The point could be important exegetically. If the shepherd leaves the ninety-nine sheep in a protected enclosure in order to go fetch the one that is lost, he is simply being portrayed as frugal. But if he (quickly) abandons them to search for the one that is lost, he is being portrayed as one who is willing to risk all he has for the sake of the one that is lost.

In the end, however, the question being posed is somewhat hypercritical. In an oriental setting the teller of the parable "keeps the central point of his teaching in the forefront, and does not concern himself about the smaller details . . . of his parable. . . . The central point is the seeking of the lost sheep, the rest of the flock are not just now in question."[26] Undoubtedly hyperbole is used, but the security of the remaining sheep is not a matter of concern in the story.[27] The hearers are called upon to think, even to let the imagination go freely. The shepherd is a metaphor for God, and God is like this particular shepherd who seeks the lost, even in a way that could seem reckless to the hearers.

The Parable in the Gospel of Matthew: Exegetical Commentary

The parable is addressed to disciples (18:1). At the narrative level chapter 18 generally has to do with instructing the disciples. But as a manual for the Christian community of the evangelist, that means that the teachings are directed to the readers as leaders in the Christian community. It contains teachings on humility (18:1-5), caring for the "little ones" and not causing them to sin or despising them (18:6-10), reconciliation (18:15-17), binding and loosing (18:18-20), and forgiveness (18:21-35).

The passage is framed by an introduction (18:10) and application (18:14) that speak of "one of these little ones." From the previous use of the phrase at 18:6, which identifies such persons as believers in Jesus, as well as at 10:42, it clearly refers in these cases, as in those, to disciples of Jesus. These verses are decisive for interpreting the parable in Matthew's Gospel. It is possible that the pre-Matthean parable, like Luke's, spoke of the joy of finding the lost. But in

---

25. BAGD 413 (2a).

26. W. O. E. Oesterley, *Parables*, 179.

27. D. Hagner, *Matthew*, 527.

Matthew's own situation that had less urgency. Transposing the story into a new key, the urgency of the moment is to restore one who has gone astray.

18:12. The parable opens with a question that in its present form (τὶ ὑμῖν δοκεῖ, "What do you think?") is Matthean (cf. its use also at 21:28; 22:42; and 26:66; cf. also 17:25; 27:17); the expression appears nowhere else in the Gospels, except at John 11:56. Addressed to the disciples (representing the Christian community for Matthew), the question sets the stage for the parable proper, which is to be given careful thought.

The verb πλανηθῇ ("goes astray") is an aorist passive subjunctive. From classical sources into the NT and beyond, the verb in its passive form means "to wander away," "to stray," even "to be deceived" or "to be misled."[28] At James 5:19 it is used to speak of the person who "wanders from the truth." In the context of Matthew 18 the verb takes on a distinct nuance. Persons are warned against causing the "little ones . . . to sin" (18:6) or to "despise" any one of them (18:10). It becomes apparent that the sheep that goes astray is a metaphor for any member of the church who is led astray from true discipleship by some deception. It is not necessarily outright apostasy,[29] but wandering into false belief that is implied. In the apocalyptic discourse warnings are given that in the latter times of testing there will be false prophets and false Christs who seek to lead many astray (24:4-5, 11, 24), "even the elect" (24:24). The imagery recalls the oracle of Jeremiah, in which he charges on behalf of the Lord that the (false) shepherds of Judah — rulers who have become corrupt — have led the people astray so that they are "lost sheep . . . upon the mountains" (πρόβατα ἀπολωλότα . . . ἐπὶ τὰ ὄρη); indeed, "Israel" is a "sheep that has wandered away" (πρόβατον πλανώμενον Ἰσραηλ) in Jeremiah 50:6, 17 (LXX 27:6, 17; cf. also Jer 23:1-4; Ezek 34:4-6).

The verb ἀφήσει ("Will he leave?") is in the future tense, fitting for a general question posed to the disciples. It expects a positive answer, whether the action is typical or not of a shepherd. While Matthew has "on the mountains," Luke has "in the wilderness." There is little difference, since the topography of the wilderness in question is very hilly, even mountainous. It is likely that whatever expression was used in his source, Matthew recalls the language of Jeremiah 50:6 (LXX 27:6).

The shepherd, having left the other sheep behind, goes and searches diligently for the one that went astray. The message to the disciples, insofar as the expression is metaphorical, is that the leader of the community is to seek out the person who has been misled. Restoration, not excommunication, is envisioned.

---

28. LSJ 1411; BAGD 665.
29. R. Gundry, *Matthew*, 365-67, speaks of the little ones as in danger of apostasy. However, there is a distinction between apostasy (rejecting the faith) and being led astray into false belief taught by false prophets and false Christs.

18:13. The "if" (ἐάν) of Matthew's version differs from Luke's "and *when* he has found it." There is contingency. As in the case of a shepherd who may not find the lost sheep, so it is possible that, despite efforts made, the one who has been misled cannot be restored back into the community. Lacking altogether in Matthew's version is the more optimistic scene of Luke's version (15:5-6), in which the shepherd places the sheep on his shoulder, returns home, and summons his friends and neighbors to rejoice with him.

The expression ἀμὴν λέγω ὑμῖν ("truly I say to you") appears no less than 29 times in the Gospel of Matthew to introduce a solemn pronouncement of Jesus. It appears in the other Gospels as well (12 times in Mark; 5 times in Luke; and 20 times in John).

Like Luke's version (15:5), this one records the rejoicing of the shepherd. But it is more explicitly personal and pastoral. Luke's version speaks of the shepherd's rejoicing over the fact of finding; Matthew's speaks of his rejoicing over the person who has been found and will be restored to the community.

18:14. The parable has ended. The application follows in this verse, introduced by "so." Whatever the wording in his source, Matthew has edited the verse for his ecclesiastical purposes. The expression "the will of your Father" echoes similar expressions at 7:21; 12:50; 21:31; and 26:42 (cf. also 6:10), and "Father in heaven" appears at seven other places (5:45; 7:21; 10:32, 33; 12:50; 18:10, 19). God's will is that none of the "little ones" (cf. 10:42; 18:6, 10) should "perish." (Cf. Jer 23:4: none of the sheep shall be missing.) At this point — and only here in the parable — Matthew uses the same verb found in Luke's version (15:4, 6), "to perish" or "to lose" (ἀπόλλυμι in its various forms). One could expect Matthew to say that it is the will of God that none of the little ones should "go astray." However, forms of the verb "to perish" were probably in the source(s) used by the two evangelists. But more to the point for theology and church, Matthew looks upon any member's going astray as ultimately leading to that person's perishing, or destruction. It is imperative that such a person be rescued and restored.

Exposition

The "little ones" are not to be despised (18:10), and it is the Father's will that none of them should perish (18:14). These verses, which precede and apply the parable, set the framework of the parable itself.

The possibility that a member of the community might go astray, or be misled, is deeply rooted in the traditions of Israel and the church. In spite of catechesis of the best sort, and valiant attempts to maintain confessional and social cohesion, there are mishaps. One in a hundred does not appear to be much of a loss (only one percent). But in the eyes of God, the loss of a single person is a tragedy. It cannot be met with resignation on the part of the faithful, and certainly not by the leader of the flock.

The only response fitting is to make valiant, even heroic, attempts to restore the one who has gone astray. The image of the shepherd leaving the ninety-nine is not to be taken as license for the leader of the community to be indifferent toward the rest of the community. A parable can do only so much. What Jesus tries to do in this parable is to open up one's horizon to see the urgency of seeking the one that has been lost. Since the time is short, the end of time is approaching, and the judgment is near, rescuing the one that has strayed is all the more urgent. To be sure, it is possible that the one who seeks the strayed one will not succeed; that is held out as a possibility by the clause, "*if* he finds it." But such realism does not undercut the seriousness of the attempt. The worst possibility of all is indifference toward the one that has strayed.

The prospect of actually having success in finding the strayed one and beginning the process of restoration is anticipated. And if the shepherd is truly a disciple of Jesus, the outcome can only be rejoicing. The rejoicing is not in the success itself, the accomplishment achieved, but "over" the *person* who has been brought back into faith and discipleship. The rejoicing is totally other-directed. It is a rejoicing that the one gone astray has now come home spiritually. There is no need to rejoice to the same degree "over" the ninety-nine who are at home already.

The whole effort is not simply for the sake of community solidarity or appearances. It is based in the will of God that none should perish.

The Parable in the Gospel of Luke: Exegetical Commentary

Luke's version of the parable (15:3-7) is set within a context that differs from that of Matthew. The larger literary context — both its larger setting in the Travel Narrative (9:51–19:27) and its more immediate setting in 15:1-2 — is taken up in Appendix 2 on "The Three Parables of Luke 15." It is sufficient here to indicate that at 15:1-2 Jesus is accused by certain scribes and Pharisees of welcoming "tax collectors and sinners" and eating with them.

The response of Jesus is called by Luke a "parable" (15:3), a designation not found in the Matthean parallel.

15:4. The opening phrase, τίς ἄνθρωπος ἐξ ὑμῶν ("What man of you?"), is used here alone in Luke's Gospel, but is similar to the simpler form, τίς ἐξ ὑμῶν ("Which of you?") that is used four other times (11:5; 12:25; 14:28; 17:7); the use of the additional word "man" in the phrase contrasts with "woman" in 15:8. Whatever wording was in Luke's source (cf. Matt 18:12), it appears that Luke has stylized the phrase. As the parable unfolds, it turns out that the person is a shepherd. It is not likely, in spite of the generalization being made, that Jesus appeals to the personal experience of his hearers here,[30] for the Pharisees and

---

30. Contra A. Plummer, *Luke*, 368.

scribes would never even have contemplated taking up the task of the shepherd.[31] Shepherds belonged to a class of despised trades.[32]

The sheep that is lost is simply one of the flock, no greater or less than the rest, in contrast to the one lost in the *Gospel of Thomas* 107. There is no implication of blame for the loss on the part of the shepherd.[33] The two verbs "lost" and "found" are key terms not only in this parable but in the other two that are to follow as well (15:8, 9 and 15:24, 32).[34]

At Matthew 18:12 the shepherd leaves the ninety-nine "on the mountains." There is actually no distinction; the wilderness in question is extremely hilly, even mountainous. It is possible that Luke's phrase recalls 1 Samuel 17:28 in the LXX (Codex Alexandrinus; missing in Vaticanus) where it is said that David had left some sheep in the wilderness (τὰ μικρὰ πρόβατα . . . ἐν τῇ ἐρήμῳ). In any case, the picture is that of the shepherd going off in a deliberate and single-minded effort to seek earnestly for the lost one until he finds it.

15:5. The portrait of a shepherd carrying his sheep (or a ram) on his shoulders has pre-Christian antecedents in the ancient Near East and the Greco-Roman world.[35] One of the most famous is the image of Hermes with a ram "upon his shoulders" (ἐπὶ τῶν ὤμων — the wording is almost identical to Luke's ἐπὶ τοῦς ὤμους) at the sanctuary at Tanagra, Greece, described by Pausanias (*Boeotia* 22.1); another is a figure on a Roman sarcophagus.[36] In addition to the depictions in art must be added the Jewish legend of Moses who, after rescuing the kid that had been lost, "placed [it] on his shoulder" and brought it home safely (a literary source from later times, but the tradition may be earlier).[37] The imagery is missing in Matthew's version of the story, as well as in the *Gospel of Thomas* and *Gospel of Truth*. Nor is it to be found in the OT either; the closest imagery is that of God as the shepherd who "will gather the lambs in his arms, and carry them in his bosom" (Isa 40:11; cf. 60:4). Here in Luke's Gospel the narrative provides an exceedingly fine touch, demonstrating the compassion and tender care of the shepherd for the one that had been lost. The shepherd goes forth to his home "rejoicing," which shows even more his exultant joy from discovering the lost one. Since the shepherd is a metaphor for God or Jesus himself as God's envoy —

31. K. Bailey, *Poet*, 147; idem, *Finding the Lost*, 65.

32. For references, cf. Joachim Jeremias, "ποιμήν," *TDNT* 6:488-89; and B. Scott, *Parable*, 413-14. A first-century text expressing the attitude is in Philo, *De Agricultura* 61. At *m. Qidd.* 4:14 the herdsman's craft is classified with that of robbers.

33. Contra K. Bailey, *Finding the Lost*, 65-67.

34. An important observation by Luke T. Johnson, *Luke*, 235.

35. Jack Finegan, *Light from the Ancient Past: The Archaeological Background of Judaism and Christianity*, 2d ed. (Princeton: Princeton University Press, 1959), 478.

36. André Grabar, *Christian Iconography: A Study of Its Origins* (Princeton: Princeton University Press, 1968), 36 and illustration #89.

37. *Exod. Rab.* 2:2; quoted from *MidR* 3:49.

and no clear distinction need be made — the message becomes clear: God de-lights in the recovery of the lost.

15:6. The verb συγκαλεῖ ("to call together") is used by Xenophon (*Cynegeticus* 8.4.1) as an invitation to a feast. Since the shepherd calls upon those invited to rejoice with him, the implication is that a feast will follow, as in the Par-able of the Prodigal Son (15:23-32). At both 15:6 and 9 (as well as at 14:12) Luke uses the term γείτονας (plural for γείτων), which is usually translated as "neigh-bors." The term is found in the NT beyond Luke's usage only at John 9:8. The more usual term for "neighbor" in the NT is πλησίον, used 17 times, including those instances which cite the commandment of love for neighbor from Leviticus 19:18 (Matt 22:39//Mark 12:31//Luke 10:27; Rom 13:9; Gal 5:14; Jas 2:8). The two Greek terms mean roughly the same, but a nuance can be detected: πλησίον means "one near by," "one close," "a neighbor," which has an emotional coloring, whereas γείτων has the simpler sense of a person from the neighborhood.[38] The shepherd therefore invites both his friends and all the others who inhabit his neighborhood without distinction. The summoning of such persons is missing in Matthew's version, as well as in the two apocryphal Gospels.

The expression συγχάρητέ μοι ("rejoice with me"), an aorist imperative, is an urgent invitation to all to enter into the shepherd's overwhelming sense of joy. An almost identical invitation (with necessary variation) is extended by the woman who found her lost coin in 15:9b; and the father of the prodigal son in-vites others to "make merry" with him on the return of his lost son (15:23, 32). (Similar language also appears at 1:58, where the friends and relatives of Eliza-beth "rejoiced with her" [συνέχαιρον αὐτῇ] at the birth of her son.) The sense of joyous merriment is the conclusion to each of the three parables of Luke 15. Along with the verbs "to lose" and "to find," the invitation to others to join in the joy of the one who has found the lost ties the three parables together. By im-plication, those who enter into the joy are thus included in the company of di-vine happiness over the recovery of the lost, while those who refuse — the Pharisees and the scribes in this case — exclude themselves. With this verse the parable itself ends; now comes the application.

15:7. The word translated here "just so" (οὕτως) introduces the applica-tion of parables on several other occasions as well, not only in Luke's Gospel (12:21; 14:33; 15:10), but also in Matthew's (13:49; 18:35; 20:16). The phrase λέγω ὑμῖν ("I say to you") appears 42 times in Luke's Gospel to introduce a sol-emn pronouncement. On seven occasions it is used to introduce the applica-tion of a parable (11:9; 15:7, 10; 16:9; 18:8, 14; 19:26); once it is used within the parable itself (14:24).

Since "heaven" is a traditional circumlocution for "God" (cf. Matt 21:25),[39] the phrase "joy in heaven" speaks of the joy of God, but it could also

38. Cf. entries for the words in LSJ 341 and 1420.
39. Various texts are cited for the circumlocution in Str-B 2:209-10.

include the angels (cf. 15:10). Although placed in the future tense ("there will be joy"), that need not refer simply to God's joy at the last judgment.[40] The verb holds out the prospect of divine joy whenever — from here on out — there is repentance; the anticipation of repentance by those who hear the good news is a prominent Lukan theme (24:47; Acts 2:38; 17:30; 20:21; 26:20). The reference to the ninety-nine without need for repentance, insofar as it is addressed to the Pharisees and scribes on the scene, must be taken as sarcastic. For Luke, the Pharisees and scribes actually do need repentance (cf. 7:30; 11:39-44; 12:1; 16:14-15). Nevertheless, and of more importance, it is a generalized saying — correlating with the ninety-nine sheep that were not lost — to heighten the focus on the divine joy over the repentance of anyone who needs to do so.

The word "repentance" (μετάνοια) should not be taken in a moralistic sense. Essentially it means a change of mind,[41] and for Luke it is above all a gift that is granted by God himself (cf. Acts 5:31; 11:18),[42] a concept arising out of Jewish wisdom tradition (cf. Wis 11:23; 12:10, 19).

Interpreters have maintained that there appears to be a discrepancy between the parable and the application in 15:7. Within the parable itself all is focused on the action of the shepherd who seeks the sheep that had been lost and his consequent joy on finding it. The sheep that is found is totally passive, the recipient of the shepherd's goodwill and effort. But now, it is said, in 15:7 there is moralizing; the person who is "found" is the sinner who repents. To be sure, there is a correlation between the one lost sheep and the single sinner, on the one hand, and between the many sheep who were not lost and the many who need no repentance on the other. But the repentance of a sinner, no matter how much moved by divine prompting, is a response and therefore an act performed; it is more than simply being found. To be consistent with both the parable itself and the introduction of 15:1-2, it would seem that the application should consist of words in which Jesus declares that, just so, he had come to seek and to save those who were lost, a saying known to Luke (19:10). Therefore it is not surprising that several major interpreters consider the saying a secondary addition to the parable itself, whether by Luke or his source.[43]

It should be said, however, that (1) the application is not likely to be entirely Lukan in composition, and (2) the application is not impossible for the parable. Concerning the first point, there are expressions in the verse that are uncharacteristic of Luke, such as the circumlocution for God. It is a possible application in that the ministry of Jesus — in which tax collectors and sinners

40. Contra J. Jeremias, *Parables*, 135-36.
41. Cf. BAGD 512.
42. D. Tiede, *Luke*, 276.
43. R. Bultmann, *HST* 171; A. Cadoux, *Parables*, 231; C. H. Dodd, *Parables*, 92; B. Smith, *Parables*, 191; N. Perrin, *Teaching*, 99; Luise Schottroff, "Das Gleichnis vom verlorenen Sohn," *ZTK* 68 (1971): 32-35, 51; and J. Fitzmyer, *Luke*, 1073. The verse is in black font (= Jesus did not say this) in R. Funk, *Five Gospels*, 355.

were drawing near, and thus giving him a hearing — was truly one in which the lost were being found. Consequently their being drawn to him, and (at least in the case of some) their response to his message of the kingdom of God, is a cause for rejoicing by God and his angels. All that would confirm the validity of the ministry of Jesus, for which he was being criticized (15:1-2). C. H. Dodd, even though suspecting that the concluding verse (15:7) may not be original to the parable as it came from Jesus, says that Luke's setting is surely right, since the parable refers to "the extravagant concern . . . which Jesus displayed for the depressed classes of the Jewish community."[44]

Whether such an interpretation is rooted in the ministry of Jesus himself — and there is no compelling reason to doubt it — that is how the parable can be understood at the level of Luke's Gospel. Jesus came not to call the righteous, but sinners, to repentance (5:32), which leads to forgiveness of sins and salvation. Wherever and whenever he was able to "find" one who was "lost," thereby opening the future of such a person for communion with God, the will of God was being done, causing great rejoicing by God and the angels in heaven.

On balance, it must be concluded that, since all that has been said here relies heavily on Luke's theological perspective, the application (15:7) is most likely a Lukan composition or at least a saying that has been given its present form by Luke. The question for the interpreter is whether such an application stands in the way of interpreting Jesus' ministry and message — indeed, whether it distorts them in some way — or "exegetes" them in a fruitful direction. The same has to be asked concerning the application at Matthew 18:14. But in terms of interpreting the parable in its Lukan version — the prime interest here — the verse must be taken as a fitting application nevertheless.

Exposition

With "all" the tax collectors and sinners drawing near to him (15:1), Jesus is open to criticism. To associate with them, even to dine with them, implies a social bonding with them with attendant risks: that he will be seen to approve of their conduct, that he might be drawn to their ways of life, and that he may in fact cut himself off from those who maintain covenant loyalty and respectability. No matter that on occasion Jesus had table fellowship with Pharisees too (Luke 7:36-50; 11:37-52; 14:1-24); his conduct is not acceptable. By his behavior he breaks solidarity with the righteous.

But in the view of Jesus, there is another way of looking at the matter. His critics and he can agree that the disreputables are in fact lost. But what is to be done? For the Pharisees and scribes on the scene, the proper course of action is to shun them. But not for Jesus. When he associates with the disreputables, he is

44. C. H. Dodd, *Parables*, 92. That Luke's context reflects the original setting of the parable is also maintained by R. Stein, *Parables*, 62; and J. Donahue, *Parable*, 148.

acting out — by means of an enacted parable — the ways of God. This can also be put into words, in a verbal parable. The ways of God are comparable to those of a shepherd who goes out, leaving behind a great flock, to seek earnestly the one that is lost. The lost are to be rescued, not rejected.

The parable has verification in Jesus' own ministry. His association with certain disreputables leads to their repentance (5:29-32; 7:36-50; 17:11-19; 19:1-9). In fact it is his will in the end that repentance and forgiveness of sins be preached in his name to all the nations (Luke 24:47).

Repentance cannot come about in persons merely on the basis of a demand. It comes about in many cases as a response to prevenient grace. Jesus' association with disreputables is precisely the enactment of such grace. Where grace is demonstrated, and when the one in need of repentance is not taken by the throat but is set free in the safety and space that grace affords, repentance has a chance. As a change of mind, repentance means to take on a new perspective, seeing things in a new way in the light of God's grace. It involves a "paradigm shift" concerning the relationship of the self before God that is possible only in light of the good news of the graciousness of a loving God. It is a response, but it is above all a gift that is granted by God himself.

God will be content with those who need no repentance (not that there is any; that is not a point that the parable is designed to make!). But God and the angels of heaven rejoice together when the one who is lost repents — just like this shepherd, who rejoices with his friends and neighbors.

Select Bibliography

Arai, Sasagu. "Das Gleichnis vom verloren Schaf: Eine traditionsgeschichtliche Untersuchung." *AJBI* 2 (1976): 111-37.

Bailey, Kenneth E. *Finding the Lost: Cultural Keys to Luke 15* (St. Louis: Concordia Publishing House, 1992).

Barton, Stephen C. "Parables on God's Love and Forgiveness (Luke 15:1-7//Matthew 18:12-14; Luke 15:8-32)." In *The Challenge of Jesus' Parables*, 199-216. Ed. Richard N. Longenecker. Grand Rapids: Wm. B. Eerdmans, 2000.

Bishop, E. F. F. "The Parable of the Lost or Wandering Sheep: Matthew 18.10-14; Luke 15.3-7." *ATR* 44 (1962): 44-57.

Bussby, Frederick. "Did a Shepherd Leave Sheep upon the Mountains or in the Desert? A Note on Matthew 18.12 and Luke 15.4." *ATR* 45 (1963): 93-94.

Derrett, J. Duncan M. "Fresh Light on the Lost Sheep and the Lost Coin." *NTS* 26 (1979): 36-60.

Dulaey, Martine. "La parabole de la brebis perdue dans l'Église ancienne: De l'exégèse à l'iconographie." *REA* 39 (1993): 3-22.

Dupont, Jacques. "Les implications christologiques de la parabole de la brebis perdue." In his *Jesus aux origines de la christologie*, 331-50. Louvain: Leuven University Press, 1975.

Gregg, Robert C. "Early Christian Variations on the Parable of the Lost Sheep." *DDSR* 41 (1977): 85-104.

Peisker, Carl H. "Das Gleichnis vom verlorenen Schaf und vom verlorenen Groschen." *EvErz* 19 (1967): 58-70.

Peterson, William L. "The Parable of the Lost Sheep in the Gospel of Thomas and the Synoptics." *NovT* 23 (1981): 128-47.

Schmidt, Wilhelm. "Der gute Hirte: Biblische Besinnung über Lukas 15,1-7." *EvT* 24 (1964): 173-77.

Schnider, Franz. "Das Gleichnis vom verloren Schaf und seine Redaktoren: Ein intertextueller Vergleich." *Kairos* 19 (1977): 146-54.

Sweet, John P. M. "A Saying, a Parable, a Miracle." *Theology* 76 (1973): 125-33.

2.4. The Lost Coin, Luke 15:8-10

[Jesus said,] 8*"Or what woman, having ten silver coins, if she loses one coin, does not light a lamp and sweep the house and search diligently until she finds it?* 9*And when she has found it, she calls together the women — friends and neighbors — saying, 'Rejoice with me, for I have found the coin that I had lost.'* 10*In the same way, I say to you, there is joy in the presence of the angels of God over one sinner who repents."*

Notes on the Text and Translation

15:8. Major Western texts (D and some Old Latin texts) simplify the syntax, substituting καὶ ἀπολέσασα μίαν ("and having lost one") for ἐὰν ἀπολέσῃ δραχμὴν μίαν ("if she loses one coin"); the latter is otherwise attested firmly.

15:9. Several witnesses, including the Majority text, have the more intensive middle voice, συγκαλεῖται ("to call to oneself"), but the active συγκαλεῖ ("to call together") is better attested.

The Greek term τὰς φίλας, a feminine plural, can be translated literally "the women friends."[1] The Greek term γείτονας can be taken along with it as a feminine plural; it is so specified by the article τάς in some manuscripts. Both terms can be translated as above: "the women — friends and neighbors." See the Commentary below for more discussion.

15:10. The preposition ἐνώπιον has been translated as both "before" (RSV, NRSV) and "among" (NEB). There is some warrant for "among."[2] Yet the basic sense (from etymology) is "in the sight of" or "in the presence of."[3] The

---

1. Cf. BAGD 861 (φίλος, 2,b), "her women friends."
2. Ibid., 270 (5.a).
3. A. F. Walls, "'In the Presence of the Angels,'" 314; and Helmut Krämer, "ἐνώπιον," *EDNT* 1:462.

context demands a correspondence to the expression "in heaven" of 15:7. Cf. also Luke 12:9. The translation "in the presence of" serves to avoid the portrayal of the angels as being simply observers (as "before" can connote), on the one hand, or limiting the rejoicing to the angels alone (as "among" can connote), on the other. Clearly the whole company of heaven is meant, including both God and the angels.

Exegetical Commentary

The parable appears only in the Gospel of Luke. The evangelist most likely derived it from his own special tradition, although some have claimed that he obtained it in a more primitive form from Q,[4] and it has even been proposed that Luke himself may have composed it as a sequel to the Parable of the Lost Sheep.[5]

The parable is generally considered a "twin" of the Parable of the Lost Sheep. The combining of parables having similarities in imagery or theme is not in itself distinctive to Luke, for one finds such combining in the Q tradition already (Mustard Seed and Leaven, Matt 13:31-33//Luke 13:18-20) and in Matthew (Hidden Treasure and Pearl, 13:44-46), as well as once again in Luke (Building a Tower and King Going to War, 14:28-33). It is somewhat typical of Luke to match a male example with one involving a woman (cf. 1:6-7; 2:36-38; 4:25, 38; 7:11-15, 36-50; 8:1-3, 19-21, 43-56; 10:38-42; 11:27; 13:10-17).[6] The extensive verbal similarities between this one and the Parable of the Lost Sheep suggest extensive reworking on Luke's part.[7]

The parable is quite remarkable, for it portrays a woman as a metaphor for God. No other parable does so. Furthermore, beside this parable's distinctiveness on that account, Luke combines parables in this instance in which there could only be negative feelings among the Pharisaic critics about the main actors — first a shepherd, now a woman.[8]

There is a (post-NT) rabbinic parable that has some resemblances to Jesus' Parable of the Lost Coin, and that deserves brief attention. Rabbi Phinehas ben Jair (a rabbi of the generation of A.D. 165-200), when commenting on Proverbs 2:4 ("If you seek [wisdom] like silver and search for it as for hidden treasures . . ."), said:

> If you seek after words of Torah as after hidden treasures, the Holy One, blessed be He, will not withhold your reward. If a man loses a *sela* or an *obol*

4. C. Montefiore, *Synoptic Gospels*, 2:984; A. Polag, *Fragmenta Q*, 26, 72.
5. R. Bultmann, *HST* 171; and Michael D Goulder, *Luke: A New Paradigm*, 2 vols. (Sheffield: JSOT Press, 1989), 2:604.
6. L. Johnson, *Luke*, 236.
7. B. Scott, *Parable*, 309.
8. K. Bailey, *Poet*, 158; idem, *Finding the Lost*, 93.

[= tiny coins] in his house, he lights lamp after lamp, wick after wick until he finds it. Now does it not stand to reason: if for these things which are only ephemeral and of this world a man will light so many lamps and lights till he finds where they are hidden, for the words of the Torah which are life both of this world and of the next world, ought you not to search as for hidden treasures?[9]

The story illustrates the motif of searching for what is lost, and how that is done with care — using "lamp after lamp, wick after wick." In Jesus' parable, however, there is an even more urgent action — the sweeping done by the woman. Incidentally, the rabbinic passage also illustrates the not unusual practice of attaching an application to a parable.

The parable presupposes much of what has been said in Appendix 2 on "The Three Parables of Luke 15" and introductory matters concerning the Parable of the Lost Sheep.

15:8. The question ἢ τίς γυνή ("Or what woman") introduces the parable without further ado, continuing a single discourse following upon the Parable of the Lost Sheep. This continuity stands in contrast to the deliberate break between these two and the Parable of the Prodigal Son that follows. The simple wording ("Or what woman?") differs slightly in syntax from the words of 15:3 ("Which one of you . . . ?"). We are to assume that both parables are addressed to men (15:1-2).

It has been observed (and objected) that the first parable is addressed to "which one of *you*?" but the second is "what woman?"; therefore when the parable is read by a woman today, it becomes clear that the woman of the parable is "someone other, someone different from the reader."[10] But the objection misses the fact that, on a literary level, the questions posed by Jesus in both 15:3 and 15:8 are to the Pharisees and scribes of 15:1-2, not to the reader of the Gospel itself.

By means of the opening question ("what woman?") there is a rather timeless, generalizing quality about the unit, resembling a similitude; and it has been classified as such.[11] Nevertheless, it can be considered a parable, for it has the specificity of a particular woman's actions. She acts in a particular and unusual way: sweeping diligently, finding, and then at the end inviting guests to rejoice with her — an action that is not simply typical. Several other parables are introduced by a question as this one is (cf. Matt 21:28; Luke 11:5; 12:42// Matt 24:45; 14:28, 31; 15:3).

The Greek term for the woman's coins is δραχμή ("drachma"), a Greek silver coin mentioned only here and in the next verse in the NT. Its value varied

9. *Cant. Rab.* 1:9; quoted from *MidR*, 9:10-11.
10. S. Durber, "The Female Reader of the Parables of the Lost," 71.
11. R. Bultmann, *HST* 171; E. Linnemann, *Parables*, 65-67; D. Via, *Parables*, 11.

at different times. It is mentioned occasionally in the LXX (Gen 24:22; Exod 39:2; Josh 7:21; 2 Esdr [= Ezra] 2:69; 8:27; Tob 5:14; 2 Macc 4:19; 10:20; 12:43; 3 Macc 3:28). In the passage from Tobit (second century B.C.) one drachma is offered by Tobit as a day's wage to a certain angelic visitor named Azarias. That would make the value of a drachma roughly equivalent to that of a denarius, a Roman coin generally considered sufficient for a day's wage for an unskilled worker.[12] This rough equivalency is confirmed by two passages in the writings of Josephus. At *Ant.* 3.8.2 (§195) Josephus says that a shekel is equal to four drachmas — at a time when a shekel was worth four denarii as well — and at *Ant.* 18.9.1 (§312) he refers to the half-shekel temple tax as a fee of two drachmas, the "double-drachma" coin (δίδραχμον; cf. Matt 17:24, where the δίδραχμον is also spoken of as the [half-shekel] temple tax). Furthermore, "there are pieces of Nero struck at Ephesus, a little earlier than the time of Josephus, upon which may be seen the word ΔΡΑΧΜΗ, and weighing 56 grains, the exact weight of the Roman *denarius*."[13]

How to estimate the value of the woman's total assets becomes speculative. She lives in a "house." Does she live alone and own it as a private dwelling (which would indicate wealth)? Is it provided for her? Does she live with others in the house, or does she have an apartment within a house? Does she have other assets? Is she a widow? All these questions are actually beside the point of a good story. Nor is it helpful in interpreting the parable to suggest that the ten coins would have been part of the woman's dowry, and that she wore them in a headdress that she could not put aside even during sleep.[14] Coins pierced for such a purpose would have little value, and the drachma was so tiny that it would not have served such a purpose very well anyway.[15] Certainly the value of ten drachmas — all that the hearer and reader are told about — would not be very much;[16] she should be considered rather poor.[17] That explains her diligent search.

In the previous parable the sheep that gets lost had gone away without the shepherd's ostensible blame, and in the Parable of the Prodigal Son the younger son leaves home apart from the will of his father. Neither the shepherd nor the father is portrayed as being at fault, although either could be in certain situations. To lose a coin is common enough as well, and it would not be fair to say that the woman is to blame for her loss. But does she implicitly blame herself in

12. BAGD 179; John W. Betlyon, "Coinage," *ABD* 1:1086. A denarius was the usual wage for a soldier or a farm laborer in the first century A.D., according to K. Harl, *Coinage,* 278-79.

13. F. Madden, *History of Jewish Coinage,* 234-35.

14. E. F. F. Bishop, *Jesus of Palestine: The Local Background to the Gospel Documents* (London: Lutterworth Press, 1955), 191; J. Jeremias, *Parables,* 134-35.

15. J. Derrett, "Fresh Light on the Lost Sheep and the Lost Coin," 40-41.

16. J. A. Fitzmyer, *Luke,* 1081.

17. J. Jeremias, *Parables,* 135; Wilhelm Pesch, "δραχμή," *EDNT* 1:354.

the words "the coin which *I* had lost" (15:9b)?[18] Whether she blames herself or not, her search for it is not a matter of pity so much as it is of recovering something of great value to her.

The threefold question ("Does [she] not light a lamp, sweep the house, and search diligently until she finds it?") works effectively; it builds up rhetorically with the expectation of a positive answer. Her lighting a lamp and sweeping the house is to be taken as an aid to her diligent searching (as in the parable of R. Phinehas cited above). It is possible that the house envisioned has no windows for natural lighting. Whatever her living arrangements, the implication is that she sweeps the entire house in which she lives. She does so ἐπιμελῶς ("diligently" or "with extreme care"), a term that is otherwise not used in the NT. The phrase "until she finds it" (cf. the shepherd in the previous parable, 15:4) implies an optimism that cannot be guaranteed in ordinary life; it signifies further the exhaustive efforts made to find what has been lost. The woman, a metaphor for God, carries out her search for the lost with extreme care.

15:9. The Greek terms in this verse for "friends and neighbors" (NRSV) are feminine, implying that the persons invited are women. The clauses correspond to what is said in 15:6: "he calls together his friends and the people from the neighborhood" (cf. a similar expression at 14:12). On the verb συγκαλεῖ ("to call together") as an invitation to a feast, cf. comment on 15:6. Since the woman calls upon those invited to rejoice with her, the implication is that a feast will follow, as in the next parable (15:23-32). At both 15:6 and 9 (as well as at 14:12) Luke uses the term γείτονας (plural for γείτων), which is usually translated as "neighbor," but for more on the nuance of the term, see comment on 15:6. Here in its feminine plural form the term means "neighbor women" or "women from the neighborhood." The woman therefore invites both her women friends and all the other women who live in her neighborhood, whether she considers them persons for whom she has a special attachment and regard or not.

The expression συγχάρητέ μοι ("rejoice with me") corresponds to that of 15:6. The woman invites her friends and the others to enter into her overwhelming sense of joy. The rest of the verse corresponds in wording closely to 15:6 as well, except for the expression that she was the one that had lost the coin, thereby possibly blaming herself, rightly or wrongly.

15:10. The Greek phrase λέγω ὑμῖν ("I say to you") is frequently attributed to Jesus in all four Gospels when he makes an authoritative pronouncement. Cf. comment on 15:7. The parable proper is in 15:8-9; now comes its application.

On joy "in the presence of the angels," see the translation note above; the phrase corresponds with "joy in heaven" in 15:7. There is a parallel to be observed between the rejoicing of the woman with her friends and neighbors and

---

18. That she is portrayed as accepting blame is the view of K. Bailey, *Finding the Lost*, 103; cf. also C. Schersten LaHurd, "Rediscovering the Lost Women of Luke 15," 68.

that of God with the angels in heaven. On "repentance," see the comment on Luke 15:7.

As with the Parable of the Lost Sheep, there appears to be a discrepancy between the parable itself and the application. The woman has joy because of her finding the lost coin, which — as an inert object — had nothing to do with its being discovered. But the repentance of a sinner is a matter of a change within and is an act performed; it is more than simply being found. Therefore it is not surprising that some interpreters consider the saying a secondary addition to the parable itself, whether by Luke or his source.[19]

The discussion at the end of the Exegetical Commentary on the Parable of the Lost Sheep applies here. The application is not impossible, but in its present form has the marks of having been shaped by the evangelist.

Exposition

Luke's setting for the parable (15:1-2) is presupposed as he relates the parable itself. "Tax collectors and sinners" were coming near to Jesus to hear him, and — so his detractors charged — he even ate with them. In the estimation of the Pharisees and the scribes alike, that would mean that disreputable people attached themselves to Jesus, and he made no objection. In fact, Jesus' critics could legitimately ask what it was about Jesus' teaching and conduct that caused them to be drawn to him. Table fellowship is a means of social bonding. Those who care about righteousness before God (as illustrated especially by the Pharisees and the Qumran community) are to avoid all who might induce them to their own way of life. Moreover, people are known by the company they keep.

Jesus defends his conduct of offering these persons a place among his followers, and even a place at his table (!), by means of the three parables of Luke 15.

According to the Parable of the Lost Coin, it can be granted that some persons are truly "lost." They have no vital faith relationship to God. But God, through Jesus — and by implication also his disciples — seeks to reach those who are lost with the good news of the kingdom. That is the good news that God is graciously disposed to them in spite of their being lost. In the Parable of the Lost Sheep the shepherd acts with brashness and energy to seek what is lost. In the Parable of the Lost Coin the woman is portrayed as a person who acts with exacting diligence and care. It is as though God cannot be portrayed simply in terms of the shepherd, a man of daring and energy, but must also be thought of in terms of a woman who is upset by her loss, and who seeks the lost coin with a fastidious, meticulous care that the tradition, androcentric by habit, is apt to forego — with some notable exceptions (cf. Isa 42:13-14, where mas-

19. R. Bultmann, *HST* 171; C. H. Dodd, *Parables,* 92; B. Smith, *Parables,* 191; J. Fitzmyer, *Luke,* 1073.

culine and feminine imagery are yoked; and 66:13, where feminine imagery appears in the midst of otherwise masculine imagery). God's mercy for the lost cannot be contained. God's desire to save them is boundless. God's joy in their being found — their awakening to his grace, resulting in repentance — overflows so as to affect even the angels.

Repentance is a gift granted by God (cf. Acts 5:31; 11:18). It is the discovery of a new perspective on one's relationship to God, who has reached out to reconcile the world already through the ministry of Jesus. Later on, beyond the earthly ministry of Jesus, Paul would say that God's reconciling work had taken place by means of Jesus' crucifixion and resurrection, leading to a new creation for those who hear and believe (2 Cor 5:17-21). The discovery of that new way of seeing and being is, in a profound sense, a being "found," like a coin discovered by a woman who sought it until she found it. The Pauline view, though different in its reference, continues an element grounded in the ministry of Jesus, as interpreted by Luke. Luke interprets, but he does not thereby falsify, an important aspect of Jesus' historical ministry, in which he befriended the despised, the "ungodly" (Rom 4:5; 5:6).

Select Bibliography

Bailey, Kenneth E. *Finding the Lost: Cultural Keys to Luke 15* (St. Louis: Concordia Publishing House, 1992).

Barton, Stephen C. "Parables on God's Love and Forgiveness (Luke 15:1-7// Matthew 18:12-14; Luke 15:8-32)." In *The Challenge of Jesus' Parables*, 199-216. Ed. Richard N. Longenecker. Grand Rapids: Wm. B. Eerdmans, 2000.

Betlyon, John W. "Coinage." *ABD* 1:1076-89.

Bivar, A. D. H. "Coins." *OEANE* 2:41-52.

Derrett, J. Duncan M. "Fresh Light on the Lost Sheep and the Lost Coin." *NTS* 26 (1979): 36-60.

Durber, Susan. "The Female Reader of the Parables of the Lost." *JSNT* 45 (1992): 59-78.

Güttgemanns, Erhardt. "Struktural-generative Analyse des Bildworts 'Die verlorne Drachme' (Lk. 15,8-10)." *LingBibl* 6 (1971): 2-77.

Harl, Kenneth W. *Coinage in the Roman Economy, 300 B.C. to A.D. 700.* Baltimore: Johns Hopkins University Press, 1996.

LaHurd, Carol Schersten. "Rediscovering the Lost Women in Luke 15." *BTB* 24 (Summer 1994): 66-76.

Lamb, R. "Ein Licht ist angezündet. Lukas 15,8-10 aus feministische-befreiungstheologischer Perspektive." *BiKi* 50 (1995): 230-34.

Madden, Frederic W. *History of Jewish Coinage and of Money in the Old and New Testament.* London: B. Quaritch, 1864; reprinted, New York: Ktav Publishing House, 1967.

Menzies, Robert. "The Lost Coin." *ExpTim* 64 (1953): 274-76.

Peisker, Carl H. "Das Gleichnis vom verlorenen Schaf und vom verlorenen Gro-schen." *EvErz* 19 (1967): 58-70.

Pesch, Wilhelm, "δραχμή," *EDNT* 1:353-54.

Walls, A. F. "'In the Presence of the Angels' (Luke XV,10)." *NovT* 3 (1959): 314-16.

2.5. The Prodigal Son, Luke 15:11-32

11*And [Jesus] said, "A certain man had two sons.* 12*And the younger of them said to [his] father, 'Father, give me the share of property that is going to be my inheritance.' And he divided his living between them.*

13*"A few days later the younger son, after converting everything [he had] into cash, went off to a distant country, and there he squandered his property by a wild and disorderly life.* 14*And when he had spent everything he had, a severe famine came upon that country, and he began to be in want.* 15*And he went and joined himself to one of the citizens of that country, and [the latter] sent him into his fields to feed pigs.* 16*And he longed to be fed from the carob pods that the pigs were eating; and no one gave him [anything to eat].*

17*"But when he came to himself, he said, 'How many of my father's hired servants have food in abundance, but here I am perishing with hunger!* 18*I shall get up and go to my father, and I'll say to him, "Father, I have sinned against heaven and before you;* 19*I am no longer worthy to be called your son; treat me like one of your hired servants."'* 20*And he got up and went to his father.*

"But while he was still at a distance, his father saw him and was moved with compassion, and he ran and embraced him and kissed him. 21*And the son said to him, 'Father, I have sinned against heaven and before you; I am no longer worthy to be called your son.'* 22*But the father said to his slaves, 'Bring quickly the best robe, and put it on him; and put a ring on his hand and sandals on his feet;* 23*and bring the fatted calf, kill it, and let us eat and celebrate;* 24*for this son of mine was dead and is alive again; he was lost, and is found.' And they began to celebrate.*

25*"Now his older son was in the field; and as he came and drew near to the house, he heard music and dancing.* 26*And when he had summoned one of the servants, he asked what this might mean.* 27*And he said to him, 'Your brother has come, and your father has killed the fatted calf, because he has received him safe and sound.'* 28*But he got angry and refused to go in. So his father went out and pleaded with him,* 29*but he answered his father, 'Look, I have been slaving away for you for so many years, and never have I disobeyed your command; but never have you given me [even] a young goat, that I might celebrate with my friends.* 30*But when this son of yours came, who has devoured your living with whores, you killed for him the fatted calf!'* 31*And [the father] said to him, 'Son, you are always with me, and all that is mine is yours.* 32*But we had to celebrate and rejoice, for this brother of yours was dead, and is alive; he was lost, and is found.'"*

Notes on the Text and Translation

15:12. The words "the share . . . that is going to be my inheritance" represent the Greek μοι τὸ ἐπιβάλλον μέρος. The verb ἐπιβάλλω ("to fall to") is used in the LXX in the sense of acquiring an inheritance (Tob 3:17; 6:12). Similar expressions exist in pre-Christian secular Greek.[1] In the Lukan context it signifies an anticipated inheritance. RSV reads, "that falls to me"; NRSV has "that will belong to me." The RSV is more literal, but the NRSV reflects the anticipation.

15:13. "A few days later" (as in NEB and NRSV) is more idiomatic than the literal expression "not many days later" (RSV). A similar expression appears at Acts 1:5.

The phrase "after converting everything [he had] into cash" represents the Greek συναγαγὼν πάντα. Cf. NEB: "turned the whole of his share into cash." The phrase may be translated "after gathering everything together," but an almost identical phrase is found in the works of Plutarch (*Cato Min.* 6.7) that unmistakably means "having converted an inheritance into silver."[2]

15:21. Some important Greek witnesses (including ℵ, B, and D), as well as the Vulgate, continue after "I am no longer worthy to be called your son," with, "treat me as one of your hired servants." But other major witnesses (including p75, A, and others) do not have it. The phrase has probably been added to correspond with the son's words in 15:19. The shorter reading is to be preferred.[3]

15:22. On the translation of δούλους as "slaves," see Appendix 3: "*Doulos* — Servant or Slave?"

15:29. The wording "I have been slaving away for you . . ." is more colloquial than most translations, but certainly fitting for an angry son to say in an outburst to his father. The main verb (δουλεύω) means "to serve as a slave" (cf. the NEB and NRSV over against the RSV).[4]

Most Greek witnesses contain the word ἔριφον, but p75 and B read ἐρίφιον. Either term can mean a young male goat, a "kid,"[5] but the latter Greek term (a diminutive of the former) emphasizes how small the gift would be. The stronger attestation of the former speaks in its favor. The latter may be due to

---

1. Cf. Diodorus Siculus, *History* 14.17.5: τὸ ἐπιβάλλον αὐτοῖς μέρος ("the share falling to them"). Cf. also Adolf Deissmann, *Light from the Ancient East: The New Testament Illustrated by Recently Discovered Texts of the Graeco-Roman World* (New York: George H. Doran, 1927), 166, who provides an inscription from a pre-Christian ostracon: ἀπέχω παρὰ σοῦ τὸ ἐπιβάλλον μοι ἐκφόριον ("I have received from you the fruit falling to me"). Still other texts are cited in BAGD 290.

2. Cf. BAGD 782 (with Greek text); MM 600; J. M. Creed, *Luke*, 199; J. Jeremias, *Parables*, 129; I. H. Marshall, *Luke*, 607; and J. Fitzmyer, *Luke*, 1087.

3. Cf. B. Metzger, *TCGNT* 164; A. Plummer, *Luke*, 375; I. H. Marshall, *Luke*, 610; and J. Fitzmyer, *Luke*, 1089-90.

4. BAGD 205.

5. Cf. entries in BAGD 309.

71

mishearing by certain scribes or by reason of their trying to make a subtle interpretive point.

15:32. Literally the Greek reads: "it was necessary to celebrate and rejoice." Cf. RSV. The subject "we" (supplied here) is not in the Greek text. But various translations (NEB, TEV, NIV, NRSV) rightly insert the pronoun, referring to the father and all others on the scene (except the older brother).

Exegetical Commentary

The parable is known generally in English usage as the "Parable of the Prodigal Son." The same equivalent is used in French tradition *(Le fils prodigue)*. In German tradition it is known best as the Parable of the Lost Son *(Der verlorene Sohn)*. In all such cases the attention fastens immediately on the younger son who left home. Yet as the parable unfolds, it is clear that the central figure is not the younger son but the father of the two sons.[6] Perhaps a more apt title would be the "Parable of the Father's Love"[7] or, even better, the "Parable of the Waiting Father," which is the title given to the English translation (but not to the German original) of a book of sermons on the parables by Helmut Thielicke.[8] Nevertheless, the traditional title is so fixed in usage that it would be virtually impossible to supplant it with another.

Frequently the text has been divided, as though the portion in 15:11-24 can be considered the main part, and 15:25-32 an appendage. But all of 15:11-32 must be taken as a unity. That is most obvious from the very first verse: "a certain man had two sons." To conclude a reading at 15:24 is premature, since nothing has been said yet about the second son.

The parable is found only in Luke's Gospel and must be attributed to his special source (L). Discussion concerning its origins (Jesus, Luke, or somewhere between?) will be taken up near the end of the exegetical section.

Luke places the parable in the broader context of 15:1-2 and the Parables of the Lost Sheep (15:4-7) and Lost Coin (15:8-10). At the level of Luke's Gospel — whatever might have been the case prior to it — the parable responds to the grumbling of the Pharisees and scribes. What is said concerning 15:1-2 in

6. Cf. J. Jeremias, *Parables*, 128 (n. 63); E. Schweizer, *Luke*, 247-48; J. Fitzmyer, *Luke*, 1084.

7. Geraint V. Jones, *The Art and Truth of the Parables: A Study in Their Literary Form and Modern Interpretation* (London: SPCK, 1964), 172; R. Stein, *Parables*, 115, calls it "The Parable of the Gracious Father."

8. Helmut Thielicke, *The Waiting Father: Sermons on the Parables of Jesus* (New York: Harper & Brothers, 1959). The title given to the book has been associated with the parable, as though Thielicke came up with it himself. Actually the German original has a quite different title, *Das Bilderbuch Gottes: Reden über die Gleichnisse Jesu* (Stuttgart: Quell-Verlag, 1957), and the parable is designated in the book by its traditional German title, *Der verlorene Sohn* (pp. 13, 33).

Appendix 2 on "The Three Parables of Luke 15" is presupposed here. The relevance of that setting, however, must be taken up again at the end of the exegesis of the parable as a whole.

The parable, the longest in the Gospels, consists of three main parts: (1) the departure of the younger son from his father to a far country where he is wasteful and eventually in want (15:11-19); (2) the homecoming of the son and his welcome by the father (15:20-24); and (3) the episode between the father and the older brother (15:25-32).

15:11-12. In the ancient world, no less than now, a person's property is normally transferred to heirs only at death. That was certainly the case in Roman law.[9] In the case of Jewish law, the relevant legislation is given in Numbers 27:8-11; 36:7-9; and Deuteronomy 21:15-17, and in each text it is assumed that property goes to heirs at the death of the one who passes it on. There is no known evidence of law or custom to suggest that it was a normal procedure to pass on one's property while still alive, nor for a potential heir to ask for it,[10] although it would not be inconceivable for a parent to initiate such a course of action.[11] Otherwise it would be impossible to account for the saying in Sirach 33:20-22 — as well as another in the Talmud[12] — that it is foolish to dispose of one's property to heirs prior to one's death. The request of the younger son, therefore, is exceedingly brash, even insolent. It is tantamount to wishing that the father were dead! Moreover, by leaving his father, he cast aside his obligation to care for him in old age. He rejected the duty of a son to honor his father and mother, as spelled out in the Decalogue (Exod 20:12; Deut 5:16). That lot fell to the older son alone.

According to the laws of inheritance in the OT (Deut 21:17), as well as in the *Mishnah*,[13] a double portion of the father's estate would normally go to the elder brother; therefore the younger one would receive one-third. That would be the "share" of the property that would be his eventual inheritance. The father in the parable was not obligated to divide his "living" among the

9. For various Roman laws concerning inheritance, cf. Fritz Schulz, *Classical Roman Law* (Oxford: Clarendon Press, 1951), 203-333. An inheritance was effective only after death. "It is incredible that a testator should ever have conveyed his whole present and future estate to somebody with immediate effect: he would then have been entirely dependent upon the goodwill of the *familiae emptor* [= the trustee of the estate]" (p. 242).

10. Nahum Levison, *The Parables: Their Background and Local Setting* (Edinburgh: T. & T. Clark, 1926), 156; J. Derrett, "Parable of the Prodigal Son," 104-6; K. Bailey, *Finding the Lost,* 112-14.

11. Cf. Wolfgang Pöhlmann, "Die Abschichtung," 194-213, who maintains that the giving of one's property in contemplation of death is illustrated in Sir 33:20-24 and Tob 8:21. Str-B 2:212 provides a rabbinic saying (ca. A.D. 320) about a king who gave portions of his goods to his sons.

12. *B. B. Mes.* 75b; text in *TalB* 21C.94.

13. Cf. *m. B. Bat.* 8:4-5; *m. Bek.* 8:9.

two sons, but did so. Verse 15:12c implies that the elder son also received his share at that moment, and at 15:31 the father declares to him that all that the father possesses belongs to the elder son, but as the story unfolds the father remains clearly the head of the household and farm, presumably as long as he is able.

Of what does the father's "living" (βίος) that is divided consist? Would it include real estate (i.e., the farm and its furnishings), as well as personal property?[14] The term βίος ("living") is virtually synonymous with οὐσία ("property") in the same verse (as well as at 15:13), and it is something that the father can "divide" (διαιρέω) between the brothers. If the scene portrayed means that the real estate is included, the younger son would then be able to sell his share (a third) of the farm before leaving home. The term βίος is a rather comprehensive word meaning one's "property" or "means" in general[15] or — perhaps better in English — his "means of livelihood."[16] The term οὐσία sometimes includes real property.[17] The term διαιρέω is used in the sense of dividing territories, estates, or a kingdom.[18] Nevertheless, even if a third of the real estate is assigned to the younger son, it is not clear that ownership in the modern sense (title to the land) and the ability to sell the land would have passed to the son. According to Jewish law, as illustrated in the *Mishnah,* neither the father nor the son could fully dispose of the land during the father's lifetime. The father could not sell it, because it has been given to the son. In regard to the son, matters are more complicated. On the one hand, it is said that a son cannot sell property given to him by his father, while the father is alive, because the father continues to have possession of it; on the other hand, it is said that he is allowed to sell it, but the buyer has no claim on it until the father dies.[19]

The economy of telling a good story need not encompass all the details of current law and custom, and it is not certain whether the law cited here (from the second century A.D.) would have been current in the first century. There is a rough parallel to this story in the works of Diogenes Laertius (third century A.D.), in which a younger son takes only the "smaller portion, which was money" of the family's property (οὐσία), in order to finance his travels far and

---

14. Interpreters are divided on the issue. According to J. Jeremias, *Parables,* 128; and R. Stein, *Parables,* 118, the land is included; according to E. Linnemann, *Parables,* 75; and Frederick H. Borsch, *Many Things in Parables: Extravagant Stories of New Community* (Philadelphia: Fortress Press, 1988), 40, it is not.

15. Diogenes Laertius, *Lives* 7.22; LXX Cant 8:7; 2 Esdr (Ezra) 7:26; Mark 12:44// Luke 21:4.

16. F. Borsch, *Many Things in Parables,* 40. M. Tolbert, "The Prodigal Son," 8, suggests "the whole of [the father's] lifetime." But it is more likely that the father's livelihood (the farm, animals, crops, and servants), not simply his life's savings, is meant.

17. Diogenes Laertius, *Lives* 9.35; LXX Tob 14:13; Josephus, *Ant.* 7.114.

18. LXX Josh 18:5; Jdt 16:24; 1 Macc 1:6; Josephus, *Ant.* 5.88.

19. *M. B. Bat.* 8:1. The speaker is R. Jose [ben Halafta] (mid-second century A.D.).

wide.[20] But in contrast to that account of an actual person, this parable — like so many others — portrays things on a grand scale. Most likely we are to assume that the son takes "everything" (15:13) coming to him and turns it into cash, including his share in the land. If this detail must remain unclear, what is more clear is that, as the story goes on, the father continues to possess the "share" that he designated for the elder son (including the farm, or a major portion of it, as 15:25, 31 imply), for he has means by which to host a grand party (15:22-24) and can tell the elder son at the end of the story that all he (still) possesses is his (15:31). The picture that emerges is that, in the case of the younger son, what is given is in effect pure gift. But in the case of the elder son, custom and law are followed by which the father assigns the remaining property to his son, but as long as the father is still alive it remains under his control.[21]

15:13-16. Going away to a distant country implies not only a geographical, but also a psychological, distancing of the son from his father, as well as from his brother and the community as a whole. The distant country would be outside Palestine (cf. 19:12), a country populated primarily by Gentiles. There the young man's life is described as "dissipated" or "wild and disorderly (ἀσώτως)"[22] — whether immoral as well (as implied later in the charge of the elder brother, 15:30) is not clear from the Greek term used — resulting in the loss of all his property. From there on, all goes downhill, including factors beyond his control or fault. A severe famine strikes, which he could not have anticipated when he left home. When he finds himself in want, he hires himself out to work for a "citizen" of that country, a Gentile who raises pigs and sends him into the fields to feed them. At this point his status is that of an indentured servant[23] — a status above that of a slave, but one that bound him by contract to work as a general laborer for his employer for a specified time. To feed pigs is degradation of the worst sort. Pigs are unclean animals in law and tradition (Lev 11:7; Deut 14:8; cf. Isa 65:4; 66:17; 1 Macc 1:47; cf. 2 Macc 6:18; 7:1). According to the *Mishnah*, from subsequent centuries, no one is allowed to rear swine, and according to the *Babylonian Talmud*, the person who does so is accursed.[24] The very idea of wishing to be fed from the "pods" eaten by pigs — and therefore being envious of the pigs! — but being refused, is even more degrading than the act of feeding the pigs itself. The type of pod (κεράτιον) referred to is the carob pod *(ceratonia siliqua)*, used as fodder for pigs.[25]

20. Diogenes Laertius, *Lives* 9.35-36.

21. Conforming here, then, to *m. B. Bat.* 8:7.

22. For translation of the adverb with these terms, cf. Werner Foerster, "ἀσώτως," *TDNT* 1:506-7.

23. Cf. J. A. Harrill, "The Indentured Labor of the Prodigal Son," 714-17.

24. *M. B. Qam.* 7:7: "None may rear swine anywhere"; *b. B. Qam.* 82b: "Cursed be the man who raises pigs."

25. BAGD 429.

15:17-19. The younger son "came to himself (εἰς ἑαυτὸν δὲ ἐλθών)." According to some interpreters, that means that the son repented.[26] But is that so? If so, why did not Luke use the conventional terms for "repentance," which he uses in noun or verb form (μετάνοια, μετανοέω) some twenty-five times in Luke-Acts, and which would have fit the narrative well? The young man is in misery not because of a sense of sin that might lead to repentance, but from his destitution. Perhaps the expression means only that he "came to his senses" (NEB, NIV) and sought how best to get himself out of his horrible situation;[27] and that would be to go home and regain his father's favor — which could be by honest remorse or by manipulation. Similar expressions are found elsewhere,[28] but none of them is a circumlocution for repentance. Augustine — no stranger to the concept of repentance — wrote that the young man had "gone away from himself" and now "he [returned] to himself" (his prior state).[29] Perhaps it is sufficient to say that the young man came to realize how foolish he had been and so "came to his senses." That is a prelude to repentance, even if not repentance itself.

The prodigal recalls that the hired servants of his father have food in abundance. The term for "hired servants" (μίσθιοι) — found in the NT only in Luke 15:17 and 19 (as well as at 15:21 in some manuscripts) — refers to day laborers, persons without steady employment who are hired (or not hired) in the morning for the day's work.[30] They had no ongoing relationship to a particular farm or

26. Tertullian, *On Repentance* 8; C. Montefiore, *Synoptic Gospels*, 2:989; J. Jeremias, *Parables*, 130, citing Str-B 2:215; E. Linnemann, *Parables*, 76; J. Creed, *Luke*, 197; L. Schottroff, "Das Gleichnis vom verlorenen Sohn," 47-49; I. H. Marshall, *Luke*, 607; E. Schweizer, *Luke*, 248; R. Aus, "Luke 15:11-32," 457; H. Hendrickx, *Parables*, 153; D. Wenham, *Parables*, 110; R. Stein, *Parables*, 120; idem, *Luke*, NAC 24 (Nashville: Broadman Press, 1992), 406; R. Culpepper, *NIB (Luke)*, 9:302; and H. Räisänen, "The Prodigal Gentile," 2:1620-21, 1633.

27. A. Jülicher, *Gleichnisse*, 2:345-46; Alfred Loisy, *L'Évangile selon Luc* (Paris: E. Nourry, 1924), 397; G. Jones, *Art and Truth of the Parables*, 182; F. Borsch, *Many Things in Parables*, 41; J. Donahue, *Parable*, 153; K. Bailey, *Poet*, 173-75; idem, *Finding the Lost*, 131; B. Scott, *Parable*, 115-16; Philip Sellew, "Interior Monologue as a Narrative Device in the Parables of Luke," *JBL* 111 (1992): 246. Cf. D. Tiede, *Luke*, 278: "He is sobered . . . , but he is primarily concerned to get something to eat." George W. Ramsey, "Plots, Gaps, Repetitions, and Ambiguity in Luke 15," *PRS* 17 (1990): 38, suggests that the phrase is "tantalizingly ambiguous," and that the reader does not know whether the son is repentant — or scheming and self-seeking (p. 42).

28. Acts 12:11 (ὁ Πέτρος ἐν ἑαυτῷ γενόμενος, "Peter came to himself" [RSV, NRSV]); *T. Jos.* 3:9 (ἦλθον εἰς ἐμαυτόν, "I came to myself"); Epictetus, *Dis.* 3.1.15 (ὅταν εἰς σαυτὸν ἔλθῃς, "when you come to yourself"); and Diodorus Siculus, *History* 13.95.2 (εἰς ἑαυτούς ἐρχόμενοι, "coming to themselves").

29. Augustine, "Sermon 46," *NPNF* 6:409.

30. Gerhard Wallis, "Lohnarbeiter," *BHH* 2:1103. Cf. use of the term in LXX Lev 19:13; Sir 7:20; 37:11. A different term is used in the Parable of the Laborers in the Vineyard (Matt 20:1-16), ἐργάτης, the more common term for "worker."

family.[31] To become such would mean that the young man was moving down the social scale from being an indentured servant (which offered some security) in the far-off country to being a servant in his homeland without any assurance of ongoing employment. That such persons would have "food in abundance" would not likely be literal or descriptive of their actual lot in life, but the young man's statement gives color to the story, emphasizing his own horrible plight and his imaginative dreams. He is headed toward death (as "I am perishing" signifies), a statement that anticipates the father's statements about his son as having died (15:24, 32). His willingness to become as one of the day laborers implies that he would have a status lower not only than sonship, but even lower than that of the slaves and servants of the household and farm (δοῦλοι and παῖδες) mentioned at 15:22, 26. He will know his father as the gracious person he really is — and himself as a son again — only when he is actually received back.[32]

The son, intent on going back home, composes and practices his homecoming speech (15:18-19). Whether truly repentant or not (there is no certainty that he is), the son rehearses by using the language of repentance for his anticipated return. In 15:18b he uses expressions that recall Hebrew tradition at various points. "I have sinned" resonates with Exod 10:16 and Ps 51:6 (LXX). The phrase "against heaven" means "against God," since the term "heaven" is occasionally a pious circumlocution for "God" (cf. Dan 4:26; 1 Macc 3:18; Matt 21:25; Luke 15:7).[33] The expression of having sinned against both God and another person or persons simultaneously has precedent in Exodus 10:16 and Numbers 21:7.

The son plans a threefold statement to his father: a confession of guilt ("I have sinned . . ."), admission of his destruction of the father-son relationship ("no longer worthy to be called your son"), and a possible resolution of the father's plight ("treat me . . ."). The son also plans to address his father as "father." Does this imply an attempt at reconciliation? Not necessarily, for it is the only proper address available.

It is not said what the young man's "sin" might be. While the modern interpreter imagines easily that it had to do with his way of life in the far country, the ancient storyteller and hearer might think otherwise. For them the sin of the younger son would more likely be his insolence in leaving home with his share of the property and therefore not providing for his father in old age, as the commandment requires.[34] Such a view becomes even more probable in light of the elder brother's statement of 15:30, in which he speaks of the younger brother's devouring "*your* property" — precisely that which was to be used to maintain the father beyond his working years when he turns the farm over to his sons.

---

31. Bruce J. Malina and Richard L. Rohrbaugh, *Social Science Commentary on the Gospels* (Minneapolis: Fortress Press, 1992), 372.

32. D. Via, *Parables*, 174.

33. Additional references are in Str-B 2:217.

34. J. Derrett, "Parable of the Prodigal Son," 109-12.

15:20-24. The homecoming scene is portrayed in highly emotional terms. When the father sees his son coming home, and while the son is still at a distance, he "has compassion" on him (15:20). The term for having compassion (σπλαγχνίζομαι) occurs a dozen times in the NT (in the Gospels only).[35] Apart from its use here and in two other parables (10:33; Matt 18:27), the term expresses the divine compassion revealed in Jesus.[36] So here, too, the compassion of the father reflects divine compassion.

Even though the father has compassion on his son, a proper response for him would be to let the young man arrive home, fall on his knees, and ask for forgiveness. Then, in the best of all circumstances, the father would respond with words of forgiveness and a review of expectations. The son would, in effect, be on probation around home for a time; perhaps he could remain there until he could earn enough to leave as an independent person once again.

But those measures of decorum are not what happen. The father *runs* to meet the son — an outlandish behavior, as emphasized by many interpreters.[37] According to tradition, the "way" a man walks "shows what he is" (Sir 19:30), and therefore a dignified man does not run. We must imagine here a prominent person wearing a long robe. In order to run, he must pull up the robe, exposing his legs, which would have been considered shameful in a Semitic culture.[38] Even in a gentile Greco-Roman context, a "proud man" makes slow steps.[39]

Prior to hearing what the son might have to say, the father embraces his son (literally the Greek reads, "he fell upon his neck," an expression found in Gen 33:4; 45:14; 46:29; 3 Macc 5:49; Acts 20:37) and kisses him. The scene recalls, above all, the reconciliation scene between Jacob and Esau, in which nearly the same language is used — Esau (a relatively young man) runs (προσέδραμεν), falls upon the neck of Jacob his younger brother (προσέπεσεν ἐπὶ τὸν τράχηλον αὐτοῦ), and kisses (ἐφίλησεν) him (Gen 33:4).[40] All takes place in the parable as though there is no time or opportunity for the son to greet his father properly, fall at his feet, and begin to make his speech. The fa-

35. Mark 1:41; 6:34//Matt 14:14; Mark 8:2//Matt 15:32; Mark 9:22; Matt 9:36; 18:27; 20:34; Luke 7:13; 10:33; 15:20.

36. Cf. Helmut Koester, "σπλάγχνον," *TDNT* 7:553-55.

37. J. Jeremias, *Parables*, 130; K. Bailey, *Poet*, 181; idem, *Finding the Lost*, 143-46; J. Donahue, *Parable*, 155; and B. Malina and R. Rohrbaugh, *Social-Science Commentary*, 372.

38. K. Bailey, *Finding the Lost*, 144-45; B. Malina and R. Rohrbaugh, *Social-Science Commentary*, 372.

39. Aristotle, *Nicomachean Ethics* 4.3.1125.10-15; cited by K. Bailey, *Finding the Lost*, 144.

40. The Greek of Luke 15:20 reads: δραμὼν ἐπέπεσεν ἐπὶ τὸν τράχηλον αὐτοῦ καὶ κατεφίλησεν αὐτόν. O. Hofius, "Alttestamentliche Motive," 246-47, is correct in pointing out that the sequence of Luke's verbs corresponds to that of the Masoretic Text of Gen 33:4 rather than to that of the LXX. The MT and Luke have the sequence "ran . . . fell . . . kissed," while the LXX has "ran . . . kissed . . . fell."

ther's running, the embrace prior to the son's speech, and the kiss — all these signify reconciliation and prevenient grace on the part of the father. The father has no clue whatsoever concerning the motives of his son or what is on his mind. The father is delightedly joyous to have his son home again.

The son's speech (15:21) — given on his feet, and in his father's arms — is word-for-word from what he practiced (15:18-19a), except that it is interrupted; he cannot get the last line out about how he should be treated as a servant (15:19b). As soon as the son says that he is no longer worthy to be called a son of his father, the father has heard more than enough. His response is to treat him as more than a son (15:22). He is a special guest! The father's bestowing on his son the "best robe" (the expression στολὴν τὴν πρώτην could just as well be translated "the foremost robe" or "the most prominent robe"[41]) signifies a status of honor, as in prior cases: Rebekah's giving one (that had belonged to Esau!) to Jacob (Gen 27:15), Pharaoh's bestowing one on Joseph (Gen 41:42), and Antiochus's presenting one to Philip (1 Macc 6:15). The giving of a "ring" recalls two of these scenes once again, signifying the granting of authority (Gen 41:42; 1 Macc 6:15; cf. also Esth 3:10; 8:2). And, not so incidentally, giving this ring to the younger son — a ring that would normally be passed on to the older son at the death of the father — means that a portentous mixture of signals is going on. Granting the ring indicates that the younger son has in effect now supplanted his older brother; yet the remainder of the property will still fall to the latter (15:31). Placing "shoes on his feet" implies not only that the son came home barefoot, but entails a twofold symbolic action. It implies the bestowal of freedom (insofar as slaves typically lacked shoes),[42] and it is an act by which the slaves — by their act of placing the shoes on his feet — acknowledge him as their master.[43] Now the son has been fully restored to the family and the community.[44] Moreover, in all the flurry of activity — the father's running to meet his son, embracing him, and presenting him with gifts (which might include his very

41. Cf. BAGD 726 (under 1, c.α). Cf. also *Jos. Asen.* 18:3, where Aseneth brings out τὴν στολὴν αὐτῆς τὴν πρώτην ("her first robe") for her marriage. For the Greek text, cf. *Joseph et Aséneth: Introduction, texte critique, traduction et notes*, ed. Marc Philonenko, SPB 13 (Leiden: E. J. Brill, 1968), 192; the English text is at 18.5 in *OTP* 2:232.

42. As various interpreters have emphasized, including J. Jeremias, *Parables*, 130; I. H. Marshall, *Luke*, 610; K. Bailey, *Poet*, 185; idem, *Finding the Lost*, 155; J. Donahue, *Parable*, 155.

43. J. Derrett, "Parable of the Prodigal Son," 113-14; B. Scott, *Parable*, 118.

44. The symbolism of the robe, ring, and shoes has been investigated thoroughly in the work of K. Rengstorf, *Die Re-Investitur des Verlorenen Sohnes*, 39-51, against the background of many texts and traditions. His thesis that the story presupposes the restoration of one on whom the legal custom of *kesasah* ("separation") has previously been enacted, however, goes beyond the evidence within the parable itself. Cf. the critique of I. H. Marshall, *Luke*, 606.

own festive garment; cf. NEB, "*my* best" robe, at 15:22) — the son is being protected by the father from hostile village reaction.[45]

Already there is enough going on to threaten the status of the elder brother. But there is more. The father orders the killing of the fatted calf, eating, and merrymaking (15:23). Any calf that has been fattened has been kept for a special event (cf. 1 Sam 28:24-25), and it would feed a very large gathering of people, including not only the immediate household but all those in the vicinity deemed significant by the father.[46] The term "to make merry" (εὐφραίνω, also in 15:24, 29, 32) is often, as here, used in connection with the merriment of banqueting (LXX Deut 14:26; 27:7; Eccl 8:15; Luke 12:19; 16:19). The father's declarations in 15:24 about his son (dead/alive again; lost/found) complete the scene. The son who had been perishing (15:17) in a far-off country, and as good as dead to a father who had been abandoned by him, can now be called alive again. The language of lost/found on the lips of the father (both here and at 15:32) links the parable to the exclamations of the shepherd and the woman in parables preceding it (15:6, 9).

15:25-32. These verses comprise the third scene of the parable, the episode of the father and his elder son. Immediately the elder son is said to be "in the field," which signifies to the hearer or reader that he is hardworking and loyal. It is strange that he was not told immediately about the return of his brother. The first he hears of it is when he approaches the house and hears what is going on ("music and dancing"). But such a detail provides for a more dramatic and emotional scene to follow. When he is told of the reason for the celebration (15:27), he becomes angry — the opposite of the rejoicing going on inside — and refuses to enter.

The father, risking humiliation and shame, leaves his guests inside the house, goes outdoors, and pleads with the elder son to come in and join the celebration. The response of the son (15:29-30) overflows with painful protest against the father's overly generous behavior toward the younger son. The father should make some demands on his wastrel son and put him on probation, but instead he has made a fool out of himself by not only accepting the fellow back home but making some kind of hero out of him! In his outburst to his father, the elder son (1) makes claims about himself as the long-standing obedient one; (2) excoriates the father for not being grateful for his obedience; and (3) humiliates the father for his foolishness. In all of this, his relationship with his father is seen to be based on law, merit, and reward rather than on love and graciousness.

---

45. Cf. B. Malina and R. Rohrbaugh, *Social Science Commentary,* 372; and K. Bailey, *Finding the Lost,* 143.

46. K. Bailey, *Finding the Lost,* 155: "the extended family and all the prominent people in town." His estimate that it would take "perhaps two hundred people to eat a fatted calf" seems extreme.

His claim to never have disobeyed a "command" of the father most certainly — at the level of Luke's Gospel — makes a not-so-veiled reference to the Pharisees and scribes present (15:2), for the term for "command" (ἐντολή) can also mean "commandment." The language of the son, οὐδέποτε ἐντολήν σου παρῆλθον ("never have I disobeyed your command") is virtually identical to that of Deut 26:13 in the LXX, οὐ παρῆλθον τὴν ἐντολήν σου ("I have not transgressed your commandment"), where "commandment," rather than "command," is required by the context. The same double meaning of the terminology would have been the case in the speech of Jesus, for in both Hebrew and Aramaic one word (מִצְוָה, miswah, and variations) serves for both "command" and "commandment" as well.[47]

In comparison to the fatted calf, the gift of a "young goat" for a celebration would be considerably less. While cattle were rather scarce and certainly expensive, goats were common and inexpensive (less than one-tenth the value of a cow);[48] and whereas the production of a fatted calf would take months of care and feeding, producing a young goat for a meal would be routine.

The charge that the younger son devoured the father's living ("*your* living," 15:30) with "whores" (either the term "harlots" or "prostitutes" is used in modern English translations, but those words are too formal for an angry outburst) is a product of the elder son's imagination. To charge that the younger son did such — and by implication say that he had had sex with "gentile whores, pigs!" — is to express utter contempt for him. Although it has been suggested that a report must have gotten back to the elder son about the conduct of the prodigal,[49] that is to historicize. It is a wonderful story as it stands.

Throughout the interchange between the father and his elder son there are elements of defiance and scorn on the part of the latter. That is obvious in the use of terminology concerning the various parties: (1) the servant announces to the elder son that his "brother" had returned and what his "father" had done (15:27); (2) the son does not address his father as "father" (in contrast to the younger son at 15:21) nor speak of his brother as his brother but pejoratively as "this son of yours" (15:29-30); nevertheless, (3) the father calls the one standing before him "son" (or "child," τέκνον, "an affectionate address to a son"[50]) and refers to the other as "this brother of yours" (15:31-32). The words of the elder brother in 15:30 (ὁ υἱός σου οὗτος, "this son of yours") are most certainly contemptuous. The response of the father with the very same turn of phrase in 15:32 (ὁ ἀδελφός σου οὗτος, "this brother of yours") must certainly

47. Cf. B. Levine, "מִצְוָה," *TDOT* 8:505-14.
48. Cf. Edwin Firmage, "Zoology," *ABD* 6:1119-20. According to him, the ratio of sheep and goats to cattle was anywhere from 2:1 to 7:1, depending on the topography, and the ratio of the value of a goat to a cow was less than 1:10. The price for a goat was two-thirds of a shekel; that for a cow ten shekels.
49. J. Creed, *Luke*, 201.
50. BAGD 808, citing Matt 21:28b; Luke 2:48; 15:31.

be deliberate.[51] It is not simply a playback to the older son, although it is that, but a reminder on the part of the father of the relationship between the two sons. In all of this the father considers both young men as his sons; and he considers them brothers, even if the elder has problems with that. Moreover, by his use of the terms "son" and "brother" he is trying to restore a family that has fallen apart.

The story closes with the father's affirmation that the elder son is "always" (15:31, in contrast to the son's "never" of 15:29)[52] with him, and that he is still heir to all that is now left. "Where the son saw himself as a faithful slave, the father views him as a *companion* ('always with me') and *co-owner* of the farm ('all that is mine is yours')."[53] Although the elder son will not have full possession of the property until the death of the father in a legal sense (so that he could dispose of it as he wishes), *de facto* the father and son hold it in common (cf. comment on 15:11-12).

Various interpreters have seized upon the father's saying in 15:31 ("you are always with me") to say that the parable does not actually fit the context of 15:1-2.[54] How can the elder son represent the Pharisees and scribes without ascribing to them an abiding fidelity to God and claiming that they are heirs of the promises of God? Yet that is to miss the true parallel: as the elder brother is unable to rejoice in the restoration of one who is lost, so, too, the Pharisees and scribes grumble over the reception of "sinners" by Jesus.[55]

The parable ends with the words of the father. Nothing more is said about either son. Did the elder finally accede to his father's wish; did the younger prosper in his new status; did the two reconcile? The parable comes to an end with the father's statements. Moreover, unlike the two before it, this one ends without a direct application. As one interpreter has said, the parable is great art, and it needs no further word "to enforce its intention."[56]

Three issues must be taken up in conclusion. First, there is the question of the parable's origins. It has been claimed that the parable, because of its theo-

---

51. T. Corlett, "This Brother of Yours," 216.

52. F. Bovon, "The Parable of the Prodigal Son," 61.

53. B. Scott, *Parable*, 121.

54. Craig A. Evans, *Luke*, NIBC 3 (Peabody, Mass.: Hendrickson Publishers, 1990), 592; H. Räisänen, "The Prodigal Gentile," 2:1623.

55. B. Scott, *Parable*, 103, denies that the elder son would have been identified with the Pharisees in the original parable of Jesus. That, he says, would imply the rejection of the son, which does not occur in the parable itself. But why a rejection? Cf. also B. Scott, "The Prodigal Son," 45-48. Scott seems to think that the Pharisees are being rejected, so the son would have to be also. This is a misreading. Both the Pharisees and the son are implicitly criticized, not rejected. Fred B. Craddock, *Luke* (Louisville: John Knox Press, 1990), 188: "The embrace of the younger son did not mean the rejection of the older; the love of tax collectors and sinners does not at all negate love of Pharisees and scribes."

56. G. Jones, *Art and Truth of the Parables*, 168.

logical compatibility with that of the Gospel of Luke as a whole, was composed by Luke himself,[57] or that only 15:11-24 came from the pre-Lukan tradition, and that 15:25-32 was composed secondarily by Luke or a predecessor (but not Jesus).[58] But such proposals have not been accepted by a good many other interpreters.[59] While it can be granted that there are Lukan stylistic touches to the whole of 15:11-32, the essentials of what is there can be attributed to pre-Lukan tradition.[60] The parable has widely been attributed to the historical Jesus,[61] but not by those who attribute it to Luke.

The source question is related to the fundamental question: Did Luke retroject his theology upon Jesus by creating this parable, or did the proclamation of Jesus in this parable and other teachings give shape to Luke's theology?

57. L. Schottroff, "Das Gleichnis vom verlorenen Sohn," 27-52; John Drury, *The Parables in the Gospels* (New York: Crossroad, 1985), 142; Jack T. Sanders, *The Jews in Luke-Acts* (Philadelphia: Fortress Press, 1987), 108 (in spite of his earlier view; cf. next note). That Luke worked with some pieces of tradition (similar to Matt 21:28-32) but essentially created the parable himself is held by J. van Goudoever, "The Place of Israel in Luke's Gospel," *NovT* 8 (1966): 121; Michael D. Goulder, *Luke: A New Paradigm*, 2 vols. (Sheffield: JSOT Press, 1989), 2:609-14; and as a possibility by Heikki Räisänen, "The Prodigal Gentile," 2:1617-36. But on the unlikelihood that the parable was created on the basis of Matt 21:28-32 (or something similar), see the exegetical commentary on the latter.

58. J. Sanders, "Tradition and Redaction in Luke xv.11-32," 433-38.

59. There are good grounds for rejecting such views. For example, the claim of L. Schottroff, "Das Gleichnis vom verlorenen Sohn," 27-52, that the parable reflects Lukan theology, especially soteriology, is facile. She claims that, for Luke, salvation is not possible without repentance, indeed, that salvation is repentance and forgiveness of sins. Then she sees these elements in the parable. But, as pointed out in the discussion of 15:17 and elsewhere, it is not clear that the younger son repents at all, and that is one of the intriguing and significant ambiguities of the parable. The father accepts the son on the basis of his own love, not the worthiness of the son.

60. J. Jeremias, "Tradition und Redaktion in Lukas 15," 172-89; idem, *Die Sprache des Lukasevangeliums: Redaktion und Tradition im Nicht-Markusstoff des dritten Evangeliums*, MeyerK (Göttingen: Vandenhoeck & Ruprecht, 1980), 248-55; J. O'Rourke, "Some Notes on Luke xv. 11-32," 431-33; I. Broer, "Das Gleichnis vom Verlorenen Sohn und die Theologie des Lukas," 459-60; C. Carlston, "Reminiscence and Redaction in Luke 15:11-32," 368-90; F. Schnider, *Der Verlorenen Söhne*, 87-88; F. Bovon, "The Parable of the Prodigal Son," 452; I. H. Marshall, *Luke*, 605-6; F. Borsch, *Many Things in Parables*, 45-46; J. Fitzmyer, *Luke*, 1085. Important here, too, are the observations of O. Hofius, "Alttestamentliche Motive," 240-48, in which he maintains that several expressions in the parable are based on the MT rather than the LXX, indicating pre-Lukan authorship and pointing to an original narrator who made use of the Hebrew OT (which he takes to be Jesus).

61. A. Jülicher, *Gleichnisreden Jesu*, 2:333-65; J. Jeremias, *Parables*, 128-32; K. Rengstorf, *Die Re-Investitur des Verlorenen Sohnes*, 61-62; J. O'Rourke, "Some Notes on Luke xv.11-32," 431-33; Roger D. Aus, "Luke 15:11-32 and R. Eliezer ben Hyrcanus's Rise to Fame," 465-69; J. Lambrecht, *Astonished*, 46-49; H. Hendrickx, *Parables*, 150; J. Fitzmyer, *Luke*, 1085. It is classified as "pink" (= Jesus probably said something like this) by the members of the Jesus Seminar; cf. R. Funk, *Five Gospels*, 356-57.

One can never know for certain. Yet it is difficult to imagine that the parable came from anyone but Jesus, whose teaching — mediated through others — influenced Luke profoundly. Both the structure and the theology of the parable are very similar to that of the Workers in the Vineyard (Matt 20:1-16),[62] which cannot be attributed to Luke. The two parables together can be considered a double attestation of the theology of Jesus himself. Those who attribute it to Luke consider it to have been created by the evangelist to address concerns of Luke's own day, not those of Jesus' day. According to one view, Luke created the parable to teach conservative Jewish Christians — represented by the elder brother — "that converted Gentiles, too, are accepted by God and should be joyously received by the community."[63] But it is precisely the identification of the younger brother with Gentiles that is a problem. His going away from his father, his coming to himself, his returning to his father — how does that correspond with the entrance of Gentiles into the Christian community? Does it not correspond more accurately with the recurring story of Israel (apostasy, repentance, and return)?[64] The younger son is not ignorant (in gentile fashion) of the father (identified with God) but is insolent toward him and wastes what has been given to him; in short, he is immoral, not ignorant. Moreover, the second half of the parable — in which the elder brother represents the Pharisees and scribes — most likely reflects Jesus' historical situation, in which actual persons in these groups protested Jesus' fellowship with the despised. That is more likely the point of origin than anything in Luke's setting, such as an alleged tension between traditional Jewish Christians and others who were accepting Gentiles; that was a non-issue in Luke's day.[65] The elder brother's anger is highly moralistic. It is directed primarily toward his father (and only indirectly toward his brother), based on the father's acceptance of one who is unworthy on moral grounds.

A second issue concerns the question: Since the parable has two distinct parts, where does the accent of its teaching lie? J. Jeremias has included this parable with others in a category of "double-edged parables," in which the emphasis falls consistently on the second half.[66] Rudolf Bultmann has included it

---

62. Petr Pokorny, "Lukas 15,11-32 und die lukanische Soteriologie," 180-81; cf. Anders Nygren, *Agape and Eros* (Philadelphia: Westminster Press, 1953), 81-91.

63. H. Räisänen, "The Prodigal Gentile," 2:1626.

64. This is a variation of the view of N. T. Wright, *Jesus and the Victory of God* (Minneapolis: Fortress Press, 1996), 126, in which the going away and return of the younger son represent exile and restoration.

65. H. Räisänen, "The Prodigal Gentile," 2:1624-27, looks to Acts 15:5 as evidence that Christian Pharisees opposed the admission of Gentiles without circumcision. But by the time that Luke wrote Luke-Acts the issue was long settled.

66. J. Jeremias, *Parables*, 131. Others in the category are the Parables of the Rich Man and Lazarus (Luke 16:19-31), the Laborers in the Vineyard (Matt 20:1-15), and the Marriage Feast (Matt 22:1-14). In the German edition the term used is *"doppelgipflige*

among those that portray an antithesis of two types of characters.[67] But in neither case do the other parables cited by Bultmann have a true break between two parts in the stark manner that this one does. They are in each case clearly a unit in which one could not possibly stop prior to the end, whereas in this one there are two distinct parts, and the history of interpretation — so often favoring an ending at 15:24 — shows how marked the break is. Nevertheless, as indicated at the outset of the discussion, this parable, too, is a unit that cannot come to an end prior to 15:32; it is about a man who had *two* sons. And one cannot escape the fact that, as it is heard or read, the emphasis falls where the story comes to an end.[68] Nevertheless, another issue must be taken up before a decision can be made.

The third issue is that of its context. Luke has placed it against the backdrop of 15:1-2, the grumbling of the Pharisees and scribes against Jesus. Could such a setting be possible in the historical ministry of Jesus? The problem with an affirmative answer is that in this parable, then, Jesus compares his opponents to the elder son, who has been obedient and is declared (again) to be an heir. Could Jesus, even for a moment, have entertained the possibility that God (symbolized by the father) considered Jesus' opponents as persons who have served God "these many years," rather than as disobedient? As already indicated, however, the point of comparison is the refusal — indeed, the complaining — of the elder son (15:31-32) and the opponents (15:2) in their respective, similar situations. To demand more parallels, and then to find fault with the correlations imagined, borders on allegorizing. There is no sufficient reason to discount the setting Luke has provided.[69] In any case, our purpose is to interpret the parable in its canonical setting.

The question must finally be asked, What is the point, or main thrust, of the parable? (1) Could it be that, by this parable, Jesus sought to illustrate the loving character of God? No earthly father loves and acts like this one, but God does.[70] (2) Could it be that Jesus sought to vindicate his message and activities (fellowship with the outcast) in reply to his critics?[71] (3) Could it be that he sought to teach his opponents that the time has arrived for celebrating the ingathering of those who are repentant and are responding to his message?[72] Certainly all three points are facets carried along by the parable. Together the vari-

---

Gleichnisse"; Joachim Jeremias, *Die Gleichnisse Jesu*, 7th ed. (Göttingen: Vandenhoeck & Ruprecht, 1965), 131.

67. R. Bultmann, *HST* 192, 196.

68. Cf. J. Jeremias, *Parables*, 131; E. Linnemann, *Parables*, 78; J. Price, "Luke 15:11-32," 67; R. Stein, *Parables*, 123; contra B. Scott, *Parable*, 105.

69. C. H. Dodd, *Parables*, 92-93; J. Jeremias, *Parables*, 131-32; E. Linnemann, *Parables*, 69; R. Stein, *Parables*, 123.

70. A. Nygren, *Agape and Eros*, 81-84.

71. J. Jeremias, *Parables*, 131; R. Stein, *Parables*, 123.

72. E. Linnemann, *Parables*, 80.

ous facets make common cause to depict the ministry of Jesus as the inauguration of the kingdom of God, a God whose love surpasses all typical expressions known to humanity, and which is celebrated by those who are caught up in the joy of the kingdom. The parable portrays the love of God in such a way that it evokes resentment in those who assume that they know all there is to know about it.

Exposition

As if the Parables of the Lost Sheep (15:4-7) and Lost Coin (15:8-10) were not sufficient to drive the point across concerning the joy of God at the restoration of the lost, Jesus tells another. Sheep go astray, and coins get lost. There is a sense of loss in each case. But that does not begin to compare to the loss and pain felt in consequence of the breakup of a home and the assault of one member upon another. As the story unfolds, each of the brothers insists upon his rights — whether property or honor — and treats the father with contempt.

If a contrast of character types is to be made, it is not only between the two brothers, but also between the brothers and their father. The brothers differ in their contrasting lifestyles — the one going away and spending all he had, the other staying home and preserving the estate. But in one major way they are very much alike and stand in contrast to the father. Both are abusive of the father, while the father remains devoted to each. There can be little doubt but what the father is the main character of the story. It is his relationship with his two sons that is the dynamic thread throughout the story.

What is so striking in his dealings with each of the sons is that he extends unconditional love prior to repentance — indeed, even *apart from* repentance on the part of either son. To be sure, the younger son comes home (but that does not in itself indicate repentance; see above), and he makes a fine speech that sounds like repentance. But the twin facts that (1) he knows he can go home and (2) the father runs and embraces him before any speech is even allowed — these two points illustrate the father's love as unconditional prior to — indeed, *apart from* — repentance. And with the unconditional love is total forgiveness. In the case of the older brother, in spite of his contemptuous comments to his father and about his brother, the father assures him that all he has belongs to him still. There is no need for the son to apologize for his harsh words to the father. According to the father, the bond between them has not been severed. The attitude of the father toward his sons is not determined by their character, but his.

Since the father clearly represents God, there is risk here in assuming or asserting that God sets aside judgment and wrath in favor of forgiveness no matter how great the offense, and no matter how sincere or insincere a person is who is moving toward change. But in so many cases it is only when the good news of divine forgiveness is offered as having been extended *already* that there is a safe enough environment for transformation to occur in a person's life. Moreover, how far is one willing to go to say that God requires repentance on our part before he can forgive our sins? To be sure, "the entire life of believers [should be] one of repentance," as Martin Luther put it in the first of his Ninety-Five Theses (1517).[73] But while that may be doctrinally correct in principle, fulfilling it may not finally be possible for many, including the most "religious," unless they are able to do so at the moment before death. Even the person who is most insistent that repentance is necessary for salvation must finally leave all to the grace of God. Within human relationships — such as relationships between members of a family in particular — forgiveness happens all the time apart from apologies; the offended person simply forgives, and life moves on. The same must be true in the divine-human relationship. If we must be repentant in order to be saved, God have mercy on us! But that's the point. When all is said and done, and even when a person has lived repentantly, he or she must leave all in the hands of a merciful and gracious God. The parable clearly portrays the love and forgiveness of God as unconditional and prevenient (= coming before human readiness to ask for them). It is not surprising that Anders Nygren, in his major study of the love that is characteristic of God (ἀγάπη, agápe), included a study of the Parable of the Prodigal Son as a prime example.[74]

What is also of immense importance in this parable is the accent on the father's rejoicing and then his telling his elder son how necessary that is (15:24, 32). Those who assert their own claims of righteousness (". . . never have I disobeyed your command") find it most difficult to rejoice when those who cannot do the same are considered equal to them. It is hard to recognize the work of God in and through such persons. Yet that is what is at stake in the parable. Those who are righteous — or think they are — are still loved by God; the difficulty is to get them to realize that others are as well. Equally difficult — perhaps even more difficult — is to get them to realize that God's grace, not their own imagined righteousness, is the basis for their own salvation as well. A moralistic view of the divine/human relationship stands in the way of one's own fellowship with God, and it impedes the imagination in regard to God's relationship with others.

Select Bibliography

Aus, Roger D. "Luke 15:11-32 and R. Eliezer ben Hyrcanus's Rise to Fame." *JBL* 104 (1985): 443-69.

---

73. Martin Luther, "Ninety-Five Theses," in *Luther's Works,* ed. Jaroslav Pelikan and Helmut T. Lehmann; 55 vols. (St. Louis: Concordia Publishing House; Philadelphia: Fortress Press, 1955-76), 31:25.
74. Cf. n. 62 above.

Bailey, Kenneth E. *Finding the Lost: Cultural Keys to Luke 15* (St. Louis: Concordia Publishing House, 1992).

————. "Jacob and the Prodigal Son: A New Identity Story: A Comparison between the Parable of the Prodigal Son and Gen. 27–35." *ThRev* 18 (1997): 54-72.

Baldwin, Robert W. "A Bibliography of the Prodigal Son Theme in Art and Literature." *BBib* 44 (1987): 167-71.

Barton, Stephen C. "Parables on God's Love and Forgiveness (Luke 15:1-7//Matthew 18:12-14; Luke 15:8-32)." In *The Challenge of Jesus' Parables,* 199-216. Ed. Richard N. Longenecker. Grand Rapids: Wm. B. Eerdmans, 2000.

Batten, Alicia. "Dishonor, Gender and the Parable of the Prodigal Son." *TJT* 13 (1997): 187-200.

Borghi, E. "Lc 15,11-32. Linee esegetiche globali." *RivB* 44 (1996): 279-308.

Bovon, François. "The Parable of the Prodigal Son, Luke 15:11-32, First Reading" and "The Parable of the Prodigal Son, Second Reading." In *Exegesis: Problems of Method and Exercises in Reading (Genesis 22 and Luke 15),* 43-73, 441-66. Ed. François Bovon and Grégoire Roullier. PTMS 21. Pittsburgh: Pickwick Press, 1978.

Broer, Ingo. "Das Gleichnis vom Verlorenen Sohn und die Theologie des Lukas." *NTS* 29 (1974): 453-62.

Brown, Colin. "The Parable of the Rebellious Son(s)." *SJT* 51 (1998): 391-405.

Carlston, Charles E. "Reminiscence and Redaction in Luke 15:11-32." *JBL* 94 (1975): 368-90.

Corlett, Tom. "This Brother of Yours." *ExpTim* 100 (1989): 216.

Crawford, Robert G. "Parable of the Atonement." *EvQ* 50 (1978): 2-7.

Dakin, Arthur. "The Prodigal Son as Literature." *ExpTim* 35 (1923-24): 330-31.

Deissmann, Adolf. "The Parable of the Prodigal Son." *RelLife* 1 (1932): 331-38.

Derrett, J. Duncan M. "Law in the New Testament: The Parable of the Prodigal Son." *NTS* 14 (1967): 56-74; reprinted as "The Parable of the Prodigal Son." In his *Law in the New Testament,* 100-125. London: Darton, Longman & Todd, 1970.

————. "The Parable of the Prodigal Son: Patristic Allegories and Jewish Midrash." In *StPat* 10/1, 219-24. Ed. Frank L. Cross. TU 107. Berlin: Akademie Verlag, 1970.

Duff, Nancy J. "Luke 15:11-32." *Int* 49 (1995): 66-69.

Dupont, Jacques. "Le fils prodigue: Lc 15,1-3.11-32." *ASeign* 17 (1969): 64-72.

Evenrud, Jerry A. "Visual Exegesis: 'The Prodigal Son.'" *Arts* 4 (1992): 4-9.

Fuchs, Ernst. "Das Fest der Verlorenen: Existentiale Interpretation des Gleichnisses vom verlorenen Sohn." In his *Glaube und Erfahrung: Zum christologischen Problem im Neuen Testament,* 402-15. Tübingen: J. C. B. Mohr (Paul Siebeck), 1965.

Grelot, Pierre. "Le père et ses deux fils: Luc, XI,11-32." *RB* 84 (1977): 321-48, 538-65.

Harrill, J. Albert. "The Indentured Labor of the Prodigal Son (Luke 15:15)." *JBL* 115 (1996): 714-17.

Harrington, Wilfrid. "The Prodigal Son." *Furrow* 25 (1974): 432-37.

Hendrickx, Herman. "A Man Had Two Sons: Lk. 15:11-32 in Light of the Ancient Mediterranean Values of Farming and Household." *EAPR* 31 (1994): 46-66.

Hiroishi, Nozomu. "Die Gleichniserzählung vom verlorenen Sohn (Lk 15,11-32). Eine form- und traditionsgeschichtliche Untersuchung der Gleichniserzählung Jesu im lukanischen Sondergut." *AJBI* 16 (1990): 71-99.

Hofius, Otfried. "Alttestamentliche Motive im Gleichnis vom verlorenen Sohn." *NTS* 24 (1977): 240-48.

Hoppe, Rudolf. "Gleichnis und Situation: Zu den Gleichnissen vom guten Vater (Lk 15:11-32) und gütigen Hausherrn (Matt 20:1-15)." *BZ* 1 (1984): 1-21.

Hurst, Antony. "The Prodigal Son." *ExpTim* 98 (1997): 274-75.

Jeremias, Joachim. "Zum Gleichnis vom verlorenen Sohn, Luk. 15,11-32." *TZ* 5 (1949): 228-31.

————, "Tradition und Redaktion in Lukas 15," *ZNW* 62 (1971): 172-89.

Klötzli, Wilfried. *Ein Mensch hatte zwei Söhne: Eine Auslegung vom Lukas 15,11-32.* Zürich: Gotthelf-Verlag, 1966.

Lees, J. G. "The Parable of the Good Father." *ExpTim* 97 (1985-86): 246-47.

Niebuhr, Karl W. "Kommunikationsebenen im Gleichnis vom verlorenen Sohn." *TLZ* 116 (1991): 481-94.

Nouwen, Henri J. *The Return of the Prodigal Son: A Meditation on Fathers, Brothers, and Sons.* New York: Doubleday, 1992.

Noyen, Carlos. "'Teilt meine Freude': Exegetische Randbemerkungen zu Lukas 15,11-32." *IKaZ* 22 (1993): 387-96.

O'Rourke, John J. "Some Notes on Luke xv.11-32." *NTS* 18 (1972): 431-33.

Parsons, Mikeal C. "The Prodigal Son's Elder Brother: The History and Ethics of Reading Luke 15:25-32." *PRS* 23 (1996): 147-74.

Patte, Daniel. "Structural Analysis of the Parable of the Prodigal Son: Toward a Method." In *Semiology and Parables: Exploration of the Possibilities Offered by Structuralism for Exegesis,* 71-149. Ed. Daniel Patte, PTMS 9 (Pittsburgh: Pickwick Press, 1976).

Pesch, Rudolf. "Zur Exegese Gottes durch Jesus von Nazaret: Eine Auslegung des Gleichnisses von Vater und den beiden Söhnen (Lk 15,11-32)." In *Jesus: Ort der Erfahrung Gottes: Festschrift für Bernhard Welte,* 140-89. Ed. Bernhard Casper. Freiburg: Herder, 1976.

Pöhlmann, Wolfgang. "Die Abschichtung des Verlorenen Sohnes (Lk 15:12f.) und die erzählte Welt der Parabel." *ZNW* 70 (1979): 194-213.

Pokorny, Petr. "Lukas 15,11-32 und die lukanische Soteriologie." In *Christus Bezeugen: Festschrift für Wolfgang Trilling zum 65 Geburtstag,* 179-92. Ed. Karl Kertelge et al. EThS 59. Leipzig: St. Benno, 1989.

Price, James L. "Luke 15:11-32." *Int* 31 (1977): 64-69.

Räisänen, Heikki. "The Prodigal Gentile and His Jewish Christian Brother: Lk 15,11-3." In *The Four Gospels 1992: Festschrift Frans Neirynck*, 2:1617-36. Ed. Frans van Segbroeck et al. BETL 100. 3 vols. Leuven: Leuven University Press, 1992.

Ramsey, George W. "Plots, Gaps, Repetitions, and Ambiguity in Luke 15." *PRS* 17 (1990): 33-42.

Rengstorf, Karl H. *Die Re-investitur des verlorenen Sohnes in der Gleichniserzählung Jesu: Luk. 15,11-32*. Cologne: Westdeutscher Verlag, 1967.

Rickards, Raymond R. "Some Points to Consider in Translating the Parable of the Prodigal Son." *BT* 31 (1980): 243-45.

Robbins, Jill. *Prodigal Son/Elder Brother: Interpretation and Alterity in Augustine, Petrarch, Kafka, Levinas*. Chicago: University of Chicago Press, 1991.

Rohrbaugh, Richard L. "A Dysfunctional Family and Its Neighbors." In *Jesus and His Parables: Interpreting the Parables of Jesus Today*, 141-64. Ed. V. George Shillington. Edinburgh: T. & T. Clark, 1997.

Sahi, Jyoti. "Reflections on the Image of the Prodigal Son." *ITS* 34 (1997): 168-84.

Sanders, Jack T. "Tradition of Redaction in Luke xv.11-32." *NTS* 15 (1969): 433-38.

Schnider, Franz. *Die Verlorenen Söhne: Strukturanalytische und historisch-kritische Untersuchungen zu Lk 15*. OBO 17. Göttingen: Vandenhoeck & Ruprecht, 1977.

Schniewind, Julius. "Das Gleichnis vom verlorenen Sohn." In his *Die Freude der Busse: Zur Grundfrage der Bibel*, 34-87. 2d ed. Göttingen: Vandenhoeck & Ruprecht, 1960.

Schottroff, Luise. "Das Gleichnis vom verlorenen Sohn." *ZTK* 68 (1971): 27-52.

Schulz, Fritz. *Classical Roman Law*. Oxford: Clarendon Press, 1951.

Schweizer, Eduard. "Zur Frage der Lukasquellen: Analyse von Luk. 15,11-32." *TZ* 4 (1948): 469-71.

Scott, Bernard B. "The Prodigal Son: A Structuralist Interpretation," *Polyvalent Narration: Semeia 9*, 45-73. Ed. John D. Crossan. Missoula: Scholars Press, 1977.

Sibinga, Joost S. "Zur Kompositionstechnik des Lukas in Lk 15:11-32." In *Tradition and Re-interpretation in Jewish and Early Christian Literature: Essays in Honour of Jürgen C. H. Lebram*, 97-113. Ed. Jan W. van Henten et al. SPB 36. Leiden: E. J. Brill, 1986.

Tissot, Yves. "Patristic Allegories of the Lukan Parable of the Two Sons, Luke 15:11-32." In *Exegesis: Problems of Method and Exercises in Reading (Genesis 22 and Luke 15)*, 362-409. Ed. François Bovon and Grégoire Roullier. PTMS 21. Pittsburgh: Pickwick Press, 1978.

Tolbert, Mary A. "The Prodigal Son: An Essay in Literary Criticism from a Psychoanalytic Perspective." *Polyvalent Narration: Semeia 9*, 1-20. Ed. John D. Crossan. Missoula, Mont.: Scholars Press, 1977.

Via, Dan O., Jr. "The Prodigal Son: A Jungian Reading." In *Polyvalent Narration: Semeia 9*, 21-43. Ed. John D. Crossan. Missoula, Mont.: Scholars Press, 1977.

Wendland, Ernest. "Finding Some Lost Aspects of Meaning in Christ's Parables of the Lost — and Found (Luke 15)." *TJ* 17 (1996): 19-65.

CHAPTER 3

Parables of Exemplary Behavior

As indicated in Chapter 1, there are four parables in the Synoptic Gospels — in the Gospel of Luke to be precise — that scholars have conventionally classified as a particular type. In German they have been called *Beispielerzählungen*,[1] which can be translated literally as "example narratives." The commonly used term in English translations is "exemplary stories."[2]

Included in this group are the Parables of the Good Samaritan (Luke 10:25-37), the Rich Fool (12:16-21), the Rich Man and Lazarus (16:19-31), and the Pharisee and the Tax Collector (18:9-14).

Although Adolf Jülicher claimed that these parables did not need interpretation, for "they are as clear and transparent as possible,"[3] that is not quite true. In the Parable of the Rich Fool, for example, interpreters differ on whether the man's flaw is that he is foolish or immoral. Or again, if the man is a negative example of human conduct (which he surely is), what is it that is to be avoided? Is it greed? Or is it a deluded sense of contentment with worldly goods? The interpreter has to make some decisions.

As in the case of other Narrative Parables, so in the case of these, creative and arresting stories are composed that have a "once upon a time" character to them. What is most characteristic about them is that they set forth examples of human conduct for the disciple of Jesus to follow or to avoid. They do not, properly speaking, provide the hearer with *comparisons* between that which is told in story form and some other reality (such as the kingdom of God). What they provide are illustrations of exemplary behavior, indeed, *examples* for the followers of Jesus to emulate in their own lives.

1. As in the work of A. Jülicher, *Gleichnisreden*, 1:114; 2:585-641.
2. R. Bultmann, *HST* 177; B. Smith, *Parables*, 18; A. Hunter, *Parables*, 11.
3. A. Jülicher, *Gleichnisreden*, 1:114.

3.6. The Good Samaritan, Luke 10:25-37

25*And behold, a lawyer stood up, testing [Jesus], saying, "Teacher, what must I do to inherit eternal life?"*

26*And [Jesus] said to him, "What is written in the law? How do you read?"*

27*And he answered, "You shall love the Lord your God with all your heart, and with all your soul, and with all your strength, and with all your mind; and your neighbor as yourself."*

28*And he said to him, "You have answered right; do this, and you will live."*

29*But he, desiring to justify himself, said to Jesus, "And who is my neighbor?"*

30*Jesus replied, "A man was going down from Jerusalem to Jericho, and he fell among robbers, who stripped him and beat him, and departed, leaving him half dead.* 31*Now by chance a priest was going down that road; and when he saw him he passed by on the other side.* 32*So likewise a Levite, when he came to the place and saw him, passed by on the other side.* 33*But a Samaritan, as he journeyed, came to where he was; and when he saw him, he had compassion,* 34*and went to him and bound up his wounds, pouring on oil and wine; then he set him on his own beast and brought him to an inn, and took care of him.* 35*And the next day he took out two denarii and gave them to the innkeeper, saying, 'Take care of him; and whatever more you spend, I will repay you on my return.'*

36*"Which of these three, do you think, proved neighbor to the man who fell among the robbers?"*

37*He said, "The one who showed mercy on him."*

And Jesus said to him, "Go and do likewise."

Notes on the Text and Translation

10:32. The entire verse is missing in codex ℵ, which is probably due to the skip of the eye on the part of a scribe from the end of 10:31 directly to 10:33 (the clause καὶ ἰδὼν ἀντιπαρῆλθεν at the end of 10:32 appears very much like καὶ ἰδὼν αὐτὸν ἀντιπαρῆλθεν at the end of 10:31). The verse appears, however, in all other ancient Greek witnesses.

In place of the wording γενόμενος κατὰ τὸν τόπον ἐλθών, two others are attested in important Greek witnesses. One lacks the participle γενόμενος, and the other lacks the participle ἐλθών. The first of the variants is supported by 𝔭75, B, and others, and it is the reading adopted by the Westcott-Hort Greek New Testament and the 25th edition of the Nestle-Aland Greek text. The second is supported by 𝔭45, D, and others. The longer reading is represented by a good many other Greek witnesses (A, C, family 13, etc.) and is the reading included in the 26th and 27th editions of the Nestle-Aland Greek text, but with the first participle in brackets, indicating doubt about its authenticity.[1]

1. For discussion about the decision, cf. B. Metzger, *TCGNT* 152-53.

The omission of either participle does not materially affect the content of the story.

Exegetical Commentary

The parable is found only in the Gospel of Luke. It is located within the Travel Narrative (9:51–19:27). More specifically, it follows the discussion between Jesus and the lawyer in 10:25-29. In that scene the lawyer asks a question (10:25); there is a recounting of the two commandments from the Torah (Deut 6:4; Lev 19:18); and then the question of who is one's neighbor (10:29).

Luke's account of the discussion prior to the parable itself (i.e., the discussion in 10:25-29) appears to be a conflation of materials from Mark and Q.[2] As evidence for the existence of a Q version, Matthew 22:35-36 and Luke 10:25 have in common, against Mark (12:28), the terms and expressions "lawyer" (νομικός), "testing him" (ἐκπειράζων αὐτόν), and "teacher" (διδάσκαλε).

The parable that follows provides an example for human behavior and can be classified as a Parable of Exemplary Behavior.[3] It is not to be taken as an account of an actual event that Jesus recalls.[4] The parable is an artful creation by a master storyteller.

10:29. Normally the term "neighbor" would refer to a fellow Jew or proselyte. That is confirmed by what is said in the context of the commandment to love the neighbor in the OT. The commandment (Lev 19:18b) is preceded by statements on how an Israelite will treat fellow Israelites ("your own people"), and that will be kind treatment (Lev 19:18a).

In asking the question about who is his neighbor, the lawyer is not seeking information (as in a definition), but to "justify" himself, that is, to vindicate himself.[5] The question really means: Where do I draw the line? How large must the circle be? If I know who my neighbor is, I also know who is not my neigh-

---

2. I. H. Marshall, *Luke*, 439-40; J. Lambrecht, *Astonished*, 64-65. According to T. W. Manson, *Sayings*, 259, the section can be attributed to Luke's tradition (L). This is agreed to by J. Fitzmyer, *Luke*, 877.

3. It is classified as a *Beispielerzählung* in the writings of A. Jülicher, *Gleichnisreden*, 1:114; R. Bultmann, *HST* 178 ("exemplary story" in English translation); B. Smith, *Parables*, 18; M. Boucher, *Parables*, 119; E. Schweizer, *Luke*, 186 ("exemplary narrative"). For a critical response, holding that originally the unit was not an example story, cf. J. Crossan, *Parables*, 65-66.

4. Contra A. Plummer, *Luke*, 285 ("not fiction, but history"); E. Bishop, "People on the Road," 2-6 (an incident the victim narrated to Jesus); C. Daniel, "Les Esséniens," 71-104 (the victim was an Essene, the robbers were Zealots, and the priest and Levite passed by because they had no sense of brotherhood with an Essene). For an example of excessive historicizing of the parable in the process of interpretation, cf. K. Bailey, *Peasant Eyes*, 41-56.

5. Cf. J. Fitzmyer, *Luke*, 886.

bor. On the other hand, whoever has love in his or her heart will know who the neighbor is.[6]

The term νομικός ("lawyer") refers to an expert in the law; it refers to that type of officer who is sometimes called a "scribe" (γραμματεύς) in other contexts, that is, a person who is trained to interpret and teach the law of Jewish tradition.

Some interpreters consider this verse to be a Lukan composition,[7] a means by which Luke the evangelist has framed the parable. Others have asserted that, whether that is so or not, the setting within Luke's Gospel is artificial; and that the parable would not have been spoken on such an occasion as Luke has it.[8] At the same time, however, it can be conceded that the parable must have been occasioned by a question or event concerning love for one's neighbor. The setting that Luke gives it, though by Luke himself, is fitting.[9]

10:30. Jesus narrates a story of a man going down from Jerusalem to Jericho. Why Jericho? Augustine allegorized the parable, saying that the descent signified the loss of immortality as the man went from the heavenly city (Jerusalem) to one that signified mortality (Jericho).[10] It is more likely, however, that Jesus chose Jericho as the destination because the road to it was known to be a treacherous and dangerous route. Anyone who has taken the road from Jerusalem to Jericho (or vice versa) can attest that one "goes down" from the former to the latter. Jerusalem is some 2,700 feet above sea level, but Jericho is 820 feet below. That means that there is a drop of over 3,500 feet, and the drop takes place within a seventeen-mile journey. In Jesus' day Jericho was located a bit southwest of modern Jericho. King Herod had a magnificent palace there, and the city served as a winter capital. It is located in a rich farming area and is sometimes called the "City of a Thousand Palms." Al-

6. T. W. Manson, *Sayings*, 262.

7. B. Smith, *Parables*, 182; I. H. Marshall, *Luke*, 447; J. Fitzmyer, *Luke*, 882; J. Lambrecht, *Astonished*, 65-66.

8. A. Jülicher, *Gleichnisreden*, 2:596-97; W. O. E. Oesterley, *Parables*, 160; J. Crossan, *Parables*, 58-62.

9. I. H. Marshall, *Luke*, 445-46.

10. Augustine, *Quaestiones Evangeliorum* 2.19: "Jericho means the moon and signifies our mortality because it is born, increases, grows old, and dies." Translated from the Latin text in *Sancti Aurelii Augustini*, ed. Almut Mutzenbecher, CChr.SL 44B (Turnholt: Brepols, 1980), 62. For other famous allegorical interpretations of the parable, see Clement of Alexandria, *Who Is the Rich Man That Shall Be Saved?* 28-29; text in *ANF* 2:599; Origen, "Homilies on Luke [Homily 34]," in *The Fathers of the Church: A New Translation*, ed. Ludwig Schopp et al., vols. still in process (Washington: Catholic University of America Press, 1947-), 94:137-41; Martin Luther, "Sermon on Luke 10:23-37," in *The Precious and Sacred Writings of Martin Luther*, ed. John N. Lenker, 31 vols. (Minneapolis: Lutherans in All Lands, 1903-10), 14:27-30; reprinted in *The Sermons of Martin Luther*, ed. John N. Lenker, 8 vols. (Grand Rapids: Baker Books, 1983), 5:27-30; the latter is discussed in detail by H. Hövelmann, "Wer Ist der Barmherzige Samariter?" 54-57.

ready in OT times it was known as the "City of Palms" (Deut 34:3; Judg 1:16; 3:13; 2 Chron 28:15).[11]

Jericho would have been familiar to Jesus. The traditional site of his baptism by John is a few miles east of the city, and the traditional site of his temptation in the wilderness is northwest of it. Even if these traditional sites are only tenuously connected with Jesus, he would have passed through Jericho during his travels from Galilee to Jerusalem.[12] Several stories are set within Jericho, although they are placed later in Luke's narrative than the present episode, such as the Healing of Blind Bartimaeus (Mark 10:46-52//Luke 18:35-43//Matt 20:29-34) and his meeting with Zacchaeus (Luke 19:1-11).

The Jericho Road was well known in antiquity for being difficult and dangerous. According to Josephus, it was "desolate and rocky,"[13] and when the Essenes traveled it, they carried arms to protect themselves from robbers.[14]

The traveler in this story met a horrible fate, one of being robbed and beaten at the hands of "robbers."[15] The meaning of the term ἡμιθανῆ ("half dead") is not clear; it is found in the NT only here. There are two possible meanings. It could mean that the man could be taken for dead, that is, that he was unconscious and looked like a corpse.[16] The other possibility is that he was injured so badly that his life was in peril, and that he needed help to survive. The latter is to be preferred for two reasons. First, the word is used elsewhere to refer to a person's being on the point of death.[17] Second, the fact that the Samaritan acts on the basis of compassion indicates that the man must have appeared alive, but in a severe condition. The consequence of this shade of meaning is that those who pass by — the priest and the Levite — simply do not come to the aid of a man who needs help. If the man can truly be taken for dead, the passersby can be excused.[18] But if he is alive, and needs help, no passerby can be exonerated. The distinction between the first two figures (the priest and the Levite) and the third (the Samaritan) is a matter of the heart and compassion, not of law and office.

11. Strabo, *Geography*, 16.2.41, provides a description from the first century A.D., including its multitude of palm trees.

12. Charles R. Page and Carl A. Volz, *The Land and the Book: An Introduction to the World of the Bible* (Nashville: Abingdon Press, 1993), 145.

13. Josephus, *J.W.* 4.8.3.

14. Ibid., 2.8.4.

15. The term used for "robber" (λῃστής) can mean a "robber," "highwayman," "bandit," or "insurrectionist." Cf. BAGD 473. There seems to be no reason to select the last of these within the context of this parable.

16. J. Jeremias, *Parables*, 203; J. Fitzmyer, *Luke*, 887; B. Scott, *Parable*, 194.

17. This meaning is clearly attested in Diodorus Siculus, *History* 12.62.5; Dionysius of Halicarnassus, *Roman Antiquities* 10.7.4; Strabo, *Geography* 2.3.4, and in the *Amherst Papyri* 2.141.13, which is cited in MM 280. Cf. also 4 Macc 4:11.

18. This seems to be the consequence of the discussions of W. O. E. Oesterley, *Parables*, 163-64, and K. Bailey, *Peasant Eyes*, 43-47.

10:31. "By chance" (κατὰ συγκυρίαν) a priest arrives on the scene. The Greek phrase appears only here in the NT. That and its use at the beginning of the sentence underscore its importance. Immediately one can expect that help has come.[19] But, no, he passes by. And as the story unfolds, the priest is without excuse for his actions. If the victim of the robbery and beating could truly be taken for dead, the priest might have a good excuse. According to the law, a priest should not touch a corpse, except that of a family member, and then he was unclean for seven days (Lev 21:1-2; Ezek 44:25-27). On the other hand, if the priest could see that the man was in need, he should help him. Saving a life overrides any other prescript of the law.[20] The verb saying that the priest "saw" the victim (καὶ ἰδὼν αὐτόν, "and when he saw him") and passed him by speaks volumes.

It is possible that the issue is of a different kind. Perhaps it is the dilemma that arises when a priest has come upon a "neglected corpse" in need of burial. On this matter rabbinic masters and schools disagreed — some holding that the priest should not defile himself by burying the apparent corpse, others saying that he should.[21] If that debate is what is at stake in this case, the priest takes the halakic fork in the road that says he should not defile himself, and so he passes. He would be justified in doing so. Yet, for reasons mentioned above, it is more fitting to conclude that the victim of the beating is a person in need, not one that appears dead. And in that case there can be no debate; the priest had a duty to save life.[22]

10:32. The next person on the scene is a Levite, a man from the tribe of Levi (Gen 29:34) and of high standing within the Jewish heritage. Both priests and Levites were actually from the tribe of Levi, but the priests were descendants of Aaron, the first of the priests, as well. Information on Levites is provided in Numbers 3–4 and 1 Chronicles 23. Essentially their function was to assist priests in sacrifices. They prepared the sacrificial animals and grains. Like the priest, the Levite passed by, which cannot be excused. To be sure, any Israelite who touches a corpse is to be considered unclean for seven days (Num 5:2; 19:11-13). But like the priest again, the man is portrayed as without excuse, neglecting one who obviously needs help. The issue is not whether to touch a corpse or not. He, too, "saw" the victim (καὶ ἰδών, "and when he saw [him]") and went on.

10:33. The third person on the scene of brutality is a Samaritan. The so-called "rule of three" of good (or at least typical) storytelling is being followed. Since there are three traditional divisions among Jews (priests, Levites, and all

19. R. A. Culpepper, *NIB (Luke)*, 9.229.

20. *B. Yoma* 82a. Cf. *m. Yoma* 8:6; *b. Ber.* 19b; *b. Meg.* 3b; *Shab.* 81b and the discussion in G. F. Moore, *Judaism*, 2:106-7.

21. For the debate, cf. *m. Nazir* 7:1; cf. also 6.5. For discussion, cf. R. Bauckham, "The Scrupulous Priest," 481-83.

22. Cf. R. Bauckham, "The Scrupulous Priest," 483.

Israel),[23] one can expect the third person to be an ordinary Israelite. But the third is a "Samaritan," and that is a surprise. Normally the Samaritans were considered apostate; the sources show that they were universally regarded as objects of contempt.[24] But here a Samaritan is the hero of the story. A Samaritan is regarded highly by Jesus in another story, and that is the healing of the ten lepers, in which the only one who returns to give thanks was a Samaritan (Luke 17:11-19). By having a Samaritan as the one who helps the man in need, Jesus breaks down the boundaries between Jew and Samaritan, to be sure, but most of all he makes the claim that whoever responds to human need is a true child of God and an example of love for the neighbor.

The origins of the Samaritans can be traced to 722 B.C., when the Northern Kingdom (Samaria) was conquered by the Assyrians. The king of Assyria brought immigrants from foreign lands to live in Samaria, and over time these inhabitants worshiped foreign gods and, in the eyes of the Jewish people, departed from Jewish customs and sensibilities regarding the law (2 Kings 17:24-41). Rejecting the OT as a whole, their only Scriptures were a particular redaction of the Five Books of Moses, the "Samaritan Pentateuch." Furthermore, they had their own temple at Gerizim (John 4:9). The Samaritans were typically regarded as Gentiles,[25] or at best a degree nearer than Gentiles, but still not full members of the house of Israel.[26] Samaritans continue to exist to the present day; in modern times it has been estimated that some 250 live in or around Nablus and another 250 at Holon near Tel Aviv.[27]

Like the priest and the Levite, this person was subject to the law of Moses (Num 5:2; 19:11-13) regarding the touching of a corpse and could just as well have passed by. If the priest and Levite could grasp excuses, so could he. But the Samaritan, "when he saw him" (καὶ ἰδών, "and when he saw [him]"), responded to the man in need.

10:33. The term for having compassion (σπλαγχνίζομαι) occurs a dozen times in the NT (in the Gospels only).[28] Apart from its use here and in two

---

23. 2 Chron 35:2-3, 18; Ezra 10:5; Neh 11:3, 20. *M. Git.* 5:8; *Hor.* 3:8.

24. Many sources are cited by Joachim Jeremias, *Jerusalem in the Time of Jesus: An Investigation into Economic and Social Conditions during the New Testament Period* (Philadelphia: Fortress Press, 1969), 352-58.

25. Joachim Jeremias, "Σαμάρεια," *TDNT* 7:91; Samuel Sandmel, *Anti-Semitism in the New Testament?* (Philadelphia: Fortress Press, 1978), 104, n. 6: "From the standpoint of the Jews, the Samaritans were of Gentile extraction." Cf. M. Gourges, "The Priest," 712: at Luke 17:18 Jesus speaks of the Samaritan as a "foreigner."

26. Theodor H. Gaster, "Samaritans," *IDB* 4:191.

27. The information is for the mid-1970s in the article "Samaritans," *The New Encyclopaedia Britannica,* ed. Philip W. Goetz, 32 vols. (Chicago: Encyclopaedia Britannica, 1987), 10:374.

28. Mark 1:41; 6:34//Matt 14:14; Mark 8:2//Matt 15:32; Mark 9:22; Matt 9:36; 18:27; 20:34; Luke 7:13; 10:33; 15:20.

other parables (10:33; Matt 18:27), the term expresses divine compassion revealed in Jesus.[29] The compassion of the Samaritan reflects divine compassion. The verb is related to the noun for entrails, the seat of emotions and sympathy (the heart in modern cultures).

10:34. Oil and wine are to ease pain and to cleanse any wounds. Oil softens; wine is a mild disinfectant. The combination of oil and wine as a curative is attested in ancient sources, both Jewish and pagan Greek.[30] The touch of verisimilitude and its accompanying irony should not be lost. Oil and wine were commonly used in sacrifices at the Temple (cf. Lev 23:13).[31] The priest and Levite could well have had them on hand for use. But it is the Samaritan who actually carries them and makes use of them.

10:35. Since a denarius, a silver coin, was worth one day's wages for a common laborer,[32] the amount given by the Samaritan is the equivalent of two days' wages. Depending on the quality and price of lodging, two denarii would be sufficient for a stay in an inn for several days. Since two denarii could provide a month's food for a healthy adult male,[33] the amount must have been sufficient to provide food, lodging, and service for well over a week, perhaps two.[34] In any case, several days are anticipated. When the Samaritan makes his return, he will pay any debt that might be outstanding.

10:36-37. The question does not correspond to the one at 10:29. The earlier question was, "Who is my neighbor?" Here the question is, "Which person proved to be neighbor?" That is a very different kind of question. At most one can say that the first question is answered indirectly: "Your neighbor is anyone in need with whom you are thrown into contact."[35] But in reality the lawyer's question is moved off the scene and replaced by one that is more fundamental. If the issue is about love of neighbor, the question one should be asking is that of how one is to express that love, not to whom it should be expressed. "One cannot define one's neighbor; one can only be a neighbor."[36]

The response of the lawyer to the question put by Jesus is very telling. He cannot say, "Samaritan," but simply, "the one who showed mercy."

29. Cf. Helmut Koester, "σπλάγχνον," *TDNT* 7:553-55.

30. Isa 1:6; *m. Shab.* 14:2; 19:2, 4; further rabbinic references in Str-B 1:428; Theophrastus, *Enquiry into Plants* 9.11.1.

31. J. Derrett, "Good Samaritan," 220; J. Donahue, *Parable*, 132.

32. John W. Betlyon, "Coinage," *ABD* 1:1086; it was the typical pay for a soldier or farm laborer in the first century, according to Kenneth W. Harl, *Coinage in the Roman Economy, 300 B.C. to A.D. 700* (Baltimore: John Hopkins University Press, 1996), 278-79.

33. K. Harl, *Coinage*, 277-78. According to D. Oakman, "Buying Power," 37, two denarii would provide food for 24 days; fewer days for both food and lodging.

34. According to J. Jeremias, *Parables*, 205, the two denarii would be enough for 24 days' stay in an inn (presumably including both food and lodging). The figure may be high.

35. J. Creed, *Luke*, 151.

36. Heinrich Greeven, "πλησίον," *TDNT* 6:317.

Not surprisingly, some interpreters have concluded that 10:36-37 as a whole is Lukan,[37] or that 10:37b, at least, can be considered a redactional comment by the evangelist Luke.[38]

What is the meaning of the parable? To ask the question by the lawyer at the outset (10:29) is also to ask, in effect, Who is *not* my neighbor? The parable teaches that one cannot justify oneself by drawing distinctions between persons, deciding who is, and who is not, one's neighbor, and using the law to do that. The question for a disciple of Jesus is not, "Who is my neighbor?" but rather, "Am I neighbor to the person in need?" The demand of the commandment to love one's neighbor as oneself knows no limit.

The Parable of the Good Samaritan is one of the most well-known and beloved parables of Jesus. It is routinely considered a parable from Jesus. Scholarly opinion is less settled. It has been attributed to a pre-Lukan Hellenistic Jewish Christian by at least one scholar.[39] Generally, however, the parable is attributed to Jesus by a considerable range of scholarly opinion.[40]

Exposition

The one who asks, "Who is my neighbor?" thinks of others in the world as classifiable commodities. One can build fences to determine who is in the circle of those to be cared for, and who is not. Then we and all others can "take care of our own," thinking that our help should be directed to those we are related to by ties of family or friendship — things based on law, rights, bloodlines, culture, or tradition.

By means of this parable Jesus calls his hearers away from a legalistic or culturally conditioned mind-set to a life of authentic love. One should not seek to define who the neighbor is, but simply be a neighbor to the one in need. That view coheres with what is said also in the Parable of the Final Judgment; the disciple of Jesus — or anyone else, for that matter — is to extend care to any and all who are the unfortunates of the world (Matt 25:31-46). The example of the Samaritan, who does good to a person in need without any apparent regard for religon or ethnicity, illustrates how authentic love pays no attention to religious, ethnic, or cultural distinctions.

The command to love God and to love one's neighbor as oneself is basic to Christian theology and ethics. The first is rooted in the ancient Shema (Deut

---

37. R. Bultmann, *HST* 178; J. Lambrecht, *Astonished,* 67-68.

38. Joachim Jeremias, *Die Sprache des Lukasevangeliums: Redaktion und Tradition im Nicht-Markusstoff des dritten Evangeliums,* MeyerK (Göttingen: Vandenhoeck & Ruprecht, 1980), 190-93; J. Fitzmyer, *Luke,* 883.

39. G. Sellin, "Lukas als Gleichniserzähler," 166-89.

40. A. Jülicher, *Gleichnisreden,* 2:598; T. W. Manson, *Sayings,* 259-60; B. Smith, *Parables,* 180; J. Jeremias, *Parables,* 202-3; J. Lambrecht, *Astonished,* 69; N. Perrin, *Teaching,* 123; I. H. Marshall, *Luke,* 440-41; K. Bailey, *Peasant Eyes,* 33; P. Perkins, *Parables,* 120; R. Funk, *Five Gospels,* 323-24 (red font used and discussion favoring authenticity).

6:4-5), a foundational and confessional statement within the Jewish tradition. The second is repeated by Paul, who says that the command to love one's neighbor as oneself is a summary of the entire moral teaching of the OT (Rom 13:8-10; Gal 5:14); elsewhere it is even called the "royal law" in Christian tradition (James 2:8). What is so fascinating about the parable discussed here is that, while a person may seek to use the law concerning love for the neighbor as a means to draw lines of distinction, its actual purpose in Jesus' view is to break down any distinctions that a person might seek to make.

Select Bibliography

Bauckham, Richard. "The Scrupulous Priest and the Good Samaritan: Jesus' Parabolic Interpretation of the Law of Moses." *NTS* 44 (1998): 475-89.

Binder, Hermann. "Das Gleichnis vom Barmherzigen Samariter." *TZ* 15 (1959): 176-94.

Bishop, Eric F. "Down from Jerusalem to Jericho." *EvQ* 35 (1963): 97-102.

———. "People on the Road to Jericho: The Good Samaritan and the Others." *EvQ* 42 (1970): 2-6.

Bowman, John W. "The Parable of the Good Samaritan." *ExpTim* 59 (1947-48): 151-53, 248-49.

Cevallos, Juan C. "The Good Samaritan: A Second Reading of the Law (Luke 10:25-37)." *ThEd* 56 (1997): 49-58.

Cranfield, C. E. B. "The Good Samaritan (Luke 10:25-37)." *TTod* 11 (1954): 368-72.

Crespy, Georges. "The Parable of the Good Samaritan: An Essay in Structural Research." *Semeia* 2 (1974): 27-50.

Crossan, John D. "The Good Samaritan: Towards a Generic Definition of Parable." *Semeia* 2 (1974): 82-112.

———. "Parable and Example in the Teaching of Jesus." *NTS* 18 (1971-72): 285-307.

Daniel, Constantin. "Les Esséniens et l'arrière-fond historique de la parabole du Bon Samaritain." *NovT* 11 (1969): 71-104.

Derrett, J. Duncan M. "Law in the New Testament: Fresh Light on the Parable of the Good Samaritan." *NTS* 11 (1964-65): 22-37. Reprinted as "The Parable of the Good Samaritan," in his *Law in the New Testament*, 208-27. London: Darton, Longman & Todd, 1970.

Diezinger, Walter. "Zum Liebesgebot Mk xii,28-34 und Parr." *NovT* 20 (1978): 81-83.

Downey, Glanville. "'Who Is My Neighbor?' The Greek and Roman Answer." *ATR* 47 (1965): 3-15.

Eichholz, Georg. "Vom Barmherzigen Samariter (Luk. 10,25-37)." In his *Gleichnisse der Evangelien*, 147-78. Neukirchen-Vluyn: Neukirchener Verlag, 1971.

Funk, Robert W. "The Good Samaritan as Metaphor." *Semeia* 2 (1974): 74-81.

———. "'How Do You Read?' A Sermon on Luke 10:25-37." *Int* 18 (1964): 56-61.

———. "The Old Testament in Parable: A Study of Luke 10:25-37." *Encounter* 26 (1965): 251-67.

———. "The Prodigal Samaritan." *JAAR* 48 (1981): 83-97.

Furness, J. M. "Fresh Light on Luke 10:25-37." *ExpTim* 80 (1968-69): 182.

Furnish, Victor P. *The Love Command in the New Testament*. Nashville: Abingdon, 1972.

Gagnon, Robert A. J. "A Second Look at Two Lukan Parables: Reflections on the Unjust Steward and the Good Samaritan." *HBT* 20 (1998): 1-9.

Gerhardsson, Birger. *The Good Samaritan, The Good Shepherd?* ConBNT 16. Lund: Gleerup, 1958.

Gollwitzer, Helmut. *Das Gleichnis vom Barmherzigen Samariter*. Neukirchen: Neukirchener Verlag, 1962.

Gordon, James C. "The Parable of the Good Samaritan (St. Luke x.25-37): A Suggested Re-orientation." *ExpTim* 56 (1944-45): 302-4.

Gourges, Michel. "The Priest, the Levite, and the Samaritan Revisited: A Critical Note on Luke 10:31-35." *JBL* 117 (1998): 709-13.

Gyllenberg, Rafael. "Den Barmhärtige Samariten." *SEÅ* 12 (1947): 163-74.

Hövelmann, Hartmut. "Wer Ist der Barmherzige Samariter? Eine ungewohnte Perspektive in Luthers Auslegung von Lk 10,23-37." *Luther* 64 (1993): 54-57.

Jones, Peter R. "The Love Command in Parable: Luke 10:25-37." *PRS* 6 (1979): 224-42.

Keesmaat, Sylvia C. "Strange Neighbors and Risky Care (Matt 18:21-35; Luke 14:7-14; Luke 10:25-37)." In *The Challenge of Jesus' Parables*, 263-85. Ed. Richard N. Longenecker. Grand Rapids: Wm. B. Eerdmans, 2000.

Kieffer, René. "Analyse sémiotique et commentaire: Quelques réflexions à propos d'études de Luc 10.25-37." *NTS* 25 (1978-79): 454-68.

Kilgallen, John J. "The Plan of the 'ΝΟΜΙΚΟΣ' (Luke 10.25-37)." *NTS* 42 (1996): 615-19.

Kingston, Michael J. "The Good Samaritan Sees It Through." *ExpTim* 103 (1992): 340-41.

Klemm, Hans G. *Das Gleichnis vom Barmherzigen Samariter: Grundzüge der Auslegung im 16./17. Jahrhundert*. Stuttgart: Kohlhammer Verlag, 1973.

Lambrecht, Jan. "The Message of the Good Samaritan." *LS* 5 (1974): 121-35.

Masson, W. J. "The Parable of the Good Samaritan." *ExpTim* 48 (1936-37): 179-81.

Mattill, A. J., Jr. "The Good Samaritan and the Purpose of Luke-Acts: Halevy Reconsidered." *Encounter* 33 (1972): 359-76.

McDonald, James I. H. "Alien Grace (Luke 10:30-36)." In *Jesus and His Parables: Interpreting the Parables of Jesus Today*, 35-51. Ed. V. George Schillington. Edinburgh: T. & T. Clark, 1997.

————. "The View from the Ditch — and Other Angles: Interpreting the Parable of the Good Samaritan." *SJT* 49 (1996): 21-37.

Oakman, Douglas E. "The Buying Power of Two Denarii." *FFF* 3/4 (December 1987): 33-38.

————. "Was Jesus a Peasant? Implications for Reading the Samaritan Story (Luke 10:30-35)." *BTB* 22 (1992): 117-25.

Patte, Daniel. "An Analysis of Narrative Structure and the Good Samaritan." *Semeia* 2 (1974): 1-26.

Sellin, Gerhard. "Lukas als Gleichniserzähler: Die Erzählung vom Barmherzigen Samariter (Lk. 10:25-37)." *ZNW* 65 (1974): 166-89.

Spicq, Ceslaus. "The Charity of the Good Samaritan — Luke 10:25-37." In *Contemporary New Testament Studies*, 218-24. Ed. M. R. Ryan. Collegeville: Liturgical Press, 1965.

Stein, Robert H. "The Interpretation of the Parable of the Good Samaritan." In *Scripture, Tradition, and Interpretation: Essays Presented to Everett F. Harrison by His Students and Colleagues in Honor of His Seventy-Fifth Birthday*, 278-95. Ed. W. Ward Gasque and William S. LaSor. Grand Rapids: Wm. B. Eerdmans, 1977.

Stenger, William R. "The Parable of the Good Samaritan and Leviticus 18:5." In *The Living Text: Essays in Honor of Ernest W. Saunders*, 27-38. Ed. Dennis E. Groh and Robert Jewett. Lanham, Md.: University Press of America, 1985.

Stern, Jay B. "Jesus' Citation of Dt 6,5 and Lv 19,18 in the Light of Jewish Tradition." *CBQ* 28 (1966): 312-16.

Thomas, Kenneth J. "Liturgical Citations in the Synoptics." *NTS* 22 (1975-76): 205-14.

Trudinger, L. Paul. "Once Again Now, 'Who Is My Neighbour?'" *EvQ* 48 (1976): 160-63.

Via, Dan O. "Parable and Example Story: A Literary-Structuralist Approach." *Semeia* 1 (1974): 105-33.

Wickham, E. S. G. "Studies in Texts: Luke x.29." *Theology* 60 (1957): 417-18.

Wilkinson, Frank H. "Oded: Proto-Type of the Good Samaritan." *ExpTim* 69 (1957-58): 94.

Wink, Walter. "The Parable of the Compassionate Samaritan: A Communal Exegesis Approach." *RevExp* 76 (1979): 199-217.

Young, Norman H. "Once Again, Now, 'Who Is My Neighbour?' A Comment." *EvQ* 49 (1977): 178-79.

————. "The Commandment to Love Your Neighbour as Yourself and the Parable of the Good Samaritan." *AUSS* 21 (1983): 265-72.

Zimmermann, Heinrich. "Das Gleichnis vom Barmherzigen Samariter: Lk. 10,25-37." In *Der Ruf Jesu und die Antwort der Gemeinde*, 58-69. Ed. Eduard Lohse. Göttingen: Vandenhoeck & Ruprecht, 1970.

3.7. The Rich Fool, Luke 12:16-21; *Thomas* 63

Luke 12:16-21

16*And [Jesus] told them a parable, saying, "The land of a rich man produced abundantly.* 17*And he thought to himself, 'What shall I do, for I have nowhere to store my crops?'* 18*And he said, 'I will do this: I will pull down my barns and build bigger ones; and there I will store all my grain and my goods.* 19*And I shall say to my soul, "Soul, you have many goods stored up for many years; take your ease, eat, drink, be merry."'* 20*But God said to him, 'Fool! This night your soul is required of you; and the things you have prepared, whose will they be?'*

21*"So is the one who stores up treasure for himself, and is not rich toward God."*

Thomas 63

Jesus said, "There was a rich man who had much money. He said, 'I shall put my money to use so that I may sow, reap, plant, and fill my storehouse with produce, with the result that I shall lack nothing.' Such were his intentions, but that same night he died. Let him who has ears hear."[1]

Notes on the Text and Translation

12:20. The Greek clause has an active verb, ἀπαιτέω, meaning "to ask for" or "demand." A literal translation would be: "they are demanding your soul from you."[2] The subject of the sentence ("they") is unspecified. Perhaps it means the angels, who carry the dead to heaven, as in 16:22.[3] Less convincingly, other interpreters claim that the expression is simply a circumlocution for God.[4] In order to avoid the difficulty, the passive is used in various English translations (KJV, RSV, NIV, NRSV).[5]

Some important Greek witnesses (including 𝔓75 and B) have αἰτοῦσιν ("ask," "ask for," "demand") rather than the otherwise slightly more widely attested (ℵ, A, et al.) ἀπαιτοῦσιν ("ask for," "demand back"),[6] but the meaning is not affected.[7]

1. Quoted from *NHLE* 133.
2. BAGD 80.
3. W. O. E. Oesterley, *Parables*, 172.
4. J. Jeremias, *Parables*, 165; E. Schweizer, *Luke*, 208; H. Hendrickx, *Parables*, 103; cf. also K. Bailey, *Peasant Eyes*, 67.
5. Exceptions are those that make the man the subject: "you must surrender your life" (NEB); and "you will have to give up your life" (TEV).
6. BAGD 25, 80, respectively.
7. For discussion of the choice, cf. B. Metzger, *TCGNT* 160.

104

Exegetical Commentary

The parable appears only in Luke among the Synoptic Gospels, and it is located there within the Travel Narrative (9:51–19:27). It has an antecedent in Jewish literature from the second century B.C. (Sir 11:18-19), although the latter is not in the form of a parable:

> There is a man who is rich through his diligence and self-denial, and this is the reward allotted to him: when he says, "I have found rest, and now I shall enjoy my goods!" he does not know how much time will pass until he leaves them to others and dies.[8]

It is possible that the parable has been inspired by this passage in some way, even if it is not directly dependent upon it. If so, the author of the parable has recomposed the material into parabolic, or pictorial, form. Both the passage from Sirach and the parable stand within the wisdom tradition of Israel, in which it is held that having or seeking wealth can be a person's downfall (cf. Ps 49:1-20; Sir 31:1-11; *1 Enoch* 97:8-10; 98:3).

The version in the *Gospel of Thomas* is shorter than Luke's. Its comparative brevity is due in part to the fact that it lacks the word of judgment from God to the rich man that is present in Luke 12:20. (A somewhat similar saying appears at the end of *Gos. Thom.* 88.) It portrays a man who plans for a long future, but fails to realize his true situation.[9] As a text for a gnostic readership, its main point seems to be that attempts at material self-sufficiency are futile.[10] The question of the source for that version is disputed. Some interpreters claim that it is a revised and shortened version of Luke 12:16-20.[11] Others hold that it is based on an independent tradition.[12] In spite of the similarities, there are sufficient differences between the two versions to conclude that they may well be based upon separate traditions.[13]

8. A somewhat similar passage appears in *1 Enoch* 97:8-10.

9. J. Crossan, *Parables*, 85.

10. H. Montefiore, "A Comparison of the Parables of the Gospel according to Thomas and of the Synoptic Gospels," in *Thomas and the Evangelists*, by H. E. W. Turner and H. Montefiore, SBT 35 (Naperville: Alec R. Allenson, 1962), 57.

11. Robert M. Grant and David N. Freedman, *The Secret Sayings of Jesus* (Garden City, N.Y.: Doubleday, 1960), 169; R. McL. Wilson, *Studies in the Gospel of Thomas* (London: A. R. Mowbray, 1960), 69, 99; E. Schweizer, *Luke*, 207. An apparent dependence (or "loose connection") is posited by Wolfgang Schrage, *Das Verhältnis des Thomas-Evangelium zur synoptischen Tradition und zu den koptischen Evangelienübersetzungen: Zugleich ein Beitrag zur gnostischen Synoptikerdeutung*, BZNW 29 (Berlin: Alfred Töpelmann, 1964), 131; and Michael Fieger, *Das Thomasevangelium: Einleitung Kommentar Systematik*, NTAbh 22 (Münster: Aschendorff, 1991), 183.

12. Stephen J. Patterson, *The Gospel of Thomas and Jesus* (Sonoma, Calif.: Polebridge Press, 1992), 47-48; R. Funk, *Five Gospels*, 508.

13. In Luke's version the man has abundant crops, but in the *Thomas* version he has

The parable in Luke's Gospel — one of Luke's four parables of exemplary behavior[14] — is framed by verses warning against covetousness (12:15) and greed (12:21), set within the even larger framework of a dispute over an inheritance (12:13-14) and a series of sayings concerning anxiety over the necessities of daily life, such as food and clothing (12:22-31). The immediate occasion for its being told is the dispute and the pronouncement of Jesus that the measure of a person's life does not consist of the abundance of his or her possessions.

12:16. The opening sentence (16:16a) is typically Lukan in style (cf. 6:39; 15:3; 19:11; 21:29). A "parable" is to follow. It is told to "them," meaning either the two brothers in the dispute over the inheritance or the crowd as a whole that is presumably present (12:13). The parable itself begins with a description of the man's land,[15] which bore abundantly. No moral judgment is made concerning the landowner.

12:17. Here an "interior monologue" on the part of the landowner commences, which is characteristic of certain parables in the Gospel of Luke (cf. 12:45; 15:17-19; 16:3-4; 18:4-5; 20:13).[16] The monologue continues through 12:19. It provides access to the man's inner thoughts, which are known to God and to the hearer of the parable. He is initially perplexed about what to do in response to an unexpected abundance of crops.

12:18-19. The monologue continues with a resolution of the man's problem. In 12:18 he spells out for himself a plan of action. He resolves to replace his existing barns with larger ones. Certainly there is nothing wrong with that. He plans to do what is right. It is in the next verse that his problem becomes apparent.[17]

One might ask questions: Where will he store his goods while the bigger barns are being built?[18] And why tear down existing barns? Why not simply build additional ones? Such questions are not dealt with in the story; it is typical for parables to portray "all-or-nothing" activity.[19]

In 12:19 the man rehearses the existential consequences of the action regarding his future. He speaks to himself, addressing himself as though talking

---

much money; in the latter there is nothing about replacing small barns with larger ones; and the man is not regarded as a fool.

14. A. Jülicher, *Gleichnisreden,* 1:114; R. Bultmann, *HST* 177-78.

15. The Greek term translated here as "land" is χώρα. BAGD 889 designate it as "land" or "farm." According to Dieter Sänger, "χώρα," *EDNT* 3:491, it simply means "cultivated land" or a "field," as in James 5:4 and John 4:35. Cf. also A. Jülicher, *Gleichnisreden,* 2:609. The term need not mean "extensive holdings, normally a district or region," as suggested by B. Scott, *Parable,* 132; cf. also M. Beavis, "The Foolish Landowner," 63.

16. Philip Sellew, "Interior Monologue as a Narrative Device in the Parables of Jesus," *JBL* 111 (1992): 239-53.

17. W. Oesterley, *Parables,* 170.

18. P. Perkins, *Parables,* 74.

19. B. Scott, *Parable,* 134.

to a separate personality ("Soul, . . ."). To do so is not unique in the scriptural tradition (cf. Pss 42:5; 103:1; 104:1, 35) and Jewish literature.[20] He assures himself that he will have plenty; that he will have no need or want for many years. The term "soul" does not designate a particular part of the man's being, but rather the entire self.

The final saying ("eat, drink, and be merry") is commonplace. Similar sayings appear elsewhere in Jewish tradition (LXX Eccl 8:15 having the same Greek verbs as here).[21]

12:20. God speaks. It is not said how (directly, by a dream, or by an intermediary, such as an angel). The man is called a "fool." The Greek term used (ἄφρων) is the very one used in the LXX version (13:1) of Psalm 14:1, "The fool (ἄφρων) says in his heart, 'There is no God,'" and the connection to the psalm is no doubt to be recognized. The term appears frequently elsewhere in the LXX for various Hebrew words — particularly in wisdom literature — to refer to someone who "rejects the order of the world articulated by the wise, that is, one who refuses to acknowledge dependence upon God." That person then becomes presumptuous in speech and behavior, damages the community, and becomes self-destructive.[22] The man's foolishness is underscored by the divine pronouncement that he must relinquish his soul "this night," which stands in sharp contrast to the man's presumption of "ample goods laid up for many years" (12:19).[23]

The question in 12:20b regarding the fate of the property at the man's death is left unanswered. As a property owner, the man must have had heirs. But the question is not one that actually seeks an answer (God would know that), but one that adds to the unsettled existence of the man. All is uncertain. The question reflects passages in the OT, such as Psalm 39:6, Ecclesiastes 2:21, and Sirach 14:15.

12:21. The verse is a secondary addition (not part of the original parable).[24] It makes a generalization, but it also makes an application that differs from the meaning of the parable alone. It makes the man an example of the wrong use of one's possessions. One ought to be generous and thereby have God's approval, "being rich in those things which are pleasing to Him."[25] The expression is comparable to those about treasures in heaven at 12:33 and 18:22.

---

20. For a prime example, cf. *Ps. Sol.* 3:1; text in *OTP* 2:654.

21. Eccl 2:24; 8:15; Isa 22:13; Tob 7:10; *1 Enoch* 98:11. For the latter text, cf. *OTP* 1:79 ("From where will you find good things that you may eat, drink, and be satisfied?"). Cf. also 1 Cor 15:32.

22. Dieter Zeller, "ἄφρων," *EDNT* 1:185.

23. A. Plummer, *Luke*, 324; R. A. Culpepper, *NIB (Luke)*, 9:256.

24. A. Jülicher, *Gleichnisreden*, 2:615; R. Bultmann, *HST* 178; A. Cadoux, *Parables*, 205; H. Hendrickx, *Parables*, 104; J. Fitzmyer, *Luke*, 971; M. Boucher, *Parables*, 127. On the other hand, I. Marshall, *Luke*, 524, concludes that the verse belongs to the original parable.

25. A. Plummer, *Luke*, 325.

Leaving the last verse aside, the parable sets forth an example of a way of living that is to be avoided. The rich fool is so preoccupied with gaining and maintaining his possessions that he is in fact idolatrous. According to the psalmist, "The fool says in his heart, 'There is no God'" (14:1). That is a form of theoretical atheism. The rich fool of the parable may or may not have such thoughts. But he places all his trust and faith in his possessions. That is a practical atheism and a form of idolatry, which is recognized as such in Jewish tradition. In the *Testament of Judah* (perhaps second century B.C.) the patriarch speaks to his children, saying that the "love of money leads to idolatry," for those who are led astray by such love "designate as gods those who are not gods." Furthermore, this love "makes anyone who has it go out of his mind."[26]

Interpreters have found other nuances for interpretation that are less persuasive. It is not likely that the parable sets forth the rich fool as a person whose fundamental flaw is that he is selfish and does not share his goods with others.[27] But sharing his goods would have been the antithesis of the life he led. Nor is there a basis for the view that the rich fool is an illustration of an oppressor who builds larger barns in order to withhold his agricultural goods and thereby raise prices and exploit the poor of the land — an example of greed.[28] That is to read extraneous details into the story,[29] making the man an example of callous and immoral behavior rather than of stupidity. The parable provides a practical model for conducting one's life before God,[30] a life that takes the reality of God into account and is sound (or healthy) in relationship to God, the self, and others.

Various interpreters regard the parable to have been composed by Jesus, even if he drew from imagery and language that was traditional.[31] There is no need to challenge that conclusion. The authenticity of the parable is supported in part by its multiple attestation, that is, its appearance in the *Gospel of Thomas* as well as in the Gospel of Luke.

---

26. *T. Judah* 19:1. Quoted from *OTP* 1:800.

27. Contra A. Jülicher, *Gleichnisreden*, 2:617; A. Cadoux, *Parables*, 205; W. Oesterley, *Parables*, 170-71; Bruce J. Malina and Richard L. Rohrbaugh, *Social-Science Commentary on the Synoptic Gospels* (Minneapolis: Fortress Press, 1992), 359; one of several flaws, according to R. A. Culpepper, *NIB (Luke)*, 9:256-57.

28. Contra M. Beavis, "The Foolish Landowner," 64-68.

29. E. Schweizer, *Luke*, 207, indicates (correctly) that there is no hint in the parable that the man, by storing his goods in larger barns, seeks to drive up prices (like the man of Prov 11:26).

30. Cf. J. Fitzmyer, *Luke*, 971.

31. A. Jülicher, *Gleichnisreden*, 2:616; T. W. Manson, *Sayings*, 271-72; W. Oesterley, *Parables*, 172. In R. Funk, *Five Gospels*, 338, the parable is in pink font (= Jesus said something like this), followed by justification for the judgment made.

Exposition

The Parable of the Rich Fool portrays a man who is in many ways exemplary. He is a person who works, plans, saves, and seeks to protect his belongings. He expects to enjoy what he has acquired and to make his future as secure as possible.

Persons who conduct their lives in such a manner, caring for themselves and for those who depend upon them, are considered prudent and good stewards of what has been entrusted to them. Persons who give no thought to the future for themselves and their loved ones are considered reckless. There is no virtue in that manner of living. The plain fact is that some courses of life are better and wiser than others. The way of work, planning, and saving is obviously better and wiser than the way of sloth, failure to plan, and waste.

The flaw that beset the rich fool, however, was not a life of work and prudence. Instead it was that he was consumed by his possessions and that the meaning and value of his life depended upon them. The man and his possessions are so intimately tied together that they are inseparable. In English translation the personal pronoun "I" shows up six times and the possessive "my" five times ("my crops," "my barns," "my grain," "my goods," and "my soul") in the six verses of the parable (RSV, NRSV).

The parable provides an example of what one ought not to be like. The person whose identity is tied up with his or her possessions, status, and/or achievements — and is driven by acquiring them — can so easily end up unaware of the call of God and the need of the neighbor. The alternative is a life that is "rich toward God," one that is devoted to serving God daily, which includes having eyes open to the needs of others.

Select Bibliography

Beavis, Mary Ann. "The Foolish Landowner (Luke 12:16b-20)." In *Jesus and His Parables: Interpreting the Parables of Jesus Today*, 55-68. Ed. V. George Schillington. Edinburgh: T. & T. Clark, 1997.

Birdsall, J. Neville. "Luke 12:16ff. and the Gospel of Thomas." *JTS* 13 (1962): 332-36.

Derrett, J. Duncan M. "The Rich Fool: A Parable of Jesus concerning Inheritance." *HeyJ* 18 (1977): 131-51.

Eichholz, Georg. "Vom reichen Kornbauern (Luk. 12,13-21)." In his *Gleichnisse der Evangelien: Form, Überlieferung, Auslegung*, 179-91. Neukirchen-Vluyn: Neukirchener Verlag, 1971.

Gaide, Gilles. "Le riche insensé Lc 12, 13-21." *ASeign* 49 (1971): 82-89.

Joüon, Paul. "La Parabole du riche insensé (Luc 12,13-31)." *RSR* 29 (1939): 486-89.

Lowery, Richard H. "Sabbath and Survival: Abundance and Self-Restraint in a Culture of Excess." *Encounter* 54 (1993): 143-67.

Malherbe, Abraham J. "The Christianization of a *Topos* (Luke 12:13-34)." *NovT* 38 (1996): 123-35.

Marion, D. "Simples et mystérieuses paraboles. VII. Paraboles de crise: le riche insensé, le riche et Lazare." *EeV* (1996): 225-30, 235-36.

Nickelsburg, George W. E. "Riches, the Rich, and God's Judgment in 1 Enoch 92–105 and the Gospel according to Luke." *NTS* 25 (1978-79): 324-32.

Reid, John. "The Poor Rich Fool: Luke xii.21." *ExpTim* 13 (1901-2): 567-68.

Seng, Egbert W. "Der reiche Tor: Eine Untersuchung von Lk. Xii 16-21 unter besonderer Berücksichtigung form- und motivgeschichtlicher Aspekte." *NovT* 20 (1978): 136-55.

Wright, Stephen I. "Parables on Poverty and Riches (Luke 12:13-21; 16:1-13; 16:19-31)." In *The Challenge of Jesus' Parables*, 217-39. Ed. Richard N. Longenecker. Grand Rapids: Wm. B. Eerdmans, 2000.

3.8. The Rich Man and Lazarus, Luke 16:19-31

[Jesus said,] 19 *"There was a rich man, and he was clothed in purple and fine linen and feasted sumptuously day by day.* 20*And at his gate a poor man named Lazarus was laid, full of sores,* 21*who desired to be fed with what fell from the rich man's table; moreover, the dogs came and licked his sores.*

22 *"The poor man died and was carried by the angels to Abraham's bosom. The rich man died also, and he was buried;* 23*and in Hades, being in torment, he lifted up his eyes and saw Abraham far off and Lazarus in his bosom.* 24*And he called out, 'Father Abraham, have mercy upon me, and send Lazarus to dip the end of his finger in water and cool my tongue; for I am in anguish in this flame.'* 25*But Abraham said, 'Son, remember that you in your lifetime received your good things, and Lazarus in like manner bad things; but now he is comforted here, and you are in anguish.* 26*And besides all this, between us and you a great chasm has been fixed, in order that those who would pass from here to you may not be able, and no one may cross from there to us.'*

27 *"And he said, 'Then I beg you, father, to send him to my father's house,* 28*for I have five brothers, in order that he may warn them, lest they also come into this place of torment.'*

29 *"But Abraham said, 'They have Moses and the prophets; let them hear them.'*

30 *"And he said, 'No, father Abraham; but if someone goes to them from the dead, they will repent.'*

31 *"He said to him, 'If they do not hear Moses and the prophets, neither will they be convinced if someone should rise from the dead.'"*

Exegetical Commentary

The parable appears only in the Gospel of Luke, and it is relatively free of issues in textual criticism. The only one necessary to discuss is that concerning the attempts to give a name to the rich man, which is taken up below.

The parable is located within the Travel Narrative (9:51–19:27). As noticed by many before, it is the only parable of Jesus with a person named within it, and that is the poor man named Lazarus, which is derived from the Hebrew name El-azar, meaning "God has helped."[1] The choice of name cannot be accidental. The man's only help is in God, rather than persons around him. A person named Lazarus appears also in the Gospel of John, the brother of Mary and Martha (11:1-44; 12:1-11). There is no reason, however, to think that the latter is being referred to within the parable.

Stories of the fate of the rich and the poor in the afterlife abound in various traditions and literatures. A story of this kind is expressed in an Egyptian tale that was probably older than the time of Jesus,[2] and there are several versions of this kind within rabbinic literature (all dated later than the NT).[3] Yet the parable is not a replica of any. While it is related to common folklore, it is a creation in its own right.

In contrast to Lazarus, the rich man has no name. But in order to remedy that seeming anomaly, various names have been attached to him. Papyrus 75 (third century, Alexandrian) gives him the name Νεύης, and the ancient writer Priscillian (d. A.D. 385) named him Finees.[4] The Vulgate (fourth century, Western) opens with the words, "homo quidam erat dives." Since the term "dives" is a Latin adjective meaning "rich," the phrase means "a certain man was rich." But it has been popularly understood as "there was a certain man, Dives." Therefore the parable has sometimes been called the Parable of Dives and Lazarus.[5]

The parable begins abruptly, but it is related to some things going before it concerning money — 16:9, 11, 13, 14-15. It is related primarily to the Pharisees (16:14). In any case, it is located within a veritable catena of passages that speak of the dangers that arise from the love of wealth.

1. According to B. Easton, *Luke*, 251, "'Lazarus' represents לְעָזָר, abbreviated . . . from אֶלְעָזָר ('Eliezar')." For etymological discussions, cf. J. Fitzmyer, *Luke*, 1131; and Raymond F. Collins, "Lazarus," *ABD* 4:265.

2. H. Gressmann, *Vom reichen Mann*; summaries in J. Jeremias, *Parables*, 183; J. Creed, *Luke*, 209-10; J. Fitzmyer, *Luke*, 1127-28; and B. Scott, *Parable*, 155-57.

3. *Ruth Rab.* 3:3; *Eccl. Rab.* 1:15:1; *y. Sanh.* 6:23c. Texts and summaries are in S. Lachs, *Rabbinic Commentary*, 313-14, and Harvey K. McArthur and Robert M. Johnston, *They Also Spoke in Parables: Rabbinic Parables from the First Centuries of the Christian Era* (Grand Rapids: Zondervan, 1990), 195.

4. On the derivation of these two names, cf. K. Grobel, "'Whose Name,'" 373-82. See further B. Metzger, *TCGNT* 165-66; J. Fitzmyer, *Luke*, 1130.

5. As in the case of W. Oesterley, *Parables*, 203, and B. Smith, *Parables*, 134.

The parable consists of two main parts. The first part (16:19-26) narrates a reversal of fortunes in the afterlife for the rich man and Lazarus. The second part (16:27-31) consists of a discussion between the rich man and Abraham, in which the rich man seeks to have his five brothers rescued by a miraculous event.

16:19-20. The rich man is not portrayed as particularly wicked; he is simply not attentive to the situation (the poor man nearby). Nor is it said that Lazarus was particularly good; he simply has no help but God alone in this world. Since Luke commonly equates poverty and piety, however, Lazarus is most likely to be understood as pious, even as his name suggests.[6]

The opening scene provides a brief social description of the two men. They are two very different men in an essentially two-tier society of "haves" and "have nots." The rich man is dressed in "purple and fine linen," signifying his belonging to royalty, or having royal favors at least, and wealth.[7] The purple garment would be worn over linen undergarments.[8] The fact that there is a "gate" at which Lazarus lay means that the rich man lives in a mansion surrounded by a wall designed to keep the "have nots" at a distance. The wall and its gate make a statement. Although he may well be aware that poverty surrounds him, the rich man does not want to see it or do anything to alleviate it.

Lazarus, on the other hand, is said to "lay" (RSV, NEB, NRSV) at the gate, or it is said that he "was laid" (KJV, NIV) there. The Greek verb is ἐβέλητο, the perfect passive of βάλλω, which is used to depict a person confined to his or her sickbed (cf. Matt 8:6, 14; 9:2; Mark 7:30).[9] The use of the verb points to his helplessness. He has to be placed at the gate every day by friends (cf. the words of the paralytic at John 5:7).

16:21. The phrase "desired to be fed" (ἐπιθυμῶν χορτασθῆναι) recalls another at 15:16 (ἐπεθύμει χορτασθῆναι, concerning the prodigal son), suggesting "a constant and unfulfilled longing."[10] What he desired amounted to mere scraps that fell from the table. It has been suggested that, in lieu of napkins, people used pieces of bread and then tossed them out.[11] But no evidence is provided for such a practice. In any case, dogs lick the sores of Lazarus. The picture portrayed is probably that of roaming street dogs that detect and taste the "fresh meat" that the sores on Lazarus would represent to them. They wait for his death (for references to dogs that consume the dead, see 1 Kings 14:11; 16:4; 21:24; Ps 16:2; Jer 5:3). The licking would be very degrading and, if done continually, would prevent the sores from healing.

6. I. H. Marshall, *Luke*, 632.

7. On purple as the color of royalty and royal favors, cf. Sir 40:4; 1 Macc 8:4; 10:20, 62, 64; 11:58; 14:43-44; 2 Macc 4:38; 1 Esdr 3:6; Mark 15:17, 20; John 19:2, 5; further, A. Jülicher, *Gleichnisreden*, 2:618.

8. A. Plummer, *Luke*, 391; J. Creed, *Luke*, 211.

9. Otfried Hofius, "βάλλω," *TDNT* 1:191.

10. J. Donahue, *Parable*, 170.

11. J. Jeremias, *Parables*, 184; C. Montefiore, *Synoptic Gospels*, 2:1,003.

16:22-23. There is a reversal of conditions at death. The poor man is carried away by angels, escorted into heaven with their aid.[12] The scene recalls the taking of Enoch to heaven by God (Gen 5:24) and the taking of Elijah to heaven in a whirlwind (2 Kings 2:11). Abraham's "bosom" is a blessed state after death, even the final resting place, comparable to dining with the patriarchs, as portrayed in 13:28-29 (cf. also 4 Macc 13:17). The contrast between the two men is stark. While Lazarus is carried to heaven by angels, the rich man dies and is simply "buried."[13] But that is not the end of the matter. Though he was buried (or at least his body was), he appears immediately in a place of torment.

It should be evident that the parable draws upon common folkloric imagery of conditions after death, and the imagery is used only here within the NT. It is not the purpose of the parable to reveal the nature of those conditions. The imagery corresponds in part to a vision of the other world in 2 Esdras 7:36 (first century A.D.): "Then the pit of torment shall appear, and opposite shall be the place of rest; and the furnace of Hell shall be disclosed, and opposite it the Paradise of delight."[14]

The term "Hades" is a transliteration of the Greek term ᾅδης. The term appears ten times in the NT and ordinarily refers to the realm of the dead.[15] Generally it is considered to be a place where the dead remain for only a short time (Acts 2:27, 31; Rev 20:13-14) prior to the final judgment (Rev 20:13). But in this verse (Luke 16:23) it appears to be a permanent abode and a place of torment (the Greek expression ἐν βασάνοις ["in torment"] referring to eschatological punishment[16]) comparable to "hell" (even having "flames" torment the man [16:24]);[17] the NIV actually translates the term as "hell." That the place is not simply an abode of the dead is clear from the fact that the rich man is there, but Lazarus is not. By implication judgment has been passed upon the rich

---

12. Cf. the ascension with the help of angels in the case of the righteous in *T. Asher* 6:5; and the description of the abode of the dead with the angels in *1 Enoch* 22:1-14; texts in *OTP* 1:818 and 1:24-25, respectively; for rabbinic parallels, cf. S. Lachs, *Rabbinic Commentary,* 314-15, in which Gabriel and Michael escort the righteous to heaven. Contra J. Fitzmyer, *Luke,* 1132, and W. Herzog, *Parables,* 120, it seems unwarranted to make the point that the body of Lazarus was left unburied. The poor man is honored by being carried by angels, which implies an ascension into heaven.

13. According to some interpreters, the implication is that there was a proper funeral, followed by an honorable burial; cf. B. Smith, *Parables,* 136; J. Fitzmyer, *Luke,* 1132; W. Herzog, *Parables,* 120. But nothing of the kind is said explicitly. It seems more likely that the words of the parable imply a "put down" (pun intended) of the rich man.

14. Quoted from *OTP* 1:538.

15. Matt 11:23; 16:18; Luke 10:15; 16:23; Acts 2:27, 31; Rev 1:18; 6:8; 20:13, 14.

16. Werner Stenger, "Βασανίζω," *EDNT* 1:200.

17. J. Creed, *Luke,* 213; C. Montefiore, *Synoptic Gospels,* 2:1,003; B. Smith, *Parables,* 137; Otto Böcher, "ᾅδης," *EDNT* 1:30-31. Contra A. Plummer, *Luke,* 393-94; J. Jeremias, *Parables,* 185; I. H. Marshall, *Luke,* 636-37; J. Osei-Bonsu, "Intermediate State," 115-30; and W. Herzog, *Parables,* 121-22.

man, and he has no way out of his situation. The persons can see one another (16:23); one is in bliss, the other in torment. The total effect is that the rich man is without hope of redemption, but he can still "look up" and see Abraham and Lazarus (16:23).

16:24-26. The rich man still tries to be in charge of things. He begins with a polite address, "Father Abraham," as if reminding Abraham of his descent from the patriarch. (Abraham responds by calling him his child in 16:25.) As part of Abraham's family, he deserves some consideration. He goes on to make three remarks in speeches to the patriarch (16:24, 27-28, 30). First, he wants Abraham to direct Lazarus to do some errands on his behalf. He wants Lazarus to provide him relief from his horrible condition — something that he would not do for Lazarus when they were on earth. The rich man suffers from thirst. That the wicked suffer thirst in the realm of the dead is traditional; it is one of their punishments.[18]

The man's wish is not granted. He has already received his share of good things (as though there is a limited supply). Moreover, the chasm between the rich man in Hades and Lazarus with Abraham is too great to cross. The fact that it is "fixed" means that it has been established by God. It is not only right that Lazarus now receive good and remain in bliss where he is rather than cross over, and it is impossible for him to make the journey in any case.

16:27-28. Having abandoned one unsuccessful approach, the rich man asks Abraham to send Lazarus to warn his five brothers. They must repent, or they will end up in the same place of torment as he.

16:29. Moses and the prophets (referring to OT books) are clear in their teaching. God's will is not difficult to figure out. One is supposed to help the poor and miserable that are nearby. The brothers are without excuse.

16:30. The rich man's third remark is argumentative. He objects to what Abraham has just said. His brothers will certainly repent if someone goes to them from the dead. That a person from the realm of the dead would visit the brothers seems at first sight to depend on post-Easter Christian imagery. But the motif is older than Christianity. Various texts speak of the dead contacting the living, especially through dreams.[19]

16:31. Even a messenger from the dead (Lazarus) would not be able to bring the five brothers to repentance. Persons who will not repent on the basis of the teachings of the Scriptures will not repent just because a resurrection from the dead takes place. Unmistakably the present wording ("if someone should rise from the dead") has been conformed to Christian language concerning the resurrection of Jesus. If persons are not converted to belief in Jesus as the Messiah on the basis of Moses and the prophets, neither will they be on

18. Cf. 2 Esdr 8:59; 15:58; texts in *OTP* 1:544, 557.
19. 1 Sam 28:6-19; 2 Kings 21:6; Isa 8:19; for rabbinic texts, cf. S. Lachs, *Rabbinic Commentary*, 315-16.

the basis of the preaching of the resurrection of Jesus.[20] The request for such a miraculous sign is itself an indication of unbelief in the word of God given in the Scriptures.

Interpreters have concluded that the main point of the parable is to be found in the second part (16:27-31).[21] That is to say, the parable is primarily a warning to persons who, like the five brothers of the rich man, still have time to repent and do the will of God. The will of God has been clearly revealed in the law and the prophets. One should pay heed to these. The one who neglects them runs the risk of indifference to the needs of the unfortunates. Such indifference will be met with punishment at the final judgment.

Scholarly opinion has divided on the question whether the parable can be attributed to Jesus of Nazareth. Some interpreters think that the parable consists essentially of a traditional, pre-Christian tale that has been attributed to Jesus.[22] Another view is that the first part (16:19-26) may well have been composed by Jesus, but the second (16:27-31) is from early Christian teaching and application.[23] Others have concluded that there is no reason to preclude its having been told by Jesus.[24] Although the parable in its present wording has clearly been transformed by Christian allegorization, it would seem that a nucleus of the parable can be attributed to Jesus. This will include the second part as well. The teaching of the parable would then be not simply that there is a reversal of conditions at death for rich and poor, but rather that the teachings of God concerning care for the poor are clear in the law and the prophets.

At the level of Luke's Gospel the parable serves to warn the rich about the peril of neglecting the needs of the poor. It also exemplifies the words of the Magnificat (1:52, God puts down the mighty and exalts those of low degree) and the Beatitudes (5:20, 24, the poor are declared blessed, and a woe is pronounced upon the rich). Although the modern reader is apt to conclude that the parable commends private charity in its modern, anonymous form, that is not the end of the matter. To be sure, the rich man allows Lazarus to have leftovers from his table, which is a form of charity, but he also knows Lazarus by name (while in Hades at least!). The parable presupposes an ancient agrarian

---

20. C. Montefiore, *Synoptic Gospels*, 2:1,006; J. Creed, *Luke*, 209; B. Easton, *Luke*, 254.

21. T. W. Manson, *Sayings*, 298, 301; J. Jeremias, *Parables*, 186; J. Fitzmyer, *Luke*, 1,128-29.

22. R. Bultmann, *HST* 203; C. Montefiore, *Synoptic Gospels*, 2:1,002; Francis W. Beare, *The Earliest Records of Jesus* (New York: Abingdon, 1962), 183; J. Donahue, *Parable*, 170; R. Funk, *Five Gospels*, 360-61 (16:19-26 in gray font; 16:27-31 in black).

23. W. Oesterley, *Parables*, 209-11; J. Crossan, *Parables*, 66-68; B. Scott, *Parable*, 142-46.

24. A. Jülicher, *Gleichnisreden*, 2:640; A. Cadoux, *Parables*, 124-28; I. H. Marshall, *Luke*, 634; J. Jeremias, *Parables*, 186; J. Fitzmyer, *Luke*, 1127; H. Hendrickx, *Parables*, 210-11; W. Herzog, *Parables*, 116.

economy in which a person like Lazarus is more than just poor. He belongs among the outcasts of society. He is the type of person about whom it would have been socially acceptable for the rich man to be indifferent.[25] The gate and wall around the rich man's mansion are outward barriers representing psychic and social barriers as well. The parable warns the well-to-do about any arrogance they may have that looks upon the unfortunates of the world as less than human.

Exposition

Since the parable is one that concerns exemplary behavior, the rich man illustrates what one is not to be like. He is not overtly wicked, but he is indifferent to the needs of the poor, including the type of person who can be written off as a companion to the stray dogs of the streets, hardly a human being. In modern times Lazarus corresponds to the person who begs, but one dare not look into his or her eyes, lest a claim is made upon one's compassion. It is acceptable to give aid to the worthy poor, but it is also socially permissible to regard some as not worthy.

But whoever is attentive to the parable, and attentive to the word of God in the Scriptures as a whole, will also be attentive to the needs of the poor and respond with help.

In spite of technological progress, poverty and the division between "haves" and "have nots" continue to exist in the world. The solution to the problems of poverty is moral and spiritual as well as — perhaps even more than — technological. It is necessary ever to ask why there is such a large number who need food aid in a world that has sufficient resources.

The parable encourages private charity. But is that all? The rich man did, after all, let Lazarus have leftovers from his table, which is a form of charity. The parable also implicitly exhorts the disciples of Jesus to "see" the conditions of those who suffer, and to see them as persons created in the image of God. Moreover, since systems (governmental and economic) are part of the cause of inequities, and then perpetuate them, those same systems are needed to fix them as well.

Select Bibliography

Barth, Karl. "Miserable Lazarus." *USQR* 46 (1921): 259-68.
Bauckham, Richard. "The Rich Man and Lazarus: The Parable and the Parallels." *NTS* 37 (1991): 225-46.
Bishop, Eric F. F. "A Yawning Chasm." *EvQ* 45 (1973): 3-5.
Cadbury, Henry J. "A Proper Name for Dives." *JBL* 81 (1962): 399-402.

25. Richard L. Rohrbaugh, *The Biblical Interpreter: An Agrarian Bible in an Industrial Age* (Philadelphia: Fortress Press, 1978), 77.

————. "The Name for Dives." *JBL* 84 (1965): 73.

Cave, C. H. "Lazarus and the Lukan Deuteronomy." *NTS* 15 (1968-69): 319-25.

Derrett, J. Duncan M. "Fresh Light on St Luke xvi: II. Dives and Lazarus and the Preceding Sayings." *NTS* 7 (1960-61): 364-80. Reprinted in his *Law in the New Testament*, 78-99. London: Darton, Longman & Todd, 1970.

Dunkerley, Roderic. "Lazarus." *NTS* 5 (1958-59): 321-27.

Evans, Christopher F. "Uncomfortable Words — V. '. . . Neither Will They Be Convinced.'" *ExpTim* 81 (1969-70): 228-31.

Glombitza, Otto. "Der reiche Mann und der arme Lazarus: Luk. xvi 19-31, Zur Frage nach der Botschaft des Textes." *NovT* 12 (1970): 166-80.

Grensted, L. W. "The Use of Enoch in St. Luke xvi.19-31." *ExpTim* 26 (1914-15): 333-34.

Gressmann, Hugo. *Vom reichen Mann und armen Lazarus.* APAW 7. Berlin: Verlag der königl. Akademie der Wissenschaften, 1918.

Griffiths, J. Gwyn. "Cross-cultural Eschatology with Dives and Lazarus." *ExpTim* 105 (1993): 7-12.

Grobel, Kendrick. "'. . . Whose Name Was Neves.'" *NTS* 10 (1963-64): 373-82.

Hanson, R. P. C. "A Note on Luke xvi.14-31." *ExpTim* 55 (1943-44): 221-22.

Haupt, Paul. "Abraham's Bosom." *AJP* 42 (1921): 162-67.

Hock, Ronald F. "Lazarus and Dives," *ABD* 4:266-67.

————. "Lazarus and Micyllus: Greco-Roman Backgrounds to Luke 16:19-31." *JBL* 106 (1987): 447-63.

Huie, Wade P. "The Poverty of Abundance: From Text to Sermon on Luke 16:19-31." *Int* 22 (1968): 403-20.

Kreitzer, Larry. "Luke 16:19-31 and 1 Enoch 22." *ExpTim* 103 (1992): 139-42.

Kvalbein, Hans. "Jesus and the Poor: Two Texts and a Tentative Conclusion." *Themelios* 12 (1986-87): 80-87.

Lorenzen, Thorwald. "A Biblical Meditation on Luke 16:19-31." *ExpTim* 87 (1975): 39-43.

Marion, D. "Simples et mystérieuses paraboles. VII. Paraboles de crise: le riche insensé, le riche et Lazare." *EeV* (1996): 225-30, 235-36.

Osei-Bonsu, Joseph. "The Intermediate State in Luke-Acts." *IBS* 9 (1987): 115-30.

Powell, W. "The Parable of Dives and Lazarus (Luke xvi,19-31)." *ExpTim* 66 (1954-55): 350-51.

Ray, Charles A. "The Rich Man and Lazarus (Luke 16:19-31)." *ThEd* 56 (1997): 77-84.

Reinmuth, Eckart. "Ps-Philo, Liber Antiquitatum Biblicarum 33,1-5 und Die Auslegung der Parabel Lk. 16:19-31." *NovT* 31 (1989): 16-38.

Rimmer, N. "Parable of Dives and Lazarus (Luke xvi.19-31)." *ExpTim* 66 (1954-55): 215-16.

Schnider, Franz, and Werner Stenger. "Die offene Tür und die unüberschreitbare Kluft: Strukturanalytische Überlegungen zum Gleichnis vom reichen Mann und armen Lazarus (Lk 16,19-31)." *NTS* 25 (1979): 273-83.

Standen, A. O. "The Parable of Dives and Lazarus and Enoch 22." *ExpTim* 33 (1921-22): 523.

Tanghe, Vincent. "Abraham, son fils et son envoye (Luc 16:19-31)." *RB* 91 (1984): 66-75.

Wehrli, Eugene S. "Luke 16:19-31." *Int* 31 (1977): 276-80.

Wright, Stephen I. "Parables on Poverty and Riches (Luke 12:13-21; 16:1-13; 16:19-31)." In *The Challenge of Jesus' Parables,* 217-39. Ed. Richard N. Longenecker. Grand Rapids: Wm. B. Eerdmans, 2000.

3.9. The Pharisee and the Tax Collector, Luke 18:10-14

9*[Jesus] also told this parable to some who trusted in themselves that they were righteous and regarded others with contempt:* 10*"Two men went up into the temple to pray, one a Pharisee and the other a tax collector.* 11*The Pharisee stood and prayed these things concerning himself: 'God, I thank you that I am not like the rest of men — thieves, swindlers, adulterers, or even like this tax collector.* 12*I fast twice a week; I pay tithes on all that I acquire.'*

13*"But the tax collector, standing far off, would not even lift up his eyes to heaven, but beat his breast, saying, 'God, be merciful to me a sinner!'*

14*"I tell you, this man went down to his house justified rather than the other; for every one who exalts himself will be humbled, but he who humbles himself will be exalted."*

Notes on Text and Translation

18:11. The wording "stood and prayed these things concerning himself" rests upon judgments in matters of textual criticism and syntax. There are five possible readings: (1) πρὸς ἑαυτὸν ταῦτα ("to/by himself these things"); (2) ταῦτα πρὸς ἑαυτόν ("these things to/by himself"); (3) simply ταῦτα ("these things"); (4) simply πρὸς ἑαυτόν ("to/by himself"); and (5) καθ' ἑαυτὸν ταῦτα ("by himself these things").

Of these, readings 1, 2, and 3 have the greatest support in the Greek witnesses. Reading 1 is represented in the 26th and 27th editions of the Nestle-Aland Greek text; reading 2 in the 25th and earlier editions, as well as in the Westcott-Hort text (1881). Reading 2 may have slightly stronger support on the basis of external evidence (p75, B, Old Latin, and others) than does reading 1 (A, W, family 13, Majority text [other than those cited already, or those in support of readings 3 through 5], and others).[1] Reading 3 has fairly strong support as well (ℵ, lectionary 844, some Old Latin and Sahidic witnesses).

1. Such is the opinion in B. Metzger, *TCGNT* 168.

118

Reading 2 is the most difficult.[2] In that reading the direct object (ταῦτα, "these things") and the prepositional phrase (πρὸς ἑαυτόν, "to himself") can be taken to mean that the Pharisee prayed "these things to himself" (as though he actually prayed to himself), which has been suggested as the meaning,[3] or that he prayed silently.[4] But neither meaning is likely. He would surely not pray to himself, for he is a stock character who parades his piety before God and those around him in the Temple. And he would not pray silently, since the usual manner of praying in antiquity is aloud. The fact that neither of these meanings is satisfactory could be the basis for selecting reading 1. Various interpreters have also supported that choice of reading by saying that the Greek prepositional phrase represents a Semitism, and that it modifies the verb "to stand" rather than the verb "to pray," emphasizing his taking a position "by himself."[5]

The question, however, from a text-critical point of view, is what Luke wrote. On the grounds of both external and internal evidence, reading 2 seems preferable. Furthermore, such a reading need not have the meanings given above. The simplest interpretation of reading 2 is to take the πρός as a "πρός of reference," which appears elsewhere in Luke-Acts (Luke 12:41; 14:6; 20:19; Acts 24:16).[6] That would mean that the Pharisee "prayed these things concerning himself."

The translation of ἄδικοι as "swindlers" seems appropriate in context; in combination with the other two words, it "is clearly not merely the opposite of δίκαιοι [= "righteous" or "just" ones], but means something like 'cheats', 'swindlers.'"[7]

18:12. Instead of the verb ἀποδεκατῶ (as in the 26th and 27th editions of the Nestle-Aland Greek text), some major witnesses have ἀποδεκατεύω. The latter is better attested (𝔭75, ℵ, B, etc.) and should be preferred, as in the 25th edition of the Nestle-Aland text, as well as in Westcott-Hort Greek text. The meaning of the verbs, however, is the same.[8]

---

2. Contra ibid.

3. J. Creed, *Luke*, 224; Walter Grundmann, *Das Evangelium nach Lukas*, THKNT, 3d ed. (Berlin, 1966), 350. Cf. TEV: "The Pharisee stood up and said this prayer to himself."

4. B. Smith, *Parables*, 177; cf. BAGD 711: "he uttered a prayer to himself."

5. Charles C. Torrey, *Our Translated Gospels: Some of the Evidence* (New York: Harper & Brothers, 1936), 75-76, 79; T. W. Manson, *Sayings*, 310; J. Jeremias, *Parables*, 140; I. H. Marshall, *Luke*, 679. Although the possibility is considered, it is finally rejected on the grounds of textual criticism by Matthew Black, *An Aramaic Approach to the Gospels and Acts*, 3d ed. (Oxford: Clarendon Press, 1967), 103.

6. On this form, cf. BDF 124-25 (#239, 6).

7. B. Smith, *Parables*, 177; cf. J. Jeremias, *Parables*, 140; I. H. Marshall, *Luke*, 679.

8. BAGD 89.

Exegetical Commentary

This parable, found only in the Gospel of Luke and typically classified as a Parable of Exemplary Behavior,[9] is one of many spoken by Jesus within the Travel Narrative of the Gospel of Luke (9:51–19:27). Immediately following this parable, Luke resumes making use of the Gospel of Mark (Luke 18:15-17//Mark 10:13-16) for the first time since 9:49-50 (//Mark 9:38-41).

The parable appears immediately after the Parable of the Unjust Judge (18:2-8), which is an exhortation to Jesus' disciples to pray without losing heart (18:1). The present parable has to do with prayer as well, even if its introduction and conclusion (18:9, 14b) speak not of prayer per se, but about one's presumed standing before God. The parable becomes an illustration of that.

18:9. The narrative introduction provides an interpretive setting. Although it has been suggested that the verse was in the pre-Lukan tradition,[10] it is more likely that Luke himself has composed it in its present form, as he does elsewhere.[11] The original parable could indeed have been addressed to persons like those described in the verse, particularly certain Pharisees,[12] but the evangelist could also have persons within the Christian communities in mind. The question whether it provides a fitting setting for the parable is debated. Some would say no.[13] But it appears that here is a case where Luke has provided an appropriate introduction, one that helps rather than hinders interpretation. The parable that follows condemns self-righteousness and commends humility in the presence of God.

18:10. Although other parables might have been addressed to Pharisees by the earthly Jesus (cf. 15:2-32), this is the only one that has a Pharisee as one of its main characters. Since a Pharisee appears in the story, one can expect that he will be portrayed in stereotypical fashion, and that is the case here. The term "Pharisee" is thought to have been derived from the Hebrew word פָּרוּשׁ (pārûš), which means "separated one."[14] The Pharisees were a movement (not a denomination

---

9. In German, a *Beispielerzählung;* cf. A. Jülicher, *Gleichnisreden,* 1:114; R. Bultmann, *HST* 177-79.

10. J. Jeremias, *Parables,* 93 (n. 13); E. Linnemann, *Parables,* 64; and R. Bultmann, *HST* 178 (n. 2), but on pp. 193 and 335 he attributes it to Luke.

11. It is typical of Luke to provide parables with settings as a framework for interpreting them. Such settings — all important for the interpretations of the parables that follow — are at 12:13-16 (for the Rich Fool), 12:41 (for the Faithful and Wise Servant), 14:15 (for the Great Banquet), 16:14-15 (for the Rich Man and Lazarus), 18:1 (for the Unjust Judge), and 19:11 (for the Pounds).

12. W. O. E. Oesterley, *Parables,* 228; J. Jeremias, *Parables,* 139; T. W. Manson, *Sayings,* 307.

13. E. Linnemann, *Parables,* 64; J. Crossan, *Parables,* 68; B. Scott, *Parable,* 93-94.

14. Rudolf Meyer, "φαρισαῖος," *TDNT* 9:12-13; Anthony J. Saldarini, *Pharisees, Scribes and Sadducees in Palestinian Society: A Sociological Approach* (Wilmington: Michael Glazier, 1988), 220-25.

in the modern sense) within Judaism devoted to observing Torah, including ritual purity, and to piety toward God.[15] According to Josephus, the Pharisees were the most observant of all the identifiable Jewish groups, and they were held in high regard among the masses of people.[16] At the same time, not only in the Gospels, but also in traditional Jewish literature, some Pharisees could be criticized by Jews (including Pharisaic Jews) as proud and self-righteous.[17]

The tax collector (τελώνης) in the parable would obviously be a Jewish person, since he goes to the Temple to pray. He would have been one of those who collect tolls, market duties, and all kinds of local taxes (sales, income, property, and inheritance),[18] making their living by overcharging people (cf. the words of Zacchaeus, 19:8), thereby preying upon them. As a tax collector, he is a figure who invites scorn.[19]

What is striking at the outset of the parable is the ease with which Jesus says that the tax collector went to the Temple to pray. While it would be customary and even expected that a Jewish man would go to the Temple for prayer, this man is a tax collector. It is not likely that he would want to be identified as such in a public way. That means that any hearer of the parable would never have heard of a tax collector going to the Temple to pray. The effect is a rather shocking spectacle within the narrative.

The two terms "Pharisee" and "tax collector" are polarities. That is demonstrated earlier in Luke's Gospel at 15:1-2, where the Pharisees criticize Jesus severely for associating with tax collectors.

18:11-12. Regarding the prayer of the Pharisee, two points can be observed — both the *manner* of his praying and the *content* of his prayer. Concerning the *manner* of prayer, 18:11 can be translated in various ways, depending on how one renders the Greek phrase σταθεὶς πρὸς ἑαυτὸν ταῦτα προσηύχετο:

15. A. Saldarini, *Pharisees, Scribes and Sadducees,* 281-97.

16. Josephus, *Ant.* 13.297-98; 18.15; *J.W.* 1.110; 2.162.

17. Cf. various passages cited by G. F. Moore, *Judaism,* 2:190-94. It is puzzling that B. Scott, *Parable,* 94, asserts that without the Lukan introduction (18:9), the reader would not think of the Pharisee as a negative caricature.

18. Fritz Herrenbrück, "Wer waren die 'Zöllner'?" *ZNW* 72 (1981): 178-94; idem, *Jesus und die Zöllner: Historische und neutestamentlich-exegetische Untersuchungen,* WUNT 41 (Tübingen: J. C. B. Mohr [Paul Siebeck], 1990); Helmut Merkel, "τελώνης," *EDNT* 3:349. This view seems to have gained support over the earlier view that the term referred primarily to toll collectors at transport and commercial centers, as in the work of John R. Donahue, "Tax Collectors and Sinners: An Attempt at Identification," *CBQ* 33 (1971): 39-61, who is followed by J. Fitzmyer, *Luke,* 469-70, 1186; and W. Herzog, *Parables,* 173, 187-88.

19. In addition to NT passages that portray tax collectors as despised, rabbinic references are cited by Joachim Jeremias, *Jerusalem in the Time of Jesus: An Investigation into Economic and Social Conditions during the New Testament Period* (Philadelphia: Fortress Press, 1969), 310-11; Greco-Roman sources are cited by John R. Donahue, "Tax Collector," *ABD* 6:337.

1. According to the RSV, the Pharisee "stood and prayed thus with himself." Here the prepositional phrase modifies the verb "to pray." The Pharisee prays in self-satisfaction. This way of translating is reflected also in the KJV ("with himself") and the TEV ("to himself"). But on the basis of syntax, such a translation is difficult. Moreover, the phrase probably does not refer to a soliloquy; in those instances a different phrase is used, ἐν ἑαυτῷ (7:39; 12:17; 16:3; cf. 15:17, εἰς ἑαυτόν).[20]

2. According to the NRSV, the Pharisee, "standing by himself, was praying thus." Here the phrase in question modifies the verb "to stand."[21] The Pharisee stands in isolation from the rest of the people. He is separated off. Although that understanding has an appeal (portraying the Pharisee as a "separated one"), it is difficult to translate the prepositional phrase as "by himself." Furthermore, since the point is made that the tax collector stood "far off" (18:13), one should understand the Pharisee as having taken up a prominent position.

3. As suggested above (Notes on Text and Translation), the prepositional phrase in question can be translated most satisfactorily as a "πρός of reference," and 18:11a can be translated: "The Pharisee stood and prayed these things concerning himself." Cf. the NIV: "The Pharisee stood up and prayed about himself."[22]

The picture is one in which the Pharisee goes to the Temple to pray, finds a place to pray, and speaks in audible tones (like all others present). These things are normal. But what is striking is that he prays a string of words about himself in which he exalts himself and denigrates others, particularly the tax collector who has come into the Temple at virtually the same time.

The *content* of the Pharisee's prayer is astonishing. It is disingenuous, self-deceptive, and mean-spirited. It begins, appropriately, with thanksgiving to God, and in fact consists of a thanksgiving all the way through.[23] It is fitting that people should thank God for what they are and what they have. But the thanksgiving is not genuine, for the Pharisee implicitly considers himself an autonomous agent of moral virtue; he is hardly dependent upon God for anything. And if he is not dependent upon God, he has no reason to give thanks to God.

Moreover, the prayer is self-deceptive, leading to a false sense of righteousness, for the Pharisee goes on to contrast himself with the worst examples of conduct — "thieves, swindlers, adulterers."

---

20. K. Bailey, *Peasant Eyes,* 148-49; J. Donahue, *Parable,* 188.

21. Cf. J. Jeremias, *Parables,* 140: "he took up a prominent position and uttered this prayer." Others who conclude that the phrase modifies the verb "to stand" include K. Bailey, *Peasant Eyes,* 147-48; B. Scott, *Parable,* 94; and W. Herzog, *Parables,* 185.

22. Cf. also J. Fitzmyer, *Luke,* 1182: "prayed thus about himself."

23. A similar prayer of thanksgiving appears at *b. Ber.* 28b.

Finally, there is a mean-spirited side to the prayer. The expression "this tax collector" is to be taken as contemptuous (cf. 15:30 for a similar one).[24]

The Pharisee goes on to speak of his good deeds. First, he fasts twice a week. That goes well beyond what was required in the law, for fasting was required on only one day per year, the Day of Atonement (Lev 16:29-34; 23:27-32; Num 29:7), a day of national repentance. Nevertheless, Jewish literature prior to the first century A.D. abounds with stories and sayings about fasting as a means of preparation for ecstatic visions, an expression of remorse and penitence, a sign of virtue, an act of mourning, and a meritorious deed.[25] Sources indicate that the Pharisees in particular observed fasting days (Mark 2:18//Matt 9:14//Luke 5:33; *Pss. Sol.* 3:8). In addition to the present text, which speaks of fasting twice a week, at least two others can be cited, which mention Mondays and Thursdays as fast days.[26] Within the parable, it appears that the Pharisee is portrayed as understanding his fasting as meritorious or vicarious — surely not as an act of repentance for himself, but possibly for the sins of Israel.

The Pharisee also pays tithes on all that he acquires. This, too, must be considered meritorious. Tithing laws were not uniform or unequivocal in Jewish tradition, for there were several kinds that originated in both Deuteronomic (14:22-27; 24:22-23) and Priestly (Lev 27:30-33; Num 18:20-32) codes.[27] Moreover, it is not clear which laws were observed in first-century-A.D. Palestine prior to the destruction of the Temple. Scribes debated over what produce of the farm and garden was to be tithed and for what purpose, seeking to harmonize the various pentateuchal laws. Entire rabbinic tractates were produced to resolve the difficulties (e.g., the *Mishnah* tractates *Demai, Maaseroth,* and *Maaser Sheni*). The scribes saw to it that all kinds of produce were tithed (cf. Matt 23:23; Luke 11:42).

That the Pharisee pays a tithe on all that he "acquires" (the basic meaning of the verb κτάομαι) does not mean that he simply pays a tithe on his entire income (contra NIV and NRSV, "all my income"). It means that he pays a tithe on everything that he brings into his household as well, including foods that he acquires by purchase, lest the tithe had not been paid by its producer, a custom that is known to have existed in antiquity.[28]

18:13. The *manner* and *content* of the tax collector's prayer are set in bold contrast to that of the Pharisee. Regarding his *manner,* there are three items listed. That he stood "far off" means that he stood at a distance from either of three things: the most holy place, the Pharisee, or others at prayer.[29] Actually if

---

24. BDF 151 (#290, 6).

25. Johannes Behm, "νῆστις," *TDNT* 4:929; G. F. Moore, *Judaism,* 2:257-66.

26. *Didache* 8.1, in reference to the "hypocrites" (= Pharisees); and *b. Ta'an.* 12a in reference to those two days as traditional (but not obligatory) fast days for some.

27. J. Christian Wilson, "Tithe," *ABD* 6:578-80.

28. Mark Wischnitzer, "Tithes," *EncJud* 15:1162.

29. A. Jülicher, *Gleichnisreden,* 2:604.

he were to be far off from any one of these, he would have been far from all three, standing in an outer courtyard of the Temple, as a sign of unworthiness before both God and others. Instead of assuming the usual posture for prayer, that is, standing with eyes and hands uplifted (Ps 123:1; John 11:41; 1 Tim 2:8),[30] the tax collector would not raise his hands or eyes. His manner is a sign of shame, based on a sense of guilt (Ezra 9:6; *1 Enoch* 13:5). That he beat his breast was a sign of extreme anguish or contrition (Luke 23:48),[31] as the words of the prayer go on to express.

Regarding the *content* of his prayer, it is not a thanksgiving, but a petition for mercy. The tax collector sees himself only in light of God's standard. He considers himself a "sinner." In contrast to the Pharisee who enumerates his good works, however, he does not elaborate on his being a sinner by listing any specific sins. The verb translated "be merciful" (ἰλάσκομαι) is found only here and at Hebrews 2:17 in the NT. In the active form it carries the sense of making atonement for sin. In the passive, however (as here, an aorist passive imperative), it has the meaning of being merciful or gracious, as already in the LXX (4 Kgdms 24:4; Lam 3:42; Dan 9:19). One would normally expect the more common verb for "have mercy" (ἐλεέω; cf. Luke 16:24; 17:13; 18:38-39), but the choice of the verb may be due to the fact that the petition is spoken in the Temple, where atonement is made.

One can expect at this point that there is no way that the tax collector, on the basis of his prayer alone, can receive forgiveness. The only way that forgiveness would be possible for him would be through true repentance, and that would entail giving up his profession and making full restitution for those whom he had defrauded, plus one-fifth of the amount owed (Lev 6:5; Num 5:7).[32] But the next verse sets all that aside.

18:14a. The perfect passive participle of δικαιόω is used, meaning that the tax collector went home "in the state of having been justified" by God (a "divine passive" is used). God has justified him, declared him to be in the right relationship with himself; the man has been "right-wised." The verb is commonly associated with the writings of the apostle Paul (Rom 3:28; 5:1; Gal 2:16, etc.). But it appears in the Gospels not only here but at other places as well (Matt 12:37; Luke 10:29; 16:15) and must have been rooted then in the teaching of Jesus.[33] That would not be surprising, since the term is found in the OT also;

30. For additional references, cf. Joachim Jeremias, "αἴρω," *TDNT* 1:185-86.

31. Cf. also Josephus, *Ant.* 7.252; *Jos. Asen.* 10:15. The beating of the chest (the location of the heart) in Middle Eastern culture is illustrated in texts quoted by K. Bailey, *Peasant Eyes*, 153.

32. It might be suggested that the story of Zacchaeus (19:1-10) could be a model. But the story does not really apply to this line of thinking. As indicated by I. H. Marshall, *Luke*, 681, "when Zacchaeus restores his ill-gotten gains . . . this follows his acceptance by Jesus and does not precede it."

33. J. Jeremias, *Parables*, 141; J. Fitzmyer, *Luke*, 1185.

forms of the verb δικαιόω are used in the LXX for various Hebrew verbs with צדק (*ṣdq*) as their root (e.g., Deut 25:1; 3 Kgdms 8:32; Ezek 16:51-52; Job 33:32; Ps 143:2 [LXX 142:2]; cf. 2 Esdr 12.7). The parable (concluding with 18:14a in particular) corresponds to the saying of Jesus in Luke 16:15. There he says to some Pharisees that they seek to justify themselves in the sight of others; but God knows their hearts. In the parable the Pharisee announces his virtues not only before God but before all who can hear. But God knows the heart of both the Pharisee and the tax collector. The expression παρ' ἐκεῖνον is to be taken in an exclusive sense[34] (KJV, RSV, NIV, NRSV: "rather than the other"), as though God had turned a deaf ear to his prayer.

By declaring the tax collector justified, Jesus assumes an authority that belongs to God alone. But what is even more striking is that what he declares here in a story he also declares elsewhere in the exercise of the forgiveness of sins (Matt 9:2-8//Mark 2:3-12//Luke 5:18-26; Luke 7:47-49). The coherence of these phenomena supports the authenticity of each. The fact that the parable is marked by many Semitisms and reflects customs of Jesus' day lends support to the common judgment that it is an authentic parable of Jesus.[35]

18:14b. The parable comes to an end at 18:14a. This portion of the verse is not part of the parable. It is generally regarded as a floating saying (cf. Luke 14:11; Matt 23:12) that Luke has attached at this point to give a generalized application of the parable. That the application is eschatological in a way that the parable is not speaks in favor of judging it to be an addition.[36]

The parable is classified as an "exemplary narrative" (or "Beispielerzählung" in German form-critical categories) or parable of exemplary behavior. The Pharisee's general conduct of life — that is, not being a thief, swindler, or adulterer; being one who fasts and tithes — is not what is condemned, nor is that of the tax collector the example to be followed. The point at which the example is to be taken is that of the contrast between the manner and content of

---

34. For other instances, cf. BAGD 611 (παρά, III, 3); Gottlob Schrenk, "δικαιόω," *TDNT* 2:215 (n. 16).

35. A. Jülicher, *Gleichnisreden*, 2:608; J. Jeremias, *Parables*, 139-40; C. Montefiore, *Synoptic Gospels*, 2:1022; N. Perrin, *Teaching*, 122; I. H. Marshall, *Luke*, 678; H. Hendrickx, *Parables*, 243. It is printed in pink font (= Jesus said something like that) in R. Funk, *Five Gospels*, 369. That the parable is not authentic, and that Luke adopted it from Hellenistic Jewish tradition, is asserted by Walter Schmithals, "The Parabolic Teachings in the Synoptic Tradition," *JHC* 4/2 (1997): 13.

36. Among those who consider it a Lukan addition here are A. Jülicher, *Gleichnisreden*, 2:607; R. Bultmann, *HST* 178-79; T. W. Manson, *Sayings*, 312; N. Perrin, *Teaching*, 122; and E. Schweizer, *Luke*, 282. Less certain — allowing that it may be original, or in Luke's source — are J. Jeremias, *Parables*, 144 (n. 62); K. Bailey, *Peasant Eyes*, 155; and J. Fitzmyer, *Luke*, 1183. But both 18:9 and 18:14b are regarded as Lukan redaction by Joachim Jeremias, *Die Sprache des Lukasevangeliums: Redaktion und Tradition im Nicht-Markusstoff des dritten Evangeliums*, MeyerK (Göttingen: Vandenhoeck & Ruprecht, 1980), 272-74.

their respective prayers. The Pharisee expects God and all in earshot to be open to hear his words of self-congratulation or self-justification; the tax collector opens himself up to the judgment of God and all who can hear him, accepting the verdict due upon him.[37] That means, too, that he relies wholly on the grace of God for healing the breach between him and God (= his salvation). The consequence is that the tax collector goes home renewed, whereas the Pharisee continues as he was.

Exposition

The modern reader or hearer of this parable, who has encountered it again and again, can easily fail to realize an important dynamic within the story and the shock that it would have caused the earliest hearers. The dynamics between the two men in the parable are revealing. The Pharisee needs those whom he despises, particularly the tax collector, to be what he is. The tax collector, on the other hand, is the person he is because of the stigma placed upon him by the Pharisees and other special persons.[38] So it is that everyone's identity is shaped by a complex of relationships, and it is by a process of distantiation that people everywhere understand who they are.

The story would have been shocking to an ancient audience. The Pharisee would have been considered by anyone as universally esteemed. Moreover, his prayer of thanksgiving affirms common values. The tax collector, on the other hand, would have been genuinely, and some might add justly, despised. Therefore he should not become an icon to be admired by the modern reader.

But the parable contains surprises. The one who is justified — stands right before God — is the tax collector, the one who is open to God, asking for mercy, rather than the Pharisee, who parades his righteousness in comparison to others. There can be no cover-ups before God — no comparisons, no contrasts — just honesty before God.

A person's presumed faithfulness to God and list of moral virtues can cause blindness regarding one's relationship to both God and other persons. God is then no longer the Holy One before whom one is ultimately and certainly accountable. Other persons can be looked upon as having lesser worth in the community and in the eyes of God. That is true especially of persons who have suffered loss for one reason or another.

The parable places a challenge on the manner and content of prayer — both private and corporate. Prayer at its best provides moments of openness

---

37. Puzzling is the assertion of B. Scott, *Parable,* 97: "There is no lesson to learn! The hearer cannot imitate the behavior of one or the other. The parable's message is simpler. . . . The parable subverts the metaphorical structure that sees the kingdom of God as temple." It is difficult to imagine that the earliest hearers would have heard the parable in that way.

38. J. Moltmann, "The Pharisee and the Tax Collector," 93-94.

before God, not cover-ups, and it leads to healing. (It should go without saying that the person who would pray, in so many words, "God, I thank you that I pray like the tax collector," misunderstands the meaning of the parable.)

The parable also offers teaching about justification. The term "justification," based on the Latin *iustificatio,* has long usage in the church, and the doctrine of justification by faith has been a subject of polemics. It is found in the letters of Paul, but even there some find it a complicated teaching. In this parable, however, it is simple. To justify means to set a person or thing in a right relationship to a larger whole. (One can think here of justifying the margin in word processing, a step by which one sets lines on the right, left, or both edges of a page in right relationship to the others.) So Jesus declares that whoever is open to the mercy of God is in a right relationship to God, who justifies the ungodly (Rom 4:5).

Select Bibliography

Bruce, F. F. "'Justification by Faith' in the Non-Pauline Writings of the New Testament." *EvQ* 24 (1952): 66-67.

Bultmann, Rudolf. "Lukas 18,9-14." In his *Marburger Predigten,* 107-17. Tübingen: J. C. B. Mohr (Paul Siebeck), 1956.

Charpentier, Étienne. "Le chrétien: Un homme 'juste' ou 'justifié'? Lc 18,9-14." *ASeign* 61 (1972): 66-78.

Downing, F. Gerald. "The Ambiguity of 'The Pharisee and the Toll-Collector' (Luke 18:9-14) in the Greco-Roman World of Late Antiquity." *CBQ* 54 (1992): 80-99.

Evans, Craig A. "The Pharisee and the Publican: Luke 18:9-14 and Deuteronomy 26." In *The Gospels and the Scriptures of Israel,* 342-55. Ed. Craig A. Evans and William R. Stegner. JSNTSup 104. Sheffield: Sheffield Academic Press, 1994.

Farris, Michael. "A Tale of Two Taxations (Luke 18:10-14b)." In *Jesus and His Parables: Interpreting the Parables of Jesus Today,* 23-33. Ed. V. George Schillington. Edinburgh: T. & T. Clark, 1997.

Feuillet, André. "Le pharisien et le publicain (Luc 18:9-14). La manifestation de la miséricorde divine en Jésus Serviteur souffrant." *EeV* 91 (1981): 657-65.

Franks, R. S. "The Parable of the Pharisee and the Publican." *ExpTim* 38 (1926-27): 373-76.

Gueuret, Agnès. "Le pharisien et le publicain et son contexte." In *Les paraboles évangéliques: Perspectives nouvelles: Congrès de l'ACFEB, Lyon, 1987,* 289-307. Ed. Jean Delorme. LeDiv 135. Paris: Cerf, 1989.

Hengel, Martin. "Die ganz andere Gerechtigkeit: Bibelarbeit über Lk 18,9-14." *TBei* 5 (1974): 1-13.

Hoerber, Robert G. "'God, Be Merciful to Me a Sinner': A Note on Lk 18:13." *CTM* 33 (1962): 283-86.

Holmgren, Fredrick C. "The Pharisee and the Tax Collector: Luke 18:9-14 and Deuteronomy 26:1-15." *Int* 48 (1994): 252-61.

Iersel, Bastiaan van. "De farizeër en de tollenaar (Lc 18,9-14)." In *Parabel-verhalen in Lucas: Van semiotiek naar pragmatiek*, 194-216. Ed. B. van Iersel et al. TFTS 8. Tilburg: Tilburg University Press, 1987.

Joji, K. "From Brokenness to Wholeness — The Jesus Way: Hermeneutical Study of Lk 18:9-14." *Vidyajyoti* 61 1997): 469-79.

Liefeld, Walter L. "Parables on Prayer (Luke 11:5-10; 18:1-8; 18:9-14)." In *The Challenge of Jesus' Parables*, 240-62. Ed. Richard N. Longenecker. Grand Rapids: Wm. B. Eerdmans, 2000.

Lorenzen, Thorwald. "The Radicality of Grace: The Pharisee and the Tax Collector (Lk 18:9-14) as a Parable of Jesus." *FaM* 3 (1986): 66-75.

Marcus, Joel. "The Pharisee and the Tax Collector." *PSB* 11/2 (1990): 138-42.

Martin, Ralph P. "Two Worshippers, One Way to God." *ExpTim* 96 (1984-85): 117-18.

Merklein, Helmut. "'Dieser ging als Gerechter nach Hause . . .': Das Gottesbild Jesu und die Haltung der Menschen nach Lk 18,9-14." *BiKi* 32 (1977): 34-42.

Moltmann, Jürgen. "The Pharisee and the Tax Collector." In *The Power of the Powerless*, 88-97. San Francisco: Harper & Row, 1983. Reprinted in *A Chorus of Witnesses: Model Sermons for Today's Preacher*, 21-33. Ed. Thomas G. Long and Cornelius Plantinga. Grand Rapids: Wm. B. Eerdmans, 1994.

Mottu, Henry. "The Pharisee and the Tax Collector: Sartrian Notions as Applied to the Reading of Scripture." *USQR* 29 (1974): 195-213.

Oke, C. Clark. "The Parable of the Pharisee and the Publican." *CJRT* 5 (1928): 122-26.

Pesch, Rudolf. "Jesus, A Free Man." In *Jesus Christ and Human Freedom*, 56-70. *Concilium* 3:10. New York: Herder and Herder, 1974.

Schlosser, Jacques. "Le pharisien et le publician (Lc 18,9-14)." In *Les paraboles évangéliques: Perspectives nouvelles: Congrès de l'ACFEB, Lyon, 1987*, 271-88. Ed. Jean Delorme. LeDiv 135. Paris: Cerf, 1989.

Schnider, Franz. "Ausschliessen und ausgescholossen werden: Beobachtungen zur Struktur des Gleichnisses vom Pharisäer und Zöllner Lk 18,10-14a." *BZ* 24 (1980): 42-56.

Schottroff, Luise. "Die Erzählung vom Pharisäer und Zöllner als Beispiel für die theologische Kunst des Überredens." In *Neues Testament und christliche Existenz*, 439-61. Ed. Hans D. Betz and Luise Schottroff. Tübingen: J. C. B. Mohr (Paul Siebeck), 1973.

Stemm, Sönke von. "Der betende Sünder vor Gott: Lk 18,9-14. Zur Rezeption von Psalm 51(50),19." In *The Scriptures in the Gospels*, 579-89. Ed. Christopher Tuckett. BETL 131. Leuven: Leuven University Press, 1992.

Strelan, John G. "The Pharisee Lurking: Reflections on Luke 18:9-14." *LTJ* 20 (1986): 116-20.

CHAPTER 4

Parables of Wisdom

Several parables are concerned about wisdom, and usually that is about being a wise disciple of Jesus. That is particularly true of the six parables that are discussed in this chapter. To be sure, there are other parables that express the theme of wisdom in one way or another, such as the Parable of the Children in the Marketplace (Matt 11:16-19//Luke 7:31-35), but in those cases other themes are stronger. The parables discussed here express the need to possess and to practice wisdom as their main thrust.

The wisdom tradition is old, broad, and perennial in biblical literature. It antedates the writing of the Scriptures, for it appears in the ancient literatures of Egypt and Mesopotamia prior to the writing of the biblical books. The tradition arose out of an international movement that was not dependent on revelation to any particular people by means of their election or by historical acts. Within the traditions of Israel its origins go back at least to Solomon, who was famous for his wisdom (1 Kings 4:29-34). The wisdom tradition was carried on primarily by sages, scribes, and officers (both religious and political) through the centuries well after the rise of Christianity.

Within the OT various literary units are classified as wisdom literature. These include the books of Proverbs, Job, Ecclesiastes, and Psalm 37. In addition, Sirach (or Ecclesiasticus) and the Wisdom of Solomon among the OT apocrypha/deuterocanonical books are considered wisdom literature.

According to Gospel traditions, Jesus of Nazareth was known to be a wise man and teacher of wisdom. In Matthew 11:28-30 he is portrayed explicitly as a teacher of wisdom. When the passage is compared with Sirach 51:23-26 concerning the call of wisdom to her pupils, the point is drawn with utmost clarity. At Luke 11:31 Jesus refers to "the wisdom of Solomon" and then declares that, by virtue of his teachings, "something greater than Solomon is here." In addition to these passages concerning Jesus as a sage, or teacher of wisdom, there are many other aphorisms and sayings of Jesus that can safely be classified as wisdom teachings, for they are not very different from those that exist in the OT wisdom literature. Several, for example, are in the Sermon on the Mount (Matt 6:19-20, 24, 34; 7:6, 13-14; etc.).

The six parables that follow have wisdom, or being wise, as a main theme. They can therefore be called "parables of wisdom."

4.10. The Wise and Foolish Builders, Matthew 7:24-27//Luke 6:47-49

Matthew 7:24-27

24[Jesus said,] *"Everyone then who hears these words of mine and puts them into practice will be like a wise man who built his house upon the rock;* 25*and the rain fell, and the floods came, and the winds blew and beat upon that house, but it did not fall, for it had been founded on rock.* 26*And every one who hears these words of mine and does not put them into practice will be like a foolish man who built his house upon sand;* 27*and the rain fell, and the floods came, and the winds blew and beat against that house, and it fell; and great was the fall of it."*

Notes on the Text and Translation

7:24. Some ancient texts have the words ὁμοιώσω αὐτόν ("I will compare him to"), which is followed by the KJV ("I will liken him unto"), instead of the verb ὁμοιωθήσεται ("[he or she] will be like"). The latter is better attested,[1] and it is represented in current translations (RSV, NEB, NIV, NRSV).

Luke 6:47-49

47[Jesus said,] *"I will show you what someone is like who comes to me, hears my words, and puts them into practice.* 48*That person is like a man building a house, who dug, went down deep, and laid a foundation upon rock; and when a flood arose, the [overflowing] river burst upon that house, and could not shake it, because it had been built well.* 49*But the person who has heard and has not put them into practice is like a man who built a house on the ground without a foundation; upon which the [overflowing] river burst, and immediately it collapsed; and the destruction of that house was great."*

1. B. Metzger, *TCGNT* 20.

Notes on the Text and Translation

6:47. The RSV represents a translation that follows the syntax of the Greek text in the opening line: "Everyone who comes to me and hears my words and does them, I will show you what he is like." The KJV and NEB have similar syntax. The syntax is complicated (consisting of a subordinate clause containing parataxis, the subject of which becomes the object of the main clause) and is regarded as Semitic.[2] The use of πᾶς with a nominative participle ("everyone who . . .") is common in Luke-Acts.[3] The translation above is better in English and is similar to those in the NIV and NRSV.

6:48. The verb προσέρηξεν (from προσρήσσω) is found only here and at 6:49 in the NT and can be translated "burst upon,"[4] indicating a violent torrent of water.

Instead of the clause translated "because it had been built well," some Greek texts have τεθεμελίωτο γὰρ ἐπὶ τὴν πέτραν ("for it had been founded upon the rock"), and that is represented in the KJV and acknowledged in marginal notes of the RSV and NRSV. That is the exact wording of Matthew 7:25, and it is probable that some scribes preferred Matthew's reason for its durability and imported it here. Superior Greek texts have the phrase represented in the translation provided here (cf. also RSV, NEB, NIV, NRSV).[5]

General Comments on the Texts

The parable is often called the Parable of the House upon the Rock.[6] Other designations include the Parable of the Two Houses,[7] the Parable of the Two Builders,[8] or the Parable of the Two Foundations.[9] The title chosen above has also been used by various interpreters.[10]

2. Klaus Beyer, *Semitische Syntax im Neuen Testament*, SUNT 1 (Göttingen: Vandenhoeck & Ruprecht, 1962), 212, 224, 267.

3. A. Plummer, *Luke*, 38.

4. BAGD 718.

5. B. Metzger, *TCGNT* 142.

6. *Synopsis Quattuor Evangeliorum*, ed. Kurt Aland, 13th ed. (Stuttgart: Deutsche Bibelgesellschaft, 1985), 99; C. Montefiore, *Synoptic Gospels*, 2:554.

7. C. H. Dodd, *Parables*, 6; J. Jeremias, *Parables*, 194; B. Smith, *Parables*, 225; J. Fitzmyer, *Luke*, 628.

8. A. Cadoux, *Parables*, 171; A. M. Hunter, *Parables*, 74; Kamal Abou-Chaar, "The Two Builders," 44-58; Hans Dieter Betz, *The Sermon on the Mount*, Hermeneia Commentary (Minneapolis: Fortress Press, 1995), 557; W. D. Davies and D. C. Allison, *Matthew*, 1:719; cf. U. Luz, *Matthew 1–7*, 450 ("The Two Housebuilders").

9. A. McNeile, *Matthew*, 97; R. Gundry, *Matthew*, 133.

10. T. W. Manson, *Sayings*, 177; George A. Buttrick, *The Parables of Jesus* (New York: Harper & Brothers, 1928), 54; R. Stein, *Parables*, 24; Georg Strecker, *The Sermon on the Mount: An Exegetical Commentary* (Nashville: Abingdon Press, 1988), 168.

It is commonly thought that both Matthew and Luke derived their respective versions of the parable from Q as a common source, even though the versions of Q available to them might have been somewhat different.[11] The wording of the two versions is quite different, however, and therefore other proposals have been made: (1) that the parable may have come to the two evangelists in their respective traditions (L and M);[12] or (2) that it came to each in Q, but also to Matthew in his special tradition.[13] Nevertheless, in spite of the differences among them, there are grounds for attributing them to a common source (Q) on the basis of form, content, and even wording.[14] The differences can be accounted for on the basis of variations in wording already in the recensions used and alterations made by the evangelists.

The imagery within the parable appears also in a rabbinic parable of the second century A.D. According to tradition from the third or fourth century, Rabbi Elisha b. Abuyah (third-generation rabbinic teacher, ca. A.D. 120-40) spoke a parable in which he compared those who study the Torah and do good deeds and those who study the Torah but do not do good deeds. Concerning the first, he said he is like someone who "builds first with stones and then with bricks," and "even though a great flood of water comes and washes against the foundations, the water does not blot them out of their place." On the other hand, the second person is like someone who "builds first with bricks and then with stones," and "even if only a little water comes and washes against the foundations, it forthwith overturns them."[15]

In both Gospels the parable closes a discourse of Jesus — either the Sermon on the Mount (Matthew 5:1–7:29) or the Sermon on the Plain (Luke 6:20-49). Its function in each case is to move the hearers of the sermon to contemplate what has been said and to act upon the teachings of Jesus.

The parable is often regarded as having originated in the proclamation of Jesus of Nazareth.[16]

11. Burnett H. Streeter, *The Four Gospels: A Study of Origins,* rev. ed. (New York: St. Martin's Press, 1930), 251, 291; T. W. Manson, *Sayings,* 177; A. Polag, *Fragmenta Q,* 38; J. Fitzmyer, *Luke,* 627; U. Luz, *Matthew 1–7,* 451; G. Strecker, *Sermon on the Mount,* 169; J. Gnilka, *Matthäusevangelium,* 1:280; W. D. Davies and D. C. Allison, *Matthew,* 1:117, 719; H. Betz, *Sermon on the Mount,* 559-60; R. Brown, *Introduction NT,* 118.

12. Francis W. Beare, *The Earliest Records of Jesus* (New York: Abingdon Press, 1962), 69.

13. E. Schweizer, *Matthew,* 190.

14. *Form:* in both versions there is a statement of a prudential thesis, followed by evidence for it; statement of an antithesis, followed by evidence for it. *Content:* in both versions there are two persons, and both hear, but one does deeds and the other does not. *Wording:* verbs of hearing, doing, building; nouns for house, rock, and flood are the same in both.

15. *Abot R. Nat.* 24:1; quoted from *The Fathers according to Rabbi Nathan: An Analytical Translation and Explanation,* trans. Jacob Neusner, BJS 114 (Atlanta: Scholars Press, 1986), 149.

16. A. Jülicher, *Gleichnisreden,* 2:267-68; K. Abou-Chaar, "The Two Builders," 44-58;

The Parable in the Gospel of Matthew

Exegetical Commentary

The parable comes specifically within the Sermon on the Mount after Jesus' saying that the expression of pious words (7:21) and even the demonstration of outstanding charismatic gifts of prophecy and exorcism (7:22) are nothing in themselves. The disciple of Jesus who is wise not only listens to Jesus' teachings but follows them as well.

7:24. The person envisioned as wise is the one who has heard "these words of mine" (μου τοὺς λόγους τούτους), that is, the instructions given throughout the Sermon on the Mount. The term translated "wise" (φρόνιμος) can also mean "prudent." It is used in three other parables (Matt 24:45//Luke 12:42; Matt 25:2, 4, 8-9; Luke 16:8) and is rooted in the wisdom tradition (cf. LXX passages Prov 3:7; 11:12, 29; 14:6; Sir 22:4). In Jewish tradition the person who is regarded as wise is observant of the Torah (Prov 2:1-2; Jer 8:8-9; Sir 9:14-16; 19:20; 38:34; 39:8; Bar 3:9-14). In this instance, the person regarded as wise is the one who observes the teachings of Jesus (hearing and putting them into practice). Furthermore, the association between possessing wisdom and building a house that will stand and is pleasing in which to dwell is a familiar metaphor (Eccl 2:4; Sir 1:16-17; 3:9; 22:16-18; cf. Prov 9:1; 14:1).

Building a house on "rock" (not "a rock") is envisioned, and that is possible in many parts of Palestine. The topography of Galilee inland from the Mediterranean Sea to Upper Galilee in the north and to the Sea of Galilee in the east includes hilly and mountainous areas of sandstone, basalt, calcareous (chalky) rock, and limestone.[17] Portions of Judea around Jerusalem have a limestone base.[18] The Temple at Jerusalem stood securely on a rock base (cf. Isa 28:16). Rock is also a metaphor for a solid, stable foundation (Ps 40:2; Sir 40:15), and frequently God is pictured as the rock on whom one can be secure (2 Sam 2:2; Ps 18:2; 31:2-3; 71:3, etc.).

7:25. Three elements of bad weather are cited: heavy rain, unexpected flash floods, and extreme winds. These are the calamities that can befall inhabitants of Palestine during the rainy season (October to April, but especially from November to February when 70 percent of the rain falls annually).[19] When rain falls in significant amounts, it comes down from the mountains and

---

U. Luz, *Matthew 1–7*, 452 (giving priority to Matthew's version). H. D. Betz, *Sermon on the Mount*, 560, considers its authenticity possible. R. Funk, *Five Gospels*, 158-59, 299, has both versions in black font (= not authentic), judged to be from common Jewish lore.

17. Claude R. Candor and Horatio H. Kitchener, *The Survey of Western Palestine: Memoirs of the Topography, Orography, Hydrography, and Archaeology*, 3 vols. (London: Palestine Exploration Fund, 1881-83), 1:143, 262-65, 358-59.

18. Ibid., 3:1-5.

19. Frank Frick, "Rain," *ABD* 5:612.

hills of upper regions (where portions of some 40 inches can fall at various times during the rainy season). It fills wadis quickly and creates streams where none existed before. Winds off the Mediterranean Sea can be fierce and do extensive damage (Job 1:19), even in modern times.

The person who hears the words of Jesus and puts them into practice is not moved or destroyed by the calamities that may come. The calamities being envisioned by means of the metaphor could be the ordinary vicissitudes of life that come to everyone. Some interpreters think that they refer to the final judgment.[20] Without discounting that view, however, the imagery of storms is often used metaphorically to indicate testing in Jewish tradition (Ps 6:10-12; 107:28-29; 2 Bar. 53:3-12), and in the NT for the testing and ordeals of the last days (symbolized in the Stilling of the Storm in Matthew's Gospel;[21] cf. also Rev 8:5; 11:19; 16:18), when many will fall away (Matt 24:10).[22] The onslaughts will then include persecution (5:10-12; 10:23) and other forms of abuse (10:16-22). But the disciple who has heard the words of Jesus and performs them will stand when the calamities come, and then stand also in the final judgment.

7:26. The "foolish" person (μωρός) stands in contrast to the wise one (as also in 25:2-3, 8). Building a house upon sand is possible in many places, particularly along the coastal plain of Palestine where sand and sand dunes extend inland for several miles at places.[23]

7:27. The first part of the verse (7:27a) repeats 7:25a verbatim. The same calamities of nature are listed. But there is no need to repeat 7:25b in a negative form. The house fell, and its fall was great (NIV: "it fell with a great crash"). The sand under a house can be washed away by the coming of streams down the hills or mountains, making it vulnerable to heavy winds.

Though not a true parallel, the scene recalls the saying: "Wisdom to a fool is like a house in ruins" (Sir 21:18).

Exposition

The rhetorical effect of the parable at the end of the Sermon on the Mount is both warning and exhortation. The disciple is warned that simply to hear the teachings of Jesus, but not to do them, is insufficient and ends in destruction.

20. J. Jeremias, Parables, 194; R. Gundry, Matthew, 133-36; G. Strecker, Sermon on the Mount, 171; D. Hagner, Matthew, 191; U. Luz, Matthew 1–7, 453; Ivor H. Jones, The Matthean Parables: A Literary and Historical Commentary, NovTSup 80 (Leiden: E. J. Brill, 1995), 189.

21. Günther Bornkamm, "The Stilling of the Storm in Matthew," in Tradition and Interpretation in Matthew, by G. Bornkamm, Gerhard Barth, and Heinz J. Held (Philadelphia: Westminster Press, 1963), 52-57.

22. B. Smith, Parables, 226-27; W. D. Davies and D. C. Allison, Matthew, 1:721-22; H. D. Betz, Sermon on the Mount, 566.

23. C. Condor and H. Kitchener, Survey of Western Palestine, 1:261.

Even though one claims to be a disciple (7:21) and can even boast of outstanding charismatic gifts (7:22), the touchstone of true discipleship is obedience to the teachings of Jesus.

There is encouragement as well, however. The one who truly hears and puts into practice the teachings of Jesus has Jesus' own promise that he will not be overcome in times of calamity. The onslaughts that can come upon a person — whether those that test one's faith or relationship to God — will not prevail wherever a person is a hearer and doer of the teachings of Jesus.

The Parable in the Gospel of Luke

Exegetical Commentary

The parable is at the very end of the Sermon on the Plain (Luke 6:20-49). More specifically it follows the question of Jesus to his hearers: "Why do you call me 'Lord, Lord,' and do not do what I tell you?" (6:46). The parable is about hearing and then *doing* what Jesus says his hearers should do. Anything less is hypocritical.

6:47. The verse is similar to its parallel (Matt 7:24), but its syntax is complex (see Note above). Moreover, it contains an additional verb (the hearer and doer "comes" to Jesus, signifying that he or she is a follower). The parable that follows is an illustration of two kinds of disciples — one sound, the other not.

6:48. As in Matthew's version the house builder builds upon rock. But greater stress is placed on his care in the building process. Three activities are cited: he dug, he went down deep, and he laid a foundation; the words of the NRSV ("who dug deeply and laid the foundation") — as well as those of the RSV, NEB, and NIV — do not capture the full sense of how hard the man worked.

While Matthew has three elements of bad weather (rain, floods, and winds), Luke has only one, a "flood" (πλήμμυρα) — a term found only here in the NT. The term refers to the overflowing of a river;[24] it is used, for instance, to refer to the annual inundation of the land along the Nile.[25] While Matthew's list of calamities corresponds more to Palestinian conditions, Luke's singular portrait of a river rising and overflowing is more fitting for a non-Palestinian setting of the author and his readers.[26] The imagery is that of a river overflowing near a house. Furthermore, that river "burst upon" (προσέρηξεν) the house.

In Matthew's account the house stands because it is built on rock. In Luke's the house not only stands but is not even shaken. The house is sturdy be-

---

24. Philo, *Op.* 58; *Leg. All.* 1.34; Plutarch, *Romulus* 3.6; *Caesar* 38.3.
25. Philo, *Abr.* 92; *Vit. Mos.* 1.202; 2.195; *POxy* 1409.17.
26. J. Fitzmyer, *Luke,* 644. According to R. Gundry, *Matthew,* 134, and I. Jones, *Matthean Parables,* 187-88, however, what is described is not impossible in a Palestinian setting.

cause it is built well as a result of extensive labor (digging, going deeply, and laying a secure foundation).

The disciple who hears and does the teachings of Jesus is compared to such a builder. That person is well prepared for the "rush of mighty waters" in a "time of distress" (Ps 32:6) and can be considered sound. The true disciple hears the words of Jesus, indeed the word of God, and does it (8:21; 11:28).

6:49. Luke uses neither the term for "wise" nor the one for "foolish" (contra Matthew), but now turns to the type of disciple who hears the teachings of Jesus but does not put them into practice. The wording and syntax are similar to those in 6:47-48a, but the participles for hearing, putting into practice, and building are all in the aorist tense. The person who is not prepared for the rigors of discipleship is one who "has not heard and not put into practice" the teachings of Jesus.

The imagery is that of a man who builds a house directly on top of the ground without a foundation. He is exceedingly careless and unprepared for any possible mishap.

The results are predictable. When the nearby river overflows its banks, it comes crashing upon the house, and the house collapses. The verb συμπίπτω ("to collapse") is found only here in the NT. It is used elsewhere in Greek literature, however, and it is used (as here) to describe the collapse of buildings due to rain or hail.[27] The term ῥῆγμα (literally, "breaking")[28] appears only here in the NT as well. The imagery is one of total destruction.

The significance of the difference between the tenses of the participles in 6:47 and 6:49 should be underscored. The present tense of the participles of the former verse indicates an openness to anyone who "comes . . . hears . . . and puts . . . into practice" the words of Jesus. The aorist tense of the participles in 6:49, however, indicates judgment. The person who has not heard and put into practice the words of Jesus is like a man who had built a house carelessly and suffered total loss.

Exposition

Discipleship that is sound and enduring is the issue addressed in this parable. Such a quality of discipleship is illustrated. The disciple who goes beyond mere lip service to Jesus (cf. 6:46) to maturity is one who lives in union with Jesus (which "who comes" implies), listens to him, and practices what he teaches.

The parable in context speaks against hypocrisy, but it also exhorts the disciple of Jesus to give care to becoming mature and strong. That is illustrated above all in the metaphors of digging, going down deep, and laying a foundation on rock (6:48). One is reminded of the Parable of the Sower, in which some

27. BAGD 779.
28. Ibid., 735.

of the plants that had been planted grew up and withered; and so some persons become believers for a short time but fall away when testing comes (8:6, 13). But how fortunate is the person who digs, goes down deeply, and lays a foundation on rock. That is a process that takes time and reflection centered in the teachings of Jesus and located within a community of faith and conversation.

Select Bibliography

Abou-Chaar, Kamal. "The Two Builders: A Study of the Parable in Luke 6:47-49." *ThRev* 5 (1982): 44-58.

Franz, Gordon. "The Parable of the Two Builders." *ABW* 3 (1995): 6-11.

Garcia, M. A. "Committed Discipleship and Jesus' Lordship: Exegesis of Luke 6:46-49 in the Context of Jesus' Discourse in the Plain." *ACS* 9 (1993): 3-10.

Jeske, Richard. "Wisdom and the Future in the Teaching of Jesus." *Dialog* 11 (1972): 108-17.

Knowles, Michael P. "'Everyone Who Hears These Words of Mine': Parables on Discipleship (Matt 7:24-27//Luke 6:47-49; Luke 14:28-33; Luke 17:7-10; Matt 20:1-16)." In *The Challenge of Jesus' Parables*, 286-305. Ed. Richard N. Longenecker. Grand Rapids: Wm. B. Eerdmans, 2000.

Nestle, Eberhard. "Matt. vii.25, 27." *ExpTim* 19 (1907-8): 237-38.

Pesch, Rudolf, and Reinhard Kratz. "Auf Fels oder auf Sand gebaut?" In *So liest man synoptisch: Anleitung und Kommentar zum Studien der synoptischen Evangelien*, 25-37. Frankfurt am Main: Josef Knecht, 1978.

Schwarz, Günther. "Er 'wird einem klugen/törichten Mann ähnlich werden'? (Matthäus 7,24b.26b)." *BibNot* 68 (1993): 24-25.

Wilson, James P. "In Matthew vii.25 Is προσέπεσαν a Primitive Error Displacing προσέκοψαν?" *ExpTim* 57 (1945-46): 138.

4.11. Building a Tower, Luke 14:28-30

28 *"For which of you, wanting to build a tower, does not first sit down and make an estimate of the cost, [and see] whether he has enough to complete it?* 29 *Otherwise, when he has laid its foundation, and is not able to finish, all who see it will begin to make fun of him,* 30 *saying, 'This man began to build, and was not able to finish.'"*

Exegetical Commentary

There are no serious problems for textual criticism or translation in regard to this parable, which is found only in Luke's Gospel. It is followed immediately by the Parable of the King Going to War (14:31-33), and the two can be considered twin parables.

137

. The two parables appear within the Travel Narrative of the Gospel of Luke (9:51–19:27). Earlier in chapter 14 Jesus tells the Parable of the Great Banquet (14:16-24), in which there is the command to go forth to "the roads and lanes" to invite all that can be found to the banquet. So God desires the kingdom to be filled with all manner of persons.

At 14:25 and following, however, there is a shift. Just as "large crowds" are following Jesus — and therefore those of "the roads and lanes" are accompanying him — he speaks harsh words by means of two sayings concerning the cost of true discipleship (14:25-27). These sayings have parallels in Matthew (10:37-38) and can be considered to have come from Q.

In the first saying Jesus says that one cannot be his disciple unless one hates one's own family, and even life itself (14:26). The use of the verb "hate" is hyperbolic, but it is also a Semitism meaning to love one thing or person less than another. At Genesis 29:30, for example, it is said that Jacob loved Rachel more than Leah, and in the next verse it is said (as in a paraphrase) that the latter was hated.[1] So also the parallel in Matthew says that one must not love family members more than one loves Jesus (10:37). In both Gospels the saying means essentially that one must disregard all others in one's loyalty to Jesus (cf. Matt 8:21-22//Luke 9:59-60).[2] A similar thought is expressed by the philosopher Epictetus (ca. A.D. 50-120) when he said that "the good is preferred above every form of kinship. My father is nothing to me, but only the good."[3] The second saying, on bearing one's cross (14:27), means that one must renounce self-serving and be willing to suffer, even die, along with Jesus to be one of his disciples.[4]

According to 14:25-27, one must be willing to make sacrifices to be a disciple. That teaching is followed by the twin parables on exercising wisdom. The verse after the two parables (14:33) is intended to be an application for both, but in thought it actually follows the sayings of 14:26-27 (verses on renunciation) better than the parables themselves (verses on being wise).[5] In fact, if the parables are dropped out, the text that remains (14:26-27, 33) reads more smoothly.[6]

14:28. The words τίς γὰρ ἐξ ὑμῶν ("for which of you") is used here and else-

---

1. Peter G. Jarvis, "Expounding the Parables: V. The Tower-Builder and the King Going to War," 196.

2. Heinz Giesen, "μισέω," EDNT 2:431.

3. Epictetus, Dis. 3.35. Quoted from Epictetus, trans. W. A. Oldfather, 2 vols. (New York: G. P. Putnam's Sons, 1926-28), 2:31.

4. Heinz-Wolfgang Kuhn, "σταυρός," EDNT 3:269; Donald R. Fletcher, "Condemned to Die: The Logion on Cross-Bearing: What Does It Mean?" Int 18 (1964): 161. In addition to this Q saying (Matt 10:38//Luke 14:27), cf. Mark 8:34//Matt 16:24//Luke 9:23.

5. Cf. C. Montefiore, Synoptic Gospels, 2:981; R. Bultmann, HST 170-71; B. Smith, Parables, 221; I. H. Marshall, Luke, 594-95; J. Fitzmyer, Luke, 1,061.

6. Cf. P. Jarvis, "Expounding the Parables," 196.

where (with minor variations) in a rhetorical question to introduce important sayings.[7] The phrase is an arresting one. It sounds as though Jesus is appealing to his hearers' personal experience. Of course that is not so, since the hearers of the parable are not likely to be in a financial position to build a tower at all. Nevertheless, the question sets the imagination into a course of pictorial thinking.

The imagery is that of building a πύργος, usually translated "tower." Some interpreters have suggested that the term means "farm building."[8] Most likely the former is to be preferred. The remains of hundreds of stone structures — circular or square, usually less than eight meters in diameter — are scattered across the Near East, including Israel. Some of them were used in antiquity for military purposes. But others, as indicated in other biblical references (Isa 5:2; Mic 4:8; Mark 12:1-2//Matt. 21:33), were for agricultural purposes. Farmers used them for the storage of agricultural equipment and produce (like modern barns, sheds, and silos), for lodging, and as lookouts to protect their crops from thieves and animals.[9] Since towers were in fact farmers' outbuildings, the term "farm building" is not to be ruled out. But the term "tower" is more fitting, as long as it is understood to be the designation of a structure that could have various purposes.

By implication the structure being contemplated is of grand size. It is typical of Jesus' parables to portray grandeur for the imagination. The farmer has to sit down and "calculate the cost" (ψηφίζει τὴν δαπάνην) or "make an estimate of the cost" of what he has in mind.

14:29-30. If the tower is only partially built, it looks ridiculous. In a culture of honor and shame, which can be presupposed here, honor is important; shame is to be avoided. The verb used here (ἐμπαίζω) means to "ridicule, make fun of, mock."[10] Used thirteen times in the Synoptic Gospels, this is the only time the verb is used in reference to a person; otherwise it is used in reference to Jesus, such as in passion predictions (Mark 10:34//Matt 20:19//Luke 18:32) and in the passion narrative itself (Mark 15:31//Matt 27:41, etc.). The verb does not signify playful teasing but mean-spirited derision.

The imagery of the parable is rooted in the wisdom tradition (cf. Prov 24:3-6),[11] and no one seems to doubt the authenticity of the parable itself.[12] It

7. Luke 11:5, 11 (//Matt 7:9); 12:25 (//Matt 6:27); 15:4; 17:7; Matt 12:11; and John 8:46.

8. The term πύργος can mean either "tower" or "farm building," according to BAGD 730. Cf. also texts and inscriptions listed in LSJ 1556 and MM 560. The term "farm building" is favored by B. Smith, *Parables*, 220 (n. 2); T. W. Manson, *Sayings*, 281; J. Jeremias, *Parables*, 196; and N. Perrin, *Teaching*, 127.

9. Edward B. Banning, "Towers," *ABD* 6:622.

10. BAGD 255.

11. Cf. J. Duncan M. Derrett, "Nisi dominus aedificaverit domum," 241-61. Derrett's claim that the parables could be the residue of a midrashic sermon, however, seems too speculative of adopt.

12. N. Perrin, *Teaching*, 127; P. Jarvis, "Expounding the Parables," 197.

is possible, however, that the meaning of the parable has undergone a slight shift from the proclamation of Jesus to its meaning in the Gospel of Luke. Clearly the parable presents the hearer or reader with a challenge; that would have been so in the preaching of Jesus no less than in Luke. In the words of Joachim Jeremias, Jesus would have been saying, in effect: "Do not act without mature consideration, for a thing half-done is worse than a thing never begun."[13] That would mean, in reference to his hearers, that one must count the cost of discipleship before making an ill-informed commitment to it.[14] Such a consideration could result in some hearers turning away. Other sayings of Jesus cohere with the thought of the parable, such as the statement, "No one who puts his hand to the plow and looks back is fit for the kingdom of God" (Luke 9:62), as well as the question, "Are you able . . . to be baptized with the baptism with which I am baptized?" (Mark 10:38).

At the level of Luke's Gospel, various interpreters have discerned essentially the same message.[15] "Jesus counsels his followers not to decide on discipleship without advance, mature self-probing."[16] "The disciple should be sure that he is able to pay the cost, lest his life should resemble a task half-completed and worthy of scorn."[17]

While it is manifestly true that the parable calls for such wisdom, or discernment, even at the level of Luke's Gospel, it is surely the case that it has a hortatory function as well, even if that is secondary. As the parable is read, it poses a challenge to the lukewarm or halfhearted person who is a disciple already. The parable is not present in Luke's Gospel to drive persons away, but to get them to consider their own situation. The hearer or reader has already crossed over into discipleship. The building of the tower has begun. It is necessary therefore to continue and complete that which has been commenced.

Exposition

Hard as it may seem, in an era in which marketing of the church is taken for granted, Jesus may well have sought to turn some prospective followers away, or at least he challenged them to look before they leaped. Discipleship is not for everyone, and certainly not possible for everyone.

As the parable is read, it poses a challenge to the hearer and reader to consider whether discipleship is a real possibility. Discipleship is costly. Just as one might not have the financial wherewithal to finish a building project, it is possi-

13. J. Jeremias, *Parables,* 196.

14. Cf. C. H. Dodd, *Parables,* 87; N. Perrin, *Teaching,* 126-28; R. Stein, *Parables,* 112-13; D. Wenham, *Parables,* 203-5.

15. Cf. E. Schweizer, *Luke,* 241; Robert H. Stein, *Luke,* NAC 24 (Nashville: Broadman Press, 1992), 396; and those referred to in the next two notes.

16. J. Fitzmyer, *Luke,* 1,062.

17. I. H. Marshall, *Luke,* 591.

ble that one does not have what it takes to be a disciple. And just as something done halfway can be ridiculous, being a halfway or halfhearted disciple can be preposterous.

Through it all there is an implicit call to committed discipleship. Whoever would be a disciple should know that discipleship involves ways of thinking and acting that do not come easily. There are times when a person must set other things aside in order to focus on what is most important. Or one must enlist what one has (time, energy, skills, and financial means) for the sake of living out a life of commitment to Jesus and his gospel. Either way, discipleship is costly. There is no such thing as easy discipleship. It involves an either/or in terms of one's primary commitment. A third possibility is excluded.

Select Bibliography

Derrett, J. Duncan M. "Nisi dominus aedificaverit domum: Towers and Wars (Lk xiv 28-32)." *NovT* 19 (1977): 241-61.

Jarvis, Peter G. "Expounding the Parables: V. The Tower-Builder and the King Going to War (Luke 14:25-33)." *ExpTim* 77 (1966): 196-98.

Knowles, Michael P. "'Everyone Who Hears These Words of Mine': Parables on Discipleship (Matt 7:24-27//Luke 6:47-49; Luke 14:28-33; Luke 17:7-10; Matt 20:1-16)." In *The Challenge of Jesus' Parables*, 286-305. Ed. Richard N. Longenecker. Grand Rapids: Wm. B. Eerdmans, 2000.

Louw, Johannes. "The Parables of the Tower-Builder and the King Going to War (Luke 14:25-33)." *ExpTim* 48 (1937): 478.

Mechie, Stewart. "The Parables of the Tower-Building and the King Going to War." *ExpTim* 48 (1936-37): 235-36.

Singer, C. "La difficulté d' être disciple. Luc 14/25-35." *ETR* 73 (1998): 21-36.

4.12. The King Going to War, Luke 14:31-33

31 *"Or what king, going to engage another king in war, will not sit down first and consider whether he is able with ten thousand to encounter him who comes against him with twenty thousand? 32And if not, while the other is yet a great way off, he sends a delegation and asks terms of peace.*

33 *"So therefore, whoever of you does not renounce all that he has cannot be my disciple."*

Notes on the Text and Translation

14:32. The Nestle-Aland text (27th ed.) follows a good number of important Greek witnesses, τὰ πρὸς εἰρήνην ("the things [or 'terms'] of peace"). Other important texts, however, read simply "for peace" (omitting τά and keeping the same preposition or using εἰς). The age and geographical extent of the Greek texts having the first reading, plus various other versions that lend support, speak in favor of the first reading. The omission of the term τά ("the things") can be explained by haplography due to a scribal eye skip; the term is preceded by the verb ἐρωτᾷ ("he asks"), which ends with the same two Greek letters (τα).

Exegetical Commentary

Like the preceding parable (14:28-30), this one is found only in the Gospel of Luke, and it is a twin parable of the one that has gone before it. Since it is so much like the Parable of Building a Tower, presupposes the same setting, and raises the same critical questions, the discussion here will presuppose familiarity with the Commentary on Luke 14:28-30.

There are some differences between the two parables. In the first the tower builder seeks to avoid shame; in the second both shame and death are possibilities for the king. Moreover, if the tower builder turns out to be foolish, he alone bears the shame. But if the king is foolish, he may be responsible for the death of up to 10,000 men. Therefore the stakes are higher in the second parable; as a story, it is more serious.

14:31. The first of the parables began with "For which of you?" (14:28); the second begins with "Or what king?" This manner of connecting parables in series occurs again in the next chapter, in which the first begins with "Which of you?" (Luke 15:4) and the second with "Or what woman?" (Luke 15:8). The first parable confronts the hearer and reader more directly ("Which of you?"); the second directs attention away from the self to consider the behavior of a king. For the sake of maximal rhetorical effect, it is hard to imagine the two parables in a reverse sequence (the same applies to 15:4, 8).

The imagery of a king preparing to go to war against another king would have been familiar to the hearers of Jesus' parable. The Scriptures express such familiarity with the words, "In the spring of the year, the time when kings go forth to battle" (2 Sam 11:1). The rallying of troops by the judges, kings, and officers of Israel's past is recounted over and again in the ancient texts (Judg 3:27; 6:34; 7:24; 2 Sam 18:1; 2 Chron 25:5, etc.). Sometimes preparations are recorded. Dozens of times the number of troops used in battles is reported (Josh 4:14; 7:3; 8:3, 12, 25; 2 Sam 8:4; 18:4; 2 Kings 13:7, etc.), and sometimes it is told how they were outfitted (1 Sam 25:18; 2 Sam 17:27-29; 1 Kings 4:27). To speak in terms of 10,000 and 20,000 soldiers in battle is not unusual in light of the military sagas of the past. Nevertheless, as in other parables (Matt 18:24; Luke 14:28), grandiose figures and imagery are used.

The picture of a king with 10,000 troops considering warfare with one having double that amount arrests one's attention. In order to be successful, such a king would have to have troops that are more highly skilled and better equipped than those of the other king; his army would have to make a surprise attack; and the courage and resolve of his soldiers would have to be higher than those of the enemy.

The term translated "to encounter" (ὑπαντάω) is sometimes translated here as "to meet" (KJV, RSV), which seems too bland, or "to oppose" (NIV, NRSV), which can imply a one-sided aggression.[1] In this context the two kings apparently meet somewhere between their points or origin: the first goes forth ("going to engage"), and the second is arriving ("coming against him").

14:32. If the king decides that a victory is impossible, and if he is wise, he must seek a way out by sending a delegation to seek peace under the best terms he can. The term for "delegation" (NIV, NRSV) is πρεσβεία and signifies an ambassador or ambassadors (so "embassy" in RSV, "envoys" in NEB).

The phrase translated "asks terms of peace" (ἐρωτᾷ τὰ πρὸς εἰρήνην) — which resembles another at 19:42 having a different verb — is similar to one in the LXX (2 Sam 8:10, ἐρωτῆσαι αὐτὸν τὰ εἰς εἰρήνην, "to ask him terms of peace"). The phrase appears within an account in which a king, named Toi, sends gifts to King David as a sign of submission; King Toi asks King David for terms of peace. For all practical purposes the phrase means to seek a truce.[2] An allusion to this particular story, however, need not be intended. A similar phrase appears in T. Judah 9.7 (αἰτοῦσιν ἡμᾶς τὰ πρὸς εἰρήνην, "they asked us for terms of peace"). What is important (for interpretation) is the phraseology.

14:33. Luke intends this verse to be an application of the twin parables. As indicated in the Commentary on 14:28-29, however, this verse continues the thought of 14:26-27, not 14:28-32. The twin parables speak not so much of renunciation of all that one has as they do about being prudent: Consider what it means to be a disciple before committing yourself to it.

As with the previous parable (14:28-30), the imagery of this one is present in the wisdom tradition (cf. Prov 24:3-6).[3] Although some interpreters have denied its authenticity,[4] there seems to be no reason to doubt that it was uttered

---

1. To "meet" or "oppose" are the only two renderings provided in BAGD 837.

2. That it means "unconditional surrender," however, seems to go beyond the meaning of the phrase, even though that could produce an important exegetical nuance (the unconditional surrender of the king corresponding to the unconditional submission of the disciple); contra Henry St. John Thackeray, "A Study of the Parable of the Two Kings," 393, 399.

3. Cf. J. Duncan M. Derrett, "Nisi dominus aedificaverit domum," 241-61. Derrett's claim that the parables could be the residue of a midrashic sermon, however, seems too speculative of adopt.

4. According to John Drury, The Parables in the Gospels: History and Allegory (New York: Crossroad, 1985), 139, the uses of the phrases εἰ δὲ μή γε and πρὸς εἰρήνην and the verb συνβάλλω are peculiar to Luke, and βουλεύομαι is used seven times by Luke (but also

by Jesus of Nazareth.[5] Moreover, the point of comparison for this parable, as for the previous one, is that one must exercise wisdom. Do you really want to become a disciple? It is possible that the earthly Jesus actually discouraged some persons from becoming disciples (cf. Luke 9:62). In any case, some did turn away (Mark 10:22//Matt 19:22). But more to the point would be that, if one contemplates discipleship, he or she should count the cost.

At the level of Luke's Gospel, however, as in the case of its parabolic twin, this parable has a rhetorical effect that goes beyond contemplating the question of discipleship. Addressed to Christian readers, the parable has a hortatory function. It challenges the disciple to examine his or her own situation. As a wise king would go out to engage another in battle only if victory seemed certain — or call it quits if defeat was sure — so one must be decisive, and be a true disciple of Jesus.

It has been suggested that the twin parables were not directed in Jesus' earthly ministry to would-be disciples, but they referred to Jesus himself. Jesus had considered the demands of 14:26-27 during his forty days in the wilderness after his baptism. The builder of the tower of 14:28-30 signifies Jesus as Builder of the Kingdom, and the king going to war of 14:31-32 represents Jesus as Warrior against evil.[6] Such allegorizing is not convincing. Within the context of the Gospel of Luke the parables are associated with sayings about discipleship, and that is the most plausible context also within the earthly ministry of Jesus.[7]

Exposition

The harsh sayings on discipleship have been uttered. The Parable of Building a Tower has been spoken. One must stop and consider the cost of undertaking discipleship.

Now comes an even more serious thought. Life and death are in the balance. Will the king go into battle, or will he seek peace? The issue is far more grave, critical, and dangerous than the first. If one is not up to the demands of discipleship, that person should not fool himself or herself. To turn away would

---

John and Paul), that is sufficient to regard the parable as a Lukan composition. That does not seem enough to go on. According to R. Funk, *Five Gospels,* 354, the Jesus Seminar concluded that the parable was derived from a fund of proverbial wisdom and was attributed to Jesus in the early church (pre-Lukan). But no instances of parallels are provided to show that it has a likeness outside the Jesus tradition. Jesus was an heir to the wisdom tradition and could certainly compose wisdom sayings and parables.

5. A. Jülicher, *Gleichnisreden,* 2:206; N. Perrin, *Teaching,* 127; P. Jarvis, "Expounding the Parables," 197. The vividness of the twin parables and the fact that 14:33 is a misunderstanding of them are the basis for Perrin's judgment.

6. J. Louw, "The Parables of the Tower-Builder and the King Going to War," 478.

7. A point made well by C. H. Dodd, *Parables,* 87; cf. also B. Smith, *Parables,* 221.

be honest, even if regrettable, as in the case of a king who seeks a truce when outnumbered. But in and through the parable the hope is expressed implicitly that one will think through the demands, get on with being a disciple, and enter the life intended for the children of God. The way to life is narrow and difficult (Matt 7:13-14; Luke 13:24), but not impossible.

The imagery of the parable is that of royal military conduct. For moderns, it is possible to envision such imagery. But athletic imagery is easier. Consider the rhetoric of an athletic coach. At the first practice session, a coach will typically exhort members of the team. He or she will say that every member must give all they have to the team's effort, and that will include showing up consistently for practice, maintaining good health habits, and so on. Then comes the line: "Now, if anyone is not willing to do all that, don't bother! Get out of here! I don't want to see you again. You do not deserve to wear the uniform!" That kind of final exhortation is meant to motivate, not to turn away. So, likewise, one purpose of the sayings and parables of Luke 14:26-33 is to get people to react and follow through.

Within the post-Easter situation, in which it is known that Jesus has gone through death and has been raised from the dead, the fainthearted Christian has the gospel of the Risen One to include as a factor in times of reflection. Discipleship is difficult, but it is discipleship to one whose teaching and manner of life have been vindicated through resurrection.

Select Bibliography

Derrett, J. Duncan M. "Nisi dominus aedificaverit domum: Towers and Wars (Lk xiv 28-32)." *NovT* 19 (1977): 241-61.

Jarvis, Peter G. "Expounding the Parables: V. The Tower-builder and the King Going to War (Luke 14:25-33)." *ExpTim* 77 (1966): 196-98.

Knowles, Michael P. "'Everyone Who Hears These Words of Mine': Parables on Discipleship (Matt 7:24-27//Luke 6:47-49; Luke 14:28-33; Luke 17:7-10; Matt 20:1-16)." In *The Challenge of Jesus' Parables*, 286-305. Ed. Richard N. Longenecker. Grand Rapids: Wm. B. Eerdmans, 2000.

Louw, Johannes. "The Parables of the Tower-Builder and the King Going to War (Luke 14:25-33)." *ExpTim* 48 (1937): 478.

Mechie, Stewart. "The Parables of the Tower-Building and the King Going to War." *ExpTim* 48 (1936-37): 235-36.

Singer, C. "La difficulté d' être disciple. Luc 14/25-35." *ETR* 73 (1998): 21-36.

Thackeray, Henry St. John. "A Study in the Parable of the Two Kings." *JTS* 14 (1913): 389-99.

4.13. The Unjust Manager, Luke 16:1-8

1*[Jesus] also said to the disciples, "There was a rich man who had a manager, and charges were brought to him that this man was wasting his goods. 2And he called him and said to him, 'What is this that I hear about you? Give an account of your management, for you can no longer be manager.'*

3*"And the manager said to himself, 'What shall I do, since my master is taking the management position away from me? I am not strong enough to dig; I am ashamed to beg. 4I have decided what to do, in order that, when I am discharged from my management position, people may receive me into their houses.'*

5*"And summoning each one of his master's debtors, he said to the first, 'How much do you owe my master?'*

6*"He said, 'A hundred measures of oil.'*

"And he said to him, 'Take your bill, and sit down quickly, and write fifty.'

7*"Then he said to another, 'And how much do you owe?'*

"He said, 'A hundred measures of wheat.'

"He said to him, 'Take your bill and write eighty.'

8*"And the master commended the dishonest manager because he had acted shrewdly; for the children of this world are more shrewd in dealing with their own generation than the children of light."*

Notes on the Text and Translation

16:5. Although the Greek expression ἕνα ἕκαστον is sometimes translated as "one by one" (as in RSV, NEB, NRSV), it actually means "each one" (as in NIV) or "every single one."[1]

16:8. It is lexically possible to translate the Greek expression ὁ κύριος either as "the master," as here (and in RSV, NEB, JB, TEV, NIV, and NRSV), or as "the Lord" (as in KJV). Either way reflects an exegetical decision. If one translates it as "the Lord," referring to Jesus (as elsewhere in Luke's Gospel, e.g., 7:13, 19; 10:1, etc.), it would mean that the parable ended with 16:7, and that 16:8 is a comment by Jesus concerning it. On the other hand, if one translates it as "the master," referring to the rich man (as at 16:5), the verse belongs within the parable. It is the rich man, or master, who commends the dishonest manager.

Exegetical Commentary

The parable appears only in the Gospel of Luke. It is located there within the Travel Narrative (9:51–19:27), in which Jesus is on his way from Galilee to Jerusalem. Although Jesus speaks the parable to his disciples (16:1), the Pharisees and the scribes have been present since 15:1-2, and the Pharisees are mentioned

1. BAGD 236.

146

again as among the listeners in 16:14. They heard everything, and they are branded as "lovers of money." The parable follows without pause from the Parable of the Prodigal Son (15:11-32).

The parable is often regarded as the most puzzling of all within the Synoptic Gospels. Why the main figure of a parable would be a dishonest person, and then, too, a model for emulation by others, seems exceedingly strange. Various interpreters have attempted to get around the problem by suggesting that the so-called dishonest manager was not dishonest at all, for he would have reduced the debts owed his master either by eliminating any hidden usurious interest they owed[2] or by eliminating the commission that he had claimed for himself previously in writing up the transactions.[3] But all such attempts are unnecessary. The manager is called dishonest (actually "wicked" would be a more literal translation) within the parable itself (16:8). Moreover, it is his cleverness, not his wickedness, that earns commendation by his employer.

The story of a subordinate outwitting a superior and being commended for it is also played out in a famous Egyptian folktale recorded by Herodotus. That is the story of Rhampsinitus (identified also as Ramses III, who ruled 1182-1151 B.C.). The builder of his treasury left a secret entrance, and after his death his two sons stole from it. One was trapped, and the other beheaded him so that he could not be identified. Subsequently, at the request of their mother, the surviving brother also obtained his brother's body by intoxicating and tricking the guards. After even further events of cunning involving an escape from the king's daughter (to whom the surviving brother had related his story during her seduction of him), the king was astonished. He admired the man's ingenuity and daring, and he gave him his daughter for a wife for his outstanding cleverness.[4]

Still other stories exist that tell of clever slaves who act as rascals and tricksters, some of whom subsequently receive praise from their masters.[5]

The parable begins at 16:1, but where does it end? Here there are various proposals. (1) Although the parable may well end earlier, its application must be included within the same unit, which ends at 16:9 ("And I tell you, make friends for yourselves by means of dishonest wealth so that when it is gone, they may welcome you into the eternal homes").[6] (2) The parable (16:1-8a) and its application (16:8b) are a unit, ending at 16:8.[7] (3) The parable ends at 16:8a

2. J. Derrett, "Parable of the Unjust Steward," 48-77; W. Herzog, *Parables*, 255-57.

3. J. Fitzmyer, *Luke*, 1098; P. Perkins, *Parables*, 167-68.

4. Herodotus, *History* 2:121. The story is related in *Herodotus*, trans. A. D. Godley; 4 vols.; LCL (Cambridge: Harvard University Press, 1920-25), 1:413-23.

5. Several are gathered in the essay by M. Beavis, "Ancient Slavery," 43-52.

6. A. Plummer, *Luke*, 380, 386; J. Wansey, "Parable of the Unjust Steward," 39-40.

7. A. Jülicher, *Gleichnisreden*, 2:505; T. W. Manson, *Sayings*, 291-92; W. Oesterley, *Parables*, 198; J. Creed, *Luke*, 201-3; J. Jeremias, *Parables*, 182; I. H. Marshall, *Luke*, 621; E. Schweizer, *Luke*, 254, 256; K. Bailey, *Poet*, 107-9; M. Lee, "Wasteful Steward," 520-28.

("because he had acted shrewdly"), and all else that follows is secondary to it.[8] (4) The parable ends at 16:7,[9] and 16:8a is already a comment, attributed to Jesus, that has been appended to the parable secondarily.

There can be no doubt that 16:9 is an interpretive application of the parable for Luke the evangelist and perhaps even within the tradition available to him. But whether the verse represents the parable's meaning from the beginning is highly questionable. It appears to be the second of two applications. Already in 16:8b there is an application about the "children of light" not being as shrewd as the "children of this age." That serves indirectly as an exhortation to those who consider themselves "children of light" to become more shrewd in spiritual matters. Verse 16:9, on the other hand, exhorts the disciples of Jesus to be generous with any wealth that they might possess.

If verse 16:9 appears to be an addition that has been attached in the transmission and application of the parable, certainly not all of 16:8 can be eliminated. The parable can hardly end with 16:7, for then no judgment is made upon the manager's action by the master who has been defrauded; the master has to come back on the scene, which he does in 16:8a. The question remaining is whether 16:8b — clearly an application — belongs with the parable from the beginning. The total lack of any application to this parable would seem unusual, and the application appears to flow out of the parable itself without difficulty.[10] What could the parable possibly have meant without it? It is difficult to imagine that the parable would have survived without some kind of significance attached to it from the beginning. Furthermore, the language used ("children of light" and "children of this age") is otherwise not found in Luke-Acts; it is terminology used in the Dead Sea Scrolls, pointing to origins in Palestinian Judaism of the first century A.D.

16:1. The parable opens with two major figures. The first is a rich man. The other is a "manager" (NIV, NRSV; called a "steward" in older translations, such as KJV and RSV) of the rich man's estate. As such, the manager has authority to carry out the business of the estate. He can make sales and loans, and he can collect, forgive, and pay off debts for his master. He earns his own living

8. B. Smith, *Parables*, 110; D. Via, *Parables*, 156-57; J. Coutts, "Unjust Steward," 54-60; Wilhelm Michaelis, *Die Gleichnisse Jesu: Eine Einführung*, 3d ed., UCB 32 (Hamburg: Furche-Verlag, 1956), 228-29; H. Hendrickx, *Parables*, 192-93; J. Donahue, *Parable*, 163; J. Fitzmyer, *Luke*, 1,105; H. Weder, *Gleichnisse*, 263-64; W. Loader, "Jesus and the Rogue," 518-32; J. Kloppenborg, "Dishonored Manager," 474-95; D. Parrott, "Dishonest Steward," 499-515; B. Scott, *Parable*, 258; R. Funk, *Five Gospels*, 358-59; W. Herzog, *Parables*, 236; T. Hoeren, "Gleichnis vom ungerechten Verwalter," 620-29; H. Binder, "Missdeutbar oder eindeutig?" 41-49.

9. R. Bultmann, *HST* 175; W. Michaelis, *Gleichnisse*, 228-29; N. Perrin, *Teaching*, 115; J. Crossan, *Parables*, 108-9.

10. T. W. Manson, *Sayings*, 291: "The point of the parable lies in v. 8; and it does not depend on anything but the story itself."

by commissions or fees resulting from various transactions.[11] As the parable unfolds, it is obvious that he had to keep careful records of all his transactions. (According to a rabbinic source, copies of transactions were customarily produced in duplicate — one for each party.[12]) In this particular case the manager deals with debtors of his master. The debtors could have been persons who had purchased goods from the estate, for which they have not yet paid.[13] Or they could have been tenant farmers who had agreed to pay a fixed amount of produce for the yearly rent.[14] In the end, one need not know precisely. What is important to observe is that the manager can deal directly with persons who are indebted to his master. Whether the latter figure is an absentee landlord, as suggested by some,[15] or not does not seem to add materially to the course or meaning of the story.

The syntax of the second clause is complicated. The Greek word οὗτος ("this") has οἰκονόμον ("manager") as its antecedent, and αὐτῷ ("him") has ἄνθρωπος ("man") as its.[16] The sense is that the manager was accused by someone of wasting his master's goods, and the charges were brought to the manager. It is not said whether the charges are true or not; one simply has to accept that they are, since he does not seek to defend himself. The wasting of the goods could imply that he had spent money on himself with total abandon (cf. the use of the same verb, διασκορπίζω, meaning "to squander," at 15:13).[17] In the end it does not matter what he was doing, except that he was wasteful with his master's goods.

16:2. The manager is summoned and dismissed from his position. The records of his management are demanded immediately. Although it is not said explicitly, he would have to leave the estate (which would have been his residence) immediately. In any case, he is an employee, not a slave, of the master.[18] If he were a slave, he would not have been dismissed but reduced to another form of work.

11. Bruce J. Malina and Richard L. Rohrbaugh, *Social-Science Commentary on the Synoptic Gospels* (Minneapolis: Fortress Press, 1992), 88-91, 373-74. Cf. also K. Bailey, *Poet,* 88-91, who dismisses the idea (originating in 1902) that the manager could simply inflate the bills to enrich himself. What was recorded would be known to the master, and if the manager had tried to inflate the bills, the debtors would know and could appeal to the master.

12. *M. B. Bat.* 10:4. Cf. also the use of duplicate copies for a transaction at Jer 32:9-15.

13. T. W. Manson, *Sayings,* 291.

14. K. Bailey, *Poet,* 94; W. Herzog, *Parables,* 247.

15. I. H. Marshall, *Luke,* 616; J. Fitzmyer, *Luke,* 1,097.

16. BDF 151 (290, 1).

17. Contra J. Crossan, *Parables,* 109-10, who suggests that the manager was lazy.

18. A. Plummer, *Luke,* 381; T. W. Manson, *Sayings,* 291; K. Bailey, *Poet,* 92; J. Fitzmyer, *Luke,* 1,097; W. Herzog, *Parables,* 241; T. Hoeren, "Gleichnis vom ungerechten Verwalter," 622-23.

16:3. In this and subsequent verses (16:4-7) the manager seeks to win friends by reducing the bills of creditors, that is, people who owe money to his boss, the rich man. As the story proceeds, it is clear that their debts are very large. The manager reduces the bills by 50 percent and 20 percent, thereby perpetuating his pattern of dishonesty.

At the outset an "interior monologue" takes place (which is characteristic of a number of parables in the Gospel of Luke),[19] in which the manager discusses his situation within his own mind; he "talks to himself." But the reader is let in on the discussion. He says that he does not have the physical strength to dig. The implication could be that, as a punishment, he would be sent away to do hard labor in a stone quarry.[20] Or it could mean digging in construction, agriculture, or landscaping. In any case, full-time digging is implied, which was considered the most difficult work in antiquity.[21] The alternative would be to go begging. That he is ashamed to beg is not surprising, since for many people of his station in life "it is better to die than to beg" (Sir 40:29).

16:4. The Greek word ἔγνων (first person, aorist, active of γινώσκω) is used here in the sense of "I have come to know."[22] What the manager has decided to do is to act as a successful rogue. He is going to go out and make friends for himself in spite of his situation. What is so attractive about him to the reader is that, as a victim of being fired (even if justly so) but nevertheless the main character of the story, he is now in the position of doing damage to his master, who can be considered extremely wealthy. Right or wrong, he is going to get even,[23] which catches the attention of the hearer or reader, for a plot to get even always makes an interesting story.

16:5. Several debtors of his master are brought in — "each one" of them, in fact. Two are given as examples in 16:5-7. Each is asked how much he owes. Of course the amount is written on the bill. But this detail is intended for the hearer or reader of the parable.

16:6. The Greek term for "measure" (applied to olive oil) is βάτος (a loan word from Hebrew, בַּת, bath), a liquid measure of approximately ten gallons (39.384 liters).[24] The amount owed (100 measures) is therefore ap-

19. Philip Sellew, "Interior Monologue as a Narrative Device in the Parables of Jesus," *JBL* 111 (1992): 239-53. In addition to this instance, other instances are at Luke 12:17, 45; 15:17-19; 18:4-5; 20:13.

20. M. Beavis, "Ancient Slavery," 49.

21. Cf. the note on this in BAGD 753 (under σκάπτω), including the line from Aristophanes, *Birds* 1432: σκάπτειν γὰρ οὐκ ἐπίσταμαι ("I do not know [how] to dig").

22. According to C. F. D. Moule, *An Idiom-Book of New Testament Greek*, 2d ed. (Cambridge: Cambridge University Press, 1959), 11, it can mean: "I found out (a moment ago)."

23. The point is made by D. Via, *Parables*, 159-60, and B. Scott, *Parable*, 263.

24. Albert Fuchs, "βάτος," *EDNT* 1:209, relying on Josephus, *Ant.* 8.57. Cf. also BAGD 137 (slightly smaller figures).

proximately a thousand gallons of olive oil, an immense amount. The bill is reduced by half.

The transactions in this verse and the next are done "quickly" (ταχέως), a detail that is important to the story. The debtors do not know that the manager has been fired. In fact, they cannot. If the transactions are going to be done at all, the debtors must assume that the manager has authority to do what he is doing.[25]

The manager offers a copy of the bill to each debtor. The bills have therefore been in his possession. Moreover, they are written up in the handwriting of each of the debtors. The situation envisioned is that the master (or the manager acting on his behalf) has handed over money or goods to each debtor. The latter have signed promissory notes acknowledging their indebtedness. When the manager hands them their notes, they can rewrite them and put in the amount that he authorizes them to write.

16:7. The Greek word translated "measure" (applied to wheat) is κόρος (another loanword from Hebrew, כֹּר, kor), a dry measure of approximately 11 bushels (393 liters).[26] Therefore the amount owed is over 1,100 bushels of wheat, which is again an immense amount. The bill is reduced by one-fifth.

16:8. The one who commends the manager is "the master" (i.e., the "rich man" of 16:1), as many commentators have concluded,[27] not "the Lord"[28] (meaning Jesus); see Notes above. (Otherwise 16:8a would have to be considered a narrator's comment, composed by Luke or a predecessor.)

Why does the master commend him? The reason is that the manager is so clever, so wise, so shrewd. He has used his wits to make friends and thereby feather his own nest in such a way that his master can only marvel at what he has done to save himself from total disaster. The manager is, for sure, a rascal, but he is a marvelously clever one![29]

In the final analysis, the master can do little else than make the most of the situation. He cannot reverse the actions of the manager. By the time he comes on the scene, all those who had had their debts reduced would have been grateful to him, and would have applauded him for his generosity if and when

---

25. K. Bailey, *Poet*, 98-100.

26. BAGD 444-45, relying on Josephus, *Ant.* 15.314.

27. A. Jülicher, *Gleichnisreden*, 2:503; R. Bultmann, *HST* 176; B. Easton, *Luke*, 242; I. H. Marshall, *Luke*, 620; J. Fitzmyer, *Luke*, 1,101; R. Stein, *Parables*, 107; K. Bailey, *Poet*, 102-4.

28. In addition to being used by the KJV, "the Lord" is favored by T. W. Manson, *Sayings*, 292; A. Cadoux, *Parables*, 132-33; B. Smith, *Parables*, 110; J. Jeremias, *Parables*, 45-46, 182; W. Michaelis, *Gleichnisse*, 227-28; N. Perrin, *Teaching*, 115; and E. Earle Ellis, *The Gospel of Luke*, NCB, rev. ed. (London: Marshall, Morgan & Scott, 1974), 199. C. H. Dodd, *Parables*, 17-18, considers it a possibility.

29. Less convincing is the view of W. Herzog, *Parables*, 257, that the master recognized that his manager was "gifted" to operate within a system of injustice.

he ever appeared in public or in their presence. If he would tell them then, or send notice to them, that the transactions done by his manager are null and void, he would have faced tremendous ridicule and anger.

The application follows. A distinction is made between the "children of this age" and the "children of light." Similar distinctions are made in Jewish literature,[30] and in the NT itself the term "children of light" is applied to the disciples of Jesus (John 12:36) and Christians (1 Thess 5:5; Eph 5:8).

The "children of this age," that is, persons driven by secular values, are clever in arranging things for themselves, and they are prudent in their dealings with one another. Generally the "children of this age" are wise and resourceful enough to get on in life quite well. Unfortunately the "children of light," that is, persons committed to the light that Jesus and his proclamation bring, do not begin to match them in their wisdom and resourcefulness in relationship to God and to one another. They do not commit themselves in the same way, and above all to the same degree, as though their well-being and future depend upon those commitments. That presents a challenge, and thereby the parable has a hortatory function, even if that is expressed indirectly.[31] As such, the parable may indeed have been addressed to the disciples, as Luke has it (16:1), but the original audience can hardly be determined with accuracy. It could have been addressed to both the disciples and others in general, or even to the disciples, the crowds, and the opponents (cf. 16:1, 15).[32] It seems less likely that it would have been addressed to Jesus' opponents only.[33]

Within the context of Luke's Gospel the parable is interpreted further. With the addition of the sayings in 16:9-13, the parable becomes an occasion to take up the use of wealth, a major theme in this gospel, which is highlighted again in the Parable of the Rich Man and Lazarus (16:19-31). Taken together, the parable and these sayings serve as a summons and challenge to discipleship, which includes the right attitude toward wealth and the use of one's resources

---

30. Cf. 1QS 1:9-10; 2:16; 3:13, 20-21, 24-25; 1QM 1:1, 7, 9, 11, 13-14. At *1 Enoch* 108:11 the distinction is between persons "born of light" and those "born of darkness"; text in *OTP* 1:89.

31. Unpersuasive is the view of some interpreters that the parable was spoken by Jesus in reference to his own ministry, that is, that the manager's canceling of debts portrays his own ministry of forgiving sins. This interpretation is offered by W. Loader, "Jesus and the Rogue," 518-32; H. Binder, "Missdeutbar oder eindeuting?" 41-49; and M. Lee, "Wasteful Steward," 520-28. The view of K. Bailey, *Poet,* 86, that the parable serves as a warning to sinners of eschatological judgment seems too restricted, especially if persons who could even remotely be called the "children of light" are being addressed.

32. According to J. Jeremias, *Parables,* 47-48, the original parable would have been addressed to the crowds, not the disciples, but it was later transformed to have a hortatory purpose in the church.

33. Contra C. H. Dodd, *Parables,* 18; A. Cadoux, *Parables,* 135-37.

in generous service to others,[34] a theme that appears elsewhere in the Gospels as well (Matt 6:19-21; Mark 10:21; Luke 12:33-34).

With few exceptions,[35] interpreters have generally attributed the parable to Jesus of Nazareth.[36] As indicated previously, the main issue among them relating to this question is how much of the present text of Luke 16:1-9 can be considered a unit from the point of the parable's origin.

Exposition

Here Jesus creates one of his most provocative stories. The manager who arranges things for himself dishonestly is so clever, so wise, that the rich man, the owner of the estate, cannot help but be amazed. One can only imagine what he might do. He might slap his knee and say: "That scoundrel! I fired him just a couple of days ago for mismanagement. But now look. He has feathered his nest among my debtors. And he has used what belongs to me to do it. What gall! But how clever! He is a rascal, but a remarkably clever one!"

The "children of this age" are generally wise in securing their own future. They try to arrange things for themselves, and many know how to do that quite well. They learn the system of rewards and punishments that goes with their choices; and they make plans for themselves and their dependents from the beginning of their working years and on into retirement. Of course readers of this parable should not think of the children of this age as people other than themselves. To some extent every reader of the parable is a child of this age and has something in common with the manager, who acts shrewdly in an emergency. That is to secure the future.

But what does the parable say to those who are not only children of this age and generation, but claim also to be children of the light on the basis of hearing the gospel? The parable places each reader or hearer under judgment and provides a challenge: the children of light do not measure up in wisdom to the children of this age. In other words, although they stand in an emergency situation before God and the final judgment to come, they do not take their situation seriously.

34. T. W. Manson, *Sayings,* 293; A. Plummer, *Luke,* 380-81; J. Derrett, "Parable of the Unjust Steward," 74-77; F. Williams, "Is Almsgiving the Point?" 293-97; D. Ireland, "History of Recent Interpretation," 293-318; I. J. du Plessis, "Philanthropy or Sarcasm?" 1-20; D. Mathewson, "Parable of the Unjust Steward," 29-39.

35. On the grounds that it contains many Lukan linguistic features, it is said to be a composition of Luke by John Drury, *The Parables in the Gospels* (New York: Crossroad, 1985), 149.

36. B. Smith, *Parables,* 109; J. Jeremias, *Parables,* 46, 182; N. Perrin, *Teaching,* 114-15; J. Derrett, "Parable of the Unjust Steward," 50, 75; I. H. Marshall, *Luke,* 614; H. Weder, *Gleichnisse,* 266-67; H. Hendrickx, *Parables,* 192-93; R. Stein, *Parables,* 106; R. Funk, *Five Gospels,* 358-59, has 16:1-8a in red font (= from Jesus).

The children of light, no less than the children of this age, give attention to many matters. But no matter is as important, or as urgent, as their relationship to God. That relationship is sound when there is daily repentance,[37] followed by selfless service to others.

Paul's message to the Thessalonians relates beautifully and appropriately to the parable. He addresses his readers as "children of light," assures them that they are "destined for salvation," and exhorts them to encourage one another and to build each other up in faith and love (1 Thess 5:5-11). Such is the way of life of those who seek to be as wise in spiritual matters as others are in the normal transactions of this world.

The exposition to this point assumes that the unit ends at 16:8, and that the verses that follow (including 16:9) are secondary expansions. The interpreter who wishes to include any of those will want to stress how generosity toward others is a specific way that the children of light exercise their way of living.

Select Bibliography

Ball, Michael. "The Parables of the Unjust Steward and the Rich Man and Lazarus." *ExpTim* 106 (1995): 329-30.

Baverstock, A. H. "The Parable of the Unjust Steward: An Interpretation." *Theology* 35 (1937): 78-83.

Beames, Frederick. "The Unrighteous Steward." *ExpTim* 24 (1912-13): 150-55.

Beavis, Mary Ann. "Ancient Slavery as an Interpretive Context for the New Testament Servant Parables with Special Reference to the Unjust Steward." *JBL* 111 (1992): 37-54.

Bindemann, Walther. "Ungerechte als Vorbilder? Gottesreich und Gottesrecht in den Gleichnissen vom ungerechten Verwalter und ungerechten Richter." *TLZ* 120 (1995): 955-70.

Binder, Hermann. "Missdeutbar oder eindeutig? Gedanken zu einem Gleichnis Jesu." *TZ* 51 (1995): 41-49.

Boyd, William F. "The Parable of the Unjust Steward (Luke xvi.1ff.)." *ExpTim* 50 (1938-39) 46.

Bretscher, Paul G. "Brief Studies: The Parable of the Unjust Steward — A New Approach to Luke 16:1-9." *CTM* 22 (1951): 756-62.

Brown, Colin. "The Unjust Steward: A New Twist." In *Worship, Theology and Ministry in the Early Church: Essays in Honor of Ralph P. Martin*, 121-45. Ed. Michael J. Wilkins and Terence Paige. JSNTSup 87. Sheffield: JSOT Press, 1992.

---

37. In the first of his 95 Theses, Martin Luther wrote that our Lord and Master Jesus Christ "willed the entire life of believers to be one of repentance"; quoted from *Luther's Works,* ed. Jaroslav Pelikan and Helmut Lehmann, 55 vols. (Philadelphia: Fortress Press; St. Louis: Concordia Publishing House, 1955-76), 31:25.

Caemmerer, Richard R. "Investment for Eternity: A Study of Luke 16:1-13." *CTM* 34 (1963): 69-76.

Clavier, Henri. 'L'Ironie dans l'enseignment de Jésus." *NovT* 1 (1956): 3-20.

Colella, Pasquale. "Zu Lk 16,7." *ZNW* 64 (1973): 124-26.

Collins, R. L. "Is the Parable of the Unjust Steward Pure Sarcasm?" *ExpTim* 22 (1910-11): 525-26.

Combrink, H. J. B. "A Social-scientific Perspective on the Parable of the 'Unjust' Steward (Lk 16:1-8a)." *Neot* 30 (1996): 281-306.

Comiskey, John P. "The Unjust Steward." *BiTod* 52 (1971): 229-35.

Compston, H. F. B. "Friendship without Mammon." *ExpTim* 31 (1919-20): 282.

Coutts, John. "Studies in Texts: The Unjust Steward, Lk. xvi,1-8a." *Theology* 52 (1949): 54-60.

Davidson, J. A. "A 'Conjecture' about the Parable of the Unjust Steward (Luke xvi,1-9)." *ExpTim* 66 (1954-55): 31.

Derrett, J. Duncan M. "Fresh Light on St Luke xvi: I. The Parable of the Unjust Steward." *NTS* 7 (1960-61): 198-219. Reprinted as "The Parable of the Unjust Steward," in his *Law in the New Testament*, 48-77. London: Darton, Longman and Todd, 1970.

———. "'Take thy Bond . . . and Write Fifty' (Luke xvi.6): The Nature of the Bond." *JTS* 23 (1972): 438-40.

deSilva, David A. "The Parable of the Prudent Steward and Its Lucan Context." *CTR* 6 (1993): 255-68.

Drexler, Hans. "Zu Lukas 16,1-7." *ZNW* 58 (1967): 286-88.

Firth, C. B. "The Parable of the Unrighteous Steward (Luke xvi.1-9)." *ExpTim* 63 (1951-52): 93-95.

Fitzmyer, Joseph A. "The Story of the Dishonest Manager (Lk 16:1-13)." *TS* 25 (1964): 23-42. Reprinted in his *Essays on the Semitic Background of the New Testament*, 161-84. Missoula, Mont.: Scholars Press, 1974.

Fletcher, Donald R. "The Riddle of the Unjust Steward: Is Irony the Key?" *JBL* 82 (1963): 15-30.

Flusser, David, "The Parable of the Unjust Steward: Jesus' Criticism of the Essenes." In *Jesus and the Dead Sea Scrolls: The Controversy Resolved*, 176-97. Ed. James H. Charlesworth. ABRL. New York: Doubleday, 1992.

Friedel, Lawrence M. "The Parable of the Unjust Steward." *CBQ* 3 (1941): 337-48.

Gächter, Paul. "The Parable of the Dishonest Steward after Oriental Conceptions." *CBQ* 12 (1950): 121-31.

Gagnon, Robert A. J. "A Second Look at Two Lukan Parables: Reflections on the Unjust Steward and the Good Samaritan." *HBT* 20 (1998): 1-9.

Gibson, M. D. "On the Parable of the Unjust Steward." *ExpTim* 14 (1902-3): 334.

Hiers, Richard. "Friends by Unrighteous Mammon: The Eschatological Proletariat." *JAAR* 38 (1970): 30-36.

Hoeren, Thomas. "Das Gleichnis vom ungerechten Verwalter (Lukas 16.1-8a)
— zugleich ein Beitrag zur Geschichte der Restschuldbefreiung." *NTS* 41
(1995): 620-29.

Hof, Otto. "Luthers Auslegung von Lukas 16,9." *EvT* 8 (1948-49): 151-66.

Ireland, Dennis J. "A History of the Recent Interpretation of the Parable of the
Unjust Steward (Luke 16:1-13)." *WTJ* 51 (1989): 293-318.

———. *Stewardship and the Kingdom of God: An Historical, Exegetical, and
Contextual Study of the Parable of the Unjust Steward in Luke 16:1-13.*
NovTSup 70. Leiden: E. J. Brill, 1992.

Kloppenborg, John S. "The Dishonored Master (Luke 16:1-8a)." *Bib* 70 (1989):
474-95.

Kosmala, Hans. "The Parable of the Unjust Steward in the Light of Qumran."
ASTI 3 (1964): 114-21.

Krüger, Gerda. "Die geistesgeschichtlichen Grundlagen des Gleichnisses vom
ungerechten Verwalter, Lk. 16,1-9." *BZ* 21 (1933): 170-81.

Lee, Martin. "The Wasteful Steward." *NBl* 78 (1997): 520-28.

Lindars, Barnabas. "Jesus and the Pharisees." In *Donum gentilicium: New Testament Studies in Honour of David Daube*, 51-63. Ed. Ernst Bammel et al.
Oxford: Clarendon, 1978.

Loader, William R. G. "Jesus and the Rogue in Luke 16,1-8a: The Parable of the
Unjust Steward." *RB* 96 (1980): 518-32.

Lunt, Ronald G. "Expounding the Parables: III. The Parable of the Unjust Steward (Luke xvi.1-15)." *ExpTim* 77 (1965-66): 132-36.

Mann, C. S. "Unjust Steward or Prudent Manager?" *ExpTim* 102 (1990-91):
234-35.

Marshall, H. S. "The Parable of the Untrustworthy Steward." *ExpTim* 39 (1927-
28): 120-22.

Marshall, I. Howard. "Luke 16:8: Who Commended the Unjust Steward?" *JTS*
19 (1968): 617-19.

Mathewson, Dave L. T. "The Parable of the Unjust Steward (Luke 16:1-13): A
Reexamination of the Traditional View in Light of Recent Challenges."
JETS 38 (1995): 29-39.

Middleton, R. D. "St. Luke XVI,9." *Theology* 29 (1934): 41.

Moore, Francis J. "The Parable of the Unjust Steward." *ATR* 47 (1965): 103-5.

Pargiter, Frederick E. "The Parable of the Unrighteous Steward." *ExpTim* 32
(1920-21): 136-37.

Parrott, Douglas M. "The Dishonest Steward (Luke 16.1-8a) and Luke's Special
Parable Collection." *NTS* 37 (1991): 499-515.

Paul, Geoffrey. "Studies in Texts: The Unjust Steward." *Theology* 61 (1958): 189-
93.

Pickar, Charles H. "The Unjust Steward." *CBQ* 1 (1939): 250-53.

Plessis, I. J. du. "Philanthropy or Sarcasm? Another Look at the Parable of the
Dishonest Manager (Luke 16:1-13)." *Neot* 24 (1990): 1-20.

Porter, Stanley E. "The Parable of the Unjust Steward (Luke 16:1-13): Irony as the Key." In *The Bible in Three Dimensions: Essays in Celebration of Forty Years of Biblical Studies in the University of Sheffield*, 127-53. Ed. David J. A. Clines et al. JSOTSup 87. Sheffield: JSOT Press, 1990.

Preisker, Herbert. "Lukas 16,1-7." *TLZ* 74 (1949): 85-92.

Schwarz, Günther. "'. . . lobte den betrugerischen Verwalter?' Lukas 16,8a." *BZ* 18 (1974): 94-95.

Scott, Bernard B. "A Master's Praise: Luke 16:1-8." *Bib* 64 (1983): 173-88.

Scott, R. B. Y. "The Parable of the Unjust Steward." *ExpTim* 49 (1937-38): 234-35.

Steele, J. "The Unjust Steward." *ExpTim* 39 (1927-28): 236-37.

Tillmann, Fritz. "Zum Gleichnis vom ungerechten Verwalter, Luk. 16,1-9." *BZ* 9 (1911): 171-84.

Topel, L. John. "On the Injustice of the Unjust Steward: Lk 16:1-13." *CBQ* 37 (1975): 216-27.

Trudinger, Paul. "Exposing the Depth of Oppression (Luke 16:1b-6a)." In *Jesus and His Parables: Interpreting the Parables of Jesus Today*, 121-37. Ed. V. George Shillington. Edinburgh: T. & T. Clark, 1997.

Via, Dan O. "The Parable of the Unjust Judge: A Metaphor of the Unrealized Self." In *Semiology and the Parables: Exploration of the Possibilities Offered by Structuralism for Exegesis*, 1-32. Ed. Daniel Patte. Pittsburgh: Pickwick Press, 1976.

Volckaert, J. "The Parable of the Unjust Steward." *CleM* 17 (1953): 332-41.

Wansey, J. C. "The Parable of the Unjust Steward: An Interpretation." *ExpTim* 47 (1935-36): 39-40.

Williams, Francis. E. "Is Almsgiving the Point of the 'Unjust Steward'?" *JBL* 83 (1964): 293-97.

Williams, Frederick J. "The Parable of the Unjust Steward (Luke xvi.1-9)." *ExpTim* 66 (1954-55): 371-72.

Wood, C. T. "Luke xvi.8." *ExpTim* 63 (1951-52): 126.

Wright, Stephen I. "Parables on Poverty and Riches (Luke 12:13-21; 16:1-13; 16:19-31)." In *The Challenge of Jesus' Parables*, 217-39. Ed. Richard N. Longenecker. Grand Rapids: Wm. B. Eerdmans, 2000.

Zimmermann, Heinrich. "Die Forderung der Gleichnisse Jesu: Das Gleichnis vom ungerechten Verwalter: Lk 16:1-9." *BibLeb* 2 (1961): 254-61.

4.14. The Faithful and Wise Slave, Matthew 24:45-51//Luke 12:42-46

Matthew 24:45-51

45 *[Jesus said,] "Who then is the faithful and wise slave, whom the master has put in charge of his household slaves, to give them their food at the proper time?*

46*Blessed is that slave whom his master, when he comes, will find so doing.* 47*Truly, I say to you, he will put him in charge of all his property.*

48*"But if that wicked slave says in his heart, 'My master is taking his time,'* 49*and begins to beat his fellow slaves, and eats and drinks with those who are drunk,* 50*the master of that slave will come on a day when he does not expect and at an hour he does not know,* 51*and will punish him with utmost severity and assign a place for him among the hypocrites; at that place there will be weeping and gnashing of teeth."*

Notes on the Text and Translation

24:45. The term οἰκετεία, used only here it the NT, signifies "the slaves in a household."[1] It is variously translated as "household" (KJV, RSV, NRSV), "household staff" (NEB), and "servants in his household" (NIV).

Luke 12:42-46

42*And the Lord said, "Who then is the faithful and wise manager whom the master will put in charge of the slaves of his household to give them their food-allowance at the proper time?* 43*Blessed is that slave whom his master, when he comes, will find so doing.* 44*Truly, I say to you, he will set him over all his property.*

45*"But if that slave says in his heart, 'My master is taking time in coming,' and begins to beat the other slaves, both men and women, and to eat, drink, and get drunk,* 46*the master of that slave will come on a day when he does not expect and at an hour he does not know, and will punish him with utmost severity and assign a place for him with the unfaithful."*

Notes on the Text and Translation

12:42. The term θεραπεία has several meanings; here it can mean "servants" or "slaves" within the household.[2] The term is used precisely in that sense in the LXX (Gen 45:16). It is commonly translated "household" (KJV, RSV), "servants" (NEB, NIV), or "slaves" (NRSV). Since the manager is referred to in the next verse as a "slave," it seems right that he would be in charge of other "slaves," which is the basis for the translation here.

General Comments on the Texts

The accounts in the Gospels of Matthew and Luke are quite similar, and similar enough, that they are commonly thought to have been derived from a common

1. BAGD 556-57.
2. BAGD 358-59.

source (Q).[3] In spite of some noticeable differences between them, they share a similar structure, and even wording is frequently identical between them. There is little need to ask which of the evangelists preserved the Q version more closely in the case of this parable, since the two versions are so much alike. Clearly each evangelist made some alterations, and these will be dealt with below.

The parable is remarkably clear, and interpreters are generally in agreement about its essential message.[4] The wise and faithful slave or manager will attend to the duties assigned by the master who is temporarily away, knowing that in the end an accounting will take place. If, on the other hand, that person abuses the trust placed in him or her, he or she will suffer severe consequences. Just so, the disciple of Jesus who is wise and faithful will attend to those duties entrusted — or face condemnation at the parousia of the Son of man. What those duties are, however, is a matter of dispute. They depend on answers to two questions: whether the parable can be traced back to Jesus, and whether the parable at its first utterance was addressed to disciples, opponents, or early Christians.

Scholarly opinion is divided on the question of authenticity. Some interpreters have been cautious and have left the question open, saying that there must be an original nucleus going back to Jesus.[5] Others have been less reserved, concluding that the parable can be attributed to Jesus,[6] or that it cannot.[7] The primary reasons for thinking that the parable is an early Christian composition, rather than from Jesus, are that (1) it presupposes the delay of the parousia, and

3. A. Jülicher, *Gleichnisreden,* 2:161; Burnett H. Streeter, *The Four Gospels: A Study of Origins,* rev. ed. (New York: St. Martin's Press, 1930), 291; T. W. Manson, *Sayings,* 117-19; A. Polag, *Fragmenta Q,* 25, 64; J. Donahue, *Parable,* 98; A. Dewey, "Prophetic Pronouncement," 99-108; Philip Sellew, "Reconstruction of Q 12:33-59," *Society of Biblical Literature 1987 Seminar Pages,* ed. Kent H. Richards, SBLSP 26 (Atlanta: Scholars Press, 1987), 622, 636-43; R. Brown, *Introduction NT,* 119.

4. With variations, cf. A. Jülicher, *Gleichnisreden,* 2:161; T. W. Manson, *Sayings,* 118; J. Jeremias, *Parables,* 56.

5. R. Bultmann, *HST* 119, 128 (possibly from Jesus); Paul Fiebig, *Die Gleichnisreden Jesu im Lichte der rabbinischen Gleichnisse der neutestamentlichen Zeitalters* (Tübingen: J. C. B. Mohr [Paul Siebeck], 1912), 160; Francis W. Beare, *The Earliest Records of Jesus* (New York: Abingdon, 1962), 170; J. Donahue, *Parable,* 99.

6. A. Jülicher, *Gleichnisreden,* 2:161; Wilhelm Michaelis, *Die Gleichnisse Jesu: Eine Einführung,* 3d ed., UCB (Hamburg: Furche-Verlag, 1956), 79; C. H. Dodd, *Parables,* 127; B. Smith, *Parables,* 158; I. H. Marshall, *Luke,* 533-35; J. Jeremias, *Parables,* 57-58; A. Weiser, *Knechtsgleichnisse,* 213-14; J. Fitzmyer, *Luke,* 987; D. Wenham, *Parables,* 76-80; B. Scott, *Parable,* 210-12; U. Luz, *Matthäus,* 3:460.

7. Erich Grässer, *Das Problem des Parusieverzögerung in den synoptischen Evangelien und in der Apostelgeschichte,* 2d ed., BZNW 22 (Berlin: Verlag Alfred Töpelmann, 1960), 90-95; J. Gnilka, *Matthäus,* 2:345; A. Dewey, "Prophetic Pronouncement," 99-108; R. Funk, *Five Gospels,* 253, 341-42; both versions of the parable are printed with black font (= not attributable to Jesus); J. Lambrecht, *Treasure,* 194.

(2) it contains allegorical elements. Yet these two points can be met. There can be no doubt that the wording in the present Matthean and Lukan versions, based on Q (where the delay of the parousia is already contemplated[8]), alludes to the delay of the parousia, and that the terms and imagery within them are to be interpreted allegorically (see below). But the parable in its origins could allude not so much to a *delay* of the parousia (as a theological construct to account for a problem), but rather to the absence of the master (metaphorically the Lord, i.e., the God of Israel) in the present — a time when the slaves are to carry on in responsible ways, and a time that will be followed by accountability in the final judgment by God. Once that is recognized, the other pieces of the parable can be accommodated metaphorically within the ministry of the historical Jesus. It shares with four other parables of Jesus the motif of a king or wealthy man leaving his slaves or managers in charge while he is away, followed by an accounting. The motif appears in the Parables of the Waiting Slaves (Mark 13:34-37//Luke 12:35-38), the Talents (Matt 25:14-30), the Pounds (Luke 19:12-27), and the Wicked Tenants (Mark 12:1-12//Matt 21:33-46//Luke 20:9-19; but lacking in *Gos. Thom.* 65–66). Three known rabbinic parables, all attributed to rabbis from times later than Jesus, share the same motif. These are indicated in the Exegetical Commentary on the Waiting Slaves.

If the parable can be attributed to Jesus, the question that follows is whether one can discern its intended hearers. Both Matthew and Luke have placed the parable within the context of Jesus' instructing his disciples. In the former Gospel the parable is located within the eschatological discourse (Matt 24–25), which is spoken by Jesus to his disciples privately (24:3; cf. 26:1). In the latter Gospel the parable is spoken in response to a question by Peter (Luke 12:41), but crowds are on the scene as well (12:1, 13). Nevertheless, various interpreters have concluded that, in the original situation, Jesus would have spoken the parable to his opponents, the religious leaders of his day.[9] While certainly possible, that conclusion is based on the general view of those interpreters concerning the function of the parables in general. It is important, however, to consider each parable as a separate case rather than to generalize. In the present instance, it is certainly possible that Jesus spoke the parable to his disciples. In such a situation he would be pressing upon them the necessity of caring for the people of Israel — a ministry of proclaiming the kingdom, healing, and casting out demons — in the time before the end, when an accounting before God will inevitably take place.[10] In those respects, the disciples of Jesus

8. B. Smith, *Parables*, 158; E. Grässer, *Das Problem des Parusieverzögerung*, 218-19.

9. C. H. Dodd, *Parables*, 127; J. Jeremias, *Parables*, 58; B. Smith, *Parables*, 158; J. Donahue, *Parables*, 99; W. Michaelis, *Gleichnisse*, 79; F. Beare, *Matthew*, 476-77. For a lengthy critique of this view, cf. A. Weiser, *Knechtsgleichnisse*, 204-13.

10. Bernhard Weiss, *Das Matthäusevangelium und seine Lucas-Parallelen* (Halle: Verlag der Buchhandlung des Weisenhauses, 1876), 524; A. Jülicher, *Gleichnisreden*, 2:161; I. H. Marshall, *Luke*, 535.

would be extending the ministry of Jesus. The parable exhorts the disciples to conduct responsible, faithful ministry. The reward for fidelity, by which the faithful slave is set over all of the master's possessions (Matt 24:47//Luke 12:44), cannot be allegorized, but its metaphorical significance cannot be missed. The imagery belongs to the story, and it signifies the eschatological blessedness of the faithful one.

Be that as it may, for the two evangelists, the saying about the coming of the master (Greek: ὁ κύριος, "the lord" or "the Lord"), presented in identical language in the two Gospels (from Q, Matt 24:50//Luke 12:46), is an allusion to the parousia of Jesus as Son of man. The wording about the master's arrival on an unexpected day and unknown hour corresponds exactly with that of sayings elsewhere about the coming of the Son of man (Matt 24:36; 25:13; cf. 24:42, 44; Luke 17:24, 26, 30). At the level of the two canonical Gospels — and perhaps already in Q — the persons being exhorted to faithful ministry would have been Christian leaders.

Another allegorical element in both Gospels is the statement that the task or duty of the slave (Matt 24:45) or manager (Luke 12:42) is to provide food for others ἐν καιρῷ ("at the proper time," Matt 24:45//Luke 12:43). The imagery recalls that of Psalm 104:27 (LXX 103:27) and 145:15 (LXX 144:15), where it is said that God provides food εὔκαιρον or ἐν εὐκαιρίᾳ (both translated in NRSV as "in due season").[11] The slave provides on behalf of God. But the food provided is to be understood metaphorically to refer to that which is needed for existence as believers, that is, proclamation and teaching. That is to be supplied in an orderly and timely fashion.

A striking similarity between the two versions is the saying near the end. There it is said that the master will punish the wicked slave with utmost severity (Matt 24:51//Luke 12:46), and in each case the verb used is διχοτομέω (literally, "to cut in two"). The word is used only here in the NT. It signifies dismemberment and can mean to punish with utmost severity.[12] The suggestion that it would mean to cut a person off from the community,[13] while appealing, is not warranted.

11. Ps 104:27 (LXX 103:27): δοῦναι τὴν τροφὴν αὐτοῖς εὔκαιρον ("to give them food in a timely manner"); Ps 145:15 (LXX 144:15): σὺ δίδως τὴν τροφὴν αὐτῶν ἐν εὐκαιρίᾳ ("you give their food in a timely manner").

12. BAGD 200; Heinrich Schlier, "διχοτομέω," TDNT 2:225: "the ancient punishment of parting asunder with the sword or saw"; cf. Sus 59; 3 Bar. 16:3, διχοτομήσατε αὐτοὺς ἐν μαχαίρᾳ ("cut them in two with the sword").

13. O. Betz, "The Dichotomized Servant," 43-58; E. Schweizer, Matthew, 463; J. Donahue, Parable, 100. For opposition to this view, cf. K. Weber, "Is There a Qumran Parallel?" 657-63.

The Parable in the Gospel of Matthew

Exegetical Commentary

The parable is located within the eschatological discourse of the Gospel of Matthew (24:1–25:46), delivered by Jesus in Jerusalem. The parable is preceded by several comments on the parousia of Jesus as the Son of man (24:3-7, 27, 37, 39). Further, various sayings of Jesus about vigilance and perseverance on the part of the disciples come before it (24:4, 6, 10, 13, 22, 31, 42). The master (for Matthew and his readers, the risen Christ) has set certain slaves over his household. Blessed is that one who cares for it properly.

24:45. The parable begins with a rhetorical question, which is characteristic of a number of Jesus' parables (Luke 11:5; 14:28; 15:4, 8; 17:7; Matt 12:11; 18:12; 21:28), by which the hearer's attention is arrested. The question concerns a slave and his relationship to his master. (At Luke 12:42 the relationship is between a manager and his master.) The slave who is faithful and wise can be expected to act in certain ways, as in the Parable of the Talents (25:21). In this particular case the duty of such a slave is "to give . . . food" (δοῦναι . . . τὴν τροφήν) to others in the "household" (οἰκετεία). The terms "food" and "household" can have metaphorical connotations,[14] and they surely do here; that becomes evident as the parable is told. Moreover, the word "slave" (δοῦλος) is often a metaphor in the NT for Christian believers (Rom 1:1; Gal 1:10, etc.). By portraying a slave in charge of other slaves within a household, and stressing the importance of his caring for the others while the master is away, the parable thereby signifies that leaders within the church are to care for the community properly between the ascension of Jesus Christ and his parousia. That proper care — feeding the household — will consist of a ministry of proclamation and teaching.

24:46-47. The Greek term for "blessed" is the one used also in the Beatitudes (i.e., μακάριος, Matt 5:3-12//Luke 6:20-23; cf. also Matt 11:6; 13:16; 16:17), signifying a person's being truly approved by his or her superior, such as God in the Beatitudes, but here the master. Metaphorically, the term signifies the verdict concerning the faithful and wise slave at the coming of the Son of man. On the slave's reward, see General Comments above.

24:48-49. Initially the verse might seem to refer to a second slave, as some interpreters have assumed or suggested that it does.[15] But that is not likely.

---

14. The Matthean word for "food" (τροφή) has such metaphorical meaning in Heb 5:12, 14; Ignatius, *Trall.* 6.1; contra R. Gundry, *Matthew*, 496, for whom the verse commends hospitality to Christian refugees on the part of "settled ecclesiastics." With Chrysostom, *Commentary on Matthew* 77.4-5, the verse concerns the just dispensing of the alms of the church; text in *NPNF* 10:467.

15. E. Schweizer, *Matthew*, 460; J. Donahue, *Parable*, 98; D. Hagner, *Matthew*, 722, 724.

What is portrayed is a second way of behaving on the part of "that slave" (ὁ δοῦλος ἐκεῖνος),[16] as he is called already in 24:46. The same slave has two ways set before him: to be faithful and wise, or to be wicked. (Luke's syntax is preferable [12:45].) A striking element in this verse is that the slave carries on a brief "interior monologue" (saying to himself, "My master is delayed"), a feature familiar in parables within the Gospel of Luke,[17] but not otherwise in the parables within the Gospel of Matthew.

To eat and drink with the drunken (24:49) implies a separation of the self from one's fellow slaves and being "taken in" by those who are opposed to the master and his will.

24:50-51. On 24:50, see General Comments above. The last line of 24:51 concerning weeping and gnashing of teeth is typically Matthean, used five other times in his Gospel (8:12; 13:42, 50; 22:13; 25:30), and only once elsewhere in the NT (Luke 13:28). The sentence is missing in Luke's account, and its composition can be attributed to Matthew in this instance.[18] To be assigned to be with the "hypocrites" means, within the Matthean context, to be placed in the company of the scribes and Pharisees (cf. 23:13-36). In Luke's parallel (12:26) those cast out are put among the "unfaithful," which may have been the term in Q (see comment on Luke 12:46 below).[19] The righteousness of every disciple is to exceed that of the scribes and Pharisees (5:20), and that will apply even more to anyone who assumes responsibility over the rest.

The Matthean rendition of the parable sets forth the importance of the disciples, and so the leaders of the church, to serve the "household" of God in accord with the will of the master, Christ himself. To "give them their food at the proper time" is a metaphorical expression signifying that the leaders are to care for those entrusted to them (their "fellow slaves" of God), teaching them to observe all that the Lord has commanded (28:20). We can imagine that the persons envisioned are leaders of house churches in the area where, and for whom, this Gospel was composed. The leaders will be accountable at the final judg-

---

16. J. Jeremias, *Parables*, 55; F. Beare, *Matthew*, 478; J. Gnilka, *Matthäus*, 2:342; J. Lambrecht, *Treasure*, 189; W. D. Davies and D. C. Allison, *Matthew*, 3:386; U. Luz, *Matthäus*, 3:460; cf. also Klaus Beyer, *Semitische Syntax im Neuen Testament*, SUNT 1 (Göttingen: Vandenhoeck & Ruprecht, 1962), 293.

17. These are the Parables of the Rich Fool (12:16-21), the Prodigal Son (15:11-32), the Unjust Steward (16:1-8), the Unjust Judge (18:1-8), the Wicked Tenants (20:9-19), and Luke's version of the Faithful and Wise Slave (12:42-46). Cf. Philip Sellew, "Interior Monologue as a Narrative Device in the Parables of Luke," *JBL* 111 (1992): 239-53.

18. A. McNeile, *Matthew*, 359; E. Schweizer, *Matthew*, 461; D. Hagner, *Matthew*, 723, 725; W. D. Davies and D. C. Allison, *Matthew*, 3:391.

19. E. Schweizer, *Matthew*, 461; R. Gundry, *Matthew*, 497; J. Gnilka, *Matthäus*, 2:342; A. Weiser, *Knechtsgleichnisse*, 202; J. Fitzmyer, *Luke*, 990; D. Hagner, *Matthew*, 723; W. D. Davies and D. C. Allison, *Matthew*, 3:391; U. Luz, *Matthäus*, 3:459; H. Fleddermann, "The Householder," 23; P. Sellew, "Reconstruction," 622, 643. Contra J. Creed, *Luke*, 177.

ment after the arrival of the Son of man. The time of his coming cannot be calculated, but the fact of his coming is certain.

Exposition

The picture before us is that of Jesus teaching his disciples in Jerusalem near the close of his earthly ministry. It anticipates the time in which those disciples, and those who come after them, will be entrusted with caring for their fellow disciples, members of the church. That responsibility is not given to all, but it is granted to certain persons. And so it continues. In many traditions, but not all, that responsibility has been passed on through history primarily by means of ordination. In any case, various persons, whether ordained or lay, are entrusted on a continuing basis with care for fellow members of the church.

To be entrusted with "feeding the flock" by means of proclamation and teaching is a serious matter. Anyone who abuses the community of faith and separates himself or herself in an arrogant manner (as in the metaphor of eating and drinking with the drunken) is liable to condemnation at the last judgment. Eating and drinking with the drunken can also imply not just arrogance, but falling in with interests within the world that are antithetical to the teachings of Jesus. Leaders, as well as other members of the church, have often been so captivated by secular movements and organizations that they have become dulled in terms of critical discernment. The clarity and precision of the teachings of Jesus have been forsaken for the good life of pleasure and ease, accommodation to the culture, and all that goes with those things.

The expectation of the person entrusted with the ministry of proclamation and teaching is that he or she will continue in fidelity, ministering to fellow members of the church continually and in a regularized manner, just like a slave who feeds his fellow slaves at the appropriate time.

One cannot calculate the time of the Lord's coming and the judgment that will follow upon one's work. Therefore it is simply necessary to be faithful now, and every day, so that when the Lord does appear, he will find that the person who has been entrusted with ministry in his name and during his absence will be carrying out that ministry wisely and faithfully.

The Parable in the Gospel of Luke

Exegetical Commentary

In Luke's Gospel (contra Matthew's) the parable is not located within the context of Jesus' ministry in Jerusalem. Instead it is within the Travel Narrative (9:51–19:27) devoted to Jesus' journey to Jerusalem. More specifically, it is located within a section of warnings to the disciples (12:1–13:9), although multitudes are present (12:1, 13, 54). In 12:35-40 (just prior to the parable) Jesus exhorts his disciples to be alert and ready for the coming (parousia) of the Son of man. But since the parable is not located within the eschatological discourse of Luke's Gospel (21:5-36), there is less sense of an impending crisis at hand than in the Gospel of Matthew.

The parable is preceded by a question of Peter (12:41) that can be attributed to Luke's own composition.[20] The question makes the reader aware that the multitudes are on the scene, and that Jesus may be speaking to them or to other hearers or readers (of the Gospel of Luke) as well as to the disciples. Peter asks concerning what was said in 12:35-40, which he calls a "parable." His question is not answered explicitly. Yet by virtue of having located that parable within the Travel Narrative (9:51–19:27), in which Jesus is instructing the Twelve for the time beyond his earthly ministry, it applies to others beyond the circle of the Twelve, including leaders of the church in Luke's own day.[21]

The actual response of Jesus is to relate an additional parable, which is told to Peter and the others among the Twelve. The cumulative effect of the first parable (12:35-40), the question of Peter (12:41), the second parable (12:42-46), and the sayings that follow (12:47-48) is to say that those who have known the will of the master, but have not carried it out, will be treated with utmost severity.

12:42. As elsewhere in Luke's Gospel,[22] and only in Luke's Gospel, Jesus is called "the Lord" within the narrative. The parable itself begins with a question, which is characteristic of many of Jesus' parables (see comment on Matt 24:45).

The question concerns a "manager" (NIV; NRSV; Greek: οἰκονόμος), or "steward" in some translations (KJV, RSV, NEB), who differs from the "slave" (δοῦλος) of Matthew 24:45. The latter may well represent the Q reading,[23] for it is found even in Luke's next verse (as well as twice more, 12:45, 46). By calling the person a "manager" at the outset (a word used by Luke in another parable at 16:1, 3), Luke implies that the person has been given a specific responsibility and position over that of other "fellow slaves" (Matt 24:49), and by using the term θεραπεία ("slaves of the household") he implies that there is a veritable "retinue" of slaves under his care.[24] The term σιτομέτριον ("portion of food") means, literally, a "measured allowance of grain" or simply a "food allowance,"[25] a term used only here in the NT. The effect is that in Luke's version the

---

20. P. Fiebig, *Gleichnisreden,* 159; W. Michaelis, *Gleichnisse,* 73-74; R. Bultmann, *HST* 193; A. Weiser, *Knechtsgleichnisse,* 216-19.

21. R. Bultmann, *HST* 193.

22. Luke 7:13; 10:1, 39, 41; 11:39; 13:15; 17:5-6; 18:6; 19:8; 22:61. Apocryphal Mark 16:19-20 has the same usage.

23. B. Smith, *Parables,* 155; E. Schweizer, *Matthew,* 460-61; idem, *Luke,* 213; R. Gundry, *Matthew,* 495; I. H. Marshall, *Luke,* 540; J. Fitzmyer, *Luke,* 989; J. Jeremias, *Parables,* 56 (n. 25); P. Sellew, "Reconstruction," 622, 637.

24. W. L. Knox, *The Sources of the Synoptic Gospels,* 2 vols. (Cambridge: Cambridge University Press, 1953-57), 2:70.

25. BAGD 752.

manager apportions food in equal amounts to a large company of slaves. The future tense of the verb (καταστήσει, "will put in charge"), as opposed to the past tense in Matthew's version (κατέστησεν, "has put in charge"), may well point allegorically forward to leaders of the church.[26]

12:43-44. The wording is virtually identical to its parallel (Matt 24:46-47), except for the reversal of two Greek words at the end of 12:43 (Luke: ποιοῦντα οὕτως; Matthew: οὕτως ποιοῦντα, meaning "so doing" in both cases) and the use of ἀληθῶς ("truly") at 12:44 instead of the Matthean ἀμήν (24:47, literally "amen," but conventionally translated "truly," as in RSV, NRSV, and above). Matthew probably reflects the Q reading here,[27] which Luke has "translated" for a predominantly gentile audience (as also at 9:27 [against Mark 9:1//Matt 16:28] and at 21:3 [against Mark 12:43]). For comment on Luke 12:43-44, see comments on the parallel passage. Luke has additional sayings concerning slaves who are "blessed" (μακάριοι) in previous verses (12:37, 38).

12:45-46. Again the wording is virtually identical to its parallel (Matt 24:48-49), but there are some differences. In Matthew's account it is possible to think that there is a second slave involved in the story, who is called the "wicked slave." But, as indicated above, that is probably not what is meant. In Luke's account the adjective κακός ("wicked") does not appear. The implication is that only one slave is involved. He can be faithful and wise, or he can be wicked.

The interior monologue of the slave is expanded by the addition of the verb ἔρχεσθαι ("to come" or, in this context, "in coming"). The verb makes more explicit the allegorical element at this point in the parable; the reference is to the delay in the *coming* of the Son of man.[28] It is probably Luke who has departed from his source in speaking of the ones beaten as both men and women slaves, reflecting his frequent inclusion of women as disciples of Jesus (8:2-3; 10:38-42; 23:49, 55-56; 24:1-12). Moreover, by using this terminology rather than that of Matthew ("fellow slaves," 24:49), Luke's "manager" is set above the other slaves in an explicit manner. Finally, in Luke's version the manager does not eat and drink with the drunken (as in Matthew's) but eats, drinks, and becomes drunk himself, which adds to his abusive behavior.

The final verse of the parable is identical in wording with its parallel (Matt 24:50-51) except for two variations. First, the master of the slave will put him "with the unfaithful" (μετὰ τῶν ἀπίστων), rather than "with the hypo-

---

26. B. Easton, *Luke*, 207; B. Smith, *Parables*, 155; I. H. Marshall, *Luke*, 541.

27. A. Jülicher, *Gleichnisreden*, 2:149; B. Smith, *Parables*, 155; I. H. Marshall, *Luke*, 541; Joachim Jeremias, *Die Sprache des Lukasevangeliums: Redaktion und Tradition im Nicht-Markusstoff des dritten Evangeliums*, MeyerK (Göttingen: Vandenhoeck & Ruprecht, 1980), 221; J. Fitzmyer, *Luke*, 990; R. Gundry, *Matthew*, 496; W. D. Davies and D. C. Allison, *Matthew*, 3:388; P. Sellew, "Reconstruction," 622.

28. E. Grässer, *Das Problem der Parusieverzögerung*, 91-92; B. Scott, *Parable*, 209.

crites" (μετὰ τῶν ὑποκιρτῶν), as in Matthew's account. Luke's term communicates better with a predominantly gentile audience,[29] but it may also have been in the common source, since "hypocrites" is so commonly used by Matthew.[30] What Luke has also serves to make a contrast and an inclusio: the slave can be "faithful" and wise (12:42), or he can be judged and placed within the company of the "unfaithful" (12:46) Second, Luke does not have the Matthean saying about the weeping and gnashing of teeth (a Matthean composition).

Luke's rendition of the parable and his placement of it within the structure of his Gospel serve to impress upon the reader or hearer the importance of fidelity and wisdom among those entrusted with leadership during the time before the parousia. More explicitly than Matthew, and probably more explicitly than his source (Q), Luke stresses the possibility of the delay of the parousia (see comment on 12:45). Nevertheless, judgment will be exercised in due course. Those entrusted with feeding others cannot presume upon the delay of the parousia and conclude that judgment upon one's accountability is remote — so remote, in fact, that one pays no heed to it. How long the delay may last is of no concern.[31] Like other disciples, those entrusted with care for others must be alert and not be caught off guard (12:37, 39-40). The one who is faithful and wise will continue in teaching and proclamation in an orderly and timely manner. In sayings that follow the parable, the emphases are upon doing the will of the Lord (12:47), that is, the risen Christ, and upon proportionate responsibility: the person to whom more has been entrusted will have to render more in return (12:48).

Exposition

The picture before us in Luke's Gospel is that of Jesus teaching his disciples, plus others, on his way to Jerusalem. The subject of the parable is a "manager," and he is entrusted with distributing rations for the crew of slaves under the control and ownership of his master, who is absent. Metaphorically, even allegorically, the parable refers to the responsibility that any leader of the church has in carrying out ministry in the name of Jesus to and with those under his or her care.

A temptation that can easily come to such a person is to revel in the absence of the master and proceed to act as though the master may never show up. Further, being the "big man" left in charge, such a person may not only fail

29. A. Jülicher, *Gleichnisreden*, 2.152.

30. Some 13 times (6:2, 5, 16; 7:5; 15:7; 22:18; 23:13, 15, 23, 25, 27, 29; 24:51). See comment on Matt 24:51 (and notation). The term appears in Mark once (7:6) and in Luke three times (6:42; 12:56; 13:15).

31. Hans Conzelmann, *The Theology of St. Luke* (New York: Harper & Brothers, 1960), 108.

to carry out his work in an evenhanded manner, but become abusive. And so it is regarding leadership in the church. The temptation is close at hand for a person to act as though the return of Christ in glory to judge the living and the dead is neither a matter of concern nor a reality with which to reckon. In the absence of the Lord, one can be tempted to lord it over others purely out of self-serving interests.

The one who is entrusted is to be faithful and wise. That means that one's ministry in the name of Jesus is to be directed outward to the care of those for whom one is responsible, proclaiming and teaching what has been received by, and entrusted to, the minister of the Word. That is ministry without illusions. Furthermore, as the verses after the parable indicate, the greater the responsibility one has, the higher the expectations are.

Select Bibliography

Bauckham, Richard J. "Synoptic Parousia Parables and the Apocalypse." *NTS* 23 (1977): 165-69.

Betz, Otto. "The Dichotomized Servant and the End of Judas Iscariot (Light on the Dark Passages: Matthew 24,51 and Parallel; Acts 1,18)." *RevQ* 5 (1964-66): 43-58.

Burnett, F. W. "Prolegomenon to Reading Matthew's Eschatological Discourse: Redundancy and the Education of the Reader in Matthew." *Semeia* 31 (1985): 96-109.

Clarke, A. K., and N. E. W. Collie. "A Comment on Luke xii 41-58." *JTS* 17 (1915-16): 299-301.

Deterding, Paul E. "Eschatological and Eucharistic Motifs in Luke 12:35-40." *ConJ* 5 (1979): 85-94.

Dewey, Arthur J. "A Prophetic Pronouncement: Q 12:42-46." *FFF* 5 (1989): 99-108.

Fleddermann, Harry. "The Householder and the Servant Left in Charge." In *Society of Biblical Literature 1986 Seminar Papers*, 17-26. Ed. Kent H. Richards. SBLSPS16. Atlanta: Scholars Press, 1986.

Hartin, Patrick J. "Angst in the Household: A Deconstructive Reading of the Parable of the Supervising Servant." *Neot* 22 (1988): 373-90.

Pesch, Rudolf, and Reinhard Kratz. "Gleichnis vom guten und bösen Knecht." In *So liest man synoptisch*, 5:561-66. 5 vols. Frankfurt am Main: Knecht Verlag, 1978.

Strobel, August. "Das Gleichnis vom heimkehrenden Hausherrn und seinem Knecht (Mt 24,45-51)." In his *Untersuchungen zum eschatologischen Verzögerungsproblem: Auf Grund der spätjüdisch-urchristlichen Geschichte von Habakuk 2,2ff.*, 215-22. NovTSup 2. Leiden: E. J. Brill, 1961.

Weber, K. "Is There a Qumran Parallel to Matthew 24,51//Luke 12,46?" *RevQ* 16 (1995): 657-63.

4.15. The Ten Maidens, Matthew 25:1-13

[Jesus said,] 1*"Then the kingdom of heaven will be like ten bridesmaids who took their lamps and went to meet the bridegroom.* 2*Five of them were foolish, and five were wise.* 3*For when the foolish took their lamps, they took no oil with them;* 4*but the wise took oil in flasks with their lamps.* 5*As the bridegroom was delayed, they all became drowsy and fell asleep.*

6*"But at midnight there was a cry, 'Behold, the bridegroom! Come out to meet him.'* 7*Then all those bridesmaids rose and trimmed their lamps.* 8*And the foolish said to the wise, 'Give us some of your oil, for our lamps are going out.'* 9*But the wise replied, 'Perhaps there will not be enough for us and for you; go rather to the dealers and buy for yourselves.'*

10*"And while they went to buy, the bridegroom came, and those who were ready went in with him to the marriage feast; and the door was shut.* 11*Afterward the other bridesmaids came also, saying, 'Lord, lord, open to us.'* 12*But he replied, 'Truly, I say to you, I do not know you.'*

13*"Watch therefore, for you know neither the day nor the hour."*

Notes on the Text and Translation

25:1, 7, 11. The Greek term παρθένος (in its plural forms) is used for the women mentioned. It is often (correctly) translated as "virgins" (KJV, NIV);[1] other versions have "maidens" (RSV), "girls" (NEB, TEV), or "bridesmaids" (JB, NAB, NRSV). The term can mean, as here, simply "young women" of marriageable age; for "the point of the parable does not depend on their 'virginity' in the strict sense."[2] Within the parable the women are attendants to the bride. The term "bridesmaids" helps to convey the sense of the text for the modern reader.

25:13. Some texts (including many Greek witnesses and the Vulgate) conclude the verse with the phrase represented in English by "in which the Son of man is coming." The phrase appears in the KJV. Superior Greek witnesses (including 𝔓35, ℵ, B, and others), however, do not contain the phrase. It has most likely been added by copyists from a similar phrase at 24:44. It is not included in the Westcott-Hort Greek text nor in the 27th edition of the Nestle-Aland Greek text. It is omitted in more recent English versions (RSV, NEB, NIV, NRSV) as well.

---

1. BAGD 627.
2. Joseph A. Fitzmyer, "παρθένος," *EDNT* 3:40.

Exegetical Commentary

The parable exists only in the Gospel of Matthew. It is located within the Eschatological Discourse devoted to events at the end of the world (Matt 24:1–25:46). Specifically it is located between two other parables that, like this one, anticipate the final judgment, the Parables of the Faithful and Wise Servant (24:45-51) and the Talents (25:14-30).

The parable presupposes Jewish marriage customs at the time of Jesus (and the evangelist Matthew). As in modern times, one can expect that there were variations in such customs, depending on the times, places, and persons involved. One can only speak of what was typical, based on sources that reflect traditions from the OT era into the age of the Tannaim (the early rabbinic period). Items in the parable itself give clues as to which customs were familiar and relevant to the hearers of the parable and therefore, in turn, important to highlight in order to illumine the parable itself.

According to the various sources, ancient Jewish customs concerning marriage typically involved two stages. The first was the *kiddushin* or *erusin* ("betrothal") at which the marriage contract was arranged by the parents (or at least with their consent) of the couple to be married,[3] in accord with ancient traditions,[4] although marriages initiated by the man are known as well.[5] The betrothal amounted to more than an engagement in modern times. (The translation "engaged" at Matt 1:18 concerning Joseph and Mary in the NRSV is unfortunate in this regard.) The betrothal was in fact a marriage contract, at which the woman was consecrated to her husband and was legally his wife from that time on,[6] and it could be broken only by divorce (a legal matter), as indicated in the story of Joseph and Mary (Matt 1:19; the NRSV translation "dismiss" is again unfortunate) and in rabbinic literature.[7]

The second stage consisted of the celebration of the marriage itself, the *nissu'in* (or *ḥuppah*), which customarily took place a year later,[8] followed by the "marriage feast." It was then (after the marriage ceremony proper and during the days of celebration) that the couple began to live together.[9] Marriages took

---

3. Cf. *m. Qidd.* 2.1; G. Moore, *Judaism*, 2:121; Victor P. Hamilton, "Marriage: Old Testament and Ancient Near East," *ABD* 4:562-63; Raymond Apple, "Marriage: The Concept," *EncJud* 11:1027.

4. Stories concerning Ishmael (Gen 21:21), Isaac (24:1-4), Joseph (37:45-46), Er (38:6), and David (1 Sam 18:21).

5. Stories concerning Esau (Gen 28:9), Judah (38:2), and David's subsequent marriages (1 Sam 25:40-42; 2 Sam 2:2-5).

6. G. Moore, *Judaism*, 2:122.

7. Cf. *m. Ketub.* 3:3; 4:2; *m. Qidd.* 1:1.

8. Cf. *m. Ketub.* 5:2; Raphael Posner, "Marriage: Marriage Ceremony," *EncJud* 11:1032.

9. Cf. *Jos. Asen.* 21:1 (composed between 100 B.C. and A.D. 135): "It does not befit a man who worships God to sleep with his wife before the wedding"; quoted from *OTP* 2:235. Cf. also *m. Ketub.* 4:5.

place while the two were usually quite young — the bride about 12 to 13 years of age,[10] the groom about 18.[11]

Three details surrounding the second stage (the marriage itself) have a direct bearing on the parable: (1) The marriage celebration was typically preceded by festival processions. There are accounts of processions of both the bride and her attendants (Ps 45:13-15; 1 Macc 9:37) and of the groom and his companions (1 Macc 9:39; cf. Matt 9:15, where the "sons of the bridegroom" are attendants).[12] (2) The marriage ceremony typically took place at the home of the groom's parents,[13] as reflected in the Parables of the Wedding Feast (Matt 22:1-14) and Great Banquet (Luke 14:16-24). Either there — and especially if it is elsewhere — it could be conducted under the traditional *ḥuppah* ("wedding canopy"), which existed prior to the Christian era (cf. Ps 19:5). (3) The marriage was followed by the "marriage feast," which by custom lasted seven days.[14]

The scene portrayed in the parable is that of the procession of the groom on his way to the wedding and wedding feast. Since the wedding festivities typically took place at the home of the bridegroom's parents, the groom is apparently expected to arrive at his parents' home where others (including the bride) are waiting, as are the bridesmaids themselves. It is possible that he has fetched the bride at the home of her parents and that she is accompanying him as he approaches his own parental home,[15] but since she is not mentioned, one should probably not read that into the parable.

Some interpreters have concluded that a very different scene is intended. According to them, the groom is expected at the home of the bride's parents, and the bridesmaids are awaiting him there. Then there are two possible scenarios: (1) the groom is going there to fetch the bride and will subsequently go

10. Cf. *b. Yebam.* 62b; *b. Qidd.* 2b; Joachim Jeremias, *Jerusalem in the Time of Jesus: An Investigation into Economic and Social Conditions in the New Testament Period* (Philadelphia: Fortress Press, 1969), 365; V. Hamilton, "Marriage," 4:562-63. According to *Jos. Asen.* 1:4, Aseneth was eighteen when she married Joseph, but that was because she had fought off suitors for many years, according to C. Burchard, "Joseph and Aseneth," *OTP* 2:203 (n. j).

11. Cf. *m. Abot.* 5:21; G. Moore, *Judaism*, 2:119; V. Hamilton, "Marriage," 4:562-63.

12. The phrase in Greek is οἱ υἱοὶ τοῦ νυμφῶνος. Although translated simply as "wedding guests" (RSV, NRSV), it actually signifies the groom's attendants; cf. BAGD 545; D. Hagner, *Matthew*, 243.

13. R. Posner, "Marriage," 11:1032. There is an account of a marriage and feasting taking place at the home of the bride (Tob 7:10-14; 8:19-21), but that is necessary since the groom is marrying her in a foreign land.

14. Gen 29:27; Judg 14:12; *Jos. Asen.* 21:8-9.

15. R. Gundry, *Matthew*, 498; D. Senior, *Matthew*, 274 (the "more likely" possibility). This way of conceiving the picture may account for the additional phrase "and the bride" in some ancient manuscripts at 25:1 (D, Θ, family 1, etc.); but it does not exist in most, nor in the most weighty, witnesses (א, B, family 13, and many others).

to his parents' home;[16] or (2) he is going there because that is where the wedding festivities are going to take place.[17] But neither of these scenarios is satisfactory. The entire story takes place at one setting, and at 25:10-12 the groom is the one who is in charge of things and prohibits the foolish bridesmaids from entering the house. The ten bridesmaids go out to meet the groom as he arrives and will accompany him to the wedding and its festivities.

25:1. The verb ὁμοιωθήσεται ("will be like," future passive of ὁμοιόω) appears also at 7:24, 26; these are the only instances in the NT. It can be translated along with its subject as above, "the kingdom of heaven will be like," followed by the parable proper.[18] The kingdom is thus not "like ten maidens," but rather it will be like the following case at its consummation,[19] in which some are admitted to the wedding feast (metaphorically understood), and others are shut out.

The women carry λαμπάδας ("lamps" in the KJV, RSV, NEB, NIV, TEV, and NRSV; "oil lamps" in the TEV; and "torches" in the NAB). The term λαμπάς appears nine times in the NT, and five occurrences are in this parable (25:1, 3, 4, 7, 8). Interpreters have debated the meaning of the term, and the translations reflect the proposals that have been offered. Some have proposed that the term means "torches" used for weddings.[20] These would have consisted of wooden poles wrapped with rags at the upper end, which were saturated with olive oil and would have been lit at the time that the groom would appear (and perhaps specifically in a dance by the women). The other view is that oil lamps made of metal or clay, furnished with wicks, are meant.[21] The former use of the word is attested in John 18:3 (μετὰ φανῶν καὶ λαμπάδων, "with lanterns and torches") and other sources,[22] and the latter in Acts 20:8 (clearly meaning indoor lamps) and other sources.[23] The choice of meaning here is difficult. When it is said that the bridesmaids "trimmed their lamps [or torches]" (25:7), it could mean that the women adjusted the wicks and added oil to their lamps, as various inter-

16. T. W. Manson, *Sayings,* 242-43; R. Smith, *Matthew,* 293; U. Luz, *Matthäus,* 3:468-69.

17. B. Smith, *Parables,* 100; E. Schweizer, *Matthew,* 467.

18. D. A. Carson, "The ὅμοιος Word-Group as Introduction to Some Matthean Parables," *NTS* 31 (1985): 278.

19. On the use of the introductory formula using words of likeness, cf. J. Jeremias, *Parables,* 101.

20. J. Jeremias, "*Lampades,*" 83-87; idem, *Parables,* 174; R. Gundry, *Matthew,* 498; U. Luz, *Matthäus,* 3:469-71.

21. A. Jülicher, *Gleichnisreden,* 2:448; Albrecht Oepke, "λάμπω," *TDNT* 4:17 (n. 2); I. Maisch, "Gleichnis," 247-59; K. Donfried, "Allegory of the Ten Virgins," 417; E. Schweizer, *Matthew,* 465-66; H. Weder, *Gleichnisse,* 241 (n. 149); Gerhard Schneider, "λαμπάς," *EDNT* 2:338; W. D. Davies and D. C. Allison, *Matthew,* 3:395-96; D. Senior, *Matthew,* 275.

22. For various references, cf. A. Oepke, "λάμπω," *TDNT* 4:16-17.

23. For various references, cf. ibid., 4:17.

preters have suggested.[24] On the other hand, it could mean that the women cut (or tore) away the outer layer of rags on their torches, dipped the remainder in oil, and lit them again.[25] By that time the foolish bridesmaids have run out of oil. A variation on the last possibility is that it is only at the arrival of the groom that the women, for the first time, seek to light their torches.[26] But since they have brought no oil, they cannot do so.

The picture is complicated by another factor. Do the women go out to meet the groom once or twice? In 25:1 it is said that the women "went out" to meet the bridegroom. Does that mean that they had gathered in a house, and then went out as a group — prior to their falling asleep (25:5) — to meet the groom? If that is so, then what does one make of 25:6? In that verse the women are summoned to come out to meet the groom as he approaches. Are we to imagine that the women had gone out once (25:1), then returned and fell asleep, and now they are called to go out again? More likely the women go out only once, and what is said in 25:1 anticipates what is said in 25:6; in short, what is said in 25:1 is an "overture" to the story that follows.

If this scenario is fitting, the story develops as follows. The ten young women gather at the place of the wedding (presumably inside the house of the groom's parents) awaiting the coming of the groom, whom they plan to meet as he comes toward the house. All ten have brought oil lamps (not torches) with them. What makes them different from one another is that the wise have brought along extra oil "in flasks" (25:4), but the foolish "took no oil with them" (25:3) except what was in their lamps already. The lamps of all ten women were lit and burned throughout the evening, as 25:8 implies, when the foolish ones say, "our lamps are going out." The trimming of the lamps in 25:7 includes pouring oil into them from flasks (not cutting away outer, burned rags). It is precisely a lack of oil that troubles the foolish women (25:8); their supply within the lamps has been consumed. As the latter go to get oil, the wise women go out, meet the bridegroom, and return with him to the wedding festivities (25:10).

25:2-4. All ten women took oil lamps with them. The difference between them is that the wise have extra oil, which they carry ἐν τοῖς ἀγγείοις (literally, "in flasks" or "in containers").[27] The phrase is translated "flasks of oil" (RSV, NEB, NRSV) or "in jars" (NIV, presumably jars made of clay). The foolish ones "took no oil with them." They obviously had oil within their lamps, as 25:8 attests. They simply did not have extra oil in additional containers. The polarity between wise and foolish recalls the Parable of the Wise and Foolish Builders (7:24-27).

---

24. A. McNeile, *Matthew,* 362; E. Schweizer, *Matthew,* 467; R. Smith, *Matthew,* 293; W. D. Davies and D. C. Allison, *Matthew,* 3:398.

25. J. Jeremias, *Parables,* 175.

26. R. Gundry, *Matthew,* 499-500; U. Luz, *Matthäus,* 3:476.

27. BAGD 6.

25:5. Why is the bridegroom delayed until midnight? One proposal is that the groom had to travel a long distance between the homes of his and her parents.[28] Another is that it took an unusual amount of time for him (and perhaps his parents) to settle financial matters with the bride's parents.[29] Such suggestions are based either on the assumption that the parable is an account of an actual event or that its composer (Jesus or whoever) would have needed a reason in case he was asked about it. Actually there is no need for a reason, except for the sake of a good story. It is an element that allows for the ten women to fall asleep and for them to be exposed later as either prepared or unprepared for the arrival of the groom.

The verb translated "became drowsy" (νυστάζω) appears only here in the NT. The translation "slumbered" (KJV, RSV) implies a deep sleep. The verb is better translated as here (and also in NIV, NRSV; cf. "dozed off," NEB).[30] The women "became drowsy and fell asleep."

25:6. With the arrival of the groom, the women are summoned to come out and meet him. Presumably this is their first venture outdoors in the darkness (see discussion above).

25:7. Various translations say that the women "trimmed their lamps" (KJV, RSV, NEB, TEV, NIV, NRSV; NAB has "got their torches ready"). The Greek verb in question is κοσμέω, which means to "put in order" or to "adorn."[31] The former is meant in this context. That would involve getting the wicks positioned rightly and adding oil (something that the foolish lack) to the lamps.

25:8-9. A sharp interchange ensues between the wise and foolish bridesmaids. The foolish ask the wise for some oil, for their lamps "are going out." The Greek verb (σβέννυμι), used here as a present passive, means simply to "go out,"[32] and so will mean that the lamps are going out one-by-one, not that they are each beginning to sputter (as torches with oil-soaked rags might do).

The wise women refuse. For them to tell the foolish women to go to the dealers to buy oil for themselves at midnight seems strange to the modern ear. Where can they find a dealer willing to sell oil in the middle of the night? But apparently they succeed in obtaining oil, as their return implies (25:10-11). (In any case, a parable, to be a good one, need not have verisimilitude in every detail.)

25:10. When the bridegroom comes, it is those who are ready (αἱ ἕτοιμοι) who are admitted to the marriage feast. (The marriage ceremony itself has not been mentioned.) The shutting of the door indicates a finality. Both the marriage feast and the shutting of the door have symbolic meanings (see below).

---

28. B. Smith, *Parables*, 100.

29. J. Jeremias, *Parables*, 172; R. Gundry, *Matthew*, 499-500.

30. BAGD 547.

31. Hermann Sasse, "κοσμέω," *TDNT* 3:867; BAGD 445; Horst Balz, "κοσμέω," *EDNT* 2:309.

32. BAGD 745.

25:11-12. The foolish bridesmaids return with oil and (presumably) have their lamps lit. The refusal to let them in is based not on whether they possess oil and have lamps burning, but on their having missed the grand moment of the groom's arrival. Their cry, "Lord, lord" is familiar in this Gospel from 7:21-23. The Greek expression κύριε, κύριε could be translated "Sir, sir" (as in NEB); but there can be little doubt that what is intended for the reader of Matthew's Gospel is a plea to the Lord (Jesus), who has the authority to close the door of the kingdom and refuse admission.

According to some interpreters, the scene of 25:10c-12 is not integral to the parable, but a Matthean addition.[33] The wording is much like that of Luke 13:25-27, and it is possible that a Q saying (Luke 13:25-27//Matt 7:22-23) was drawn upon by the evangelist.[34] It is more likely, however, that the traditional ending of the parable stands behind these verses, and that it has been reworked by the evangelist in light of the Q saying.[35] As the first to put the parable into writing, Matthew can be expected to have drawn phrases from the larger Gospel tradition. Without the ending represented by these verses (25:10c-12), the parable lacks the consequences of being foolish on the part of the five left out.

25:13. The Greek imperative verb γρηγορεῖτε can be translated "keep awake" (NRSV), but it can also be translated "be on the alert" or "be watchful."[36] In this particular case the term should be translated as "watch" (RSV) or "keep watch" (NIV). That they fell asleep was not the problem of the foolish women; even the wise had done that. Here the verb must mean to be vigilant, ready at all times for the coming of the bridegroom.

A similar saying appears at 24:42 (cf. also 24:36). In the latter case it means that the day of the parousia of the Son of man may be very soon. But here it means that it might be later than expected.[37] The verse is commonly assigned to Matthew and not regarded as integral to the parable itself.[38]

Within its present Matthean context the parable signifies that the disciples of Jesus are to be wise, as the five maidens were, in some respect. That is that Jesus as the Bridegroom may be delayed, even though his coming is certain.

33. J. Gnilka, Matthäus, 2:348-49; J. Lambrecht, Treasure, 205; W. D. Davies and D. C. Allison, Matthew, 3:393. According to A. McNeile, Matthew, 363, Matt 25:11-12 is Matthean; according to T. W. Manson, Sayings, 242, all of 25:10-12 is Matthean.

34. Luke 13:25-27//Matt 7:22-23 is regarded as Q by A. Polag, Fragmenta Q, 25, 68.

35. U. Luz, Matthäus, 3:468.

36. BAGD 167.

37. Cf. E. Schweizer, Matthew, 468; D. Hagner, Matthew, 730; contra Frederick H. Borsch, Many Things in Parables: Extravagant Stories of New Community (Philadelphia: Fortress Press, 1988), 85-86, who says that the parable opposes the thought that the judgment is far off in the future; instead, it will come soon.

38. B. Smith, Parables, 104; J. Lambrecht, Treasure, 205; J. Gnilka, Matthäus, 2:348-49; W. D. Davies and D. C. Allison, Matthew, 3:400.

No one can know when that will be. The coming may be later than expected.[39] Therefore, the disciples of Jesus should be ready for the long haul.

The parable fits within an interesting chain of sayings, all of which are part of an eschatological discourse by Jesus: (1) no one knows the day nor the hour of the coming of the Son of man (24:36-44); (2) it is incumbent upon the disciples of Jesus not to abandon their obligations but to fulfill them (24:45-51); (3) it is also necessary for them to be wise about these things and realize that the coming of the Son of man (or Lord) may be later than expected (25:1-13); (4) it is urgent in the interval to give of one's best in serving the Lord who is to come (25:14-30); and (5) with the coming of the Son of man the judgment will be carried out, based on whether or not one has served the unfortunates of the world (25:31-46).

Could such a parable have been uttered by Jesus? There is wide disagreement concerning its origins, and three positions are most prominent: (1) that the parable was uttered by Jesus;[40] (2) that it was an allegory from the beginning, composed in the early church;[41] or (3) that it was composed as an allegory by the evangelist Matthew himself.[42] A decision on the matter is extremely difficult.

The parable contains a number of allegorical features. Some interpreters go so far as to call it an allegory (rather than a parable), claiming that it was an allegory from the moment of its composition.[43] Allegorical features that are apparent at the Matthean level include the following: (1) the marriage feast represents the gathering of the Messiah and his people, as elsewhere in the NT (Matt 22:1-14; Rev 19:9; nonnuptial feasting, Matt 8:11-12; Luke 14:15-24) and in rabbinic literature;[44] (2) the bridegroom represents Christ (Mark 2:19-20// Matt 9:15; John 3:29-30; 2 Cor 11:2; Eph 5:25-27; Rev 19:7, 9; 21:9); (3) his delay and eventual coming represent the delay and yet the certainty of the parousia (2 Cor 11:2; Rev 19:7-9; 21:2); (4) in light of all that, the closing of the

---

39. E. Schweizer, *Matthew*, 468; D. Hare, *Matthew*, 286; D. Hagner, *Parables*, 727.

40. A. Jülicher, *Gleichnisreden*, 2:457; C. H. Dodd, *Parables*, 137; B. Smith, *Parables*, 103-4; J. Jeremias, *Parables*, 52-53; A. McNeile, *Matthew*, 360; Werner G. Kümmel, *Promise and Fulfilment: The Eschatological Message of Jesus*, SBT 23 (Naperville: Alec R. Allenson, 1957), 56-58; R. Stein, *Parables*, 38; J. Gnilka, *Matthäus*, 2:353-54; H. Weder, *Gleichnisse*, 246-47; A. Puig i Tàrrech, *La parabole des dix vierges*; J. Lambrecht, *Astonished*, 161-63; idem, *Treasure*, 209-11; W. D. Davies and D. C. Allison, *Matthew*, 3:392-94; U. Luz, *Matthäus*, 3:471-72.

41. R. Bultmann, *HST* 119, 176; G. Bornkamm, "Verzögerung der Parusie," 125; E. Linnemann, *Parables*, 126-27; E. Grässer, *Das Problem*, 125-27; B. Scott, *Parable*, 70-72; R. Funk, *Five Gospels*, 253-55, with gray font (not from Jesus, even if some ideas in it may be close to his own).

42. K. Donfried, "Allegory," 415-28; R. Gundry, *Matthew*, 497; F. Beare, *Matthew*, 481; D. Senior, *Matthew*, 274.

43. P. Perkins, *Parables*, 104; J. Donahue, *Parables*, 101-5.

44. Cf. *b. Pesah* 119b; *Exod. Rab.* 25:10.

door represents the final judgment; and (5) the wise and foolish women symbolize those who are prepared at the final judgment (true Christians) and those who are not. The figure of the bride as the church, however, does not appear as it does elsewhere in the NT (Eph 5:25-27; Rev 18:23; 19:7; 21:9; cf. 2 Cor 11:2).

In light of so many allegorical features, the authenticity of the parable can surely be questioned. On the other hand, in spite of their evident christological associations in the post-Easter era, the allegorical elements are traditional Jewish symbols, and it is not necessary to conclude that the symbolism presupposes the rise of Christianity. The imagery of God as Israel's husband is common enough as a basis for the parable (Isa 54:5-8; 62:5; Jer 31:32; Ezek 16:8-14; Hos 2:1-23), and the imagery of a marriage feast and feasting as metaphors for the kingdom is commonplace in the proclamation of Jesus (cf. Matt 8:11//Luke 13:29; Matt 22:1-10; Luke 12:37; 22:16). It is possible that Jesus used the traditional imagery within a parable, in which he set forth the need for his disciples to be prepared, and therefore wise, at the coming of the kingdom in its fullness, a time that is associated with judgment, exclusion of some, and feasting by those who are admitted.[45]

Exposition

No one knows the timing of the end, the coming of the Lord. For most persons, the encounter with him will be at death. But there is also the end of all things, the beginning of the new, with the coming of Christ. The NT pictures it both as soon and as distant. No one can know. It might be soon: so one should take care today and be ready. But it might be far: so do not grow weary in doing good. In any case, near or far, one must come to terms with living in the world, the place God has given for human habitation. For modern Christians, that includes care of the earth and making peace for the sake of future generations. It is imperative to plan for the long haul, remain faithful, and be wise and strong.

The Parable of the Ten Maidens is assigned regularly for reading late in the church year in lectionaries most commonly used in modern times; in the past it was even assigned for reading on the last Sunday of the church year. Within hymnody, however, this parable has been alluded to in a beautiful Swedish hymn for the Season of Advent, known in English as "Rejoice, Rejoice, Believers," by Laurentius Laurentii (1660-1722). The second stanza sets forth the entirely positive side of the parable's message, in which the believing community holds firm to the conviction that they are among the "wise" who are going to meet the groom:

---

45. With nuances, the view also of A. Jülicher, *Gleichnisreden,* 2:448; C. H. Dodd, *Parables,* 137; J. Jeremias, *Parables,* 175; R. Stein, *Parables,* 57; J. Lambrecht, *Treasure,* 209-11.

The watchers on the mountain
  Proclaim the bridegroom near;
Go forth as he approaches
  With alleluias clear.
The marriage feast is waiting;
  The gates wide open stand.
Arise, O heirs of glory;
  The bridegroom is at hand.[46]

From this it can be seen that the parable can strike the hearer in two ways. On the one hand, it provides a warning. Be wise and prepared for the long haul. On the other hand, what wondrous good news it is to know that the Bridegroom will come and gather in all those who are his.

Select Bibliography

Argyle, Aubrey W. "Wedding Customs at the Time of Jesus." *ExpTim* 86 (1974-75): 214-15.

Batey, Richard A. *New Testament Nuptial Imagery.* Leiden: E. J. Brill, 1971.

Blinzler, Josef. "Bereitschaft für das Kommen des Herrn! Mt 25,1-13." *BiLi* 37 (1963-64): 89-100.

Bornkamm, Günther. "Die Verzögerung des Parusie: Exegetische Bermerkungen zu zwei synoptischen Texten." In *In Memoriam Ernst Lohmeyer,* 116-26. Ed. Werner Schmauch. Stuttgart: Evangelisches Verlagswerk, 1951. Reprinted in his *Geschichte und Glaube,* 1:46-55. 2 vols. BEvT 48. Munich: Chr. Kaiser Verlag, 1968-71.

Büchler, Adolf. "The Introduction of the Bride and the Bridegroom into the הופה in the First and Second Centuries in Palestine." In *Livre d'hommage à la mémoire du Dr. Samuel Poznanski,* 82-132. Ed. Committee of the Grand Synagogue. Warsaw: Committee of the Grand Synagogue, 1927.

Burkitt, F. C. "The Parable of the Ten Virgins: Mt 25.1-13." *JTS* 30 (1929): 267-70.

Donfried, Karl P. "The Allegory of the Ten Virgins (Matt. 25:1-13) as a Summary of Matthean Theology." *JBL* 93 (1974): 415-28.

———. "The Ten Virgins (Mt. 25:1-13)." *TD* 2 (1975): 106-10.

Duff, Nancy J. "Wise and Foolish Maidens: Matthew 25:1-13." *USQR* 40/3 (1985): 55-58.

Feuillet, André. "Les éspousailles messianiques et les références au Cantique des cantiques dans les évangiles synoptiques." *RThom* 84 (1984): 399-424.

———. "La parabole des vierges." *VS* 75 (1946): 667-77.

---

46. Quoted from *Lutheran Book of Worship* (Minneapolis: Augsburg Publishing House, 1978), hymn 25.

Ford, J. Massingberd. "The Parable of the Foolish Scholars (Matt. xxv 1-13)." *NovT* 9 (1967): 107-23.

France, Richard T. "On Being Ready (Matthew 25:1-46)." In *The Challenge of Jesus' Parables*, 177-95. Ed. Richard N. Longenecker. Grand Rapids: Wm. B. Eerdmans, 2000.

Gerhardsson, Birger. "Mashalen om de tio bröllupstärnorna (Matt 25:1-13)." *SEÅ* 60 (1995): 83-94.

Goudge, Henry L. "The Parable of the Ten Virgins: Mt 25.1-13." *JTS* 30 (1929): 399-401.

Granqvist, Hilma. *Marriage Conditions in a Palestinian Village*, 2 vols. Helsingfors: Centraltryckeriet, 1931-35.

Jeremias, Joachim. "*Lampades* in Matthew 25:1-13." In *Soli Deo Gloria: New Testament Studies in Honor of William Childs Robinson*, 83-87. Ed. J. McDowell Richards. Richmond: John Knox Press, 1968.

Légasse, Simon. "La parabole des dix vierges (Mt 25,1-13): Essai de synthèse historico-critique." In *Les paraboles évangéliques: Perspectives nouvelles*, 349-60. LeDiv 135. Paris: Cerf, 1989.

Lövestam, Evald. "The Parable of the Ten Virgins." In *Spiritual Wakefulness in the New Testament*, 108-22. LUÅ 1.55.3. Lund: Gleerup, 1963.

Lohfink, Norbert. "Vom Täufer Johannes und den Törichten Jungfrauen: Das Evangelium und seine sozialen Konsequenzen." *BiKi* 50 (1995): 26-31.

Maisch, Ingrid. "Das Gleichnis von den klugen und törichten Jungfrauen." *BibLeb* 11 (1970): 247-59.

Puig i Tàrrech, Armand. *La parabole des dix vierges (Mt 25,1-13)*. AnBib 102. Rome: Biblical Institute Press, 1983.

Reid, James. "The Parable of the Ten Virgins." *ExpTim* 37 (1926): 447-51.

Rosenblatt, Marie-Eloise. "Got into the Party After All: Women's Issues and the Five Foolish Virgins." *Continuum* 3 (1994): 107-37.

Schrenk, Wolfgang. "Auferweckung der Toten oder Gericht nach den Werken: Tradition und Redaktion in Matthäus xxv 1-13." *NovT* 20 (1978): 278-99.

Schwarz, Günther. "Zum Vokabular von Matthäus XXV.1-12." *NTS* 27 (1981): 270-76.

Sherriff, J. M. "Matthew 25:1-13: A Summary of Matthean Eschatology?" *Studia Biblica 1978, II: Papers on the Gospels*, 301-5. Ed. Elizabeth A. Livingstone. JSNTSup 2. Sheffield: JSOT Press, 1980.

Staats, Reinhart. "Die törichten Jungfrauen von Mt 25 in gnostischer und antignostischer Literatur." In *Christentum und Gnosis*, 98-115. Ed. Walther Eltester. BZNW 37. Berlin: Alfred Töpelmann, 1969.

Strobel, August. "Das Gleichnis von den zehn Jungfrauen (Mt 25,1-13)." In *Untersuchungen zum eschatologischen Verzögerungsproblem auf Grund der spätjüdischurchristlichen Geschichte von Habakuk 2,2FF*, 233-54. NovTSup 2. Leiden: E. J. Brill, 1961.

—————. "Zum Verständnis von Mt 25,1-13." *NovT* 2 (1958): 199-227.

CHAPTER 5

Parables of Life before God

The essential message of a dozen parables within the Synoptic Gospels serves primarily to warn, encourage, or exhort the hearer. They appear in all three Gospels. At the level of those Gospels they are directed toward the life of the Christian *coram deo* ("in the presence of God").

When these parables are gathered into a collection, as in this chapter, the collection might well be called a parabolic miscellany, for the parables have to do with a wide range of themes or topics. Some function to exhort the disciples of Jesus (and therefore Christians in the time after the life of the earthly Jesus) to pray without giving up and earnestly, such as the Friend at Midnight, the Father's Good Gifts, and the Unjust Judge. Others emphasize the importance of carrying out one's duties prior to the coming of Christ again, such as the Sower, the Slave at Duty, and the Waiting Slaves. Still others emphasize the right use of what has been entrusted to the follower of Jesus, such as the Talents and the Pounds.

That Jesus spoke parables for hortatory and didactic purposes has been challenged by some interpreters in modern times. It is sometimes assumed or asserted that Jesus' parables took on such purposes only after they had been edited in the early church, particularly by the evangelists, to fulfill those very purposes.[1] But to assume or to assert that Jesus would not have taught in parables (for a didactic purpose) or preach in parables (for a hortatory purpose) is to take him out of the culture and religious tradition in which he had been raised. One must also say that Jesus had nothing to say about discipleship to his disciples. To be sure, not all that is attributed to Jesus of Nazareth must necessarily have been spoken by him. But there are several parables that speak of the disciple's life before God. They appear in all strands of the Synoptic tradition (Mark,

---

1. The most insistent example is in J. Jeremias, *Parables,* 33-66 *et passim.*

Q, M, and L). It seems most likely that the responsible life before God would be a common theme in the teaching and preaching of Jesus.[2]

5.16. The Sower and Its Interpretation, Mark 4:3-8, 13-20// Matthew 13:3-8, 18-23//Luke 8:5-8, 11-15; *Thomas* 9

Mark 4:3-9, 13-20

[Jesus said,] 3"Listen! A sower went out to sow. 4And as he sowed, one seed fell along the path, and the birds came and devoured it. 5Another seed fell on rocky ground, where it had not much soil, and immediately it sprang up, since it had no depth of soil; 6and when the sun rose it was scorched, and since it had no root it withered away. 7And another seed fell among thorns, and the thorns grew up and choked it, and it yielded no grain. 8And other seeds fell into good soil and brought forth grain, growing up, increasing, and yielding — one thirtyfold, one sixtyfold, and one a hundredfold."

9And he said, "Let the person having ears to hear hear." . . .

13And he said to them, "Do you not understand this parable? How then will you understand all the parables?

14"The sower sows the word. 15And these are the ones along the path, where the word is sown; and when they hear, Satan immediately comes and takes away the word which is sown in them.

16"And these are the ones sown upon rocky ground who, when they hear the word, immediately receive it with joy; 17and they have no root in themselves, but endure for a while; then when tribulation or persecution arises on account of the word, immediately they fall away. 18And others are the ones sown among thorns; they are those who have heard the word, 19but when the cares of the world, the delight in riches, and the desire for other things enter in, they choke the word, and it is unfruitful. 20But those that were sown upon the good soil are the ones who hear the word, accept it, and bear fruit — one thirtyfold, one sixtyfold, and one a hundredfold."

Notes on the Text and Translation

4:4. While modern English versions (KJV, RSV, NEB, NAB, NIV, and NRSV) all read "some," "some seed," or the like here, signifying plural, and continue with plurals in 4:5, 7, the text has singular terms (Greek demonstrative pronoun ὅ, "the one" [4:4] and the substantive ἄλλο, "another" [4:5, 7]). The plural form

---

2. Cf. the balanced and helpful discussion of the parables that is provided by Amos N. Wilder, *The Language of the Gospel: Early Christian Rhetoric* (New York: Harper & Row, 1964), 79-96.

ἄλλα ("others") is not used until 4:8. The singular ("one" and "another") ought to be maintained prior to 4:8.[1]

4:8, 20. The readings of the 26th and 27th editions of the Nestle-Aland Greek text (ἓν τριάκοντα καὶ ἓν ἑξήκοντα καὶ ἓν ἑκατόν, "one thirtyfold, one sixtyfold, and one a hundredfold") replaces its major competitor, which existed in the 25th edition and also in the Westcott-Hort text (εἰς τριάκοντα καὶ ἐν ἑξήκοντα καὶ ἐν ἑκατόν). In the latter reading three prepositions (εἰς . . . ἐν . . . ἐν) exist in place of the numerals (ἓν . . . ἓν . . . ἓν) and cannot be translated literally. Still other Greek readings are possible. By far most texts have some form of εν . . . εν . . . εν, to which markings can be added — the earliest uncials being unmarked — to get either the prepositions ἐν . . . ἐν . . . ἐν or the numerals ἓν . . . ἓν . . . ἓν. The reading adopted in the 26th and 27th editions has fairly good support, and it is the only one that makes good sense.[2]

Matthew 13:3-9, 18-23

3And [Jesus] told them many things in parables, saying: "A sower went out to sow. 4And as he sowed, some seeds fell along the path, and the birds came and devoured them. 5Other seeds fell on rocky ground, where they had not much soil, and immediately they sprang up, since they had no depth of soil, 6but when the sun rose they were scorched; and since they had no root they withered away. 7Other seeds fell upon thorns, and the thorns grew up and choked them. 8Other seeds fell on good soil and brought forth grain, some a hundredfold, some sixty, some thirty. 9Let the person having ears hear." . . .

18"Hear then the parable of the sower. 19When any one hears the word of the kingdom and does not understand it, the evil one comes and snatches away what is sown in his heart; this is what was sown along the path. 20As for what was sown on rocky ground, this is he who hears the word and immediately receives it with joy; 21yet he has no root in himself, but endures for a while, and when tribulation or persecution arises on account of the word, immediately he falls away. 22As for what was sown among thorns, this is he who hears the word, but the cares of the world and the delight in riches choke the word, and it proves unfruitful. 23As for what was sown on good soil, this is he who hears the word and understands it; he indeed bears fruit and yields, in one case a hundredfold, in another sixty, and in another thirty."

1. Cf. BAGD 585 (ὅς, II, 2); BDF 131 (#250); F. Hahn, "Gleichnis," 134-36; J. Marcus, *Mystery*, 42 (n. 98); R. Gundry, *Mark*, 192; J. Gnilka, *Markus*, 1:156; Robert A. Guelich, *Mark 1-8:26*, WBC 34A (Dallas: Word Books, 1989), 187-88. There is no basis, contra V. Taylor, *Mark*, 252, for translating ὅ as "a part," nor "this portion of seed," as in Robert G. Bratcher and Eugene A. Nida, *A Translator's Handbook on the Gospel of Mark*, HeTr 2 (Leiden: E. J. Brill, 1961), 129.

2. For more discussion, cf. V. Taylor, *Mark*, 254; B. Metzger, *TCGNT* 83.

Luke 8:5-8, 11-15

[Jesus said,] 5*"A sower went out to sow his seed; and as he sowed, some fell along the path, and was trodden under foot, and the birds of the air devoured it. 6And some fell on the rock; and as it grew up, it withered away, because it had no moisture. 7And some fell among thorns; and the thorns grew with it and choked it. 8And some fell into good soil and grew, and yielded a hundredfold." As he said this, he called out,* 9*"Let the person having ears to hear hear." . . .*

11*"Now the parable is this: The seed is the word of God.* 12*The ones along the path are those who have heard; then the devil comes and takes away the word from their hearts, that they may not believe and be saved.* 13*And the ones on the rock are those who, when they hear the word, receive it with joy; but these have no root, they believe for a while and in a time of testing fall away.* 14*And as for what fell among the thorns, they are those who hear, but as they go on their way they are choked by the cares and riches and pleasures of life, and their fruit does not mature.* 15*And as for that in the good soil, they are those who, hearing the word, hold it fast in a noble and good heart, and bring forth fruit with patient endurance."*

Thomas 9

Jesus said, "Now the sower went out, took a handful (of seeds), and scattered them. Some fell on rock, did not take root in the soil, and did not produce ears. And others fell on thorns; they choked the seed(s) and worms ate them. And others fell on the good soil and it produced good fruit: it bore sixty per measure and a hundred and twenty per measure."[3]

General Comments on the Texts

The parable appears in all three Synoptic Gospels and in the Coptic *Gospel of Thomas*. Other than items mentioned in the Notes above (all related to the Gospel of Mark) and one very minor translation item at Luke 8:5 (taken up below), there are no serious textual and translation matters that need further comment.

On the basis of verbal similarities, it can be concluded that Matthew's version is based on Mark's, but it has been revised significantly. Luke's version, shorter than the other two, appears to be based on Mark's as well.[4] Although there are some differences (primarily the addition of "trodden under foot" [8:5] and the substitution of "because it lacked moisture" for lack of soil [8:6]), these are not significant enough to claim a different, or additional, source other

3. Quoted from *NHLE* 127.
4. Cf. I. H. Marshall, *Luke,* 317-18; J. Fitzmyer, *Luke,* 700. The possibility that Luke's version is based on an independent tradition is entertained in R. Funk, *Five Gospels,* 54, 305. B. Scott, *Parable,* 350, suggests that Luke's version may be dependent on both Mark and an independent tradition.

Table 1
Comparative Chart: The Parable of the Sower
Mark 4:3-9//Matthew 13:3-9//Luke 8:4-8//*Gospel of Thomas* 9

Bold font indicates features distinctive to a particular Synoptic version.
Italic font indicates features distinctive to the Thomas version.

	Destination of First Seed(s)	Destination of Second Seed(s)	Destination of Third Seed(s)	Destination of Fourth Seed(s)	Yield of Grain
Mark	One seed along the path; birds devoured it.	**One** seed on the rocky ground; lacked depth of soil, sprang up, withered away.	**One seed** in the thorns; it was choked by thorns.	Other seeds in good soil; they brought forth grain, **growing up, increasing, and bearing**.	**30** fold, 60 fold, **100** fold.
Matthew	**Some seeds** along the path; birds devoured them.	**Other seeds** on the rocky ground; lacked depth of soil, sprang up, withered away.	**Other seeds** in the thorns; they were choked by thorns.	Other seeds in good soil; they brought forth grain.	**100** fold, 60 fold, **30** fold.
Luke	One seed along the path; it was **trodden under foot**, and birds devoured it.	**Another** on **the rock**; it withered away **because it lacked moisture.**	**Another** in the thorns; it was choked by thorns.	**Another** in good soil; it grew and produced fruit.	**100** fold.
Thomas	[None comparable is mentioned.]	*Some* on rock; *did not take root and did not produce ears.*	*Others* in thorns; they choked the seeds *and worms ate them.*	*Others* in good soil; it produced good fruit.	*60 per measure and* 120 per measure.

than the Gospel of Mark. The differences among the four versions of the parable can be seen in Table 1, and they are discussed below.

Whether the *Gospel of Thomas* 9 is derived from a tradition independent of the Synoptic versions is possible, even likely. To be sure, there are some similarities between the parable in the Coptic version of the *Gospel of Thomas* and the parable in the Coptic (Sahidic) version of Mark's Gospel that provide grounds for claiming dependence.[5] Nevertheless, the differences between the *Thomas* version

5. Wolfgang Schrage, *Das Verhältnis des Thomas-Evangeliums zur synoptischen Tradition und zu den koptischen Evangelienübersetzungen: Zugleich ein Beitrag zur gnostischen Synoptikerdeutung*, BZNW 29 (Berlin: Alfred Töpelmann, 1964), 45-47; Craig L. Blomberg, "Tradition and Redaction in the Parables of the Gospel of Thomas," in *The Jesus Tradition outside the Gospels*, ed. David Wenham (Sheffield: JSOT Press, 1985), 184-86; Christopher Tuckett, "Thomas and the Synoptics," *NovT* 30 (1988): 153-56.

and the Synoptic versions are so many that interpreters have generally attributed the origins of the *Thomas* version to an independent tradition.[6] Insofar as that is the case, the Thomas version provides additional witness to the great age of the parable. It goes without saying, however, that it also provides witness to a gnosticized version. The seed symbolizes the light, or enlightenment, which is strewn about, but which is not received by ordinary persons. The good soil represents the Gnostic, who alone can bring forth good fruit.[7]

The parable receives an interpretation in the three Synoptic Gospels (Mark 4:13-20//Matt 13:18-23//Luke 8:11-15), but not in the *Gospel of Thomas.* The differences among the three versions are illustrated in Table 2 (p. 186) and are discussed below.

Even a quick review of differences among texts highlighted in the two tables shows an immediate problem in interpreting the parable. Setting the *Thomas* version aside, there are six texts to deal with (three versions of the parable, and three versions of its interpretation), and it is difficult to follow the symbolic significance of the seeds. (Actually the word "seed" does not appear within Mark's and Matthew's versions in either the parable or its interpretation, even though its presence is implied. It does appear in Luke's and Thomas's versions, however.) Do the seeds represent the word of God, or do they symbolize people, for example? (Sometimes they can symbolize both in the same piece of literature, e.g., at 2 Esdr 8:41 [seed = people] and 9:31 [seed = the law].) What is the significance of the singular and plural? In hortatory contexts (within the three Synoptic interpretations) is the seed or the soil exemplary? All these questions have to be dealt with case by case, text by text.

The imagery of the parable is familiar in Jewish culture, as illustrated in a passage from *2 Esdras,* usually regarded as coming from the first century A.D.:

> For just as the farmer sows many seeds in the ground and plants a multitude of seedlings, and yet not all that have been sown will come up in due season, and not all that were planted will take root; so also those who have been sown in the world will not all be saved. (2 Esdr 8:41)

Here the picture of a farmer sowing seeds, the failure of many seeds to take root and grow, but the growth nevertheless of some is identical to what one finds in the parable. The accent on only a few being saved, however, is not in the parable. On the other hand, another passage speaks of the great abundance that can come from sowing:

6. J. Crossan, "Seed Parables," 24-51; idem, *Parables,* 39; Jacques-É. Ménard, *L'Évangile selon Thomas,* NHS 5 (Leiden: E. J. Brill, 1975), 91; J. Horman, "The Source," 326-43; B. Scott, *Parable,* 350; Michael Fieger, *Das Thomasevangelium: Einleitung Kommentar Systematik,* NTAbh 22 (Münster: Aschendorff, 1991), 53; Stephen J. Patterson, *The Gospel of Thomas and Jesus* (Sonoma, Calif.: Polebridge Press, 1992), 22-23; R. Funk, *Five Gospels,* 54, 478.

7. M. Fieger, *Thomasevangelium,* 54.

Table 2
Comparative Chart: The Interpretation of the Parable of the Sower
Mark 4:13-20//Matthew 13:18-23//Luke 8:11-15

	Comparison #1	Comparison #2	Comparison #3	Comparison #4
Mark	Some people are like terrain along a path where seeds are stolen by birds; they are robbed of the word by Satan.	Some people are like plants on rocky ground that lack roots; they fall away during tribulation or persecution.	Some people are like a field with thorns in it; they are lovers of the world, and cares, delights, and desires choke the word, and it is unfruitful.	Some people are like good soil; they hear the word, accept it, and bear fruit.
	Analogy: people and terrain.	*Analogy:* people and plants.	*Analogy:* people and a field.	*Analogy:* people and good soil.
Matthew	One type of person is like a seed sown along a path, stolen by a bird; that one does not understand the word and is a victim of the evil one.	Another type of person is like a seed sown on rocky ground; that one hears the word, receives it with joy, but falls away due to tribulation or persecution.	Another type of person is like a seed sown in thorns; that one hears the word, but cares and delights choke it, and it is unfruitful.	Another type of person is like a seed sown in good soil; that one hears the word, understands it, and bears fruit.
	Analogy: a [type of] person and a seed.	*Analogy:* a [type of] person and a seed.	*Analogy:* a [type of] person and a seed.	*Analogy:* a [type of] person and a seed.
Luke	Some persons are like terrain along a path where seeds are stolen by birds; they are robbed of the word by the devil.	Some persons are like plants on a rock that lack roots; they fall away during testing.	Some people are like a seed sown among thorns; they hear the word but are choked by cares, riches, and pleasures of life.	Some people are like a seed sown in good soil; they hear and hold fast the word and bear fruit.
	Analogy: people and terrain.	*Analogy:* people and plants.	*Analogy:* people and a seed.	*Analogy:* people and a seed.

For a grain of evil seed was sown in Adam's heart from the beginning, and how much ungodliness it has produced until now — and will produce until the time of threshing comes! . . . When heads of grain without number are sown, how great a threshing floor they will fill! (2 Esdr 4:30-32)

The abundance appears particularly at the harvest.

The point is made by Joachim Jeremias that the parable contains remarkable realism. He claims that an important detail can be seen against the background of ancient Palestinian life where sowing preceded plowing. The sower in the parable, according to Jeremias, sows "on the path" (which he regards as the correct translation, rather than "along the path"), upon rocky soil, and among the thorns, because he will plow it all up when he is done.[8] The viewpoint of Jeremias is often repeated. What it yields is the conclusion that the sower is portrayed not as a wasteful person, but as a man who follows an ancient custom.

There are problems with that view, however. If one were to follow Jeremias's line of thinking, the conclusion would be that once the plowing is done, there should be an abundant harvest indeed — not just from the seeds that fell on the good soil, but also from all that fell in other places, since all the land would be turned over by the plow. But that is precisely what does not happen. The seeds get eaten by birds, scorched, and choked. Perhaps the imagery presupposed is that of sowing prior to plowing.[9] But it is going too far to say that the imagery implies that some seeds are deliberately sown "on the path" and in the other places in order to be plowed under later. Second, the translation of παρὰ τὴν ὁδόν as "on the path" instead of as "along the path" is forced, and it should be rejected.[10]

In all versions of the parable the yield from the seeds falling into good soil is abundant.[11] The critical question is whether the yield (using any of the figures) is overwhelming or typical. Several interpreters have stressed that the yield is indeed marvelous, thereby symbolizing the fullness of divine blessing eschatologically.[12] Other interpreters have maintained that the yield, while abundant, is rather typical.[13]

8. J. Jeremias, *Parables,* 11-12; cf. also V. Taylor, *Mark,* 252. Matthew Black, *An Aramaic Approach to the Gospels and Acts,* 3d ed. (Oxford: Clarendon Press, 1967), 162, indicates that an Aramaic retroversion of the Greek phrase would be ambiguous; it could mean either on or alongside the path.

9. That is the sequence in *Jub.* 11:11, where crows eat seeds prior to the plowing under of the seeds; text in *OTP* 2:78. The sequence may be presupposed at *m. Shab.* 7:2, but the evidence is exceedingly slim. The sequence is challenged by K. D. White, "Parable of the Sower," 300-307; and according to P. Payne, "Order of Sowing," 123-29, neither Jeremias nor White can be confident that he is right. At Isa 28:24; Jer 4:3 it appears that plowing normally preceded sowing.

10. BAGD 553-54 (ὁδός, 1, a, with additional references to Matt 20:30; Mark 10:46; Luke 18:35) favors "along the road." On the other hand, BAGD 611 (παρά, III, 1, d) allows for "on the road" as well. For other items that speak against the translation "on the road," cf. J. Crossan, "Seed Parables," 245 (n. 3).

11. In the Synoptic accounts it is the seeds in the good soil that yield such; in the *Gospel of Thomas* 9 it is the field that does so.

12. J. Jeremias, *Parables,* 150; V. Taylor, *Mark,* 251, 257; N. Dahl, "Parables of Growth," 160-62; E. Schweizer, *Mark,* 90-91; J. Donahue, *Parables,* 34; A. Wilder, "Telling from Depth to Depth," 93.

13. E. Linnemann, *Parables,* 181 (n. 13); K. White, "Parable of the Sower," 300-307; B. Scott, *Parable,* 357-58; R. Guelich, *Mark,* 195.

According to Gustav Dalman, a hundredfold yield is possible within the Jordan Valley, and therefore Jesus remains within the realm of the possible in the parable.[14] But his figures, adopted by others, have been severely challenged. It has been argued that even a thirtyfold yield would have been considered miraculous in ancient Palestine.[15] In any event, such computations are beside the point. It is doubtful whether anyone, including Jesus or his original hearers, would have sat down and counted how many seeds are produced in an ear of grain (e.g., wheat) from one seed any more than the hearer or reader does today. The sheer piling up by the "rule of three" in the parable — 30, 60, 100 (Mark 4:8) or 100, 60, 30 (Matt 13:8) — and reaching a veritable crescendo in Mark's account, or even the straightforward "hundredfold" in Luke (8:8a), signifies an extraordinary, magnificent abundance. Furthermore, the imagery is related to the story of Isaac, who sowed and reaped a hundredfold (Gen 26:12), which is taken to be a sign of blessing and wealth.

The essential meaning of the story — leaving the canonical interpretations aside for the time being — must be found in the huge contrast between the indiscriminate, so often useless-in-effect, sowing of the sower, on the one hand, and the abundant yield of the few seeds on the other. But even if that is agreed upon, there remain various possible meanings.[16] Two commend themselves in particular: (1) the parable is linked to the ministry of Jesus and his disciples, and it provides encouragement to the disciples for sowing (= proclamation) in spite of obvious rejection of the message;[17] or (2) it anticipates the coming of the kingdom of God in spite of small beginnings.[18]

The problem with the latter is that the term "kingdom of God" is nowhere to be found in the parable (nor in its interpretation). Yet, since the kingdom was indeed at the heart of Jesus' proclamation, and because the harvest was a common figure for the arrival of the kingdom in its fullness, the parable cannot be detached from Jesus' proclamation of the kingdom. That means that an either/or is not necessary. The parable can be understood within the historical ministry of Jesus to have been a word of encouragement in proclaiming the kingdom. In spite of the proclamation's seeming failure, illustrated by the "rule of three" (the pathway, the rocky ground, and the thorns), there will be an abundant harvest in due course. The present is not therefore a time to be fainthearted. The ministry of proclamation must go on.

---

14. Gustaf Dalman, *Arbeit und Sitte in Palästina,* 7 vols. (Gütersloh: Verlag C. Bertelsmann et al., 1928-41), 3:153, 163, respectively.

15. R. McIver, "One Hundred-Fold Yield," 606-8.

16. Four are listed by V. Taylor, *Mark,* 250-51; four (different ones) are listed by W. D. Davies and D. C. Allison, *Matthew,* 2:375-76; six are discussed by E. Linnemann, *Parables,* 181-84 (n. 15).

17. W. Oesterley, *Parables,* 39-41; B. Smith, *Parables,* 126; J. Jeremias, *Parables,* 150-51; J. Gnilka, *Markus,* 1:161.

18. N. Dahl, "Parables of Growth," 160-62; N. Perrin, *Teaching,* 156.

Regarding the question whether the parable can be attributed to the historical Jesus, there is widespread agreement that it can.[19] One reason for the claim is its abundance of Semitisms,[20] which does not in itself establish authenticity, but it does indicate an early origin.

Regarding the interpretation (Mark 13-20//Matt 13:18-23//Luke 8:11-15), which is lacking in the *Gospel of Thomas,* interpreters have been divided over the question whether it is an early Christian composition or whether it originated with Jesus. The view that the interpretation is not integral and that it is an early Christian composition is based on three main points: (1) while the parable is replete with translation Greek from Aramaic in Mark's Gospel, the interpretation is in common Greek; (2) the interpretation contains imagery and themes already in Mark's version that express Christian concerns (such as sowing the seed as sowing the word,[21] persecution as occurring on account of the word, and falling away from faith after once hearing the word [= the gospel] with joy[22]), to which further expansions are added in the other two Gospels (illustrated below); and (3) while the parable encourages proclamation of the word in spite of obstacles, the interpretation takes up and presses the question of the readiness of the recipients to hear the word and let it transform them.

The last point is the most difficult for the view that the interpretation originated at the same time as the parable. If the interpretation is not integral to the parable, that speaks in favor of its being from a later stratum of tradition. Several interpreters have argued that the parable and its interpretation are indeed integral, and that that would have been so from their point of origin, whether from Jesus or the early church.[23] Some have maintained that the inter-

19. M. Black, *Aramaic Approach,* 63; V. Taylor, *Mark,* 250; C. E. B. Cranfield, "St. Mark 4.1-34," 405-12; N. Perrin, *Teaching,* 156; P. Payne, "Authenticity," 1:162-207; Hans-Josef Klauck, *Allegorie und Allegorese in synoptischen Gleichnistexten,* NTAbh 13 (Münster: Aschendorff, 1978) 186-98, 206; J. Lambrecht, *Astonished,* 102; H. Weder, *Gleichnisse,* 108-11. If *Gospel of Thomas* 9 can be considered dependent on a tradition independent of the canonical Gospels, it provides evidence of an early tradition. For J. Crossan, "Seed Parables," 246, the pre-Markan parable consisted of 4:3-5a, 6a, 7-8a. In R. Funk, *Five Gospels,* 54, 478 (Mark and Thomas versions, respectively), the parable is printed in pink (= Jesus said something like this), and the *Thomas* version is considered closer to the original.

20. Cf. Matthew Black, *Aramaic Approach,* 63; V. Taylor, *Mark,* 250; P. Payne, "Seeming Inconsistency," 564-68.

21. N. T. Wright, *Jesus and the Victory of God* (Minneapolis: Fortress Press, 1996), 232-33, refers to Isa 55:10-11 as an illustration of sowing seed as a metaphor (in parallelism) for proclamation of the word. But the parallel is actually between rain and snow from heaven and the word (of God) from God.

22. The verb is σκανδαλίζω, which is used frequently to refer to a person's falling away from faith, going astray to his or her ruin. The reference here is to persons who have already accepted the gospel with joy, but go astray in light of persecution. Cf. Gustav Stählin, "σκάνδαλον," *TDNT* 7:349.

23. B. Gerhardsson, "Parable of the Sower," 187; C. F. D. Moule, "Mark 4:1-20," 111;

pretation can essentially be attributed to Jesus himself.[24] But when the three points against authenticity mentioned are taken together, it is likely that the interpretation is an early Christian composition.[25]

The Parable in the Gospel of Mark

Exegetical Commentary

The parable is located relatively early in Mark's Gospel. It is situated in the Galilean ministry of Jesus, and it is spoken to a large crowd beside the Sea of Galilee (4:1-2).

The parable shows a contrast regarding what happens when (1) most seeds scattered about do not produce; they are devoured, withered, or choked (4:4-7); but (2) some do produce abundantly (4:8). Table 1 shows what is distinctive in Mark's version of the parable.

4:3. This is the only parable that is introduced by the imperative, "Listen" (not in parallels, Matt 13:3//Luke 8:5). Others may be introduced by other devices, such as "Who among you?" or the like. The direct form of speech is characteristic of Jesus' parables (see chapter 1, "The Parables of Jesus: An Introduction"). Its closest biblical analogue would be commands to hear in the OT and other sources (Deut 6:4; Judg 9:7; Isa 28:23; Ezek 20:47; 2 Esdr 9:30; 1 Enoch 37:1).[26]

The "sower," though essential for the story, is nondescript. He comes on the scene to do his sowing, but then the attention shifts to the seeds sown and the outcome of their conditions.

4:4-7. As indicated above in the Notes, single seeds are mentioned in Mark's version of the parable in these verses. One falls here, one there, and so on. As the interpretation will make clear, the seed is the word of God (4:14). It falls here and there, and it gets different responses. The various seeds that are scattered clearly are not persons in Mark's account (but they become such in Matthew's interpretation).

D. Wenham, "The Interpretation," 305; M. Boucher, *Mysterious Parable*, 49-53; P. Payne, "Authenticity," 1:162-207; idem, "Seeming Inconsistency," 564-68; M. Knowles, "Abram and the Birds," 149; N. T. Wright, *Jesus*, 238-39.

24. A. McNeile, *Matthew*, 195-96; C. F. D. Moule, "Mark 4:1-20," 113; R. Brown, "Parable and Allegory Reconsidered," 326-33; N. T. Wright, *Jesus*, 230-39.

25. Those maintaining that the interpretation is a Christian composition include A. Jülicher, *Gleichnisreden*, 2:524, 532-33; C. H. Dodd, *Parables*, 145; A. Cadoux, *Parables*, 20-24; B. Smith, *Parables*, 125, 128; V. Taylor, *Mark*, 258-62; J. Jeremias, *Parables*, 77-79; E. Linnemann, *Parables*, 117-19; J. Crossan, "Seed Parables," 247-51; idem, *Parables*, 41-42; E. Schweizer, *Mark*, 96-98; J. Fitzmyer, *Luke*, 711; F. Borsch, "Waste and Grace," 202; H.-J. Klauck, *Allegorie*, 204-6; J. Lambrecht, *Astonished*, 97; H. Weder, *Gleichnisse*, 111-14; J. Gnilka, *Markus*, 1:161; R. Guelich, *Mark*, 218.

26. M. Boucher, *Mysterious Parable*, 45.

4:4. The picture is that of a seed falling alongside a footpath — not upon it (see discussion above).

4:5-6. The fate of another seed being cast is to land on τὸ πετρῶδης ("rocky ground," Mark 4:5//Matt 4:5). The expression probably does not mean that a seed or seeds (Matthew's version) fell upon ground with rocks in it, but refers to rocky ground over which a thin layer of soil is spread ("where it did not have much soil," Mark 4:5).[27] The problem with the seed is that, once it began to germinate, it could not grow into a plant since it could not develop roots. The figure is surely metaphorical, and it is traditional: "The children of the ungodly put out few branches; they are unhealthy roots on sheer rock" (Sir 40:15).

4:7. Before sowing, one should clear the land of thorns (Jer 4:3), or it will be unproductive. But a seed falls there too.

4:8. Some seeds — now the plural is used — fall upon the good soil. They are highly productive. There is a crescendo: one seed produces thirtyfold, one sixtyfold, and one a hundredfold. It is not the case that three kinds of persons are meant, each one producing at different levels. The reality being referred to is the outcome of the word when it falls on good soil; it produces abundantly. The focus is still on the sowing and its results, not on the seed or the soil.

4:9. All three versions of the parable conclude with the saying (slight variations) that the person with ears ought to listen (Mark 4:9//Matt 13:9//Luke 8:8b). The admonition — but not the exact wording — comes from Ezekiel 3:27, where the prophet speaks on behalf of God to the rebellious people: "Let whoever hears hear [LXX, ὁ ἀκούων ἀκουέτω], and let whoever refuses to hear, refuse; for they are a rebellious house." This is the only place where the three have the statement in common. But it appears five times in the Synoptic Gospels elsewhere (Mark 4:23; 8:18; Matt 11:15; 13:43; Luke 14:35). The saying can probably be attributed to Jesus, but it became a free-floating saying that was attached to various teachings within the transmission of the Gospel tradition. Whether it was attached by Jesus to the parable, or was attached subsequently, the saying does not actually belong to the parable itself.

The meaning of the parable within the Gospel of Mark runs as follows. Jesus, God's envoy, proclaims the word. Unfortunately, as history has shown, his message was and has been unfruitful in many cases, but it also produces an abundance. This is encouragement for the church. The church is to be faithful in proclamation of the word. In spite of how ineffectual the word is in so many cases, it does produce in surprising, abundant ways.

4:10-12. For comment on these intervening verses, see Appendix 1, "The Purpose of the Parables according to the Evangelists."

4:13-20. The interpretation is allegorical, providing a meaning for several items in the parable. Two things are immediately apparent. First, there is a switch to the use of plurals all the way through; now it is batches of seeds that

---

27. BAGD 655.

have been thrown into the various places mentioned in the parable, not just individual seeds. A second point that is apparent is that there is a lack of precision. Comparisons are made between what happens to seeds and what happens to persons, to be sure. But the comparisons are not equivalencies. They are exceedingly loose. That makes the correlation between the parable and its interpretation difficult. The comparisons are followed in the discussion that ensues, and they are illustrated in shorthand in Table 2.

While the perspective of the parable was focused on the sowing of the seeds and the outcome of it all, the perspective of the interpretation is radically different. Now the imagery is recast, and another angle of vision is employed. The perspective is from the receiving end of the process, and what transpires in the interpretation is an analysis of the circumstances that caused the seeds to fail or to produce.

The syntax of the sentences lacks clarity. For example, 4:15 begins, "these are the ones along the path." Who are the "these" that are intended? The verse goes on to speak of persons who hear the word, but Satan takes it from them. Circumlocutions are necessary for each comparison made, verse-by-verse:

4:15. There are persons who hear the word, but Satan robs them of it. They are like the terrain along a path where a seed falls, but a bird grabs it before it is productive. Here the analogy is between persons and a type of soil.

4:16-17. There are persons who hear the word, and rejoice in it, but they fall away under persecution. They are like seeds that fall on rocky ground, but they lack roots and therefore cannot endure. Here the analogy is between persons and plants that cannot grow for lack of roots.[28] The reference to persecution is an indicator that the interpretation is from the post-Easter church.

4:18-19. There are persons who hear the word, but they are so in love with the world that the word is overwhelmed, and they are unproductive. They are like a field that contains thorns, into which a seed is sown, but it gets choked by the thorns and is unproductive. Here the comparison is between persons and a field that cannot provide a place for a seed to grow because of the thorns.

4:20. There are persons who hear the word, accept it, and bear fruit. They are like a field of good soil, which produces abundantly. Here the comparison is between persons and good soil.

As can be seen, the use of metaphors is inconsistent. Analogies are made between people and the terrain, plants, a thorn-infested field, and good soil. By use of all the various pictures in the interpretation, the evangelist places a challenge before his readers and community. Readers are challenged to consider whether they are receptive (hear the word) and bear fruit or not. The sad fact is that many persons have opportunities for discipleship cut short by the assaults

---

28. Here is where the thesis put forth by P. Payne, "Seeming Inconsistency," 564-68, breaks down, that is, that the participle σπειρόμενοι consistently means soil sown with seeds in Mark 4:16, 18, 20.

of Satan, from weakness during persecution, or from love of the world. On the other hand, where the word is heard and accepted, there is a response that is comparable to an abundant yield of fruit. Therein lies a challenge to hear the word, accept it, and thus bear fruit that befits a true disciple.

Exposition

The interpreter has various possibilities for exposition. One might seek to interpret what he or she discerns to have been the message of Jesus when he spoke the parable in his time and place. That is a somewhat tricky task beset with a level of speculation. The other possibilities are to deal with Mark's parable alone or to deal with Mark's parable and interpretation.

If one sticks to the parable alone, the message is primarily one of encouragement. By the time the reader has reached this portion of the gospel, Jesus has called his disciples, has launched his public ministry, and has already met opposition. So he teaches the parable before the crowds gathered and sets forth a prognosis of the proclamation of the word of God. There is both abject failure and surprising fruition in store. But one does not allow failures to rule the day. The mission of proclamation will, in the end, bring about an abundant yield. God will bring about an ending that is beyond human calculation. That message is needed for the church of every generation.

The interpreter who includes the interpretation within the scope of exposition will go beyond the emphasis on the course of the word of God in the world to make a theological analysis of its recipients. Here the four comparisons become the tool (see Table 2). The accent will now be upon people as recipients of the word and what happens to them. Those are unfortunate who are victimized by Satan, who have no spiritual roots (or foundations), and who are enamored of the world and its empty promises. How fortunate, however, are those hear the word, accept it, and bear fruit.

The Parable in the Gospel of Matthew

Exegetical Commentary

Matthew gives a name to the parable. For him, as for most persons ever since, it is "the parable of the sower" (13:18). He gives a name to a parable at one other place in his Gospel, and that is "the parable of the weeds of the field" (13:36). The process of giving names to the parables of Jesus began therefore in the first century. The parable appears as the first of seven in the Parable Discourse of Matthew's Gospel (13:1-50).

Matthew has integrated the parable (13:3-9) and the interpretation (13:18-23) thoroughly. As will be seen below, and can also be seen in Table 2, the allegorical interpretation makes clear connections between particular seeds and categories of persons. It appears that the evangelist may have been as frustrated as any subsequent reader in trying to align elements in Mark's interpretation with the parable. Matthew has gone on to make clearer connections between the two sections.

While Mark has individual seeds being cast into various places, Matthew has them as plurals in 13:4-8a. However, it is clear that his allegorical interests have taken over by the time he writes 13:8b. There he switches over to "one" (Greek ὅ), meaning one seed (contra the RSV and the NRSV, which read "some"). The idea is that one produces "a hundredfold, one sixtyfold, and one thirtyfold." No doubt he has individual persons in mind.[29]

13:5. Regarding "rocky ground," see the comment on Mark 4:5.

13:8. The figures are reversed in comparison to Mark's version. Now they read in the descending order of 100, 60, and 30. Although interpreters have offered suggestions why the figures have been reversed, there seems to be no clear reason. One suggestion, which does not seem plausible, is that a Hebrew acrostic is involved.[30] More plausible is the view, shared by several, that Matthew sought to shift the focus of attention away from the ascending order to a variegated outcome. His major concern is to indicate that there are various degrees of fruit-bearing among hearers of the word, and that can be done better by avoiding the climactic structure.[31] Along with rearranging the sequence of numbers, Matthew omits Mark's verbs about the seed's growing up and increasing.

13:9. For comment on this verse, see comment on Mark 4:9.

13:10-17. For comment on the intervening material, see Appendix 1, "The Purpose of the Parables according to the Evangelists."

13:18-23. Matthew does not begin the interpretation (13:18-23) as Mark does (who has, "The sower sows the seed," 4:14) but begins with the words, "When anyone hears the word . . . and does not understand" (13:19). More dramatically than in Mark's version, the attention shifts away from the *sower sowing the seed* (Mark) to *the recipient* of the proclamation (the one who hears but does not "understand"); that person is "the one sown along the path."

In Matthew's version of the interpretation, there is a remarkable consistency. All four parts of the interpretation contain exact equivalencies, in which each seed (singular) is identified as a particular type of person. For Matthew, the seeds are various categories of people. Each produces to a different degree — or fails to do so. See Table 2 for the comparisons being made.

29. A. McNeile, *Matthew,* 188-89; J. Kingsbury, *Matthew 13,* 53; E. Schweizer, *Matthew,* 301.

30. J. Bernardi, "'Cent, soixante et Trente,'" 398-402.

31. A. McNeile, *Matthew,* 188-89; C. Carlston, *Parables,* 25; Margaret Pamment, "The Kingdom of Heaven according to the First Gospel," *NTS* 27 (1981): 218; J. Gnilka, *Matthäus,* 1:478.

13:19. A person who hears the word of the kingdom but does not *under-stand* it is bereft of the word, for the "evil one" snatches it away. That person is like a seed sown by the pathway, which a bird will devour. The verb συνίημι ("to understand") appears nine times in Matthew's Gospel (twice in quotations from Isaiah, viz., 13:14, 15), including six times in chapter 13 alone (13:13, 14, 15, 19, 23, 51; 15:10; 16:12; 17:13). The disciples of Jesus are asked whether they understand the seven parables of Matthew 13 (13:51), to which they say yes. Jesus told his parables for the sake of understanding (13:13). Twice more it is said that the disciples understood Jesus' teaching (16:12; 17:13). A disciple ("one who is taught") is one who does not simply listen but understands the teachings of Jesus (takes them to heart). The term can also be translated "to grasp" or "to comprehend."[32] The lack of understanding is the basis for allowing "the evil one" opportunity to take away what has been sown, a feature that is distinctive to Matthew's version.[33]

The use of ὁ πονηρός ("the evil one") for Satan (Mark 4:15) or the devil (Luke 8:12) is distinctive of Matthew (cf. 5:37; 6:13; 13:38).

13:20-21. A person who has no root falls away during trouble. The analogy is that of a seed that is sown on rocky ground.

13:22. A person who is overcome by cares of the world and the delight in riches is unfruitful. That type of person is comparable to a seed falling among the thorns in a field.

13:23. A person who hears and *understands* the word bears fruit. This type of person is comparable to a seed that fell into good soil. The result is that the teaching of Jesus becomes a matter of the heart (13:19), and the person transformed by his teaching seeks to do the will of God (15:18-19). But not every person is alike. There are even varying degrees of fruit-bearing, as the threefold use of the demonstrative pronoun indicates. One produces to this extent, another to that, and so on.

There is now a consistency between the parable and its interpretation. To be sure, there is a difference in emphasis: whereas in the parable the emphasis is upon sowing the seed, in the interpretation the focus of interest is upon the persons who hear the word. But there is a connection. As seeds sown differ in their fate, so, too, do persons in the church who hear the word. Some lack "understanding" or are victimized by external or internal problems. They are unproductive. But those who hear and "understand" bear fruit. For the evangelist Matthew, his Gospel, and his community, the interpretation exhorts persons in the church to be careful lest they be like the unfortunate seeds. The kind of seed that one ought to be is spelled out in 13:23: Hear the word and gain understanding of it; then you will bear fruit, that is, you will be a true disciple.

32. Horst Balz, "συνίημι," *EDNT* 3:307-8.
33. R. Gundry, *Matthew*, 259.

Exposition

What was said in the Exposition concerning Mark's version of the parable and its interpretation has a bearing here. The interpreter using Matthew's text will most likely find the task of following the argument easier. The transition from the parable to its interpretation works more smoothly. While it is likely that the original parable was about proclaiming the word, that the imagery of casting the seed had to do with proclamation, and that the seeds corresponded to the word, the imagery has now been transformed in such a way that the focus is upon people and their reaction to the preaching and teaching of the word.

The distinctions made among persons are that there are some who do not understand, some who are weak in faith, some who are worldly (for lack of a better term), and some who hear God's word, understand it, and bear fruit. Persons of those types must have been evident within the community of Matthew the evangelist. (The fact that Matthew speaks of them one by one makes the types even more evident.) The types are actually perennial. The fourth type is what all Christians should be. It is not enough simply to hear the Christian message. It is imperative to "understand" it in the sense of grasping hold of it, considering it in depth, pondering it, and embedding it into one's very being by living it out. It is not a matter of understanding all the mysteries of the faith (the Trinity, etc.), but of contemplating what it means to be a disciple of Jesus — what he teaches, asks, points toward for one's daily life. That is what leads to true discipleship and life in its most fulfilling sense.

The Parable in the Gospel of Luke

Exegetical Commentary

The evangelist Luke reduces the length of the parable and its interpretation drastically, even though he adds some touches to it. The parable proper (8:5-9) consists of some 30 words fewer in Luke's version compared to Mark's (68 words verses 98 words, respectively, in Greek; about 70 percent the length of Mark's). The parable is placed within the larger framework of Jesus' ministry conducted primarily in Galilee (4:14–9:50). Up to this point in the narrative, Jesus has already called the Twelve (6:13; 8:1), cast out demons (4:31-37, 40-41), healed the sick (5:12-13, 18-26; 6:6-10; 7:1-17), and taught the crowds, including the Sermon on the Plain (6:17-49). But by this time he had also run into considerable opposition for his words and deeds (4:28-30; 5:21; 6:1-11; 7:39). Both positive and negative reactions have been expressed. He has many followers (8:3), but an opposition is forming.

8:5-8. As in Mark, Luke has a single seed falling into the various destinations. But he is more consistent than Mark. Even that which falls into the good soil is a single seed (8:8), whereas in Mark's version it is "others" (= seeds), a plural, which is also the case in Matthew's version (13:8). See Table 1 for Synoptic comparisons.

8:5. The verse is based on Mark 4:4, but it contains some alterations. Luke alone among the evangelists says explicitly that the sower sowed "his seed" (τὸν σπόρον αὐτοῦ), which is only implicit in the other two Gospels. Moreover, Luke alone has the term κατεπατήθη ("it was trampled under foot"). If the seed were alongside the path, why would it be trampled on? The term is also a metaphor for disdain.[34] The phrase "the birds of the air" (as in the RSV, NIV, and NRSV) is a translation of the Greek τὰ πετεινὰ τοῦ οὐρανοῦ (literally, "birds of heaven," which could imply birds within heaven to the modern reader, but ordinary birds are meant). KJV has "fowls of the air," and NEB and TEV simply have "birds."

8:6. This verse represents a major abridgment of Luke's source. Instead of the seed falling on "rocky ground," it simply fell upon the "rock" (ἐπὶ τὴν πέτραν). For Mark, the seed had four things against it: lack of soil, no depth of soil, the scorching of the heat, and no root. For Luke, the seed merely lacked moisture. The result was that it withered away or was dried up (ἐξηράνθη); in the parallels it was scorched (ἐκαυματίσθη, Mark 4:6//Matt 13:6).

8:8a. The singular seed (plural in Matthew and Mark) that fell into good soil produced a hundredfold. Luke's version lacks the other numerical figures (thirty and sixty). He goes straight to the highest of the numbers, indicating the abundant yield within the good soil.

8:8b. For comment, see comment on Mark 4:9.

8:9-10. For comment on these intervening verses, see Appendix 1, "The Purpose of the Parables according to the Evangelists."

8:11-15. Like the parable, the interpretation is shorter in Luke's Gospel (104 words in Greek) than in Mark's (132 words), slightly less than 80 percent the length of the latter. (It is also shorter than Matthew's version of 128 words.) As in the other Gospels, so here the interpretation is allegorical. See Table 2 for Synoptic comparisons.

8:11. Again (as at 8:5) Luke alone uses the word "seed," and he identifies it explicitly as the word of God. But that identification causes problems for what is to follow. The logic becomes tortuous.

8:12. Having started with the singular seed, Luke now switches to the plural, "those along the path." If the reader ignores what has just been said (8:11), one can expect that the term "those along the path" refers to seeds. But that is not possible, for it has just been established in the previous verse that the seed is the word of God. Whatever "those" are, they signify a category of persons who hear the word, but the devil takes it from them — right out of their hearts. The analogy must be then, as in Mark's version, between the terrain along the path (on which seeds are sown, but where they are also vulnerable) and persons in this group. That is a strict analogy, but it is exceedingly cumbersome.

34. BAGD 415.

Luke substitutes ὁ διάβολος ("the devil") for Mark's "Satan." In addition, the result of the devil's stealing the word from the hearts of the people is that they cannot believe and be saved.

8:13. Again, one is inclined at first to read "those on the rock" as seeds (cf. 8:6), but that does not work if the seed is the word of God. What is clear in the verse is that those on the rock represent another category of persons, and that is persons who hear the word (= the seed), receive it with joy, but fall away in temptation. They lack roots. But now the analogy is between plants that will not grow on rocks (for they have no roots) and persons whose commitments are ephemeral, and who then fall away "in a time of testing." In the final analysis, then, the analogy is between plants and persons.

Luke's verb ἀφίστανται (from ἀφίστημι) is translated "fall away" in the RSV, NIV, and NRSV, but it really means "to desert" (NEB) or "become apostate."[35] The combination of this verb with the phrase ἐν καιρῷ πειρασμοῦ ("in a time of testing") is the language of the church for becoming apostate due to testing of the church.

8:14. Here the analogy is clear. The seed (singular in Greek) among the thorns represents that category of persons who hear the word, but are choked by cares, riches, and the pleasures of life. The analogy is straightforward between a seed and a group of persons.

8:15. Again the analogy is clear. The seed (singular) that fell into good soil represents that category of persons who hear the word, hold it fast in an honest and good heart, and bear fruit with ὑπομονή ("patient endurance"). The analogy is between a seed and a group of persons. The term translated "patient endurance" is found only here and one other time in the Gospels (Luke 21:19), but often in the letters of Paul, expressing Christian endurance related to hope (e.g., Rom 5:3-4; 8:25; 15:4; 2 Cor 1:6-7). There is no reference to the "hundredfold" yield of 8:8 (whereas Mark 4:20 and Matt 13:23 repeat the figures earlier in each, Mark 4:8; Matt 13:8).

Luke's version of the parable and its interpretation is much like Mark's. He does, however, add some touches that bring out features of meaning. First, there is a more abrupt contrast between the three seeds that have failed endings (8:5-7) and the single one that brings forth a great yield — a hundredfold; nothing short of that is contemplated. Second, within the interpretation the vocabulary of the church is used to a higher degree — "word of God," "to believe," "to be saved," "to fall away" (or "become apostate"), and "patient endurance" (8:11-12, 13, 15). And third, Luke has an accent on the word being possessed in the heart (8:12), indeed held fast "in a noble and good heart" (8:15). It becomes clear that the center of Luke's attention is the cluster of Christian themes within the interpretation rather than the parable itself.

35. Ibid., 126.

Exposition

Since the correlations between the parable and its interpretation are difficult (as in Mark's version), the interpreter may want to refrain from trying to make them explicit. In any case, Luke's version, including the interpretation, contains a straightforward message. There are essentially two ways set before anyone. The one leads to destruction by the devil, by lack of any depth of commitment that fails in a time of testing, or by cares, riches, or the pleasures of life. The other leads to faith, salvation, and good works.

The reference to a noble and good heart as the only place in which the word of God is secure (held fast) is of interest. One could conclude that only those persons who have integrity and character are therefore eligible to hear the word of God, hold it fast, and be productive. And that would mean, in addition, that a person must cultivate the heart prior to hearing the word of God; there must be a "preparation" for the gospel *(praeparatio evangelii)*. But that is probably pushing details too far. The gospel itself transforms the heart. And wherever the gospel does its transforming work, the heart becomes purified. But when and where that transformation will take place is the decision of God, who is ever an electing God. The human factor in the entire transaction is the proclamation of the word of God. That leads one back to the imagery at the outset of the parable.

Select Bibliography

Arida, Robert M. "Hearing, Receiving, and Entering ΤΟ ΜΥΣΤΗΡΙΟΝ/ΤΑ ΜΥΣΤΗΡΙΑ: Patristic Insights Unveiling the Crux Interpretum (Isaiah 6:9-10) of the Sower Parable." *SVTQ* 38 (1994): 211-34.

Bacon, Benjamin W. "The Matthean Discourse in Parables, Mt 13.1-32." *JBL* 46 (1927): 237-65.

Bailey, Mark L. "The Parable of the Sower and the Soils." *BiblSac* 155 (1998): 172-88.

Bernardi, Jean. "'Cent, soixante et trente': Matthieu 13,8." *RB* 98 (1991): 398-402.

Boobyer, G. H. "The Redaction of Mark 4,1-34." *NTS* 8 (1961-62): 59-70.

Borsch, Frederick H. "Waste and Grace: The Parable of the Sower." *HMPEC* 53 (1984): 199-208.

Boucher, Madeleine. *The Mysterious Parable: A Literary Study.* CBQMS 6 (Washington: Catholic Biblical Association of America, 1977).

Bowker, John W. "Mystery and Parable: Mark 4:1-20." *JTS* 25 (1974): 300-317.

Brown, Raymond E. "Parable and Allegory Reconsidered." In his *New Testament Essays*, 321-33. Milwaukee: Bruce Publishing Company, 1965.

Bultmann, Rudolf. "Die Interpretation von Mk. 4,3-9 seit Jülicher." In *Jesus und Paulus: Festschrift für Werner Georg Kümmel zum 70. Geburtstag*, 30-34.

Ed. E. Earle Ellis and Erich Grässer. Göttingen: Vandenhoeck & Ruprecht, 1975.

Carlston, C. E. *The Parables of the Triple Tradition*. Philadelphia: Fortress, 1975.

Cranfield, C. E. B. "St. Mark 4.1-34." *SJT* 5 (1951): 398-414; 5 (1952): 49-62.

Crossan, John D. "The Seed Parables of Jesus." *JBL* 92 (1973): 244-66.

Dahl, Nils A. "The Parables of Growth." *ST* 5 (1951): 132-66. Reprinted in his *Jesus in the Memory of the Early Church*, 141-66. Minneapolis: Augsburg Publishing House, 1976.

Dalman, Gustav. "Viererlei Acker." *PJ* 22 (1926): 120-32.

Drury, John. "The Sower, the Vineyard, and the Place of Allegory in the Interpretation of Mark's Parables." *JTS* 24 (1973): 367-79.

Essame, William G. "Sowing and Plowing." *ExpTim* 72 (1960): 54.

Evans, Craig A. "On the Isaianic Background of the Sower Parable." *CBQ* 47 (1985): 464-68.

Fay, Greg. "Introduction to Incomprehension: The Literary Structure of Mark 4:1-34." *CBQ* 51 (1989): 65-81.

Fusco, Vittorio. *Parola e regno: La sezione delle parabole (Mc. 4,1-34) nella prospettiva marciana*. Aloisiana 13. Brescia: Morcelliana, 1980.

Garnet, Paul. "The Parable of the Sower: How the Multitudes Understood It." In *Spirit within Structure: Essays in Honor of George Johnston on the Occasion of His 70th Birthday*, 39-54. Ed. Edward J. Furcha. PTMS 3. Allison Park: Pickwick Publications, 1983.

Gealy, F. D. "The Composition of Mark IV." *ExpTim* 48 (1936): 40-43.

Geischer, H.-J. "Verschwenderische Güte: Versuch über Markus 4,3-9." *EvT* 38 (1978): 418-27.

Gerhardsson, Birger. "The Parable of the Sower and Its Interpretation." *NTS* 14 (1967-68): 165-93.

Grayston, K. "The Sower." *ExpTim* 55 (1943-44): 138-39.

Hagner, Donald A. "Matthew's Parables of the Kingdom (Matthew 13:1-52)." In *The Challenge of Jesus' Parables*, 102-24. Ed. Richard N. Longenecker. Grand Rapids: Wm. B. Eerdmans, 2000.

Hahn, Ferdinand. "Das Gleichnis von der ausgestreuten Saat und seine Deutung (Mk iv.3-8, 14-20)." In *Text and Interpretation: Studies in the New Testament Presented to Matthew Black*, 133-42. Ed. Ernest Best and R. McL. Wilson. Cambridge: Cambridge University Press, 1979.

Heil, John P. "Reader-Response and the Narrative Context of the Parables about Growing Seed in Mark 4:1-34." *CBQ* 54 (1992): 271-86.

Hooker, Morna D. "Mark's Parables of the Kingdom (Mark 4:1-34)." In *The Challenge of Jesus' Parables*, 79-101. Ed. Richard N. Longenecker. Grand Rapids: Wm. B. Eerdmans, 2000.

Horman, John. "The Source of the Version of the Parable of the Sower in the Gospel of Thomas." *NovT* 21 (1979): 326-43.

Jeremias, Joachim. "Palästinakundliches zum Gleichnis vom Säemann (Mark. IV 3-8 Par.)." *NTS* 13 (1966): 48-53.

Keegan, Terence. "The Parable of the Sower and Mark's Jewish Leaders." *CBQ* 56 (1994): 501-18.

Knowles, Michael P. "Abram and the Birds in Jubilees 11: A Subtext for the Parable of the Sower?" *NTS* 41 (1995): 145-51.

Kodell, Jerome. "'The Word of God Grew': The Ecclesial Tendency of Logos in Acts 1,7 [*sic*; read 6:7]; 12,24; 19,20." *Bib* 55 (1974): 505-19.

Kosmala, H. "The Three Nets of Belial: A Study in the Terminology of Qumran and the New Testament." *ASTI* 4 (1965): 91-113.

Lindemann, Andreas. "Die Erzählung vom Sämann und der Saat (Mk 4,3-8) und ihre Auslegung als allegorisches Gleichnis." *WuD* 21 (1991): 115-31.

Longenecker, Richard N. "Luke's Parables of the Kingdom (Luke 8:4-15; 13:18-21)." In his *The Challenge of Jesus' Parables*, 124-47. Grand Rapids: Wm. B. Eerdmans, 2000.

Luck, Ulrich. "Das Gleichnis von Sämann und die Verkündigung Jesu." *WuD* 11 (1971): 73-92.

McIver, Robert K. "One Hundred-Fold Yield — Miraculous or Mundane? Matthew 13.8, 23; Mark 4.8, 20; Luke 8.8." *NTS* 49 (1994): 606-8.

Marcus, Joel. "Blanks and Gaps in the Markan Parable of the Sower." *BibInt* 5 (1997): 247-62.

———. *The Mystery of the Kingdom of God.* SBLDS 90. Atlanta: Scholars Press, 1986.

Marshall, I. Howard. "Tradition and Theology in Luke (Luke 8:5-15)." *TynB* 20 (1969): 56-75.

Moule, C. F. D. "Mark 4:1-20 Yet Once More." In *Neotestamentica et Semitica: Studies in Honour of Matthew Black*, 95-113. Ed. E. Earle Ellis and Max Wilcox. Edinburgh: T. & T. Clark, 1969.

Neil, William. "Expounding the Parables: II. The Sower (Mk 4:3-8)." *ExpTim* 77 (1965-66): 74-77.

Newman, B. M. "To Teach or Not to Teach (A Comment on Matthew 13:1-3)." *BT* 34 (1983): 139-43.

Payne, Philip B. "The Authenticity of the Parable of the Sower and Its Interpretation." In *Studies of History and Tradition in the Four Gospels*, 1:162-207. Ed. R. T. France and David Wenham. 2 vols. Sheffield: JSOT Press, 1980-81.

———. "The Order of Sowing and Ploughing in the Parable of the Sower." *NTS* 25 (1978): 123-29.

———. "The Seeming Inconsistency of the Interpretation of the Parable of the Sower." *NTS* 26 (1980): 564-68.

Peters, Donald. "Vulnerable Promise from the Land (Mark 4:3b-8)." In *Jesus and His Parables: Interpreting the Parables of Jesus Today*, 69-84. Ed. V. George Shillington. Edinburgh: T. & T. Clark, 1997.

Robinson, William C., Jr. "On Preaching the Word of God (Luke 8:4-21)." In *Studies in Luke-Acts: Essays Presented in Honor of Paul Schubert*, 131-38. Ed. Leander E. Keck and J. Louis Martyn. Nashville: Abingdon Press, 1966.

Sellin, Gerhard. "Textlinguistische und semiotische Erwägungen zu Mk. 4.1-34." *NTS* 29 (1983): 508-30.

Swanson, Richard W. "Parables and Promises Not Kept: An Investigation of the Literary Function of the Sower in the Gospel of Mark." Th.D. diss., Luther Northwestern Theological Seminary, 1991.

Tolbert, Mary Ann. "How the Gospel of Mark Builds Character." *Int* 47 (1993): 347-57.

Vorster, Willem S. "Meaning and Reference: The Parables of Jesus in Mark 4." In *Text and Reality: Aspects of Reference in Biblical Texts*, 27-65. Ed. Bernard C. Lategan and W. S. Vorster. Semeia Studies. Atlanta: Scholars Press, 1985.

Weeden, Theodore J. "Recovering the Parabolic Intent in the Parable of the Sower." *JAAR* 47 (1979): 97-120.

Wenham, David. "The Interpretation of the Parable of the Sower." *NTS* 20 (1974): 299-319.

Westendorf, Craig. "The Parable of the Sower (Luke 8:4-15) in the Seventeenth Century." *LQ* 3 (1980): 49-64.

White, K. D. "The Parable of the Sower." *JTS* 15 (1964): 300-307.

Wilder, Amos N. "The Parable of the Sower: Naiveté and Method in Interpretation." *Semeia* 2 (1974): 134-51.

———. "Telling from Depth to Depth: The Parable of the Sower." In his *Jesus' Parables and the War on Myths: Essays on Imagination in the Scriptures*, 89-100. Ed. James Breech. Philadelphia: Fortress Press, 1983.

Wilckens, Ulrich. "Die Redaktion des Gleichniskapitels Mark 4 durch Matth." *TZ* 20 (1964): 305-27.

5.17. Children in the Marketplace, Matthew 11:16-19//Luke 7:31-35

Matthew 11:16-19

16*[Jesus said,] "But to what shall I compare this generation? It is like children sitting in the marketplaces and calling to others,* 17*'We played the flute for you, and you did not dance; we sang a dirge, and you did not mourn.'* 18*For John came neither eating nor drinking, and they say, 'He has a demon.'* 19*The Son of man came eating and drinking, and they say, 'Behold, a glutton and a drunkard, a friend of tax collectors and sinners!' Yet wisdom is vindicated by her deeds."*

Notes on the Text and Translation

11:16. Some ancient witnesses (G, 700, plus Latin and Sahidic equivalents) have ἑταίροις ("friends") instead of ἑτέροις ("others") at the end of the verse, but the latter is attested far more in superior texts. The RSV reads "playmates," which is helpful for the reader. NIV has "others," which is literal. NRSV has "one another," which is actually what appears in the Lukan parallel (7:32, ἀλλήλοις).

11:17. The expression "we played the flute" (NIV, NRSV) is superior to "we piped" (KJV, RSV, NEB). It is a literal translation of the verb αὐλέω,[1] and it is less archaic than "piped."

Likewise the expression "we sang a dirge" (NIV, NAB, JB ["sang dirges"]) is superior to "we wailed" (RSV, NEB ["wept and wailed"], NRSV) or "we mourned" (KJV). The Greek verb θρηνέω can be translated in these various ways, but in the present context it refers to an act of inciting a mournful response, as the singing of a dirge would do.[2]

11:19. In place of τῶν ἔργων ("works"), some ancient witnesses (B [as altered by a scribe], C, D, and many others) have τῶν τέκνων ("children"), which is undoubtedly a scribal harmonization with Luke 7:35.[3] The former is attested in superior texts (including B, ℵ, and various others).

Luke 7:31-35

31 *[Jesus said,]* *"To what then shall I compare the people of this generation, and what are they like?* 32 *They are like children sitting in the marketplace and calling to one another, 'We played the flute for you, and you did not dance; we sang a dirge, and you did not weep.'* 33 *For John the Baptist has come neither eating bread nor drinking wine; and you say, 'He has a demon.'* 34 *The Son of man has come eating and drinking; and you say, 'Behold, a glutton and a drunkard, a friend of tax collectors and sinners!'* 35 *Yet wisdom is vindicated by all her children."*

Notes on the Text and Translation

7:32. On "we played the flute" and "we sang a dirge," see on Matthew 11:17.

7:33. A few ancient witnesses (D, families 1, 13; some Old Latin and Syriac texts) lack "bread" and "wine." Other major texts (including ℵ and B) include the words. The omission can be attributed to harmonization with Matthew's version.

---

1. BAGD 121.
2. Ibid., 363: "sing a dirge" (with reference to Matt 11:17//Luke 7:32).
3. B. Metzger, *TCGNT* 30.

General Comments on the Texts

Interpreters are widely agreed that the parable existed in Q, and that Matthew and Luke made use of that source here,[4] although each evangelist made some redactional alterations.

In both Gospels the parable is spoken by Jesus within his Galilean ministry. It follows a series of sayings concerning John the Baptist (Matt 11:2-15// Luke 7:18-30), who is currently imprisoned by Herod Antipas (Matt 11:2; Luke 3:20) at Machaerus,[5] a fortress-palace near the Dead Sea. In both cases Jesus speaks the parable to the crowds and in the presence of his disciples (Matt 11:7// Luke 7:24).[6] In part, the message of the parable is that the crowds had understood neither John nor Jesus. As in the case of John, who was executed by order of a political official, King Herod Antipas (Matt 14:10 //Mark 6:27//Luke 9:9), so, too, Jesus' fate will be execution on orders of the governor, Pilate (Matt 27:26//Mark 15:15//Luke 23:25).

Interpreters of various approaches consider the parable to have originated with Jesus,[7] and that judgment seems sound, although there are those who discount it.[8]

Various interpreters have concluded that the application in Matthew 11:18-19//Luke 7:33-35 does not actually fit the parable itself and can be considered an early Christian composition.[9] Against that, two points favor the view that the application can be attributed to Jesus (setting aside the vexing question whether the term "Son of man" is authentic or not):[10] (1) the fact that the saying places Jesus and John on the same plane is more likely due to Jesus than to the early church;[11]

---

4. Burnett H. Streeter, *The Four Gospels: A Study in Origins,* rev. ed. (New York: St. Martin's Press, 1930), 291; T. W. Manson, *Sayings,* 67-71; B. Smith, *Parables,* 174; A. Polag, *Fragmenta Q,* 23, 42; J. Fitzmyer, *Luke,* 677; D. Hagner, *Matthew,* 309; W. D. Davies and D. C. Allison, *Matthew,* 2:235; U. Luz, *Matthäus,* 2:183; R. Brown, *Introduction NT,* 118. Against Q as a source here is T. Brodie, "Again Not Q," 2-32.

5. Josephus, *Ant.* 18.119.

6. Contra W. Allen, *Matthew,* the parable need not have been addressed to the Pharisees alone, although they may have been the primary target, as suggested by A. Plummer, *Matthew,* 163.

7. R. Bultmann, *HST* 172; C. H. Dodd, *Parables,* 15-16; J. Jeremias, *Parables,* 160-62; N. Perrin, *Teaching,* 120; U. Luz, *Matthäus,* 2.184.

8. A. Cadoux, *Parables,* 31; in R. Funk, *Five Gospels,* 180, 302, the texts have gray font (= not likely from Jesus, though it contains ideas close to his), and the saying at the end of Matt 11:19 is in black (= not from Jesus).

9. R. Bultmann, *HST* 172; A. Cadoux, *Parables,* 32; J. Gnilka, *Matthäus,* 1:423; W. Cotter, "Parable of the Children," 293; idem, "Children Sitting in the Agora," 31-35.

10. Those who hold that the application can be attributed to Jesus include C. H. Dodd, *Parables,* 15-16, 88; J. Jeremias, *Parables,* 160-62; B. Smith, *Parables,* 175-76; I. H. Marshall, *Luke,* 298; N. Perrin, *Teaching,* 120-21; U. Luz, *Matthäus,* 2:184.

11. N. Perrin, *Teaching,* 120.

and (2) that it contains an insulting remark about Jesus makes its origins in an early Christian community unlikely. Further, two closely related arguments speak in favor of the parable and the application as having been a unit from the beginning: (1) the parable simply needs an explanation;[12] one must show how the present generation can be compared to children at play in the marketplace; and (2) it is difficult to imagine that the parable would have survived without an explanation.[13]

The explanation, however, is not clear. How can one compare the present generation to children at play in the marketplace? There have been various answers to the question.[14] Two approaches appear to be the most widely held. The first follows the procedure of parable interpretation elsewhere in cases where "it is like" actually means "it is the case with . . . as with. . . ."[15] Then the comparison need not be between the present generation and the children per se but, more generally, between the one group of children (the flute players) and Jesus, and the other group of children (the dirge singers) and John. The opening lines (Matt 11:16//Luke 7:31-32) can be understood to mean: "The present generation can be compared to what follows." Both Jesus and John have cried out, and continue to cry out, to their contemporaries (surely not to each other, for that would put a negative construction on each), but to no avail. People will neither "dance" nor "mourn," metaphorically speaking, that is, neither rejoice nor repent.[16]

The second comparison is between the "present generation" and the children sitting in the marketplace, who complain that no one responded to their flute playing and singing of dirges. The point of comparison would be that, just as children will spend time and energy taunting others for not joining their activities (dancing and mourning, i.e., playing mock weddings and funerals), so the people of the present generation are obstinate and so preoccupied by frivolous attitudes, petty disputes, and criticism that they are unable to see the work of God being done through the ministries of John and Jesus. They are like disorderly children who quarrel among themselves and taunt each other rather than get together to play games.[17]

---

12. U. Luz, *Matthäus*, 2:184.

13. B. Smith, *Parables*, 176.

14. Surveys, which are by no means alike, can be found in A. Jülicher, *Gleichnisreden*, 2:30-33; I. H. Marshall, *Luke*, 300-301; U. Luz, *Matthäus*, 2:184-88; D. Zeller, "Bildlogik," 252-57, surveys three approaches.

15. J. Jeremias, *Parables*, 101.

16. Interpreters who go in this direction (with obvious variations) include D. Zeller, "Bildlogik," 252-57; E. Schweizer, *Matthew*, 264; J. Fitzmyer, *Luke*, 679-80; R. A. Culpepper, *NIB (Luke)*, 9:166; and the Jesus Seminar, according to R. Funk, *Five Gospels*, 180, 303.

17. Interpreters who go in this direction (with obvious variations) include A. Jülicher, *Gleichnisreden*, 2:31-33; A. Plummer, *Matthew*, 163; idem, *Luke*, 207; J. Jeremias, *Parables*, 161-62; B. Easton, *Luke*, 104; M. J. Suggs, *Wisdom*, 44; O. Linton, "Parable of the Children's Game," 177; I. H. Marshall, *Luke*, 300-301; P. Perkins, *Parables*, 44;

In order to produce a satisfactory interpretation, it is important to keep in mind that the parable is employed to pass judgment upon the "present generation." Immediately — a point important in the oral telling of a parable — the present generation is compared to certain children and their behavior. The children are calling out and making a complaint about others who do not join in their games. Since that is so, it is not likely that Jesus and John should be compared to the complaining children. But it is fitting to compare the people of the present generation with them. In the midst of their preoccupations and sullen manner, they look upon John as possessed and upon Jesus as a glutton and a drunkard and thereby miss what is being offered through the ministries of these figures. But finally Jesus and John will be vindicated, as well as the children of wisdom (see comment on Matt 11:19//Luke 7:35 below). The people of "this generation" are not among them.

The last line of Matthew 11:19//Luke 7:35 ("wisdom is vindicated . . .") is sometimes considered secondary, a product of the Q community.[18] The reading in Q would most likely have been that wisdom is vindicated "by her children" (as in Luke), rather than "by her deeds" (as in Matthew).[19] Who are those children? Would they be members of the Q community, which considered itself composed of wisdom's children?[20] Or are the children of wisdom Jesus and John?[21] The question will be taken up in the Exegetical Commentary on each Gospel.

The Parable in the Gospel of Matthew

Exegetical Commentary

As in Luke's Gospel, the parable is spoken by Jesus during his Galilean ministry. Within the Matthean context, John the Baptist had already been imprisoned (11:2), a detail not mentioned at this place in Luke's account (but registered already at 3:20). The rejection of John has meant that the kingdom of heaven has suffered violence (11:12).

11:16. The wording "to what shall I compare" is a typical formula introducing a parable, as illustrated in rabbinic parables.[22] The expression "this genera-

---

R. Gundry, *Matthew*, 212; D. Hagner, *Matthew*, 310-11; W. D. Davies and D. C. Allison, *Matthew*, 2:262; H. Kee, "Jesus," 383-84; Douglas R. A. Hare, *Matthew* (Louisville: John Knox Press, 1993) 124; U. Luz, *Matthäus*, 2:188. W. Cotter, "Parable of the Children," 289-304, goes essentially in this direction and interprets the unit in terms of its meaning within the Q community.

18. D. Zeller, "Bildlogik," 252.

19. A. McNeile, *Matthew*, 158; M. J. Suggs, *Wisdom*, 33; O. Linton, "Parable of the Children's Game," 165; A. Polag, *Fragmenta Q*, 42; J. Fitzmyer, *Luke*, 679; W. D. Davies and D. C. Allison, *Matthew*, 2:264; U. Luz, *Matthäus*, 2:188.

20. U. Luz, *Matthäus*, 2:184.

21. M. J. Suggs, *Wisdom*, 35.

22. For examples, cf. Wilhelm Bacher, *Die exegetische Terminologie der jüdischen*

tion" (ἡ γενεὰ αὕτη) appears eighteen times in the Synoptic Gospels,[23] referring to Jesus' contemporaries as the last generation before the end, just prior to the approaching final judgment, and it is always a negative (or pejorative) expression.[24] Similar expressions about the present generation are that it is "adulterous" (Mark 8:38), "evil" (Matt 12:45; Luke 11:29), and "faithless" (Matt 17:17//Mark 9:19). The concept of a whole generation as being corrupt appears already in the OT (Deut 32:5, 20; Judg 2:10; Pss 78:8; 95:10) and Jewish tradition.[25]

11:17. The couplet recalls Ecclesiastes 3:4: "a time to weep, and a time to laugh; a time to mourn, and a time to dance." The last word in 11:17 is ἐκόψασθε, an aorist of the verb κόπτω, which in this context would mean to "beat one's breast" as a sign of mournng.[26] Luke's parallel has simply ἐκλαύσατε, an aorist of the verb κλαίω, meaning to "weep" or "cry."[27] Matthew probably represents the Q reading,[28] attesting the ancient Palestinian custom, but Luke has altered the terminology for the non-Palestinian reader.

11:18. The parable has ended; this verse and the next are an application. John and Jesus shared the same fate, that is, rejection. John was an ascetic, but Jesus was not. What they had in common was not their manner of life but their message. And that was most vehemently resisted. John's ascetic appearance has been described at 3:4.

The charge that John has a demon will be leveled at Jesus as well when his opponents say that he is possessed by Beelzebul (12:24; cf. John 10:20).

11:19. The charge that Jesus is a "glutton and a drunkard" is extremely serious. It is characteristic of the 'rebellious son' in the OT, who is worthy of being stoned to death (Deut 21:20-21). It is not clear, however, that there is an allusion to the Torah at this point (the wording differs greatly from that of the LXX);[29] it can probably be attributed to a slogan actually applied to Jesus in his day. It is hardly a saying that would have originated in the early church.[30]

Traditionsliteratur, 2 vols. (Darmstadt: Wissenschaftliche Buchgesellschaft, 1965 [reprinted from the Leipzig ed., 1899-1905]), 1:121.

23. Matt 11:16; 12:41, 42, 45; 23:36; 24:34; Mark 8:12, 38; 13:30; Luke 7:31; 11:29, 30, 31, 32, 50, 51; 17:25; 21:32. To this list can be added Acts 2:40; Heb 3:10.

24. Victor Hasler, "γενεά," *EDNT* 1:241.

25. *1 Enoch* 93:9; *Jub.* 23:16; 1QpHab 2:6.

26. BAGD 444.

27. Ibid., 433.

28. A. Polag, *Fragmenta Q,* 42.

29. The LXX has συμβολοκοπῶν οἰνοφλυγεῖ at Deut 21:20. According to U. Luz, *Matthäus,* 2:188 (n. 37), the formulation is too different from Deut 21:20 for it to refer back to it; likewise, J. Fitzmyer, *Luke,* 681, says that the formulation "scarcely reflects the LXX." The allusion is affirmed by J. Jeremias, *Parables,* 160; R. Gundry, *Matthew,* 213; D. Hagner, *Matthew,* 310. Often cited as a companion text is Prov 23:20-21: the wise father instructs his son to avoid gluttony and drunkenness.

30. That the saying is traditional and can be assigned to critics of Jesus in his lifetime is held by, among others, Günther Bornkamm, *Jesus of Nazareth* (New York: Harper

Jesus had been labeled a friend of tax collectors and sinners previously in this Gospel and its parallels (9:10-11//Mark 2:15-16//Luke 5:29-30). Such persons were counted among the despised. Tax collectors seem to have been well-to-do persons, including Jews, who paid for the privilege of collecting tolls and various local taxes (sales, income, property, and inheritance).[31] They made their own income by overcharging people (Luke 19:8), thereby taking advantage of them. Scorn for them is attested not only in the NT but also in rabbinic writings and secular literature of antiquity.[32] The term "sinners" was applied to all who, in the eyes of their critics, had abandoned the law and for all practical purposes denied God's covenant with Israel.[33] It is the tax collectors and sinners with whom Jesus consorted, as though they, not the presumed righteous, are the ones whom God truly loves.

As indicated above, the ending of 11:19 has probably been altered by Matthew from Q, which would have more likely have wisdom being vindicated "by her children" (as at Luke 7:35) than "by her works" (ἀπὸ τῶν ἔργων). Here the preposition ἀπό is equivalent to ὑπό ("by") in connection with a passive verb.[34] The verb ἐδικαιώθη (aorist passive of δικαιόω) is a gnomic aorist (an aorist used in Greek for a proverbial saying).[35] The result of Matthew's alteration is to make a connection with the "works of the Messiah" (τὰ ἔργα τοῦ Χριστοῦ) spoken of at 11:2, that is, the miracles that Jesus performs; Jesus is thus the personification of wisdom.[36] Even though Jesus and his message are rejected by the

---

& Brothers, 1960), 50, 80; N. Perrin, *Teaching*, 119-21; Hans Conzelmann, *Jesus* (Philadelphia: Fortress Press, 1973), 32, 67.

31. Fritz Herrenbrück, "Wer waren die 'Zöllner'?" *ZNW* 72 (1981): 178-94; idem, *Jesus und die Zöllner: Historische und neutestamentlich-exegetische Untersuchungen*, WUNT 41 (Tübingen: J. C. B. Mohr [Paul Siebeck], 1990); Helmut Merkel, "τελώνης," *EDNT* 3:349.

32. Rabbinic references are cited by Joachim Jeremias, *Jerusalem in the Time of Jesus: An Investigation into Economic and Social Conditions during the New Testament Period* (Philadelphia: Fortress Press, 1969), 310-11; secular sources in John R. Donahue, "Tax Collector," *ABD* 6:337.

33. E. P. Sanders, "Jesus and the Sinners," *JSNT* 19 (1983): 5-36.

34. BAGD 88 (ἀπό, V, 6).

35. BDF 171 (#333).

36. M. J. Suggs, *Wisdom*, 56-57; Felix Christ, *Jesus Sophia. Die Sophia-Christologie bei den Synoptikern*, ATANT 57 (Zurich: Zwingli Verlag, 1970), 76; Fred W. Burnett, *The Testament of Jesus-Sophia: A Redaction-Critical Study of the Eschatological Discourse in Matthew* (Lanham, Md.: University Press of America, 1981), 88-92; P. Perkins, *Parables*, 44-45; R. Gundry, *Matthew*, 213; U. Luz, *Matthäus*, 2:189. According to Reginald H. Fuller, "Christology in Matthew and Luke," in *Who Is This Christ? Gospel Christology and Contemporary Faith*, by R. H. Fuller and Pheme Perkins (Philadelphia: Fortress Press, 1983), 85, one should not speak of Jesus as the "incarnation" of wisdom in Matthew's Gospel (since that implies preexistence), but rather that Jesus "embodied" or "incarnated" wisdom; wisdom was "operative in Jesus."

foolish generation of his day, he is vindicated by the ministry that he exercises. Those who fail to respond to him as the envoy of God do so because of their preoccupations and negative attitudes. For those who can see the truth, however, Jesus personifies the divine wisdom; he does the deeds of the Messiah. Or to put it the other way, his doing the deeds of the Messiah (11:5-6) vindicates who he is, the Messiah and bearer of the divine wisdom.

Exposition

The problem with John and Jesus, in the eyes of the public, was that John "was too gloomy . . . , an eccentric ascetic," and, on the other hand, Jesus was "too worldly — not even giving due regard to the difference between the righteous and sinners"; so John and Jesus were "extremes which are to be avoided."[37]

John (in his austerity) and Jesus (in his message of the kingdom and its joy) were both too intense for most people. The people who saw and heard them could not get them either to lighten up (in the case of John) or to become more restrained (in the case of Jesus). They were like children sitting in the marketplaces playing flutes and singing dirges to get a response, but failed. But then, who should be responding to whom? In actuality the present "generation" has failed to respond.

Every generation throughout history can be comparable to the one of which the parable speaks. Generations within the OT, and generations since the NT, have balked at, resisted, and even killed those whom God has sent. Jesus, proclaimer of the kingdom and the friend of tax collectors and sinners, was resisted and even crucified.

But the saying that wisdom will be vindicated by her deeds has, for Christian faith, been confirmed. The resurrection is the vindication of the crucified one, who performed the messianic deeds and personified the divine wisdom.

The Parable in the Gospel of Luke

Exegetical Commentary

The parable is located by Luke within the Galilean ministry of Jesus. The last place marker prior to it is at 7:11 where Jesus and his disciples are at Nain, which was some twenty-five miles southwest of Capernaum. Immediately prior to the parable there are sayings concerning John the Baptist (7:18-30), whose imprisonment has been referred to much earlier (3:20). John had been a controversial figure. Some, even tax collectors, had been baptized by him and praised God, but the "Pharisees and lawyers" had rejected John and his baptism, and therefore God's purpose for themselves (7:30).

---

37. G. Bornkamm, *Jesus*, 50.

A great deal of the Lukan parable and its application is identical to what appears in Matthew's version. Since there is no need to repeat comments already made, the reader should review comments on Matthew's version above.

7:31. Luke has "the people" (οἱ ἄνθρωποι) of "this generation," which is probably an addition by him to the Q version.[38]

The double question ("To what then shall I compare the people of this generation, and what are they like?"), however, which is not in Matthew, was probably present in Q.[39] It represents a familiar Semitism (cf. Isa 40:18).

7:32. The children call to "one another" (ἀλλήλοις; simply to "others" at Matt 11:16). Does this mean that there are two groups of children who yell back and forth antiphonally to one another? Or does it simply mean that the children, in chaotic fashion, call out to one another, but not to other persons outside their circle? The matter is not clear, but the relative pronoun "who" (Greek: ἅ) refers to the children in general. It seems that readers are to imagine the hubbub of a (single) group of children shouting out to one another. In any case, Matthew's wording probably represents the Q reading.[40]

Concerning the use of the verb for weeping, see the comment on Matthew 11:17. By portraying two groups more explicitly, Luke tends to equate them with Jesus and John, plus their disciples, respectively. But the children cannot represent these. They represent the present generation.

7:33. The saying about John's not eating and drinking is longer in Luke than in Matthew due to the additional words "bread" and "wine." Luke also calls John "the Baptist," which is not in Matthew's version. These are probably additions by Luke over against his source (Q).[41] In this verse and the next Luke has the verbs in second person plural (λέγετε, "you say"), whereas in Matthew's version (11:18-19) they are in third (λέγουσιν, "they say"). It is commonly thought that Luke has made the alteration.[42] The effect is that Jesus accuses his hearers directly — the people of "this generation" — of rejecting both John and himself.

John's not eating bread and drinking wine underscore his extreme asceticism. His not eating "bread" is borne out by his having a diet of locusts and wild honey, but that detail is recorded only in the other two Synoptic Gospels (Mark 1:6//Matt 3:4). That John would drink no "wine" had been foretold in the prophecy of his father Zechariah (1:15; cf. Judg 13:4-5 regarding Samson). The "wild honey" mentioned refers to a drink of honey in water, a substitute for wine.[43] The charge of demon possession is applied to Jesus at 11:15.

38. A. Polag, *Fragmenta Q,* 42; J. Fitzmyer, *Luke,* 679.

39. A. Jülicher, *Gleichnisreden,* 2:24; A. Polag, *Fragmenta Q,* 42.

40. B. Smith, *Parables,* 175; A. Polag, *Fragmenta Q,* 42; contra R. Gundry, *Matthew,* 211-12.

41. J. Creed, *Luke,* 108; B. Smith, *Parables,* 174; J. Fitzmyer, *Luke,* 678, 680; A. Polag, *Fragmenta Q,* 42; contra R. Gundry, *Matthew,* 212.

42. J. Fitzmyer, *Luke,* 678.

43. O. Bother, "Ass Johannes der Täufer kein Brot?" 90-92.

7:34. The verse is identical to its parallel (Matt 11:19) except for three minor alterations (perfect tense verb [ἐλήλυθεν] instead of aorist; use of second person; and reversal of two words [φίλος τελωνῶν]). See comment on the parallel.

7:35. Wisdom is vindicated by her children because they listen to God's messengers.[44] Besides the difference between Luke's "children" and Matthew's "works" (which is probably Matthew's alteration; cf. General Comments above), Luke has inserted the word "all" (πάντων), as in "all the people" of 7:29. Whereas in Matthew's version the expression concerning the works of wisdom refers to the deeds of Jesus the Messiah, here the children of wisdom are those who listened to John and now listen to Jesus as envoys of the divine wisdom; they are different from the "people of this generation" (7:31). The divine wisdom is vindicated by a following of persons who find God's revelation disclosed in the message of Jesus.

Exposition

The coming of John and Jesus into the midst of their own generation was divisive. So in this parable a sharp distinction is made between the people of "this generation" and the "children" of "wisdom."

John and Jesus can be seen to represent two aspects of the biblical message. John the austere one calls for repentance. Jesus the joyous one announces the good news of the kingdom. To be sure, each could do and did what the other did; John could proclaim good news (3:18), and Jesus could urge repentance (13:3, 5). But in this passage the two aspects are portrayed as virtual opposites, and they are assigned to the two figures independently.

The divide between the unrepentant and the faithful is drawn sharply in the Gospel of Luke. It can be shocking, and history has seen enough of those who would divide the world into the children of light and the children of darkness. Yet the division between the present generation and the children of wisdom stands in this parable as a challenge to its readers to take stock of where they are as they stand in the presence of God. A person can reject the message of John and Jesus, and even kill the messenger. Or one can listen, repent, and be counted among the children of wisdom.

Select Bibliography

Bother, Otto. "Ass Johannes der Täufer kein Brot (Luk. vii. 33)?" *NTS* 18 (1971): 90-92.

Brodie, Thomas. "Again Not Q: Luke 7:18-35 as an Acts-orientated Transformation of the Vindication of the Prophet Micaiah (1 Kings 22:1-38)." *IBS* 16 (1994): 2-30.

44. J. Creed, *Luke,* 109.

Cotter, Wendy J. "Children Sitting in the Agora." *FFF* 5 (1989): 63-82.

———. "The Parable of the Children in the Marketplace, Q (Lk) 7.31-5." *NovT* 29 (1987): 289-304.

Donahue, John R. "Tax Collectors and Sinners." *CBQ* 33 (1971): 39-61.

Edwards, Richard A. "Matthew's Use of Q in Chapter Eleven." In *Logia: Les paroles de Jésus — The Sayings of Jesus: Memorial Joseph Coppens,* 257-75. Ed. Joël Delobel et al. BETL 59. Leuven: Leuven University Press, 1982.

Feuillet, André. "Jésus et la Sagesse divine d'après les Évangiles synoptiques." *RB* 62 (1955): 161-96.

Kee, Howard C. "Jesus: A Glutton and a Drunkard." *NTS* 42 (1996): 374-93.

Kloppenborg, John S. "Wisdom Christology in Q." In *LTP* 34 (1978): 129-47.

Leivestad, Ragnar. "An Interpretation of Matt 11,19." *JBL* 71 (1952): 179-81.

Linton, Olof. "The Parable of the Children's Game." *NTS* 22 (1976): 159-79.

Ljungmann, Henrik. "En Sifre-text till Matt. 11.18f. par." *SEÅ* 22-23 (1957-58): 238-42.

Mussner, Franz. "Der nicht erkannte Kairos (Mt. XI:16-19 = Lk. VII:31-35." *Bib* 40 (1959): 599-612.

Sahlin, Harald. "Traditionskritische Bermerkungen zu zwei Evangelienperikopen." *ST* 33 (1979): 69-84.

Suggs, M. Jack. *Wisdom, Christology, and Law in Matthew's Gospel.* Cambridge, Mass.: Harvard University Press, 1970.

Waters, Mark. "Matthew 11:16-19." *RevExp* 90 (1993): 565-67.

Zeller, Dieter. "Die Bildlogik des Gleichnisses Mt 11 16f./Lk 7 31f." *ZNW* 68 (1977): 252-57.

5.18. The Two Debtors, Luke 7:41-43

40*Jesus . . . said to [Simon the Pharisee], "Simon, I have something to say to you."*

And [Simon] answered, "Tell [me], Teacher."

41*"A certain moneylender had two debtors; one owed five hundred denarii, and the other fifty.* 42*When they could not pay, he forgave them both. Therefore which of them will love him more?"*

43*Simon answered, "The one, I suppose, to whom he forgave more."*

And [Jesus] said to him, "You have judged correctly."

Exegetical Commentary

There are no serious textual critical problems, and there are no major issues concerning the translation of the text.

The parable appears within the midst of a conflict story (Luke 7:36-50), and it is told in response to the setting of that larger story, often called the Sinful Woman at a Pharisee's House. The story appears only in the Gospel of Luke. Conversely a story that is quite similar, the Anointing at Bethany, appears in the other two Synoptic Gospels (Mark 14:3-9//Matt 26:6-13) and the Gospel of John (12:1-8), but not in Luke's Gospel. In spite of the similarities,[1] the story at Luke 7:36-50 can be regarded as having an origin independent of the Anointing at Bethany.

It appears, however, that Luke has incorporated materials from Mark's story of the Anointing at Bethany into his account and added further details. These include the clauses "[she] brought an alabaster jar flask of ointment" (7:37), "and [she] anointed them [= his feet] with the ointment" (7:38), the follow-up statement about her having anointed him with ointment (7:46), the concluding pronouncement and dialogue about forgiveness (7:48-50),[2] and the name "Simon" three times over (7:40, 43, 44).[3] When those materials are removed, a coherent story remains. It is no longer the story of an anointing of Jesus' feet with ointment, but of a penitent woman who entered a Pharisee's house where Jesus was reclining for a meal, wept at his feet, and then wiped her tears from his feet with her hair and kissed them. Her action aroused the indignation of the Pharisaic host since she was known to be a "sinner." His words of criticism are spoken "to himself" (7:39, or literally, "within himself," ἐν ἑαυτῷ) — another instance of "interior dialogue" within the Gospel of Luke[4] — but the reader is to understand that his consternation was obvious. In any case, the reader is filled in on the situation, as though no words were necessary within the story itself. Thereupon Jesus replies with his Parable of the Two Debtors (7:41-43) in defense of the woman and her activity, as well as in defense of himself for allowing her to touch him. This is followed by statements of Jesus to the Pharisee. Jesus contrasts the behavior of the woman and the Pharisee (7:44-45), and he declares that the person who is forgiven much will love more than the one who has been forgiven little (7:47).[5]

1. Similarities between Mark 14:3-9//Matt 26:6-13 and Luke 7:36-50 include: (1) the host's name is Simon; (2) the event takes place in a house; (3) Jesus reclines at table; (4) an uninvited woman enters; and (5) she brings an alabaster jar of ointment.

2. These verses are attributed to Lukan composition also by A. Jülicher, *Gleichnisreden*, 2:299-300; R. Bultmann, *HST* 21; and J. Fitzmyer, *Luke*, 685.

3. This proposed reconstruction is based on further work in Arland J. Hultgren, *Jesus and His Adversaries: The Form and Function of the Conflict Stories in the Synoptic Tradition* (Minneapolis: Augsburg Publishing House, 1979), 84-87. Proposals by other scholars (Pierre Benoit, André Legault, Raymond E. Brown, Barnabas Lindars, Georg Braumann, and Robert Holst) are reviewed on p. 97 (n. 82).

4. Other instances are at Luke 12:17; 15:17; 16:3; 18:4, 11.

5. The translation of 7:47 is notoriously difficult. It is clear that an antithetical parallelism is intended; the great love of the woman is in consequence of having been forgiven much (not prior to it), just as the one forgiven little loves less. The NRSV rendering expresses the parallelism: "Therefore, I tell you, her sins, which were many, have been forgiven; hence she has shown great love. But the one to whom little is forgiven, loves little." The ὅτι-clause

7:41. The imagery is that of a moneylender and two persons who owe money. The term δανιστής ("moneylender," "creditor"), found only here in the NT, has no special significance; the person is one of substantial means who has loaned money. Within a theological context, however, the moneylender will be a metaphor for God, to whom everyone is indebted. This is confirmed by the view that "debts" is a metaphor for sins against God.[6]

The debtors differ. The one owes ten times that of the other. The first owes five hundred denarii. Since a denarius (δηνάριον) is the equivalent of a day's wages for a common laborer,[7] the total envisioned is equivalent to the wages due a common laborer for about a year and a half (allowing for the inclusion of sabbaths). The other debtor owes fifty denarii. The equivalent envisioned here would be wages for about two months (allowing for the inclusion of sabbaths).

7:42a. The debtors (rather than the debts they owed) are forgiven. The outward means by which they are forgiven is that their debts are cancelled. But at a deeper level the debtors themselves are forgiven. The reason for their being forgiven as debtors is simply their inability to pay what they owe (contrast the slave's plea in the Parable of the Unforgiving Slave, Matt 18:26, "Lord, have patience with me, and I will pay you everything"). The forgiveness is pure grace. Forgiving debts purely on the grounds of the debtors' inability to pay is "rather unheard of, which drives home the point of the parable."[8] The verb used for forgiveness (χαρίζομαι) can be used in a legal sense, as in granting property to another person, but it can also signify forgiveness and showing favor to another.[9]

7:42b-43. The story line of the parable has ended. It is not followed by a statement, but by a question addressed to the Pharisee, an answer, and a concluding statement by Jesus. In this respect, the parable concludes like the Parable of the Good Samaritan, in which Jesus asks the lawyer a question, the lawyer responds, and there is a closing statement by Jesus (10:36-37).

The dialogue establishes that the debtor who owed the 500 denarii will love the moneylender more than the one who owed 50. The greater the forgiveness, the greater the level of appreciation in return. It has been suggested that the verb ἀγαπάω need not mean "to love" (as in KJV, RSV, NEB, NIV,

can be taken to speak of evidence for her forgiveness, according to C. F. D. Moule, *An Idiom-Book of New Testament Greek*, 2d ed. (Cambridge: Cambridge University Press, 1959), 147; cf. I. H. Marshall, *Luke*, 313; J. Fitzmyer, *Luke*, 686-87.

6. Within the NT, cf. Matt 6:12; 18:23-35; in rabbinic literature, cf. *Exod. Rab.* 31; additional references in Str-B 1:798-99, 800-801; discussion in G. F. Moore, *Judaism*, 2:95.

7. John W. Betlyon, "Coinage," *ABD* 1:1086.

8. J. Fitzmyer, *Luke*, 690.

9. BAGD 876-77; Klaus Berger, "χαρίζομαι," *EDNT* 3:456-57. According to Berger, the use of the term to express forgiveness does not appear in the LXX, but first in Josephus, *Ant.* 6.144. Within the NT it has such a meaning at Col 3:13.

NRSV). Joachim Jeremias has written: "Hebrew, Aramaic, and Syriac have no word for 'thank' and 'thankfulness.'" So other verbs are used. In this particular case the question of Jesus means: "Which of them will feel the deepest thankfulness?"[10] Be that as it may, as a translation "to love" is fitting. It coincides with the action of the woman and the statement of 7:47. And within the parable itself the debtors' gratitude is suffused with genuine, and demonstrative, affection. That will be more in the case of the one than the other. In Near Eastern fashion, the one who is forgiven more will make more ado about the matter and make more of a public demonstration of affection to the moneylender than the other one will.

The Parable of the Two Debtors is the only parable found exclusively in the Gospel of Luke that is located outside of his travel narrative (9:51–19:27); it is placed in what is sometimes called Luke's "little interpolation" (6:20–8:3). The parable is also distinctive in that it is the only one told to a particular person, rather than to the crowds, a group of opponents, or the disciples. There is no indication in the narrative that others are supposed to be present besides Jesus, the Pharisee, and the penitent woman. Finally, the parable arises out of a specific occasion. That is not distinctive, for specific occasions elicit other parables as well (such as the Parable of the Good Samaritan in response to a lawyer's question and the three parables of Luke 15 in response to the criticism of some scribes and Pharisees). But both its reason for being and its message are dependent upon the narrative in which it is embedded.

The last point has a bearing on the question of the origins of the parable. Since the parable is so utterly dependent upon its narrative, it could be secondary to it,[11] and that could speak against its having been spoken by Jesus of Nazareth.[12] On the other hand, that need not be the case. It is surely possible that the parable arose out of a specific situation in the ministry of the earthly Jesus, a situation that is related in Luke's narrative. That would mean that the parable and its narrative setting were told together from the beginning.[13] After having heard Jesus proclaim the forgiveness of God, and having experienced such forgiveness, a woman followed Jesus into the home of a person, possibly a Pharisee, and expressed herself through the acts related. The host's response was one of shock and indignation. The woman had stepped over the line. It would have been appropriate enough for Jesus to have proclaimed that God forgives sins, a

10. J. Jeremias, *Parables,* 127; cf. H. J. Wood, "The Use of ἀγαπάω," 319-20; I. H. Marshall, *Luke,* 311.

11. J. Fitzmyer, *Luke,* 690.

12. The parable is attributed to Luke himself by B. Smith, *Parables,* 216; and in R. Funk, *Five Gospels,* 304. All of Luke 7:36-50 is viewed as a Lukan composition, but based on oral tradition, by Vincent H. Stanton, *The Gospels as Historical Documents,* 3 vols. (Cambridge: Cambridge University Press, 1903-20), 2:298-99.

13. V. Stanton, *Gospels as Historical Documents,* 2:298-99; H. Drexler, "Die grosse Sünderin," 165-66; U. Wilckens, "Vergebung für die Sünderin," 398-402.

teaching familiar enough in Jewish tradition. Further, it would have been appropriate for the woman — known to be a "sinner" (for whatever reasons)[14] — to hear and accept such good news. But for her to assume, or to conclude, that she personally had actually been forgiven, and for her to express her gratitude by her loving gesture, was to go beyond the bounds of propriety. The only way that one could possibly qualify for receiving God's forgiveness is repentance and some obvious change of behavior, tested over time. The host would have considered her temerity to enter the house and to perform her gesture in front of the invited guests to be an act of spiritual arrogance, to say nothing of social disgrace. The obvious consternation of the host was then met by means of the parable. Although it is possible that the entire episode and the parable within it have been composed by a storyteller in the early church, it is certainly plausible that they are rooted in the ministry of the earthly Jesus.[15] They cohere with other known traditions about Jesus' behavior and words, as well as of those around him — both opponents and followers.

Interpreters have disagreed concerning the meaning of the parable. Two major proposals have been made. One is that Jesus used the parable to speak of the inconceivable goodness of God.[16] The other is that by means of the parable Jesus taught that the greater the amount of forgiveness one experiences, the greater the amount of gratitude one will have.[17] The proposals do not cancel each other out. If indeed the parable was spoken within the context of the woman's action and the indignant response of the Pharisaic host, it would have driven home the point that God's forgiveness is greater than human reckoning normally conceives or allows, and that the one who experiences its abundance is like the person who has been forgiven an enormous debt (in comparison to one forgiven only a little by comparison). The parable is therefore both didactic and polemical, as it must be. Just as it is necessary to clear a field of weeds in order to make room for planting grain, so it is necessary to clear away human misunderstandings and even opposition in order for the gospel of divine favor to be heard. The Pharisee loves little because he has not experienced divine

14. Various commentators conclude that "woman of the city" means that she is a prostitute; cf. A. Jülicher, *Gleichnisreden*, 2:290; J. Jeremias, *Parables*, 127; E. Schweizer, *Luke*, 139.

15. The authenticity of the parable is affirmed by A. Jülicher, *Gleichnisreden*, 2:302; J. Jeremias, *Parables*, 127, 145; G. Braumann, "Schuldner und die Sünderin," 487-93; U. Wilckens, "Vergebung für die Sünderin," 416-22.

16. This is expressed, with variations, by W. M. Macgregor, "Parable of the Money-Lender," 346; J. Jeremias, *Parables*, 145; G. Braumann, "Schuldner und die Sünderin," 492; K. Bailey, *Peasant Eyes*, 12; H. Drexler, "Die grosse Sünderin," 166; E. Schweizer, *Luke*, 140-41.

17. This is expressed, with variations, by A. Jülicher, *Gleichnisreden*, 2:298-99, 302; A. Plummer, *Luke*, 212; A. Cadoux, *Parables*, 140; B. Smith, *Parables*, 211; J. Creed, *Luke*, 111; B. Scott, *Parable*, 213.

grace; and he has not experienced divine grace because of his presumed lack of its need. But those who know their need are able to receive it. Divine forgiveness is more abundant than human piety will normally allow. Right at the point where human piety is affronted, that is the threshold at which one can begin to get a glimpse at the abundance of divine grace.

Exposition

Deep within the heart and mind of nearly everyone there lurks a sense of justice on a cosmic scale. One can speak of it as a sense of divine justice. And there are consequences to such a sense within. One is that, from childhood on, judgments are made about other persons, and those judgments are writ large, projected unto the big screen of reality. The judgments of God are thought to be much like our own.

It is then thought that there are persons who are so far removed from the realm of right living that they are "beyond the pale." They do not deserve forgiveness from God, and they do not deserve "a place at the table" among respectable persons or in the church.

But what happens if such persons, without any outward signs of reform, appear within the company of Jesus, that is, for worship or some other fellowship activity in the church? The exclamation "Look who's coming to dinner!" comes to mind. It happens again and again. People stare and feel awkward. There is an uneasy feeling that such persons should work their way into the community of faith over time by some tangible, apparent signs of repentance and amendment of life.

Could it be that divine forgiveness precedes repentance? Could it be that it is more important for the company of Jesus to show signs of acceptance and joy than for the one who has come into its midst to demonstrate qualities of worthiness? The answer to both questions is an unqualified yes.

Awkwardness, not knowing what to do, even a sense of disgust in the presence of the unworthy one — these emotions coupled with the teaching and remembered behavior of Jesus can elicit new ways of thinking about divine love and grace.

Select Bibliography

Braumann, Georg. "Die Schuldner und die Sünderin Luk. VII.36-50." *NTS* 10 (1963-64): 487-93.

Brodie, Thomas L. "Luke 7:36-50 as an Internalization of 2 Kings 4:1-37: A Study in Luke's Use of Rhetorical Imitation." *Bib* 64 (1983): 457-85.

Drexler, Hans. "Die grosse Sünderin Lucas 7,36-50." *ZNW* 59 (1968): 159-73.

Holst, Robert. "The One Anointing of Jesus: Another Application of the Form-critical Method." *JBL* 95 (1976): 435-46.

Kilgallen, John J. "A Proposal for Interpreting Luke 7:36-50." *Bib* 72 (1991): 305-30.

———. "Forgiveness of Sins (Luke 7:36-50)." *NovT* 40 (1998): 105-16.

Macgregor, W. M. "The Parable of the Money-Lender and His Debtors (Luke vii.41-47)." *ExpTim* 37 (1925-26): 344-47.

Reid, Barbara E. "'Do You See this Woman?' Luke 7:36-50 as a Paradigm for Feminist Hermeneutics." *BR* 40 (1995): 37-49.

Resseguie, James L. "Luke 7:36-50." *Int* 46 (1992): 285-90.

Thibeaux, Evelyn R. "'Known to be a Sinner': The Narrative Rhetoric of Luke 7:36-50." *BTB* 23 (1993): 151-60.

Wendland, Ernst R. "A Tale of Two Debtors: On the Interaction of Text, Cotext, and Context in a New Testament Dramatic Narrative (Luke 7:36-50)." In *Linguistics and New Testament Interpretation,* 101-43. Ed. David A. Black et al. Nashville: Broadman Press, 1992.

Wilckens, Ulrich. "Vergebung für die Sünderin (Lk 7,36-50)." In *Orientierung an Jesus: Zur Theologie der Synoptiker: Für Josef Schmid,* 394-424. Ed. Paul Hoffmann et al. Freiburg: Herder, 1973.

Wood, H. G. "The Use of ἀγαπάω in Luke viii. [sic] 42, 47." *ExpTim* 66 (1954-55): 319-20.

5.19. The Two Sons, Matthew 21:28-32

[Jesus said,] 28*"What do you think? A man had two sons. And he went to the first and said, 'Son, go and work in the vineyard today.' 29And he answered, 'I am not going to'; but later he felt remorse and went. 30And [the father] went to the other [son] and said the same; and he answered, 'I am going, sir,' but did not go. Which of the two did the father's will?"*

They said, "The first."

Jesus said to them, "Truly, I say to you, the tax collectors and the prostitutes precede you into the kingdom of God. 32For John came to you in the way of righteousness, and you did not believe him, but the tax collectors and the prostitutes believed him; and you, even when you saw [that happen], did not afterward repent and believe him."

Notes on the Text and Translation

The passage has a major textual problem. There are three major textual traditions (all in Greek witnesses) concerning the sequence of responses from the two sons to their father. These are as follows:

1. Reading Number One. The first son says yes to his father but does nothing, and the second says no but then changes his mind. The hearers agree that the latter did the father's will. This is represented in some important

manuscripts (B, Θ, family 13, and others). It is the reading accepted in the Westcott-Hort edition (1881) and the 25th edition of the Nestle-Aland Greek text (1963), as well as in some modern versions (NEB, NAB).

2. Reading Number Two. The first son says no to his father but afterward changes his mind, and the second son says yes but does nothing. The hearers agree that the latter did the father's will. This is represented in one important Greek witness (D) and various Old Latin and Syriac texts. No modern editions represent this reading.

3. Reading Number Three. The first son says no to his father but afterward changes his mind, and the second son says yes but does nothing. The hearers agree that the first of the sons did the father's will. This reading is attested in some important manuscripts (א, C, some Old Latin and Vulgate texts, and some Syriac texts). It is the reading accepted in the 26th and 27th editions of the Nestle-Aland Greek text (1979 and 1993, respectively) and most modern English versions (KJV, RSV, TEV, JB, NIV, NRSV). It is represented in the translation above.

The third reading is to be preferred, since it has better support in the ancient texts.[1] The second reading makes no sense and has not been adopted by modern versions.[2] The first reading is possible, and it is favored by some,[3] but it may be due to an allegorical alignment of the parable with the sequence of salvation history by later scribes, in which the Jewish people by and large (= the first son) say no, and Christians (= the second son) say yes.[4]

21:29, 32. The verb μεταμέλομαι has a range of meanings: "feel regret," "repent," "change one's mind," or "feel remorse."[5] It does not always have to mean "repent": "μετανοεῖν ['to repent'] implies that one has later arrived at a

---

1. For a thorough discussion of text-critical matters and judgments by various critics, and reasons for support of Reading Number Three, cf. Kurt Aland and Barbara Aland, *The Text of the New Testament,* 2d ed. (Grand Rapids: Wm. B. Eerdmans, 1989), 312-16. Cf. also the discussion and same conclusion in B. Metzger, *TCGNT* 55-56.

2. That it is the text original to Matthew is held, however, by A. Cadoux, *Parables,* 117-18; J. Ramsey Michaels, "The Parable of the Regretful Son," 15-26. Michaels understands the use of the verb ἀπέρχομαι as meaning to "go away" from the father, instead of to go off into the vineyard. While that is a possible understanding of the verb, the reading is very limited in textual support; the other readings have much weightier evidence. B. Scott, *Parable,* 80-85, considers this version to be based on oral tradition but not favored by Matthew's "ideology." Apparently Scott would conclude that the reading is not Matthean, but nevertheless pre-Matthean (the earliest, or original, also?).

3. B. Smith, *Parables,* 209-10; J. Derrett, "The Parable of the Two Sons," 109-16; J. Lambrecht, *Treasure,* 93-94; W. Langley, "The Parable of the Two Sons," 230, seems to favor this version, but in the end (p. 243) he declares that it makes no difference, for both sons are disobedient in one respect — either in word or deed.

4. B. Metzger, *TCGNT* 55-56; J. Gnilka, *Matthäusevangelium,* 2:219; D. Hagner, *Matthew,* 611-12; U. Luz, *Matthäus,* 3:204-5; D. Senior, *Matthew,* 237.

5. BAGD 511; *EDNT* 2:414-15.

different view of something (νοῦς), μεταμέλεσθαι that one has a different feeling about it (μέλει). But it is easy for the two ideas to come together."[6] Although some versions use "repented" in 21:29 (KJV, RSV), others use other terms — which are preferable — such as "changed his mind" (NEB, TEV, NIV, NRSV), "thought better of it" (JB), or "regretted it" (NAB). That he simply changed his mind is too bland. That he "felt remorse" is used above to capture the sense of regret. The use of "did not repent" seems fitting in 21:32, however, as in various translations (KJV, RSV, NAB, NIV). Others have "did not change your minds" (NEB, TEV, NRSV) and "refused to think better of it" (JB).

Exegetical Commentary

The parable appears only in Matthew's Gospel. It is located within the Jerusalem setting of Jesus' ministry, which begins at 21:1. It follows upon the Entry into Jerusalem (21:1-11), the Cleansing of the Temple (21:12-17), the Cursing of the Fig Tree (21:18-22), and the conflict story on the Question of Authority, in which the opponents of Jesus (the chief priests and elders) will not answer his question about the origins of John's baptismal ministry (21:23-27). The situation is one of conflict. The immediate audience to whom the parable is told is the chief priests and elders (21:23), and it is established in both the conflict story and the parable that they refused to accept John and his message (21:27, 32).

The parable is the first within a series of three parables that depict the unfaithfulness of the chief priests and elders. The other two, which follow immediately, are the Wicked Tenants (21:33-44) and the Wedding Banquet (22:1-11).

The parable and its application consist of three parts: the introductory material and the interaction between the father and the first son (21:28-29), the interaction between the father and the second son (21:30), and the application (21:31-32).

21:28-29. The parable is introduced by the question: "What do you think?" which appears also at the outset of the Parable of the Lost Sheep (18:12) and elsewhere (17:25; 22:17, 42; 26:66; John 11:56; cf. Luke 10:36), and it is probably redactional (an original parable could begin without it). It is an arresting phrase, asked in this case of the opponents of Jesus. It does not allow their previous silence (21:27) to go unchallenged.

The first son refuses to work for his father. The refusal is not only an outright rejection of the father's request, but an act of rebellion as well, which is an affront to the father. Later, however, that son changes his mind and goes to work in the vineyard. So the initial refusal is followed by actual obedience after all. On the meanings of the verb μεταμέλομαι, see Notes above.

The parable has allegorical features. The father is here, as elsewhere

6. Otto Michel, "μεταμέλομαι," *TDNT* 4:626.

(21:37; 22:2; Luke 11:11; 15:11), a metaphor for God, and the vineyard is here, as elsewhere (Isa 5:1-7; Matt 21:33-43), a metaphor for Israel. Each of the sons is a metaphor for the obedient and disobedient within Israel, as will be developed as the parable unfolds.

21:30. The second son assents to his father's request, but he fails to do what he was asked to do. Nothing is said about his changing his mind; that is not needed. He simply fails to carry out what he is supposed to do. But at a deeper level, he also breaks a promise.

The latter son actually calls his father "lord" (κύριος, "sir" in modern versions, e.g., KJV, RSV, NIV, and NRSV), which the first son does not do. So he is all words, not deeds — all talk, not obedience. Clearly the term κύριος has a metaphorical significance. Many are those who say κύριε, κύριε ("Lord, Lord"), but do not do the will of God (7:21).

21:31a-b. The narrative from Jesus is over; now there is a question and a response. By saying that "the first" son did the father's will, the chief priests and elders (21:23) pass judgment upon themselves. They correspond to the second son in that they claim to be workers in the vineyard, but they have failed in their duties.

21:31c-32. By way of application, Jesus links his opponents explicitly with the second son. They had given assent to God's law and prophets (and were therefore like people who say yes), but they refused John, the greatest of the prophets. On the other hand, the tax collectors and prostitutes made no claims of accepting the law and the prophets, but accepted the preaching of John.

Even though they "saw" the response of the tax collectors and prostitutes to the preaching of John, they did not "change their minds" and believe him (and his message). And those who reject John reject Jesus.

The tax collectors and prostitutes "precede" (προάγουσιν) the Pharisees into the kingdom. The phrase "tax collectors and prostitutes" is found only here and in the following verse (21:32) within the NT; the more usual phrase is "tax collectors and sinners" (Matt 9:10-11//Mark 2:15-16//Luke 5:30; Matt 11:19//Luke 7:34; Luke 15:1). The two may be linked primarily — already in the tradition prior to Matthew — because both were regarded as major collaborators with the occupying Roman forces. On this matter the tax collectors were infamous; the prostitutes can be included because they worked near Roman military camps.[7]

It has been argued that the verb προσάγω ("precede") means that, while the tax collectors and prostitutes enter the kingdom, the chief priests and elders are excluded.[8] But actually the verb (used 20 times in the NT) normally

---

7. J. Gibson, "Hoi telonai kai hai pornai," 430-31 (with references to Josephus, Ant. 19.356; B. Shab. 33b; B. Abod. Zar. 18a).

8. J. Jeremias, Parables, 125; Günther Bornkamm, Jesus of Nazareth (New York: Harper & Brothers, 1960), 79; W. D. Davies and D. C. Allison, Matthew, 3:169-70.

means a temporal or spatial sequence ("to go before"), not exclusion.[9] Therefore the door is left open for the Pharisees finally to repent and enter the kingdom — but they shall be at the end of the line. The phrase "kingdom of God" (instead of the more common "kingdom of heaven," used 32 times in Matthew) is used, besides here, only at 12:28; 19:24; 21:43. Here it is probably embedded in the tradition that Matthew has received (although that is not a proof for a pre-Matthean origin, since the same phrase is used at 21:43, which is redactional).

21:32. The verse serves as a "proof" of the application (21:31). Independently of it, Luke claims also that tax collectors were baptized by John, that the Pharisees refused, and that they therefore rejected God's purpose (7:29-30). Matthew's verse includes both tax collectors and prostitutes.

The phrase "the way of righteousness" is enigmatic. The term δικαιοσύνη ("righteousness") — used seven times in this Gospel (3:15; 5:6, 10, 20; 6:1, 33; 21:32) — can refer simply to that standard of moral conduct which is demanded by God (5:20; 6:1). On this basis, "the way of righteousness" could be taken to refer to a way of life or conduct that God demands,[10] as in the NIV ("to show you the right way to live") and TEV ("showing you the right path to take") and in some ancient texts (LXX, Job 24:13; Prov 21:16, 21; 2 Peter 2:21; plural "ways of righteousness" in LXX, Prov 8:20; 12:28). But that is not likely the meaning here; it is too narrow. The term δικαιοσύνη is used in connection with John the Baptist at 3:15 also, where it is said that the baptism of Jesus by John was to fulfill all righteousness, that is, to conform to the will and purpose of God.[11] The "way of righteousness" in the present verse refers back to John, and it designates John as one who followed the path of the purpose of God.[12] That such is the meaning is likely in light of the related statement in Luke 7:30 in which it is said that the Pharisees, by rejecting John, rejected the purpose of God (τὴν βουλὴν τοῦ θεοῦ). Moreover, accepting the way of righteousness (21:32) relates in a positive way to doing the father's will (21:31).

9. A. McNeile, *Matthew*, 306; Jan-Adolf Bühner, "προάγω," *EDNT* 3:150-51; Werner G. Kümmel, *Promise and Fulfilment: The Eschatological Message of Jesus*, SBT 23 (Naperville: Alec R. Allenson, 1957), 78; U. Luz, *Mattäus*, 3:211.

10. W. Allen, *Matthew*, 227; J. A. Kleist, "Greek or Semitic Idiom," 196; Robert Bratcher, "Righteousness in Matthew," *BT* 40 (1989): 234; Georg Strecker, *Der Weg der Gerechtigkeit: Untersuchung zur Theologie des Matthäus*, FRLANT 82 (Göttingen: Vandenhoeck & Ruprecht, 1962), 187; Charles H. H. Scobie, *John the Baptist* (Philadelphia: Fortress Press, 1964), 85; H. Weder, *Gleichnisse*, 238; W. D. Davies and D. C. Allison, *Matthew*, 3:170.

11. Karl Kertelge, "δικαιοσύνη," *EDNT* 1:329.

12. Benno Przybylski, *Righteousness in Matthew and His World of Thought*, SNTSMS 41 (Cambridge: Cambridge University Press, 1980), 94-96; Donald A. Hagner, "Righteousness in Matthew's Theology," in *Worship, Theology and Ministry in the Early Church: Essays in Honor of Ralph P. Martin*, ed. Michael J. Wilkins and Terence Paige (Sheffield: JSOT Press, 1992), 117-18.

It has been maintained that 21:32 is an independent saying that does not fit its context well, and that it must have been added to the rest of the application either by Matthew[13] or by a pre-Matthean editor.[14] The reason for this view is that the parable proper has to do with obedience to the will of the father (therefore God), but the application in 21:32 has to do with a positive or negative attitude toward John the Baptist. In this view, 21:31 is a fitting application of the parable. Others would include 21:31c (beginning with "Jesus said . . .") as secondary along with 21:32, which would mean that the parable had no application attached whatsoever.[15]

Although that is possible, it would seem that the material in 21:31c-32 is pre-Matthean in any case. The language of 21:31c is traditional, not Matthean, in its use of "tax collectors and prostitutes" and "kingdom of God." Moreover, if the "way of righteousness" (21:32) exemplified in the ministry of John is in fact the purpose and plan of God, all of 21:31c-32 is fitting as an application. The point of comparison would be that those who have not professed to be obedient (the tax collectors and prostitutes) — thereby corresponding to the son who said no but then entered the vineyard — have in fact responded to the purposes of God, beginning with the ministry of John, while those who claim to be obedient (the chief priests and elders) — corresponding to the disobedient son — have not. Further, even when the latter saw the phenomenon of repentance among the tax collectors and prostitutes, they did not themselves repent. They have thus decided against John and his ministry twice.[16] The fact that believing John is so strongly emphasized twice (21:32a, c), thereby putting a very high estimate upon him, casts doubt on whether the saying was created within a Christian community. It must have originated in the earliest stratum of the tradition, reflecting the attitude of Jesus himself.[17]

Several interpreters have maintained that the parable was composed by Matthew.[18] On the other hand, the authenticity of the parable itself (21:28b-31b) — apart from the introductory question (21:28a) and its specific applica-

13. R. Bultmann, *HST* 177; T. W. Manson, *Sayings*, 223; W. L. Richards, "Another Look at the Parable of the Two Sons," 5-14; J. Donahue, *Parable*, 88.

14. J. Jeremias, *Parables*, 80-81; N. Perrin, *Teaching*, 119.

15. A. Jülicher, *Gleichnisreden*, 2:382-33; H. Weder, *Gleichnisse*, 231-33; J. Gnilka, *Matthäusevangelium*, 2:219-20; J. Lambrecht, *Treasure*, 95-99; U. Luz, *Matthäus*, 3:205-7.

16. W. D. Davies and D. C. Allison, *Matthew*, 3:171.

17. Martin Dibelius, *Die urchristliche Überlieferung von Johannes dem Täufer*, FRLANT 15 (Göttingen: Vandenhoeck & Ruprecht, 1911), 20-21; Walter Wink, *John the Baptist in the Gospel Tradition*, SNTSMS 7 (Cambridge: Cambridge University Press, 1968), 18, considers it among a cluster of sayings concerning John, many of which are authentic. N. Perrin, *Teaching*, 75, seems to consider 21:32 authentic, but placed where it is in the pre-Matthean tradition (p. 119).

18. H. Merkel, "Das Gleichnis von den 'ungleichen Söhnen,'" 254-61; R. Gundry, *Matthew*, 422-24; M. E. Boring, *Matthew (NIB)*, 8:411; R. Cameron, "Matthew's Parable," 191-209; R. Funk, *The Five Gospels*, 231-33 (21:28a, 32 black font; 21:28b-31 gray font).

tion (21:31c-32) — is held to be a probability by others.[19] Although there are many stylistic features of Matthew within it,[20] there are also traditional expressions (as pointed out above), and it seems that there is no compelling need to exclude it from the preaching of Jesus.

Occasionally it is suggested that this parable was the basis for the Parable of the Prodigal Son (Luke 15:11-32).[21] In spite of their similarity in narrating stories of a father and his two sons, there is no basis for the suggestion. The most obvious difference between them, at a fundamental structural level, is apparent in the responses of the sons. If the first son in Matthew's parable is assumed to be the oldest, his initial insolence does not correspond to the always deferential older son in Luke's parable. Surely Jesus could have spoken parables concerning fathers and sons on more than one occasion.

Exposition

Doing the will of God is more than a matter of words; it has to do with deeds (7:21-27; 25:31-46). And when words are uttered as promises, and those promises are not kept, the words are more than empty platitudes; they are corrupt.

The parable does more, however, than speak against the hypocrisy of uttering pious words that are not consonant with behavior. It also speaks against the view that the ways and will of God are always evident to those who presume to be the custodians of the tradition — and that they are always obscure to those outside. New occasions may in fact demand new duties. God may be doing a new thing. The sending of John was such, and who knows what else? To reject the new and unfamiliar may be right. But there may also be occasions where God is beckoning his children to serve in the kingdom in unexpected ways or places.

What is so intriguing is that God often gets a hearing and response in the lives of people whom the righteous despise. These are people who make no claims of being righteous or religious, but who carry on daily tasks given them by God. Precisely when people do not try to be religious, but simply do the will

---

19. H. Weder, *Gleichnisse*, 230-35; E. Schweizer, *Matthew*, 410; J. Gnilka, *Matthäusevangelium*, 2:219-20; J. Lambrecht, *Treasure*, 98-100; U. Luz, *Matthäus*, 3:207-8; W. D. Davies and D. C. Allison, *Matthew*, 3:165. According to A. Jülicher, *Gleichnisreden*, 2:385, the parable is definitely authentic.

20. R. Gundry, *Matthew*, 422, provides a survey.

21. J. van Goudoever, "The Place of Israel in Luke's Gospel," *NovT* 8 (1966): 121; Michael D. Goulder, *Luke: A New Paradigm*, JSNTSup 20, 2 vols. (Sheffield: JSOT Press, 1989), 2:609; it is a possibility, according to Jack T. Sanders, *The Jews in Luke-Acts* (Philadelphia: Fortress Press, 1987), 108. This is held as a possibility by Heikki Räisänen, "The Prodigal Gentile and His Jewish Christian Brother: Lk 15,11-32," *The Four Gospels 1992: Festschrift Frans Neirynck*, ed. Frans van Segbroeck et al., BETL 100, 3 vols. (Leuven: Leuven University Press, 1992), 2:1,631, 1,636. On the other hand, R. Gundry, *Matthew*, 422, suggests that Matthew composed the parable as a "counterpart" to the Parable of the Prodigal Son.

of God through the normal course of living, they respond to God's call. That can include anyone who hears the parable within the Christian fellowship, and it may include those who do not. God's dominion takes place and gets done beyond the bounds of church activity in many corners of the world, even where the gospel has not been heard. That should be good news even for those who consider themselves the bearers of the gospel.

Select Bibliography

Bratcher, Robert G. "Righteousness in Matthew." *BT* 40 (1989): 228-35.

Cameron, Ron. "Matthew's Parable of the Two Sons." *FFF* 8/3-4 (1992): 191-209

Derrett, J. Duncan M. "The Parable of the Two Sons." *ST* 25 (1971): 109-16.

Gibson, J. *"Hoi telonai kai hai pornai."* *JTS* 32 (1981): 429-33.

Guy, Harold A. "The Parable of the Two Sons." *ExpTim* 51 (1939-40): 204.

Kleist, James A. "Greek or Semitic Idiom: A Note on Mt. 21,32." *CBQ* 8 (1946): 192-96.

Langley, Wendell E. "The Parable of the Two Sons (Matthew 21:28-32) against Its Semitic and Rabbinic Backdrop." *CBQ* 58 (1996): 228-43.

Macgregor, W. M. "The Parable of the Two Sons." *ExpTim* 38 (1926-27): 498.

Martens, Allan W. "'Produce Fruit Worthy of Repentance': Parables of Judgment against Jewish Religious Leaders and the Nation (Matt 21:28–22:14, par.; Luke 13:6-9)." In *The Challenge of Jesus' Parables*, 151-76. Ed. Richard N. Longenecker. Grand Rapids: Wm. B. Eerdmans, 2000.

Merkel, Helmut. "Das Gleichnis von den 'ungleichen Söhnen' (Matth. xxi.28-32)." *NTS* 20 (1974): 254-61.

Michaels, J. Ramsey. "The Parable of the Regretful Son." *HTR* 61 (1968): 15-26.

Ogawa, Akira. "Paraboles de l'Israël véritable? Reconsidération critique de Mt 21.28–22.14," *NovT* 21 (1979): 121-49.

Read, David H. C. "When What You Believe Is What You Do." *ExpTim* 90 (1979): 367-68.

Richards, W. L. "Another Look at the Parable of the Two Sons." *BR* 23 (1978): 5-14.

Schmid, Josef. "Das textgeschichtliche Problem der Parabel von den zwei Söhnen, Mt 21.28-32." In *Vom Wort des Lebens: Festschrift für Max Meinertz*, 68-84. Ed. Nikolaus Adler. Münster: Aschendorff Verlag, 1951.

5.20. The Friend at Midnight, Luke 11:5-8

5*And [Jesus] said to them, "Which of you will have a friend; and [you] will go to him in the middle of the night and say to him, 'Friend, lend me three loaves of bread,* 6*since a friend of mine has arrived from a journey, and I have nothing to set before him.'*

7 *"And that friend will answer from inside and say, 'Do not bother me. The door is already locked and my children are in bed with me. I am not able to get up and give [anything] to you'?*

8 *"I tell you, even if he does not get up and give anything to him because he is his friend, he will get up and give him [who has come for help] as much as he needs at least on account of his troublesome persistence."*

Notes on the Text and Translation

11:5. The syntax of the verbs is difficult. Since the verb πορεύσεται ("[he] will go") is in future indicative, one would expect the same for the next verb in the same clause instead of the verb εἴπῃ ("say" in aorist subjunctive).[1] Various texts (A, D, and several others) have the future indicative (ἐρεῖ, "[he] will say"). The weightiest texts, however, have the subjunctive, which is also the more difficult reading, and it is to be preferred.

Other difficulties of translation due to syntax are taken up in the Exegetical Commentary below.

11:7. In the phrase for "in bed," one should expect the use of the preposition ἐν instead of εἰς, but the latter often appears for the former (the local sense of "in") within the NT.[2]

11:8. The phrase εἰ καὶ οὐ δώσει ("even if he will not give") is equivalent to ἐὰν καὶ μὴ δῷ in classical Greek (protasis for a general condition).[3]

The particle γέ is often not translated, but can mean "at least" or "yet" at 11:8 and 18:5.[4] The inclusion of "at least" implies that the "troublesome persistence" is that of the person making the call, not that of the man inside the house.

The term ἀναίδεια (translated here as "troublesome persistence") appears only here in the NT. Its meaning and translation are disputed. Etymologically it means to be without αἰδώς ("modesty" or "respect"). It is translated variously in lexicons as "persistence," "impudence," (most literally) "shamelessness,"[5] "audacity," and "obtrusiveness."[6] English versions of the NT translate it as "importunity" (KJV, RSV), "shamelessness" (NEB), or "persistence" (JB, NAB, NIV, NRSV). Although "importunity" has long usage in English translations (cf. Tyndale's "importunite"), that word is virtually obsolete (except for its use in this verse) and does not carry with it the sense of presumptuousness that the Greek does. The word "persistence" standing alone does not fit either, since it

---

1. BDF 185 (#366, 1).
2. Ibid., 110 (#205).
3. Ibid., 221 (#428, 1).
4. BAGD 152.
5. Ibid., 54, has all three terms. LSJ 105 has "shamelessness."
6. *EDNT* 1:81 has "shamelessness" and then the two latter terms for Luke 11:8.

lacks the same nuance. In context the man's action is somewhat "audacious," but "audacity" seems too strong. There seems to be no one English word that fits well; "troublesome persistence" is used here to catch the breadth of its meaning in this particular context.

Exegetical Commentary

The parable appears only in the Gospel of Luke. Although some interpreters have claimed that it was derived by Luke from Q (and Matthew simply did not reproduce it),[7] it is more likely to have come from Luke's special tradition.[8] Its larger context is the Travel Narrative (9:51–19:27), in which Jesus instructs his followers on a wide range of topics. The immediate context is a series of events and sayings on prayer. Jesus had been praying, but ceased (11:1a). Then follows the request of one of his disciples to teach the disciples how to pray (11:1b). This is followed by the Lukan version of the Lord's Prayer (11:2-4) and further instructions on prayer (11:5-13). The parable has been placed within that larger context of instruction, coming immediately after the Lord's Prayer. Thematically it has similarities to another parable also distinctive to Luke, the Unjust Judge (18:2-8), which illustrates persistence in prayer.

The syntax of the parable is extremely awkward, as can be seen in more literal English translations (e.g., KJV and RSV) and in the Greek text. Part of the problem is that, in Greek, all of 11:5-7 is in the form of a question. But there is also uncertainty about the subject of various clauses. A rather literal translation would be: "Which of you will have a friend and he will go to him . . . and say to him . . . ?" Is the one who goes and speaks to another the hearer (or reader) of the parable, or is it the hearer's friend? The difficulty of trying to unravel the syntax is apparent in English versions of the NT. Two examples are given here (with emphasis supplied to highlight the differences):

> NIV: "Suppose one of you has a friend, and *he goes* to him at midnight and *says*. . . ."
> NRSV: "Suppose one of you has a friend, and *you go* to him at midnight and *say*. . . ."

The translation of Joseph Fitzmyer appears to give still another nuance: "Suppose one of you has a friend, and *he comes* at midnight and *says*. . . ."[9] Here it

---

7. Wilfred L. Knox, *The Sources of the Synoptic Gospels,* 2 vols. (Cambridge: Cambridge University Press, 1953-57), 2:30; B. Easton, *Luke,* 177-78; David R. Catchpole, "Q and the Friend at Midnight," 407-24; idem, "Q, Prayer, and the Kingdom: A Rejoinder," 377-88.

8. C. Tuckett, "Q, Prayer, and the Kingdom," 367-71.

9. J. Fitzmyer, *Luke,* 909.

appears that the friend is portrayed as arriving at the hearer's (or reader's) own home. But at 11:7 the Fitzmyer translation indicates (correctly) that the person being visited is someone other than the hearer. Usually the NEB is excellent in its use of English, but in this case it is very confusing: "Suppose one of you has a friend *who comes* to him . . . and *says.* . . ." To whom does the friend come? Does he come to the hearer or to someone else?

What is portrayed in the narrative and parable is the following: Jesus asks his hearers a general question and individualizes it ("Which *one* of you?"). The individual hearer is then spoken of as having a friend to whom he goes at midnight and makes a request for three loaves of bread. In other words, the antecedent of the verb "to go" is "one of you" (as in the NRSV), not the "friend."[10] The person who goes calling (the hearer of the parable) has become a host in need of loaves to feed an unexpected guest. Surely the friend called upon at midnight will not refuse the person who comes calling (again, the hearer of the parable). To be sure, he could grumble and say that everyone is in bed, but he will not. He will help out. And the reason for helping will not actually be on the basis of friendship, but rather because of the troublesome persistence of the one who comes calling upon him at that hour of the night — after he and his family have gone to bed and have been there for some time. It is important to help whoever is at the door at that time of night, friend or not. He will get up and give whatever is needed.

11:5. The opening phrase, "Which of you" (τίς ἐξ ὑμῶν), appears here for the first time in the Gospel of Luke, but it will appear again to introduce parables.[11] It is an arresting phrase that introduces a rhetorical question. The question runs from here to the end of 11:7. Several modern translations (NEB, NIV, and NRSV) begin with the less literal "Suppose one of you," which helps simplify the syntax in modern English. The implied answer to the question in this parable, as it unfolds, is, "No one." Surely the friend who is approached for help will supply what is needed.

The verb ἕξει is literally future ("will have") and can be translated that way here, even though it is customarily translated present ("has," RSV, NEB, NIV, and NRSV). The friend is one to whom the hearer or reader of the parable can go for help. One can go to him even at midnight. The Greek term μεσονύκτιον need not be taken literally and precisely as meaning "midnight" (twelve o'clock). In a non-Western, non-modern culture the term can have the more general meaning of "the middle of the night."[12] In any case, arriving in the middle of the night would be unusual.[13]

---

10. Contra J. Jeremias, *Parables*, 158; and J. Creed, *Luke*, 157-58.

11. Luke 11:11 (//Matt 7:9); 15:4; 17:7; cf. also 12:25 (//Matt 6:27); Matt 12:11; and John 8:46.

12. Raymond Rickards, "The Translation of Luke 11.5-13," 240.

13. K. Bailey, *Poet*, 121.

The host who goes to his friend for help requests a loan of three loaves. The reason for "three" loaves is not clear. Perhaps the loaves envisioned are small, so three are necessary for a meal.[14] Or they could be large enough so that one alone would suffice, and so three would signify abundance and generosity. Or again, perhaps three loaves are requested so that (on the biblical model) there is one for the host and two for the traveling friend (one immediately, and one left over; cf. 1 Sam 10:3-4). In any case, it is not likely that the loaves would be the sum total of the meal to be served, even though they would be essential for it. Pieces of the loaves would be broken off and used for dipping into dishes or scooping other food items.[15] The verb χρῆσον ("lend," aorist imperative form for κίχρημι) is found only here in the NT.

11:6. The reason for the petitioner's request is hospitality. It is unthinkable not to receive a traveling friend into one's home, even in the middle of the night. Hospitality was considered a sacred duty throughout the Mediterranean world of antiquity, even when the visitor was a stranger.[16] In this particular case, hospitality is required on two grounds: the visitor is not only a stranger but a friend as well.

11:7. The verse says exactly what the person called upon during the middle of the night would *not* do. Surely he would not call out in this manner, making four statements: (1) do not bother me; (2) the door is locked; (3) my children and I are in bed; and (4) I cannot get up and help you.

Each of the four statements is a statement of refusal. To be called upon in the middle of the night is troublesome for anyone, friend or not; the expression κόπους πάρεχε commonly means "to cause trouble" for someone,[17] and it shows up again in a similar parable at 18:5. Once the door has been "already locked," it is most cumbersome and noisy to open it. The house is portrayed as a small one. It has only one door, and the family shares the same sleeping area. No reference is made to the man's wife, but the children are mentioned as being in bed, which is not an insignificant detail. If the man inside the house gets up to unlock the door, the children (or at least the smaller ones) will most likely wake up, cry, and not go to sleep again readily. Finally, in regard to the fourth statement, "here, as so often, 'I cannot' camouflages 'I will not.'"[18]

11:8. Nothing recorded in the previous verse will actually happen. Although it is conceivable in normal life, things like that simply do not occur in the usual course of events. The man inside the house will surely get up and tend to the needs of the one who comes calling upon him. He will disregard the time

14. J. Jeremias, *Parables*, 157.

15. K. Bailey, *Poet*, 123.

16. Cf. Vernon H. Kooy, "Hospitality," *IDB* 2:654; John Koenig, "Hospitality," *ABD* 3:299-301.

17. BAGD 443 with various references (LXX, Josephus, papyri, and Matt 26:10; Mark 14:6; Luke 18:5; Gal 6:17).

18. T. W. Manson, *Sayings*, 267.

of night, the noise, and possibly even waking the children in order to do his duty. In fact, he will do his duty not because the visitor is a friend, but because of the latter's ἀναίδεια ("troublesome persistence"; see Note above).

At this point a major exegetical issue arises. Is the ἀναίδεια actually that of the visitor, or is it that of the man inside the house? A number of interpreters have concluded that the term refers to the man inside.[19] There are three main reasons for such a view: (1) In the cultural world of the parable, wherein hospitality is so important, the man inside the house (and perhaps his whole family) would suffer shame if he did not help. "Thus the petitioner threatens to expose the potential shamelessness of the sleeper. By morning the entire village would know of his refusal to provide hospitality. He thus gives in to avoid public exposure as a shameless person."[20] (2) The central figure within the parable is actually the man inside the house, not the man who comes visiting. The parable is about God who responds readily to prayer, not about persistence in prayer. This is corroborated by a third point. (3) The man who comes calling is not really troublesome or persistent at all. He makes only one request, and he is doing what a person in his situation ought to do.

Other interpreters — either routinely (in light of the tradition) or by deliberation — consider the term to refer to the manner of the man who comes calling.[21] In spite of the difficulties posed, this seems to be correct. The verse can be outlined as follows, placing a question mark [?] for the unknowns (which man is being referred to in each case?) and employing the most widely used translation of the Greek term ἀναίδεια within the scholarly literature — and the most neutral one for our purposes here — namely, "shamelessness."

1. If he [= the man inside] . . . will not give to him [= the man outside],
2. because he [= ?] is his [= ?] friend,
3. because of his [= ?] shamelessness at least,
4. he [= the man inside] . . . will give to him [= the man outside] as much as he [= the man outside] needs.

19. Anton Fridrichsen, "Exegetisches zum Neuen Testament," SO 13 (1934) 40-43 (cited by Jeremias); J. Jeremias, Parables, 158-59; Eberhard Jüngel, Paulus und Jesus: Eine Untersuchung zur Präzisierung der Frage nach dem Ursprung der Christologie, HUTh 2 (Tübingen: J. C. B. Mohr [Paul Siebeck], 1962), 156; N. Perrin, Teaching, 128-29; K. Bailey, Poet, 125-33; E. W. Huffard, "The Parable of the Friend at Midnight," 156; B. Scott, Parable, 89-91; Bruce J. Malina and Richard L. Rohrbaugh, Social-Science Commentary on the Synoptic Gospels (Minneapolis: Fortress Press, 1992), 351; R. A. Culpepper, NIB (Luke), 8:236. I. H. Marshall, Luke, 465, expresses some uncertainty but inclines toward this view.

20. B. Malina and R. Rohrbaugh, Social-Science Commentary, 351.

21. A. Jülicher, Gleichnisreden, 2:273-75; W. Oesterley, Parables, 221-22; A. Cadoux, Parables, 34-35; T. W. Manson, Sayings, 268; B. Smith, Parables, 147; J. Crossan, Parables, 84, 107; P. Perkins, Parables, 194-95; D. Wenham, Parables, 181; J. D. M. Derrett, "The Friend at Midnight," 82-85; J. Fitzmyer, Luke, 912; W. Liefeld, "Parables on Prayer," 251.

In this outline the "he" of line two (the first causal clause) could be either of the two men (the one outside or the one inside); the clause makes perfectly good sense either way.[22] But the man referred to in line three by the oblique "his" (the second causal clause) must be the man outside (i.e., the petitioner). If honor and shame are at stake for the man inside the house, and he acts on that basis, there should be terminology that makes that point. But that is precisely not what motivates him in this case. The term used — ἀναίδεια, "shamelessness" (i.e., being or acting without sensibility to shame or disgrace) — does not work as a means of action for a person who is trying to avoid being shamed by others. How could he possibly act "shamelessly," that is, without regard to shame, if being a shameful person is precisely what he seeks to avoid in the eyes of his neighbors? The term ἀναίδεια is pejorative, and cannot be made into its opposite so as to mean that the man inside acted to avoid being shamed.[23] In order to make line three refer to the man inside, one interpreter actually has to translate the word ἀναίδεια as "shame" instead of "shamelessness" ("yet because of the sleeper's shame").[24] If the issue at stake is the avoiding of shame, or (in other words) maintaining the honor of the man inside the house, the clause should read διά γε τὴν τιμὴν αὐτοῦ ("because of his honor at least") or something similar. In any case, acting shamelessly does not avoid shame but can actually incur it.

The most plausible meaning of 11:8 is therefore that the "shamelessness" (or "troublesome persistence") spoken of is that of the person who comes calling. The three points of the alternative interpretation do not hold up. (1) To say that the man inside the house acts without regard to shame is the opposite of what the alternative interpretation requires. (2) The view that the main figure in the parable is the man inside the house, who acts with shamelessness or impertinence, and that the parable is primarily about God (who — in the alternative interpretation — apparently does not want to be

22. So the verse could read either way: "because the man outside is the friend of the man inside" or "because the man inside is the friend of the man outside."

23. It appears only once in the LXX at Sir 25:22, but related words appear more often, such as ἀναιδής (Deut 28:50; 1 Kgdms 2:29; Prov 7:13; 25:23; Eccl 8:1; Sir 23:6, 11; 40:30; Isa 56:11; Jer 8:5; Bar 4:15; Dan 8:23) and ἀναιδῶς (Prov 21:29). All these terms are negative in one way or another. The term appears ten times in the writings of Josephus (*J.W.* 1.224, 276, 504, 616; 6.199; *Ant.* 17.119; 20.181, 357; *Apion* 2.22, 26), always in a negative sense.

24. B. Scott, *Parable*, 89. But on p. 87 and elsewhere Scott has "shamelessness." Cf. also J. Jeremias, *Parables,* 158, who paraphrases the term to mean "so that he may not lose face in the matter," which would mean to avoid shame. Avoiding shame and acting with shamelessness are virtual opposites. The fellows of the Jesus Seminar end up in the same contradiction with the paraphrase: "because you'd be ashamed not to." Cf. R. Funk, *Five Gospels*, 327. N. Perrin, *Teaching,* 128-29, follows Jeremias. K. Bailey, *Poet,* 131, manages to convert the word into "blamelessness" by saying that the wrong word appears in the Greek text (some form of ἀναίτιος ["innocent"] would be the correct one)!

shamed), does not pay much of a compliment to God. (3) And the man at the door, who arouses the man inside, is in fact somewhat of a irritant, even as 11:7 attests; at a basic human level the man in bed is indeed justified in thinking and acting the way 11:7 records. The man who comes calling in the middle of the night is right to seek help so that he can offer hospitality to his friend who has just arrived. But he nevertheless is troublesome, an utter nuisance, to the man who has gone to bed. The latter must finally "accept the bothersome inevitability of what must be done."[25] He will get up and serve the visitor at the door not on the basis of their friendship, but because he is obliged to do so even in an annoying situation.[26]

The parable is set within a series of sayings on prayer. Following the Lord's Prayer, it sets forth the message that one ought to call upon God persistently in prayer, even though that might seem impertinent, for God will indeed respond. The seemingly troublesome person gets the attention and response of God. Following the parable, the thought is drawn out by additional sayings: "Ask, and it will be given you; search, and you will find; knock, and the door will be opened for you" (11:9). The parable, in short, exhorts the hearer and reader to pray. In this regard the parable is much like that of the widow before the Unjust Judge (18:2-8) in both content and function.

It is sometimes maintained that the parable and its setting in Luke's Gospel do not match well. Joachim Jeremias, in fact, says that "the point of the parable has been distorted" by Luke's placing it where he did.[27] The original meaning of the parable, he says, was that "God helps as unconditionally as the friend did," but Luke has turned the parable into a lesson on how persistently one ought to pray.[28]

The distinction made by Jeremias is overly subtle. Rhetorically the parable invites the hearer or reader to pray persistently, based on the prior confidence that God will respond, just as the man inside the house did.

There are details within the parable that give it its vitality but that should not be pressed too far. For example, the parable does not teach that shamelessness, impertinence, or audacity is necessary to get God's attention. The real point of the parable is that people ought most certainly to pray and do so with persistence, for God responds to the prayers of his children. In regard to the

25. J. Crossan, *Parables*, 84.

26. The view of W. Herzog, *Parables*, 201, that the man inside is honored to be called upon seems to run against the plain meaning of the text. His view that in this parable Jesus speaks of and encourages a shameless boundary-breaking hospitality among peasants to foreshadow a different social order (pp. 212-14) goes far beyond what is envisioned in the parable. The parable can be understood only in light of a given social order, and it is in that light that it works as a parable on prayer, as Luke has it.

27. J. Jeremias, *Parables*, 105.

28. Ibid., 105; cf. 158-59.

question of its authenticity, there seem to be no challenges of note.[29] The parable is regarded as characteristic of the teaching of Jesus.

Exposition

Almost every hearer of this parable has been awakened at a late hour or early in the morning by a knock on the door, a ring of the doorbell, or a telephone call. Most can also recall having to make such a visit or phone call as well.

When one is on the receiving end, it is difficult to know whether the arousal from sleep will eventuate in something rather trivial (such as a wrong number in a phone call) or something of great importance. The latter is feared unless good news is expected (like the birth of a child), and the former is unwanted. In either case the usual and normal response is to find out what is wanted. The door is opened or the phone receiver is picked up.

If a person is at the door, and he or she makes a reasonable request (one that can be met), the response is to take care of the matter. It may be annoying to have to do so, but it will be done.

God is portrayed here in a rather ordinary way. A human analogy is at work. Within some parables God is portrayed in extraordinary ways in terms of his dealing with his children, but not always — and not here. Here God is portrayed as a person who is awakened and bothered by someone at the door, and who responds because of the persistence of the visitor who comes calling. Likewise, God responds to the prayers of his persistent children, and therefore they are encouraged to pray unrelentingly. It may seem impertinent to do so. In fact, from the human side, such behavior could appear as "troublesome persistence." But like the man who goes to the neighbor for a legitimate need even in the middle of the night, the children of God should approach God in prayer without reservations.

Select Bibliography

Catchpole, David R. "Q and the Friend at Midnight." *JTS* 34 (1983): 407-24.
———. "Q, Prayer, and the Kingdom: A Rejoinder." *JTS* 40 (1989): 377-88.
Derrett, J. Duncan M. "The Friend at Midnight: Asian Ideas in the Gospel of St. Luke." In *"Donum gentilicium": New Testament Studies in Honour of David Daube,* 78-87. Ed. Ernst Bammel et al. Oxford: Clarendon Press, 1978.
Güttgemanns, Erhardt. "Struktural-generative Analyse der Parabel 'Vom bittenden Freund' (Lk. 11,5-8)." *LingBibl* 2 (1970): 7-11.

29. That the parable originated with Jesus is affirmed or implied in the works of A. Jülicher, *Gleichnisreden,* 2:276; T. W. Manson, *Sayings,* 267; J. Jeremias, *Parables,* 159-60; N. Perrin, *Teaching,* 128-29; W. Herzog, *Parables,* 194-214. The parable is printed in pink in R. Funk, *Five Gospels,* 327, indicating that the parable most likely originated with Jesus.

Huffard, Evertt W. "The Parable of the Friend at Midnight: God's Honor or Man's Persistence?" *ResQ* 21 (1978): 154-60.

Johnson, Alan. "Assurance for Man: The Fallacy of Translating *anaideia* by 'Persistence' in Luke 11:5-8." *JETS* 22 (1979): 123-31.

Liefeld, Walter L. "Parables on Prayer (Luke 11:5-10; 18:1-8; 18:9-14)." In *The Challenge of Jesus' Parables,* 240-62. Ed. Richard N. Longenecker. Grand Rapids: Wm. B. Eerdmans, 2000.

Martin, A. D. "The Parable concerning Hospitality." *ExpTim* 37 (1925-26): 411-14.

Rickards, Raymond R. "The Translation of Luke 11.5-13." *BT* 28 (1977): 239-43.

Snodgrass, Klyne. "*Anaideia* and the Friend at Midnight (Luke 11:8)." *JBL* 116 (1997): 505-13.

Tuckett, Christopher M. "Q, Prayer, and the Kingdom." *JTS* 40 (1989): 367-76.

5.21. The Father's Good Gifts, Matthew 7:9-11//Luke 11:11-13

Matthew 7:9-11

9*[Jesus taught them, saying,]* "Or which person is there among you, if his son asks him for a loaf of bread, will give him a stone? 10*Or if he asks for a fish, he will give him a serpent?* 11*If you then, who are evil, know how to give good gifts to your children, how much more will your Father who is in heaven give good things to those who ask him!*"

Notes on the Text and Translation

7:9-10. The Greek syntax is difficult. The verses can be translated: "Or which man of you, whom his son will ask for bread, will give him a stone? Or also he will ask for a fish, will give him a serpent?" In both questions the Greek μή is used to anticipate a negative answer (not to express "will not give him a stone/ serpent"). The protasis is made up of two clauses (one interrogative, the second relative), and that is said to be "un-Greek" and Semitic.[1] A better Greek construction would translate as: "Which of you will give a stone to your son, if he asks for bread?"[2]

---

1. Klaus Beyer, *Semitische Syntax im Neuen Testament,* SUNT 1 (Göttingen: Vandenhoeck & Ruprecht, 1962), 287-93.
2. BDF 246 (#469); a sentence in Greek is proposed.

THE FATHER'S GOOD GIFTS

Luke 11:11-13

11 *[Jesus said to them,] "And what father among you, if his son asks for a fish, and he will give him a serpent in place of a fish;* 12 *or also if he asks for an egg, will give him a scorpion?* 13 *If you then, who are evil, know how to give good gifts to your children, how much more will the Father give the Holy Spirit from heaven to those who ask him!"*

Notes on the Text and Translation

11:11-12. As in the case of the Matthean parallel (see above), the syntax (two clauses in the protasis — one interrogative, the other relative) is Semitic.[3]

11:11. Some important Greek witnesses read that the "son asks for bread, will give him a stone" prior to "asks for a fish," so that there are three items listed (bread, fish, egg). The shorter reading is attested in papyri (45, 75) and B, however, and the addition can be attributed to harmonization with Matthew 7:9-10. The shorter reading is to be preferred.[4]

The καί is replaced in some Greek witnesses by μή, and the 25th edition of the Nestle-Aland Greek text followed them, thereby replacing a Semitism with a Greek interrogative particle expecting a negative answer. The 26th and 27th editions follow the papyri (45, 75) and B, which is preferred.[5]

11:12. The interrogative particle μή is inserted in some Greek witnesses, but is lacking in the papyri (45, 75) and B, and the omission is to be preferred.[6]

11:13. Following "how much more will," four readings are attested in Greek and other witnesses: (1) "the Father in heaven give the Holy Spirit" (the textual preference for Nestle-Aland; followed in RSV, NEB, NRSV as "the heavenly Father give the Holy Spirit); (2) "the Father give the Holy Spirit from heaven" (reflecting 𝔭75, ℵ, and other witnesses); (3) "your heavenly Father give the Holy Spirit" (reflecting 𝔭45 and others); and (4) "your Father in heaven give the Holy Spirit." Of these, the last is least well attested, and the third may be a harmonization with Matthew 7:11. The second is best attested on external grounds and is the shorter and more difficult reading. It should be preferred.

General Comments on the Texts

What to call this unit in Matthew and Luke is a problem. We actually have twin sayings in each Gospel, and only one is common to both — the illustration concerning the son asking for a fish (Matt 7:10//Luke 11:11). Even though three illustrations are used in the two Gospels (asking for bread, fish, egg), the unit is

---

3. Ibid., 246 (#469); K. Beyer, *Semitische Syntax*, 287-93.
4. B. Metzger, *TCGNT* 157.
5. Ibid.
6. Ibid.

often spoken of comprehensively as a single entity, such as the Parable of the Son Asking for Bread.[7] That may be fitting in the case of the first illustration in Matthew's version (7:9), but not in the second (asking for a fish, 7:10), and not at all in Luke's case; there the son asks for a fish and an egg. Other names used are the Parable of the Father and the Child,[8] the Asking Son,[9] the Father and His Children's Requests,[10] or Good Gifts.[11] Since the focus is on the father who gives good gifts, the title used above seems fitting.

There is no narration as in a narrative parable. Therefore the unit can be classified as a similitude,[12] but one that contains two illustrations within it.

It is generally held that both evangelists made use of a common text before them, Q, which each has modified.[13] But there are other possibilities. Some interpreters have suggested that the source shared by Matthew and Luke contained three illustrations — bread/stone; fish/serpent; and egg/scorpion — and that Matthew made use of the first two, and Luke the last two.[14] Another possibility is that Matthew and Luke had two different recensions of Q, each containing the illustrations that the two evangelists used.[15] Any of these views is possible.

In each Gospel the similitude consists of only two verses (Matt 7:9-10// Luke 11:11-12) — two questions, which are to be answered by an emphatic negative reply — followed by an application (Matt 7:11//Luke 11:13). The application completes (as in an *inclusio*) the theme of asking in prayer expressed earlier (Q, Matt 7:7//Luke 11:9).

It has been claimed that the parable and its application do not actually fit well within their contexts. The reason given is that the verses leading up to it (Matt 7:7-8//Luke 11:9-10) have to do with assurance that God responds to those who ask, while the parable gives assurance that God does not give what is detrimental or useless.[16] The point is an exceedingly fine one. The use of a father-son relationship by means of a parable is surely fitting, and the *inclusio* at the end seems to obviate the point. It is not more likely that the editor of Q fused the sayings together than that Jesus would have done so.

7. C. H. Dodd, *Parables*, 6.

8. J. Jeremias, *Parables*, 144.

9. A. Hunter, *Parables*, 68; R. Stein, *Parables*, 25.

10. D. Wenham, *Parables*, 179.

11. John D. Crossan, *In Fragments: The Aphorisms of Jesus* (San Francisco: Harper & Row, 1983), 343.

12. C. H. Dodd, *Parables*, 6.

13. Burnett H. Streeter, *The Four Gospels: A Study of Origins,* rev. ed. (New York: St. Martin's Press, 1930), 291; A. Polag, *Fragmenta Q,* 50; J. Fitzmyer, *Luke,* 913; U. Luz, *Matthew 1–7,* 421; W. D. Davies and D. C. Allison, *Matthew,* 1:681; D. Goldsmith, "'Ask and it will be given,'" 254; R. Brown, *Introduction NT,* 118.

14. T. W. Manson, *Sayings,* 81; Francis W. Beare, *The Earliest Records of Jesus* (New York: Abingdon, 1962), 162-63; K. Bailey, *Poet,* 136-37.

15. A. McNeile, *Matthew,* 92; I. H. Marshall, *Luke,* 469.

16. A. Cadoux, *Parables,* 75-76; R. Piper, "Matthew 7:7-11 par. Luke 11:9-13," 134.

Interpreters have generally concluded that the parable can ultimately —
in some form — be attributed to Jesus,[17] and there seems to be no compelling
reason to oppose that view.

The Parable in the Gospel of Matthew

Exegetical Commentary

Just prior to the parable (7:7-8) Jesus tells his hearers to pray (ask, search, and
knock). Such persons will receive, find, and have doors opened for them. The
sayings of Jesus appear to promise more than one can expect. By means of this
parable Jesus seeks to show that such is not the case.

7:9-10. The opening question is asked of those who are hearers of the Sermon on the Mount, which include the disciples in the foreground (5:1) and the
crowds nearby (5:1; 7:28). There is no reason to say that the opening formula
(τίς ἐστιν ἐξ ὑμῶν, "which person is there among you") means that the parable
is addressed by Jesus to his opponents.[18] There are instances in which the same
formula is used for parables and sayings that are clearly addressed to the disciples (Q, Matt 6:27//Luke 12:25; Luke 11:5; 17:7) or the crowds in general (Luke
14:28).

Bread and fish have been two basic foods in Palestine from antiquity (indeed, around the world) until the present. The association of a loaf of bread —
flat, round, and tan — and stone — also flat, round, and tan — is easy, since
they are similar in appearance (cf. 4:3, where the command to make stones into
loaves of bread presupposes a similarity too). The same is true for a fish and
some species of snakes.[19]

7:11. The phrase "being evil" is used in reference to human beings. It need
not have a moral connotation,[20] as though Jesus' hearers are wicked. It can be
regarded, rather, as a comparative term in which a contrast is made between
God, who is absolutely good, and human beings, who are not.[21] "There is only
one who is good," namely, God (Matt 19:17).

The term "good gifts" differs from Luke's "Holy Spirit." Interpreters differ

---

17. A. Jülicher, *Gleichnisreden*, 2:40, 43; H. Greeven, "Wer unter euch . . . ?" 86-101;
U. Luz, *Matthew 1–7*, 421. It is printed in pink (= Jesus said something like that) in
R. Funk, *Five Gospels*, 155, in its Matthean form, but in gray (= not from Jesus, but ideas
close to his own) in its Lukan form (p. 328).

18. Contra A. Cadoux, *Parables*, 76-77; J. Jeremias, *Parables*, 145.

19. K. Bailey, *Poet*, 137, drawing upon other sources, suggests a possibility here: the
"barbut" *(clarias macamcracanthus)* in the Sea of Galilee has characteristics of a fish but is
able to crawl on land.

20. Contra Hans-Dieter Betz, *The Sermon on the Mount*, Hermeneia Commentary
(Minneapolis: Fortress Press, 1995), 506.

21. BAGD 691 (πονηρός, 1, b).

on which term would have been more original. It is possible that Matthew made the substitution so that there is a parallel between the two clauses of 7:11 (δόματα ἀγαθά ["good gifts"] in 7:11a and ἀγαθά ["good things"] in 7:11b).[22] That would mean that Luke's version is older. But there are better reasons to maintain that Matthew's "good gifts" is older in the tradition, for it is the more general and could include spiritual gifts, while the gift of the Spirit is more specific and reflects Luke's particular interest in the Holy Spirit.[23] Moreover, in light of the parables that go before, which have to do with physical needs (bread and fish), it would seem that physical needs would be included in the closing statement.[24]

Within the parable a familiar form of argumentation is used, the *qal wahomer* (*a minori ad maius,* "from the lesser to the greater"):[25] If an ordinary father knows how to give good gifts to his children, how much more will God, who is good, give good things to those who ask. The saying marks a switch from an appeal to experience to an appeal to reason.[26] Moreover, not just anything is promised, but only that which is good.

Exposition

The promise of Jesus that God will respond to those who ask, seek, and knock on the door in prayer is grand. Surely that is not the way it is. God is not a cosmic bellhop who can be at the beck and call of anyone — not even a committed disciple — to care for whims or perceived needs on the spot. Even the apostle Paul admits that he could not get the desired effects of prayer (2 Cor 12:8-9).

There is a qualification to the statement about prayer in 7:11: God gives "good things," not just anything, to those who ask. One finds the promises concerning prayer to be qualified by certain conditions elsewhere in the NT as well; compare John 17:7 (one must abide in Christ); 1 John 3:22 (we must keep the commandments and do what is pleasing to God); 5:14-15 (we must ask for what accords with God's will).

Yet God is extremely good. The person who persists in prayer so often finds, even if late in life, that things turn out better than one might expect. Life

---

22. Contra R. Gundry, *Matthew,* 124-25.

23. A. Jülicher, *Gleichnisreden,* 2:44; A. McNeile, *Matthew,* 92; J. Creed, *Luke,* 158; T. W. Manson, *Sayings,* 81-82; E. Earle Ellis, *The Gospel of Luke,* rev. ed., NCB (London: Marshall, Morgan, & Scott, 1974), 166; J. Fitzmyer, *Luke,* 913, 915-16; D. Hagner, *Matthew,* 173. Cf. W. D. Davies and D. C. Allison, *Matthew,* 1:685: the "good things" are "all that is required to live the life of faithful discipleship."

24. R. Piper, "Matthew 7:7-11 par. Luke 11:9-13," 135.

25. On the use of the *qal wahomer* in Scripture and rabbinic works, cf. Louis Jacobs, "Hermeneutics," *EncJud* 8:367.

26. R. Piper, "Matthew 7:7-11 par. Luke 11:9-13," 134.

is more interesting than one could plan, and it is richer by far than what one could desire.

The relationship presupposed by Jesus is similar to that of a father and his children. The person who trusts God and asks for that which is good is rightly related and in the position to receive all that God is so willing to give. It is surely true that "faith in God stands at the beginning of this parable and is not its result."[27]

The Parable in the Gospel of Luke

Exegetical Commentary

In Luke's Gospel the parable is related more directly to prayer. It follows immediately after Jesus' teaching the Lord's Prayer (11:1-4) and the Parable of the Friend at Midnight (11:5-8). All these are addressed to his disciples (11:1-2, 5). As in Matthew 7:9-11, the parable is preceded by the promises of Jesus that those who ask, seek, and knock will receive a response. The promises seem too great. Therefore a parable follows.

11:11-12. The question is formulated in a different manner than in Matthew's Gospel. The one being asked is to imagine himself a "father" whose "son" asks for a fish or an egg. These (as in the case of Matthew's bread and fish) are common foods. No father would give his son a "snake" in place of a fish or a "scorpion" (σκορπίος) in place of an egg. The possibilities of endangerment are greater in Luke's version than in Matthew's. The scorpion (of which there are some 800 species, ranging from one-half inch to seven inches in length) has an elongated and segmented tail with a stinger at the end that produces a poisonous venom (usually resulting in a local irritation, but a few species release a neurotoxin that causes death). Commentators point out that a scorpion is somewhat egg-shaped when its limbs are closed around it.[28] In biblical literature the scorpion is symbolic of evil and harm (Deut 8:15; Ezek 2:6; Luke 10:19; Rev 9:3, 5, 10).[29]

11:13. The expression πονηροὶ ὑπάρχοντες ("being evil") is equivalent to Matthew's, but the use of the verb in the sense of "to be" is a stylistic touch familiar in Luke-Acts (31 times; no cases in Matthew and Mark). On the expression that fathers are evil, the use of the qal waḥomer form of argumentation, and the use of "Holy Spirit" instead of "good things," see comment on Matthew 7:11.

In Luke's Gospel the parable teaches confidence in prayer for the Holy Spirit. For Luke, the Spirit "is the ultimate gift of answered prayer."[30] It is the

27. U. Luz, *Matthew 1–7*, 422.
28. A. Plummer, *Luke*, 300; J. Fitzmyer, *Luke*, 914.
29. BAGD 757.
30. Jacob Kremer, "πνεῦμα," *EDNT* 3:121.

basis for joy, strength, and courage for witness,[31] and it is operative for every new initiative taken in the life of the early church.[32]

Exposition

Although modern persons are somewhat uneasy about petitioning God in prayer, the parable and its application are not. Part of the boldness set forth rests on the fact that what is being asked for is the gift of the Holy Spirit. That is a gift for which many have never thought about asking.

The thought lying behind the parable and its application is the very obvious view that God seeks the good of his children. God will in no way give evil gifts. Prayer for the Spirit is the most appropriate prayer imaginable. The one who prays thereby endorses the work of God in human lives and history through the Spirit, and that person becomes open to the work of God in his or her own life.

Select Bibliography

Goldsmith, Dale. "'Ask, and it will be given . . .': Toward Writing the History of a Logion." *NTS* 35 (1989): 254-65.

Greeven, Heinrich. "Wer unter euch . . . ?" *WuD* 3 (1952): 86-101.

Hjerl-Hansen, Börge. "Le rapprochement poisson-serpent dans la prédication de Jésus (Mt. VII,10 et Luc. XI,11)." *RB* 55 (1948): 195-98.

Kraeling, Carl H. "Seek and You Will Find." In *Early Christian Origins: Studies in Honor of Harold R. Willoughby,* 24-34. Ed. Allen Wikgren. Chicago: Quadrangle, 1961.

McEleney, Neil J. "The Unity and Theme of Matthew 7:1-12." *CBQ* 56 (1994): 490-500.

Piper, Ronald A. "Matthew 7:7-11 par. Luke 11:9-13: Evidence of Design and Argument in the Collection of Jesus' Sayings." In *The Shape of Q: Signal Essays on the Sayings Source,* 131-37. Ed. John S. Kloppenborg. Minneapolis: Fortress Press, 1994. Reprinted from *Logia: Les paroles de Jésus: The Sayings of Jesus: Memorial Joseph Coppens,* 411-18. Ed. Joel Delobel et al. BETL 59. Leuven: Leuven University Press, 1982.

Rickards, Raymond R. "The Translation of Luke 11,5-13." *BT* 28 (1977): 239-43.

Tuckett, Christopher M. "Q, Prayer, and the Kingdom." *JTS* 40 (1989): 367-76.

31. E. Schweizer, *Luke,* 192.

32. Stephen S. Smalley, "Spirit, Kingdom and Prayer in Luke-Acts," *NovT* 15 (1973): 64.

5.22. The Barren Fig Tree, Luke 13:6-9

6And [Jesus] spoke this parable: "A man had a fig tree planted in his vineyard; and he came seeking fruit on it and found none.

7"And he said to the caretaker of the vineyard, 'Look, it has been three years now that I have come seeking fruit on this fig tree, and I keep finding none. Cut it down; why should it use up the soil?'

8"And he answered him, 'Leave it alone, sir, this year also, till I dig about it and put on manure. 9And if it bears fruit next year, well and good; but if not, you can cut it down.'"

Notes on the Text and Translation

13:9. The verse has both textual and translation problems. The reading above represents that of some very important Greek witnesses (𝔭75, ℵ, B, and others), in which the adverbial phrase εἰς τὸ μέλλον ("next year") modifies the first "if" clause. An alternative in some other major witnesses (including 𝔭45, A, D, W, Θ, families 1 and 13, and others) has the phrase modify the second "if" clause, so that the entire sentence would read: "And if it bears fruit, well and good; but if not, next year you can cut it down." The latter reading is reflected in the KJV. Although evidence is strong for either reading, the former has greater support,[1] and is the choice in modern Greek editions and is reflected in modern English versions (RSV, NEB, NIV, NRSV).

The Greek adverbial expression (found only here and at 1 Tim 6:19 in the NT) can be translated literally as "unto that which is to come" or idiomatically "for the future" and in this context "next year."[2]

The first "if" clause (protasis) is not followed by an apodosis in the Greek text; it simply reads in translation: "And if it bears fruit next year." The phrase "well and good" in the translation above has been supplied (as in modern versions, RSV, NEB, and NRSV; NIV supplies "fine"). The suppression of the first of two apodoses, as in this case, has been called "classical"[3] since it is found in classical Greek sources, but it is also found in Hebrew and Aramaic texts.[4] It could be expressed as "so much the better."[5]

1. B. Metzger, TCGNT 162.
2. BAGD 501 (μέλλω, 2).
3. BDF 237 (#454, 4).
4. Cf. Klaus Beyer, Semitische Syntax im Neuen Testament, SUNT 1 (Göttingen: Vandenhoeck & Ruprecht, 1962), 97-98.
5. BDF 237 (#454, 4).

Exegetical Commentary

The parable is found only in the Gospel of Luke among the canonical Gospels. A version of it does appear, however, in the (Ethiopic) *Apocalypse of Peter* 2,[6] which is usually dated from the second century A.D. There are major differences between the two versions, and it can be regarded as based on an independent Gospel tradition (not on Luke's).[7]

Similar stories appear in other texts. One, vaguely similar, appears within the pre-Christian *Story of Ahikar* 8.35, in which the request to allow an unfruitful tree to stand for another year is refused.[8] Another, again vaguely similar, appears in rabbinic literature. It is a parable attributed to Rabbi Simeon ben Jehozadak concerning God's repenting of destroying Israel after the golden calf incident. The parable is about a king who converted an uncultivated field into a vineyard. But the vineyard produced only wine that was sour. He decided to destroy the vineyard. But a workman persuaded him to give the young vineyard more time. So, too, Moses pleaded on behalf of Israel, which had come from a pagan (uncultivated) culture and was a young nation. He said, "Be patient with them yet awhile and go with them, and they will yet perform good deeds before Thee." And God did not destroy the people.[9]

Closely associated with the parable is the miracle story of the Cursing of the Fig Tree in the other two Synoptic Gospels (Mark 11:12-14, 20-21//Matt 21:18-19). Interpreters have conjectured whether there is a relationship between the two passages. Some have suggested that the miracle story is a secondary reconstruction of this or a similar parable, thereby turning a story into an event.[10] That issue is not germane to the discussion here; suffice it to say that the suggestion has been contested and found wanting.[11] Why the miracle story is lacking in Luke's Gospel remains a puzzle. Perhaps Luke preferred to include the parable, rather than the miracle story, since the former allows for a time of grace and an opportunity for repentance, which the miracle story does not.[12]

6. The text of the parable is printed in *New Testament Apocrypha*, ed. Wilhelm Schneemelcher, rev. ed., 2 vols. (Louisville: Westminster/John Knox Press, 1991-92), 2:626.

7. Richard Bauckham, "The Two Fig Tree Parables in the Apocalypse of Peter," *JBL* 104 (1985): 280-83.

8. Text in *The Apocrypha and Pseudepigrapha of the Old Testament*, ed. Robert H. Charles, 2 vols. (Oxford: Clarendon Press, 1913), 2:775.

9. *Exod. Rab.* 43:9. Text in *MidR.* 3:504-6; quotation from 3:505.

10. Erich Klostermann, *Das Markusevangelium*, 4th ed., HNT 3 (Tübingen: J. C. B. Mohr [Paul Siebeck], 1950), 116; V. Taylor, *Mark*, 459; Günther Bornkamm, *Jesus of Nazareth* (New York: Harper & Brothers, 1960), 206 (n. 24).

11. William R. Telford, *The Barren Temple and the Withered Tree: A Redaction-Critical Analysis of the Cursing of the Fig-Tree Pericope in Mark's Gospel and Its Relation to the Cleansing of the Temple Tradition*, JSNTSup 1 (Sheffield: JSOT Press, 1980), 233-37.

12. Ibid., 231. An alternative has been proposed by B. Kinman, "Lucan Eschatology and the Missing Fig Tree," 669-78: whereas Mark's account could be interpreted as an end

The parable is located within the Travel Narrative of Luke's Gospel (9:51–19:27). Jesus is speaking to the crowds (12:54), and the parable itself is preceded by a response by Jesus to some who were concerned about the recent execution of Galileans by Pilate (13:1). Jesus takes that incident, plus another from Jerusalem, as an opportunity to speak of the need for his hearers to repent.

The parable that follows contains the image of a fig tree (Greek συκῆ, the *ficus carica*). The fig tree is referred to some sixty times in the Bible. Typically it grows to a height of some fifteen feet. It can actually be expected to produce fruit twice a year. The winter figs (Rev 6:13) are small, hard, and not edible. The summer figs (Mark 13:28//Matt 24:32//Luke 21:29) are the main crop, however. They ripen each year in August and September, "the season for figs" (Mark 11:13), and they are eaten fresh, dried, or in fruitcakes. The image of sitting under one's vine and fig tree symbolizes prosperity and peace (Mic 4:4; Zech 3:10).[13] By itself the fig tree can also represent Israel (Hos 9:10; Joel 1:7).

13:6. The picture of a fig tree within a vineyard is striking. Why is the fig tree planted there? Actually the picture is not unusual at all. Fig trees, as well as other fruit trees, were often placed within vineyards in antiquity,[14] as well as in subsequent times.[15]

13:7. The owner does not find fruit for three years. The meaning of the three years is debated. There are four possibilities: (1) It is now the third year since the tree had been planted. Normally it would take that long for the tree to grow sufficiently to produce fruit. The owner had come each of the three years since he had planted the tree — twice to inspect it, and now to gather its anticipated fruit. (2) It is now the sixth year since the tree had been planted. The first three years would have been the time that, according to Jewish law, the fruit was forbidden (Lev 19:23); the owner of the tree has thus been coming for three subsequent years (after the third) seeking fruit.[16] (3) It is now the ninth year since the tree had been planted. The first three years were a time for the tree simply to grow; the next three years were the years of forbidden fruit; and the owner has been coming for three subsequent years seeking the fruit.[17] (4) The

---

to national Israel in A.D. 70, Luke expected a future for it, replacing it with the words of Jesus in 19:41-44.

13. Roland K. Harrison, "Fig; Fig Tree," *ISBE* 2:301-2; Irene Jacob and Walter Jacob, "Flora," *ABD* 2:807; John C. Trever, "Fig Tree, Fig," *IDB* 2:267; Michael Zohary, "Flora," *IDB* 2:286-87.

14. For references in rabbinic texts, cf. Str-B 1:873; cf. also Martin Noth, *The Old Testament World* (Philadelphia: Fortress Press, 1966), 36, who refers to grapevines growing within the branches of fig trees. Although not explicit, certain OT texts imply both growing together (1 Kings 4:25; Jer 5:17; 8:13; Hos 2:12; Joel 1:7, 12; Mic 4:4; Zech 3:10).

15. Gustaf Dalman, *Arbeit und Sitte in Palästina,* 7 vols. (Gütersloh: Verlag C. Bertelsmann et al., 1928-41), 1:161, 378; 4:315-16, 327-28.

16. J. Jeremias, *Parables,* 170; M. Boucher, *Parables,* 131.

17. K. Bailey, *Peasant Eyes,* 82.

date of planting (obviously more than three years ago) is irrelevant to the story. Whatever its age, the tree is obviously unproductive. For three years in a row, it has failed to produce figs, and most likely it will not in the future.[18] The time has come to cut it down.

The syntax of the clause implies that it has been three years since the time that the owner first became responsible for the tree (presumably by ownership).[19] The parable does not begin by saying that the owner "planted" the tree, but that he had a vineyard with a tree planted in it (already). The first explanation of the three years can be excluded on the basis of Jewish law. The second and third presuppose that the owner had planted the tree and that that detail is important for the story. But it is not. The simplest reading of the text favors the last of the four meanings.[20]

The owner of the vineyard orders that the tree be cut down. There are two reasons: (1) it is unfruitful; and (2) it takes up valuable space. The destruction of a fig tree (which grows slowly) would mean a serious economic loss for most landowners (cf. Ps 105:33; Jer 5:17; Hos 2:13; Amos 4:9). As an OT metaphor, it signifies an impending national distress (Jer 5:17; 8:13; Hos 2:12; Joel 1:7, 12; Amos 4:9).

13:8-9. The caretaker intercedes for the tree. He asks for another year, which would be the minimum time for it to bear fruit. In the meantime, he will loosen up the soil around the tree and apply fertilizer (κόπρια, "manure"). To apply fertilizer to a fig tree would be unusual, a sign of extraordinary care for the tree. The imagery of cutting down the tree recalls the preaching of John the Baptist in 3:8-9 where the same verb for cutting down (ἐκκόπτω, 3:9) appears. John had proclaimed that "even now the axe is laid to the root of the trees; every tree therefore that does not bear good fruit is cut down and thrown into the fire" (3:9). So now in the ministry of Jesus the time is at hand for repentance; the alternative is to perish in the final judgment.

The parable does not end with the landowner's giving consent to the caretaker's request, although that is implied. There is also no application appended to it.

The essential message of the parable is that it is necessary for the people of Israel to repent — the time is running short — but there is still a period of grace.[21] God is merciful as well as just. Luke the evangelist has set the parable

---

18. A. Plummer, *Luke*, 340; Claus-Hunno Hunzinger, "συκῆ," *TDNT* 7:755 (n. 43); W. Telford, *Barren Temple*, 226.

19. The Greek expression ἀφ' οὗ represents ἀφ' τοῦ χρονοῦ οὗ ("from the time which"); cf. BAGD 87 (ἀπό, II, 2, c). A. Plummer, *Luke*, 340, offers as a literal translation: "It is three years from the time when I continue coming."

20. Cf. B. Easton, *Luke*, 213: "The three years indicate simply a long time (Lev 19:23-25 is irrelevant)."

21. So, with various nuances, A. Jülicher, *Gleichnisreden*, 2:442; W. Oesterley, *Parables*, 16; B. Smith, *Parables*, 115-16; T. W. Manson, *Sayings*, 275; J. Jeremias, *Parables*, 170-

within the context of a call for repentance (13:3, 5). That does not appear to be arbitrary. If the parable was spoken by Jesus, that would have been the most likely setting for it.

The parable most likely originated in the ministry of Jesus himself.[22] If indeed the version in the *Apocalypse of Peter* 2 can be regarded as based on independent tradition, that lends support (multiple attestation) to that view.

Not surprisingly, some interpreters have claimed that the parable contains allegorical elements. The three years have been understood by Luke and his readers to have alluded to the three-year ministry of Jesus,[23] but that is unlikely since the three-year chronology is Johannine, and there is no hint that Luke was aware of it. Neither is it likely that the caretaker of the vineyard represents Jesus as an intercessor over against God (as the landowner).[24] The two figures within the story can easily represent the two sides of God — judgment and mercy, clothed here in parabolic form.[25] T. W. Manson has stated the matter well: "The conversation between the owner of the vineyard and his workman is reminiscent of Rabbinical passages in which the attributes of God debate, the attribute of justice and the attribute of mercy."[26]

Exposition

Set within the broader context of Luke 13:1-5, the Parable of the Barren Fig Tree is laden with a tone of urgency. Pilate's attack on the Galileans (13:1-3) was an atrocity carried out upon innocent persons — persons, at any rate, who were no better and no worse than anyone else. And the killing of the eighteen in Jerusalem, when the tower of Siloam fell upon them, was random, killing persons neither better nor worse than anyone else. Nevertheless, these incidents show how fragile and unpredictable life is. Therefore it is necessary for everyone to repent, lest they be caught off guard and perish.

The present moment is a time of pure grace and divine forbearance. God is like the landowner who comes looking for fruit continually. When none is

---

71; A. Hunter, *Parables*, 82; I. Marshall, *Luke*, 556; J. Fitzmyer, *Luke*, 1,005; M. Boucher, *Parables*, 131-33; R. A. Culpepper, *NIB (Luke)*, 9:271.

22. A. Jülicher, *Gleichnisreden*, 2:443-44; J. Jeremias, *Parables*, 170-71; C. Montefiore, *Synoptic Gospels*, 2:965; E. Schweizer, *Luke*, 220; K. Bailey, *Peasant Eyes*, 81-82. In R. Funk, *Five Gospels*, 345, the parable is printed in pink font (= Jesus probably said something like this).

23. Theodor Zahn, *Introduction to the New Testament*, 3 vols. (New York: Charles Scribner's Sons, 1909), 3:169 (and n. 2).

24. Contra J. Jeremias, *Parables*, 170.

25. E. Schweizer, *Luke*, 220: "Something of the mystery of Jesus can be seen in the image of God against God in order that grace may be offered to all."

26. T. W. Manson, *Sayings*, 275.

found, the wrath of God is stirred. But the other side of God, the all-merciful side, prevails for the time.

The apostle Paul wrote that the forbearance, patience, and kindness of God are meant to lead people to repentance (Rom 2:4). Unfortunately these attributes of God lead people to think that God is indulgent. Paul's response was that, no, God's wrath is being stored up and will be revealed at the final judgment (2:5). Such thinking is also expressed in the final words of the caretaker to the landowner in the parable that if there is no fruit next year, "you can cut it down."

The life of the Christian disciple is to be characterized by continual, daily repentance and renewal. Each day is a day of grace, allowing a fresh opportunity for repentance and a renewed life of discipleship, living out the fruits of repentance.

Select Bibliography

Derrett, J. Duncan M. "Figtrees in the New Testament." *HeyJ* 14 (1973): 249-65.
Gourgues, Michel. "Regroupement littéraire et équilibrage théologique: Le cas de Lc 13,1-9." In *The Four Gospels 1992: Festschrift Frans Neirynck*, 2:1591-1602. Ed. Frans van Segbroeck et al. 3 vols. BETL 100. Leuven: Leuven University Press, 1992.
Hedrick, Charles W. "Prolegomena to Reading Parables: Luke 13:6-9 as a Test Case." *RevExp* 94 (1997): 179-97.
Kahn, Jean G. "La parabole du figuier stérile et les arbres récalcitrants de la Genèse." *NovT* 13 (1971): 38-45.
Kinman, Brent R. "Lucan Eschatology and the Missing Fig Tree." *JBL* 113 (1994): 669-78.
Martens, Allan W. "'Produce Fruit Worthy of Repentance': Parables of Judgment against Jewish Religious Leaders and the Nation (Matt 21:28-22:14, par.; Luke 13:6-9)." In *The Challenge of Jesus' Parables*, 151-76. Ed. Richard N. Longenecker. Grand Rapids: Wm. B. Eerdmans, 2000.
Schottroff, Luise. "Von den Bäumen lernen, dass Gott nahe ist: Exegetische Überlegungen zu Lk 13,1-9 und Mk 13,28-33." In *Abscheid vom Männergott: Schöpfungsverantwortung für Frauen und Männer Catherina Halkes zum 75 Geburtstag*, 262-71. Ed. Johanna Jäger-Sommer. Lucerne: Edition Exodus, 1995.
Shirock, Robert J. "The Growth of the Kingdom in Light of Israel's Rejection of Jesus: Structure and Theology in Luke 13:1-35." *NovT* 35 (1993): 15-29.
Young, Franklin W. "Luke 13:1-9." *Int* 31 (1977): 59-63.

5.23. The Slave at Duty, Luke 17:7-10

7[*Jesus said,*] *"Will any one of you, who has a slave plowing or keeping sheep, say to him when he has come in from the field, 'Come at once and sit down to eat'?* 8*Will he not rather say to him, 'Prepare supper for me, and gird yourself and serve me while I eat and drink; and afterward you shall eat and drink'?* 9*Does he thank the slave because he did what was commanded?*

10*"So you also, when you have done all that is commanded you, say, 'We are unworthy slaves; we have only done what was our duty.'"*

Notes on the Text and Translation

17:7. The words "will any one of you" represent the Greek expression, τίς δὲ ἐξ ὑμῶν (literally, "and which of you"), which also appears at Luke 11:5, 11; 12:25; 14:28; cf. also 15:4. The translation here is identical to that of the RSV. Alternatives are: "Which of you?" (KJV), "Who among you?" (NRSV), or various circumlocutions, as in NEB and NIV, both of which have "Suppose one of you." But that expression lessens the interrogative force that is present in the Greek.

The translation "sit down to eat" (as in NIV) represents the Greek ἀνάπεσε, an aorist imperative of ἀναπίπτω, which means "to recline," that is, to recline at a meal.[1]

17:8. Here the Greek term ἕως, followed by subjunctive verbs, means "while" (NEB, NIV), not "until" (or "till," KJV, RSV).[2]

Exegetical Commentary

The parable appears only in the Gospel of Luke. Although it has been claimed that Luke derived the parable from Q,[3] that can hardly be established. Instead the parable can be attributed to Luke's special tradition.[4]

The parable is located within the Travel Narrative (9:51–19:27) of the Gospel of Luke. More specifically it stands in a collection of sayings of Jesus to his disciples. Jesus warns them against causing the "little ones" to stumble (17:1-2); he teaches them that they are to forgive to an unlimited extent (17:3-4); and then he tells them that even if they have only a little faith, comparable in size to a mustard seed, they are capable of mighty works (17:5-6). The Parable of the Slave at Duty follows in order to impress upon them the understanding that a disciple does all that is commanded. The unit under dis-

---

1. BAGD 59.
2. Ibid., 334 (ἕως, I, 2, b).
3. According to A. Weiser, *Knechtsgleichnisse*, 112, 118, Luke derived the parable from Q, but Luke himself composed 17:8.
4. T. W. Manson, *Sayings*, 302; I. H. Marshall, *Luke*, 646; J. Fitzmyer, *Luke*, 1145.

cussion here (17:7-10) consists of the parable itself (17:7-9) and its application (17:10).

17:7. The parable opens with a question, as do several other parables,[5] addressed in this case to Jesus' disciples. Its directness catches the attention of the hearer immediately. The question is hypothetical (there is no reason to think that any of the disciples possessed farmland and had slaves!). Anyone who would ask the question posed would expect a negative reply: "No one!" To invite a slave, who has been plowing or tending sheep, to join in a meal would imply equality of status or honor to a guest.[6] Contrary to various other parables, which portray characters that are larger than life (kings, rich landowners, and masters of many slaves), here the details are on a small scale. What is pictured is the owner of a small farm who seems to have only one slave, and that slave has to do both farmwork and housework.

17:8. The question asked in this verse begs for a positive response. The master will order the slave to do what is required — prepare supper, serve it to the master, and only then give thought to having his own supper.

The verse sets forth the opposite of what is said at 12:37 concerning a master within the Parable of the Waiting Slaves. There a master returns from a wedding banquet, fastens the belt around his garment, takes up the (unlikely) role of a slave himself, and serves his slaves. What is portrayed in 17:8 is what one should expect.

According to some interpreters, 17:8 is a composition by Luke. Two reasons have been given: (1) certain stylistic features can be attributed to Luke;[7] and (2) the verse serves only to intensify the question posed in 17:7 and so is unnecessary.[8] But neither reason is convincing. Apart from the phrase μετὰ ταῦτα ("afterwards"), there is nothing about the verse to consider it Lukan in origin on linguistic or stylistic grounds.[9] Moreover, it does more than intensify. It advances the story. It makes clear that a slave who finishes in the field and then comes into the house is not yet done; his duties do not end at the doorway. The slave must now take up some additional duties. That is to prepare and serve supper for the master. Only when that task is done can the slave settle down and have his own supper.

---

5. Matt 24:45//Luke 12:42; Matt 18:12; 21:28; Luke 11:5, 11; 14:28; 15:4. The latter four in Luke's Gospel have the same form: "Which of you?"

6. There is, however, a saying in *y. B. Qam.* 8:5 concerning Rabbi Johanan ben Zakkai (late first century A.D.) to the effect that he had his slaves dine with him. The text is cited by S. Lachs, *Rabbinic Commentary,* 318.

7. A. Weiser, *Knechtsgleichnisse,* 109-10.

8. Ibid., 112. J. Crossan, *Parables,* 108, considers the verse secondary, but does not necessarily attribute it to Luke. I. H. Marshall, *Luke,* 646, allows for the possibility of Lukan composition but leaves the question open.

9. Joachim Jeremias, *Die Sprache des Lukasevangeliums: Redaktion und Tradition im Nicht-Markusstoff des dritten Evangeliums,* MeyerK (Göttingen: Vandenhoeck & Ruprecht, 1980), 263; cf. J. Fitzmyer, *Luke,* 1,145.

17:9. A third question is asked. As in 17:7, a negative response is expected. If a slave does what is required, there is no need for the master to thank him or her. Doing one's duty is doing simply what is expected.

17:10. Two shifts take place with this verse. First, the attention shifts from the probable thoughts and actions of the master to those of the slave. Second, the words "so you also" shift attention to those who are listening to the parable (the disciples of Jesus), providing an application. The disciples of Jesus are obligated to be faithful and to do the will of the master, Jesus himself. When that has been done, there should be no thought of a reward due or even thanks.

Attention has been given to the word ἀχρεῖος, which has been translated variously as "unprofitable" (KJV), "unworthy" (RSV, NIV), or even "worthless" (NRSV). The word appears only one other time in the NT (Matt 25:30), again in connection with a slave, and there it can mean "worthless" or "useless." But here the clause that follows, which speaks of having done one's duty, rules out that meaning. Clearly it is an expression of modesty; so it has the sense of being "unworthy" of receiving some reward for service.[10] Similar expressions of modesty before God appear elsewhere in Scripture (Job 22:2-3; 35:7; Isa 40:13-14; Rom 11:33-36).

Some interpreters have concluded that the application has been composed and attached secondarily by Luke or a predecessor.[11] It must be said, however, that on linguistic and stylistic grounds there is no reason to attribute the verse to Luke the evangelist.[12] Moreover, the parable simply needs an application if it is to say anything at all, and in this case it draws out the meaning in a precise manner.[13]

Two sayings recorded in rabbinic literature are somewhat like this one in Luke's Gospel. The first is attributed to the sage Antigonus of Soko, who lived long before the time of Jesus (he is usually placed in the third century B.C.): "Be not like slaves that minister to the master for the sake of receiving a bounty, but be like slaves that minister to the master not for the sake of receiving a bounty; and let the fear of Heaven be upon you."[14] The other is attributed to Rabbi

10. BAGD 128; I. H. Marshall, *Luke*, 647; J. Kilgallen, "What Kind of Servants?" 549-51 ("servants to whom no favor is owed"). Less persuasive is the view of B. Smith, *Parables*, 184, that an epithet is being used ("good-for-nothing slaves"), signifying the class to which a slave belongs. Even less satisfactory is the view of A. Plummer, *Luke*, 402, that the word means "'unprofitable,' because nothing has been *gained* by them for their master."

11. B. Easton, *Luke*, 258; P. Minear, "A Note," 82-83. A. Jülicher, *Gleichnisreden*, 2:22, and E. Schweizer, *Luke*, 264, incline toward this view.

12. I. H. Marshall, *Luke*, 646. Except for the use of πάντα τά, which can be assigned to Luke, the verse is assigned to tradition by J. Jeremias, *Sprache*, 264. J. Fitzmyer, *Luke*, 1,145, concludes that the verse was probably in Luke's source.

13. R. Bultmann, *HST* 170.

14. *M. Abot* 1:3; quoted from *The Mishnah*, ed. Herbert Danby (Oxford: Oxford University Press, 1933), 446.

Johanan ben Zakkai (late first century A.D.): "If thou hast wrought much in the Law, claim not merit for thyself, for to this end wast thou created."[15]

According to various interpreters, the parable can be attributed to Jesus of Nazareth, who spoke it to his disciples,[16] although that is not a universal judgment.[17] Clearly the most questionable part, in terms of authenticity, is 17:10. Yet there seems to be no convincing reason to deny its origins with Jesus. Its opening verse is expressed in Semitic style,[18] and the imagery and theological thrust of the parable seem to be consistent with the message of Jesus elsewhere.

The parable is addressed to the disciples of Jesus (specifically, the "apostles" have been mentioned at 17:5). If spoken by Jesus, it could have been spoken to them, as Luke has it,[19] although some interpreters have suggested that it may have been spoken to the crowds in general,[20] or to his opponents.[21]

For the evangelist Luke and his readers, the parable would most likely function to instruct members of the church, and especially its leaders, that their service does not entitle them to rewards. That view is likely, since in its present form the parable mentions three functions that were carried out particularly by the early Christian leaders, such as apostles, and those who succeeded them. These include, most obviously, the work of shepherding (Mark 6:34; Luke 12:32; John 21:16; Acts 20:28; 1 Cor 9:7; Eph 4:11; 1 Peter 5:2-3) and service (Rom 15:25); but even the metaphor of plowing is used for apostolic work (Luke 9:62; 1 Cor 9:10). Those involved in apostolic work, therefore, cannot expect special rewards from God. What they do in service to the community, and therefore to God, is simply what should be expected of them.[22] The same viewpoint would apply to every Christian.

15. *M. Abot* 2:8; quoted from *The Mishnah,* ed. H. Danby, 448.

16. A. Jülicher, *Gleichnisreden,* 2:15, 18; R. Bultmann, *HST* 170; Wilhelm Michaelis, *Die Gleichnisse Jesu: Eine Einführung,* UCB 32, 3d ed. (Hamburg: Furche-Verlag, 1956), 182; A. Weiser, *Knechtsgleichnisse,* 114-17; I. H. Marshall, *Luke,* 646; J. Dupont, "Le maître," 233-51; idem, "Master," 343-46. According to J. Crossan, *Parables,* 107-8, only 17:7 can be attributed to Jesus; the remainder is a Lukan composition.

17. In R. Funk, *Five Gospels,* 363, the passage is printed in black font (= not spoken by Jesus).

18. Klaus Beyer, *Semitische Syntax im Neuen Testament,* SUNT 1 (Göttingen: Vandenhoeck & Ruprecht, 1962), 287-93.

19. A. Jülicher, *Gleichnisreden,* 2:18; K. Bailey, *Peasant Eyes,* 114; J. Dupont, "Le maître," 233-51; idem, "Master," 343-46. According to P. Minear, "A Note," 83, the parable would have been spoken specifically to the "apostles" (meaning the Twelve).

20. A. Plummer, *Luke,* 401. According to M. Boucher, *Parables,* 112, it could have been spoken to either the disciples or a general audience.

21. A. Cadoux, *Parables,* 220-21; J. Jeremias, *Parables,* 193, concludes that it is addressed to the opponents of Jesus or perhaps to the crowd.

22. So, with some variations, A. Weiser, *Knechtsgleichnisse,* 117-20; P. Minear, "A Note," 84-85; I. H. Marshall, *Luke,* 645; J. Fitzmyer, *Luke,* 1,145-46; J. Dupont, "Le maître," 233-51; idem, "Master," 343-46; contra E. Schweizer, *Luke,* 264, for whom there is no refer-

Exposition

Like other parables, this one does not present a full-blown view of God or the life of the disciple of Jesus. It presents only facets of each. God is somewhat analogous to the master who awaits the coming in of his slave, but only in part. The likeness is that God is the one who is to be served; God is the one to whom the disciple of Jesus is responsible.

The disciple is somewhat analogous to the slave that enters the house. A person may well be inclined to think that, if he or she has done what is commanded, a reward should follow. But there can be no grounds for such thinking. No person should think, even for a moment, that he or she is worthy of God's praise or reward. No one, no matter how virtuous or hardworking, can ever put God in his or her debt. When one has done what God expects, he or she is only doing his or her duty. The one who loves God and seeks to do his will knows that one's duty is never done.

The parable also has importance for Christian humility regarding social action. Our good works and programs of human betterment, as important as they most certainly are, are never sufficient under the judgment of God. In spite of all our efforts, there is always that "eschatological reserve," the "not yet." When we have done our best, we are still "unworthy servants" who have "only done our duty" (17:10), if that much, standing before God with clay feet, subject to God's judgment and grace.

Select Bibliography

Derrett, J. Duncan M. "The Parable of the Profitable Servant." In his *Studies in the New Testament*, 4:157-66. 4 vols. Leiden: E. J. Brill, 1977-95.

Dupont, Jacques. "Le maître et son serviteur (Luc 17,7-10)." *ETL* 60 (1984): 233-51.

—————. "The Master and His Servant." *TD* 33 (1986): 343-46.

Houzet, Pierre. "Les serviteurs de l'Évangile (Luc 17,5-10) sont-ils inutiles? Ou un contresens traditionnel." *RB* 99 (1992): 335-72.

Kilgallen, John J. "What Kind of Servants Are We?" *Bib* 63 (1982): 549-51.

Minear, Paul S. "A Note on Luke 17:7-10." *JBL* 93 (1974): 82-87.

Shelton, Robert M. "Luke 17:1-10." *Int* 31 (1977): 280-85.

Ward, A. Marcus. "Uncomfortable Words: IV. Unprofitable Servants." *ExpTim* 81 (1969-70): 200-203.

---

ence here to community leaders. The view of P. Minear, "A Note," 85 (against J. Creed, *Luke*, 216) that τὰ διαταχθέντα cannot refer to "all our duties" as Christians, but refers specifically to the three duties assigned to apostles, is too restrictive. Cf. A. Plummer, *Luke*, 401 ("ordinary duties of the Christian life"); J. Fitzmyer, *Luke*, 1,146-47 (comments against Minear's view).

5.24. The Unjust Judge, Luke 18:2-8

1*And [Jesus] told them a parable to show them that it is necessary to pray at all times and not give up. 2He said, "In a certain city there was a judge who neither feared God nor had respect for anyone; 3and there was a widow in that city who kept coming to him and saying, 'Vindicate me against my adversary.' 4For a while he refused; but afterward he said to himself, 'Though I neither fear God nor respect anyone, 5yet because this widow bothers me, I will vindicate her, lest she wear me out by her continual coming.'"*

6*And the Lord said, "Hear what the unrighteous judge says. 7And will not God obtain justice for his elect who cry out to him day and night? Does he even delay over them? 8I tell you, he will vindicate them speedily. Nevertheless, when the Son of man comes, will he find faith on earth?"*

Notes on the Text and Translation

There are no serious problems in textual criticism. The text of the 27th edition of Nestle-Aland is followed here.

18:1. The phrase πρὸς τὸ δεῖν (a preposition followed by an articular infinitive) expresses purpose.[1] The difficulty of translation is illustrated in modern English versions: "to this end" (KJV), "to the effect that" (RSV), "about their need" (NRSV), and "to show that" (NEB, NIV), which is followed above.

The phrase μὴ ἐγκακεῖν is translated here, as in the NIV, "not to give up," which is more colloquial than "not to lose heart" (RSV, NRSV; cf. NEB, "never lose heart"). Etymologically the word ἐγκακέω means "to act badly." But then it comes to mean "to fail" and "to grow weary."[2] It is used here and elsewhere with a negative particle in exhortations and requests (Gal 6:9; Eph 3:13; 2 Thess 3:13).

18:2. The Greek phrase ἄνθρωπον μὴ ἐντρεπόμενος has been translated "nor regarded man" (RSV). The NRSV attempts inclusive language with "nor had respect for people." The translation above seeks to preserve the singular of the Greek expression.

18:5. The verb ὑπωπιάζω, translated here as "to defame," is discussed in the Commentary below.

Exegetical Commentary

The parable appears only in Luke's Gospel, and it is located at a relatively late point in the Travel Narrative (9:51–19:27). A few verses previously (17:11)

---

1. BDF 207-8 (#402, 5).
2. Walter Grundmann, "ἐγκακέω," *TDNT* 3:486. On Luke 18:1, BAGD 215 has "become weary, tired."

Luke gives notice that Jesus was on his way to Jerusalem. Jesus heals ten lepers (17:12-19), responds to a question of the Pharisees concerning the coming of the kingdom (17:20-21), and speaks to his disciples concerning the parousia of the Son of man (18:22-37). Two parables follow concerning prayer. The Parable of the Unjust Judge (18:2-8) is spoken to the disciples. Jesus teaches them not to "lose heart" (18:1) in light of the coming crisis, but to pray boldly. The second parable, that of the Pharisee and the Publican (18:10-14), is addressed to a wider audience of those who trusted in themselves for righteousness and despised others.

In both form and content the Parable of the Unjust Judge is a twin of the Parable of the Friend at Midnight (11:5-8): (1) it portrays a person in need going to another for assistance; (2) that person goes with one degree or another of impertinence; (3) the other person (the one being visited) becomes annoyed; but (4) he does actually provide the assistance; (5) there is a linguistic similarity between 18:5 and 11:7 (see below); and (6) in each case the parable has to do with the theme of prayer.

The parable itself is contained within 18:2-5. Critical opinion concerning the composition and significance of the verses surrounding it (18:1, 6-8) will be taken up after all the verses receive comment.

18:1. The verse, composed by Luke,[3] provides a setting and an interpretive framework for the parable to follow. The parable is told specifically to Jesus' disciples (cf. 17:22). The purpose of the parable is stated at the outset. It is told "to show them that it is necessary to pray at all times and not give up." The emphasis on praying continuously is not distinctive to this parable. It appears also at 21:36 and Romans 12:12 (cf. 1 Thess 5:17).

18:2. The judge being portrayed is ruthless by any human estimation but particularly in light of Jewish law and custom. The clause used to describe him — that he neither feared God nor respected anyone — corresponds closely to one used by Josephus in describing King Jehoiakim: "he was unjust and wicked by nature, and was neither reverent toward God nor kind to man."[4]

That the judge does not "fear God" is contrary to a primary expectation. The obligation to fear God is to be learned by every Israelite (Lev 19:14, 32; Deut 4:10; 6:13; 14:23; 17:13; 19:20). Fearing God and keeping the commandments are linked, as though fearing the Lord is a presupposition for keeping the commandments (Deut 5:29; 8:6; 10:12; 13:4; 31:12); at other times keeping the commandments is a way to learn how to fear God (Deut 6:2; 17:19). Above all,

---

3. The expression λέγειν . . . παραβολήν ("to tell a parable") as an introduction to a parable is found only in the Gospel of Luke (5:36; 6:39; 12:16, 41; 13:6; 14:7; 15:3; 18:9; 19:11; 20:9; 21:29).

4. Josephus, *Ant.* 10.83, μήτε πρὸς θεὸν ὅσιος μήτε πρὸς ἀνθρώπους ἐπιεικής; quoted from *Josephus*, trans. Henry St. John Thackeray et al., LCL, 10 vols. (Cambridge: Harvard University Press, 1961-81), 6:202-3.

and most relevant for this parable, the fear of the Lord is the antithesis of injustice (Lev 25:17, 36, 43) and the basis of rendering a wise judgment (Ps 111:10). A judge who does not fear God cannot be just in his judgment. Yet righteous judgment on a part of a judge is mandated by the Torah (Deut 1:16; 16:18-20; cf. Zech 7:9).

The judge is also portrayed as one who does not have respect for anyone. The verb ἐντρέπομαι ("to respect," "to have regard for")[5] appears here and again in the parable at 18:4. In context the expression does not mean that he simply lacked respect for others, but that he had outright contempt for those who came before him. Such an attitude is in direct contrast to the ideal judge portrayed at Sirach 35:12-15 (speaking of God as judge). The ideal judge is righteous. He will not show partiality; he will listen to the one who is wronged; and he will not ignore the "supplication of the fatherless, nor the widow when she pours out her story" (35:14). In the parable, however, that is precisely what the judge does; he ignores the supplications of the widow. In 18:6 he is called an "unrighteous judge."

Some interpreters suggest that such a judge portrayed as this one is would be subject to bribery.[6] That may be true, but that is not said explicitly, and enough has been said already to indicate that he is not a judge from whom justice can be expected. He cares nothing about justice before God, and he cares not at all about those who appear before him, nor about the merits of their cases.

18:3. The one who comes before the judge is a woman, specifically a widow. Within the Torah and other books widows enjoy, or are expected to enjoy, a particular regard or respect. God protects them and executes justice for them (Deut 10:17-18; Pss 68:5; 146:9), which should therefore be enacted upon earth. The commandment in the Torah not to afflict widows (Exod 22:22) is complemented by others that speak of care for them (Deut 14:29; 24:17; 26:12-13; 27:19). Elsewhere there are exhortations not to mistreat them (Isa 10:2; Jer 7:6; 22:3; Ezek 22:7; Zech 7:10) but indeed to defend them (Isa 1:17, 23).

The widow comes to the judge to have her case settled over against an adversary. Who could that be, and what is the issue between them? We are not told. Most likely it would be a money matter.[7] Possibly she has a lawsuit against one of the heirs of her husband's property, or perhaps she is being evicted from her home, as widows sometimes were (cf. 20:47). Though not technically an heir under Jewish law, she has the right of continued support from her husband's estate and the right to continue dwelling in his home as long as she re-

5. BAGD 269.
6. T. W. Manson, *Sayings*, 306; J. Jeremias, *Parables*, 153; K. Bailey, *Peasant Eyes*, 133-34; W. Herzog, *Parables*, 226-27.
7. J. Jeremias, *Parables*, 153; K. Bailey, *Peasant Eyes*, 133.

mains a widow.[8] In any case, she seeks what she considers to be rightfully her own. She is not seeking revenge but simple justice. Furthermore, since it would have been extremely unusual for a woman to appear in court, she must not have a brother, son, or other person to serve as an advocate. She has to take the case to court herself.

18:4. The judge has no sense of justice, nor does he abide by the commandments and exhortations to take up the widow's cause. He delays for a time. But finally he does come around. As in certain other Lukan parables (12:16-21, 42-46; 15:11-32; 16:1-8; 20:9-19), an "interior monologue" follows in which the thoughts of the judge are revealed to the hearer and reader of the parable, but not to the widow herself.[9] He speaks of himself in terms exactly like those in the narration (18:2).

18:5. The judge responds purely because of the woman's persistence. She bothers him. The Greek expression παρέχειν . . . κόπον ("to bother") appears also in the Parable of the Friend at Midnight (11:7) — a feature of their similarity as twin parables. The use of the verb ὑπωπιάζω (translated here as "wear out") presents lexical and syntactical puzzles. It is related to the noun ὑπώπιον, meaning the "part of the face under the eyes"; the verb itself means "to strike someone on the face (under the eyes) in such a way that he gets a 'black eye' and is disfigured as a result."[10] It is possible that in this parable the judge fears that the woman will literally strike him in the face. More likely, the verb is to be understood in a metaphorical way. It is used only one other time in the NT (1 Cor 9:27), and there too it is used in a metaphorical sense, meaning to "punish" (NRSV) or "discipline" one's body. But something else is intended within the parable.

The verb is accompanied by the adverbial modifier εἰς τέλος. This can mean "in the end, finally,"[11] a temporal meaning. If that is the sense here, the verse could refer to some future action that the woman is capable of doing (rather than simply the conclusion of what she has been doing). She will give the judge a black eye; metaphorically, she will make him look bad in public. She will "defame" (so ὑπωπιάζω might be translated) him for not responding to her continual coming for vindication.[12]

But the adverbial phrase need not be temporal in reference. The phrase εἰς τέλος can mean "completely, fully, absolutely,"[13] the sense of the completion

---

8. Ben-Zion Schereschewsky, "Widow: In Jewish Law," *EncJud* 16:491.

9. Philip Sellew, "Interior Monologue as a Narrative Device in the Parables of Luke," *JBL* 111 (1992): 247-48.

10. Konrad Weiss, "ὑπωπιάζω," *TDNT* 8:590.

11. BAGD 812 (εἰς τέλος, 1, γ), "in the end, finally."

12. The choice of "defame" would be close to those suggested by J. Duncan M. Derrett, "Law in the New Testament: The Parable of the Unjust Judge," 190: "he has slandered me" or ". . . disgraced me," possibly by her spreading rumors about him.

13. BAGD 228-29 (εἰς τέλος, 3); favored by BDF 112 (207, 3).

of a thought or action. The main verb in this clause is a present (not aorist) subjunctive (ὑπωπιάζῃ), and the participle is also in the present tense (ἐρχομένη). These things speak in favor of a continuing action of the woman (rather than some future, separate action). The verb can thus be translated "to annoy greatly, to wear out,"[14] as in various versions ("wear me out," RSV, NEB, NIV, NRSV).[15] A very literal translation might be: "in order that she may not gradually wear me out completely by her continued coming."[16]

18:6. The parable has ended. Now comes an application. The term "Lord" (κύριος) refers to Jesus as elsewhere in Lukan compositions, the earthly Jesus.[17] The English "unrighteous judge" represents a Semitism in Luke's text, literally "the judge of unrighteousness" (ὁ κριτὴς τῆς ἀδικίας). Cf. similar Semitisms at 16:8-9.[18]

18:7. The verse consists of two questions. The first (18:7a) — with its οὐ μή plus subjunctive (ποιήσῃ) construction — implies an emphatic yes for an answer:[19] "will not God do justice for his elect who cry out to him day and night?" The second clause (18:7b) has a simple present tense, but its meaning is not simple, as a comparison of translations will show:

KJV: "though he bear long with them?"
RSV: "and delay long over them?"
NEB: "while he listens patiently to them?"
NAB: "Will he delay long over them?"
NIV: "Will he keep putting them off?"
NRSV: "Will he delay long in helping them?"

The verb is μακροθυμέω, which essentially means "to have patience, wait" or "to delay."[20] In that case, the clause can mean, "and delay over them?" Putting it together with 18:7a, the two questions then take two different answers: (1) yes, God will vindicate his elect; and (2) no, God will not delay in regard to them.

18:8. The first part of the verse (18:8a) affirms that God will indeed vindicate his elect, and that will be ἐν τάχει ("quickly"), which ratifies the answer to the statement of 18:7b (that God will not delay).

14. LSJ 1,904; BAGD 848.
15. Cf. also J. Jeremias, *Parables*, 154; E. Linnemann, *Parables*, 185; I. H. Marshall, *Luke*, 673; B. Scott, *Parable*, 185. The term is not dealt with precisely by W. Herzog, *Parables*, 230; he does not translate it but has it signify the woman's aggressive behavior and her calling the judge to account.
16. Quoted from BDF 112 (207, 3).
17. Luke 7:13, 19; 10:1, 39, 41; 11:39; 12:42; 13:15; 17:5, 6; 19:8; 22:61.
18. On the adjectival genitive as a Semitic idiom, cf. C. F. D. Moule, *An Idiom-Book of New Testament Greek*, 2d ed. (Cambridge: Cambridge University Press, 1960), 174-76.
19. BDF 184 (#365, 40).
20. BAGD 488.

The second part of the verse (18:8b) returns to the theme of the coming of the Son of man in 17:22-37. Will he find faith on earth?[21]

The question of the unity of 18:1-8 is disputed. Clearly 18:1 is Luke's introduction. Clearly also the parable consists at least of 18:2-5.[22] The next two and a half verses (18:6-8a) are an application. The final saying (18:8b) is an addition, either from tradition or due to composition by the evangelist, to the foregoing material. Since Luke does not otherwise compose Son of man sayings, this one can most likely be considered to have been derived from pre-Lukan tradition.[23]

Critical opinion concerning the origins and unity of 18:2-8a differs widely. Three positions are typically held: (1) the entire composition (18:2-8a or even 18:2-8) is a unity that originated in the proclamation of Jesus;[24] (2) the entire pericope is indeed a unity, but none of it originated in Jesus' proclamation;[25] (3) although 18:2-5 may or may not be authentic, 18:6-8 must be considered neither authentic nor integral to the parable from its origins.[26] That does not mean that 18:6-8 is a Lukan composition; some hold it to be pre-Lukan in origin.[27]

There is no really good reason to exclude the parable (18:2-5) from the tradition coming from the proclamation of Jesus. Its emphasis on prayer (as in

21. The use of the article (τὴν πίστιν) need not necessitate "'the faith,' i.e. the faith of the Christian Church," as claimed by J. Creed, *Luke*, 224; cf. also A. Plummer, *Luke*, 415. The use of the article is unusual, but not impossible in connection with an abstract noun. Cf. BDF 134 (#258). The definite article is also used with "faith" at Matt 23:23. In Aramaic the word for faith would have had the definite article (so *haimanutha*), according to Charles C. Torrey, *The Four Gospels: A New Translation*, 2d ed. (New York: Harper & Brothers, 1947), 312.

22. J. Fitzmyer, *Luke*, 1176-77, includes 18:6 in the parable on the grounds that it is necessary for the argument from minor to major. J. Donahue, *Parable*, 181, follows him. But the verse is a hortatory pronouncement, initiating an application of the parable itself.

23. J. Jeremias, *Parables*, 155 (n. 15).

24. Ibid., 155-56; Werner G. Kümmel, *Promise and Fulfilment: The Eschatological Message of Jesus*, SBT 23 (Naperville: Alec R. Allenson, 1957), 59; G. Delling, "Das Gleichnis vom gottlosen Richter," 1-25; R. Deschryver, "La parabole du juge malveillant," 355-66; I. H. Marshall, *Luke*, 669-71. According to D. Catchpole, "The Son of Man's Search for Faith," 81-104, the whole of 18:2-5, 7-8 was a unity from the beginning, reflecting the voice of the earthly Jesus.

25. E. Linnemann, *Parables*, 187-88 (n. 14); E. Freed, "The Parable of the Judge and the Widow," 38-60. W. Kümmel, *Promise and Fulfilment*, 59 (n. 126) cites an essay by Ernst Fuchs in the journal *Verkündigung und Forschung* of 1947-48 (p. 77), which is not available to me, in which Fuchs ascribes 18:1-8 to the primitive church.

26. A. Jülicher, *Gleichnisreden*, 2:284, 289; R. Bultmann, *HST* 175; B. Smith, *Parables*, 152-53; N. Perrin, *Teaching*, 129; H. Paulsen, "Die Witwe und der Richter," 13-39; B. Scott, *Parable*, 176-77; W. Herzog, *Parables*, 215. In R. Funk, *Five Gospels*, 368, 18:2-5 is pink (Jesus said something like that); 18:6-8 is black (not authentic, composed by Luke).

27. H. Paulsen, "Die Witwe und der Richter," 13-39; J. Fitzmyer, *Luke*, 1,177; J. Donahue, *Parable*, 181; and all who consider 18:2-8 as authentic.

Matt 6:5-15; 7:7-11; Luke 11:1-13; 22:40, 46), its use of a woman as the main figure (as in Luke 15:8-10), and even its outlandish form of argument from the behavior of an unjust judge to an assertion about God speak for its essential authenticity. Although these items do not in themselves prove its authenticity, there is nothing to preclude its authenticity either.[28]

The authenticity of the application in 18:6-8a is more controversial. But it must be said at the outset that without an application of some kind the parable is a torso at best. Some comment is called for — either by Jesus or the tradition.

If the application of 18:6-8a is removed, commentators propose what the parable was about. According to some interpreters, for example, the parable could not have had to do with persistence in prayer. According to William Herzog, the parable illustrates how strongly sanctioned social boundaries contribute to oppression, and how these boundaries must be broken for the sake of justice.[29] On the other hand, for Bernard Scott the parable has to do with the kingdom of God. The woman's continued coming and wearing down of the judge is a metaphor for the kingdom; the kingdom keeps coming regardless of honor or justice.[30] He also claims that the judge is not a metaphor for God since the judge does not act on the basis of simple justice.[31]

But these views are not totally persuasive. The point that the judge is not a metaphor for God is correct in the sense that other figures are within various parables, such as fathers and kings. To press the analogy of the unjust judge and God would result in a portrait of God in the parable that is extremely problematic.[32] But the parable rests not upon a portrait of God at that point but rather on the argument of *qal waḥomer* (*a minori ad maius*, "from the lesser to the greater"):[33] If an unrighteous judge could not withstand the supplications of this widow, all the more would God's lack of response be unthinkable.

But the parable is surely one about prayer. At the center of the story is the woman who keeps persisting to obtain justice. She finally prevails. In like manner, the children of God are to persevere in prayer. And in spite of the seeming

---

28. The arguments of E. Linnemann, *Parables*, 187-88 (n. 14) are not persuasive. These are that (1) the applications of parables are frequently secondary; (2) the application is sharply separated from the parable; and (3) the concept of the elect is found nowhere in the teachings of Jesus, but it is in early Christianity. Concerning points 1 and 2, the secondary origin of an application does not preclude the authenticity of a parable; and on point 3 (which also concerns the application), it is possible that "the elect" is secondary to a more general term at the beginning, such as "his people."

29. W. Herzog, *Parables*, 232.

30. B. Scott, *Parable*, 187.

31. Ibid., 175, 186-87.

32. That is evident in the work of J. Derrett, "The Parable of the Unjust Judge," 187; and W. Herzog, *Parables*, 216-17, 220.

33. On the use of the *qal waḥomer* in Scripture and rabbinic works, cf. Louis Jacobs, "Hermeneutics," *EncJud* 8:367.

lack of response on God's part, nevertheless God will not delay forever in making a response.

The parable is at home in the world of Jesus and his ministry. There is a famous parallel referred to, and sometimes quoted, in many commentaries that illustrates aspects of the parable. It is a story from the end of the nineteenth century. A visitor to Nisibis, Iraq, observed an incident at a court of justice in which the crowds were milling about, making noise, and paying bribes to the underlings of the judge (the *Kadi*). In the midst of the fray a poor woman appeared and kept screaming for justice. The story continues:

> She was sternly bidden to be silent, and reproachfully told that she came there every day. "And so I will," she cried out, "till the *Kadi* hears me." At length . . . the judge impatiently demanded, "What does that woman want?" Her story was soon told. Her only son had been taken for a soldier, and she was alone, and could not till her piece of ground; yet the tax-gatherer had forced her to pay the impost, from which as a lone widow she could be exempt. The judge asked a few questions, and said, "Let her be exempt." Thus her perseverance was rewarded. Had she had money to fee a clerk, she might have been excused long before.[34]

The Parable of the Unjust Judge reflects a world of bribes and brutality, a world of injustice for the poor — or at least justice delayed or gained only by force, which is injustice too. The only decent figure is the woman. The parable fits indeed within the context of teaching about persistence in prayer, as Luke has it.

Within the Lukan context the parable serves to encourage the disciples of Jesus to persist in prayer. Just prior to the parable there are sayings concerning the kingdom and the coming of the Son of man (17:20-37). Soon Jesus and his disciples will be in Jerusalem. That could mean disaster, even death, for Jesus and his followers. But within such perilous times one should not lose heart. God will not only care for his own, but even vindicate them. Therefore the disciples should persist in prayer and faith.

The final comment (18:8b) is a postscript that addresses the readers of Luke's Gospel. Jesus asks whether there will be faith, that is, persons faithful to him, at the time of the coming of the Son of man. The judgment will be universal. Only as persons persist in prayer will they persist in faith — a living relationship with God.

Exposition

After the birth narratives in the Gospels of Matthew and Luke and the story of Jesus in the Temple at the age of twelve, we hear no more about Joseph. It is

34. Henry B. Tristram, *Eastern Customs in Bible Lands* (London: Hodder & Stoughton, 1894), 228; quoted from B. Smith, *Parables,* 150.

quite possible that Mary became a widow before Jesus had fully matured. In any case, Jesus was surely aware of the plight of widows in his day. They could easily become victimized by unscrupulous persons, even members of their own family.

The picture of a widow seeking justice for herself (and sometimes for her children along with her) would have been common enough for the creation of a parable. In order to instruct his followers on prayer, Jesus needed an illustration. He fastened on to this one to show that, if a wicked rogue judge will help out a woman who keeps pestering him, surely God will respond to the needs of his children who cry out to him. It is a wonderful illustration. Other examples can be shown from modern times. The saying that "the squeaking wheel gets the most grease" illustrates well that those who ask — and do so persistently — are more likely to receive than those who do not.

The church is reminded by this parable and its application not only of the need to be persistent in prayer, but also to be accountable. The Son of man will come in judgment. The question of "faith on earth" will be paramount. Evidence for faith on earth will be a church that prays with persistence, even in the face of possible persecution.

Select Bibliography

Benjamin, Don C. "The Persistent Widow." *BiTod* 28 (1990): 213-19.

Bindemann, Walther. "Die Parabel vom unrechten Richter." In *Theologische Versuche 13*, 91-97. Ed. Joachim Rogge et al. Berlin: Evangelisches Verlagsanstalt, 1983.

———. "Ungerechte als Vorbilder? Gottesreich und Gottesrecht in den Gleichnissen vom 'ungerechten Verwalter' und 'ungerechten Richter.'" *TLZ* 120 (1995): 955-70.

Binder, Hermann. *Das Gleichnis von dem Richter und der Witwe: Lk 18,1-8.* Neukirchen-Vluyn: Neukirchener Verlag, 1988.

Bovon, François. "Apocalyptic Traditions in the Lukan Special Material: Reading Luke 18:1-8." *HTR* 90 (1997): 383-91.

Catchpole, David R. "The Son of Man's Search for Faith (Luke 18:8)." *NovT* 19 (1977): 81-104.

Cranfield, C. E. B. "The Parable of the Unjust Judge and the Eschatology of Luke-Acts." *SJT* 16 (1963): 297-301.

Delling, Gerhard. "Das Gleichnis vom gottlosen Richter." *ZNW* 53 (1962): 1-25.

Derrett, J. Duncan M. "Law in the New Testament: The Parable of the Unjust Judge." *NTS* 18 (1971-72): 178-91.

Deschryver, Richard. "La parabole du juge malveillant (Luc 18,1-8)." *RHPR* 48 (1968): 355-66.

Freed, Edwin D. "The Parable of the Judge and the Widow." *NTS* 33 (1987): 38-60.

Haacker, Klaus. "Das Gleichnis von der bittenden Witwe (Lk 18,1-8)." *TBei* 25 (1994): 277-84.

Hicks, John M. "The Parable of the Persistent Widow." *ResQ* 33/4 (1991): 209-23.

Huhn, Karl. *Das Gleichnis von der "bittenden Witwe": Gebetsaufruf Jesu an die Gemeinde der Endzeit.* Hamburg: Verlagbuchhandlung Bethel, 1946.

Iersel, Bastiaan van. "De rechter en de weduwe (Lc 18,1-8)." In *Parabelverhalen in Lucas: Van seiotiek naar pragmaatiek,* 168-93. Ed. Bastiaan van Iersel et al. TFTS 8. Tilburg: University Press, 1987.

León, Domingo Muñoz. "Jesus y la apocaliptica pesimista (a proposito de Lc 18:8b y Mt 24:12)." *EstBib* 46/4 (1988): 457-95.

Liefeld, Walter L. "Parables on Prayer (Luke 11:5-10; 18:1-8; 18:9-14)." In *The Challenge of Jesus' Parables,* 240-62. Ed. Richard N. Longenecker. Grand Rapids: Wm. B. Eerdmans, 2000.

Ljungvik, Herman. "Zur Erklärung einer Lukas-Stelle (Luk. XVIII,7)." *NTS* 10 (1964): 289-94.

Meecham, H. G. "The Parable of the Unjust Judge." *ExpTim* 57 (1946): 306-7.

Paulsen, Henning. "Die Witwe und der Richter (Lk 18,1-8)." *TGl* 74 (1984): 13-39.

Porcile Santiso, Maria Teresa, and Angelica Ferreira. "The Parable of the Importunate Widow." In *Stories Make People: Examples of Theological Work in Community,* 75-82. Ed. Samuel Amirtham. Geneva: WCC Publications, 1989.

Riesenfeld, Harald. "Zu μακροθυμεῖν (Lk 18,7)." In *Neutestamentliche Aufsätze: Festschrift für Josef Schmid zum 70. Geburtstag,* 214-17. Ed. Josef Blinzler. Regensburg: Verlag Friedrich Pustet, 1963.

Robertson, J. A. "The Parable of the Unjust Judge (Luke xviii.1-8)." *ExpTim* 38 (1927): 389-92.

Ru, G. de. "De gelijkenis van de onrechtvaardige rechter (Lucas 18:1-8)." *NTT* 225 (1971): 379-92.

Sabbe, Maurits. "Het eschatologisch gebed in Lukas 18,1-8." *CBG* 1 (1955): 361-69.

Sacchi, Alessandro. "Pazienza di Dio e Ritardo Della Parousia." *RivB* 36 (1988): 299-327.

Sahlin, Harald. *Zwei Lukas-Stellen: Lk 6:43-45; 18:7,* 9-20. SBU 4. Uppsala: Wretman, 1945.

Spicq, Ceslaus. "La Parabole de la veuve obstinee et du juge inerte aux decisions impromptues (Lc. XVIII,1-8)." *RB* 68 (1961): 68-90.

Stählin, Gustav. "Das Bild der Witwe: Ein Beitrag zur Bildersprache der Bibel und zum Phänomenon der Personifikation in der Antike." *JAC* 17 (1974): 5-20.

Strong, L. Thomas. "The Importunate Widow and the Pharisee and the Publican (Luke 18:1-14)." *ThEd* 56 (1997): 85-92.

Tyson, Kenneth H. "Faith on Earth." *ExpTim* 88 (1977): 111-12.

Via, Dan O. "The Parable of the Unjust Judge: A Metaphor of the Unrealized Self." In *Semiology and Parables: Exploration of the Possibilities Offered by Structuralism for Exegesis*, 1-32. Ed. Daniel Patte. Pittsburgh: Pickwick Press, 1976.

Vogt, Hermann J. "Die Witwe als Bild der Seele in der Exegese des Origenes." *TQ* 165/2 (1985): 105-18.

Warfield, Benjamin B. "The Importunate Widow and the Alleged Failure of Faith." *ExpTim* 25 (1913-14): 69-72, 136-39.

Wifstrand, Albert. "Lukas xviii.7." *NTS* 11 (1964-65): 72-74.

Zimmermann, Heinrich. "Das Gleichnis vom Richter und der Witwe (Lk 18,1-8)." In *Die Kirche des Anfangs: für Heinz Schürmann*, 79-95. Ed. Rudolf Schnackenburg et al. EThS 38. Leipzig: St. Benno Verlag, 1977.

5.25. The Waiting Slaves, Mark 13:34-37//Luke 12:35-38

Mark 13:34-37

34[*Jesus said*,] *"It is like a man away on a journey; when he left his house and had put his slaves in charge, each with his work, he commanded the doorkeeper to be on the watch.*

35*"Watch therefore, for you do not know when the master of the house will come — in the evening, or at midnight, or at cockcrow, or in the morning —* 36*lest he come suddenly and find you asleep.* 37*And what I say to you, I say to all: 'Watch.'"*

Notes on the Text and Translation

13:34. The Greek text has the conjunction καί ("and") before ἐνετείλατο ("he commanded"). Its presence is reflected in various translations (RSV, NIV, NRSV). But its presence is exceedingly awkward. Either it should not be there if the verb is finite, or if it is present, the verb in question should be a participle. Perhaps the usage reflects a Semitism.[1] In any case, it can remain untranslated in order to bring out the force of the verb.

Luke 12:35-38

35[*Jesus said*,] *"Be dressed for action, and have your lamps burning;* 36*and be like those who are waiting for their master to come home from the wedding banquet, in order that they may open to him at once when he comes and knocks.* 37*Blessed are those slaves whom the master finds awake when he comes. Truly, I say to you, he will fasten his belt and have them recline at the table, and he will come*

1. Cf. V. Taylor, *Mark*, 523.

and serve them. 38*If he comes in the second watch, or in the third, and finds them so, blessed are they!"*

Notes on the Text and Translation

12:35. The Greek says literally, "Let your loins [or waist] be girded" (RSV). The figure of speech is a call to be ready for action, such as a journey. Typically a garment was worn without a belt at home, and a belt was put on for outside activity or travel.[2] But the figure of speech means nothing today. We follow the NRSV here: "Be dressed for action" (cf. NIV: "Be dressed ready for service").

12:37. In the second sentence the Greek says literally, "he will gird himself." The expression is lost on the modern ear. The NRSV is followed here again, "he will fasten his belt."

12:38. Some major Greek witnesses (including A, families 1 and 13, and the Majority Text) read οἱ δοῦλοι ἐκεῖνοι ("those slaves," as at the outset of 12:37) at the very end of this verse. That reading is reflected in the RSV and NRSV. Other witnesses (including 𝔭75, B, and D) read simply ἐκεῖνοι ("those persons").[3] The most difficult reading in still other witnesses (in Greek ℵ and in Latin equivalents in some Old Latin texts and Irenaeus) has no demonstrative adjective or noun, simply reading μακάριοί εἰσιν ("blessed are they"). That is the reading of the Nestle-Aland 27th edition, and it is reflected in the NIV. The noun and/or demonstrative adjective are more likely to have been added than eliminated. Therefore the last reading cited is to be preferred.

General Comments on the Texts

The two texts cited are enough alike to be treated together. They are brief, and they share a similar story line involving the departure of the master of a household, who leaves his slaves in charge of his home and then returns to find them awake or asleep. Being awake is essential for their being treated well by their master.

There is, however, no literary relationship between the two texts. The Lukan version of the parable is generally considered to have been derived from his own special tradition (L),[4] although some interpreters have contended that it was derived from Q,[5] even though there is no parallel to it in the Gospel of

---

2. BAGD 587 (under ὀσφῦς).

3. This is the reading preferred by J. Fitzmyer, *Luke,* 983, 989.

4. C. H. Dodd, *Parables,* 130 (n. 2); C. Carlston, *Parables,* 84-85; J. Fitzmyer, *Luke,* 984. This view seems to be favored also by E. Lövestam, *Spiritual Wakefulness,* 79-80, 92.

5. J. Creed, *Luke,* 176; T. W. Manson, *Sayings,* 115-16; I. H. Marshall, *Luke,* 533 (but with uncertainty). For a survey of views pro and con (and taking the pro position), cf. Philip Sellew, "Reconstruction of Q 12:33-59," *Society of Biblical Literature 1987 Seminar Papers,* ed. Kent H. Richards, SBLSP 26 (Atlanta: Scholars Press, 1987), 630-31.

Matthew. The parable has double attestation in the tradition (Mark and L), but it has been developed in those respective traditions in such a way that only the common story line remains apparent.

The theme of a wealthy man leaving servants or slaves in charge while away is a popular one. It appears in four parables from Jesus — the Faithful and Wise Slave (Matt 24:45-51//Luke 12:42-46), the Talents (Matt 25:14-30), the Pounds (Luke 19:12-27), and the Wicked Tenants (Mark 12:1-12//Matt 21:33-46//Luke 20:9-19; but lacking in *Gos. Thom.* 65–66). Three known rabbinic parables, all attributed to rabbis from times later than Jesus, tell of a king or a man entrusting money with others as well. According to one of these, a king left a deposit of money with a man of his realm, and the latter was anxious for his responsibility to end so that he could return the sum to the king. The parable was told late in the first century A.D. by Rabbi Eleazar ben Arak to Rabbi Johanan ben Zakkai after the death of the latter's son, meaning that he should be comforted for returning to God the trust unimpaired.[6] Another parable was spoken by Rabbi Simeon ben Eleazar (late second century) about a king who entrusted straw to one person but silver and gold to another. If one cannot be entrusted with straw, neither can one be entrusted with silver and gold. The point is then made that the sons of Noah could not observe even seven commandments, so how could they possibly have been entrusted with more?[7] Finally there is a parable from much later (A.D. 600 or later) in which a man entrusts a small amount of money to his wife, departs for a while, and returns to find that the sum has been increased. The parable is spoken to praise the careful preservation of the Torah by Israel.[8]

A parable of this kind is considered to have been uttered by the historical Jesus by various interpreters,[9] but others oppose such a view.[10] Luke's rendition of it has some features that actually appear more primitive than those in Mark's account, such as the admonition to all the slaves to stay awake (not just the

---

6. *Abot R. Nat.* 14:6; text cited and summarized in Harvey K. McArthur and Robert M. Johnston, *They Also Taught in Parables: Rabbinic Parables from the First Centuries of the Christian Era* (Grand Rapids: Zondervan Publishing House, 1990), 34-35.

7. *Mek. Bachodesh* 5:81-92; text summarized in ibid., 52-53.

8. *Cant. Rab.* 7:14:1; text summarized in ibid., 187.

9. C. H. Dodd, *Parables*, 131-32; J. Jeremias, *Parables*, 55; C. Carlston, *Parables*, 87 (but see the next note); J. Crossan, *Parable*, 99; E. Schweizer, *Luke*, 212; I. H. Marshall, *Luke*, 535; J. Fitzmyer, *Luke*, 987; A. Weiser, *Knechtsgleichnisse*, 144-51; Hans-Josef Klauck, *Allegorie und Allegorese in synoptischen Gleichnistexten*, NTAbh 13 (Münster: Aschendorff, 1978), 336.

10. A. Jülicher, *Gleichnisreden*, 2:171; R. Bultmann, *HST* 118, 205; B. Smith, *Parables*, 107-8; J. Donahue, *Parable*, 58-60; B. Scott, *Parable*, 213. According to J. Lambrecht, *Astonished*, 137, it was probably composed by Mark. Both versions of the parable are printed in gray font (not likely from Jesus) in R. Funk, *Five Gospels*, 114, 341. While C. Carlston, *Parables*, 87, has written that an original form of the parable represented in Luke's Gospel could have come from Jesus, he concludes that Mark composed his own version at 13:34-37 (pp. 200-202).

doorkeeper, which appears to be a strange intrusion into Mark's account, since all the slaves left at home are in charge), the three watches in the night, and the telling of the parable uninterrupted by an application. These details are discussed below.

Interpreters give different answers to the question to whom an authentic parable of Jesus would have been spoken and, in turn, its meaning. Within the Gospels of Mark and Luke it is addressed to the disciples (Mark 13:3; Luke 12:22). In spite of that, Joachim Jeremias concluded that it was most likely addressed to the scribes, and Jesus warned them of the crisis to come with the arrival of the Son of man.[11] Other interpreters, however, have concluded that the parable would indeed have been addressed to the disciples, exhorting them to be faithful (spiritually awake) at the coming of the Son of man, the coming of the kingdom of God, or the coming of God in judgment.[12] The metaphor of remaining awake at night, used in both versions of the parable, has been interpreted in various ways. Perhaps the most satisfactory is that for anyone to slumber means to become spiritually dulled and absorbed by the world and its indifference to the divine claim upon oneself.[13] To be awake means then to be prepared for the coming of the Son of man, the kingdom, or God himself into one's life.

The Parable in the Gospel of Mark

Exegetical Commentary

The parable is located at the close of the eschatological discourse of Mark 13 and is, in fact, the last parable within the Gospel of Mark. It is sometimes called the Parable of the Doorkeeper.

Prior to this parable there is a string of prophetic and apocalyptic sayings of Jesus. They consist of declarations about the defilement and destruction of the Temple (13:1-2, 14-20), warnings about the coming of false messiahs, persecutions, and natural disasters (13:4-8, 9-13, 21-23), and a prophecy concerning the coming of the Son of man (13:24-27). Then comes a series of sayings just prior to this parable: the sayings on the budding fig tree as a lesson on the signs of the times (13:28), the imminent coming of the Son of man and the consummation (13:29-31), and the need for constant vigilance, since one knows neither the day nor the hour of the coming of the Son of man (13:32-33).

11. J. Jeremias, *Parables*, 55.

12. E. Lövestam, *Spiritual Wakefulness*, 91, 95; I. H. Marshall, *Luke*, 535; A Weiser, *Knechtsgleichnisse*, 144-51. According to C. H. Dodd, *Parables*, 129-32, the parable was spoken either to the disciples or to the general public concerning the "crisis" of Jesus' coming (in history).

13. E. Lövestam, *Spiritual Wakefulness*, 91, 95; he reviews other interpretations on pp. 83-90.

Form critically the parable is limited to only one verse, 13:34. The remaining three verses (13:35-37) are an application. In fact, the single-verse parable is fractured and interrupted by the sayings that follow. The verse sets out to make a comparison ("it is like"), contains two subordinate clauses, and then completes the comparison by means of a main verb, ἐνετείλατο ("he commanded"), narrating that the master of the house commands the doorkeeper to be on guard. That is the end of the comparison. But then the application follows in which the hearers of the parable are addressed: *you* (plural) must therefore be watchful, for the man may return at any time. The telling of the man's return at an unpredicted time should actually be part of the parable itself, as in Luke's version, but it has been incorporated into the application.

The first two verses of the application (13:35-36) are dependent upon the parable. They can be considered to be derived from traditional material, but reformulated here by Mark. The final verse (13:37) appears to be an appended admonition composed by Mark to address the readers of his Gospel.

13:34. The brief parable begins simply with ὡς ("[it is] like"). The antecedent of "it" (required by English usage) is the καιρός ("time") of the coming of the Son of man and the consummation of all things (13:26, 29-31). The comparison being set up is not simply between the Son of man and the man who arrives after having been away for some time, but, more loosely, between the timing of the coming of the Son of man and that which follows in the story. As the timing of the man's return is unpredictable, so is the timing of the coming of the Son of man.

The adjective ἀπόδημος ("away on a journey") is found only here in the NT. It appears, however, in other ancient sources (classical texts, Josephus, and papyri).[14] The verb form (ἀποδομέω, "go on a journey") is used in other parables with similar beginnings (Mark 12:1//Matt 21:33//Luke 20:9; Matt 25:14, 15).

The man who leaves assigns to each of his slaves specific duties while he is away. Everyone knows what is to be done while he is away. He gives a special command to the θυρωρός ("doorkeeper"). Although the usual duty of a doorkeeper is to keep out possible intruders,[15] here his assignment is to watch for the man's return and to open the door when he arrives. Envisioned here is a massive door to a grand house, which is locked from inside. The doorkeeper becomes especially important in what follows, for in 13:36 it is his analogue, the disciple of Jesus, who is to remain vigilant. Watching is all-important since the doorkeeper must be awake and ready at all times to open the door when his master returns.[16] As indicated above, however, that the doorkeeper alone

14. BAGD 90 (with references).
15. References from the OT, Josephus, and rabbinic works are provided by E. Lövestam, *Spiritual Wakefulness*, 80-81.
16. V. Taylor, *Mark*, 523; E. Schweizer, *Mark*, 280.

should be on guard at night seems awkward. It is a detail that may have been added to the original parable.[17] One would expect, as in Luke's account, that all the slaves should be vigilant. Although the doorkeeper is given a special responsibility, he has no special accountability in the end. He disappears from the scene. In the end the admonition to watch is applicable to "all" (13:37).

13:35. The exhortation to watch (γρηγορεῖτε, second person plural in Greek) is addressed to the disciples, who alone make up the audience for the words of Jesus in Mark 13. Various forms of the verb for watching (γρηγορέω) appear in several NT texts of diverse origins as a metaphor for spiritual vigilance (Matt 24:42//Mark 13:35; Matt 26:41//Mark 14:38; Mark 13:37; Matt 25:13; Acts 20:31; 1 Cor 16:13; 1 Thess 5:6; 1 Peter 5:8; Rev 3:2-3; 16:15). The metaphor also appears in the Apostolic Fathers.[18] Moreover, in this verse the one who returns is not simply the "man" (ἄνθρωπος) of 13:34, but the "master of the house" (ὁ κύριος τῆς οἰκίας), and the metaphorical significance of ὁ κύριος ("the master," but also "the Lord") cannot be missed. The circumstances of the church in the evangelist's own day are being addressed: members of the church must be spiritually vigilant, or prepared, for the coming of the Lord.

The four references to time (evening, midnight, cockcrow, and morning) correspond to the four Roman watches of the night (cf. Matt 14:25//Mark 6:48); at Luke 12:38 there are three watches, corresponding to the more customary Jewish reckoning of time.[19]

13:36. The Son of man may come "suddenly" (ἐξέφνης), meaning here not "soon" but "unexpectedly."[20] To be found asleep is the worst of possibilities. Metaphorically the term can mean to be spiritually lazy or indifferent.[21] Here it more likely has a slightly different nuance, meaning to be spiritually unprepared.

13:37. The admonition of Jesus to his disciples (that they should watch) is said "to all," that is, to all who hear him. For Mark that will mean the readers of his Gospel as well.

Exposition

Most Christians do not give much thought, if any, to the second coming of Christ. Moreover, the declaration that Christ will come in glory is taken by many as a threat rather than as a promise of something good to anticipate. That sense of threat, and dread, is engendered by this and other NT passages.

17. E. Schweizer, *Mark*, 279.

18. Ignatius, *Pol.* 1.3; *Didache* 16.1.

19. For references to the literature, cf. BAGD 867-68 (φυλακή, 4); LSJ 1,960. Various references are given in A. Jülicher, *Gleichnisreden*, 2:168; see comment on Luke 12:38 as well.

20. BAGD 272 (under the more common spelling, ἐξαίφνης).

21. BAGD 388.

Yet the affirmation that "he will come again to judge the living and the dead," as expressed in the Apostles' Creed, belongs to the structure of Christian faith. It is indispensable. The triumph of God in raising Jesus from the dead cannot go unattended; it must be accompanied antiphonally by the parousia. It is only after the parousia that all things will be subjected to God, and God will be "all in all" (1 Cor 15:27-28).

The challenge deriving from this passage in Mark's Gospel is that all who claim the name of Christ should be constantly vigilant, awaiting his coming. That will not mean that the Christian will be oblivious to life in this world. Quite the contrary is true. As each of the slaves was given his own work to do during the absence of the master, so each follower of Jesus has tasks to do between the time of Jesus' resurrection and his coming again. Furthermore, this world is the place that God has given for human habitation. If one is faithful to one's calling, the matter of the timing of the Lord's coming is of no consequence.

The force of the need to be vigilant means that the Christian will be ever open to the advent of God and always prepared for the coming of Christ. That will be, first of all, a spiritual readiness that allows for the presence and reign of God and Christ in one's daily life. And that, in turn, implies a readiness for Christ's return in glory.

The Parable in the Gospel of Luke

Exegetical Commentary

Luke's rendition of the parable is not located within the eschatological discourse (21:5-36), as it is in Mark's Gospel, but rather in a section of warnings to the disciples (12:1–13:9) set within the larger framework of the Travel Narrative (9:51–19:27). Jesus has just spoken to his disciples about not being anxious (12:22-31) and about the true treasures that one might have, that is, treasures in heaven (12:32-34). The Parable of the Waiting Slaves (12:35-38) comes at that point, and it is followed by a parabolic saying concerning the thief, corresponding to the coming of the Son of man (12:39-40) and the Parable of the Faithful and Wise Manager (12:42-46), which also alludes to the coming of the Son of man. Both the context and the content of the Parable of the Waiting Slaves alert the disciples to be ready for the parousia.

12:35. On the translation and meaning of the figure of speech (literally, "gird up your loins"), here translated "be dressed for action," see Notes above. It is a traditional expression indicating readiness for some task (Exod 12:11; 1 Kings 18:46; 2 Kings 4:29; 9:1; Job 38:3; 40:7; Jer 1:17; Eph 6:14; cf. Isa 5:27; Luke 17:8; 1 Peter 1:13). Moreover, "the long eastern robe must be caught up round the waist if it is not to hinder action."[22] The expression "have your lamps

22. J. Creed, *Luke*, 175-76.

burning" is, metaphorically, an exhortation to watchfulness, as shown in the following verses, but also by means of comparable imagery in the Parable of the Ten Maidens (e.g., Matt 25:1-13), even though the Greek word for "lamp" differs there (λαμπάς) from here (λύχνος). Both expressions (girding loins/having lamps burning) are found in *Didache* 16:1 (not obviously dependent on Luke, since different verbs are used). Both expressions are also applied already to the "capable wife" (as she is called in the NRSV) at Proverbs 31:17-18.

12:36. The parable itself begins with this verse. The disciples are exhorted to be "like" the persons who act in a certain way, which is illustrated in the following parable. These men (but called "slaves" in 12:37, 38) are in expectation of their "master" (κύριος, which can also be translated as "lord" or "Lord"), who has left them during his absence, while he has been at a wedding banquet. If the slaves are truly awaiting his coming, they will be able to open the door of the house (from inside) when he comes and knocks. Metaphorically the master and the slaves correspond to Christ (or the Son of man) and his disciples. At this place, as well as at 14:8 (as opposed to Isa 25:6; 2 Esdr 2:38; Rev 19:7, 9), the imagery of a wedding banquet probably has no reference to a messianic feast; it is simply a place from which the master comes.[23] He could just as well come home from a journey. Although the image of the man knocking at the door corresponds with that of Christ knocking at the door elsewhere (Rev 3:20), that is not likely to be the meaning here;[24] the man simply returns home and seeks admission to his house by knocking (cf. Luke 13:25; Acts 12:13, 16).

12:37. The Greek term translated as "blessed" (μακάριος) signifies receipt of favor, in this case from the returning master, which metaphorically signifies receipt of favor from the Son of man at his parousia. They are "blessed" ones, since they are found to be "awake" (translated from a participial form of the verb γρηγορέω), that is, spiritually vigilant. On the use of the metaphor in the NT, see comment on Mark 13:35 above.

Jesus makes a pronouncement about the behavior of the master who has returned and found his slaves awake and alert. He will take up the (unlikely!) role of a slave himself and serve them, even if it is midnight or beyond! Such an action is not something that a master would normally do; the opposite is in fact to be expected (the slave should serve the master; cf. Luke 17:7-10). The scene recalls that of John 13:4-5 (though it is not dependent upon it), in which Jesus girds himself and washes the feet of his disciples as a sign of eschatological hospitality.[25] Whether this detail of the parable can be attributed to Jesus is difficult to establish, for it could be an allegorical item based on the Christian view

23. C. Carlston, *Parables,* 86; I. H. Marshall, *Luke,* 536; E. Schweizer, *Luke,* 213; J. Fitzmyer, *Luke,* 988; contra B. Easton, *Luke,* 205.

24. Contra J. Fitzmyer, *Luke,* 988.

25. Cf. Arland J. Hultgren, "The Johannine Footwashing (13:1-11) as Symbol of Eschatological Hospitality," *NTS* 28 (1982): 539-46.

of Jesus as a servant of others (Mark 10:45; Luke 22:27), who is also the host of the eschatological banquet (Rev 19:9).[26] On the other hand, the "concept [of Jesus as one who serves] is so firmly anchored in the teaching and activity of Jesus that there is no reason to suspect that the early church has imported the idea here."[27] Its very radical (not to mention delightful) twist speaks in favor of its having come integrally with the rest of the parable from Jesus.

12:38. Rather than four watches of the night, as at Mark 13:35 (corresponding to the Roman reckoning), here only three are envisioned (and the first of the three is past already), in accord with Jewish tradition.[28] The beatitude ("blessed") is repeated. Regardless of what time the master returns, even up to 6:00 a.m. (the end of the third watch),[29] the slaves are expectant and watchful. So it is expected that Christians will be vigilant at all times, even if the Lord seems to be delayed in his coming.

Exposition

Luke's rendition of the parable, though much like Mark's, is more positive about the parousia of the Son of man and less threatening and foreboding. Twice the slaves who are awake at the coming of their master are called "blessed" (12:37, 38). So the disciples of Jesus are exhorted to be awake, that is, spiritually vigilant, at the coming of the Lord in glory. To be sure, such an exhortation can be threatening. But the news of the coming of the Lord is presented more as a joyous promise than a threat, for the expectation is that the disciples of Jesus will in fact be ready, and he will entertain them at his table, signifying eschatological blessing and joy.

As indicated in the Exposition on the text from Mark 13:34-37, the expectation of the second coming of Christ belongs to the structure of Christian faith. It is integral to it. If that is so, the Christian will live in constant expectation, knowing that he or she will be accountable in the final judgment, but also rejoicing in the promise of being in the eternal presence of God, Christ, and all those whom God has chosen to dwell with himself eternally. Spiritual vigilance is the only human response that is fitting, for it certifies one's belief in the promises of God. Lack of such vigilance is a denial of the promises and amounts to living in an illusion.

---

26. B. Smith, *Parables*, 107; J. Jeremias, *Parables*, 53-54; B. Easton, *Luke*, 205; A Weiser, *Knechtsgleichnisse*, 169-71.

27. I. H. Marshall, *Luke*, 537.

28. Three watches (first, second, and third) are mentioned explicitly by Josephus, *J.W.* 5.510. Various OT passages speak of the middle (Judg 7:19) or morning (Exod 14:24; 1 Kings 11:11) watch. See comment on Mark 13:35 for further details.

29. Presumably the three watches of the night would have run roughly 6:00–10:00 p.m., 10:00 p.m.–2:00 a.m., and 2:00–6:00 a.m.

Select Bibliography

Bauckham, Richard. "Synoptic Parousia Parables and the Apocalypse." *NTS* 23 (1977): 165-69.

Deterding, Paul E. "Eschatological and Eucharistic Motifs in Luke 12:35-40," *ConJ* 5 (1979): 85-94.

Dupont, Jacques. "La parabole du maître qui rentre dans la nuit (Mc. 13, 34-36)." In *Mélanges bibliques en hommage au R. P. Béda Rigaux*, 89-116. Ed. Albert Descamps and André de Halleux. Gembloux: Duculot, 1970.

Joüon, Paul. "La Parabole du Portier qui doit veiller (Marc XIII,33-37) et la Parabole des Serviteurs qui doivent veiller (Luc XII,35-40)." *RSR* 30 (1940): 365-68.

Kollmann, Bernd. "Lk 12,35-38 — ein Gleichnis der Logienquelle." *ZNW* 81 (1990): 254-61.

Lövestam, Evald. *Spiritual Wakefulness in the New Testament.* LUÅ 1.55.3. Lund: Gleerup, 1963.

Weiser, Alfons. "Von der Predigt Jesu zur Erwartung der Parusie: Überlieferungs-geschichtliches zum Gleichnis vom Türnhüter." *BibLeb* 12 (1971): 25-31.

5.26. The Talents, Matthew 25:14-30

[Jesus said,] 14 *"For it is as when a man going on a journey called his slaves and entrusted to them his property;* 15 *to one he gave five talents, to another two, to another one, to each according to his ability. Then he went away.*

16 *"The one who had received the five talents went at once and traded with them; and he made five talents more.* 17 *So also, he who had the two talents made two talents more.*

18 *"But the one who had received the one talent went and dug in the ground and hid his master's money.*

19 *"After a long time the master of those slaves came and settled accounts with them.* 20 *And the one who had received the five talents came forward, bringing five talents more, saying, 'Master, you delivered to me five talents; behold, I have made five talents more.'*

21 *"His master said to him, 'Well done, good and faithful slave; you have been faithful over a little; I will set you over much; enter into the joy of your master.'*

22 *"And the one who had the two talents came forward also, saying, 'Master, you delivered to me two talents; behold, I have made two talents more.'*

23 *"His master said to him, 'Well done, good and faithful slave; you have been faithful over a little; I will set you over much; enter into the joy of your master.'*

24 *"The one who had received the one talent came forward also, saying, 'Master, I knew you to be a hard man, reaping where you did not sow, and gathering*

where you did not scatter [seed]; 25*so I was afraid, and I went and hid your talent in the ground. Behold, you have what is yours.'*

26*"But his master answered him, 'You wicked and lazy slave! You knew that I reap where I have not sowed, and gather where I have not scattered?* 27*Then you ought to have invested my money with the bankers, and at my coming I should have received what was my own with interest.* 28*So take the talent from him, and give it to him who has the ten talents.*

29*"For to every one who has will more be given, and he will have abundance; but from the one who has not, even what he has will be taken away.* 30*And cast the worthless slave into the outer darkness; there people will weep and gnash their teeth."*

Notes on the Text and Translation

25:14, 19, 21, 23, 26, 30. On the translation of δοῦλος as "slave" (as in the NRSV) rather than "servant" (as in the KJV, RSV, and NIV), see Appendix 2.

25:15-16. In some ancient witnesses (including A, C, D, and the Majority text) the adverb εὐθέως ("immediately," "at once") is made to modify the verb ἀπεδήμησεν ("went away") of 25:15. Superior texts (including ℵ and B), however, have it modify πορευθείς ("went") of 25:16. The KJV ("straightway took his journey") reflects the former. The RSV, NEB, NIV, NRSV, and others reflect the latter. This also makes better sense. There is no point to the immediate departure of the master, but there is a point for the first, diligent slave to go to work.[1]

Exegetical Commentary

The parable has a close parallel in the Gospel of Luke, the Parable of the Pounds (19:12-27). Yet the two parables are different. Some of the major differences are as follows:

1. The major figure in Matthew's account is a man (25:14); in Luke he is a nobleman (19:12).
2. The amounts of money are very different. In Matthew eight talents are divided (unequally) between three slaves (25:15); in Luke ten pounds (a considerably smaller amount) is divided evenly among ten slaves (19:13).
3. The number of slaves is different. In Matthew there are three; in Luke there are ten.
4. The master's purpose in leaving is not indicated in Matthew's account; in Luke's it is to receive a kingdom (19:12).
5. Matthew's account narrates what the slaves did (or did not do) with the

1. For further discussion, cf. B. Metzger, *TCGNT* 63.

amounts entrusted to them (25:16-18); this feature is missing in Luke's account.

6. The results of the slaves' activities differ. In Matthew's account the first two slaves double the amount entrusted (25:20, 22); in Luke's they do much better (the first makes a tenfold increase, and the second a fivefold one, 19:16, 18).

7. The rewards differ. In Matthew's account the slaves who increase the amounts are simply given greater responsibilities (25:21, 23); in Luke's they are set over ten cities or five cities, respectively (19:17, 19).

Since the two are so different in detail, they can be considered to have come from the special Matthean (M) and special Lukan (L) traditions, respectively,[2] rather than from Q.[3] To be sure, there are some striking linguistic similarities: (1) at the outset where the master calls his slaves and gives to each a sum of money (Matt 25:14//Luke 19:13); (2) near the end where the master orders that the third slave be deprived of his sum and that it be given to the first (Matt 25:28//Luke 19:24); and (3) the saying that follows (Matt 25:29//Luke 19:26). But these three similarities can be accounted for. The first and the second belong to the very foundation of the story and its telling. And the third, a saying, is found elsewhere in the Gospel tradition, as indicated in the Exegetical Comment on 25:29 below, and could have been part of a parable that originated with Jesus of Nazareth.

Two other theories on the question of a literary relationship between the Matthean and Lukan texts have been suggested. According to one, Jesus told two different parables at different times and places.[4] According to the other, Matthew derived his version from his own tradition, while Luke derived his from Q.[5] Either is possible, but neither can be demonstrated. Finally,

2. T. W. Manson, *Sayings*, 245, 313; C. H. Dodd, *Parables*, 114; J. Jeremias, *Parables*, 59-60; J. Dupont, "La parabole des talents," 376-91; J. Crossan, *Parables*, 100-101; A. Weiser, *Knechtsgleichnisse*, 256; D. Hagner, *Matthew*, 733; U. Luz, *Matthäus*, 3:495; J. Wohlgemut, "Entrusted Money," 105; R. France, "On Being Ready," 184; accepted as a possibility by W. D. Davies and D. C. Allison, *Matthew*, 3:376.

3. Contra Burnett H. Streeter, *The Four Gospels: A Study of Origins*, rev. ed. (New York: St. Martin's Press, 1930), 291; J. Fitzmyer, *Luke*, 1,230-33; A. Polag, *Fragmenta Q*, 26, 80-83; J. Donahue, *Parable*, 105; J. Lambrecht, *Astonished*, 19, 167-68; *Treasure*, 20, 217-18; H. Weder, *Gleichnisse*, 193; J. Gnilka, *Matthäus*, 2:356; R. Funk, *Five Gospels*, 255; and R. Brown, *Introduction NT*, 119. A bibliography on the issue of sources for the two parables is provided by John S. Kloppenborg, *Q Parallels: Synopsis, Critical Notes, and Concordance* (Sonoma, Calif.: Polebridge Press, 1988), 200.

4. A. Plummer, *Luke*, 437; idem, *Matthew*, 348; W. Oesterley, *Parables*, 143-44; Craig L. Blomberg, *Interpreting the Parables* (Downers Grove, Ill.: InterVarsity Press, 1990), 220; Leon Morris, *The Gospel according to Matthew* (Grand Rapids: Wm. B. Eerdmans, 1992), 626.

5. Entertained as a possibility by W. D. Davies and D. C. Allison, *Matthew*, 3:376.

according to Eusebius, a version of the parable also appeared in the apocryphal *Gospel of the Nazarenes,* and Eusebius cites it in one of his works (otherwise it does not exist), but it appears to have been based primarily on Matthew's version.[6]

As indicated in the Exegetical Commentary on the Parable of the Waiting Slaves (Mark 13:34-37//Luke 12:35-38), the theme of a king or wealthy man leaving some of his slaves or servants in charge while being away is a popular motif, which appears in that parable, this one, and three others (the Faithful and Wise Slave, Matt 24:45-51//Luke 12:42-46; the Pounds, Luke 19:12-27; and the Wicked Tenants, Mark 12:1-12//Matt 21:33-46//Luke 20:9-19) and within some rabbinic parables as well.

It is possible that both versions of the parable attest to an earlier form, which has been adapted and edited in the course of transmission. Such an "original" can be, and is often, called the Parable of Money in Trust.

The parable appears with the eschatological discourse of Matthew 24–25. It is the third in a string of parables concerning events at the end. The first was the Parable of the Faithful and Wise Slave (24:45-51), and the second was the Ten Maidens (25:1-13). Those parables had to do more obviously with wisdom. To some degree this one does, too, in the sense that two slaves act wisely, but a third is foolish. The first two parables had to do more precisely with the responsibility of leaders in the church and the responsibility of all, respectively, while this one has to do with the use of the gifts given to various persons.

25:14. The opening words (ὥσπερ γάρ, "for as") seem to link the parable to the saying of 25:13, in which the hearer or reader is exhorted to be watchful for the coming of the day of judgment. More likely, however, the linkage is to the whole of 25:1-13, resuming the theme of the kingdom of heaven (cf. the text of the KJV).[7] The kingdom therefore is like, or can be imagined to be like, the following situation, in which a man entrusts his property to his slaves while he goes away on a journey. The wording of 25:14 is similar to that of Mark 13:34 at the outset of the Parable of the Waiting Servants (13:34-37//Luke 12:35-39) and may indeed be affected by it.

25:15. The sums distributed to the three slaves are enormous. In the first century A.D. of the Greco-Roman world a τάλαντον ("talent") was equivalent to about 6,000 denarii.[8] Since a denarius was a day's wages for a com-

---

6. For the text, cf. *New Testament Apocrypha,* rev. ed., ed. Wilhelm Schneemelcher, 2 vols. (Louisville: Westminster/John Knox, 1991-92), 1:161-62 (#18); the text is taken from Eusebius, *Theophania* on Matt 25:14-15.

7. A. McNeile, *Matthew,* 364; W. D. Davies and D. C. Allison, *Matthew,* 3:404. According to E. Schweizer, *Matthew,* the link is to 25:13.

8. Marvin A. Powell, "Weights and Measures," *ABD* 6:907-8; Kenneth W. Harl, *Coinage in the Roman Economy, 300 B.C. to A.D. 700* (Baltimore: Johns Hopkins University Press, 1996), 482. Originally the term "talent" referred to a weight that varied in differing

mon laborer, and since such a person might work some 300 days per year, a talent would be worth nearly twenty years' wages.[9] Five talents would be worth approximately 30,000 denarii or a hundred years' wages; two talents would be worth about 12,000 denarii or forty years' wages. The amounts entrusted are based on the "ability" (δύναμις) of each slave (contra Luke's account, in which each of the ten receives an equal amount). The giving of property to three different slaves provides the way for the "rule of three" of good storytelling to operate. The hearer or reader expects that the third slave will be an object of scorn or derision.

In modern English the word "talent" has come to refer almost exclusively to a mental endowment, skill, aptitude, or physical ability that a person might have. The modern understanding is based on this parable. Apparently it appeared for the first time in the fifteenth century.[10] The English usage has become important in the interpretation of the parable in modern times (an issue to be taken up later).

25:16-18. The three slaves do what they can (or are willing to do). The first two take risks and double the amount entrusted to them. The phrase ἠργάσατο ἐν αὐτοῖς in 25:16 means "he worked with them,"[11] meaning that he worked with the talents at his disposal, and in this case it will mean specifically that he engaged in business,[12] although we are not told what kind. The same would be true for the second person who received two talents (25:17). (That the two may have simply made wise investments is ruled out by what is said to the third slave at 25:27.) We are not told how much time their dealings took, except that a great deal of time is meant (25:19). The third slave is the odd man out. He places the talent entrusted to him in a safe place; he can think only of security and must rule out risk. To place money into the ground for safekeeping was not unusual in the world of Jesus. It is illustrated already at 13:44. Furthermore, when the Romans had conquered Jerusalem in A.D. 70, for example, they dis-

---

parts of the Near East. In Greco-Roman times it amounted to ca. 42.5 kilograms (ca. 93.7 pounds). By virtue of its weight, a talent could designate value; a talent of gold or silver, for example, would have a customary value. But in the first century A.D. the term customarily referred to a monetary unit equivalent to 6,000 denarii.

9. The figures can be only approximate. The textual notes for the RSV and NRSV say that a talent was "more than fifteen years' wages of a laborer." That appears somewhat conservative. The textual note in the NIV reads, "A talent was worth more than a thousand dollars," which is surprisingly meager, even to the point of being misleading.

10. *The Oxford English Dictionary,* 2d ed., ed. J. A. Simpson and E. S. C. Weiner, 20 vols. (Oxford: Clarendon Press, 1989), 17:580. Cf. Benedikt Schwank, "τάλαντον," EDNT 3:332, who cites first usage in the sixteenth century.

11. BAGD 307.

12. The verb has the specific connotation of engaging in business at LXX Prov 31:18; Rev 18:17; cf. also the related noun form ἐργασία ("business") at Acts 16:16, 19; 19:24-25.

covered hoards of gold, silver, and other treasured articles that had been stored underground prior to the war.[13]

25:19. The man who entrusted his property to his slaves and returns is now designated for the first time as "master" (κύριος in Greek) or "lord." This appears to be, at the Matthean level at least, a term capable of an allegorical meaning in which "lord" is heard and read as "Lord," and his return "after a long time" is heard and read as the parousia of Christ, which has been delayed.

25:20-23. Since the slaves belong to the master, their earnings do too. Accounts settled with the first two are very favorable to the master. The two have doubled the amount entrusted to them. The master commends each one by using exactly the same words in each case (25:21, 23). He calls them "good and faithful," gives each one more authority on the basis of their having been faithful in "little," and invites each into his joy. The rewards are identical, even though the values brought back by the two slaves are not the same; the increases are proportional to the original amounts, but the yield of the first slave's work is much larger than that of the other. The fidelity of the two to their respective tasks, not the amounts gained, is what is important.[14] The fact that the amounts entrusted are called "little," when in fact talents are huge, indicates that Matthew has inflated the amounts given in an earlier version of the parable.[15]

25:24-25. The response of the third slave is entirely different. His action of burying the talent entrusted to him was on the basis of fear of the master. That does not actually make him "wicked" (which he is called at 25:16), but he is judged so, apparently, because he does not do what his master would do. In any case, the metaphors of reaping without sowing and gathering without broadcasting seed (25:24) indicate that the master enriches himself at the cost of others.[16]

25:26-28. The judgment is pronounced. The words "wicked and lazy" in 25:26 stand in antithesis to "good and faithful" in 25:21, 23. The master admits that he is known to be ruthless and rapacious in business. Therefore, in his mind at least, the slave should have acted in the same manner as the master would have — and as the other two slaves did. Moreover, if he was not able to take risks, he ought minimally to have invested the funds with bankers (who can take some risks at least) and earned some interest. In disgust, the master orders that the talent, which the slave has, must be taken immediately and be given to the one who took the greatest risk, and that is the one who has ten.

---

13. Josephus, *J.W.* 7.115; text quoted from *Josephus,* trans. Henry St. John Thackeray et al., LCL, 10 vols. (Cambridge: Harvard University Press, 1961-81), 3:539.

14. J. Meier, *Matthew,* 299. The fact that at the end of the story (25:28) the first slave receives even more does not contradict the matter of equal rewards in the final judgment.

15. W. D. Davies and D. C. Allison, *Matthew,* 3:403.

16. A. McNeile, *Matthew,* 366.

25:29. The saying is similar to its parallel at Luke 19:26. It is also similar to one at Mark 4:25//Matthew 13:12//Luke 8:18) and still another within the *Gospel of Thomas* (Logion 41).[17] The saying is difficult and appears to be unfair. The basic idea is that only the person who has been tested in small matters can be entrusted with larger ones. It is located here to extend and explain the thought of 25:28: one dare not fail, for the master is impatient. Although the verse is often considered to represent an authentic saying of Jesus,[18] various interpreters regard it as not belonging to the original parable.[19] The reason is that within the parable the slave was deprived of his talent not because he had little, but because he had not increased the value of what had been entrusted to him. Yet that is not the only possible conclusion to make. The fact that a similar (though not identical) saying appears at the end of Luke's version (19:26) indicates that such a saying was present within the parable before the two streams of tradition (M and L) had gone their separate ways. Furthermore, the sayings referred to above that are very similar are attributed to Jesus; here the saying is attributed to the master within the parable, and thus only indirectly to Jesus. To attribute an otherwise dominical saying to a figure within a parable, rather than as an appendage to it, lends some weight to its originality within the parable. In the final analysis, whether it was spoken by Jesus himself in the telling of the parable, or was added to it by early transmitters of the tradition, cannot be determined. In a more general way, and in its metaphorical and theological sense, the verse can be seen to cohere with the parable. That is that wherever God's gift has already borne fruit, God gives in greater abundance; where it has been fruitless, it is lost completely.[20]

25:30. The third slave is to be cast into the darkness. That a person would weep and gnash his or her teeth in such a place shows that the verse is heavily laden with symbolic meaning. Virtually the same saying appears at 8:12 and 22:13 and similar ones at 13:42, 50; 24:51. The wording is Matthean in its present form.[21]

Clearly the parable contains many allegorical elements.[22] The phrase "Enter into the joy of your master" (25:21, 23), while ostensibly referring to the joy of

17. "Jesus said, 'Whoever has something in his hand will receive more, and whoever has nothing will be deprived of even the little he has.'" Quoted from *NHLE* 131.

18. J. Donahue, *Parable*, 105.

19. A. McNeile, *Matthew*, 367; B. Smith, *Parables*, 167; R. Bultmann, *HST* 176; C. H. Dodd, *Parables*, 116-18; J. Jeremias, *Parables*, 62; D. Via, *Parables*, 114; A. Weiser, *Knechtsgleichnisse*, 267; J. Lambrecht, *Treasure*, 230-32; W. D. Davies and D. C. Allison, *Matthew*, 3:410.

20. E. Schweizer, *Matthew*, 472.

21. According to W. Oesterley, *Parables*, 149, T. W. Manson, *Sayings*, 248, and R. Bultmann, *HST* 176, the verse did not belong to the parable that Matthew received.

22. Agreed upon by various interpreters, including C. H. Dodd, *Parables*, 115-20; J. Jeremias, *Parables*, 63; E. Schweizer, *Matthew*, 473; W. D. Davies and D. C. Allison, *Matthew*, 3:402; U. Luz, *Matthäus*, 3:506, 509.

the master in the story, carries with it the meaning of the entering of the faithful into the eschatological kingdom of Christ, the κύριος ("Master," "Lord") of the Christian community (cf. Rom 14:17). The casting of the worthless slave "into the outer darkness" with subsequent gnashing of teeth carries with it reference to eschatological judgment, as elsewhere (8:12; 22:13; cf. 13:42, 50; 24:51). The master's return "after a long time" (25:19, μετὰ πολὺν χρόνον) is unmistakably a metaphor for the delay of the parousia.[23] Even the slaves themselves then become metaphors for Christians, to whom much has been given. For Matthew and his intended readers, then, the parable has to do with Christian responsibility prior to the parousia and final judgment. The man on a journey (called the κύριος in 25:19-24, 26) is a metaphor for Christ, who has gone, but will come again and judge. The giving of the talents to each according to his ability must signify not only the different gifts given but also the different levels of responsibility each person has been given. What is given is what the master considers appropriate. Nothing is given that is more than one can manage.

The meaning of the parable at the Matthean level must be discerned in light of the allegorical elements within it. The accent is upon the disciple's being faithful in his or her use of the gift given, regardless of how much has been entrusted.[24] In fact, even the disciple who thinks that he or she has little to employ in the service of Christ must use what has been given. One enlists what one has. Each one is given according to his or her ability (25:15). To be afraid or to refuse to use one's gift signifies failure, and the final judgment will disclose that. The type of gift that one might have to employ is not specified; to limit a person's gift to the modern sense of a "talent" is too restrictive; to exclude such in a modern interpretation would be too restrictive, too. At the Matthean level, however, such an understanding of the word "talent" would not have been in view.[25] "The parable sets the responsibility of the servants in terms of money ('talents'), but the symbolism points to something obviously more comprehensive."[26]

Whether the parable can be attributed to Jesus or not is debated. According to some interpreters, it can be attributed to him in some "original" form.[27]

23. J. Jeremias, *Parables*, 63.

24. So, with slight nuances, C. Montefiore, *Synoptic Gospels*, 2:747; E. Schweizer, *Matthew*, 472-74; J. Donahue, *Parable*, 109; H. Weder, *Gleichnisse*, 208-9; J. Gnilka, *Matthäus*, 2:364; D. Hagner, *Matthew*, 737; W. D. Davies and D. C. Allison, *Matthew*, 3:403-4.

25. T. W. Manson, *Sayings*, 246; R. Gundry, *Matthew*, 510.

26. D. Hagner, *Matthew*, 733.

27. A. Jülicher, *Gleichnisreden*, 2:482; T. W. Manson, *Sayings*, 245; C. H. Dodd, *Parables*, 117; B. Smith, *Parables*, 168; J. Jeremias, *Parables*, 61-62; D. Via, *Parables*, 115; E. Schweizer, *Matthew*, 472; A. Weiser, *Knechtsgleichnisse*, 259-72; J. Lambrecht, *Astonished*, 183-84; idem, *Treasure*, 232-36; J. Gnilka, *Matthäus*, 2:363; W. D. Davies and D. C. Allison, *Matthew*, 3:403; U. Luz, *Matthäus*, 3:497-98. The parable (minus 25:29-30 and the closing statements of 25:21, 23) is in pink font (= Jesus said something like this) in R. Funk, *Five Gospels*, 255-56; cf. also W. Herzog, *Parables*, 155.

The fact that it is doubly attested gives weight to such a conclusion. The "original" would have been more like Matthew's than Luke's version,[28] except that the amounts of money entrusted in Matthew's version (in talents!) reflect that evangelist's penchant for the grandiose. As indicated above, the three slaves are hardly faithful in "a little" (25:21, 23), since talents amount to so much. The original parable would have been a parable addressed by Jesus to his disciples in which the allegorical elements would be fewer and not at all explicitly christological. It would be a parable in which those elements (the man on a journey, the gifts given) would refer to God's giving gifts that are to be used in the service of God; the commendation of the first two slaves would signify their salvation at the final judgment, while the word to the third would signify condemnation. Rhetorically the parable would then function as an exhortation to use the gifts one has been given for the sake of the kingdom of God. Concern for one's own personal security is ruled out; the disciple who is faithful will take risks for the kingdom, that is, in service to God. There is no basis for claiming that, in an original situation, the parable would have been spoken by Jesus against his opponents, so that the third slave represents either the Pharisaic Jew who "seeks personal security in a meticulous observance of the Law"[29] or the scribes, who have been entrusted with the Word of God but have not used it properly, "for they had frustrated the operation of the divine word by self-seeking and careless neglect of God's gift."[30] Nor is there a sound basis for the view that in its original setting the parable was in some way a critique of exploitation of the poor by the rich and powerful.[31]

Exposition

The Parable of the Talents reminds the Christian community that God has bestowed various gifts, and gifts in various measure, to all. That is spelled out elsewhere in the NT, as when Paul speaks of the "gifts that differ according to the grace given to us" (Rom 12:6; cf. 1 Cor 12:4) and when the writer of Ephesians writes concerning the various gifts given for the sake of ministry and building up the body of Christ (4:11-12). Strictly speaking, the talents doled out to the three slaves were not gifts, but money entrusted to them. But then all the gifts of God are temporary; they are like funds entrusted to people but for a while.

The parable addresses the individual reader or the congregation hearing it

28. B. Smith, *Parables*, 162; E. Schweizer, *Matthew*, 472-73; B. Scott, *Parable*, 223; J. Wohlgemut, "Entrusted Money," 106.

29. C. H. Dodd, *Parables*, 119.

30. J. Jeremias, *Parables*, 62; cf., for a similar view, B. Smith, *Parables*, 168-69; J. Lambrecht, *Treasure*, 234-35 (against both scribes and Pharisees).

31. As in the work of W. Herzog, *Parables*, 150-68, and R. Rohrbaugh, "A Peasant Reading," 32-39. For an incisive review and criticism of these works, cf. J. Wohlgemut, "Entrusted Money," 103-20.

in such a way that it exhorts each and all to make use of those gifts that God has given. The tradition of identifying those gifts as "talents" (abilities) that one has (rather than money) need not be ruled out, although limiting one's thinking to that alone would be too restrictive and, as indicated above, the understanding of the term in that sense was surely not in view for the evangelist Matthew. Such gifts are normally considered natural endowments given by the Creator in creation (abilities in music, finances, the arts, and so on). But there are also particular spiritual gifts given by the Spirit (proclamation, teaching, works of mercy, and so on, as spelled out in Rom 12:6-8 and 1 Cor 12:7-11). In any case, all gifts entrusted are to be enlisted in the service of Christ. The metaphor of doing business in such a way that the amount is doubled (25:16) is powerful, signifying great efforts in the use of the gifts one has. On the other hand, the burying of that which has been entrusted (25:18) signifies lack of use, acting in such a way that nothing has been entrusted at all. The parable functions as an exhortation to "serve one another with whatever gift each . . . has received" (1 Peter 4:10).

The note of judgment is clear on the one who buries that which has been entrusted (25:26-30). But there is also within the parable much that can be celebrated. The very idea of risk taking runs counter to a form of calculation that assumes that there is only one way to please God. Taking risks is also the work of faith in action. When it comes to serving Christ, one should be bold and not be afraid of risks. That is another way of saying something like the famous slogan of Martin Luther: "Sin boldly, but believe and rejoice in Christ even more."[32] The words of promise from Jesus, inviting disciples into the joy of his kingdom, are meant to be heard by all who do not worry too much about securing their own lives, but get on with lives of self-abandon and witness, knowing that the grace of God in Christ will more than compensate for any mistakes they might make.

Select Bibliography

Brisman, L. "A Parable of Talent." *RelArts* 1 (1996): 74-99.

Candlish, Robert. "The Pounds and the Talents." *ExpTim* 23 (1911-12): 136-37.

Dauviller, Jean. "La Parabole des mines ou des talents et le #99 du code Hammourabi." In *Mélanges dédiés à M. le professeur Joseph Magnol*, 153-65. Ed. J. Dauviller. Paris: Recueil Sirey, 1948.

Derrett, J. Duncan M. "Law in the New Testament: The Parable of the Talents and Two Logia." *ZNW* 56 (1966): 185-95. Reprinted as "The Parable of the Talents and Two Logia," in his *Law in the New Testament*, 17-31. London: Darton, Longman & Todd, 1970.

32. The passage is in a letter from Luther to Philip Melanchthon: "pecca fortiter, sed fortius fide et gaude in Christo." The letter appears in an edition of Luther's works published at Jena (1556), 1:345. Quoted from *The Oxford Dictionary of Quotations*, 3d ed. (Oxford: Oxford University Press, 1979), 320.

Didier, Marcel. "La parabole des talents (Mt 25,14-30)." *ASeign* 93 (1965): 32-44.

Dietzfelbinger, Christian. "Das Gleichnis von den anvertrauten Geldern." *BTZ* 6 (1989): 222-33.

Dupont, Jacques. "La parabole des talents (Mt 25,14-30) ou des mines (Lc 19,12-27)." *RTP* 19 (1969): 376-91.

Fiedler, Peter. "Die übergegebenen Talente: Auslegung von Mt 25,14-30." *BibLeb* 11 (1970): 259-73.

Flusser, David. "Aesop's Miser and the Parable of the Talents." In *Parable and Story in Judaism and Christianity,* 9-25. Ed. Clemens Thoma and David Wyschogrod. New York: Paulist, 1989.

Fortna, Robert. "Reading Jesus' Parable of the Talents through Underclass Eyes: Matt 25:14-30." *FFF* 8 (1992): 211-28.

France, Richard T. "On Being Ready (Matthew 25:1-46)." In *The Challenge of Jesus' Parables,* 177-95. Ed. Richard N. Longenecker. Grand Rapids: Wm. B. Eerdmans, 2000.

Harrington, Daniel J. "Polemical Parables in Matthew 24–25." *USQR* 44 (1991): 287-98.

Joüon, Paul. "La parabole des mines (Lc 19,12-27) et la parabole des talents (Mt 25,14-30)." *RSR* 29 (1939): 489-93.

Lys, Daniel. "Contre le salut par les oeuveres dans la prédication des talents." *ETR* 64 (1989): 331-40.

Manns, Frédéric. "La parabole des talents: Wirkungsgeschichte et racines juives." *RSR* 65 (1991): 343-62.

Marion, D. "Simples et mystérieuses paraboles. VIII. Paraboles de crise (2): Mt 25,14-30: les talents." *EeV* 30-33 (1996): 241-45, 252-55.

Martin, F. "Parabole des talents. Matthieu 25, 14-30." *SémBib* 84 (1996): 14-24.

McCullough, W. "The Pounds and the Talents." *ExpTim* 23 (1911-12): 382-83.

McGaughy, Lane C. "The Fear of Yahweh and the Mission of Judaism: A Postexilic Maxim and Its Early Christian Expansion in the Parable of the Talents." *JBL* 94 (1975): 235-45.

Mutch, John. "The Man with the One Talent." *ExpTim* 42 (1930-31): 332-34.

Naegele, J. "Translation of *talanton* 'talent.'" *BT* 37 (1986): 441-43.

Resenhöfft, Wilhelm. "Jesu Gleichnis von den Tenenten, ergänzt durch die Lukas-Fassung." *NTS* 26 (1979-80): 318-31.

Rohrbaugh, Richard. "A Peasant Reading of the Parable of the Talents/Pounds: A Text of Terror?" *BTB* 23 (1993): 32-39.

Ross, J. M. "Talents." *ExpTim* 89 (1978): 307-9.

Steinmetz, David C. "Matthew 25:14-30." *Int* 34 (1980): 172-76.

Tillich, Paul. "Riddle of Iniquity." *USQR* 13 (May 1958): 3-9.

Wohlgemut, Joel R. "Entrusted Money (Matt. 25:14-28)." In *Jesus and His Parables: Interpreting the Parables of Jesus Today,* 103-20. Ed. V. George Shillington. Edinburgh: T. & T. Clark, 1997.

See also the Bibliography for the Parable of the Pounds.

5.27. The Pounds, Luke 19:12-27

12 *[Jesus] said therefore, "A nobleman went into a distant country to receive a kingdom for himself and then return.* 13*Calling ten of his slaves, he gave them ten minas and said to them, 'Trade with these till I come.'*

14 *"But his citizens hated him and sent a delegation after him, saying, 'We do not want this man to rule over us.'*

15 *"When he returned, having received the kingdom, he commanded these slaves, to whom he had given the money, to be called to him, that he might know what they had gained by trading.*

16 *"The first came before him, saying, 'Lord, your mina has produced ten more.'*

17 *"And he said to him, 'Well done, good slave! Because you have been faithful in a very little, you shall have authority over ten cities.'*

18 *"And the second came, saying, 'Lord, your mina has produced five more.'*

19 *"And he said to him, 'And you are to be over five cities.'*

20 *"Then another came, saying, 'Lord, here is your mina, which I kept laid away in a piece of cloth;* 21*for I was afraid of you, because you are a severe man; you take up what you did not lay down, and reap what you did not sow.'*

22 *"He said to him, 'I will condemn you out of your own mouth, you wicked slave! You knew that I was a severe man, taking up what I did not lay down and reaping what I did not sow?* 23*Why then did you not put my money into the bank, and at my coming I should have collected it with interest?'*

24 *"And he said to those who stood by, 'Take the mina from him, and give it to him who has the ten minas.'*

25 *"And they said to him, 'Lord, he has ten minas!'*

26 *" 'I tell you, that to every one who has will more be given; but from him who has not, even what he has will be taken away.* 27*But as for these enemies of mine, who did not want me to rule over them, bring them here and slay them before me.'"*

Notes on the Text and Translation

19:12, 15. The term βασιλεία can mean "kingdom" (RSV) or "kingship." The NRSV translates it "royal power." To be sure, the noun can have the abstract meaning of "royal power."[1] But within this parable the term most likely means "kingdom" since it follows a saying concerning the kingdom of God (19:11), and it is from the holdings of his kingdom that the nobleman distributes cities as rewards (19:17, 19).

19:13, 16, 18, 20, 24-25. The term "mina" is used in the translation, which is a transliteration of the Greek μνᾶ, a Semitic loanword that is used only here

---

1. Ulrich Luz, "βασιλεία," *EDNT* 1:201.

in the NT. Except for the NIV, which uses the transliteration, modern translations generally prefer "pound," but the value of a pound in modern times (of which the best known is British) hardly begins to match that of a mina. As difficult as the term is, it is no more so than the "talent" used in the Parables of the Talents and the Unforgiving Slave, even if less familiar.

19:23. The phrase ἐπὶ τράπεζαν is translated "into the bank" (KJV, RSV, NRSV), "in the bank" (JB, TEV), or "on deposit" (NEB, NIV). Literally it would mean "upon a table," but by NT times the noun had already come to mean "the table on which money-changers display their coins."[2] Somewhat similarly, the English word "bank" — used in connection with an institution for the deposit and lending of money — is an extension of the word for a money dealer's "bench."[3] Within the context of the parable, the slave is scolded for not investing the money with money dealers. More than a "deposit" for safekeeping is involved. For the modern ear, "into the bank" seems the best translation of the phrase in question.

19:25. The verse is missing in two important ancient Greek witnesses (D, W) and some Old Latin, Syriac, and Coptic versions. It is an expendable element as far as the story goes; if it is dropped, the story flows very well. But it is widely attested in other sources, and the very fact that it makes the reading more difficult makes its presence from the beginning a likelihood.[4]

Exegetical Commentary

The parable is known as the Parable of the Pounds. For the North American reader of the NT the term "pounds" is not associated immediately with money but rather with a particular weight. For the British or other reader who is familiar with the "pound" as a type of currency there is another problem, and that is the value involved. In modern times ten pounds does not amount to anything like the value of the currency referred to in the parable. See the discussion below. Yet the designation of the parable as the Parable of the Pounds is so widely used and so familiar that it will no doubt continue to be used, and is used here.

There is a similarity between this parable and the Parable of the Talents in the Gospel of Matthew (25:14-30). Yet the parables are quite dissimilar in many respects. In this one, for example, ten slaves are involved in the story, and ten equal amounts of money are given to each. In the Parable of the Talents only three slaves are involved, and three unequal amounts of money are given to each. The two parables are not likely to have come from a common source used by the two evangelists (i.e., Q), but from two independent traditions (special

---

2. BAGD 824.

3. Cf. *The Oxford English Dictionary,* 2d ed., ed. J. A. Simpson and E. S. C. Weiner, 20 vols. (Oxford: Clarendon Press, 1989), 1:930-31.

4. Cf., for more discussion on this verse, B. Metzger, *TCGNT* 169.

Matthean and special Lukan traditions). For discussion, see the Exegetical Commentary on the Parable of the Talents.

The Parable of the Pounds differs particularly from the Talents by having within it what some interpreters have called an independent parable, that is, the Parable of the Throne Claimant, which is said to lie behind 19:12-14, 24a, 27.[5] But the material there can be accounted for on other grounds (see below on 19:12, 14) and attributed to Lukan composition.[6]

The theme of a king, powerful man, or rich man leaving servants or slaves in charge while away is a popular one in the parables of Jesus, as well as in rabbinic parables. It appears in four other parables from Jesus besides this one — the Waiting Slaves (Mark 13:34-37//Luke 12:35-38), the Faithful and Wise Slave (Matt 24:45-51//Luke 12:42-46), the Talents (Matt 25:14-30), and the Wicked Tenants (Mark 12:1-12//Matt 21:33-46//Luke 20:9-19; but missing in *Gos. Thom.* 65–66). Three known rabbinic parables, all attributed to rabbis from times later than Jesus, share the same theme. These are indicated in the Exegetical Commentary on the Waiting Slaves.

The parable has been set by Luke within the Travel Narrative of 9:51–19:27 and is, in fact, the very last pericope within that section of Luke's Gospel. More specifically, the parable has been placed by Luke where Jesus and his disciples (mentioned in 18:31) were coming near to Jerusalem. They have arrived at Jericho (19:1) and are still there or have set out upon the seventeen-mile journey uphill toward Jerusalem. The disciples begin to wonder whether "the kingdom of God was to appear immediately" (19:11), either before or when they arrive in Jerusalem. Jesus had been quizzed earlier by the Pharisees concerning the time of the kingdom's arrival (18:20) as well. What follows is called a "parable" by Luke the evangelist (19:11). It appears here to hold in check the view that the kingdom is to appear imminently.[7]

19:12, 14. The nobleman goes off for a specific purpose (a feature missing in Matthew's account). Although the going and coming of the nobleman are no doubt an allegorical feature within the parable, alluding to the ascension of Je-

5. These interpreters include A Jülicher, *Gleichnisreden,* 2:486-87; E. Easton, *Luke,* 282; J. Jeremias, *Parables,* 59; M. Zerwick, "Parabel vom Thronanwärter," 654-74; F. Weinert, "Parable of the Throne Claimant," 505-15; P. Perkins, *Parables,* 146-47; J. Crossan, *Parables,* 100, 103; M. Boucher, *Parables,* 140.

6. A. Jülicher, *Gleichnisreden,* 2:486-88; J. Creed, *Luke,* 232; R. Bultmann, *HST* 176; T. W. Manson, *Sayings,* 313; A. Weiser, *Knechtsgleichnisse,* 229-31; J. Lambrecht, *Astonished,* 174-76; J. Fitzmyer, *Luke,* 1231; B. Scott, *Parable,* 223.

7. A. Jülicher, *Gleichnisreden,* 2:486; C. H. Dodd, *Parables,* 115; T. W. Manson, *Sayings,* 314; J. Jeremias, *Parables,* 59; I. H. Marshall, *Luke,* 702; J. Fitzmyer, *Luke,* 1,229; Hans Conzelmann, *The Theology of St Luke* (New York: Harper & Brothers, 1960), 113; H. Weder, *Gleichnisse,* 209; J. Lambrecht, *Astonished,* 188-89; M. Boucher, *Parables,* 143. According to L. Johnson, "Lukan Kingship Parable," 139-59, the parable confirms the expectation of Luke 19:11.

sus and his parousia, various interpreters have suggested that the verses might recall a well-known event decades before the writing of Luke's Gospel.[8] After the death of Herod the Great in 4 B.C., his son Archelaus (heir to Judea, Samaria, and Idumea) traveled to Rome to acquire the title of king. But a delegation of fifty persons (Jews and Samaritans), sent by people opposed to Archelaus, went to Rome to try to prevent that from happening. The result was that Archelaus was granted the title of ethnarch, not king.[9] (Additional stories of men traveling to Rome in order to acquire royal titles and positions exist.[10]) The suggestion is a sound one since these details are not necessary for the structure of the parable itself. Matthew's version, for example, simply has a wealthy man entrust money to his servants; he goes away, and then returns. The same could have been said here. But the recollection of the event (if indeed it is that event and not another) adds color to the story. The final saying in 19:14 would have been heard by Luke's readers as a reference to the rejection of Jesus.

19:13. The Greek term μνᾶ is sometimes translated as "pound" (KJV, RSV, NEB, NRSV), but it can also be transliterated as "mina" (NIV). The value of a mina was equivalent to one hundred denarii.[11] Since the denarius was worth a day's wages for common laborers,[12] ten minas (= 1,000 denarii) was worth wages for 1,000 days for a common laborer, that is, wages for about three years and four months. (In modern times ten British pounds would be minuscule in comparison.) As the story unfolds, it is clear that the ten minas are distributed evenly among the ten slaves; that is, each receives one mina. In Matthew's account the amounts distributed are uneven (five talents, two talents, and one talent) and "to each, according to his ability" (25:15).

In comparing the value of the minas given in this parable with the talents given to the slaves in Matthew 25:14, each mina was worth about one-sixtieth of a talent.[13] Therefore the amounts referred to in this parable are considerably smaller. Another difference is that in this version of the parable the nobleman gives explicit directions to his slaves; they are to do business with the amounts given until he returns. The verb used is an imperative form (aorist, second person, plural) of πραγματεύομαι, meaning to "do business" or "conduct trade" (used only here in the NT).[14]

8. B. Smith, *Parables,* 163; T. W. Manson, *Sayings,* 313; I. Marshall, *Luke,* 701, 703-4; J. Lambrecht, *Astonished,* 174-75; J. Fitzmyer, *Luke,* 1235. The connection is refuted by B. Scott, *Parable,* 223.

9. Josephus, *Ant.* 17.299-320; *J.W* 2.80-100.

10. Josephus, *Ant.* 14.302; 18.244.

11. BAGD 524; "μνᾶ," *EDNT* 2:434.

12. A denarius was commonly the wage of a soldier or farm worker in the first century A.D., according to Kenneth W. Harl, *Coinage in the Roman Economy, 300 B.C. to A.D. 700* (Baltimore: Johns Hopkins University Press, 1996), 278-79.

13. Cf. "μνᾶ," *EDNT* 2:343.

14. BAGD 697.

19:15. The nobleman returns after obtaining the kingdom that he had wanted and makes his slaves accountable. At the level of Luke's Gospel the verse takes on an allegorical meaning, referring to the parousia of Christ and the final judgment.

19:16-19. The verses recount the successful dealings of the first two slaves. They have multiplied the value of the amounts entrusted to them, and they are rewarded for their efforts. The first of the two, who has multiplied the amount tenfold, is commended to a degree that the second one, who has made half as much, is not. He alone is addressed as a "good slave" and commended with the words "well done." He has fulfilled what his master had commanded him to do. Then he is given charge of ten cities, presumably located within the master's kingdom. The second slave is simply given charge of five cities. The greater the amounts gained, the greater the rewards.

19:20-23. The third slave, who returns the amount given, had wrapped it in a σουδάριον, a Latin loanword (sudarium) variously translated as a "napkin" (KJV, RSV), "handkerchief" (NEB, TEV), or "piece of cloth" (NIV, NRSV). The latter is preferable; typically the term refers to a piece of cloth used for wiping perspiration off the face and neck,[15] a bandanna. In light of the command of his master in 19:13 ("trade with these"), the slave's action is not simply a matter of neglect but of disobedience. Furthermore, in light of a saying in the Mishnah, in which a contrast is made, on the one hand, between wrapping money in cloth and carrying it over one's back and, on the other, proper safekeeping,[16] the saying makes the man reckless or careless.

The slave calls his master a "severe" or "strict" (αὐστηρός) man. The term (used only here in the NT) is not as stinging as in Matthew's account, in which the master is a "harsh" or "cruel" person (σκληρός, 25:24). Luke's term need not have an adverse meaning at all.[17] But as in Matthew's account, so here, he is described as a man who enriches himself at the expense of others.[18] In any case, the master considers his slave "wicked" (πονηρός, 19:22) because he did not trade with the money entrusted to him. The slave is scolded for not trading in the manner that is fitting for a slave of this type of man. If he did not have the adventurous courage that was required, he could at least have invested the money with the money dealers, obtained the interest, and turned it over to the master. To be sure, the interest gained would probably be modest. The money dealers themselves, to whom the slave would entrust the investment, could lend the money out — legally — at four to six percent per annum.[19] Since they would profit from their loans, they would pay the slave even less. But it would at least be something.

---

15. BAGD 759; LSJ 1859.
16. *M. B. Mes.* 3:10.
17. BAGD 122.
18. F. Brightman, "Αἴρεις," 158.
19. Bruce W. Frier, "Interest and Usury in the Greco-Roman Period," *ABD* 3:423-24.

19:24-26. It has been maintained that the parable ended at 19:23.[20] If so, that would mean that the words uttered by the nobleman in 19:24-27 were appended. The usual reason for claiming that a parable has come to an end, even though related sayings of application follow, is that there was a tendency in the early church to attribute interpretations or applications to Jesus. That viewpoint is then applied across the board, even though it has been shown that an application (in Hebrew the *nimshal*) typically follows in known Jewish parables from antiquity.[21] In the present parable (as well as in its Matthean parallel) the words are spoken not by Jesus but by the nobleman; they are internal and integral to the parable.

The bystanders (19:24) seem to appear out of nowhere. They could simply be persons of the realm, subjects of the master, or they could be the other nine slaves to whom money had been entrusted (19:13). More likely, they are additional personnel in the master's company, that is, personal attendants, bodyguards, and the like (cf. 1 Kings 9:22; 10:8). In any case, the nobleman gives them orders. In his haste he makes a simple mistake in mathematics. Although the first slave is said to have ten minas, he actually has eleven (the original one, plus the ten more that he made); now he shall have twelve. Even the slaves make the mathematical mistake in their choral declaration (19:25). The latter verse is widely regarded as a secondary addition to the parable (either pre-Lukan or Lukan);[22] it is rightly placed in parentheses in some modern versions (KJV, RSV, NRSV), since the master continues to speak in the next verse. Moreover, the giving of the extra mina to the first slave, who has not only eleven others but ten cities as well, seems to be a condescending pittance to the first slave. The giving of jurisdiction over cities to the first two slaves appears now to be a secondary addition. It is a detail missing in Matthew's account, whereas the taking of the sum from the third and giving it to the first slave is present in the parallel (Matt 25:28).

The next-to-final verse (19:26) is similar to a parallel in Matthew's account (25:29) and somewhat similar to still other sayings (Mark 4:25//Matt 13:12//Luke 8:18; *Gos. Thom.* 41). The saying cannot simply be regarded as a free-floating one that has been attached to the parable. Its connection with the parable must have existed from early on, perhaps with Jesus himself. See the Exegetical Commentary on Matthew 25:29.[23]

20. B. Smith, *Parables,* 167; A. Cadoux, *Parables,* 68. According to J. Crossan, *Parables,* 102, the original parable ended at Luke 19:24.

21. Harvey K. McArthur and Robert M. Johnston, *They Also Spoke in Parables: Rabbinic Parables from the First Centuries of the Christian Era* (Grand Rapids: Zondervan, 1990), 99, 111-12; David Stern, *Parables in Midrash: Narrative and Exegesis in Rabbinic Literature* (Cambridge, Mass.: Harvard University Press, 1991), 8, 16, 21-22.

22. J. Creed, *Luke,* 235; J. Jeremias, *Parables,* 62; B. Easton, *Luke,* 283; C. Montefiore, *Synoptic Gospels,* 2:1031; I. H. Marshall, *Luke,* 708; A. Weiser, *Knechtsgleichnisse,* 251-52; E. Schweizer, *Luke,* 295; J. Fitzmyer, *Luke,* 1238.

23. According to A. Plummer, *Luke,* 443, and E. Schweizer, *Luke,* 295, Jesus makes

19:27. The enemies of the nobleman, who had not wanted him to reign over them (19:14), are now brought on the scene, and their execution is ordered. According to some interpreters, the verse refers to divine vengeance against those who had rejected Jesus, that is, the Jews of first-century Palestine in general, or the Jewish leaders.[24] If Jews in general are meant, the charge of anti-Judaism can be leveled against Luke's Gospel (or both his source and the Gospel) at this point. Yet it is possible that only the leaders of the Jewish people are meant. In either case, as a referent to persons after the time of Jesus' ministry, it cannot be attributed to Jesus himself. The earliest form of the parable that can be recovered on the basis of Synoptic comparison would have ended with 19:26.[25] The verse stands as the second part of an *inclusio* with 19:13-14 and is fitting for an ending from a literary point of view. But it is a horrible ending if the nobleman who has returned after obtaining a kingdom is related allegorically to Jesus at his parousia. He is portrayed in the fashion of a despotic king who slays his enemies (cf. 1 Sam 15: 33); one has to understand it metaphorically as an allusion to judgment by the Son of man.

The Parable of the Pounds is in some ways very much like the Parable of the Talents in the Gospel of Matthew in regard to its teaching, but not exactly. The Parable of the Talents is more obviously allegorical and moralistic; it has more explicit christological features and emphasizes more strongly the need for the disciples of Jesus to use gifts entrusted to them prior to the parousia of Christ.

The difference between the two parables becomes immediately evident by noticing the location of the Parable of the Pounds within the Gospel of Luke. It has been located in such a way that it makes a response to popular eschatological expectations, that is, that the kingdom of God is imminent (19:11). Furthermore, the third slave, who is condemned, is more deserving of being called "wicked" (19:22), since he did not do what his master had told him to do, that is, to do business with what had been entrusted to him (19:13). Although less explicit than in Matthew's account, allegorical elements are present: the nobleman's going away to a far country and then returning, which represents the departure of Jesus from this world through his ascension and his return by his subsequent parousia; the addressing of the nobleman by his slaves as "lord" (κύριος, 19:16, 18, 20, 25); and the nobleman/lord as carrying out a final reckoning, corresponding to the final judgment. All of these features serve to open the parable to interpretation in a particular way at the level of the Gospel of

---

the reply here. But that is not satisfactory since the speech of the master continues in 19:27.

24. A. Jülicher, *Gleichnisreden*, 2:487; A. Plummer, *Luke*, 443; J. Creed, *Luke*, 235; B. Easton, *Luke*, 283; C. Montefiore, *Synoptic Gospels*, 2:1,030-31; J. Sanders, "Parable of the Pounds," 660-68; J. Fitzmyer, *Luke*, 1,233.

25. R. Bultmann, *HST* 176; T. W. Manson, *Sayings*, 317.

Luke. That is that during the absence of the ascended Christ each of his disciples is expected to carry on with his or her duties of Christian mission, seeking to do the most that can be done. Two temptations are to be avoided. The first temptation is that, in light of the expected return of the risen and ascended Christ, a disciple may withdraw from engaging the world with the gospel and do essentially nothing with it. The second is that, in light of the apparent delay in the coming of Christ, a disciple will postpone such engagement and be preoccupied with other things. Either way, the disciple's behavior is comparable to hiding a sum of money in a piece of cloth.

There is, to be sure, a second theme running through Luke's rendition of the Parable of the Pounds. That is the matter of judgment upon those who reject Jesus. In fact, one might suggest that, for Luke, that is the main theme, since he as redactor has inserted the material that gives rise to it (19:14, 27). But that is not the only approach to take. The theme of rejection and consequent judgment makes its appearance to anticipate the cross and the parousia. But that is surely secondary to the stress of the parable on faithful obedience to the Lord in the interim. The coming of the master to carry out the final reckoning with his servants, particularly the third, is central. Other details are subordinate.[26] Not to be forgotten, too, is that the parable follows the situation described at 19:11, the expectation of some that the kingdom was imminent.

On the possible setting and meaning of an "original" parable within the ministry of Jesus of Nazareth, see the conclusion to the Exegetical Commentary on the Parable of the Talents.

Exposition

The parable sets forth the view that, in the end, all the disciples of Jesus are accountable to him. To each has been given a gift for creative and vigorous use until Jesus comes again. The command to do business with those gifts given is not to be taken lightly. The first two slaves are presented as examples of persons willing to take risks and thereby receive the commendation of the Lord at his return.

Many are the gifts entrusted to the disciples of Jesus. One can make a list of those things entrusted and how they have been and are used. The gifts of musical composition and performance, theological insight and expression, missionary work of outstanding persons, the use of the arts, and benevolences to support all of these — these and much more are items that one can come up with to illustrate how gifts have been used for the sake of the ministry of Jesus.

But the focus of the parable is upon the third slave. The third slave is condemned by his master. The master's action is unusually harsh. From the point of view of the slave, his reticence to do business was that he was fearfully timid.

---

26. J. Creed, *Luke*, 232; C. H. Dodd, *Parables*, 118; J. Jeremias, *Parables*, 61; H. Weder, *Gleichnisse*, 209.

If he were to carry on business with money entrusted to him, he might lose a portion, or even all, of it. Then what would the master do? He would be enraged, and there is no telling what might happen.

The slave played it safe. He placed the money in a piece of cloth. For him, that was sufficient. But it was a rather careless thing to do. A bank would have been much safer, and the sum would have increased with interest.

From the point of view of the master, the slave was wicked. He was not only careless, but above all disobedient. He had not followed the command of the master to do business with the money until he should return.

The lives of many Christians are characterized by playing it safe in the use of things entrusted to them. After all, the result could be failure or ridicule. But is it truly a matter of playing it safe, or is it disobedience? The Bible knows nothing of "playing it safe" in the service of God and in discipleship.

Select Bibliography

Brightman, F. E. "S. Luke 19,21: Αἴρεις ὃ οὐκ ἔθηκας." *JTS* 29 (1927-28): 158.

Candlish, Robert. "The Pounds and the Talents." *ExpTim* 23 (1911-12): 136-37.

Derrett, J. Duncan M. "A Horrid Passage in Luke Explained." *ExpTim* 97 (1985-86): 136-38.

Didier, Marcel. "La Parabole des talents et des mines." In *De Jésus aux évangiles: Tradition et rédaction dans les évangiles synoptique*, 2:248-71. Ed. Ignace de la Potterie. 2 vols. BETL 25. Gembloux: J. Duculot, 1967.

Dupont, Jacques. "La Parabole des talents (Mat 25:14-30) ou des mines (Luc 19:12-27)." *RTP* 19 (1969): 376-91.

Holdcroft, I. T. "The Parable of the Pounds and Origen's Doctrine of Grace." *JTS* 24 (1973): 503-4.

Johnson, Luke T. "The Lukan Kingship Parable." *NovT* 24 (1982): 139-59.

Joüon, Paul. "La Parabole des Mines (Luc 19,13-27) et la Parabole des Talents (Matthieu 25,14-30)." *RSR* 29 (1939): 489-94.

Kamlah, Ehrhard. "Kritik und Interpretation der Parabel von den anvertrauten Geldern Mt. 25:14ff.; Lk. 19:12ff." *KuD* 14 (1968): 28-38.

McCullough, W. "The Pounds and the Talents." *ExpTim* 23 (1911-12): 382-83.

McGaughy, Lane C. "The Fear of Yahweh and the Mission of Judaism: A Postexilic Maxim and Its Early Christian Expansion in the Parable of the Talents." *JBL* 94 (1975): 235-45.

Panier, Louis. "La parabole des mines: Lecture sémiotique (Lc 19,11-27)." In *Les paraboles évangéliques: Perspectives nouvelles*, 333-47. Ed. Jean Delorme. Paris: Cerf, 1989.

Puig i Tàrrech, Armand. "La parabole des talents (Mt 25,14-30) ou des mines (Lc 19,11-28)." *RCT* 10 (1985): 269-317.

Reinert, Francis. "Parable of the Throne Claimant (Lk 19:12, 14-15a, 27) Reconsidered." *CBQ* 39 (1977): 505-14.

Resenhöfft, Wilhelm. "Jesu Gleichnis von den Talenten, ergänst durch die Lukas-Fassung." *NTS* 26 (1979-80): 318-31.

Sanders, Jack T. "The Parable of the Pounds and Lucan Anti-Semitism." *TS* 42 (1981): 660-68.

Simpson, J. G. "The Parable of the Pounds." *ExpTim* 37 (1925-26): 299-302.

Stock, Eugene. "The Pounds and the Talents." *ExpTim* 22 (1910-11): 424-25.

Weinert, Francis D. "The Parable of the Throne Claimant (Luke 19:12, 14-15a, 27) Reconsidered." *CBQ* 39 (1977): 505-14.

Zerwick, Max. "Die Parabel vom Thronanwärter." *Bib* 40 (1959): 654-74.

See also the Bibliography for the Parable of the Talents.

CHAPTER 6

Parables of Final Judgment

Many of the parables within the Synoptic Gospels refer to the final judgment. For example, within the Parable of the Rich Man and Lazarus (Luke 16:19-31) a judgment takes place; the rich man goes to Hades after he dies, while the poor man is carried by the angels to the bosom of Abraham. Other examples occur as well. The Unforgiving Slave (Matt 18:23-35) — who had been forgiven a huge debt, but would not forgive a fellow servant a small amount — was cast into prison; he thereby becomes an illustration of a person's obligation to forgive others. And the casting out of the man without a garment at the end of the Parable of the Wedding Feast (Matt 22:1-14) refers to the final judgment as a counterpoint to the themes of grace and gathering.

Nevertheless, in spite of the appearance of the theme of final judgment in various other parables, it is the dominant theme in three of them. All three are in the Gospel of Matthew. They can be called Parables of Final Judgment.

6.28. The Weeds in the Wheat and Its Interpretation, Matthew 13:24-30, 36-43; *Thomas* 57

Matthew 13:24-30, 36-43

Another parable [Jesus] put before them, saying, "The kingdom of heaven has become like a man who sowed good seed in his field; 25but while people slept, his enemy came and sowed weeds among the wheat and went away. 26So when the plants came up and bore grain, then the weeds appeared also.

27"And the slaves of the householder came and said to him, 'Sir, did you not sow good seed in your field? From where then did it get weeds?'

28"He said to them, 'An enemy did this.'

"The slaves said to him, 'Then do you want us to go and gather them?'

29 *"But he said, 'No, lest in gathering the weeds you root up the wheat along with them.* 30 *Let both grow together until the harvest; and at harvest time I will tell the reapers, "Gather the weeds first and tie them in bundles to be burned, but gather the wheat into my barn."'"* . . .

36 *Then he left the crowds and went into the house. And his disciples came to him, saying, "Explain to us the parable of the weeds of the field."*

37 *He answered, "The one who sows the good seed is the Son of man;* 38 *the field is the world, and the good seed means the children of the kingdom; the weeds are the children of the evil one,* 39 *and the enemy who sowed them is the devil; the harvest is the close of the age, and the reapers are angels.* 40 *Just as the weeds are gathered and burned with fire, so will it be at the close of the age.* 41 *The Son of man will send his angels, and they will gather out of his kingdom all obstacles to faith and those who commit lawlessness,* 42 *and they will throw them into the furnace of fire; at that place there will be weeping and gnashing of teeth.* 43 *Then the righteous will shine like the sun in the kingdom of their Father. Let whoever has ears listen."*

Notes on the Text and Translation

13:27-28. On the translation of δοῦλοι as "slaves" (as in the NRSV) rather than as "servants" (as in the KJV, RSV, TEV, and NIV), see Appendix 3.

13:36. Some important Greek witnesses have ὁ Ἰησοῦς ("Jesus") as the subject of the sentence (as in the KJV). The most weighty, however, lack it, so that the subject is simply "he," as represented in the 27th edition of the Nestle-Aland Greek text and modern English versions.

Thomas 57

Jesus said, "The kingdom of the father is like a man who had [good] seed. His enemy came by night and sowed weeds among the good seed. The man did not allow them to pull up the weeds; he said to them, 'I am afraid that you will go intending to pull up the weeds and pull up the wheat along with them.' For on the day of the harvest the weeds will be plainly visible, and they will be pulled up and burned."[1]

Exegetical Commentary

The parable and its interpretation appear only in the Gospel of Matthew within the NT — and then at the *Gospel of Thomas* 57. It appears as the second in a collection of seven parables in Matthew 13. At 13:36 it is called "the parable of the weeds in the field," which illustrates that names were given to parables as far back as the first century (cf. also the "parable of the sower" at Matt 13:18).

1. Quoted from *NHLE* 132.

293

Various interpreters have suggested that the parable was composed either by the evangelist Matthew (or perhaps a predecessor or predecessors in the Matthean community) on the basis of the Parable of the Seed Growing Secretly in Mark 4:26-29.[2] If that is so, the parable cannot be attributed to Jesus.

At least four reasons have been advanced for making such a claim. First, the parable appears sequentially parallel to the Seed Growing Secretly (Mark 4:26-29) and could therefore be a substitute for it. Second, there are words in this parable that correspond to those in Mark's: ἄνθρωπος ("man," Mark 4:26// Matt 13:24), καθεύδω ("sleep," Mark 4:27//Matt 13:25), σῖτος ("wheat," "grain," Mark 4:28//Matt 13:25, 29, 30), βλαστάνω ("sprout," "come up," Mark 4:27// Matt 13:26), χόρτος ("stalk," "plants," Mark 4:26//Matt 13:26), καρπός ("grain," Mark 4:29//Matt 13:26), and θερισμός ("harvest," Mark 4:29//Matt 13:30, 39). Third, there are parallels in plot. In both parables a man sows seed, sleeps (implied in Matthew's account; he would sleep at the same time as others) while the plants are growing, and initiates the reaping at harvest time. Finally, there can be no doubt that there is a major Matthean theme expressed in the parable to make it appear as though it could be a Matthean composition. That is the theme of the church as a mixed body *(corpus mixtum),* made up of good and bad, a situation that will be resolved only at the final judgment. That theme is expressed also in the Parables of the Dragnet (13:47-50), the Wedding Feast (22:1-14), and the Final Judgment (25:31-46), all of which appear only in the Gospel of Matthew.

On the other hand, the differences between this parable and the Seed Growing Secretly are substantial. In spite of the similarities of terminology, pointing to a common agricultural motif, the stories are certainly different. As C. H. Dodd has put it, "the Matthean parable stands on its own feet."[3] It is possible that its similarity to Mark's parable led Matthew to place it where it is.[4] Several major interpreters therefore consider it to have been transmitted as an independent parable.[5] The most likely explanation of the similarities and dif-

2. A. Jülicher, *Gleichnisreden,* 2:562-63; Benjamin W. Bacon, *Studies in Matthew* (New York: Henry Holt, 1930), 85, 97, 216-17; T. W. Manson, *The Teaching of Jesus: Studies of Its Form and Content* (Cambridge: Cambridge University Press, 1935), 222-23; idem, *Sayings,* 192; Charles W. F. Smith, "The Mixed State of the Church in Matthew's Gospel," *JBL* 82 (1963): 150-51; Hans-Josef Klauck, *Allegorie und Allegorese in synoptischen Gleichnistexten,* NTAbh 13 (Münster: Aschendorff, 1978), 227; R. Gundry, *Matthew,* 276 (a conflation of this plus the Sower); U. Luz, *Matthäus,* 2:322-23; F. Zeilinger, "Redaktion in Mt 13,24-30," 105; D. Senior, *Matthew,* 153. B. Scott, *Hear Then the Parable,* 68-70, attributes the parable to the early Christian community, and maintains that the Matthew and *Thomas* versions are independent of one another.

3. C. H. Dodd, *Parables,* 147.

4. A. McNeile, *Matthew,* 196.

5. A. McNeile, *Matthew,* 196; E. Schweizer, *Matthew,* 302; H. Weder, *Gleichnisse,* 123-24; R. Stein, *Parables,* 143; J. Gnilka, *Matthäus,* 1:490; D. Hagner, *Matthew,* 382; W. D. Davies and D. C. Allison, *Matthew,* 2:407 (n. 1), 409.

ferences is that Matthew edited an existing parable, making use of Mark's location and elements from his parable.[6] The question whether it can be attributed to Jesus will be taken up below.

The version in the *Gospel of Thomas* is most likely an abbreviation of — and therefore dependent upon — Matthew's, as various scholars have concluded,[7] although some hold to its independence.[8] The reasons for claiming dependence and abbreviation are that it presupposes details in Matthew's version that are necessary for it to make sense as a story; otherwise it is too enigmatic. These include, above all, the attempted intervention of the slaves (simply "them," who appear out of nowhere in *Gos. Thom.* 57), plus the lack of other elements of the story that are presupposed: sowing the seed, its initial stages of growth, and the explicit command to allow both to grow together until the harvest. The gnostic tendency of the *Thomas* version can be seen in the elimination of the explicit command for coexistence between the wheat and the weeds, which would call for the intolerable coexistence of the Gnostic, on the one hand, and the person of the material world (or even the ordinary Christian!) on the other.

13:24. The phrase "another parable he set before them" or "said to them" is typically Matthean (cf. 13:31, 33; 21:33). The verb ὡμοιώθη (aorist passive of ὁμοιόω) appears also at 18:23 and 22:2, introducing the Parables of the Unforgiving Slave and the Wedding Feast. It is found only in Matthean introductions. Although it is common to translate the clause as "the kingdom of heaven may be compared" (RSV, NRSV), it is more properly translated as "the kingdom of heaven has become like," followed by the parable proper.[9] The kingdom is thus not "like a man," but rather it has already dawned in the ministry of Jesus and

6. F. W. Beare, *Matthew*, 303; J. Lambrecht, *Treasure*, 165.

7. Hugh Montefiore, "A Comparison of the Parables of the Gospel according to Thomas and of the Synoptic Gospels," in *Thomas and the Evangelists*, by H. E. W. Turner and H. Montefiore, SBT 35 (Naperville: Alec R. Allenson, 1962) 51-52; Robert M. Grant and David N. Freedman, *The Secret Sayings of Jesus* (Garden City, N.Y.: Doubleday, 1960), 165; Bertil Gärtner, *The Theology of the Gospel according to Thomas* (New York: Harper & Brothers, 1961), 45-46; Wolfgang Schrage, *Das Verhältnis des Thomas-Evangelium zur synoptischen Tradition und zu den koptischen Evangelienübersetzungen: Zugleich ein Beitrag zur gnostischen Synoptikerdeutung*, BZNW 29 (Berlin: Alfred Töpelmann, 1964), 124; Jacques-É. Ménard, *L'Évangile selon Thomas*, NHS 5 (Leiden: E. J. Brill, 1975), 159; Michael Fieger, *Das Thomasevangelium: Einleitung Kommentar Systematik*, NTAbh 22 (Münster: Aschendorff, 1991), 169-72. J. Crossan, "Seed Parables," 261, regards dependence a possibility.

8. Stephen J. Patterson, *The Gospel of Thomas and Jesus* (Sonoma, Calif.: Polebridge Press, 1992), 45; Charles W. Hedrick, *Parables as Poetic Fictions: The Creative Voice of Jesus* (Peabody, Mass.: Hendrickson Publishers, 1994), 249-51.

9. D. A. Carson, "The ὅμοιος Word-Group as Introduction to Some Matthean Parables," *NTS* 31 (1985): 278; J. Lambrecht, *Treasure*, 165-66; W. D. Davies and D. C. Allison, *Matthew*, 2:411.

has become like the following case,[10] in which weeds and wheat, metaphorically understood, grow together in the same field.

That which is sown is "good seed." Later we learn it is wheat (13:25, 29, 30).

13:25. An enemy plants weeds (mentioned also in 13:26, 26, 29, 30). The Greek term translated "weeds" is ζιζάνια, sometimes translated "tares" (KJV) or "darnel" (NEB).[11] It is the *lolium temulentum,* a troublesome plant for the farmer. It is similar in appearance to wheat and can be identified easily only when it is ripe. Then if it is harvested with the wheat, and the two are milled together, the flour will be spoiled.[12]

13:26-28. The good and bad are allowed to grow until the harvest. There is a dialogue between the slaves and the householder. The slaves ask questions concerning (1) what the owner of the field did, (2) where the weeds might have come from, and (3) what to do. No one knows who can be blamed for sowing the weeds, except that it was an enemy.

The slaves address the master as κύριε ("sir" or "lord"), which may go beyond polite address to christological significance in preparation for the equivalence of the householder and the Son of man in the interpretation (13:37).[13] On the other hand, that form of address is the only possible one for the slaves to use.

13:29. The master forbids the slaves to pull up the weeds growing among the wheat. One can only imagine the damage that the slaves would do to wheat plants by going into the field. But actually more is at stake. The roots of the weeds are intertwined with those of the wheat, which presupposes that some time has already passed since the planting of the wheat. Furthermore, the weeds look very much like the wheat plants, so a person cannot always distinguish between them.

13:30. There is a surprising twist. Although one might expect, as the story unfolds, that the slaves will have a further role to play, that is not to be. The householder tells his slaves that, instead of them, he will send "reapers" into the field to do the harvesting. It is the reapers who will resolve the problem by separating the weeds and the wheat. Moreover, their work of separating will take place at the harvest, not before. The slaves are heard from no more, and they have nothing more to do. The burning of the bundles of weeds may refer to their use as fuel.[14]

---

10. On the use of the introductory formula using words of likeness, cf. J. Jeremias, *Parables,* 101.

11. BAGD 339 translates the word as "darnel, cheat." J. Jeremias, *Parables,* 224: "a weed which, botanically, is closely related to bearded wheat, and in the early stages of growth is hard to distinguish from it."

12. Irene Jacob and Walter Jacob, "Flora," *ABD* 2:816.

13. W. D. Davies and D. C. Allison, *Matthew,* 2:413.

14. J. Jeremias, *Parables,* 225. R. Gundry, *Matthew,* 265, considers the imagery of col-

The imagery of a harvest is a biblical symbol for the final judgment (Isa 27:12; Hos 6:11; Joel 3:13; 2 Esdr 4:28-32; 9:17, 31-35; Mark 4:29; Matt 3:12// Luke 3:17; Rev 14:15), and burning by fire a symbol for divine punishment (Jer 29:22; 2 Esdr 7:36; *1 Enoch* 108:3; Matt 3:10//Luke 3:9; Matt 13:50; 18:8-9; 25:41; Luke 9:54; John 15:6; Heb 10:27; Jude 7, 23; Rev 19:20; 20:9; 21:8).

[13:31-35. The interpretation is separated from the parable by three units: the Parable of the Mustard Seed (13:31-32), the Parable of the Leaven (13:33), and the Reason for Parables (13:34-35).]

13:36. The scene shifts to the privacy of a house for Jesus and his disciples. Jesus explains the "parable of the weeds of the field," as it is called here, to his disciples alone. The verb διασαφέω ("explain") is used only here and at 18:31 in the NT.

13:37-39. What follows is an allegorical exposition, beginning with a word list. The reader is provided with an item-by-item key to the interpretation of the parable. Significant elements of the parable become symbols for Christ and the Christian faith. Seven equivalencies are set up:

1. The sower = the Son of man (Jesus).
2. The field = the world.
3. The good seed = the children of the kingdom.
4. The weeds = the children of the evil one.
5. The enemy = the devil.
6. The harvest = the end of the age (or this world).
7. The reapers = the angels.

13:37. Jesus is here the Son of man in his earthly ministry. At the end of the pericope (13:41) he is the apocalyptic Son of man. Both uses of the christological title appear in Matthew's Gospel, including Matthean redaction (cf. Matt 16:13, 28 against Mark 8:29; 9:1).

13:38. The field is the κόσμος ("the world"). The imagery is that of a world in which the children of the kingdom and the children of evil reside together. The Son of man is responsible for the existence of the former, and the devil of the latter. Within the parable, however, it is said that the kingdom "has become like" the following story in which the Son of man has (already) planted the good seed, and the sowing of the bad seed is an intrusion into it. Thus the parable allows for a sequence of the two sowings, but the interpretation does not.

---

lecting and binding the weeds into bundles to be burned to be unreal to Palestinian custom; the practice was to burn the tares and remaining stalks of wheat in the open field. He cites a dictionary article ("Agriculture," in *Dictionary of Life in Bible Times,* ed. Willy Corswant [New York: Oxford University Press, 1960], 24) as evidence. But the article says that cattle ate the tares, and the straw was "usually" burned in the field. Certainly there need not have been only one custom. Why ruin a good story?

13:40-43. Having provided the allegorical lexicon, an application is made, and that is the fate of the good and the bad at the final judgment. There is no reference to the gathering of the wheat as in the parable itself (13:30). The only gathering to be done is the collecting of the weeds (which is reflected in the name of the parable, "the *weeds* in the field") by the Son of man. He comes to condemn, not to save. The righteous are the residue of the harvest, not its yield.

13:40. The weeds are thrown into the furnace of fire, a symbol of final punishment (see comment on 13:30). The expression "the close of the age" is Matthean, used four other times (13:39, 49; 24:3; 28:20) and only once in the NT outside this book (Heb 9:26). This verse provides the central thrust of the interpretation of the parable (according to the passage called the interpretation).

13:41. The reigning Son of man sends the angels to do the harvesting, the collecting of "all obstacles to faith and those who commit lawlessness." (At 24:31 the Son of man sends the angels also, but to gather the elect.) The word σκάνδαλα (translated here as "obstacles to faith") refers to anything that is either an obstacle to coming to faith or a cause of going astray in it,[15] and the evangelist uses it four other times (16:23; three times at 18:7). Here it is personified along with those who commit lawlessness.[16] The latter are persons who reject the will of God (7:21). "Among the evangelists Matthew alone speaks of human ἀνομία"[17] ("lawlessness," 7:23; 23:28; 24:12).

13:42. The words "they will throw them into the furnace of fire" are virtually identical to those in LXX Daniel 3:6, and they appear again at 13:50. The expression "weeping and gnashing of teeth," found only once outside this Gospel in the NT (Luke 13:28), is used six times by Matthew and can be regarded as a typically Matthean refrain (8:12; 13:50; 22:13; 24:51; 25:30).

13:43. The fortune of the righteous is to shine like the sun in the Father's kingdom. The imagery signifies blessedness (Judg 5:31; 2 Sam 23:3-4) and sharing in divine glory (Dan 12:3; Sir 50:7; *1 Enoch* 39:7; 104:2; Matt 17:2; Rev 1:16; 10:1).[18] The term "righteous" (δίκαιος) is used frequently in this Gospel to designate those who will be saved (10:41; 13:49; 25:37, 46).

The interpretation (13:36-43) does not follow immediately upon the parable (13:24-30). Between them are three units: the Parable of the Mustard Seed (13:31-32), the Parable of the Leaven (13:33), and the Reason for Parables (13:34-35). Why the material has been arranged in this fashion remains a puzzle, and its solution may be bound up with the solution to the larger puzzle of

---

15. Gustav Stählin, "σκάνδαλον," *TDNT* 7:345.

16. The term is also personified in the Symmachus recension of Zeph 1:3, based on the MT.

17. Meinrad Limbeck, "ἀνομία," *EDNT* 1:106.

18. The imagery is also in rabbinic literature, as illustrated by Str-B 1:673-74.

the editing of chapter 13 as a whole, for which there are various theories.[19] In any case, it is clear that there are major differences in meaning between the parable and the interpretation, and each must therefore be considered separately.

Among various interpreters it is widely agreed that the parable alone (without the interpretation) emphasizes patience.[20] The master tells his slaves that they must await the harvest for the separation of the wheat and the weeds. For now the wheat and the weeds will coexist. There can be little doubt but that, on the Matthean level, the wheat represents believers or at least true believers (Christians). But it is not so clear what the weeds represent. John Chrysostom asserted that they are Christian heretics. Jesus, he said, does not forbid silencing them, but when he says that one should not uproot the weeds, he forbids killing them.[21] A second possibility is that the weeds represent unbelieving Israel, and the message of the parable is that "the Church is not now to pronounce judgement on unbelieving Israel by evoking a formal withdrawal from it."[22] A third is that the weeds represent persons *within* the church, and these would be persons who willfully disregard the standard of righteousness expected within the church.[23] It is the last that is the most likely within the Matthean text, for in the interpretation (which builds upon the parable) the weeds are associated with those who commit lawlessness (13:41). But to these should be added still another group of persons, and they are those who cause others to fall away or go astray, those who are included in the designation "all obstacles to faith" (an impersonal designation that refers nevertheless to persons), a significant presence and threat to the Matthean community (18:6-7, 12-14).

The parable thus teaches that the church is a *corpus mixtum* while on earth. There will be discipline (18:15-20), even cases where persons must be removed from the community (22:11-14). But an unbridled zeal to create a community that is pure is held in check. Nevertheless, that is not the only or last word of the parable. The judgment will take place in God's good time, and then the ambiguities of life will be overcome.

The question can be raised here concerning the authenticity of the parable, leaving the interpretation (13:36-43) aside for the time being. All who consider Matthew to have composed it from Mark 4:26-29 (and possibly other materials) would answer the question negatively. Others would regard it as not

19. Birger Gerhardsson, "The Seven Parables of Matthew XIII," *NTS* 19 (1972-73): 16-37; David Wenham, "The Structure of Matthew XIII," *NTS* 25 (1978-79): 516-22; U. Luz, *Matthäus*, 2:291-95; W. D. Davies and D. C. Allison, *Matthew*, 2:370-72; D. Hagner, *Matthew*, 361-65.

20. J. Jeremias, *Parables*, 226; J. Kingsbury, *Matthew 13*, 74; E. Schweizer, *Matthew*, 303; H. Hendrickx, *Parables*, 60; R. Stein, *Parables*, 144; J. Lambrecht, *Treasure*, 165.

21. John Chrysostom, *Homilies on Matthew* 46; text in *NPNF* 10:289.

22. J. Kingsbury, *Matthew 13*, 75.

23. E. Schweizer, *Matthew*, 304; H. Weder, *Gleichnisse*, 127; H. Hendrickx, *Parables*, 63; F. W. Beare, *Matthew*, 305; U. Luz, *Matthäus*, 2:325.

from Jesus on other grounds. Adolf Jülicher, for example, considered it an allegory, and therefore concluded *a priori* that it could not have come from Jesus,[24] and others think that it reflects concerns that are post-Easter, not from the ministry of Jesus.[25] Some are willing to attribute it to Jesus virtually as it appears in the Gospel of Matthew, allowing, however, for some Matthean redaction.[26] Others have suggested that at least a nucleus of the present parable can be attributed to Jesus, to which pre-Matthean and Matthean redactional materials have been added. Jack Kingsbury attributes 13:24b-26 to Jesus.[27] Hans Weder suggests 13:24b, 26, 30b.[28] And Eduard Schweizer assigns 13:24b, 26, 28b-29 to the original nucleus.[29]

There are good grounds for maintaining that the parable originated with Jesus, albeit in briefer form than what Matthew provides. It fits plausibly within the ministry of Jesus, although plausibility is not proof. The movement inaugurated by Jesus had not brought about a purified Israel nor even a pure community within it. From various narratives in the Gospels it is clear that Jesus had fellowship with persons both good and bad (tax collectors, sinners, etc.), and that he had a following that was mixed, persons regarded as good and bad alike. Within those circumstances he was challenged, as various passages illustrate (Matt 11:19//Luke 7:34; Mark 2:15; Matt 9:10-11; Luke 15:1-2).

The parable fits into a setting in which a challenge is made, either from Jesus' disciples or a wider circle of followers. That is the question whether the community around Jesus should be pure, or be purified. Other societies, such as the Pharisees and the Qumran community, had dedicated themselves to purity among their members. In a Pharisaic psalm usually dated from the first century B.C. the psalmist prays that the Lord will raise up a messiah who will "drive out the sinners from the inheritance," "smash the arrogance of sinners," "condemn sinners," and "gather a holy people whom he will lead in righteousness" (*Pss. Sol.* 17:23-26).[30] If indeed the kingdom is coming into being, or is imminent, it seems that the ingathering of persons into "a holy people" should be taking place, and sinners should be driven out.

The teaching of the parable is that, no, the followers of Jesus are a mixed group, and they will be that way up to the end. Good and bad look much alike,

---

24. A. Jülicher, *Gleichnisreden,* 2:562-63; cf. also T. W. Manson, *Sayings,* 193.

25. In R. Funk, *Five Gospels,* 194, the parable is printed in gray (= not likely from Jesus) on the grounds that it "reflects the concern of a young Christian community attempting to define itself over against an evil world, a concern not characteristic of Jesus."

26. C. H. Dodd, *Parables,* 148; B. Smith, *Parables,* 198; J. Jeremias, *Parables,* 227 (n. 90); R. Stein, *Parables,* 143; J. Lambrecht, *Treasure,* 165.

27. J. Kingsbury, *Matthew 13,* 65.

28. H. Weder, *Gleichnisse,* 123-24. A similar view is held by D. Catchpole, "John the Baptist," 369: Matt 13:24b, 26b, 30b.

29. E. Schweizer, *Matthew,* 303.

30. Quoted from *OTP* 2:667.

and in fact every person is neither totally one or the other. Each person is a mixture, and each community is a mixture. No disciple or follower of Jesus can presume always to know the difference between the good and the bad in the present. The judgment will come at the end of time, and it will be carried out not by the zealous but by those appointed to the task, like reapers at the harvest. In the meantime God cares providentially for good and bad alike (5:45).

The teaching in the interpretation (13:36-43) is quite different. Gone now is the theme of patient waiting for the final judgment to take place and its corollary that for now the good and the bad coexist. It is given over almost entirely to the final judgment. It functions as an exhortation, an eschatological warning; all evildoers will be cast into the furnace of fire. To a lesser degree it offers the promise of salvation to the righteous, who will finally shine like the sun.

It is widely held by interpreters of diverse perspectives and approaches that the interpretation is Matthew's own composition,[31] and that judgment is inescapable. (Some prefer to attribute it to a pre-Matthean composer, but still not to Jesus.[32]) There are several reasons for that. To begin with, the interpretation cannot be by the same composer as the parable. It knows nothing of the major point of the parable, that is, that there should be no premature judgment and separation.[33] Second, the interpretation, as an allegorical interpretation, reflects the post-Easter church, its theology, and its concerns. For example, it has an implicit Christology that portrays Jesus as both the Son of man on earth (13:37) and as the apocalyptic Son of man in charge of the angels at the last judgment (13:41). That it was composed by the evangelist Matthew is most likely on the grounds that these views of the last judgment and Christology reflect his own and that, in addition, the pericope is infused with Matthean terminology. This has been seen above already, but more can be said. Joachim Jeremias has listed some thirty-seven Greek terms within the interpretation that are characteristic of the Gospel of Matthew.[34]

As soon as the interpretation of 13:36-42 is added, and it is accepted that this material is Matthean, one must consider the parable once again at the level of Matthew's Gospel. Now it becomes clear that the parable has been put to service within the Matthean Gospel and community for a purpose and with a message somewhat different from the original. Now, when the two units are

31. J. Jeremias, *Parables*, 81-85; B. Smith, *Parables*, 200; F. W. Beare, *Matthew*, 303; J. Lambrecht, *Treasure*, 169; R. Gundry, *Matthew*, 274; W. D. Davies and D. C. Allison, *Matthew*, 2:426-27; U. Luz, *Matthäus*, 2:338-39. R. Funk, *Five Gospels*, 196, prints the text with black font (= not from Jesus). Notable exceptions contending for authenticity are M. de Goedt, "L'explication," 32-54; D. Wenham, *Parables*, 65. It could be either from Matthew's special source or be Matthew's own creation in the view of D. Hagner, *Matthew*, 392.

32. H. Weder, *Gleichnisse*, 122-24; H. Hendrickx, *Parables*, 64; J. Gnilka, *Matthäus*, 1:499.

33. J. Jeremias, *Parables*, 81; J. Lambrecht, *Treasure*, 165.

34. J. Jeremias, *Parables*, 82-84.

read together (and one cannot read the interpretation without the parable), hearers and readers are warned, which is the primary thrust, but also given hope. They are warned that evildoers — those who commit lawlessness — will go into the furnace of fire, but the righteous will be in the kingdom of the Father. So everyone is to take heart (13:43b) and observe the law of Moses as interpreted by Jesus.

Exposition

The interpreter must decide whether to focus on the parable alone or on the parable and its interpretation. There will be a considerable difference in the outcome.

Leaving the interpretation of 13:36-43 aside for the moment, and concentrating on the parable alone, the parable is a marvelous text on Christian forbearance and community. The church is made up of all sorts of people; it always has been. Sometimes there are those who, in their zeal for righteousness, want the church to be pure in every respect. In order to achieve that goal, it is necessary for the church to rid itself of those who do not measure up to the standards deemed appropriate. But the parable teaches all such persons the need for patience. Even the most discerning are not always good at making judgments; one does not know the heart. The weeds and the wheat look very much alike. And sometimes an attempt to clean house causes great harm among those who seem good (the wheat). The judgment will take place at the end, supervised by Christ. Let that be sufficient.

But the interpreter can apply the parable in another way, taking the Matthean interpretation of 13:36-43 into account. That is that all within earshot — all who have ears to hear — should heed the warning. All who claim to be among the righteous must live up to what they profess and do the will of God (cf. 7:21-23).

The interpreter will have to make a choice of how much of the text to use in a teaching or preaching situation. The question arises, "But what is the right thing to do?" Clearly the evangelist knew. But does that mean that the interpreter of today cannot focus simply on the parable itself, which has a higher claim to contain the teaching of Jesus? There the accent would be more on patience than warning. Here is a place where the Scriptures leave the interpreter with a dilemma. What kind of response is to be made when a member or members of a congregation do not live up to, and even live counter to, basic Christian norms and what is being professed? Are patience and restraint the answer, or judgment and warning? One is left here in the position of needing the Spirit and the skill of discernment. It should be realized that, in either case, one is dealing with canonical material, and the interpreter should listen with care and deal with the themes with integrity. Both patience and warning are canonical themes.

302

Select Bibliography

Bacq, Philippe, and Odile Ribadeau Dumas. "Reading a Parable: The Good Wheat and the Tares (Mt 13)." *LV* 39 (1984): 181-94.

Carlston, Charles E. "A Positive Criterion of Authenticity?" *BR* 7 (1962): 33-44.

Catchpole, David. "John the Baptist, Jesus and the Parable of the Tares." *SJT* 31 (1978): 557-70.

Crossan, John D. "The Seed Parables of Jesus." *JBL* 92 (1973): 244-66.

Doty, William G. "An Interpretation: Parable of the Weeds and Wheat." *Int* 25 (1971): 185-93.

Goedt, Michel de. "L'explication de la parabole de l'ivraie (Mt. xiii,36-43)." *RB* 66 (1950): 32-54.

Homes-Gore, V. A. "The Parable of the Tares." *Theology* 35 (1937): 117.

Houseman, Hubert G. "The Parable of the Tares." *Theology* 3 (1921): 31-35.

Jeremias, Joachim. "Die Deutung des Gleichnisses vom Unkraut unter dem Weizen (Mt 13,36-43)." In his *Abba*, 261-65. Göttingen: Vandenhoeck & Ruprecht, 1966.

Luz, Ulrich. "Vom Taumellolch im Weizenfeld." In *Vom Christentum zu Jesus: Festschrift für Joachim Gnilka*, 154-71. Ed. H. Frankemölle and Karl Kertelge. Freiburg: Herder, 1989.

McIver, Robert K. "The Parable of the Weeds among the Wheat (Matt 13:24-30, 36-43) and the Relationship between the Kingdom and the Church as Portrayed in the Gospel of Matthew." *JBL* 114 (1995): 643-59.

Smith, Charles W. F. "The Mixed State of the Church in Matthew's Gospel." *JBL* 82 (1963): 149-68.

Strelan, Richard E. "A Ripping Yarn: Matthew 13:24-30." *LTJ* 30 (1996): 22-29.

Wiches, Dean R. "Note on Matthew 13,30 and Matt. 6,30 = Luke 12,28." *JBL* 42 (1923): 251.

Zeilinger, Franz. "Redaktion in Mt 13,24-30." In *Christus Bezeugung: Festschrift für Wolfgang Trilling zum 65. Geburtstag*, 102-9. Ed. Karl Kertelge et al. EThS 59. Leipzig: St. Benno Verlag, 1989.

6.29. The Dragnet and Its Interpretation, Matthew 13:47-50

Matthew 13:47-50

[Jesus said,] 47 *"Again, the kingdom of heaven is like a net that was cast into the sea and gathered [sea creatures] of every kind; 48when it was full, [men] drew it upon the shore, and having sat down, they gathered the good ones into containers but threw away those that were worthless.*

49 *"So it will be at the close of the age. The angels will come out and separate*

the evil from the midst of the righteous, 50and throw them into the furnace of fire; in that place there will be weeping and gnashing of teeth."

Notes on the Text and Translation

13:47. The term "sea creatures" is not in the Greek text. The text simply says that the net "gathered of every kind" or "species," not indicating what part of the animal kingdom is meant. Most translations supply the word "fish," which is not in the text either. See further discussion below.

13:50. Some important Greek witnesses (including ℵ, D, and family 13) have the present tense, βάλλουσιν ("[they] throw") instead of the future tense, βαλοῦσιν ("[they] will throw"). The present tense would rob the verse of its future orientation toward the final judgment. The future is to be preferred for three reasons: (1) it is more widely attested in Greek witnesses, (2) the other two verbs in the sentence are in future tense (represented by "will come out" and "[will] separate," and (3) the difference in pronunciation is so slight that copyists could more easily write the more familiar present tense of the verb.

Exegetical Commentary

The parable appears only within the Gospel of Matthew in the NT. There it is the last in a series of seven within the Parable Discourse (13:3-52). Like the Parable of the Weeds among the Wheat and its Interpretation (13:24-30, 36-43), it directs its hearers and readers to the final judgment, when the righteous and the wicked will be separated. The theme will be picked up again in the Parable of the Final Judgment (25:32).

A similar parable appears within the *Gospel of Thomas* (logion 8), the Parable of the Wise Fisherman. Although the two are similar in some respects in regard to imagery (fisherman, net, sea, fish, and separation), and they are sometimes treated together, they are not actually the same parable.[1] The latter is discussed in the chapter, "Parables in the *Gospel of Thomas*."

The parable proper is contained in 13:47-48. That is followed by an interpretation at 13:49-50. The parable presupposes that the hearer is familiar with scenes of fishing at the Sea of Galilee (e.g., Mark 1:16-20; Luke 5:2-10). Ancient writers commented on the fishing industry along that body of water and on the variety of fish to be found in it.[2]

1. J. Jeremias, *Parables*, 201; N. Perrin, *Teaching*, 90; contra W. G. Morrice, "Parable of the Dragnet and the Gospel of Thomas," 269-73. According to T. Baarda, "'Chose' or 'Collected,'" 373-97, the *Gospel of Thomas* 8 cannot be considered a precanonical version of the same parable in Matt 13:47-50.
2. Strabo, *Geography* 16.2.45; Josephus, *J.W.* 3.508, respectively. For a survey of fishing sites around the Sea of Galilee, cf. Wilhelm H. Wuellner, *The Meaning of "Fishers of Men"* (Philadelphia: Westminster Press, 1967), 26-36.

13:47. The introductory phrase "again, the kingdom of heaven is like" corresponds exactly with the opening of the Parable of the Pearl of Great Price immediately before it (13:45). If the term πάλιν ("again") is dropped, the rest of the phrase is found at 13:31, 33, 44 as well. The comparison being made here is between the kingdom and the story that follows, not the net alone. As the net catches sea creatures of every kind, and they must be sorted, so it is with the kingdom.

The net being cast into the sea is the σαγήνη, which can be translated "dragnet,"[3] a term used only here in the NT. It was a large net used on the Sea of Galilee that could be cast into the sea with the help of a boat swinging around in a semicircle. It was supported by floats and held in place by sinkers. After a time it was drawn to shore with long ropes.[4] This net differs from the more familiar casting net, the ἀμφίβληστρον, which was cast by hand from shore (Mark 1:16//Matt 4:18) or, if the generic δίκτυον ("net") is the same, from a boat (Luke 5:2, 4-6; John 21:6, 8).[5]

That which is caught in the net is ἐκ παντὸς γένους ("of every kind" or "species"). That would include many species of fish, of which there are some two dozen — the exact figures vary[6] — in the Sea of Galilee. But surely other sea creatures would be included as well, including eels and crustaceans.[7] The gathering of the sea creatures by nets is an eschatological symbol. In an eschatological vision Ezekiel beheld the netting of fish (with the σαγήνη-type of net in the LXX) of many kinds, like the fish of the Great Sea (Mediterranean), on the shore of the Dead Sea (Ezek 47:10).

13:48. What is caught in the net is both καλά ("good") and σαπρά ("those that are worthless"). The good would be fish that are considered clean (by Levitical law), edible, and marketable. The worthless would be any creatures that are not clean, edible, and marketable. These include fish (e.g., catfish) and any other creatures of the sea without fins and scales, for they are considered unclean and inedible by law (Lev 11:9-12; Deut 14:9). The basic meaning of the term σαπρός is "decayed, rotten," but "rotten fish" is not the meaning here,

3. BAGD 739.

4. Gustaf Dalman, *Sacred Sites and Ways: Studies in the Topography of the Gospels* (New York: Macmillan, 1935), 135; W. Stewart McCullough, "Net," *IDB* 3:540.

5. For a survey of terms, cf. W. Wuellner, *Meaning of "Fishers of Men,"* 232-38.

6. According to Edwin Firmage, "Zoology," *ABD* 6:1146, there are19 species of fish "native" to the Sea of Galilee. The figures of species actually existing are higher in the work of Gustaf Dalman, *Arbeit und Sitte in Palästina,* 7 vols. (Gütersloh: Verlag C. Bertelsmann et al., 1928-41), 6:351. According to him, at the time of writing his multivolume work there were 24 species in the Sea of Galilee, 11 in the Jordan River, 78 along the coast of the Mediterranean Sea, and 12 in Lake Huleh.

7. Lacking in the expression is the specific reference to *fish,* as in the phrase of Josephus, *J.W.* 3.508, γένη δ' ἰχθύων . . . διάφορα ("and different species of fish").

since the catch would be fresh. On the basis of the first meaning, the term can also refer to anything that is "unfit" or "unusable."[8]

The good fish are placed into ἄγγη ("containers"). The term is used generally to designate containers for oil (cf. Matt 25:4) or other items, including fish.[9] The worthless are thrown away (into a heap of refuse, not into the sea).

13:49. The interpretation begins with wording in Greek and English versions that is exactly the same as in 13:40b (the interpretation of the Weeds in the Wheat): "so it will be at the close of the age."

The picture of the angels coming out (from heaven) clashes with the picture of the fishermen sitting upon the shore and sorting their catch. The portrait is drawn from typical apocalyptic language (4 Macc 4:10; Mark 8:38; Matt 13:41; 24:31; 25:31; Rev 20:1), which has taken over.

Now the distinction is not between the good and the unusable but between the δίκαιοι ("righteous") and the πονηροί ("evil" or "wicked ones"), who are removed from the righteous.

The separating of the evil from the righteous means, as at 13:41, that the evil are taken, and the righteous are left. The accent is not on saving the righteous, which would be proper on the basis of the parable — placing the good fish into the security of containers (13:48) — but upon the destruction of the wicked. The righteous are the residue of the process of judgment and punishment. See the contrast at 24:31, where the Son of man sends his angels to gather the elect.

13:50. The verse reads in Greek and English versions exactly like 13:42. The words "they will throw them into the furnace of fire" are virtually identical to those in LXX Daniel 3:6. The imagery of "weeping and gnashing of teeth" is used six times by Matthew and can be regarded as a typically Matthean refrain that concludes solemn declarations of judgment on the part of Jesus (8:12; 13:42; 22:13; 24:51; 25:30). Otherwise it is found only once in the NT (Luke 13:28). Cf. the phrase "into eternal punishment" at 25:46.

The Parable of the Dragnet is related thematically to the Parable of the Weeds in the Wheat and its Interpretation (Matt 13:24-30, 36-43). There are elements present in the latter, however, that are not present in this parable, including an emphasis upon patient waiting for the final resolution of the mixed state of the good and the bad, dialogue, the origin of evil with the devil, and the promise of gracious rewards to the righteous.[10]

Considering the parable alone (13:47-48) without its appended interpretation (13:49-50), the emphasis is upon the casting of the net and gathering all kinds, sorting, and then preserving the good — and casting out the worthless. At the Matthean level, however, this positive note is blunted immediately by the

8. BAGD 742; Otto Bauernfeind, "σαπρός," TDNT 7:94-97.
9. BAGD 6-7 (with references).
10. For additional differences, cf. J. Kingsbury, *Matthew 13*, 117-18.

306

interpretation. The message is that there is a final judgment to come, and that the fate of evil persons is the fiery furnace, eternal torment.[11] In the meantime, to be sure, both good and evil ones coexist. But not a word is heard that that condition should remain. The point is that the seeming contradiction will be resolved at the final judgment. This will also mean that the parable serves as a warning to those who profess to be disciples of Jesus. Since the judgment is certain, and the evil ones will be taken from the fellowship of the righteous, it is essential for each member of the community to remain faithful and to do the will of God, as interpreted by Jesus.

The question whether any of the material originated with Jesus is debated. Critical opinion is divided on the question whether the parable (13:47-48) can be attributed to Jesus. Some maintain or simply assume that it can.[12] Others regard it as a composition by the evangelist Matthew that is based on a traditional saying of Jesus about gathering followers indiscriminately (cf. Mark 2:17//Matt 9:13) and comparable to gathering fish into a net (cf. Mark 1:17// Matt 4:19).[13] Still others consider it a Matthean composition entirely.[14] The decision is a difficult one. But the fact that there is a difference between the interpretation and the parable itself is significant. The parable by itself goes in the direction of gathering, or inclusion, and salvation — with casting out of the wicked as an allied thought. The interpretation goes in the direction of judgment and casting out of the evil ones — with no word about the salvation of the righteous.

If that is so, the parable in its most primitive form would have been a statement of Jesus concerning the kingdom in which he indicates that he and his disciples must cast their "net" of proclamation (their mission) widely, preaching to all sorts of persons. Fishing metaphors for the ingathering of people are found widely in pre-Christian and non-Christian traditions.[15] It would not be unusual, therefore, for Jesus to speak of his own ministry with such a metaphor, which is confirmed by its use also at Matthew 4:19//Mark 1:17.[16] No

11. Such is the traditional interpretation. Cf. John Chrysostom, *Homilies on Matthew* 47; text in *NPNF* 10:294.

12. A. Jülicher, *Gleichnisreden*, 2:569; C. H. Dodd, *Parables*, 150-52; B. Smith, *Parables*, 201; J. Jeremias, *Parables*, 225-27 (and n. 90); C. W. F. Smith, "Mixed State," 154; J. Derrett, "Jesus' Fishermen," 128-30; H. Weder, *Gleichnisse*, 144; J. Gnilka, *Matthäus*, 1:508-9.

13. E. Schweizer, *Matthew*, 313; B. Scott, *Parable*, 313-16; Ivor H. Jones, *The Matthean Parables: A Literary and Historical Commentary*, NovTSup 80 (Leiden: E. J. Brill, 1995), 357-58; D. Hagner, *Matthew*, 398; U. Luz, *Matthäus*, 2:357-58. T. W. Manson, *Sayings*, 197-98, and W. Morrice, "Parable of the Dragnet," 270, 272, limit the original to 13:47 alone.

14. R. Gundry, *Matthew*, 279; R. Funk, *Five Gospels*, 197.

15. For a survey of metaphors in Greco-Roman, Ancient Near Eastern, biblical, and postbiblical literary traditions, cf. W. Wuellner, *The Meaning of "Fishers of Men*," 64-133.

16. For a survey of metaphors in Christian literature, cf. ibid., 134-231.

one is to be neglected. No judgment is to be made of who is worthy and who is not worthy of the kingdom prior to the proclamation. A judgment will be made in due course, but it must not be made before persons have an opportunity to hear the message. A parable of that kind would certainly have been possible in the ministry of Jesus of Nazareth.

The parable in its present form still bears the marks of the primitive one, but it has been expanded to include Matthean language, such as the antithesis of καλός and σαπρός in 13:48 (cf. 7:18; 12:33). The appended interpretation (13:49-50) bears many marks of being a Matthean composition, as various interpreters have held.[17]

Exposition

As with the Parable of the Weeds in the Wheat and its Interpretation (13:24-30, 37-43), the interpreter must decide where to focus and put the emphasis. If one focuses upon the parable alone, the accent will be upon the indiscriminate character of the mission of the church. No prejudgment is to be made concerning who is worthy to receive the gospel and who is not. The work of evangelization is like casting a net into the sea, which gathers every kind of creature that is available.

If, however, one seeks to be comprehensive, as the evangelist clearly was, the interpretation of the parable has to be included. Now there is a bifocal message. Without loss of the one just mentioned, the matter of final judgment is inescapable. Members of the church are given notice that they are finally accountable before God, and that there will be a reckoning at the final judgment to come. The gathering of all kinds of people into the church is fit and proper, as illustrated also in the Parable of the Wedding Feast, in which both good and bad are gathered in (Matt 22:10). But by means of catechesis and assimilation into the community, a transformation is expected of any persons who do not know the will of God, as taught by Jesus. In the end a judgment will take place, and those who have not allowed a transformation to happen will be cast out (cf. 22:11-14). That is information about the end, to be sure, but it is a warning to all; everyone should learn and observe what Jesus has commanded (28:20).

17. T. W. Manson, *Sayings*, 198; J. Jeremias, *Parables*, 85; C. W. F. Smith, "Mixed State," 154-55; F. W. Beare, *Matthew*, 315; R. Gundry, *Matthew*, 280; H. Weder, *Gleichnisse*, 143; J. Gnilka, *Matthäus*, 1:508-10; W. D. Davies and D. C. Allison, *Matthew*, 2:442; D. Hagner, *Matthew*, 398; U. Luz, *Matthäus*, 2:357. R. Stein, *Parables*, 142, considers it either a Matthean composition or an expansion on the words of Jesus. R. Bultmann, *HST* 173, however, considers it to have been original along with the parable.

Select Bibliography

Archbald, P. "Interpretation of the Parable of the Dragnet (Matthew 13:47-50)." *VR* 48 (1987): 3-14.

Baarda, Tjitze. "'Chose' or 'Collected': Concerning an Aramaism in Logion 8 of the Gospel of Thomas and the Question of Independence." *HTR* 84 (1991): 373-97.

Derrett, J. Duncan M. "'ΗΣΑΝ ΓΑΡ' ΑΛΙΕΙΣ (Mk. I 16): Jesus' Fishermen and the Parable of the Net." *NovT* 22 (1980): 108-37.

Jacobson, Delmar. "An Exposition of Matthew 13:44-52." *Int* 29 (1975): 277-82.

Morrice, William G. "The Parable of the Dragnet." *ExpTim* 85 (1984): 281-82.

———. "The Parable of the Dragnet and the Gospel of Thomas." *ExpTim* 95 (1984): 269-73.

Quispel, Gilles. "Jewish-Christian Gospel Tradition." In *Gospel Studies in Honor of Sherman Elbridge Johnson*, 112-16. ATRSS 3. Evanston: Anglican Theological Review, 1974.

6.30. The Final Judgment, Matthew 25:31-46

[Jesus said,] 31 *"And when the Son of man comes in his glory, and all the angels with him, then he will sit upon his glorious throne.* 32*And all the nations will be gathered before him, and he will separate them from one another as a shepherd separates the sheep from the goats,* 33*and he will place the sheep at his right, and the goats at his left.*

34*"Then the King will say to those at his right, 'Come, O blessed of my Father, inherit the kingdom prepared for you from the foundation of the world;* 35*for I was hungry and you gave me [food] to eat; I was thirsty and you gave me [something] to drink; I was a stranger and you took me into your home,* 36*naked and you clothed me, sick and you took care of me; I was in prison and you came to me.'*

37*"Then the righteous will answer him, saying, 'Lord, when did we see you hungry and feed you, or thirsty and give you drink?* 38*And when did we see you a stranger and take you in, or naked and clothe you?* 39*And when did we see you sick or in prison and come to you?'*

40*"And the King will answer them, 'Truly, I say to you, insofar as you did it to one of the least of these, my brothers and sisters, you did it to me.'*

41*"Then he will say to those at his left, 'Depart from me, you cursed, into the eternal fire which is prepared for the devil and his angels;* 42*for I was hungry and you did not give me [food] to eat; I was thirsty and you did not give me [something] to drink;* 43*I was a stranger and you did not take me in, naked and you did not clothe me, sick and in prison and you did not take care of me.'*

44*"Then they also will answer, saying, 'Lord, when did we see you hungry or thirsty or a stranger or naked or sick or in prison, and we did not minister to you?'*

45 "Then he will answer them, saying, 'Truly, I say to you, insofar as you did it not to one of the least of these, you did it not to me.'
46 "And these will go away into eternal punishment, but the righteous into eternal life."

Notes on the Text and Translation

25:40. According to BAGD 289 (ἐπί, III, 3), the expression ἐφ' ὅσον here and at 25:45 is to be translated as "to the degree that" or "insofar as." The expression is found only at these places and Rom 11:13 in the NT. The KJV has "inasmuch." The simple "as" of the RSV and "just as" of the NRSV are exceedingly weak. The phrase introduces a causal clause.[1] The phrase "insofar as" linked with an aorist verb conveys the causal expression as a completed action in the past (cf. JB, "in so far as").

Some ancient witnesses omit τῶν ἀδελφῶν μου ("my brothers and sisters"). These include Codex B, Clement of Alexandria (d. ca. 215), and other witnesses. The omission may be due to harmonization with 25:45 (or an eye skip by a scribe), where the words are lacking. The term in the plural can be translated (as in the NRSV) inclusively, "brothers and sisters."

The NEB reads: "for one of my brothers *here*" (emphasis added) at 25:40, but not at 25:45. The addition of "here" implies the presence of the brothers/sisters on the scene, but that is not necessarily to be implied (see comment below).

25:41. Instead of "which is prepared for," some manuscripts read "which my Father prepared." Such a reading provides a contrast to 25:34, where the Father is mentioned in connection with the righteous ones who inherit the kingdom prepared for them. But the former is more firmly attested.

Exegetical Commentary

The unit is not truly a parable. It is actually an apocalyptic discourse with a parabolic element in 25:32b-33 — the simile of a shepherd separating the sheep from the goats. Yet it is often called (even if miscalled) "The Parable of the Sheep and the Goats" or "The Parable of the Last Judgment," and exegesis of it is commonly included in studies of the parables of Jesus.[2]

The passage appears only here within the Gospels. It is located within the

---

1. Archibald T. Robertson, *A Grammar of the Greek New Testament in the Light of Historical Research*, 5th ed. (New York: Harper & Brothers, 1931), 963.

2. J. Jeremias, *Parables*, 206-10; R. Stein, *Parables*, 131-40; P. Perkins, *Parables*, 158-65; J. Donahue, *Parable*, 109-25; Jan Lambrecht, *Astonished*, 196-235; idem, *Treasure*, 249-84. Discussion of it is not included in the works of A. Jülicher, B. T. D. Smith, C. H. Dodd, E. Linnemann, and B. Scott.

context of Matthew 24–25, the so-called Eschatological or Apocalyptic Discourse, bringing that section to a close. The discourse of these two chapters is the last of the five discourses of Jesus in the Gospel of Matthew (chapters 5–7, 10, 13, 18, 24–25). It is addressed to Jesus' disciples alone.

The Apocalyptic Discourse contains a number of smaller units: the Prediction of the Destruction of Jerusalem (24:1-2), Sayings on Signs before the End (24:3-8), Persecution (24:9-14), the Desolating Sacrilege (24:15-22), Warnings against False Prophets (24:23-28), the Coming of the Son of man (24:29-31), the saying about the Fig Tree (24:32-36), the saying about the Flood and the Exhortation to Watchfulness (24:36-44), the Parable of the Faithful and Wise Servant (24:45-51), the Parable of the Ten Maidens (25:1-13), and the Parable of the Talents (25:14-30).

25:31. The unit opens with a scene of the last judgment. The Son of man is seated on his glorious throne (literally, in Greek, "upon his throne of glory"), and "all the angels" are present. Whether the company of angels includes the angels of the devil (25:41) is not said; presumably "the devil and his angels" are not present. Therefore "all the angels" should have been more properly written as "all *his* [= the Son of man's] angels," as at 16:27 and 24:31. As it is, the phrase is identical to LXX Zechariah 14:5, which speaks of the coming of the Lord "and all the angels with him."

The scene recalls other apocalyptic texts in which the Son of man is seated upon a throne.[3] Since he is seated upon a throne, he is portrayed as a regal figure, which permits the use of the title "king" for him in 25:34.

25:32-33. Although "all the nations" are present for the judgment to take place, the judgment has to do not with entire nations but with individual persons on the scene; the "them" (αὐτούς in Greek) individualizes.[4] So the NRSV does well to render the passage, "he will separate people one from another," rather than "he will separate *peoples* one from another."

It is only after speaking of the judgment that the analogy of a shepherd separating his sheep from his goats comes into play. In that respect, the analogy is rather incidental to the passage as a whole. In any case, familiar scenes of the Middle East, ancient and modern, are brought forth. Sheep and goats are often herded together. But they must be separated when goats are milked and sheep are sheared. Placing the sheep on the right is a sign of their being in a place of honor. Therefore, as the image is continued, it functions to signify that the righteous will be at a place of honor at the final judgment. On the other hand, being placed on the left signifies condemnation in this context.[5]

---

3. *1 Enoch* 61:8; 62:2-3, 5; 69:29; cf. Dan 7:13-14; Matt 19:28; Rev 1:13; 20:11.

4. Cf. the same at 28:19. Although πάντα τὰ ἔθνη is a neuter plural, the baptizing and teaching is directed to individual persons, αὐτούς ("them," masculine plural).

5. The metaphor is common to various cultures. Plato, *Republic* 10.614c-d, relates the dream of a warrior who envisioned a judgment scene. After the judges passed judg-

The meaning of the phrase πάντα τὰ ἔθνη (usually: "all the nations") — the designation of those gathered before the Son of man — is disputed.[6] The full Greek phrase is found also at Matt 24:9, 14; 28:19.[7] There has been a good deal of discussion as to whether the term ἔθνη means "nations" (including the Jewish people) or "Gentiles" (excluding the Jewish people from consideration here). Both are possible translations of the Greek term. Modern translations (RSV, NRSV, NEB, NIV, JB) render the phrase "all the nations" (rather than "Gentiles"). The term "nations" (including the Jewish people) is favored by several scholars,[8] but "Gentiles" or "gentile nations" by others.[9]

The Greek expression πάντα τὰ ἔθνη is found in secular Greek sources referring to nations (ethno-political groups) within a region (e.g., within Greece as a whole) or of the known world.[10] It frequently refers to "all the nations" (of

---

ment, the souls of the righteous passed through portals into heaven on the right, and the unjust to the left. Various rabbinic texts (*Midr. Num.* 22:9; *Midr. Cant.* 1:9:1; and *b. Shab.* 88b) are cited by J. M. Court, "Right and Left," 224-26.

6. The following possibilities among interpreters are listed by S. Gray, *The Least of My Brothers*, 255-57: (1) all of humanity, (2) Christians (only), (3) all non-Christians and non-Jews, (4) all non-Christians, and (5) all non-Jews (= Gentiles). The first and fifth have been argued most powerfully, and they alone are discussed here.

7. The simple singular or plural term ἔθνος or ἔθνη ("nation" or "nations") appears at 4:15; 6:32; 10:5, 18; 12:18, 21; 20:19, 25.

8. Karl L. Schmidt, "ἔθνος," *TDNT* 2:369-70; A. T. Cadoux, "The Parable of the Sheep and the Goats," 561; Wolfgang Trilling, *Das wahre Israel: Studien zu einer Theologie des Matthäusevangeliums*, 3d ed., SANT (Munich: Kösel Verlag, 1964), 26-28; Günther Bornkamm, "End-Expectation and Church in Matthew," in *Tradition and Interpretation in Matthew*, by Günther Bornkamm, Gerhard Barth, and Heinz J. Held (Philadelphia: Westminster Press, 1963), 23; Ulrich Wilckens; "Gottes geringste Brüder," 382; John P. Meier, "Nations or Gentiles in Matthew 28:19?" *CBQ* 39 (1977): 99-101; P. Christian, *Jesus und seine geringsten Brüder*, 36, 39, 56; E. Schweizer, *Matthew*, 478; F. Beare, *Matthew*, 493; J. Donahue, "The 'Parable' of the Sheep and the Goats," 14-16; J. Lambrecht, *Treasure*, 275-76 (but in his earlier work, *Astonished*, 222-23, only Gentiles is meant); D. Catchpole, "The Poor of the Earth and the Son of Man in Heaven," 387; D. Hagner, *Matthew*, 742-43; U. Luz, "The Final Judgment," 294; C. E. B. Cranfield, "Who Are Christ's Brothers?" 31-39.

9. T. W. Manson, *Sayings*, 250; J. Jeremias, *Parables*, 209; Douglas R. A. Hare and Daniel J. Harrington, "'Make Disciples of All the Gentiles' (Mt 28:19)," *CBQ* 37 (1975): 363; J. Lambrecht, *Astonished*, 222-23, 227; but in his *Treasure*, 275-76 (written later), the term means "all nations"; J. Friedrich, *Gott im Brüder?* 252-56; J. M. Court, "Right and Left," 229; Graham Stanton, *A Gospel for a New People: Studies in Matthew* (Louisville: Westminster/John Knox Press, 1993), 212-14; and Nikolaus Walter, "ἔθνος," *EDNT* 1:383.

10. Various instances with the full phrase in Greek fragments are listed in *TLG* (citing texts from *Inscriptiones Graecae* 2/2.1134.a-b.62; *Fouilles de Dephes: Epigraphie* 3.2.69.44; *Tituli Asiae Minoris* 5.1180.6; *Orientalis Graeci Inscriptiones Selectae* 199.61.377.1; 199.62.377.1; 199.63.377.3; and *Corpus Inscriptionum Graecarum* 9061.6). Herodotus, *Hist.* 9.106, uses the term to refer to "the Greek nations." Appian, *Bell. Civ.* 2.106, uses the phrase ἐν ἔθνεσιν ἅπασι to refer to "all the provinces" of Rome; cf. 2.13.

the world, as known) in the Septuagint,[11] the writings of Josephus,[12] and early Christian literature.[13] But it can also refer to "all the Gentiles" in the Septuagint[14] and in the NT, such as the writings of Paul.[15]

Most important is the use of the term in the Gospel of Matthew itself. There are instances in Matthew where the term ἔθνη (lacking πάντα, "all") refers clearly to "Gentiles" (4:15; 6:32; 10:5, 18; 12:18, 21; 20:19).[16] On the other hand, at 21:43 and at 24:7 (twice in the latter verse) the use of the (singular) noun ἔθνος means a "nation" or a "people." Besides the verse under consideration here (25:32), the full phrase πάντα τὰ ἔθνη (or oblique cases) appears three more times in Matthew (24:9, 14; 28:19), and the most natural meaning in each is "all the nations."[17] Likewise, the phrase in 25:32 should be read to mean "all the nations," including the Jewish people. For Matthew, the judgment is universal (24:30-31), and the picture painted here is one of broad sweep: all of humanity stands before the Son of man awaiting judgment. To translate the passage as "all the Gentiles will be gathered before [the Son of man]" leaves the question, Where are the people of Israel?

The usual (but erroneous) reason for interpreting the passage to mean "all the Gentiles" (not the "nations") is that, in Matthew's perspective, the Jews have already been judged, condemned, and rejected,[18] based in part on a particular interpretation of 21:43 ("Therefore I tell you, the kingdom of God will be taken away from you and given to a people that produces the fruits of the kingdom").[19] Yet that verse does not speak of the rejection of Israel or the Jewish people. It speaks rather of the taking away of the kingdom from its presumed custodians, those to whom Jesus was speaking — the chief priests and elders

11. Scores of occurrences. Cf. Gen 18:18; 22:18; 26:4; Exod 23:27; Deut 29:23; Josh 4:24; Pss 47:1; 49:1; 113:4; 117:1; Jdt 3:8; Isa 66:18; Amos 9:12; Dan 3:7; 7:14; Joel 3:2, 11-12; 1 Macc 2:19. In some cases, however, Israel is not included within the expression "all the nations"; the latter are those that surround Israel (e.g., Joel 3:2, 11-12), that is, the "gentile nations."

12. Josephus, Ant. 11.215.

13. Matt 24:9, 14; 28:19; Mark 11:17 (quoting Isa 56:7); 13:10; Luke 12:30; 21:24; 24:47; Acts 14:16; Rev 12:5; 14:8; 15:4; 18:3, 23; 1 Clem. 59.4; and 2 Clem. 13.2.

14. For example, Tob 14:6 (2x); 1 Macc 1:42; 5:38, 43; 3 Macc 7:4.

15. Rom 15:11 (quoting Ps 117:1 to support the gentile mission); 16:26; Gal 3:8; and probably (deutero-Pauline) 2 Tim 4:17.

16. Possibly 12:18, 21; and 20:25 have that meaning too.

17. Cf. John P. Meier, "Nations or Gentiles in Matthew 28:19?" CBQ 39 (1977): 94-102.

18. That view is examined and rejected by Amy-Jill Levine, The Social and Ethnic Dimensions of Matthean Salvation History, SBEC 14 (Lewiston: Edwin Mellen Press, 1988), 233-39.

19. Cf., for example, J. Lambrecht, Astonished, 222-23. But in idem, Treasure, 275-76, Lambrecht has departed from that view; the term in question includes all the nations, not simply the Gentiles.

(21:23, 45).[20] The church, as Matthew knew it, was made up of Jews and Gentiles together.

25:34. The king calls those on the right εὐλογημένοι ("blessed ones"), a perfect passive participle. The expression differs from the adjective μακάριοι ("blessed") in the Beatitudes (5:3-11; cf. also 11:6; 13:16; 16:17; 24:46). There appears to be no major difference in meaning, but it corresponds in form with the perfect passive participle in 25:41, κατηραμένοι ("cursed"), its opposite in meaning. The blessed ones are invited to "inherit the kingdom," an expression found also in the letters of Paul (1 Cor 6:10; 15:50; Gal 5:21; cf. Eph 5:5) and James (2:5). In each case it is used in reference to the final judgment; those who have a positive outcome are heirs of the kingdom, that is, enter into eternal life (cf. 19:29; 25:46; Mark 10:17). "From the foundation of the world" — a common expression in ancient Jewish and Christian literature — is equivalent to "from the creation of the world"; that the kingdom "has been prepared" for the righteous since then indicates divine decision before time began.[21] Was the decision about persons, as in election (predestination), or about the establishing of the kingdom for those who will go there? Syntax suggests the latter, as well as the fact that human responsibility is assumed in the verses that follow.

25:35-36. The things accredited to those on the right are actions performed to alleviate typical problems of the unfortunate — hunger, thirst, being an alien, lacking clothes, illness, and imprisonment. The actions spoken of are not mandated by law, religious or secular, nor do they ensue from a person's conforming to typical virtues, such as the classical virtues (wisdom, courage, temperance, and justice).[22] They arise rather out of love and compassion. They correspond most closely to what are called in rabbinic tradition the *gemiluth hasadim,* the "deeds of lovingkindness,"[23] which the good person does to the unfortunates encountered. Moreover, the deeds listed are certainly not unknown in the OT and/or postbiblical Jewish tradition, as indicated in comment on each. In addition to the specific deeds mentioned, various OT texts and passages within Jewish literature commend the more general virtue of giving to the needy (Deut 15:7-11; Isa 58:7-10; Pss 37:21; 41:1; Tob 4:16; Sir 7:32; 2 Esdr 2:20; *T. Iss.* 3:8; *T. Zeb.* 7:4; *Vision of Ezra* 7, 31; *Lev. Rab.* 34:9-11; *Ruth Rab.* 5:9; and *b. Sukk.* 49b) and speak against oppressing them (Zech 7:9-10).

The list of six actions done to alleviate conditions of need is not exhaustive; that would have had to include actions to care for persons who are victims of assault, of robbery, of grief from a loved one's death, and so on. The actions listed must be considered representative, even "symbolic stageprops . . . used to

20. Cf. D. Hagner, *Matthew,* 623.
21. Otfried Hofius, "καταβολή," *EDNT* 2:255-56.
22. Cf. Plato, *Republic* 4.427e; *Laws* 1.631c-d; 12.965d.
23. *M. Abot* 1:2; *b. Sukk.* 49b; *b. Sot.* 14a. Cf. *b. Shab.* 127a.

convey the primary meaning of the parable."[24] Moreover, the list has been cast into symmetrical parallelism, with two items in each of three groupings: (1) giving food and drink to the hungry and thirsty, (2) providing shelter for the stranger and clothing for the naked, and (3) visiting the sick and the imprisoned.[25]

Feeding the hungry is the most basic act of kindness. It is one of the most often listed of such acts, and often at the head of the list in Scripture and Jewish tradition (Isa 58:7; Job 22:7; Prov 25:21; Ezek 18:7, 16; Tob 1:17; 4:16; *T. Iss.* 7:5; *T. Jos.* 1:5; and *Sifre* 118). Here giving food to the hungry is said to be giving it to Jesus. The thought is similar to that in rabbinic literature where God says to Israel, "My sons, whenever you give food to the poor, I impute it to you as though you gave me food."[26]

Giving a drink to the thirsty is the second most basic act of kindness and can be listed, as here, as the companion to feeding the hungry (Job 22:7; Prov 25:21) or with other acts of kindness (*T. Jac.* 2:23).

The third act of kindness has some ambiguity about it. The term ξένος can mean either "stranger" (as in the NRSV) or "alien," and the meaning of the verb συνηγάγετε is hardly exhausted by "you welcomed me" (NRSV). In the Septuagint and other sources the verb means to receive a person into one's own home.[27] The modern distinction between an alien (a noncitizen) and a stranger would not have been so clear-cut. The stranger would be from another locality, virtually an alien, certainly "foreign" in the estimation of the person giving the welcome,[28] and perhaps having a different manner and accent. To express the sense of the clause, one could translate it as: "I was a complete stranger to you, and you took me into your home." The act of bringing the homeless poor into one's home is commended in Job 31:32, Isaiah 58:7, and in various Jewish texts (*T. Jac.* 2:23; *Vision of Ezra* 31; *b. Sabb.* 127a). A saying on the importance of hospitality is attributed to Rab (= Rabbi Abba Arika, third century A.D.): "Hospitality to wayfarers is greater than welcoming the presence of the *Shekinah*."[29]

Clothing the naked is commended in various OT and Jewish texts as well (Isa 58:7; Ezek 18:7, 16; Tob 1:17; 4:16; 2 Esdr 2:20; *T. Zeb.* 7:1; *T. Jac.* 2:23; *Vision of Ezra* 7; *b. Sot.* 14a).

24. Cf. S. Gray, *The Least of My Brothers*, 353; D. Hagner, *Matthew*, 744.
25. R. Gundry, *Matthew*, 513.
26. Quoted from G. F. Moore, *Judaism*, 2:169. The source from which Moore quotes is *Midrasch Tannaim zum Deuteronomium* (Berlin, 1908-9), 83 (on Deut 15:9), which is not available to me.
27. Cf. BAGD 782 (συνάγω, 5). Deut 22:2; Judg 19:18; and 2 Kgdms 11:27 are included from the LXX.
28. Cf. Johannes Friedrich, "ξένος," *EDNT* 2:486.
29. *B. Shab.* 127a; quoted from *BabT* 2/2:632. The term "shekinah" means the divine presence.

Visiting the sick is the fifth act of kindness listed. The clause "I was sick" translates the verb ἠσθένησα. The present tense of the verb (ἀσθενέω) can mean simply "to be weak," but in its aorist form (as here), it means "to be sick."[30] Forms of the term ἐπεσκέψασθε ("you visited me," aorist form of ἐπισκέ-πτομαι) appear eleven times in the NT. Two of the eleven occurrences are in this pericope (25:36, 43). Here and in other sources the verb means to visit the sick.[31]

Visiting (or caring for) the sick is listed as a religious duty in various texts, both Jewish and Christian.[32] Among pre-Christian Jewish sources is Sirach 7:35 (2d century B.C.): "Do not hesitate to visit the sick (ἐπισκέπτεσθαι ἄρρωστον ἄνθρωπον), because for such deeds you will be loved." In the *Letter of Polycarp* (2d century A.D.) the presbyters of the church are called upon to visit (care for) the sick (ἐπισκεπτόμενοι πάντας ἀσθενεῖς),[33] and various other early Christian texts use the same verb to commend the visitation of the sick as well.[34] Many rabbinic texts can be cited.[35] Among them are sayings attributed to various rabbinic teachers concerning visiting the sick: a saying of (first century A.D.) Johanan ben Zakkai lists visiting the sick among six religious duties;[36] first/second century Rabbi Hama commended visiting the sick as a way of imitating the Shekinah;[37] the second-century Rabbi Akiba said that the person who does not visit the sick is like one who sheds blood;[38] and Rab (= Rabbi Abba Arika, second/third century) said that the one who visits the sick will be delivered from the punishments of Gehenna.[39]

Visiting the imprisoned is the last of the six activities mentioned. Such an act was not only possible, but often necessary for the very survival of prisoners. Prisons in the Greco-Roman world were for detention, not for long-term incarceration as a means of punishment,[40] and prisoners were often dependent upon relatives and friends to supply them with food, water, and other necessi-

30. BAGD 115 (ἀσθενέω, 1a).

31. Sir 7:35; Josephus, *Ant.* 9.112, 178; and Pol. *Phil.* 6:1. Closely related is Jas 1:27: "religion that is pure and undefiled . . . is this: to visit (ἐπισκέπτεσθαι) orphans and widows in their affliction. . . ." For additional references, cf. LSJ 656.

32. For Jewish texts, cf. Sir 7:35; 2 Esdr 2:21; *T. Jos.* 1:6; *T. Jac.* 2:23; *b. Shab.* 127a; *b. Sota* 14a; *b. Ned.* 39b, 40a.

33. Pol. *Phil.* 6:1.

34. Athanasius, *Epistula encyclica* 5; *Herm. Man.* 8.10; *Ps. Clem. H.* 3.67; *Const. App.* 3.19.7. These and other texts are cited in *PGL* 531.

35. Str-B 4/1:573-78 provides 17 excerpts together with many other quotations and references.

36. *B. Shab.* 127a.

37. *B. Sot.* 14a.

38. *B. Ned.* 40a.

39. Ibid.

40. Adolf Berger and Andrew Lintott, "Prison," *OCD* 1248; Karel van der Toorn, "Prison," *ABD* 5:468-69.

ties.[41] Visiting a person in prison as a benevolent act is mentioned in Jewish sources,[42] as well as in other Christian texts.[43] Within the Babylonian Talmud there is a story in which Rabbi Akiba is in prison, and he is attended by a friend who has to supply his basic need of water.[44] Many texts in the NT presuppose that those in prison can be, and were, visited and cared for by friends (Matt 11:2; Phil 3:25; 4:18, 21; 2 Tim 1:16-17; 4:11, 21; Heb 13:3), which is amply illustrated also in classical sources.[45]

25:37-40. A dialogue ensues. These people know nothing about all this (doing good works for the king). The king has to explain it: that by doing good for others, they were doing good to him. The king represents Christ metaphorically.

Who would qualify as "one of the least of these my brothers and sisters" (25:40)? Within current scholarship there are three major proposals, and each has a direct bearing on the interpretation of the pericope. The three are: (1) any persons in need, the unfortunates of the world; (2) the disciples of Jesus; or (3) early Christian missionaries. These options will be discussed below; at this point the focus is on terminology.

The term ἐλάχιστος ("least") — actually the superlative of ἐλαχύς ("small," "little") — functions as the superlative form for μικρός ("small," "little"), meaning "smallest" or "least." In the NT it is used 14 times; in reference to persons five times (Matt 5:19; 25:40, 45; 1 Cor 15:9; Eph 3:8). To the three instances in Matthew must be added two similar terms: (1) the fourfold use of μικρός (10:42; 18:6, 10, 14), used each time in the plural within the rather formalized phrase ἕνα τῶν μικρῶν τούτων ("one of these little ones"), referring to vulnerable disciples of Jesus; and (2) the use of the comparative μικρότερος ("smaller," "lesser") at 11:11 ("the one who is of lesser significance in the kingdom of heaven is greater" than John the Baptist), referring to the disciple of Jesus.[46]

The term ἀδελφός ("brother"; plural at 25:40, 45, "brothers and sisters") is used frequently in the Gospel of Matthew (as elsewhere in the NT) to mean "brother" in a spiritual sense, that is, those devoted to one another on the basis of their devotion to Jesus (5:22-24; 7:3-5; 12:49-50; 18:15, 21, 35; 23:8; 28:10). The Twelve (minus Judas) are specified as the "brothers" of Jesus at 28:10.

41. Detailed information on prison life and conditions is provided in the chapter on "Prisons in the Ancient Roman World," in Craig S. Wansink, *Chained in Christ: The Experience and Rhetoric of Paul's Imprisonments*, JSNTSup 130 (Sheffield: Sheffield Academic Press, 1996), 27-95.

42. *T. Jos.* 1:6; *b. Erub.* 21b.

43. Heb 10:34; 13:3; Ignatius, *Smyrn.* 6.2.

44. *B. Erub.* 21b.

45. Perhaps best known: Plato, *Apology* 37c; *Crito* 43a.

46. E. Schweizer, *Matthew*, 261: "If John is 'more' than all the prophets, it is because he stands on the threshold of this new age; therefore, even the least of those who stand beyond the threshold is greater than he."

25:41-43. The king speaks to those on the left. Again, what they have not done is to attend to typical problems of the unfortunate. They are condemned to eternal fire.

25:44-45. A dialogue takes place with these persons. It is parallel to that with the people on the right. But there is a major distinction between 25:34, "the kingdom prepared for you from the foundation of the world," and 25:41, "the eternal fire prepared for the devil and his angels." The latter has not been prepared for humanity! It is an unnatural place.

25:46. The separation will take place, and it is final.

The interpretation of the passage in recent years goes primarily in three directions, as indicated above. For purposes of analysis, we shall state them briefly, leaving aside various nuances (as well as still other interpretations).[47] According to the various views, the pericope portrays the last judgment, but the basis on which the judgment is to be made differs:

1. The judgment will be based on how people have dealt with the unfortunates of the world — those who are hungry, ill-clothed, imprisoned, etc.[48] Here the term "least" has special significance; it applies particularly to the unfortunates of the world, who are also Jesus' brothers (and sisters). Usually, in this interpretation, all who are being judged include both Christians and non-Christians alike. This interpretation prevails in various studies of NT ethics.[49]

2. The judgment will be based on how the people of the world have

---

47. These are dealt with by S. Gray, *The Least of My Brothers*.

48. Among those who hold this position are A. McNeile, *Matthew*, 368-71; A. Cadoux, "The Parable of the Sheep and the Goats," 559-62; J. Jeremias, *Parables*, 206-10; idem, *New Testament Theology: The Proclamation of Jesus* (New York: Charles Scribner's Sons, 1971), 113; Floyd V. Filson, *A Commentary on the Gospel according to St. Matthew*, 2d ed., BNTC (London: Adam & Charles Black, 1971), 266-68; J. A. T. Robinson, "The 'Parable' of the Sheep and the Goats," 236-37; Werner G. Kümmel, *Promise and Fulfilment: The Eschatological Message of Jesus*, SBT 23 (Naperville: Alec R. Allenson, 1957), 94-95; R. Bultmann, "Sermon (Matthew 25,31-46)," 47-51; G. Bornkamm, "End-Expectation and Church in Matthew," 23-24; E. Schweizer, *Matthew*, 478-80; U. Wilckens, "Gottes geringste Brüder," 363-83; P. Perkins, *Parables*, 163-64; F. Beare, *Matthew*, 495-96; D. Catchpole, "The Poor of the Earth and the Son of Man in Heaven," 389-95; J. Meier, *Matthew*, 304; J. Lambrecht, *Treasure*, 273-82; F. Watson, "Liberating the Reader," 57-84; D. Hare, *Matthew*, 288-91; C. E. B. Cranfield, "Who Are Christ's Brothers?" 31-39; R. France, "On Being Ready," 191-93; and others. S. Gray, *The Least of My Brothers*, 257-62, lists 305 scholars (for whom "all nations" means "all mankind") in this category, and on p. 267 another ten (for whom "all nations" means "all non-Christians and non-Jews").

49. Wolfgang Schrage, *The Ethics of the New Testament* (Philadelphia: Fortress Press, 1988), 44, 82-83, 145; Eduard Lohse, *Theological Ethics of the New Testament* (Minneapolis: Fortress Press, 1991), 46-47, 54, 124-25; and Richard B. Hays, *The Moral Vision of the New Testament: Community, Cross, New Creation: A Contemporary Introduction to New Testament Ethics* (San Francisco: Harper Collins, 1996), 106-7, 464. Cf. also Victor P. Furnish, *The Love Command in the New Testament* (Nashville: Abingdon Press, 1972), 79-84.

treated Jesus' disciples, that is, Christians.[50] Here the term "brothers" has special significance; it applies particularly (as elsewhere in Matthew) to the disciples of Jesus. Because of persecution, they suffer the various misfortunes listed. In this interpretation those being judged are necessarily the non-Christians of the world; how they have treated Christians is decisive. A variation on this is that, while the original version of the parable (from Jesus) had to do with the treatment of the needy, the evangelist Matthew revised it so that it has to do with the treatment of Jesus' disciples.[51]

3. The judgment will be based on how the people of the world have responded to a particular subgroup of Jesus' disciples, namely, his missionaries.[52] Here the term "brothers" has special significance too, but the six types of misfortunes listed (four times over: 25:35, 37-39, 42-43, 44) are brought in for emphasis as misfortunes typically experienced by traveling missionaries. In this interpretation those being judged are, again, usually regarded as the non-Christians of the world.

The third of these is in many ways compelling. The six types of misfortunes can be found, for example, as types of suffering experienced by Paul in his travels as an apostle: being hungry and thirsty (1 Cor 4:11; 2 Cor 6:5; 11:27), naked (2 Cor 11:27; cf. 1 Cor 4:11), homeless (1 Cor 4:11; 3 John 5-6), ill (or weak, 1 Cor 4:10), and imprisoned (Acts 16:23; 2 Cor 6:5; 11:23; Phlm 1, 9). Moreover, in the Gospel of Matthew itself it is known that the missionaries of

---

50. Included here are G. E. Ladd, "The Parable of the Sheep and the Goats in Recent Interpretation," 197-99; S. Gray, *The Least of My Brothers*, 358; R. Gundry, *Matthew*, 511-16; William L. Kynes, *A Christology of Solidarity: Jesus as the Representative of His People in Matthew* (Lanham, Md.: University Press of America, 1991), 145-59 (esp. p. 151); G. Stanton, *Gospel for a New People*, 214-21; D. Hagner, *Matthew*, 744-46; J. Donahue, "The 'Parable' of the Sheep and the Goats," 25-28; and idem, *Parable*, 120. Donahue says that the phrase in question refers "primarily to Christian disciples or missionaries, which for Matthew are virtually the same" (p. 120). S. Gray (pp. 262-63) lists 86 names (for whom "all nations" = "all mankind") in this category and (p. 267) 15 more (for whom "all nations" means "all non-Christians and non-Jews").

51. M. E. Boring, *NIB (Matthew)*, 8:456. For J. Lambrecht, *Astonished*, 219-27, the parable originated with Jesus and dealt with the needy, but Matthew revised it so that it has to do with receiving the missionaries of Jesus.

52. T. W. Manson, *Sayings*, 251 (disciples of Jesus in their apostolic work); J. R. Michaels, "Apostolic Hardships and Righteous Gentiles," 27-37 (specifically, "preachers and teachers of the Word," 30); L. Cope, "Matthew xxv:31-46," 32-44; J. Mánek, "Mit wem identifiziert sich Jesus?" 15-25; R. Stein, *Parables*, 130-40; J. Lambrecht, *Astonished*, 226-27 (but in his *Treasure*, 275-82, he rejects this view in favor of the first view listed; see above); Ulrich Luz, *The Theology of the Gospel of Matthew* (Cambridge: Cambridge University Press, 1995), 129-31; idem, "The Final Judgment," 302-3; idem, *Matthäus*, 3:535-42; D. Senior, *Matthew*, 283-84. S. Gray, *The Least of My Brothers*, 263-64, lists 13 scholars in this category (for whom "all nations" = "all humankind"), and on p. 267 another seven (for whom "all nations" means "all non-Christians and non-Jews").

Jesus are to travel without provisions, always depending for food and drink on those who receive them (10:8-10, 42). Some will experience persecution (and presumably imprisonment, 10:17; 23:34); they will be hated because of the name of Jesus (10:22). How the various people treat the missionaries decides their fate. Whoever receives a missionary receives Jesus (10:40); whoever rejects the missionary will be held accountable in the final judgment (10:14-15).

The second of the proposed interpretations is essentially a modified, reduced version of the third. Interpreters in this case tend to look upon the persons in need simply as disciples of Jesus, that is, Christians, who would be involved in mission. But to make a distinction between Christian disciples in general and Christian missionaries is unnecessary and unfounded.[53]

While these proposals are extremely attractive — based as they are on linguistic and comparative study — there are good reasons to maintain that the first interpretation cited is the most satisfactory for the following reasons:

(1) The passage is located at the conclusion of the lengthy eschatological discourse of 24:1–25:46 and follows upon material that is thoroughly hortatory in function (24:32–25:30). The discourse contains warnings directed at the disciples regarding the final judgment and their responsibilities prior to the coming of the Son of man and the judgment that he will exercise. The discourse contains parables, just prior to this passage, that make demands on the disciples. They are to be faithful (24:45-51), wise (25:1-13), and resourceful (25:14-30).

The question must be asked how the discourse concerning the final judgment in 25:31-46 would have functioned rhetorically within its context and for its ancient audience, the Matthean community. In order to take the view that, for this passage, the peoples of the world will be judged on how they respond to Jesus' missionary disciples, one must at the same time adopt the view that the text functioned to encourage the members of the Matthean church in the truth of their mission (or that of their missionaries). The missionaries will be vindicated, regardless of the hardships they suffer in the present. But such an overall view does not fit the literary context of the pericope nor the rhetorical strength of Matthew 24:1–25:46. Better it is to view the passage as another in a series on the responsibility of the disciples prior to the judgment. They are to be faithful (24:45-51), wise (25:1-13), resourceful (25:14-30) — and merciful to the needy whom they encounter (25:31-46). In this case, the pericope would have functioned rhetorically to provide a warning: the members of the Matthean community, as well as everyone else in the world, will be judged on the basis of their care (or failure to care) for the unfortunates whom they encounter. In other words, one has to ask: Does the passage provide consolation or warning to the disciples of Jesus? Certainly the passage has the marks of being paraenetic. The final judgment is to be taken with utmost seriousness. It is the righteous (οἱ

53. J. Donahue, *Parable*, 120, may be regarded as representative: The "least" are "Christian disciples or missionaries, which for Matthew are virtually the same."

320

δίκαιοι) who — on the basis of their actions — will be declared "blessed" and enter into eternal life (25:37, 46). The others will be condemned to eternal torment (25:41, 46). The passage affects the members of its audience rhetorically to move them to care for the unfortunates.[54]

(2) There is nothing within the passage itself that requires the narrower meaning (that the six categories refer to Jesus' disciples). One comes to that only by way of making connections between terms that appear in the passage ("least of these" and "brothers and sisters") and similar ones that occur elsewhere in the Gospel of Matthew. While cross-referencing is essential in the study of terms, it should be subservient to the study of the overall structure and content of the text at hand. "No one, reading Matt. 25.31-46 in isolation, would suppose that its subject is the treatment of Christian evangelists."[55]

(3) The phrase "one of the least of these, my brothers and sisters" (25:40) and its briefer form (25:45) have an antecedent. They refer back to any and all of the six examples of the unfortunates listed in 25:35-36. To link the phrase up with designations for the disciples in earlier portions of the Gospel is a difficult stretch. The last time that Jesus has called any of his disciples "my brothers" (οἱ ἀδελφοί μου) was in an enigmatic statement about his disciples (and it is not clear whether that means the Twelve or his followers in general) thirteen chapters earlier (12:49). The next instance is in the postresurrection scene (28:10).

(4) To make the link on linguistic grounds, that is, the use of ἐλάχιστος ("least"), is extremely difficult. When related terminology is used regarding the disciples, they are called by terms that sound to the ear and appear to the eye as quite different. They are called the μικροί ("little ones," 10:42; 18:6, 10, 14) or (in the singular) the μικρότερος ("the lesser one," 11:11). Why would Matthew use the relatively rare superlative here?[56] The word μικροί would have worked perfectly well in the phrase (so: ἑνὶ τούτων τῶν ἀδελφῶν μου τῶν μικρῶν, "to one of these little ones, my brothers and sisters"). The only other time that ἐλάχιστος is used for a disciple is at 5:19, and there the term has a very negative meaning. One must entertain the strong possibility that, by use of the superlative in this pericope, Matthew actually intended to *distinguish* the unfortunates from the disciples of Jesus; it is not simply the latter who are to be recipients of acts of mercy.[57]

54. Cf. D. Catchpole, "The Poor of the Earth and the Son of Man in Heaven," 396: "the discourse voices demand rather than consolation," and R. Bultmann, "Sermon (Matthew 25,31-46)," 51: "And there is no doubt that the ultimate purpose of our text is [Jesus'] admonition."

55. F. Watson, "Liberating the Reader," 65.

56. Cf. Eduard Schweizer, "Matthew's Church," in *The Interpretation of Matthew*, ed. Graham Stanton, IRT 3 (Philadelphia: Fortress Press, 1983), 138: "Matthew is unlikely to have chosen a different phrase if he had meant the same as he means when elsewhere he uses the phrase 'these little ones' so emphatically."

57. J. Lambrecht, *Treasure*, 278.

(5) The contexts for Matthew's use of the terms μικροί and μικρότερος are decidedly ecclesiastical. The context for his use of ἐλάχιστος in this passage is not. The scene here has a "sweeping universalism" that the others do not.[58]

(6) The term ἐλάχιστος is sometimes used in contrasts, as at Matt 5:19 ("least"/"great") and elsewhere.[59] It is also used to designate the "least" within a collective in order to emphasize the overwhelming power and grace of God operative in history or in a person's life,[60] a concept that is rooted in various OT passages as well.[61] While "the least" could refer to a disciple (one in whom God is at work), its more fitting referent is any and all of those listed as persons in need, those who make up the collective of unfortunates. In this way of thinking, it is precisely because they are *not* his disciples in any obvious way that Jesus can call them "the least" of his "brothers." They are "the least" purely because of God's special favor for them, which Jesus here declares. It is certainly much simpler — looking for the plainest meaning of the text — to consider "the least" as referring to persons who are actually and continuously despised and neglected in the course of common life, and then declared to be Jesus' brothers by grace alone, than to think of them as disciples of Jesus, who may or may not be despised at any time or place.

(7) The persons on the right and left are astonished to hear that they have, or have not, served the king who speaks to them (25:37-39, 44). If the persons on the right had served the representatives of the king — feeding them, clothing them, welcoming them (regardless of their being strangers), and visiting them while sick or in prison — and if the representatives had been missionary disciples of Jesus, why would those on the right find that out only at the last judgment? If we are to adopt the view that "the least" are disciples, it follows that the last judgment passage portrays a scene in which the Son of man rewards those who knowingly served him in the world, that is, those who had received and served disciples who came in his name. But that is precisely what we do not have. Those on the right are completely surprised; they *did not know* the one whom they served. They do not ask simply, "When *were* you hungry?" but "When did *we see* you hungry?"[62] They served those in need close at hand. The same applies to those on the left. They *did not know* that the persons they neglected to serve came to them in the name of Jesus. And if the unfortunates never identified themselves, how are they to be distinguished from any other unfortunates of the world?

58. J. Meier, *Matthew,* 304.

59. LXX Isa 60:22; Wis 6:6; *SIG* 888, 58.

60. So Bethlehem is the "least" among the rulers (Matt 2:6; contrast Matthew's ἐλάχιστος with ὀλιγοστός at LXX Mic 5:1). Paul calls himself the "least of the apostles" (1 Cor 15:9). Cf. the deutero-Pauline "least of all the saints" (Eph 3:8).

61. Magne Saebo, "צָעִיר," *TWAT* 6:1086-87. The term ἐλάχιστος appears 13 times in the LXX. In five of seven cases where it translates Hebrew, the Hebrew adjective is צָעִיר. The remaining six cases are in LXX books that lack a Hebrew base.

62. D. Catchpole, "The Poor of the Earth and the Son of Man in Heaven," 381.

(8) Neglecting to serve those in need is the only offense mentioned of those on the left. If they had rejected the missionary disciples of Jesus, it would seem that their offenses would have been more overt than simple neglect. The six misfortunes do not begin to coincide with the activities of the persecutors known in this Gospel, namely, the slandering, killing, and flogging of the disciples (5:11; 23:34). The offense is more likely simple neglect of the unfortunates by those who have the means to relieve their suffering.

(9) In keeping with Matt 10:14-15, it would be fitting that the last judgment be based on how persons respond to the *message* of the missionary disciples of Jesus. That it should be based on how persons respond to their *condition* has no other basis in this Gospel (or any other early Christian literature).

(10) If "the least" are Christians, and if the peoples of the world are to be judged on the basis of their receiving them, one of the six items listed seems out of place. That is visiting the imprisoned. Visiting the imprisoned is not a matter of "receiving" people or responding to their apparent needs. It is an overt act that involves seeking a person out. Furthermore, if a person were placed in prison on the basis of missionary work, and if it were known why that person was imprisoned, it is difficult to imagine any non-Christian risking a visit.[63] In this particular instance, visiting a person in prison appears rather to be simply an act of kindness and support, regardless of the reason why that person had been placed there.

(11) According to the perspective of the Gospel of Matthew, "righteousness" is characterized in part by mercy. That is spelled out in texts characteristic of this Gospel (5:7; 18:33; 23:23; cf. 12:7). It is therefore to be expected in the present context that the one who will be accounted righteous in the final judgment is the one who has shown mercy to persons in need.

(12) The conditions of those called "the least" are typical, though not exhaustive, of those suffered by human beings the world over and in every age. It is not unusual for ancient writers to list a number of them in what can be called form-critically a "catalog of misfortunes." Such lists are found, for example, in the OT (e.g., Isa 58:6-7: the oppressed, the hungry, the homeless, and the naked; Zech 7:9-10: "the widow, the orphan, the alien, or the poor"). They are found in both Greco-Roman literature[64] and Jewish pseudepigraphical works.[65] There is nothing about the list in our pericope, given four times over (25:35-36, 37-39, 42-43, 44), that characterizes the suffering of missionary disciples alone. Such an interpretation is certainly narrower than required by the text.

---

63. G. Stanton, *Gospel for a New People*, 220, grants the difficulty but does not consider it decisive.

64. Epictetus, *Dis.* 3.3.17-18 (grief, exile, and poverty); 3.10.9 (sickness, thirst, and hunger); 3.24.29 (sickness, being assaulted, hunger, and exile); and 4.6.23 (hunger, thirst, and cold).

65. *T. Jac.* 2:23 (thirst, exile, sickness, and nakedness); *T. Jos.* 1:5-7 (hunger, exile, sickness, and imprisonment).

Just as the misfortunes are typical of those that the unfortunates of the world experience, so there are texts that contain lists of typical acts of kindness toward them — and which commend these acts — in various literatures of the world. In the eighth-century-B.C. Akkadian "Counsels of Wisdom" a sage teaches that one should give food, drink, and clothing to those in need.[66] Other literatures include the Egyptian *Book of the Dead* (125: A person being judged says, "I have given bread to the hungry, water to the thirsty, clothes to the naked and a boat to him who was boatless"), the Mandaean *Ginza* (2.36.13-17: "If you see one who hungers, feed him, someone who thirsts, give him to drink; if you see one naked, place a garment on him and clothe him. If you see a prisoner, who is believing and upright, obtain a ransom and free him"), and more.[67] Lists of acts of kindness abound in the OT and Jewish literature, most notably Isaiah 58:6-7, which commends freeing the oppressed, giving bread to the hungry, providing hospitality to the homeless poor, and covering the naked. Other OT and deuterocanonical texts contain similar lists (Job 22:7; 31:16-19, 32; Prov 25:21; Ezek 18:5-9, 16; 2 Esdr 2:20-23; Tob 4:16), as does other ancient Jewish literature.[68] One of the most notable is in the *Testament of Jacob*, where the person is declared blessed who does acts of mercy: giving drink (to the thirsty), taking in strangers, visiting the sick, and clothing the naked (2:23). Another is the list of the needs of the unfortunate given in the *Testament of Joseph* (1:5-7) and spoken of by Joseph in a manner similar to that of Jesus in Matt 25:35-36: "I was taken into captivity . . . overtaken by hunger . . . was alone . . . was in weakness . . . was in prison"; in each case God alone was his helper.[69] Encompassed before, after, and around by so many texts of its kind, the list of the unfortunates of Matthew 25:31-46 (provided four times over) must be considered a typical — and therefore not exhaustive but suggestive — listing of those whom "the righteous" are expected to care for, the needy that they encounter.

It has been said that the interpretation favored here — often thought to be "traditional," and sometimes called "universalistic" — is actually not very old, and that it became important only in the nineteenth century.[70] That in itself would not be cause for rejecting it. But it should be pointed out that it has been expressed from early times, for example, in the writings of Cyprian, Commo-

66. For text, cf. *ANET* 426.

67. Quoted from *The Ancient Egyptian Book of the Dead*, rev. ed., trans. Raymond O. Faulkner (New York: Macmillan, 1985), 32, and *Ginza, der Schatz, oder das grosse Buch der Mandäer*, trans. Mark Lidzbarski (Göttingen: Vandenhoeck & Ruprecht, 1925), 36 (English trans. mine), respectively. Other works are referred to by R. Bultmann, *HST* 124.

68. Several texts considered relevant by D. Catchpole, "The Poor of the Earth and the Son of Man in Heaven," 390-91, are: Tob 1:16-17; *T. Ben.* 4:4; *2 Enoch* 9:1; *Der. Er. Rab.* 2:21; *Midr. Tehillim* 118:9; and *Midr. Tann.* 15:9. The most exhaustive collection of rabbinic parallels is in Str-B 4/1:559-610.

69. Quoted from *OTP* 1:819.

70. U. Luz, "The Final Judgment," 279-80; idem, *Matthäus*, 3:525.

dianus, and John Chrysostom, in the *Rule* of St. Benedict, and occasionally in the works of Jerome.[71] When writers such as Augustine and (usually) Jerome take "the least" to refer to Christians,[72] that does not mean that they have made a conscious decision to restrict the meaning of the term; it only means that their extant texts serve catechetical and homiletical purposes, instructing Christians to care for one another, including the unfortunates, in a world that, for all practical purposes in their times and places, was totally Christian.

Whether this parabolic discourse can be considered to have been uttered by Jesus is, like much else about it, contested. If the passage has to do with providing welcome, hospitality, and aid to the disciples of Jesus (i.e., Christian missionaries), the likelihood of its authenticity is severely diminished.[73] While some scholars contend, on the grounds of (1) vocabulary and syntax and (2) the interests of the passage, that it must be a Matthean composition,[74] both of these have been taken into account by others who consider the evangelist to have taken it primarily from pre-Matthean tradition and edited it thoroughly.[75] The latter view is the more persuasive. That usually means, too, that the one who is the king and carries out the judgment would have been God (the Father) in the original version.

There can be no doubt that the Parable of the Final Judgment portrays a scene in which Jesus is Son of man, Shepherd, King, and Judge of humanity. It is thoroughly Christianized. Yet that does not mean that the account is a Christian composition from the outset. As indicated above, there is nothing particularly Christian about the six works of kindness that those on the right have done; they belong to the world of moral reflection and behavior in various cultures, including those prior to the ministry of Jesus. There is merit in the suggestion that originally the parable would have come from Jesus, but the King who carries out the judgment was understood to be God (not Jesus).[76] The only

71. Cf. S. Gray, *The Least of My Brothers,* 27-28, 29, 50-53, 65-69, 104, 333. Gray's comments on Cyprian point in two directions, but it appears that most texts speak of care for all persons, Christian and non-Christian alike.

72. Cf. ibid., 65-72.

73. Cf. W. Kümmel, *Promise and Fulfilment,* 94-95.

74. L. Cope, "Matthew xxv:31-46," 42-44; R. Gundry, *Matthew,* 511; J. Lambrecht, *Treasure,* 274-75; and others.

75. J. Jeremias, *Parables,* 206-10; J. A. T. Robinson, "The 'Parable' of the Sheep and the Goats," 225-37; I. Broer, "Das Gericht des Menschensohnes über die Völker," 288; U. Wilckens, "Gottes geringste Brüder," 372-82; J. Friedrich, *Gott im Brüder?* 283-97; S. Brown, "Faith, the Poor and the Gentiles," 171-81; and U. Luz, "The Final Judgment," 288-92. U. Luz, *Matthäus,* 3:521, suggests that the parable originated with unknown Jewish-Christian disciples of Jesus (rather than from Jesus himself).

76. Among others, cf. J. Lambrecht, *Astonished,* 219 (but in his *Treasure,* 274-75, he considers the parable a Matthean composition); A. Cadoux, "The Parable of the Sheep and the Goats," 560. S. Brown, "Faith, the Poor and the Gentiles," 171-81, considers it authentic as well.

other time "king" is used metaphorically by Jesus in the Gospels it refers to God (Matt 5:35), and in the Parable of the Wedding Feast the king can be considered a symbol for God as well (22:2-14). Theologically the discourse on the Final Judgment coheres with the Parable of the Rich Man and Lazarus in the Gospel of Luke (16:19-31); in both cases the criterion at the final judgment is whether or not a person has cared for the one in need. Luke did not create that parable, nor did Matthew create the discourse on the Final Judgment. It is probable that both have origins in the preaching ministry of Jesus.

Exposition

Christ the King and Son of man is portrayed as sharing in the glory of God at the final judgment. He even executes judgment on behalf of God.

But as the account unfolds, it becomes clear that at one time that glorified Christ was in and among the unfortunates of the earth. He appeared in a form totally opposite of what he was to become.

Matthew 25:31-46 had a major impact on the ministry of Mother Teresa (1910-97). At one time she said that her work is done for, with, and to Jesus: "We serve him in the neighbor, see him in the poor, nurse him in the sick; we comfort him in his afflicted brothers and sisters."[77] And at her own funeral she was eulogized for having exemplified 25:31-46 in ministering to the needs of the unfortunates.[78] For her and others, Christ is seen in the disfigured faces of the despised.

The passage, therefore, has a motivating dimension. Among Christians of all times, it has provided inspiration for doing works of mercy. The way to serve Christ is through serving the neighbor. He is the one who lived among us as hungry, thirsty, and without a home. He knows about these problems of human suffering. He identifies with the poor and the homeless, the suffering. The proper response of God's people is to work for the betterment of the poor, the sick, the homeless, the suffering. Doing good for them is one form of service to Christ.

But there is something even more profound about the passage. If Christ is seen clearly in the disfigured faces of the unfortunates, one may indeed be moved to serve him. But, in fact, according to this passage, Christ is actually hidden in those faces; his face is obscured by the faces of the unfortunates. People therefore do not know that it is Christ whom they serve — or fail to serve. Gone is the view here that the only way one can serve Christ (or God) is a prior commitment to him. The old argument that one must be religious

---

77. Quoted from Edward Le Joly, *Mother Teresa of Calcutta: A Biography* (San Francisco: Harper & Row, 1983), 162-63.

78. Kenneth L. Woodward, "Requiem for a Saint," *Newsweek* 130/12 (September 22, 1997): 27. The eulogy was given by Cardinal Angelo Sodano, Vatican Secretary of State.

in order to be moral — and so religious faith becomes only instrumental to ethics — goes by the board. The down-to-earth service of the person in need — without any sense of religious obligation or motivation — *that* is service to Christ! Christ's true servants, then, know nothing about him, but seek only to serve the neighbor.

That will mean that Christians can freely join up with other groups and organizations (religious or not) in doing good for refugees and prisoners, the poor, the sick, and the homeless. Such groups are doing service unto Christ, whether they know it or not. In the end Christ will acknowledge their service as well as that of Christians. What makes Christians different is that they are aware of the service to others as being service to Christ ahead of time.

The theological question must be raised and dealt with: Does this passage teach works righteousness? Does it teach that good works are not only necessary for salvation, but are in fact the very basis for it? Does it nullify faith in Christ as the basis?

To ask of any parable or parabolic discourse a full and unified theology is to demand too much. Parables illumine aspects of the truth; they do not give all that one might want or expect. Who could possibly provide any parable that would do such? This particular parable does not provide teaching about salvation (soteriology) per se. Its focus is rather upon human responsibility in face of the destitution of fellow human beings. How is a person's life to be judged? It can only be judged outwardly by what that person does. (What is inside is known only to God.) Moreover, the grace of God is greater than anyone can possibly conceive. But for the time being, before the judgment, one stands responsible and accountable. The person who acts to alleviate human misery and suffering, and does so without thought of reward and makes no claims of righteousness or right belief, is the one whose life is whole and approved by God. In a sermon on this text, Rudolf Bultmann once remarked: "The judgment of the Lord does not depend upon your conscious confession of faith, but on the faith which is working unconsciously in your behaviour."[79]

Or to put it another way: Those who live in Christ, and whose destiny is to be among the sheep of Christ, have no need to seek a reward. By means of good works they simply enact what they are. And this discourse challenges them to do such.

Select Bibliography

Berger, Adolf, and Andrew W. Lintott. "Prison." *OCD* 1248.
Beyer, Hermann W. "ἐπισκέπτομαι." *TDNT* 2:599-622.
Bligh, Philip H. "Eternal Fire, Eternal Punishment, Eternal Life (Mt 25,41-46)." *ExpTim* 83 (1971-72): 9-11.

79. R. Bultmann, "Sermon (Matthew 25,31-46)," 49.

Bonnard, Pierre. "Matthieu 25,31-46. Questions de lecture et d'interpretation." *FV* 76/5 (1977): 81-87.

Brändle, Rudolf. "Jean Chrysostome: L'importance de Matth 25:31-46 pour son éthique." *VC* 31 (1977): 47-52.

————. *Matth. 25,31-46 im Werk des Johannes Chrysostomos.* BGBE 22. Tübingen: J. C. B. Mohr (Paul Siebeck), 1979.

————. "Zur Interpretation von Mt 25:31-46 im Matthäuskommentar des Origenes." *TZ* 36 (1980): 17-25.

Brandenburger, Egon. *Das Recht des Weltenrichters: Untersuchung zu Matthäus 25,31-46.* SBS 99. Stuttgart: Katholisches Bibelwerk, 1980.

Broer, Ingo. "Das Gericht des Menschensohnes über die Völker: Auslegung von Mt 25,31-46," *BibLeb* 11 (1970): 273-95.

Brown, Schuyler. "Faith, the Poor and the Gentiles: A Tradition-Historical Reflection on Matthew 25:31-46." *TJT* 6 (1990): 171-81.

Bultmann, Rudolf. "Sermon (Matthew 25,31-46)." In *Hören und Handeln: Festschrift für Ernst Wolf zum 60. Geburtstag,* 47-51. Ed. Helmut Gollwitzer and Hellmut Traub. Munich: Chr. Kaiser Verlag, 1962.

Burney, Charles F. "St Matthew xxv 31-46 as a Hebrew Poem." *JTS* 14 (1913): 414-24.

Cadoux, Arthur T. "The Parable of the Sheep and the Goats (Mt. xxv.31-46)." *ExpTim* 41 (1930): 559-62.

Catchpole, David R. "The Poor of the Earth and the Son of Man in Heaven: A Re-Appraisal of Matthew xxv.31-46." *BJRL* 61 (1979): 355-97.

Christian, Paul. *Jesus und seine geringsten Brüder: Mt 25,31-46 redaktionsgeschichtlich untersucht.* EThS 12. Leipzig: St. Benno Verlag, 1975.

Cope, Lamar. "Matthew xxv:31-46: 'The Sheep and the Goats' Reinterpreted." *NovT* 11 (1969): 32-44.

Court, John M. "Right and Left: The Implications for Matthew 25.31-46." *NTS* 31 (1985): 223-33.

Cranfield, C. E. B. "Diakonia: Mt 25,31-46." *LQHR* 30 (1961): 275-81.

————. "Who Are Christ's Brothers (Matthew 25.40)?" *Metanoia* 4/1-2 (1994): 31-39.

Derrett, J. Duncan M. "Unfair to Goats (Mt 25:32-33)." *ExpTim* 108 (1997): 177-78.

deSilva, David A. "Renewing the Ethics of the Eschatological Community: The Vision of Judgment in Matthew 25." *Koinonia* 3 (1991): 168-94.

Donahue, John R. "The 'Parable' of the Sheep and the Goats: A Challenge to Christian Ethics." *TS* 47 (1986): 3-31.

Farahian, Edmond. "Relire Matthieu 25:31-46." *Gregorianum* 72 (1991): 437-57.

Feuillet, André. "Le caractère universel du jugement et la charité sans frontières en Mt 25,31-46." *NRT* 102 (1980): 179-96.

Forrest, R. G. "Judgment." *ExpTim* 91 (1979): 48-49.

Frahier, Louis-Jean. *Le jugement dernier. Implications éthiques sur le bonheur de l'homme, Mt 25,31-46.* ReMo 17. Paris: Cerf, 1992.

France, Richard T. "On Being Ready (Matthew 25:1-46)." In *The Challenge of Jesus' Parables,* 177-95. Ed. Richard N. Longenecker. Grand Rapids: Wm. B. Eerdmans, 2000.

Friedrich, Johannes. *Gott im Brüder? Eine methodenkritische Untersuchung von Redaktion, Überlieferung und Traditionen in MT 25,31-46.* CThM 7. Stuttgart: Calwer, 1977.

Gay, George. "The Judgment of the Gentiles in Matthew's Theology." In *Scripture, Tradition and Interpretation: Essays Presented to Everett F. Harrison by His Students and Colleagues in Honor of His Seventy-Fifth Birthday,* 199-215. Ed. W. Ward Gasque and William S. LaSor. Grand Rapids: Wm. B. Eerdmans, 1978.

Grassi, Joseph A. "'I Was Hungry and You Gave Me to Eat' (Matt 25:35ff.): The Divine Identification Ethic in Matthew." *BTB* 11 (1981): 81-84.

Gray, Sherman W. *The Least of My Brothers: Matthew 25:31-46: A History of Interpretation.* SBLDS 114. Atlanta: Scholars Press, 1989.

Heil, John P. "The Double Meaning of the Narrative of Universal Judgment in Matthew 25:31-46." *JSNT* 69 (1998): 3-14.

Herrmann, Volker. "Anmerkungen zum Verständnis einer Paralleltexte zu Mt 25:31ff aus der altägyptischen Religion." *BibNot* 59 (1991): 17-22.

Hutter, Manfred. "Mt 25:31-46 in der Deutung Manis." *NovT* 33 (1991): 276-82.

Ingelaere, Jean-Claude. "La parabole du jugement dernier (Mattieu 25:31-46)." *RHPR* 50 (1970): 23-60.

Jurgens, David W. "The Least: Contemporary Interpretations of the Judgment in Matthew 25:31-46." *RefRev* 39 (1986): 128-29.

Kornfeld, Walter. "Die Liebeswerke Mt 25,35f, 42f in alttestamentlicher Überlieferung." In *Theologia Scientia Eminens Practica: Fritz Zerbst zum 70. Geburtstag,* 225-65. Ed. Hans-Christoph Schmidt-Lauber. Vienna: Herder, 1979.

Kratz, Reinhard, "φυλακή." *EDNT* 3:441.

Ladd, George E. "The Parable of the Sheep and the Goats in Recent Interpretation." In *New Dimensions in New Testament Study,* 191-99. Ed. Richard N. Longenecker and Merrill C. Tenney. Grand Rapids: Zondervan, 1974.

Lapoorta, Japie J. "'. . . whatever you did for one of the least of these . . . you did for me' (Matt. 25:31-46)." *JTSA* 68 (1989): 103-9.

Luz, Ulrich, "The Final Judgment (Matt 25:31-46): An Exercise in 'History of Influence' Exegesis." In *Treasures New and Old: Contributions to Matthean Studies,* 271-310. Ed. David R. Bauer and Mark A. Powell. SBLSS 1. Atlanta: Scholars Press, 1996.

Maddox, Robert. "Who Are the 'Sheep' and the 'Goats'? A Study of the Purpose and Meaning of Matthew XXV:31-46." *AusBR* 13 (1965): 19-28.

Mánek, Jindrich. "Mit wem identifiziert sich Jesus? Eine exegetische Rekonstruction ad Matt. 25:31-46." In *Christ and Spirit in the New Testament: In Honour of Charles Francis Digby Moule,* 15-25. Ed. Barnabas Lindars and Stephen S. Smalley. Cambridge: Cambridge University Press, 1973.

Michaels, J. Ramsey. "Apostolic Hardships and Righteous Gentiles: A Study of Matthew 25:31-46." *JBL* 84 (1965): 27-37.

Mitton, Charles L. "Expository Problems: Present Justification and Final Judgment — A Discussion of the Parable of the Sheep and the Goats." *ExpTim* 68 (1956-57): 46-50.

Panier, Louis. "Le Fils de l'Homme et les nations." *SémBib* 69 (1993): 39-52.

Pregeant, Russell. "The Matthean Undercurrent: Process Hermeneutic and the 'Parable of the Last Judgment.'" In *Society of Biblical Literature 1975 Seminar Papers,* 2:143-59. Ed. George W. MacRae. 2 vols. SBLSP 9. Missoula: Scholars Press, 1975.

Robinson, John A. T. "The 'Parable' of the Sheep and the Goats." *NTS* 2 (1956): 225-37.

Schillebeeckx, Edward C. "A Glass of Water for a Fellow Human Being (Matt. 25,31-46)." In his *God among Us: The Gospel Proclaimed,* 59-62. New York: Crossroad, 1983.

Smith, T. C., David L. Bartlett, Charles E. Booth, and Paul M. Nagano. "Claims of Christ: Parable of the Sheep and Goats: An Exegesis of Matthew 25:31-46." *Foundations* 19 (1976): 206-22.

Turner, H. E. W. "Expounding the Parables — The Parable of the Sheep and the Goats (Mt 25:31-46)." *ExpTim* 77 (1965-66): 243-46.

Via, Dan O. "Ethical Responsibility and Human Wholeness in Matthew 25:31-46." *HTR* 80 (1987): 79-100.

Watson, Francis. "Liberating the Reader: A Theological-Exegetical Study of the Parable of the Sheep and the Goats (Matt 25:31-46)." In *The Open Text: New Directions in Biblical Studies?* 57-84. Ed. F. Watson. London: SCM Press, 1993.

Weber, Kathleen. "The Image of the Sheep and Goats in Matthew 25:31-46." *CBQ* 59 (1997): 657-78.

Wengst, Klaus. "Wie aus Böcker Ziegen Wurden (Mt 25,32f): Zur Entstehung und Verbreitung einer Forschungslegende oder: Wissenschaft als 'stille Post.'" *EvT* 54 (1994): 491-500.

Weren, Wilhelm J. C. *De broeders van de Mensenzoon. Mt 25,31-46 als toegang tot de eschatologie van Matteüs.* Nijmegen: Catholic University of Nijmegen, 1979.

Wilckens, Ulrich. "Gottes geringste Brüder — zu Mt 25,31-46." In *Jesus und Paulus: Festschrift für Werner Georg Kümmel zum 70. Geburtstag,* 363-83. Ed. E. Earle Ellis and Erich Grässer. Göttingen: Vandenhoeck & Ruprecht, 1975.

Winandy, Jacques. "La scène du Jugement Dernier (Mt 25:31-46)." *ScEc* 18 (1966): 169-86.

CHAPTER 7

Allegorical Parables

As indicated in Chapter 1, it is not possible to make a sharp distinction between parable and allegory in the world of Jesus, nor is it possible to assert that Jesus taught parables but not allegories and that any of the latter must be early Christian (post-Easter) constructions.

Three parables within the Synoptic Gospels are decidedly allegorical through and through. They are discussed in this chapter. Each of the three can be considered allegorical insofar as an allegory is "an extended or continued metaphor."[1] Within these three, more than any of the others, meanings can be assigned to all the major details presented. In the present, canonical renditions of these parables the details relate quite clearly to the history of salvation in its Christian expression.

Allegorical elements appear in other parables as well, and they are plentiful. Even within one of the briefest parables, the Parable of the Waiting Slaves (Mark 13:34-37//Luke 12:35-38), one can discern allegorical elements.[2] Discussion of other parables in previous chapters, especially some in the Gospel of Matthew — such as the Ten Maidens (Matt 25:1-13), the Weeds in the Wheat (13:24-30), and the Dragnet (13:47-50) — has illumined allegorical elements. Those elements have to be identified by the interpreter and dealt with exegetically. But in each of the parables mentioned here, there are other themes that draw attention away from the allegorical elements themselves.

The following three parables are so carefully embroidered with allegorical detail that they can be recognized instantly as allegories or, more precisely, allegorical parables. They sketch out the history of salvation and the place of the

---

1. *The Oxford English Dictionary,* 2d ed., ed. J. A. Simpson and E. S. C. Weiner, 20 vols. (Oxford: Clarendon Press, 1989), 1:333.

2. As pointed out by A. Cadoux, *Parables,* 191; C. Carlston, *Parables,* 197.

ministry and significance of Jesus (or of Jesus and his followers during or after his earthy ministry) within it.

7.31. The Great Banquet, Luke 14:16-24; *Thomas* 64

Luke 14:16-24

16*But [Jesus] said to him, "A certain man prepared a great banquet, and invited many;* 17*and he sent his slave at the time for the banquet to say to those who had been invited, 'Come; for it is now ready.'*

18*"But they all alike began to make excuses. The first said to him, 'I have bought a field, and I must go out and see it; I ask you to excuse me.'* 19*And another said, 'I have bought five yoke of oxen, and I go to examine them; I ask you to excuse me.'* 20*And another said, 'I have married a wife, and therefore I cannot come.'*

21*"So the slave came and reported these things to his master. Then the owner of the house got angry and said to his slave, 'Go out quickly to the streets and alleys of the city, and bring in the poor, the crippled, the blind, and the lame.'* 22*And the slave said, 'Sir, what you commanded has been done, and still there is room.'*

23*"And the master said to the slave, 'Go out to the highways and hedges, and compel people to come in, that my house may be filled.* 24*For I tell you, none of those who were invited shall taste my banquet.'"*

Notes on the Text and Translation

14:17. Various modern versions read *"all"* is ready (KJV, RSV) or "everything" is ready (NEB, NIV, NRSV), instead of "it" is ready. In doing so, they follow those ancient witnesses that include πάντα (including A, D, and the Majority text). But the term does not appear in other very important ancient witnesses (e.g., 𝔭75, B, ℵ). Since it appears in its Matthean parallel (22:4), it has probably been imported into Luke's text for consistency.[1] For reasons of (1) ancient witnesses, (2) the Matthean parallel, and (3) the fact that the shorter reading is to be preferred, the term should not be included or translated.

14:18. The adverbial expression ἀπὸ μιᾶς is found only here in the NT. Various meanings have been assigned: "unanimously," "with one accord," "alike," and "in concert."[2] Less likely is "at once" or "immediately" (based conjecturally on a possible Semitism).[3]

---

1. B. Metzger, *TCGNT* 164.
2. BDF 126 (#241 [6]); BAGD 88 (ἀπό, VI).
3. Matthew Black, *An Aramaic Approach to the Gospels and Acts*, 3d ed. (Oxford: Clarendon Press, 1967), 113.

The expression "I ask you to excuse me" (both here and in 14:19) is better English than a literal translation would be: "I ask you, have me excused."

Thomas 64

Jesus said, "A man had received visitors. And when he had prepared the dinner, he sent his servant to invite the guests. He went to the first one and said to him, 'My master invites you.' He said, 'I have claims against some merchants. They are coming to me this evening. I must go and give them my orders. I ask to be excused from the dinner.' He went to another and said to him, 'My master has invited you.' He said to him, 'My master invites you.' He said to him, 'My friend is going to get married, and I am to prepare the banquet. I shall not be able to come. I ask to be excused from the dinner.' He went to another and said to him, 'My master invites you.' He said to him, 'I have just bought a farm, and I am on my way to collect the rent. I shall not be able to come. I ask to be excused.' The servant returned and said to his master, 'Those whom you invited to the dinner have asked to be excused.' The master said to his servant, 'Go outside to the streets and bring back those whom you happen to meet, so that they may dine.' Businessmen and merchants [will] not enter the places of my father."[4]

Exegetical Commentary

The Parable of the Great Banquet in the Gospel of Luke is much like the Parable of the Wedding Feast in the Gospel of Matthew (22:1-14) and logion 64 of the *Gospel of Thomas*. The three have the following things in common:

1. Each has a banquet setting to which persons have been invited previously (according to typical Near Eastern custom).

2. The host sends a slave/slaves to announce to the guests that the banquet is ready (again, according to typical Near Eastern custom).

3. The invited guests reject the invitation.

4. The slave/slaves are sent by the host to bring in replacements from the streets without regard for their social, economic, and religious standing.

These four items have to be intact for a complete story in an ancient setting. One might argue that only three are necessary (invitation, refusal, and replacements), dispensing with the second item (the host sending word that the banquet is ready), but in a day when the exact timing of a meal would have been virtually impossible to predict, that element belongs within the story as well.[5]

Although these similarities can be granted, there are significant differ-

---

4. Quoted from *NHLE* 133-34.

5. Cf. Esth 6:14; Philo, *Op.* 78; *Lam. Rab.* 4:2; T. W. Manson, *Sayings*, 225; J. Jeremias, *Parables*, 176, 188.

Table 3
The Parables of the Wedding Feast and Great Banquet

	Matthew	Luke	Thomas
Meal	Wedding feast for a son	Banquet for friends	Banquet for friends
Host	A king	A rich man	A rich man
Sending of slave or slaves	Three times (22:3, 4, 9-10)	Two times (14:17, 21)	Two times
Number of slaves	Several (22:3, 4, 8)	One (14:17, 22)	One
Number of exits from the scene or excuses	Two exits — to farm, to business (22:5)	Three excuses — land, oxen, or wife (14:18-20)	Four excuses — to meet merchants, care for a house, arrange a dinner, or collect rent
"Additions" in Matthew	Killing of slaves (22:6); burning the city (22:7); good and bad (22:10); and the sequel (22:11-14)		
Setting	Jerusalem	Journey on the way to Jerusalem, home of a Pharisee (14:1, 12)	None said
Audience	Chief priests and Pharisees (21:45; 22:15)	A Pharisee and an un-named guest (14:1, 12, 15)	None said

ences between them (with the versions in Luke and the *Gospel of Thomas* most alike), which are illustrated in Table 3.

Both the similarities and differences between the Matthean and Lukan versions are striking, and both have to be weighed in answer to the question whether the two versions are based on a common source (Q) or on independent traditions (M and L). Some interpreters have asserted or concluded that Matthew and Luke derived their parables from Q and edited them in significant ways (leaving Matt 22:11-14 aside).[6] Others consider the two versions so di-

---

6. A. Polag, *Fragmenta Q*, 70; Hans Conzelmann, *The Theology of St. Luke* (New York: Harper & Brothers, 1960), 111; J. Fitzmyer, *Luke*, 78, 1052; H. Weder, *Gleichnisse*, 177-78; H. Hendrickx, *Parables*, 131; J. Donahue, *Parable*, 93, 141; L. Schottroff, "Gleichnis vom grossen Gastmahl," 192; Ivor H. Jones, *The Matthean Parables: A Literary and Historical Commentary*, NovTSup 80 (Leiden: E. J. Brill, 1995), 401; D. Hagner, *Matthew*, 627; H. Klein, "Botschaft für viele," 427-37; R. Brown, *Introduction NT*, 119. According to T. W.

verse that the evangelists must have drawn their respective parables from their own special traditions (M and L).[7] The latter judgment is accepted here. As indicated above, some of the similarities simply belong to the essential structure of a banquet parable. The differences are therefore more important in this regard. They seem sufficiently significant to warrant the view adopted here.

As seen from the table above, the version in the *Gospel of Thomas* is in various respects close to that in the Gospel of Luke. Whether it can be considered to be based on a tradition independent of the Synoptic versions is a matter of debate. While a good number of interpreters have concluded that the version in the *Gospel of Thomas* is dependent on one or both Synoptic versions,[8] others hold that it is based on independent tradition.[9] A good reason for claiming independence is that in the *Gospel of Thomas* the excuses are greater in number than in the Synoptic versions and are made for different reasons.[10] In any case, the parable is quite different in its metaphors and significance. Gone now is Luke's nuance in which the persons compelled to come in are the underprivileged members of society (14:21-23). Gone, too, is Matthew's collection of persons brought in, "both bad and good" (22:10). To be sure, there are replacements of those originally invited, but they are persons generally considered worthy of having a place at the dinner. The parable closes with a comment against persons engaged in com-

Manson, *Sayings,* 129-30, 224-26, portions of Matt 22:1-10 are considered to have come from Q and to have been conflated with other materials.

7. Burnett H. Streeter, *The Four Gospels: A Study in Origins,* rev. ed. (London: Macmillan, 1930), 243-44; A. Plummer, *Luke,* 359; C. H. Dodd, *Parables,* 93; B. Smith, *Parables,* 203; J. Jeremias, *Parables,* 63; E. Linnemann, *Parables,* 166 (n. 20); J. Gnilka, *Matthäus,* 2:234-35; W. D. Davies and D. C. Allison, *Matthew,* 3:194; U. Luz, *Matthäus,* 3:233; A. Weiser, *Knechtsgleichnisse,* 59-60 (although he allows Q as a possible source). Two different parables are involved, according to A. Plummer, *Matthew,* 300; idem, *Luke,* 359-60.

8. Robert M. Grant and David N. Freedman, *The Secret Sayings of Jesus* (Garden City: Doubleday, 1960), 170; Michael Fieger, *Das Thomasevangelium: Einleitung Kommentar Systematik,* NTAbh 22 (Münster: Aschendorff, 1991), 187 (a "free retelling" ["freie Nacherzählung"] of the Synoptic versions). Apparent dependence, but no certainty, is held by Wolfgang Schrage, *Das Verhältnis des Thomas-Evangelium zur synoptischen Tradition und zu den koptischen Evangelienübersetzungen: Zugleich ein Beitrag zur gnostischen Synoptikerdeutung,* BZNW 29 (Berlin: Alfred Töpelmann, 1964), 134-35; H. Weder, *Gleichnisse,* 185; Craig L. Blomberg, "Tradition and Redaction in the Parables of Jesus," in *The Jesus Tradition outside the Gospels,* ed. David Wenham (Sheffield: JSOT Press, 1985), 187-89.

9. J. Jeremias, *Parables,* 24; N. Perrin, *Teaching,* 111-14; Robert McL. Wilson, *Studies in the Gospel of Thomas* (London: A. R. Mowbray, 1960), 100, 147; J. Fitzmyer, *Luke,* 1,051; Stephen J. Patterson, *The Gospel of Thomas and Jesus* (Sonoma, Calif.: Polebridge Press, 1992), 77-78; R. Funk, *Five Gospels,* 352; W. D. Davies and D. C. Allison, *Matthew,* 3:195.

10. A thorough discussion of differences can be found in the essay by Hugh Montefiore, "A Comparison of the Parables of the Gospel according to Thomas and of the Synoptic Gospels," in *Thomas and the Evangelists,* by H. E. W. Turner and H. Montefiore, SBT 35 (Naperville: Alec R. Allenson, 1962), 61-62.

merce. Buying and selling lead persons astray; commerce is incompatible with the contemplative life required of the true Gnostic.[11]

While Matthew's parable is located within a section where Jesus is in Jerusalem and in the presence of opponents (21:23, 45, 46; 22:15), Luke's version appears within the Travel Narrative (9:51–19:27), and it is told while Jesus is a guest at the home of a Pharisee (14:1) and in response to a fellow guest (14:15).

14:16. The person who gives a dinner is ἄνθρωπός τις, which is translated variously as "a man" (RSV, NEB, TEV, JB, NAB), "a certain man" (KJV, NIV), or "someone" (NRSV). The expression appears also at 10:30; 12:16; 14:2; 15:11; 16:1, 19; 19:12; 20:9; Acts 9:33, but nowhere else in the NT. Except for two cases (Luke 14:2; Acts 9:33), the expression stands at the outset of a parable. It can be considered typically Lukan in terminology,[12] but it represents the tradition Luke received, providing a narrative introduction.

The Greek term for a banquet used here and at 14:24 is δεῖπνον, which signifies either the main meal of the day (toward evening) or a banquet.[13] But in this parable it also has metaphorical significance as an eschatological image (cf. Rev 3:20; 19:9), which is rooted in the OT and Jewish tradition (Isa 25:6; 2 Esdr 2:37-41; Matt 8:11//Luke 13:29).[14] The term used in the Matthean parallel is γάμος ("wedding feast"), which has the same metaphorical significance (see commentary on Matt 22:3).

14:17. As indicated above, the persons invited had been invited long ago, but the precise time had not been given. Now the meal is ready, and it is time for the host to send out his slave ("slaves" in Matthew's version) to summon those who had been invited.

14:18-20. The persons invited were "many," according to 14:16. The excuses of only three are given in these verses, following the "rule of three" of good storytelling.[15] Each is, in effect, a flat refusal to come to the banquet that has been prepared. Their refusals are extremely offensive since they had accepted the invitation previously.[16] And what kind of excuses are they? One

---

11. R. M. Grant and D. N. Freedman, *Secret Sayings,* 171; H. Montefiore, "Comparison," 53.

12. Contra Joachim Jeremias, *Die Sprache des Lukasevangelium: Redaktion und Tradition im Nicht-Markusstoff des dritten Evangeliums,* MeyerK (Göttingen: Vandenhoeck & Ruprecht, 1980), 191.

13. BAGD 173. Cf. Luke 14:2, where both this term and ἄριστον ("meal") are used; on the latter term, cf. BAGD 106.

14. For additional sources, cf. *1 Enoch* 62:14; *2 Enoch* 42:5; *2 Bar.* 29:1-8; texts, respectively, in *OTP* 1:44, 168, 630-31; various rabbinic references are given by Johannes Behm, "δεῖπνον," *TDNT* 2:35.

15. Cf. the Parable of the Pounds (19:12-27), which has to do with ten slaves, but only three are called forth in the story to render an accounting of their activities.

16. Cf. A. Plummer, *Luke,* 360, and K. Bailey, *Peasant Eyes,* 95-99, who supply considerable information about Near Eastern customs.

could go out to see one's newly purchased field or oxen on another day. And having married a wife (who is apparently not invited) and therefore being not able to come seems to be an odd excuse (or is the banquet to go on through the night or for several days?).[17] The time of feasting from the wedding must now be past since the man is at home. OT law exempts a man from military service and business for a year (Deut 20:5-7; 24:5), but that is not what is at stake here.

The dynamics of the parable to this point must carry allegorical meanings. But what can they mean? The first invitation to the banquet, which had gone out previously, most likely corresponds to an earlier era of proclamation of the kingdom, which was done by the prophets. The second invitation, carried by a lone slave from the master to those invited, could correspond to the ministry of Jesus himself (including his disciples).[18] The refusal of the final summons would then correspond to the refusal of those who had been invited to the preaching of Jesus. The master who prepares the banquet and declares a judgment at the end on those who made excuses would thereby represent God.[19]

14:21. The host of the banquet is called both "master" (κύριος) of the slave and "owner of the house" (οἰκοδεσπότης). Angered by the report of his slave, he commissions him to take on a new task. That is to go into the "streets and lanes" of the city and to "bring in," not simply call or invite, the "poor, the crippled, the blind, and the lame." These are the same categories of persons listed in 14:13, persons who ought to be invited to a meal but usually are not. For Luke, "the poor and those with bodily infirmities symbolize all who need God's help."[20] The list has probably been inserted here by Luke. The "streets" (πλατεῖαι) and "alleys" (ῥῦμαι) in this commissioning are located within the city. The list of the kind of persons to be invited recalls those listed at 7:22, who are the beneficiaries of the ministry of the Messiah Jesus. They are the kind of persons, on the other hand, who were not eligible for full participation in the life of the community, including the meals, at Qumran.[21]

17. That 14:20 is a later addition is maintained unpersuasively by E. Linnemann, *Parables*, 89.

18. A. Jülicher, *Gleichnisreden*, 2:416; C. Montefiore, *Synoptic Gospels*, 2:977; B. Easton, *Luke*, 228; T. W. Manson, *Sayings*, 129; N. Perrin, *Teaching*, 113. The reference is to John the Baptist and Jesus, according to A. Plummer, *Luke*, 360. An allegorical reference on this matter is denied by J. Fitzmyer, *Luke*, 1055. J. Creed, *Luke*, 191: one should not ask who is represented by the slave.

19. A. Jülicher, *Gleichnisreden*, 2:415-16; T. W. Manson, *Sayings*, 129; B. Smith, *Parables*, 205; contra A. Plummer, *Luke*, 363, J. Creed, *Luke*, 192, and J. Jeremias, *Parables*, 177, for whom the speaker in 14:24 represents Jesus.

20. E. Schweizer, *Luke*, 238.

21. 1QSa 2:6-10; cf. 1QM 7:4-6; cited by J. Donahue, *Parable*, 144.

22. J. Fitzmyer, *Luke*, 1,057.

14:22. That has been done. Such persons did not refuse. They have been gathered into the banquet hall already. "Still there is room," declares the slave to his master. If the allegorical elements have been identified correctly to this point, this is the declaration of Jesus concerning the divine mission.

14:23. The master commissions his slave a second time. Now he is to go outside the city to the "highways and hedges." In this version of the parable the slave is commanded to "compel" (ἀνάγκασον) people to come in, which is much stronger than the expression in Matthew's version; there the slaves are to "invite" as many as they find (22:9). It may well be necessary to "compel" these persons in because of their modesty.[22] That will not mean that they are to be mistreated. They are to be urged, but not abused.

The term "highways" (ὁδοί) refers to main roads outside the city in this instance. The term translated "hedges" (φραγμοί) refers to hedges that enclosed yards and fields; they were places where the homeless could seek shelter and where beggars could hide.[23]

Is there any significance to two commissionings? According to some interpreters, the two indicate a mission to Israel first, and then to the Gentiles.[24] In light of Luke's view of salvation history,[25] that is possible. Moreover, it is possible, then, that those who had been invited in the first place are the "religious aristocracy," especially the Pharisees, and the two latter groups would be Jews of a lower class (outcasts among them) and Gentiles, respectively.[26] Another possibility (favored here), however, is that the two commissionings are derived from the pre-Lukan stages of tradition and simply point to the all-encompassing and thorough impulses of the divine mission. No area of possible habitation is to be left out.

14:24. The parable ends with a word of judgment upon those who had originally been invited but then made excuses. They are excluded. Oddly, the Greek word for "you" in the opening phrase of this verse is plural (ὑμῖν; see notations in the RSV and NRSV). It should be singular (σοί) if the master is speaking to his slave. Although the saying is the master's, it has been conformed to the familiar pronouncement formula of Jesus elsewhere (and in all four strands of the Synoptic tradition: Mark 3:28; 8:41; 13:37; Matt 5:20; 6:2; 18:10; Luke 12:4, 37; 13:24; 16:9; Q, Matt 13:7//Luke 10:24; Matt 18:3//Luke 15:7, and many other instances in all four). Rhetorically the verse is effective for oral reading. In a sense, the master "steps as it were on to the apron of the stage and addresses the audience."[27]

23. BAGD 865.

24. C. Montefiore, *Synoptic Gospels,* 2:977; R. Bultmann, *HST* 175; B. Smith, *Parables,* 205; B. Easton, *Luke,* 229; C. H. Dodd, *Parables,* 94; J. Jeremias, *Parables,* 64; F. Hahn, "Gleichnis vom der Einladung," 51-82; E. Schweizer, *Luke,* 238-39; J. Fitzmyer, *Luke,* 1,053.

25. Cf. Acts 13:44-67; 18:5-6; 28:23-28.

26. T. W. Manson, *Sayings,* 130; cf. N. Perrin, *Teaching,* 113.

27. E. Linnemann, *Parables,* 90.

The parable is generally attributed to Jesus of Nazareth.[28] Less certain are the circumstances in which it would have been spoken. According to one point of view, it was spoken by Jesus against his opponents, telling them that they have been shut out of the kingdom.[29] But that seems too negative in light of the very positive thrust of the parable as a whole. The parable could have been spoken to a more general audience, including not only Jesus'critics but also his disciples. According to Luke, the parable was spoken in the presence of Pharisees, within the confines of a house, and in response to a statement made by one of the guests. But the statement is by no means hostile or critical of Jesus. It is a beatitude, spoken by a person with good intentions (14:15, "Blessed is anyone who will eat bread in the kingdom of God!"). From there, as a "teaching moment," Jesus goes into the parable and teaches that there are persons who refuse God's invitation to the kingdom, even though they have been invited by way of the teachings of the Scriptures and the traditions that enrich their lives concerning the reality and promises of God. But God will not be constrained or limited. Even within the ministry of Jesus himself, that is apparent. Those who are considered the lost and unworthy within his generation are precisely those who are responding to the gospel of the kingdom.

For the evangelist Luke and his community, another facet can be seen. The parable speaks about the inclusive nature of the Christian community. When the church has its own gatherings for fellowship, particularly at the Lord's Supper, it is to be inviting and inclusive, having a place at the table for those who would not normally be invited.[30]

Exposition

"Still there is room!" That phrase stands out as a commentary on the divine economy throughout the ages. The mission of God seems never to be complete. Grace, like nature, abhors a vacuum.

Not only the phrase but also the placing of the phrase within the parable is significant. In an ideal world, those who were invited ought to arrive at the banquet, and the host ought to notice that "still there is room" so he can fit in some more. But the phrase does not come at such a point in the story, for those who had been invited never come. Nor does the phrase appear after they refuse

28. A. Jülicher, *Gleichnisreden*, 2:407; T. W. Manson, *Sayings*, 130; B. Easton, *Luke*, 230; B. Smith, *Parables*, 203; J. Jeremias, *Parables*, 69; A. Weiser, *Knechtsgleichnisse*, 64; E. Linnemann, *Parables*, 90-92; N. Perrin, *Teaching*, 113; H. Hendrickx, *Parables*, 133; H. Weder, *Gleichnisse*, 185-90; I. H. Marshall, *Luke*, 586-87; J. Fitzmyer, *Luke*, 1,053; K. Bailey, *Peasant Eyes*, 105. The text (14:16-23) is in pink font (= Jesus probably said something like this) in R. Funk, *Five Gospels*, 351-52 (14:24 is in black [= not authentic]).

29. J. Jeremias, *Parables*, 176; E. Linnemann, *Parables*, 91; cf. B. Smith, *Parables*, 203 (against the "professedly religious"); M. Boucher, *Parables*, 104 (against Jesus' "critics").

30. J. Donahue, *Parable*, 144.

to come. Instead it comes after the poor, the crippled, the blind, and the lame have already been brought into the banquet. Those who would not ordinarily be invited have been brought in. That should be enough. But "still there is room." The master and the slave have started down that road of bringing such persons in, and there is no end to it.

The mission of God through Jesus is resolute and comprehensive. The biblical drama reveals a God who is determined to have fellowship with his children and to save any and all from perishing. The ministry of Jesus and his disciples may well face resistance. But resistance does not impede it. A riverbank may come crashing down into a river and thereby offer resistance. But the river is not impeded; it is simply diverted. So, too, the mission of God may meet resistance and thereby be diverted, but it will not be impeded forever.

The parable presents a challenge to the hearer or reader. The question it poses is whether one who hears it makes excuses in the present era, turning down the call of God in contemporary proclamation. Are other things more important than God's call to discipleship in the kingdom?

Excuses, resistance, and refusal are common and are to be expected. But that is not the main theme of the parable. The element of refusal is the means by which to make the main point of the parable come to light. The parable centers in the good news of God, who seeks to embrace those who have nothing to offer, who must in fact be urged to come to the banquet, the feast of eschatological salvation.

Select Bibliography

Aalen, Sverre. "St Luke's Gospel and the Last Chapters of I Enoch." *NTS* 13 (1966-67): 1-13.

Ballard, Paul H. "Reasons for Refusing the Great Supper." *JTS* 23 (1972): 341-50.

Bultmann, Rudolf. "Lukas 14,16-24." In his *Marburger Predigten,* 126-36. Tübingen: J. C. B. Mohr (Paul Siebeck), 1956.

Carey, W. Gregory. "Excuses, Excuses: The Parable of the Banquet (Luke 14:15-24) within the Larger Context of Luke." *IBS* 17 (1995): 177-87.

Derrett, J. Duncan M. "The Parable of the Great Supper." In his *Law in the New Testament,* 126-55. London: Darton, Longman and Todd, 1970.

Dormeyer, Detlev. "Literarische und theologische Analyse der Parabel Lk. 14, 15-24." *BibLeb* 15 (1974): 206-19.

Glombitza, Otto. "Das grosse Abendmahl: Luk. 14:12-24." *NovT* 5 (1962): 10-16.

Hahn, Ferdinand. "Das Gleichnis von der Einladung zum Festmahl." In *Verborum Veritas: Festschrift für Gustav Stählin zum 70. Geburtstag,* 51-82. Ed. Otto Böcher and Klaus Haacker. Wuppertal: Theologischer Verlag Brockhaus, 1970.

Haenchen, Ernst. "Das Gleichnis vom grossen Mahl." In his *Die Bibel und wir: Gesammelte Aufsätze II*, 135-55. Tübingen: J. C. B. Mohr (Paul Siebeck), 1968.

Klein, Hans. "Botschaft für viele — Nachfolge von wenigen. Überlegungen zu Lk 14,15-35." *EvT* 57 (1997): 427-37.

Martens, Allan W. "'Produce Fruit Worthy of Repentance': Parables of Judgment against Jewish Religious Leaders and the Nation (Matt 21:28-22:14, par.; Luke 13:6-9)." In *The Challenge of Jesus' Parables*, 151-76. Ed. Richard N. Longenecker. Grand Rapids: Wm. B. Eerdmans, 2000.

Navone, John. "The Parable of the Banquet." *BiTod* 1 (1964): 923-29.

Norwood, Frederick A. "'Compel Them to Come In': The History of Luke 14:23." *RelLife* 23 (1953-54): 516-27.

Palmer, Humphrey. "Just Married, Cannot Come (Matthew 22, Luke 14, Thomas 44, Dt. 29)." *NovT* 18 (1976): 241-57.

Pesch, Rudolf, and R. Kratz. "Gleichnis vom grossen Gastmahl." In *So liest man synoptisch*, 39-60. Frankfurt am Main: Knecht Verlag, 1978.

Sanders, James A. "The Ethic of Election in Luke's Great Banquet Parable." In *Essays in Old Testament Ethics (J. Philip Hyatt, In Memoriam)*, 245-71. Ed. James I. Crenshaw and John T. Willis. New York: Ktav, 1974.

Schlier, Heinrich. "The Call of God." In his *The Relevance of the New Testament*, 249-58. New York: Herder and Herder, 1968.

Schottroff, Luise. "Das Gleichnis vom grossen Gastmahl in der Logienquelle." *EvT* 47 (1987): 192-211.

Swartley, Willard M. "Unexpected Banquet People (Luke 14:16-24)." In *Jesus and His Parables: Interpreting the Parables of Jesus Today*, ed. V. George Shillington, 177-90. Edinburgh: T. & T. Clark, 1997.

Vine, Victor E. "Luke 14:15-24 and Anti-Semitism." *ExpTim* 102 (1990-91): 262-63.

Wegenast, Klaus. "Freiheit ist lernbar: Lukas 14,15-24 im Unterricht." *EvErz* 40 (1988): 592-600.

7.32. The Wedding Feast, Matthew 22:1-14

1*And again Jesus spoke to them in parables, saying,* 2*"The kingdom of heaven has become like a king who gave a marriage feast for his son,* 3*and sent his slaves to call those who were invited to the marriage feast; but they would not come.*

4*"Again he sent other slaves, saying, 'Tell those who are invited, "Behold, I have made ready my dinner; my oxen and my fat calves are killed, and everything is ready; come to the marriage feast."'* 5*But they paid no attention and went off, one to his farm, another to his business,* 6*while the rest seized his slaves, treated them shamefully, and killed them.*

7 *"The king was angry, and he sent his troops and destroyed those murderers and burned their city.*

8 *"Then he said to his slaves, 'The wedding is ready, but those invited were not worthy. 9Go therefore to the thoroughfares, and invite to the marriage feast as many as you find.' 10And those slaves went out into the streets and gathered all whom they found, both bad and good; so the wedding hall was filled with guests.*

11 *"But when the king came in to look at the guests, he saw there a man who had no wedding garment; 12and he said to him, 'Friend, how did you get in here without a wedding garment?' And he was speechless. 13Then the king said to the attendants, 'Bind him hand and foot, and cast him into the outer darkness; at that place there will be weeping and gnashing of teeth.' 14For many are called, but few are chosen."*

Notes on the Text and Translation

22:10. One must make a choice between two ambiguous words, both of which have strong attestation in ancient Greek witnesses. Either it was the γάμος or the νυμφών that was filled. The first of these usually means a "wedding," a "banquet," or a "wedding banquet," as elsewhere in the parable itself (22:2, 3, 4, 8, 9, 12).[1] The second usually means a "wedding hall" or a "bridal chamber."[2] The latter Greek term appears in some excellent Alexandrian witnesses (e.g., ℵ and B) and in the 25th edition of the Nestle-Aland text. The former appears in significant witnesses (e.g., D, W, Θ, the Majority Text, and more). It is the more difficult reading. If it is to mean "wedding hall," this is the only place in the NT where it is used in that way.[3] The suggestion has been made that the Alexandrian scribes made the alteration from the inappropriate term γάμος to the more fitting νυμφών.[4] The decision is difficult, but that reasoning may well be correct.

Exegetical Commentary

The Parable of the Wedding Feast resembles in many ways the Parable of the Great Banquet in the Gospel of Luke (14:16-24) and logion 64 of the *Gospel of Thomas*. The similarities and differences among them — and the question of possible interrelationships — are discussed in the section on the Parable of the Great Banquet.

If the three versions of the parable have a common origin (and are not simply three parables told on three occasions), it is clear that Matthew's has

1. BAGD 151.
2. Ibid., 545.
3. Ibid., 151.
4. B. Metzger, *TCGNT* 58.

been developed allegorically more than the other two. For Matthew, the parable is a parable of the kingdom. It is about a king, not simply a wealthy man. The king has several slaves, as a king indeed ought to. There are more instances of sending out slaves. There is violence against the slaves, even to the point of the death of some. And it includes the burning of the city in which the banquet is being held. In addition to these elements, Matthew's version has a sequel, the story of the man without a wedding garment (22:11-14), which is not included in Luke's parable. It must have an allegorical significance as well. Questions concerning its literary background and its meaning will be taken up below.

22:1. The parable that follows is addressed to the chief priests and Pharisees (21:45; 22:15). It stands as the third of three parables that, among other things, cast a very negative light upon the opponents of Jesus. The Parable of the Two Sons (21:28-32) castigates the opponents as disobedient to the will and purposes of God. The Parable of the Wicked Tenants (21:33-46) speaks of judgment to come upon those who have killed the son of the owner of the vineyard. Within the context of Matthew's Gospel the son unmistakably represents Jesus, and the owner of the vineyard is a metaphor for God. These parables set a tone for the passage that follows, the Parable of the Wedding Feast, which ends on a note of harsh judgment. But the judgment this time is not upon the opponents of Jesus (see below). As will be seen, the Matthean parable provides a sweeping overview of the history of salvation.

22:2. The verb ὡμοιώθη (aorist passive of ὁμοιόω, "has become like") appears also at 13:24 and 18:23, introducing the Parables of the Weeds among the Wheat and the Unforgiving Slave. It is found only in Matthean introductions to parables and can be translated along with its subject as above ("the kingdom of heaven has become like"), followed by the parable proper.[5] The kingdom is thus not "like a king," but rather it has already dawned in the ministry of Jesus and has become like the following case,[6] in which a king — metaphorically understood as God[7] — summons persons to a wedding banquet (another metaphor), and in light of the reactions he gets, he has to resort to drastic action.

For Matthew and his readers, ancient or modern, the son refers allegorically to Jesus,[8] who is the bridegroom (cf. 9:15; 25:1-13; Rev 19:7, 9). This feature may well be an addition to an earlier version of the parable that speaks simply of a great banquet, as in the parallels (Luke 14:16; Gos. Thom. 64). On the other hand, if one does not look for allegorical features in every facet, the son need not be Jesus. If a king (as a metaphor for God) gives a wedding feast

---

5. D. A. Carson, "The ὅμοιος Word-Group as Introduction to Some Matthean Parables," NTS 31 (1985): 278.

6. On the use of the introductory formula containing words of likeness, cf. J. Jeremias, Parables, 101.

7. So various interpreters, for example, W. D. Davies and D. C. Allison, Matthew, 3:197.

8. Ibid., 3:198-99.

(as a metaphor for the kingdom), it would have to be for someone close, which would most likely be a son.

22:3. The wedding banquet is a metaphor for the eschatological messianic kingdom and its joys (Isa 25:6; 62:1-5; 2 Esdr 2:37-41; Rev 19:7-9; cf. Isa 54:5; Matt 25:10).[9] Invitations to the kingdom had gone out previously, apparently in the preaching of the prophets, including John the Baptist. Now the kingdom is at hand; it has become realized in the time of Jesus and his disciples. But those who should be prepared for it turn down the final summons, which can be considered an extreme offense since they had made a provisional acceptance previously. Although in Luke's version the persons give reasons for turning down the summons (14:18-20; this is true also of *Gos. Thom.* 64), here they simply go away without explanation. Even though it is not narrated, it is to be understood that the group of slaves returned to the king with their report.

22:4. A second delegation of slaves (different persons) is sent out to those who had been invited. They explain the urgency of coming immediately. The food is ready and will spoil if it is not consumed by those invited. The summons has some similarities to Wisdom's call to her guests in Proverbs 9:1-6. It corresponds also to the double sending of slaves in the Parable of the Wicked Tenants (21:34, 36), which precedes this one.

22:5-6. Among those summoned, some "paid no attention" (ἀμε-λήσαντες)[10] to the summons and left for their farms and businesses. Others seized, mistreated, and killed the slaves. Within the ministry of Jesus, such actions can allude to the seizing, mistreating, and killing of prophets up to and including John the Baptist (14:1-12).

For the evangelist Matthew, these acts correspond allegorically to the arrests, mistreatments, and killing of Jesus and early Christian messengers (Stephen, the apostle James, etc.) prior to the composition of his gospel.

The significance of two sendings of slaves to those invited is debated. Luke has only one. Several proposals have been made: (1) they represent the former and latter prophets;[11] (2) the first delegation represents the prophets of Israel, and the second represents John the Baptist, Jesus, and his disciples;[12] (3) while the first delegation indeed represents the prophets, the second represents the apostles and missionaries of the early church;[13] (4) the first group rep-

---

9. Imagery of a banquet is associated with the coming of the Messiah in later writings as well, such as the second-century-A.D. *2 Bar.* 29:1-8 and the rabbinic *Exod. Rab.* 15:31 (on 12:2), commenting on the marriage between God and Israel spoken of in Isa 54:5: "The actual marriage ceremony will take place in the Messianic days"; quoted from *MidR.* 3:204.

10. Cf. BAGD 44-45 (on ἀμελέω); the NIV, KJV, RSV, and NRSV have "made light of it"; NEB has "took no notice."

11. R. Gundry, *Matthew,* 437.

12. D. Hagner, *Matthew,* 630.

13. A. Jülicher, *Gleichnisreden,* 2:421; J. Jeremias, *Parables,* 68; A. Weiser, *Knechtsgleich-nisse,* 66-69; M. Boucher, *Parables,* 104; J. Gnilka, *Matthäus,* 2:238; U. Luz, *Matthäus,* 3:240.

resents John the Baptist, Jesus, and his disciples, and the second group represents Christian apostles and missionaries;[14] and (5) no such coordination is intended; the point is simply that God has sent many messengers, some of whom have been ignored, others killed.[15] Any of these is possible. The fact that the meaning is not obvious causes one to pause. It is surely possible that, as one reads the entire parable, one should notice that there are actually three sendings (22:3, 4, 10), thus employing the "rule of three" for dramatic effect. The telling of three emphasizes the efforts of God to get a response and to include as many persons as possible within the kingdom.

22:7. The king's wrath, the killing of the murderers by armies, and the burning of the city allude rather obviously and allegorically to the destruction of Jerusalem by the Romans in A.D. 70 (on fire as a sign of divine judgment, see Isa 5:24-25).[16] The verse, which has no parallel in Luke's Parable of the Great Banquet, is an addition and composition by Matthew (unless it was already in some post-70 source that the evangelist used) and not from the proclamation of Jesus. While the destruction is going on, the dinner that has been freshly prepared (22:4) is still ready when the warfare is over (22:8)! Equally absurd, if one is looking for verisimilitude, is that after all the mayhem is over there are still people available to invite and a place to have a feast. One can conclude that 22:6-7 breaks what seems to be an original connection between 22:5 and 22:8.[17]

22:8-9. The invitation to those first invited is now void due to the refusal of the would-be guests to come. Now a third group of slaves is sent out (those of group two have been killed [22:6]). These are to go into the "thoroughfares" (διεξόδους τῶν ὁδῶν; "main streets," NRSV) and extend invitations to whomever they find. The "thoroughfares" are those roads leading into the country.[18] This effort is no doubt an allegorical allusion to the Christian mission,[19] which for Matthew is a mission to the "lost sheep of the house of Israel" (10:6; 15:24) and the Gentiles (28:16-20) alike.[20] The slaves are told

14. A. McNeile, *Matthew*, 314-15.

15. B. Smith, *Parables*, 204; by implication, so also J. Lambrecht, *Treasure*, 133.

16. Such is the view of many: A. McNeile, *Matthew*, 315; W. Oesterley, *Parables*, 126; B. Smith, *Parables*, 205; J. Jeremias, *Parables*, 33, 68; E. Linnemann, *Parables*, 96, 165 (n. 17); H. Weder, *Gleichnisse*, 191; J. Lambrecht, *Parables*, 133; B. Scott, *Parable*, 163; W. D. Davies and D. C. Allison, *Matthew*, 3:201; U. Luz, *Matthäus*, 3:242. The view is opposed, discounted, or challenged by T. W. Manson, *Sayings*, 225; K. Rengstorf, "Die Stadt der Mörder," 106-29; R. Gundry, *Matthew*, 436-37; D. Hare, *Matthew*, 628, 630; I. Jones, *Matthean Parables*, 403-4. For the ancient view that the destruction of Jerusalem is evidence of God's punishment for the crucifixion and for not accepting the gospel, cf. Eusebius, *Eccl. hist.* 2.5.

17. J. Jeremias, *Parables*, 68; E. Schweizer, *Matthew*, 418.

18. BAGD 194; Wilhelm Michaelis, "ὁδός," *TDNT* 5:108.

19. J. Lambrecht, *Treasure*, 135.

20. Some interpreters look upon this as a mission to Gentiles only, basing their view

to "invite" (καλέσατε) people in; at Luke 14:23 the slave is told to "compel" (ἀνάγκασον) people to enter.

22:10. The slaves obey. They bring in both "bad and good" (πονηρούς τε καὶ ἀγαθούς).[21] The expression "bad and good" echoes similar ones previously in this Gospel — using either the same words (5:45, πονηρὸς καὶ ἀγαθούς) or synonyms (13:48, καλά . . . σαπρά). In the present era God's embrace of humanity is universal; there is no "sorting out" ahead of time of who shall be welcome into the kingdom. (There is an implicit sorting out if one is to recognize both bad and good and include them, but the rhetorical effect is that the slaves are not to pass by those commonly considered bad; cf. also 13:47-48.) The circumstances will be resolved only in the final judgment. The result of this mission is that the wedding hall was filled.

At the Matthean level the expression "bad and good" designates the church as a "corpus mixtum" (a "mixed body" of persons both bad and good),[22] at least in its outreach efforts. Its missionaries do not make judgments ahead of time, but seek to win all who are willing to receive the invitation.

22:11-13. These verses — which have no parallel in Luke's Parable of the Great Banquet — speak of a man without a wedding garment, who is cast out. This is not a separate parable,[23] even though it is somewhat like a rabbinic parable,[24] for it presupposes the material in 22:2-10. It can be regarded as a composition by the evangelist, as various interpreters have concluded on the basis

---

on the fact that those invited originally were the Jewish people, and that that invitation is now withdrawn. Included here are A. Jülicher, *Gleichnisreden*, 2:423; Wilhelm Michaelis, *Die Gleichnisse Jesu: Eine Einführung*, 3d ed. UCB 32 (Hamburg: Furche-Verlag, 1956), 159; A. Weiser, *Knechtsgleichnisse*, 62; H. Hendrickx, *Parables*, 126. But such a view (excluding Jews) is not necessary. The Matthean community was undoubtedly mixed Jewish and Gentile, and it is difficult to imagine that persons of Jewish heritage would not have continued to be incorporated. Cf. E. Schweizer, *Matthew*, 419; Warren Carter, "The Parables in Matthew 21:28–22:14," in *Matthew's Parables: Audience-Oriented Perspectives*, by W. Carter and John P. Heil, CBQMS 30 (Washington: Catholic Biblical Association of America, 1998), 175.

21. The sequence "bad and good," which is in Greek, is preserved in the KJV, RSV, and NAB; curiously, the NEB, TEV, and NIV have "good and bad."

22. J. Donahue, *Parable*, 94.

23. Contra A. Cadoux, *Parables*, 64; A. Plummer, *Matthew*, 302; W. Oesterley, *Parables*, 127; A. McNeile, *Matthew*, 316; C. H. Dodd, *Parables*, 94; T. W. Manson, *Sayings*, 224; J. Jeremias, *Parables*, 65, 68, 187; E. Linnemann, *Parables*, 96; E. Merriman, "Matthew xxii.1-14," 61; D. Via, *Parables*, 129; E. Schweizer, *Matthew*, 416; J. Crossan, *Parable*, 70; M. Boucher, *Parables*, 104. J. Gnilka, *Matthäus*, 2:236-37, attributes the verses of 22:11-13 to oral tradition, which the evangelist has reduced to writing.

24. The parable is attributed to Rabbi Johanan ben Zakkai (late first century A.D.) and is recorded in *b. Shab.* 153a. The parable is about wise and foolish servants at a king's banquet. The wise were properly clothed. They were admitted to the banquet. The foolish wore soiled clothing. They had to stand and watch the wise enjoy the banquet.

of its many Matthean terms and expressions,[25] which has been composed and appended in order to check any misunderstanding that could be derived from the parable. The parable ends with the saying that all are to be gathered in and admitted, "both bad and good" (22:10). But surely, for Matthew, once the "bad" have been admitted, they must be found worthy of their place in the kingdom.

The king's coming in to inspect the guests is an allegorical reference to the last judgment. It has to be, because why else would he be surprised to find a man without a wedding garment? His slaves have rounded up people off the streets; therefore, no one should be wearing a wedding garment. Are we to imagine that all the others have wedding garments? From whence did they obtain them, especially in a burned-over city?

Interpreters have made various suggestions concerning the allegorical significance of the wedding garment that the man lacks. Already in antiquity, Irenaeus interpreted the wearing of a wedding garment as a person's being "adorned with the works of righteousness."[26] Modern interpreters have suggested that the wearing of such signifies any of the following: (1) as with Irenaeus, good works: "a life lived in conformity with the Christian Law,"[27] "evidential works of righteousness" (but not "works meriting salvation"),[28] "the deeds of Christian discipleship,"[29] or similar expressions concerning righteousness or moral rectitude:[30] (2) symbolism of membership within the redeemed community, that is, to be clothed in the garments of salvation,[31] or to live in a new mode of existence;[32] (3) repentance, which Jesus' opponents lack;[33] (4) "the resurrection body or its garment of glory, which were typically imagined to be luminous and angelic";[34] and (5) the "bad" invitees of 22:10 and the Jewish leaders (as the interpreter thinks they are) signified in 22:3-6.[35] In light of Matthew's rigorous emphasis on righteousness elsewhere (5:6, 10, 20; 6:33), the reference to the "bad" being brought in at 22:10, and the fact that other Matthean parables close with a note of judgment and the casting out of the bad (13:30, 41-43, 47-50), a moral meaning appears to be close at hand. Although

25. R. Bultmann, *HST* 175, 195; F. Beare, *Matthew*, 436; R. Gundry, *Matthew*, 167; J. Lambrecht, *Treasure*, 134; B. Scott, *Parable*, 163 (n. 11); R. Funk, *Five Gospels*, 235; W. D. Davies and D. C. Allison, *Matthew*, 3:194. This is considered a possibility by E. Schweizer, *Matthew*, 419.

26. Irenaeus, *Against Heresies* 4.36.6; text in *ANF* 1:517.

27. B. Smith, *Parables*, 206.

28. R. Gundry, *Matthew*, 439.

29. J. Donahue, *Parable*, 96.

30. W. Dawson, "Gate Crasher," 304-6; D. Hagner, *Matthew*, 631; I. Jones, *Matthean Parables*, 406; R. Funk, *Five Gospels*, 235.

31. J. Jeremias, *Parables*, 189.

32. E. Schweizer, *Matthew*, 420.

33. W. Michaelis, *Gleichnisse*, 162.

34. W. D. Davies and D. C. Allison, *Matthew*, 3:204.

35. D. Sim, "The Man without the Wedding Garment," 165-78.

both "bad and good" are brought into the fellowship of the church, there will be a final judgment. The passage thus serves a hortatory function for the Matthean community. Though the efforts of the church in its mission will be as inclusive as possible, those who are its members, or become so, are to seek that level of righteousness which is expected by Christ and his community.

The address "friend" (22:12, the vocative form ἑταῖρε), as in the Parable of the Workers in the Vineyard (20:13) and the address of Jesus to Judas in Gethsemane (26:50), is used where the person being addressed is insolent (as here) or deceitful (as in the case of Judas) and is being confronted and exposed.

At 22:13 the Greek term διάκονος ("servant" or, as above, "attendant") is used rather than the word δοῦλος ("slave" or "servant"), which is otherwise used in the parable (22:3, 4, 6, 8, 10). The former noun is used only three times by Matthew (20:26; 22:13; 23:11), but the latter thirty times. Although this could indicate Matthew's use of a source having the term,[36] it is more likely due to the fact that the servants spoken of here are table servants, who are typically designated by διάκονος.[37] The command to "cast . . . into the outer darkness" where "there will be weeping and gnashing of teeth" is typically Matthean. The expressions are found, respectively, at 8:12; 25:30 and 8:12; 13:42, 50; 24:51; 25:30; and Luke 13:28.[38]

22:14. This verse can be considered an addition by Matthew[39] by which he supplies a summary for the entire parable, even though it does not quite fit. Within the parable, to be sure, many are called, but none of those who enter the wedding hall at the end (22:10) can actually be designated as "chosen" (ἐκλεκτοί) persons. They have simply been rounded up. On the other hand, since one person without a proper garment is selected for dismissal (22:11-14), one could say in a loose sense that those remaining are "chosen." The verse is puzzling. At Revelation 17:14 the words "called," "elect," and "faithful" are full equivalents. In Matthew, in any case, the verse functions to say that one's status can never be taken for granted; it "is continually to be set afresh under the judgment and grace of God."[40]

According to various interpreters, a nucleus of the parable (minus the obvious additions, including 22:11-14 above all) can be attributed to Jesus of Nazareth.[41] If so, the suggestion has been made that it was spoken to certain Phari-

---

36. A. Cadoux, *Parables*, 65.

37. Alfons Weiser, "διακονέω," *TDNT* 1:302.

38. The expression is virtually identical to one at *1 Enoch* 10:4, where God commands the angel Raphael: "Bind Azaz'el hand and foot (and) throw him into the darkness"; quoted from *OTP* 1:17.

39. It has some similarity to a saying at 2 Esdr 8:3, but is not based upon it. For similar sayings, cf. 2 Esdr 9:15; *2 Bar.* 44:15.

40. Karl L. Schmidt, "κλητός," *TDNT* 3:495.

41. T. W. Manson, *Sayings*, 130; J. Jeremias, *Parables*, 69; E. Schweizer, *Matthew*, 420; A. Weiser, *Knechtsgleichnisse*, 64; H. Weder, *Gleichnisse*, 185-90; J. Lambrecht, *Treasure*,

sees, telling them that it is now "too late" for them to enter into the kingdom, and that the despised and ungodly are taking their place.[42]

Yet such a negative message hardly captures the positive note of the parable. It is fitting that an original parable of Jesus would have been spoken by Jesus to his opponents, but within the hearing of his disciples, to illumine his own ministry. Those who have heard the call of God through the scriptural traditions of Israel are rejecting the good news and gift of the kingdom when it is now being offered, and it is precisely those who had heretofore been outcasts and despised who are accepting the good news and the gift. In spite of the designs of those who reject Jesus and his message, the kingdom will come into being, and the despised are the ones who will be gathered into it.

Exposition

The story leads up to 22:9-10, the commission to universal mission. The mission of God through Christ and his church is to all people without regard for their socioeconomic status, their ethnic identity, their religious standing, or their presumed moral condition. The mission is, significantly, to both "bad and good," not the reverse. No one has problems with going to the "good" people; it is the "bad" that are avoided. But here the "bad" are mentioned first, so that they cannot be overlooked or avoided. Judgments are not to be made ahead of time as to who shall be part of the community of faith.

The history of Israel and the church is replete with disobedience to God's call and even with persecution of those sent as messengers from God. Much of that is illustrated allegorically within the parable. But in spite of all that, God has a desire to call people of all sorts into his kingdom and eternal fellowship. The parable illustrates both judgment and grace. Those who should be expected to accept are the ones who refuse to come, and they lose the opportunity they have. The unexpected ones are gathered in, for they are open to accepting the invitation of the slaves who come to them.

The ending of the parable should not be overlooked. It is too easy to view 22:1-10 as a summary of the history of salvation and leave the happy ending alone. But 22:11-14 reminds the reader or hearer that the invitation to the banquet, received in good faith, has implications beyond mere feasting and rejoicing with the king. The warning remains. One could still be excluded. Throughout one's life there should be constant and rigorous efforts toward the higher righteousness to which Christ calls his disciples (5:20).

130-31; J. Gnilka, *Matthäus*, 2:243; D. Hagner, *Matthew*, 629; W. D. Davies and D. C. Allison, *Matthew*, 3:195; U. Luz, *Matthäus*, 3:236.

42. J. Jeremias, *Parables*, 176-80. With similar views, but nuanced: J. Lambrecht, *Treasure*, 131.

Select Bibliography

Bauckham, Richard, "The Parable of the Royal Wedding Feast (Matthew 22:1-14) and the Parable of the Lame Man and the Blind Man *(Apocryphon of Ezekiel)*." *JBL* 115 (1996): 471-88.

Beare, Francis W. "The Parable of the Guests at the Banquet: A Sketch of the History of Its Interpretation." In *The Joy of Study: Papers on the New Testament and Related Subjects Presented to Honor Frederick Clifton Grant*, 1-7. Ed. Sherman E. Johnson. New York: Macmillan, 1951.

Boissard, Edmond. "Many Are Called, Few Are Chosen." *TD* 3 (1955): 46-50.

Cripps, K. R. J. "A Note on Matthew xxii.12." *ExpTim* 69 (1957-58): 30.

Dawson, W. Selwyn. "The Gate Crasher." *ExpTim* 85 (1974): 304-6.

Eichholz, Georg. "Vom grossen Abendmahl (Luk. 14,16-24) und von der königlichen Hochzeit (Matth. 22,1-14)." In his *Gleichnisse der Evangelien: Form, Überlieferung, Auslegung*, 126-47. Neukirchen-Vluyn: Neukirchener Verlag, 1971.

Hasler, Victor. "Die köningliche Hochzeit, Matth. 22,1-14." *TZ* 18 (1962): 25-35.

Lemcio, Eugene E. "The Parables of the Great Supper and the Wedding Feast: History, Redaction and Canon." *HBT* 8 (1986): 1-26.

Lewis, Agnes S. "Matthew xxii.4." *ExpTim* 24 (1912-13): 427.

Linnemann, Eta. "Überlegungen zur Parabel vom grossen Abendmahl, Lc 14,15-25 / Mt 22,1-14." *ZNW* 51 (1960): 246-55.

Martens, Allan W. "'Produce Fruit Worthy of Repentance': Parables of Judgment against Jewish Religious Leaders and the Nation (Matt 21:28-22:14, par.; Luke 13:6-9)." In *The Challenge of Jesus' Parables*, 151-76. Ed. Richard N. Longenecker. Grand Rapids: Wm. B. Eerdmans, 2000.

Matura, Thaddee. "Les invités à la noce royale (Mt 22,1-14)." *ASeign* 58 (1974): 16-27.

Merriman, E. H. "Matthew xxii.1-14." *ExpTim* 66 (1954-55): 61.

Meyer, Ben F. "Many (= All) Are Called, but Few (= Not All) Are Chosen." *NTS* 36 (1990): 89-97.

Musurillo, Herbert. "Many Are Called, but Few Are Chosen." *TS* 7 (1946): 583-89.

Rengstorf, Karl H. "Die Stadt der Mörder (Mt. 22:7)." In *Judentum, Urchristentum, Kirche: Festschrift für Joachim Jeremias*, 106-29. Ed. Walther Eltester. Berlin: Alfred Töpelmann, 1960.

Schottroff, Luise. "Das Gleichnis vom grossen Gastmahl in der Logienquelle." *EvT* 47 (1987): 192-211.

Selbie, William B. "The Parable of the Marriage Feast (Matthew xxii.1-4)." *ExpTim* 37 (1925-26): 266-69.

Sim, David C. "The Man without the Wedding Garment (Matthew 22:11-13)." *HeyJ* 31 (1990): 165-78.

————. "Matthew 22.13a and 1 Enoch 10.4a: A Case of Literary Dependence?" *JSNT* 47 (1992): 3-19.

Sutcliffe, Edmund F. "Many Are Called but Few Are Chosen." *ITQ* 28 (1961): 126-31.

Trilling, Wolfgang. "Zur Überlieferungsgeschichte des Gleichnisse vom Hochzeitsmahl Mt 22,1-14." *BZ* 4 (1960): 251-65.

Via, Dan O. "The Relationship of Form to Content in the Parable: The Wedding Feast." *Int* 25 (1971): 171-84.

Vögtle, Anton. "Die Einladung zum grossen Gastmahl und zum könligichen Hochzeitsmahl: Ein Paradigma für den Wandel des geschichtlichen Verständnishorizonts." In his *Das Evangelium und die Evangelien*, 171-218. Düsseldorf: Patmos, 1971.

Wainwright, Elaine. "God Wills to Invite All to the Banquet, Matthew 22:1-10." *IRM* 77 (1988): 185-93.

7.33. The Wicked Tenants, Mark 12:1-12// Matthew 21:33-46//Luke 20:9-19; *Thomas* 65–66

Mark 12:1-12

1And [Jesus] began to speak to them in parables. "A man planted a vineyard, set a hedge around it, dug a pit for the wine press, built a tower, let it out to tenants, and went into another country. 2At harvest time he sent a slave to the tenants in order to obtain from them some of the fruit of the vineyard. 3And they took him, beat him, and sent him away empty-handed.

4"Again he sent to them another slave, and they struck him on the head and treated him shamefully. 5And he sent another, and they killed him; and so with many others, some they beat and some they killed.

6"He had still one other, a beloved son; finally he sent him to them, saying, 'They will respect my son.'

7"But those tenants said to one another, 'This is the heir; come, let us kill him, and the inheritance will be ours.' 8And they took him, killed him, and cast him out of the vineyard.

9"What will the owner of the vineyard do? He will come and destroy the tenants, and give the vineyard to others.

10"Have you not read this passage in scripture:
'The very stone which the builders rejected has become the head of the corner; 11this was the Lord's doing, and it is marvelous in our eyes'?"

12And they tried to arrest him, but feared the multitude, for they perceived that he had told the parable against them; so they left him and went away.

Notes on the Text and Translation

12:1. Those to whom the vineyard is entrusted are γεωργοί, which is translated as "husbandmen" (KJV), "tenants" (RSV, NRSV), "vine-growers" (NEB), or "farmers" (NIV). The term essentially means one who tills the soil,[1] so it can refer to either one who owns land or one who works on it. The latter is meant here; therefore, "farmers" is not a good term to use. For consistency, the term is translated here as "tenants" throughout the pericope.

12:2. "At harvest time" (NIV) is the sense of the Greek τῷ καιρῷ (literally, "at the right time").[2] Matthew improves on Mark by having, "when harvest time drew near" (21:34).

12:4. Some manuscripts include stoning (λιθοβολήσαντες), as reflected in the KJV: "and at him they cast stones, and wounded him in the head. . . ." Superior texts do not contain the term, nor do modern versions (RSV, NEB, NIV, and NRSV) translate it. Stoning is included at Matthew 21:35, and it is probably from there that the term has been taken by later scribes.

Matthew 21:33-46

33 *[Jesus said,] "Hear another parable. There was a householder who planted a vineyard, set a hedge around it, dug a winepress in it, built a tower, let it out to tenants, and went into another country.* 34 *When harvest time drew near, he sent his slaves to the tenants, to obtain his fruit;* 35 *and the tenants took his slaves and beat one, killed another, and stoned another.*

36 *"Again he sent other slaves, more than the first; and they did the same to them.*

37 *"Finally he sent his son to them, saying, 'They will respect my son.'*

38 *"But when the tenants saw the son, they said among themselves, 'This is the heir; come, let us kill him and have his inheritance.'* 39 *And they took him and cast him out of the vineyard, and killed him.*

40 *"When therefore the owner of the vineyard comes, what will he do to those tenants?"*

41 *They said to him, "He will put the evildoers to a miserable death and lease the vineyard to other tenants who will give him the fruits in their seasons."*

42 *Jesus said to them,*

"Have you never read in the scriptures: 'The very stone which the builders rejected has become the head of the corner; this was the Lord's doing, and it is marvelous in our eyes'? 43 *Therefore I tell you, the kingdom of God will be taken away from you and given to a nation producing the fruits of it."*

45 *When the chief priests and the Pharisees heard his parables, they perceived*

1. BAGD 157.
2. Ibid., 395 (2, a).

that he was speaking about them. 46*But when they tried to arrest him, they feared the multitudes, because they considered him a prophet.*

Notes on the Text and Translation

21:33. On γεωργοί as "tenants," see Note on Mark 12:1.

21:34. The RSV and NRSV are very literalistic in translating the opening phrase as "when the season of fruit drew near." But "harvest time" expresses the meaning better in current English (cf. NIV: "when the harvest time approached").

21:39. The word order differs in the Western textual tradition (D, Old Latin, and other witnesses), so that the son is killed and then cast out. This is most likely due to assimilation to Mark 12:8. Superior texts have the son cast out and then killed.[3]

21:43. The term ἔθνος is translated here as "a people" (as in the NRSV), rather than as "a nation" (as in the KJV, RSV, and NIV). The latter term can be confused too easily with the concept of a nation-state or construed as a particular ethnic group. The people envisioned consists of both Jews and Gentiles within the Christian community. See Comment below.

21:44. The verse is missing in some highly regarded Greek manuscripts (D, 33), as well as in most Old Latin texts, Syriac Sinaiticus, and texts cited by Origen and Eusebius. On the other hand, it is included in other highly regarded Greek, Latin, and Syriac witnesses (ℵ, B, families 1 and 13; Old Latin, Vulgate, some Syriac, and Coptic texts). It is printed in brackets in the 27th edition of the Nestle-Aland Greek text (as well as in the 25th and 26th editions), meaning that there is considerable doubt about its authenticity. The editors of the United Bible Societies Greek text considered the verse "an accretion"[4] and placed it in double brackets in their printed edition (= the verse is a later addition to the text of Matthew's Gospel). The verse was included in the KJV, but it is relegated to a footnote in the RSV and NEB. The NIV and NRSV include it in the text; the NRSV renders it as follows: "The one who falls on this stone will be broken to pieces; and it will crush anyone on whom it falls."

The verse has no parallel in Mark but is found in virtually identical wording at Luke 20:18. In neither case is the verse a quotation from the OT, but it is a composite made up of words and phrases that appear in Isaiah 8:14-15 and Daniel 2:34-35, 44-45. The text-critical rule probably applies here that, when a reading is stable in one of the Synoptic Gospels (Luke in this case), but unstable in another (Matthew here), the latter is highly suspect.[5] The best arguments in

3. Cf. B. Metzger, *TCGNT* 57.
4. Ibid., 58.
5. The authenticity of the verse is maintained by J. Jeremias, *Parables,* 77 (n. 7); K. Snodgrass, *Parable of the Wicked Tenants,* 66-68; R. Gundry, *Matthew,* 430-31; D. Senior,

favor of its authenticity are three: (1) the verse appears in some very important witnesses; (2) the wording is not exactly like that of Luke 20:18; (3) its omission from some texts may be due to haplography (both 21:44 and 21:45 begin with καί ["and"], and so an eye skip could miss 21:44); and (4) one might expect an interpolation to appear more likely after 21:42, not 21:43. But the following speak more strongly against it: (1) its absence in early and diverse witnesses; and (2) since it is not in Mark, its presence would have to be due to composition by Matthew from the same composite texts that Luke used from the OT (independently of one another), Matthew's use of a common source, such as Q (which is unlikely), or Matthew's drawing upon a special Matthean tradition that happens to have identical wording in Luke.

Luke 20:9-19

9*And [Jesus] began to tell the people this parable: "A man planted a vineyard, let it out to tenants, and went away for a long time.* 10*At harvest time he sent a slave to the tenants, in order that they might give him some of the fruit of the vineyard. But the tenants beat him and sent him away empty-handed.*

11*"And he proceeded to send another slave. They also beat and treated him shamefully and sent him away empty-handed.*

12*"And he proceeded to send a third; this one they wounded and cast out.*

13*"Then the owner of the vineyard said, 'What shall I do? I will send my beloved son; perhaps they will respect him.'*

14*"But when the tenants saw him, they deliberated with one another, saying, 'This is the heir; let us kill him, in order that the inheritance may be ours.'* 15*And they cast him out of the vineyard and killed him.*

"What then will the owner of the vineyard do to them? 16*He will come and destroy these tenants, and give the vineyard to others."*

When they heard this, they said, "God forbid!"

17*But he looked at them and said, "What then is this that has been written:*

'The very stone which the builders rejected has become the head of the corner'?

18*"Every one who falls on that stone will be broken to pieces; but when it falls on any one it will crush him."*

19*The scribes and the chief priests tried to lay hands on him at that very hour, but they feared the people; for they perceived that he had told this parable against them.*

Matthew, 241. It is placed in brackets but commented on by D. Hagner, *Matthew*, 616-17, 623. It is rejected by A. Jülicher, *Gleichnisreden*, 2:401; W. Allen, *Matthew*, 233; A. McNeile, *Matthew*, 313; A. Plummer, *Matthew*, 299; C. Carlston, *Parables*, 45 (n. 28); E. Schweizer, *Matthew*, 415; R. Smith, *Matthew*, 254; and W. D. Davies and D. Allison, *Matthew*, 3:175, 186 (n. 65).

Notes on the Text and Translation

20:9. On γεωργοί as "tenants," see Note on Mark 12:1.

20:10. "At harvest time" translates the Greek expression καιρῷ. See Note on Mark 12:2.

The verse has a purpose clause using the future indicative δώσουσιν ("in order that they might give") rather than the more common (and proper, by classical standards) aorist subjunctive δῶσιν. Some texts have the latter. But superior texts have the former, and the form is attested elsewhere in the NT.[6]

20:14. Some very important Greek witnesses read δεῦτε ἀποκτείνωμεν αὐτόν ("come, let us kill him"), exactly as do Mark 12:7 and Matthew 21:38. Other very important witnesses omit δυῖτε ("come"). Its presence is likely due to scribal assimilation.

Gospel of Thomas 65–66

He [= Jesus] said, "There was a good man who owned a vineyard. He leased it to tenant farmers so that they might work it and he might collect the produce from them. He sent his servant so that the tenants might give him the produce of the vineyard. They seized his servant and beat him, all but killing him. The servant went back and told his master. The master said, 'Perhaps he did not recognize them.' He sent another servant. The tenants beat this one as well. Then the owner sent his son and said, 'Perhaps they will show respect to my son.' Because the tenants knew that it was he who was the heir to the vineyard, they seized him and killed him. Let him who has ears hear."

Jesus said: "Show me the stone that the builders have rejected. That one is the cornerstone."[7]

General Comments on the Texts

As indicated, the parable appears not only in all three Synoptic Gospels but also in the *Gospel of Thomas*. As usual, the version in the *Gospel of Thomas* has no narrative setting. In the Synoptic Gospels the telling of the parable is set in Jerusalem. Mark and Luke have it immediately after the conflict story on the Question of Authority (Mark 11:27-33//Luke 20:1-8), and Matthew has it near at hand; only one brief pericope appears between the Question of Authority (21:23-27) and the Wicked Tenants, namely, the Parable of the Two Sons (21:28-32). According to Mark, Jesus spoke the parable within the temple to the chief priests, scribes, and elders in the hearing of the crowd. Matthew has much the same setting but omits the scribes and adds the Pharisees (21:23, 45). Ac-

6. BDF 186-87 (#369, 2).
7. Quoted from *NHLE* 134.

cording to Luke, Jesus spoke the parable to the people in the hearing of the chief priests, scribes, and elders (Luke 20:1, 9, 19). For all three evangelists, the unit is a "parable" (Mark 12:1; Matt 21:33; Luke 20:9).

The versions of the parable in Matthew and Luke are usually considered to be literarily dependent on that in Mark. However, there are three other proposals:

(1) It has been contended that, in addition to Mark's version, a Q version stands behind the other two Synoptic Gospels.[8] The main argument is that there are similarities between Matthew 21:39, 44//Luke 20:15, 18 over against Mark. But the first of these verses can be accounted for as an easy, even obvious, step in allegorizing (in both cases) of material taken from Mark 12:8; and the second collapses on the basis of textual criticism (see above).

(2) It has been suggested that the earliest of all versions existed in the special Matthean tradition, which Matthew combined with materials from Mark and Q.[9] This rests on a number of observations, among them the fact that Matthew alone contains the saying of Jesus in 21:43. This view (Mark + Q + M = Matthew) is not persuasive. The Matthean version can be accounted for on the basis of Matthew's use of Mark, plus redactional, allegorical elaborations. The saying in 21:43, for example, could have been composed by Matthew and added to Markan material.

(3) It has been held that a version of the parable existed in the special Lukan tradition, which Luke conflated with material from Mark.[10] That such a version existed is plausible, but it is not certain. Three main points stand in favor of such a view, but none is persuasive. First, the account in Luke contains significant differences from Mark's (the number of sendings, the simplicity of the opening lines, etc.). But these can be considered alterations by the evangelist himself. Second, Luke's account contains a Hebraism twice (the use of προστίθημι, "to proceed to," followed by an infinitive, 20:11, 12). But that expression is found elsewhere and can be attributed to Lukan style (cf. 19:11; Acts 12:3). Finally, there is the omission of words paralleled in Mark 12:11, on the one hand, and the addition of 20:18, on the other. But a theory of a Lukan source is not a prerequisite for these differences. In the end, it can be said that, attractive as the possibility of an independent Lukan version is, the grounds for its existence are insufficient.[11]

Whether the version in the *Gospel of Thomas* is dependent upon one or more of the Synoptic versions is debated. This question will be taken up later.

8. A. Cadoux, *Parables*, 40-41.

9. K. Snodgrass, *Parable of the Wicked Tenants*, 56-71.

10. Tim Schramm, *Der Markus-Stoff bei Lukas: Eine literarkritische und redaktions-geschichtliche Untersuchung*, SNTSMS 14 (Cambridge: Cambridge University Press, 1971), 154-67. On p. 164 Schramm limits traces of the special tradition to Luke 20:9-15a. On pp. 150-51 he includes 20:17b-18 as special to Luke as well.

11. Cf. C. Carlston, *Parables*, 78-79; and J. Fitzmyer, *Luke*, 1278, for the same conclusion.

The four versions differ widely in regard to a number of details. These are summarized in the Table 4, which focuses on three main areas of difference: (1) the number of sendings of emissaries, the identity of the persons who are sent by the owner of the vineyard, and their fate; (2) the landowner's reaction to what happens to his emissaries; and (3) the closing comment of Jesus. Some words are in bold print, signifying features that make a version distinctive in additional ways.

Features that are distinctive of each of the Synoptic versions will be taken up below. At this point comment is made that applies to the parable in two or more versions.

In all three Synoptic versions the parable is rich in allegorical detail.[12] The various items and their referents are easily identified:

1. The vineyard. The opening lines of the versions in the Gospels of Mark and Matthew recall the Song of the Vineyard of Isaiah 5:1-7 (a feature that is all but lacking in Luke 20:9; "a man planted a vineyard" is all that is there, and it is totally lacking in the *Gos. Thom.* 65). Several words and phrases in the parable appear to be drawn directly from the LXX version of Isaiah.[13] Furthermore, vineyard imagery appears elsewhere in OT and rabbinic literature to symbolize Israel.[14]

God is portrayed in Isaiah 5:1-7 as one who has planted and cared for a vineyard, doing all that one could possibly do to make it yield a good crop. But the vineyard failed. The only recourse of the owner is to destroy it. The Isaiah passage closes by identifying the vineyard as "the house of Israel" and the vines as "the people of Judah." Their failure is a lack of justice and righteousness.

Recalling the Song of the Vineyard prompts immediately the question about a referent in the parable. One interpreter has suggested that the vineyard represents the kingdom of God, for how could the nation of Israel be taken away from its caretakers and be granted to others?[15] It should be seen, however, that while in the Isaiah text the owner's (= God's) problem is with the *vineyard,*

12. That the parable is not allegorical, but codifies the seizure of land and the futility of rebellion — and thereby questions those activities — is maintained by W. Herzog, *Parables,* 98-113. According to J. Hester, "Socio-rhetorical Criticism," 27-57, the allegorical detail covers up an original parable that portrays revolt, and Jesus then asks the audience "how they feel about it" (p. 55). Against the assumption of Herzog and Hester that the tenants are to be understood as impoverished peasants, for they can be commercial farmers of considerable means, cf. C. Evans, "Jesus' Parable of the Tenant Farmers," 65-83. All of the allegorical details can be attested as current in Jewish exegetical traditions prior to A.D. 70, according to J. de Moor, "The Targumic Background of Mark 12:1-12," 63-80.

13. These include the following phrases from Isaiah 5:2: φραγμὸν περιέθηκα ("set a hedge around it"), ἐφύτευσα ἄμπελον ("planted a vineyard"), ᾠκοδόμησα πύργον ("built a watchtower"), and προλήνιον ὤρυξα ("dug a pit").

14. Cf. Ps 80:8-13; Jer 2:21 and other texts cited by Johannes Behm, "ἄμπελος," *TDNT* 1:342.

15. W. Oesterley, *Parables,* 120.

Table 4
The Sendings

Mark	Matthew	Luke	*Thomas*
1. One slave, beaten	1. Slaves, one beaten, one killed, one stoned	1. One slave, beaten	1. One slave, beaten
2. Another slave, wounded in head, mistreated	2. More slaves, more than before, same outcome	2. Another slave, beaten	2. Another slave, beaten
3. Another slave, killed		3. A third slave, wounded and cast out	
4. Many others, some beaten, some killed			
5. **Beloved** son, **killed**, **cast out**	3. Son, cast out, killed	4. **Beloved** son, cast out, killed	3. Son (heir), killed

Responses of the Landowner

Mark	Matthew	Luke	*Thomas*
1. **Destroy** tenants	1. **Kill** tenants	1. **Destroy** tenants	None given
2. **Give** the vineyard to others	2. **Let out** the vineyard to others **who will render fruits**	2. **Give** the vineyard to others	

Comment by Jesus

Mark	Matthew	Luke	*Thomas*
1. Ps 118:22-23	1. Ps 118:22-23	1. Ps 118:22	1. Paraphrase of Ps 118:22
	2. **The kingdom taken, given to another**		

the owner's problem in the parable is with the *tenants* who are supposed to care for the vineyard. This subtle shift allows the vineyard to continue to refer to the Jewish people (as in Isaiah); and it also means that the vineyard is the object of God's continuing care. God as owner of the vineyard does not come to destroy the vineyard, and God as owner does not plant a new vineyard (signifying Christian supersessionism). It is the tenants, the leadership of the people of God, that are the problem. When the tenants do not fulfill their obligations, they have to be replaced.

2. The owner of the vineyard. On the basis of the Isaiah passage and the content of the parable itself, the owner is God.

3. The slaves. The slaves that are sent and mistreated by beatings, stonings, and killings (not that all three elements are present in all three Synoptic Gospels) are the prophets.[16] NT passages that allude to such are the Q passages of Luke 11:49//Matthew 23:34 and Luke 13:34//Matthew 23:37, and Hebrews 11:37. These are all based on information derived from the OT, in which prophets and their messages are rejected (2 Chron 24:19; Jer 7:25-26; 25:4), beaten (Jer 20:2), and killed (Neh 9:26; Jer 26:21-23).

4. The tenants. Those to whom the vineyard is entrusted, the tenants, are usually designated the leaders of Israel in Jerusalem:[17] the chief priests, scribes, and elders (Mark 11:27; 12:12). It is not likely that they represent all Israel (the Jewish people).[18]

5. The son. One interpreter has maintained that the son has no "specifiable referent."[19] But surely within the post-Easter Gospels the "son" (Matt 21:37; *Gos. Thom.* 65) or "beloved son" (Mark 12:6; Luke 20:13) represents Jesus, as virtually all interpreters have asserted.[20] The term "beloved son" (Greek: υἱὸς ἀγαπητός) appears elsewhere in the Synoptic tradition to refer to Jesus specifically (Mark 1:11//Matt 3:17//Luke 3:22; Mark 9:7//Matt 12:18//Luke 9:35), and never to anyone else.

Within the preaching of the earthly Jesus, however, the "son" would not necessarily have the same referent. Some interpreters have claimed that the term would have referred to John the Baptist.[21] Such an interpretation is thought to have the advantage of reducing the allegorical character of the parable — making it less christological and eliminating a supersessionist interpreta-

16. A. Weiser, *Knechtsgleichnisse,* 51-57.

17. C. H. Dodd, *Parables,* 98; W. Oesterley, *Parables,* 119; J. Jeremias, *Parables,* 70; J. Crossan, *Parables,* 91; R. Gundry, *Mark,* 684.

18. Contra Wolfgang Hackenberg, "γεωργός," *EDNT* 1:246. According to C. Carlston, *Parables,* 185, the tenants represent Israel by the time the story ends, but that is not so.

19. A. Milavec, "A Fresh Analysis of the Parable of the Wicked Husbandmen in Light of Jewish-Christian Dialogue," 104.

20. C. H. Dodd, *Parables,* 99-100; J. Jeremias, *Parables,* 70; V. Taylor, *Mark,* 472, and too many other commentaries to mention. For an unpersuasive attempt to reject this view, cf. Jane E. Newell and Raymond R. Newell, "The Parable of the Wicked Tenants," 226-37; they understand the parable as directed against Zealots (= the wicked tenants) who seek to take the land of Israel by force and whose end will be death.

21. M. Lowe, "From the Parable of the Vineyard to a Pre-Synoptic Source," 257; D. Stern, "Jesus' Parables from the Perspective of Rabbinic Literature," 65.

tion of it — and rendering it more likely authentic. The primary basis for the proposal is that the passage follows immediately upon Jesus' reference to John in Mark 11:27-33. But the suggestion is far from persuasive on several grounds: (1) the well-known facts about the death of John do not correspond with those of this text; he was killed by Herod Antipas (Mark 6:14-29), not the Jewish officials mentioned at the close of the parable; (2) the son who is killed is an "heir" to the vineyard (Mark 12:7 par.), which appears to have christological significance, and it is difficult to see how John could be spoken of in such a manner; (3) the casting of the son out of the vineyard has no referent in the case of John, but does in the case of Jesus; and (4) although the use of Psalm 118:22-23 may not be integral to the original parable, its use is surely christological. More will be said on the identity of the son below.

6. The punishment. This element is missing in the *Gospel of Thomas* version, but it is present in all Synoptic versions. Those punished are the tenants, the leadership of the people. The vineyard itself, however, is not destroyed (contra Isa 5:5-6). The punishment is due to the leadership's rejection of the prophets and even the son, whom God had sent.

7. The "others." Some interpreters have claimed that the "others" to whom the vineyard will be given are the "Gentiles";[22] others suggest, more precisely, the "gentile church"[23] or "the early Christian community."[24] However, if the vineyard is Israel, it is difficult to see how it could be given to Gentiles, the gentile church, or the Christian community. It is more fitting that the "others" are a new or renewed leadership other than the Jerusalem leaders. If the parable is authentic, that could consist of the Twelve,[25] Jesus and the Twelve,[26] or at least a new leadership that God shall raise up that accepts the proclamation of Jesus. On the other hand, if the parable is an early Christian composition, the apostolic leadership of the church could be envisioned here.

Since the parable is allegorical in so many of its details, the question of its authenticity comes to the fore immediately. According to Adolf Jülicher, it is an allegory constructed by the early church, "a product of primitive Christian theology," reflecting upon the death of Jesus.[27] Rudolf Bultmann concluded that it is "a community product" (not from Jesus), which is intelligible only as an allegory.[28] It must be admitted that, since the parable sets forth in outline the

---

22. Irenaeus, *Against Heresies* 4.36.2 [text in *ANF* 1:515]; John Chrysostom, *Homilies on the Gospel of Matthew* 68.1 [text in *NPNF* 10:415]; E. Schweizer, *Mark,* 241; J. Crossan, *Parables,* 91; Morna D. Hooker, *A Commentary on the Gospel according to St. Mark,* BNTC (London: A. & C. Black, 1991), 276; R. Funk, *Five Gospels,* 101.

23. J. Jeremias, *Parables,* 70. On p. 76, however, Jeremias identifies them as the poor.

24. J. Donahue, Parable, 56.

25. A. Milavec, "A Fresh Analysis of the Parable of the Wicked Husbandmen," 107.

26. R. Gundry, *Mark,* 688-89.

27. A. Jülicher, *Gleichnisreden,* 2:406.

28. R. Bultmann, *HST* 177; cf. p. 205.

Christian drama of salvation, its authenticity is highly suspect, as various other interpreters have held.[29] All that notwithstanding, the authenticity of the parable in a reduced, less allegorized form has been accepted by a wide range of interpreters whose perspectives and methodologies differ from one another very widely.[30] Here one should notice that the most allegorical of all the parables of Jesus is being considered, and various interpreters across the spectrum have concluded that it is authentic at its core.

It can be granted that there have been allegorical elaborations in the Synoptic texts. But when these texts are reduced to their essentials and compared with that in the *Gospel of Thomas,* a basic four-part structure appears that can be interpreted without reference to the entire Christian history of salvation; allegorical elements remain, but they fit as understandable referents within the ministry of Jesus prior to his crucifixion:

(1) The owner of the vineyard (= God) leases a vineyard (= Israel) to tenants (= Israel's leaders, the priests, scribes, and elders, i.e., the Sanhedrin) and expects produce; the imagery is based on Isaiah 5:1-7. Furthermore, the motif of a king or wealthy man leaving servants or slaves in charge while away is a popular one in the parables of Jesus, as well as in rabbinic parables. It appears in four other parables of Jesus besides this one (although it is conspicuously lacking in the Wicked Tenants of the *Gospel of Thomas* [logia 65-66]) — the Waiting Slaves (Mark 13:34-37//Luke 12:35-38), the Faithful and Wise Slave (Matt 24:45-51//Luke 12:42-46), the Talents (Matt 25:14-30), and the Pounds (Luke 19:12-27). Three known rabbinic parables, all attributed to rabbis from times later than Jesus, share the same theme. These are indicated in the Exegetical Commentary on the Parable of the Waiting Slaves.

(2) The owner of the vineyard sends his slaves (= the prophets) to gather fruits, but they are rejected. The popular "rule of three" could have been employed, which would require the sending of one slave and then two others, fol-

29. Erich Klostermann, *Das Markusevangelium,* 2d ed., HNT (Tübingen, 1926), 135; C. Montefiore, *Synoptic Gospels,* 1:273-75; W. Kümmel, "Das Gleichnis von den bösen Weingärtnern," 207-17; and C. Carlston, *Parables,* 181-88. That the parable is a community product ("Gemeindebildung") is held as a possibility by U. Luz, *Matthäus,* 3:218-20.

30. C. H. Dodd, *Parables,* 96-102; A. Cadoux, *Parables,* 41; J. Jeremias, *Parables,* 72-73; V. Taylor, *Mark,* 472; D. Via, *Parables,* 134; X. Léon-Dufour, "La parabole des vignerons homicides," 365-96; M. Hengel, "Das Gleichnis von den Weingartnern," 1-39; J. Crossan, *Parables,* 86-96; A. Weiser, *Knechtsgleichnisse,* 50-51; P. Perkins, *Parables,* 194; Hans-Josef Klauck, *Allegorie und Allegorese in synoptischen Gleichnistexten,* NTAbh 13 (Münster: Aschendorff, 1978), 308-9; J. Lambrecht, *Astonished,* 129-31; idem, *Treasure,* 113-15; Craig L. Blomberg, *Interpreting the Parables* (Downers Grove, Ill.: InterVarsity Press, 1990), 251; T. Schmeller, "Der Erbe des Weinbergs," 183-201; C. Evans, "Jesus' Parable of the Tenant Farmers," 65-83; E. Horne, "Parable of the Tenants," 113. According to R. Funk, *Five Gospels,* 101, "the Fellows of the [Jesus] Seminar were of the opinion that a version of this parable, without allegorical overtones, could be traced to Jesus." The text is printed in gray (= not spoken by Jesus, but its ideas are close to his own) in that volume.

lowed by the sending of the son (as in Luke), or (more likely) the sending of one slave, then another, followed by the son (as in the *Gospel of Thomas*).

(3) The owner sends his son (= Jesus), who is rejected, treated shamefully, and killed. This need be only an implicit Christology. Since his baptism by John, Jesus has a sense of filial relationship to God; his vocation is to continue the work of the prophets and bring finality to it all.

(4) New tenants (= those who will lead Israel aright, rather than the Sanhedrin) are necessary. The vineyard must and will surely be given to them and their care.

That a four-part structured parable such as this could have originated with Jesus is plausible. The sending of the slaves builds up to a climax, the sending of the son. A hearer of the parable would not have to be hearing the final sending as the sending of the Son of God, the Messiah. C. H. Dodd is correct in saying that "a climax of iniquity is demanded by the plot of the story," and "it is the logic of the story, and not any theological motive, that has introduced this figure."[31] At the same time, if the parable was told in Jerusalem and in the presence of leading figures of the Sanhedrin, Jesus could well have sensed that his own death was inevitable. By means of the parable, Jesus would then have pronounced judgment upon the present leadership, which rejects him as its predecessors had rejected the prophets; and standing at the end of the long line of prophetic figures, who were rejected, he could anticipate the rejection of himself as God's final envoy.

There are features of the story that seem bizarre, even absurd. The most absurd is that the owner of the vineyard would send his son alone after the tenants had mistreated some of his servants (and had even killed some others, according to Mark and Matthew). Another feature is the seeming stupidity of the tenants, who think that they can acquire the vineyard by killing the heir. Are not these absurdities proof enough that the parable is based on the drama of Christian history? They are not. Those elements are characteristic of good storytelling. Moreover, they are actually quite plausible in an ancient setting. In regard to the first point, it is not clear that the son was sent alone; he could have been accompanied by a retinue. But whether alone or with others, he would have been sent to get the matter cleared up once and for all; the sending of servants has not sufficed, so it is time to send someone with more authority. And in regard to the second point, the tenants could have assumed one of two possibilities: (1) the absentee owner of the vineyard had died, and his son (the "heir") had come to claim it; therefore, if they killed him, the land would be ownerless, and they could possess it;[32] or (2) the absentee landowner had as-

---

31. C. H. Dodd, *Parables*, 100-101.

32. J. Jeremias, *Parables*, 75-76; R. Gundry, *Mark*, 687; Bruce Malina and Richard L. Rohrbaugh, *Social Science Commentary on the Synoptic Gospels* (Minneapolis: Fortress Press, 1992), 255.

signed the land to his "heir," and so the tenants could wrest it from the son by killing him.[33]

Up to this point nothing has been said about the use of Psalm 118:22-23 (or 118:22 alone in Luke, and only a paraphrase of 118:22 in *Gos. Thom.* 66). Is it integral to the parable?[34] Four considerations weigh against its being original with the parable itself: (1) the narration surely does not require it as an ending; the parable ends properly with the punishment of the evil tenants by the landowner; (2) the use of these lines from the psalm turn the parable from being a pronouncement of judgment upon the leaders of the Sanhedrin into a declaration of the divine vindication of Jesus; (3) the lines from the psalm were most likely attached to the parable not only to allude to the resurrection of Jesus but to give it a scriptural proof as well; and (4) these verses from the Psalms were commonly used in early Christian proclamation (Acts 4:11 and 1 Peter 2:6-8).[35] The wording in the canonical Gospels is exactly that of the LXX (Ps 117:22-23).

The view that the psalm verses must have been attached to the parable from the beginning by Jesus, because in a Semitic context the reference to the rejection of the "son" (בֵּן, *ben*) would immediately suggest the rejection of a "stone" (אֶבֶן, *'eben*) — and hence the recollection and use of the psalm — demands too much subtlety on the part of both the composer and the first hearers of the parable.[36] Moreover, assuming that Jesus spoke Aramaic, the actual term for "son" in that language (בַּר, *bar*) would not suggest the word for "stone" (אֶבֶן, *'eben*, in both Hebrew and Aramaic) in any case.

The connection between the parable and the psalm verses is not "son" and "stone." The connection can be accounted for in light of parallel acts: the rejecting of the son and the rejecting of the stone (as is the case also in Acts 4:10-11).[37] The use of Psalm 118:22-23 is a proof from Scripture that the re-

---

33. J. Derrett, "The Parable of the Wicked Vinedressers," 306.

34. That the quotation is an addition to the parable is claimed by many, including A. Jülicher, *Gleichnisreden,* 2:405; R. Bultmann, *HST* 177; C. H. Dodd, *Parables,* 99; J. Jeremias, *Parables,* 73-74; C. Carlston, *Parables,* 180-81; J. Donahue, *Parable,* 53; and J. Lambrecht, *Treasure,* 110. V. Taylor, *Mark,* 473, 476-77, says that Mark has appended it here, although Jesus may have used the psalm to attack authorities. That the quotation is integral to the parable is maintained by R. Gundry, *Mark,* 690.

35. It is not clear that Ps 118:22-23 ever had messianic significance prior to the NT era. According to Str-B 1:876, it had a messianic meaning in Rashi's commentary on Micah 5:1, but Rashi is very late (A.D. 1040-1105). According to S. Lachs, *Rabbinic Commentary,* 355, the Messiah is compared to a stone in *Esth. Rab.* 3:1. But that document is dated from ca. A.D. 500, according to Herman L. Strack and Günter Stemberger, *Introduction to the Talmud and Midrash* (Edinburgh: T. & T. Clark, 1991), 346.

36. The research is covered comprehensively by K. Snodgrass, *Parable of the Wicked Tenants,* 63, 113-18, who accepts the wordplay thesis.

37. Barnabas Lindars, *New Testament Apologetic: The Doctrinal Significance of the Old Testament Quotations* (Philadelphia: Westminster Press, 1961), 170, says regarding the

jected son (= Jesus) would become the cornerstone of the new temple (the people of God).

The use of the psalm at this point could have arisen from its wider use in early Christianity. In 1975-76 the hill of Calvary was uncovered, exposing what had been a hill thirteen meters high alongside what had been a stone quarry from the eighth or seventh century B.C. By the first century A.D., however, the hill and quarry had been transformed into a refuse dump and place for executions and burials.[38] If in fact Golgotha was known to be a rejected stone quarry, it is possible that early Christians came there, made the association between the rejected stone of the quarry and Jesus, and recited Psalm 118:22-23.[39]

The parable clearly begins at Mark 12:1b//Matthew 21:33b//Luke 20:9b. But where does it end? As indicated, the psalm quotation is probably not a part of the original. Some interpreters suggest that the parable would have ended with the narration of the killing of the son (Mark 12:8//Matt 21:32//Luke 20:15a) with no further ado.[40] Others say that the parable ends with the question at Mark 12:9a//Matthew 21:40//Luke 20:15.[41] Still others would include the answer (Mark 12:9b//Luke 20:16a) that Jesus gives to his own question[42] (but which Matthew has taken from the mouth of Jesus and put into the mouth of his hearers [21:41], plus further elaboration). Strictly speaking, if a parable consists of narration alone — which it does in the narrowest sense — the parable ends without the questions and answers. On the other hand, the fact that rhetorical questions and answers appear frequently in rabbinic parables[43] encourages the conclusion that the parable was transmitted with such an ending. Rhetorical questions and answers are by no means out of place in the parables of Jesus (cf. the endings to the Parables of the Good Samaritan, Luke 10:36-37; the Two Sons, Matt 21:31; and the Servant at Duty, Luke 17:9), so the question

---

use of Ps 118:22-23, "The emphasis falls on the element of *rejection*" (emphasis his). Another proposal, probably less likely, is that the connection is to be found in the catchwords between Isa 5:1-2 and Ps 118, the building of a tower and the stone rejected by the builders; cf. G. J. Brooke, "4Q500 1 and the Use of Scripture," 287-89.

38. Christos Katsimbinis, "The Uncovering of the Eastern Side of the Hill of Calvary," *SBF* 27 (1977): 197-208. Photos are printed in Gaalyah Cornfeld, *The Historical Jesus: A Scholarly View of the Man and His World* (New York: Macmillan, 1982), 202, and a description of the site is provided on pp. 209-10.

39. The suggestion is put forth by James H. Charlesworth, *Jesus within Judaism: New Light from Exciting Archaeological Discoveries* (New York: Doubleday, 1988), 123-25.

40. J. Jeremias, *Parables,* 74; C. Carlston, *Parables,* 180; B. Scott, *Parable,* 248.

41. R. Bultmann, *HST* 177; C. H. Dodd, *Parables,* 97; B. Smith, *Parables,* 224; V. Taylor, *Mark,* 476.

42. J. Donahue, *Parable,* 53-56; J. Lambrecht, *Treasure,* 111-12.

43. For various examples, plus the claim that some 12 percent of known rabbinic parables contain rhetorical questions and answers, cf. Harvey K. McArthur and Robert M. Johnston, *They Also Taught in Parables: Rabbinic Parables from the First Centuries of the Christian Era* (Grand Rapids: Zondervan, 1990), 31, 47, 69, 90, 125-27.

and answer need not be out of place here either. They could indeed have come appended to the parable as part of a larger unit based on an actual pronouncement of Jesus in the presence of his adversaries.

The question whether the version in the *Gospel of Thomas* is independent in origin has not received an agreed-on answer. As can be expected, some interpreters have contended that it is altogether independent in origin;[44] others have concluded that it is dependent on at least one of the Synoptic accounts.[45] The primary reason for claiming independence (in addition to a more general view of the independence of the *Gospel of Thomas* as a whole) is that the account is simpler and less allegorical than the Synoptic accounts. But there are weighty reasons to conclude that in this case dependence is apparent. Its simplicity (sending of only two servants, then the son) can be due to simplifying and streamlining disparate, disagreeing sources, and its less allegorical character (no clear allusion to Isa 5:1-2) could be modeled on Luke 20:9.

Within the parable itself there are elements that appear to show dependence. First, the sending of the first servant presupposes that the owner of the vineyard is away, but that has not been narrated (contra the Synoptic accounts); it is simply taken for granted, presupposing knowledge of a more extensive account. Second, there are two verbal similarities between the parable in the *Gospel of Thomas* and Luke's Gospel. The expression "that the tenants might give him [the slave] the produce of the vineyard" appears to be dependent on Luke 20:10 ("that they [the tenants] should give him some of the fruit of the vineyard"), in contrast to the wording of Mark and Matthew; and the clause "perhaps they will show respect to my son" in the *Gospel of Thomas* 65 appears to be dependent on Luke 20:13 ("perhaps they will respect him [= my son]"). The Greek word ἴσως ("perhaps") appears only here in the entire NT (and only once

---

44. J. Jeremias, *Parables*, 24, 70-72; Gilles Quispel, "The Gospel of Thomas and the New Testament," *VC* 11 (1957): 205-6; Hugh Montefiore, "A Comparison of the Parables of the Gospel according to Thomas and of the Synoptic Gospels," in *Thomas and the Evangelists*, by H. E. W. Turner and H. Montefiore, SBT 35 (Naperville: Alec R. Allenson, 1962), 62-63; Jacques-É. Ménard, *L'Evangile selon Thomas*, NHS 5 (Leiden: E. J. Brill, 1975), 167; John D. Crossan, "The Parable of the Wicked Husbandmen," 461; idem, *Parables*, 91-96; Helmut Koester, "Three Thomas Parables," in *The New Testament and Gnosis: Essays in Honor of Robert McL. Wilson*, ed. A. H. B. Logan and A. J. M. Wedderburn (Edinburgh: T. & T. Clark, 1983), 199-200; W. G. Morrice, "The Parable of the Tenants and the Gospel of Thomas," 104-7; and J. Fitzmyer, *Luke*, 1280.

45. Robert M. Grant and David N. Freedman, *The Secret Sayings of Jesus* (Garden City, N.Y.: Doubleday, 1960), 172; Wolfgang Schrage, *Das Verhältnis des Thomas-Evangelium zur syoptischen Tradition und zu den koptischen Evangelienübersetzungen*, BZNW 29 (Berlin: Alfred Töpelmann, 1964), 137-45; K. Snodgrass, "The Parable of the Wicked Husbandmen," 142-44; idem, *The Parable of the Wicked Tenants*, 52-54; Michael Fieger, *Das Thomasevangelium: Einleitung Kommentar und Systematik*, NTAbh 22 (Münster: Aschendorff, 1991), 188-94.

in the LXX, 1 Sam 25:21); its equivalent in the *Gospel of Thomas* 65 has the appearance of dependence on Luke.

Perhaps more important is the Synoptic-like sequence of logia 65 and 66. As indicated above, the use of Psalm 118:22-23 is secondary to the parable, an addition provided by interpreters, perhaps Mark himself. The location of logion 66 (alluding to Ps 118:22) is best explained as due to dependence on the Synoptic accounts in which the connection has already been established. Furthermore, logion 66 is the only passage in the *Gospel of Thomas* composed of OT material.[46] But it is not likely to have been composed on the basis of direct usage of the OT (which Gnostics generally rejected). It is more likely to have been composed out of the Synoptic materials at hand. Moreover, in Gnostic fashion, it has been transformed so that there are no markers to identify it as an OT quotation (it is called "Scripture" in Mark 12:10//Matt 21:42; it is introduced by "this that has been written" at Luke 20:17). The explanation that fits best is that logion 65 is a mosaic composed from the Synoptic accounts; and that both the location and wording of logion 66 are dependent on the canonical Gospels, not from similar (and coincidental) editing for its location, and not from direct use of the OT for its content. As such, the parable sets forth a gnostic point of view: the son represents the living Jesus (the light, cf. logion 77), who comes into the material world to gather the fruits of the vineyard, thereby rekindling within Gnostics remembrance of their belonging to the realm of light and being rejected by the people of the world (the tenants). The parable breaks off there with the admonition to the Gnostic, "Let him who has ears hear."[47]

As often indicated by interpreters, the basic details of the parable reflect the realities of first-century Palestine. That a landowner would plant a vineyard, leave it in the care of tenants, and go abroad would not be unusual. Further, it would not be unusual for the rights of the landowner, the tenants, and the son as heir to be disputed with the passing of time. According to J. N. D. Derrett, the possession of the vineyard by the tenants would increase the presumption of ownership more and more as the years passed. By the fourth year the landowner would have had to assert his authority or perhaps suffer loss of the land to those who possessed it. That accounts for the sending of his son.[48] It is not necessary, however, to understand the various sendings as annual events,

---

46. This becomes apparent from examining the section called "Scriptural Parallels and Echoes," in *The Gospel according to Thomas: Coptic Text Established and Translated*, by A. Guillaumont et al. (New York: Harper & Brothers, 1959), 59-62. Six logia (3, 21, 25, 37, 66, and 111) are listed as having OT parallels and echoes. Aside from logion 66, however, the echoes are very faint and can be accounted for from materials in the NT or from sayings attributed to Jesus that have some vague commonality to OT imagery. No quotations are cited from the OT.

47. Cf. M. Fieger, *Das Thomasevangelium*, 193-94.

48. J. Derrett, "The Parable of the Wicked Vinedressers," 296-306.

as Derrett does. According to traditional Jewish law, the fruit is not to be eaten for the first three years; in the fourth year it is to be offered to the Lord; and only in the fifth year is it to be enjoyed (Lev 19:23-25). The series of sendings may therefore all occur in the fourth or even fifth year. This makes the action of the tenants against the heir even more credible. In their view, any reassertion of authority and claim by the landowner at this late date must be denied, and that is carried out by their killing of his son.

The Parable in the Gospel of Mark

Exegetical Commentary

The foregoing General Comments are presupposed for what is provided here.

12:1. Jesus began to speak ἐν παραβολαῖς ("in parables"). But there is only one parable that follows. The same phrase appears at 3:23; 4:2, 11. The phrase does not mean that a string of parables is to follow; it refers to Jesus' manner of speaking ("parabolically," one might say).

Drawing on the imagery of Isaiah 5, the point being made is that everything was done properly and with care to protect the vineyard so that it might yield its fruit for the owner. The hedge would keep out predators, both animals and people. The tower would be a vantage point to watch for intruders.[49] Moreover, the man dug a ὑπολήνιον ("trough" or "vat") for storing juice beneath his wine press; the word appears only here in the NT (LXX Isa 5:2 has προλήνιον, meaning "vat," as well;[50] Matt 21:33 has the simpler ληνός, "wine press").

Rhetorically the opening verse raises high expectations; the owner has given such great care to his estate prior to leaving that one can expect that he wants it to produce, and the tenants to be good stewards of it.

12:2-5. The phrase τῷ καιρῷ ("at the proper time")[51] means "at harvest time" in connection with produce.[52] Three slaves are sent in succession, and each is mistreated. The kind of mistreatment grows from bad to worse: beaten, wounded in the head, killed (12:2-5a). Then in 12:5b there is a summary of additional beatings and killings.

The slave wounded in the head (12:4) is unique to Mark's version. It has been suggested that this is a reference to John the Baptist, who was beheaded (6:27).[53] But being struck on the head and being beheaded are quite different,

---

49. Cf. Edward B. Banning, "Towers," ABD 6:622-24.

50. LSJ 1488: "vat in front of a wine press." Only LXX Isa 5:2 is cited for usage of the term.

51. BAGD 395 (καιρός, 2,a).

52. Jörg Baumgarten, "καιρός," EDNT 2:233.

53. J. Crossan, Parables, 87; W. J. Bennett, "The Herodians in Mark's Gospel," NovT 17 (1975): 12-13.

and the slave is not actually killed. The verb κεφαλιόω ("to strike on the head") appears only here in the NT.

The summary in 12:5b has been called "intrusive."[54] The "law of three" is satisfied without it by means of 12:3-5a (one servant beaten, another wounded, another killed). Moreover, the killing of various slaves in 12:5b reduces the climactic impact of the decision to kill the son in 12:7. On the other hand, the verse "heightens the tension by magnifying the risk in sending the son."[55] Further, the killing of certain prophets was common knowledge in the story of Israel's past. In any case, Mark's version of the parable contains more instances of the owner's sending of slaves and their mistreatment than do the others. The history of violence against those whom God has sent throughout history is underscored vividly. Violence against Jesus, the Son of God, is one more instance of that history.

12:6. The clause "he had still another" leads one to expect the sending of another slave. But, using asyndeton, the evangelist introduces the "beloved son," which could only mean for Mark's readers a messianic title (cf. 1:11; 9:7). The word "finally" (ἔσχατον) has eschatological significance: at the end of the long history of the sending of the prophets, God has finally sent his beloved Son. The clause "they will respect my son" heightens the tension.

12:7-8. The treatment of the son is worse than that given to any of the servants. The tenants recognize him as the κληρονόμος ("heir"). Although the term is used christologically elsewhere (cf. Heb 1:2), and that cannot be excluded from one's hearing in this instance, its literal sense is primary here. The tenants think that by killing him the inheritance will be theirs; and this is simply assumed by the narrator, regardless of what the law (or lack thereof) prescribed.[56] After killing him, they cast his body out of the vineyard, that is, did not provide a burial (Matt 21:39//Luke 20:15 reverse the sequence of the verbs), so that his body would have to be placed in a common grave (cf. Jer 26:23).

12:9. Jesus asks a question and answers it (contrast Matt 21:41, where the hearers respond). The Greek behind "owner of the vineyard" is literally "the lord (ὁ κύριος) of the vineyard," which can figuratively refer to the Lord of Israel. The verb for "destroy" (Greek ἀπόλλυμι), with persons as its object, means "to kill, put to death."[57] Figuratively the verse speaks of the judgment of God upon the leaders of Israel and their condemnation. The "others" to whom the

54. A. Cadoux, *Parables,* 39.

55. R. Gundry, *Mark,* 686.

56. S. Lachs, *Rabbinic Commentary,* 355, has suggested that the legal situation presupposed is that the landowner was a proselyte, that he had died intestate, and that his property thus became ownerless. Lachs then refers to *b. Qidd.* 17b as the legal basis for that to happen. But there is nothing in the parable to hint that the landowner is to be considered a proselyte, and the Talmudic text hardly supports such a thesis.

57. BAGD 95.

vineyard will be given is therefore a new leadership. For Mark and his readers the new leaders would be leaders within the Christian church.

12:10-11. The quotation of Psalm 118:22-23 agrees verbatim with LXX 117:22-23. The imagery of the rejected "stone" that becomes "head of the corner" refers to the crucified and resurrected Jesus. The term "head of the corner" (κεφαλὴ γωνία) applies to the cornerstone of a building, "the foundation-stone . . . with which a building is begun."[58] The risen Jesus is designated the foundation of the new temple (the people of God; cf. Eph 2:20; 1 Peter 2:4-10). The exaltation of the crucified Jesus is the Lord's doing, a thing of wonder (12:11); the word for "marvelous" (θαυμαστός) is used in biblical literature only in reference to the "marvelous" deeds of God.[59]

12:12. There is no need for Jesus to add an application (the *nimshal*: "likewise . . ."). The officers of the Sanhedrin (chief priests, scribes, and elders, 11:27; 12:1) understood the parable as applying to themselves (being compared to the wicked tenants). What he says by means of the parable is, at least according to Mark, offensive enough for the officers to arrest him, which will not occur until 14:46. The offense is not clear. Most likely it is his speaking of divine judgment and the consequent destruction of the leadership of Israel (12:9). The officers do not arrest him, however, "because they feared the multitude." The word ὄχλος ("multitude") is used thirty-seven times in Mark's Gospel. Except for scenes in the Passion Narrative where the "multitude" is moved to hostility by the leaders of the Sanhedrin (14:43; 15:8, 11, 15), the "multitude" is overwhelmingly favorable to Jesus and responsive to his teaching. The people of Israel are therefore portrayed in a positive way. It is the leaders who are portrayed negatively. So strongly are the people disposed toward Jesus that the leaders are unable to seize him and destroy him — both earlier (cf. 11:18, 32) and now.

The passage anticipates events to come in the narrative of Mark's Gospel. The officers will soon arrest Jesus and seek to have him killed. Furthermore, for the evangelist and his community — in their time and place — the vindication of the Son of God has occurred; the leadership has been replaced by "others" in consequence of divine judgment upon the officers.

Exposition

The parable sets forth images of divine care, human treachery, resurrection, and responsibility. God has called forth a people, the people of Israel, and has

58. Helmut Krämer, "γωνία," *EDNT* 1:268. The alternative of "capstone" used at the apex of an arch, sometimes suggested, is disputed by Krämer and others, including R. J. McKelvey, "Christ the Cornerstone," *NTS* 8 (1961-62): 352-59; and John R. Donahue, *Are You the Christ? The Trial Narrative in the Gospel of Mark*, SBLDS 10 (Missoula: Society of Biblical Literature, 1973) 126 (n. 1).

59. BAGD 352.

cared for them as the owner of a vineyard would do. The owner portrayed here is not just any owner, but one who is exceedingly careful concerning the protection and envisioned prosperity of the vineyard.

In light of divine election and such providence, one should be able to anticipate that God's elect will produce the good fruits, the righteousness, that God expects. But that is not the way that the parable unfolds. On the contrary, it comes into alignment with the actual facts of human history. History is full of instances both of neglecting to do God's will and outright resistance to doing it. Worse yet, time and again the leaders of the people are the ones who coordinate the resistance and then focus it on God's messengers; the crucifixion of Jesus of Nazareth is the most obvious case. Nevertheless, God has vindicated Jesus, the rejected one, through resurrection from the dead.

Since that first Easter event the vineyard that was Israel alone consists of all those, Jew and Gentile, whom God has added and gathered into his elect. The question facing all who have responsibilities for the people of God is whether they will carry out the will of God and lead others to do so as well. If not, divine judgment will be visited upon them in due course.

The parable speaks of judgment. Does it speak of, or even hint at, hope or grace? If we consider 12:9 the ending of the parable and can go no further, there is little room for either; the parable functions as an exhortation to responsibility. But at the level of the Gospels, and of the canon in general, the parable unit goes on and does in fact open up grounds for hope. The vindication of the Son, his resurrection, is borne witness to by means of the psalm quotation. Even though the Son was killed by his adversaries, he was raised from death by God. The good news of Easter cries out as a response to the treachery of the crucifixion. A new creation is inaugurated by which God has a new future in store for his people.

The Parable in the Gospel of Matthew

Exegetical Commentary

Much of what appears in the Matthean account is based on Mark's, but it is more allegorized, historicized, and moralized. This is the third of three vineyard parables in succession within the Gospel of Matthew — the Workers in the Vineyard (20:1-16) and the Two Sons (21:28-32) being prior to it.

21:33. The expression ἄλλην παραβολήν ("another parable") is fitting, since this parable comes almost immediately after the Parable of the Two Sons (21:28-32), but it is also a typically Matthean connecting device found elsewhere (13:24, 31, 33). As in the Gospel of Mark, the parable is spoken in the Jerusalem temple and in the presence of the chief priests and elders (21:23). Unlike Mark, Matthew mentions no scribes, and Pharisees are added (cf. 21:45). It appears that for Matthew the term "scribe" can refer to Christian scribes (13:52;

23:34), and therefore they are sometimes removed from the scene. Antagonism against the Pharisees, on the other hand, is heightened in this Gospel.

The term "man" (who planted the vineyard) in Mark 12:1 is now called an οἰκοδεσπότης (a "householder"), a term used seven times in Matthew's Gospel, particularly to portray a stock character in parables (in addition to this one, in the Weeds in the Wheat and the Workers in the Vineyard, 13:27; 20:1, 11). In each of the parables, as here, the "householder" represents God. The linking of ἄνθρωπος ("a man") and οἰκοδεσπότης is a Matthean expression and redactional peculiarity found, besides here, twice more (13:52; 20:1).

At first the phrase "he dug a wine press (ληνός) in [the vineyard]" appears secondary to Mark's "he dug a vat" (12:1). Would one dig a "wine press" (rather than a "vat" for a wine press) into the *ground?* Excavations have uncovered both wine presses and vats that are in fact hewn into limestone, including one in Nazareth: the winepress is a bed-sized level area cut into the limestone for squashing grapes, and a vat is cut into the limestone below for collecting the runoff juice. The area also has the bases of five watchtowers.[60]

21:34-36. The expression "when the harvest time drew near" (ὅτε δὲ ἤγγισεν ὁ καιρός) increases the sense of impending final judgment; it is an eschatological expression (cf. 26:18), more allegorized than the more realistic expression in Mark 12:2.

The sending of two delegations of slaves may symbolize the former and latter prophets.[61] The symbolism (slaves = prophets) is highlighted in two further respects distinctive to Matthew: (1) the use of the plural "slaves" (versus singular "slave" in Mark and Luke) and (2) the fact that one of the slaves is stoned (21:35), as were the prophets (cf. the Q saying, Matt 23:37//Luke 13:34 and the stoning of Zechariah at 2 Chron 24:21). Quite similar allegorical symbolism is used in the Parable of the Wedding Feast; there, too, the mistreating of slaves symbolizes the persecution of the prophets (22:6). It is only in Matthew's account that stoning occurs (21:35).

In 21:34, Matthew has made the matter of collecting the fruits more earnest. The slaves come to collect "his" (= the landowner's) fruits, all of them, instead of the implied "some" in Mark's version (12:2).

60. Taken from an Associated Press article, "Threatened Nazareth Excavations Unearth Clues to Jesus' Boyhood," published in the [Minneapolis] *Star Tribune* 16/263 (December 23, 1997), A16. The site was discovered in 1997 by Stephen Pfann on the grounds of the Nazareth hospital. Cf. also the article by Ze'ev Herzog, "Michal, Tel," *OEANE* 4:20-22 with photo of two wine presses with vats (p. 21). In this case they are dug out of the ground and plastered. Tel Michal is located in the southern part of the Sharon coastal plain. Additional descriptions of wine presses cut into rock in central Galilee and Tiberias are provided by Claude R. Condor and Horatio H. Kitchener, *The Survey of Western Palestine: Memoirs of the Topography, Orography, Hydrography, and Archaeology,* 3 vols. (London: Committee of the Palestine Exploration Fund, 1881-83), 1:223, 418.

61. So R. Gundry, *Matthew,* 425-26; D. Hagner, *Matthew,* 621.

21:37-38. Here Matthew follows Mark (12:6-7) more closely. The adverb ὕστερον ("finally") in 21:37 is Matthean (used seven times in his Gospel), indicating within the allegory a new stage of salvation history, and αὐτοῦ ("his"), modifying "son," heightens the christological ring of the clause (as in Gal 4:4, "God sent forth his Son"). In 21:38 two stylistic changes are made: the addition of "when [they] saw [the son]" (ἰδόντες; also in Luke 20:14) and "let us have his inheritance."

21:39. The sequence of Mark 12:8 is altered so that the son is cast out and then killed. This conforms to the leading of Jesus out of the city and his crucifixion at Golgotha (cf. 27:31-33; cf. John 19:17-18; Heb 13:12).

21:40. Mark 12:9 is transformed and supplemented. The phrase "when therefore the owner (ὁ κύριος) of the vineyard comes" seems at first to have language that alludes to the parousia.[62] But that cannot be the meaning here. It is eschatological language, to be sure, but it refers not to the coming of Jesus but to the judgment of God upon the wicked tenants for the killing of the son.

21:41. In contrast to Mark (and Luke), Matthew has Jesus' question of 21:40 answered by the hearers of the parable rather than by Jesus himself. Their reply is intensified by the use of two words of nearly the same spelling in succession (a literary technique called "paronomasia" and common in classical Greek[63]), an adjective (κακούς, "evil ones") and an adverb, (κακῶς, "evilly"), "he will put the evildoers to a miserable death."[64] Matthew no doubt has the destruction of Jerusalem (A.D. 70) in mind (as he surely does at 22:7). Furthermore, what Mark has as simply "[he will] give the vineyard to others" (12:9) is made much more explicit: "[he will] lease the vineyard to other tenants, who will give him the fruits in their seasons." Allegorically this means (1) that Israel will be placed under the leadership and care of others, and (2) the latter will be expected to produce the faithfulness and righteousness that God demands. On fruit-bearing as a metaphor for right, productive, and life-giving conduct in Matthew, cf. 3:8, 10; 7:16-20; 12:33; 21:43. It is not clear whether the hearers who answer the parable are simply people in general within the temple who are listening, or whether they are Jesus' opponents. But as in the preceding parable (21:31), it is probably the opponents who are meant. By answering the question, they condemn themselves.

21:42. As in Mark, the quotation is identical to that of the LXX (Ps 117:22-23). As always in Matthew, the plural "scriptures" is used (22:29; 26:54, 56) over against Mark's singular "this passage in scripture" in this instance.

21:43. The verse is unique to Matthew. In place of Matthew's usual phrase "kingdom of heaven" (32 times), the phrase employed is "kingdom of God" (as also at 12:28; 19:24; 21:31). But what does it mean? There is no basis for saying

62. R. Gundry, *Matthew*, 428.
63. BDF 258 (#488, 1, a).
64. BAGD 95.

that it is equivalent to the vineyard.[65] The contents of 21:41 and 21:43 are not actually parallel, as can be seen (with suggested allegorical referents):

21:41	21:43
The vineyard (Israel)	The kingdom of God (= ?)
[is taken away from	is taken away from
the wicked tenants	from you
(former leaders)]	(former leaders)
and leased	and given
to new tenants	to a people producing fruits
(Christian leaders)	(the Christian church)

The question (signified by "=?" above) is the meaning of the term "kingdom of God." It cannot be Israel (the Jewish people), since Israel is not "given" to the church. Rather, the "kingdom of God" — something that one can possess in this case — must here signify the blessing of salvation that can be given to a people, as elsewhere in Matthew's Gospel (13:44-46; 25:34).[66]

It is not accurate, then, to say on the basis of this parable that Matthew has a "supersessionist" view of history,[67] that is, that the history of Israel has reached its end with the Christ event, and that the church has replaced Israel as the people of God. The "vineyard" (Israel) is not destroyed, ended. It is given new leadership in order that it may continue. The kingdom of God (salvation) is not taken away from Israel but from its presumptive leaders and granted to the community of disciples, who produce the righteousness that God demands, a "people" (ἔθνος) or community made up of Jews and Gentiles.[68] The election of Israel itself is not thereby denied. To be sure, "the vineyard" (God's elect people) has been placed under the care of the new leaders, which for Matthew would mean the apostolic leadership. And "the kingdom" (the blessing of salva-

---

65. Contra various interpreters, for example, Charles A. Briggs, *The Messiah of the Gospels* (New York: Charles Scribner's Sons, 1894), 116-17; W. Allen, *Matthew*, 231; W. Oesterley, *Parables*, 120; A. McNeile, *Matthew*, 312; R. Gundry, *Matthew*, 430; D. Hare, *Matthew*, 248-49; B. Scott, *Parable*, 242; and J. Lambrecht, *Treasure*, 119.

66. Ulrich Luz, "βασιλεία," *EDNT* 1:203-4; idem, *Matthäus*, 3:226-27.

67. The supersessionist view (though not the term itself) seems to have been obvious to some interpreters at the dawn and early years of the twentieth century; see, for example, C. Briggs, *Messiah of the Gospels*, 116-17; A. Plummer, *Matthew*, 297; and A. McNeile, *Matthew*, 311. M. Boring, *NIB (Matthew)*, 8:415, refers to the "false understanding of supersessionism" that some derive from the passage.

68. Cf. Wolfgang Trilling, *Das wahre Israel: Studien zur Theologie des Matthäusevangeliums*, EThS 7 (Leipzig: St. Benno-Verlag, 1962), 43-44; C. Carlston, *Parables*, 45; Kenzo Tagawa, "People and Community in the Gospel of Matthew," *NTS* 16 (1970): 161; O. Lamar Cope, *Matthew: A Scribe Trained for the Kingdom*, CBQMS 5 (Washington: Catholic Biblical Association, 1976), 85-86; D. Hagner, *Matthew*, 623; W. D. Davies and D. Allison, *Matthew*, 3:190; and D. Senior, *Matthew*, 243.

tion) has been extended thereby to a wider fellowship consisting of all those who produce the fruits of it.

21:45-46. The basic information is taken from Mark. Matthew, however, identifies the hearers clearly: "the chief priests and the Pharisees." He also indicates why the "multitude" was so committed to Jesus: "because they considered him a prophet." That was the estimation of the people also at 21:11, the triumphal entry. (There are parallel sayings concerning John the Baptist at 14:5 and 21:26.) Mark's statement that now "they left him and went away" is postponed until 22:22.

Exposition

What was said in the Exposition of Mark 12:1-12 is by and large applicable here. But there are some new emphases to track. It is clear that Matthew's version is "more allegorized, historicized, and moralized" (see the Exegetical Commentary). Its more specific alignment of details with the history of Israel opens the way ever more easily for the interpreter of today to highlight the evils of the Israelites and to castigate the Jewish leaders of Jesus' day in a very bad light for crucifying him.

A thoughtful Jewish interpreter of this parable could agree with its metaphorical assertion that the story of Israel is one of human failure and divine grace. Such a person would most likely agree that the death of Jesus was a tragic event.

But where does one go from there? The Christian interpreter should not ignore the fact that the passage does signify judgment on the Jewish leaders (but not the Jewish people in general) and the end of their legitimacy. And yet the passage is within the Christian canon, addressed to Christian readers and hearers — particularly Christian readers and hearers who are leaders. Moreover, this account raises the stakes for Christian leaders above what is portrayed already in Mark's account. They are now all the more clearly responsible for bringing forth good fruits from the people of God (21:41).

Matthew's version of the parable sets forth in miniature a history of salvation schema. It ends up (21:42) by asserting that the rejected, crucified Jesus has been vindicated. Through him the kingdom has been given to the community of those who claim him as Lord. In spite of human resistance and outright wickedness toward God and his Son, God has the last word. And the last act is sure to come by which God vindicates his people. In the meantime, the responsibility of Christian leadership is to tend to the nurture of the community, so that it bears good fruits.

The Parable in the Gospel of Luke

Exegetical Commentary

Like Mark and Matthew, Luke has Jesus tell the parable within the Jerusalem temple. On Luke's version as dependent on Mark, see General Comments above.

20:9. Luke alone says that Jesus spoke the parable to "the people," but even he has it spoken in the presence of the chief priests, scribes, and elders, and they hear it as spoken against themselves, as in the other Gospels (20:1, 19).

Immediately it is apparent that Luke has trimmed the parable of several details from Isaiah 5:1-7. Gone are all those items in Mark's version that speak of the great care given to the vineyard by its owner. What is left is that "a man planted a vineyard" prior to letting it out to tenants. Nevertheless, the allegorical elements are not stripped away entirely. One still hears metaphors for God and Israel in the opening words.

The owner went away χρόνους ἱκανούς (literally, "for considerable times"; RSV, NEB, NIV, and NRSV: "for a long time"). That he went to "another country" (RSV, NRSV) could be implied, but it is not stated explicitly in the text. The verb used (ἀποδημέω) means simply to "go away on a journey" or "be absent."[69] The emphasis in Luke is the amount of time, not the amount of distance.[70] Does this symbolize Luke's theme of the delay of the parousia, as some interpreters have maintained?[71] Since the owner represents God, not Jesus, that is not the case. The long time can refer to the long era of the history of Israel. At best the phrase alludes to the long-suffering and patience of God in the face of the disobedience of his people.[72]

20:10-12. On καιρῷ ("at harvest time"), see Note on 20:10 and Comment on Mark 12:2. In regard to the sending of the slaves, Luke has a more simplified sequence. Only three are sent, one at a time. Over against Mark (12:5) and Matthew (21:36), none of the slaves is killed; that is reserved for the son alone. But as in Mark's account, there is a progression in the severity of mistreatment: the first is beaten, the second beaten and treated shamefully, and the third wounded and cast out. As the severity of shameful treatment increases, the drama of the story is heightened.

Along with Luke's simplicity of storytelling, however, there is a corresponding lessening of allegorization in comparison with the other two Gospels. The sendings in Matthew and Mark clearly correspond to God's sendings of the

---

69. BAGD 90.

70. C. Carlston, *Parables,* 77.

71. Erich Grässer, *Das Problem der Parusieverzögerung in den synoptischen Evangelien und in der Apostelgeschichte,* 2d ed., BZNW 22 (Berlin: Verlag Alfred Töpelmann, 1960), 113; and C. Carlston, *Parables,* 77.

72. Cf. J. Fitzmyer, *Luke,* 1283; D. Tiede, *Luke,* 340; R. Stein, *Luke,* 492.

prophets. That correspondence is still present in Luke's version, but it is less evident.

In 20:10 Luke has revised the clause of Mark 12:2 ("in order to obtain some of the fruit of the vineyard from them") to read, "in order that they should give him some of the fruit of the vineyard" (cf. similar wording in *Gos. Thom.* 65). The result is that the owner appears less aggressive; the tenants are expected to respond freely of their own accord and without pressure from the slave of the owner.

In 20:11-12 Luke employs a Hebraism in his twofold use of the expression προσέθετο . . . πέμψαι ("he proceeded to send"), namely, the use of the verb προστίθημι plus infinitive (a form of expression used in the LXX, e.g., at Gen 8:12; Judg 3:12; 4:1; 10:6; 1 Sam 18:29; also at Acts 12:3).[73]

20:13. In light of what has happened to his slaves, the owner of the vineyard must take stronger action. That is to send his "beloved son" (as in Mark) — a term applied to Jesus at his baptism (3:22). Only in Luke is there a soliloquy in which the landowner deliberates, "What shall I do?" etc., in direct discourse. This is another instance of "interior monologue," which appears in several parables in Luke — and only in Luke's parables (for other instances, cf. 12:17; 15:17-19; 16:3)[74] — and the question "What shall I do?" has been heard in Lukan parables before (12:17; 16:3). The use of "perhaps" (only here in the NT, but also in *Gos. Thom.* 65 at this place) in the statement about sending the son may well be Luke's way of softening the prediction; God cannot err in thinking that respect for his Son is assured.[75] It is not said, contra Mark and Matthew, that the owner does actually send his son, but that is implied in the next verse. The son signifies God's Son, as in the other Gospels.

20:14. The verse is based on Mark 12:7, but Luke has heightened its style by use of the expression διελογίζοντο πρὸς ἀλλήλους λέγοντες ("they deliberated with one another, saying")[76] in place of Mark's πρὸς ἑαυτοὺς εἶπαν (literally, "said to themselves," which must be improved in English to "said to one another," as in the RSV, NEB, NIV, and NRSV). Luke makes a second improvement by creating a purpose clause: "in order that the inheritance may be ours." On the legal situation, see "General Comments on the Texts."

20:15. As in the Gospel of Matthew (21:39), the sequence differs from that in Mark 12:8; the son is first cast out, and then killed, which corresponds to the sequence in the Passion Narrative, in which Jesus was led out of the city and then crucified (23:25-26, 33; cf. John 19:17-18; Heb 13:12).

73. BDF 225 (#435, a).

74. Philip Sellew, "Interior Monologue as a Narrative Device in the Parables of Luke," *JBL* 111 (1992): 248-49.

75. A. Jülicher, *Gleichnisreden*, 2:391-92. But it is only "a dramatic touch," according to J. Fitzmyer, *Luke*, 1284.

76. The expression appears otherwise only in the Gospel of Mark in other contexts (8:16; 11:31).

20:16. The first sentence of this verse is exactly like that of Mark 12:9 (see Commentary on that verse), except for inclusion of "these" (so, "these tenants"; cf. the literal translation of the KJV and the NEB; but "those tenants" in RSV, NIV, and NRSV). What is most distinctive to Luke is the reply of the hearers: μὴ γένοιτο, which can be translated literally as "May it not be!" (cf. "May this never be!" NIV), but "God forbid" expresses the emotion of the expression better (cf. KJV, RSV, and NRSV). The expression is used by Paul some thirteen times in his letters,[77] but it appears only here in the Gospels. The hearers making the exclamatory response are "the people" (20:9),[78] not the temple officers. Their response underscores the sense of dread that the parable conveys. Furthermore, at this point Luke makes a sharp distinction between the officers of the Sanhedrin and "the people." In the thirty-six references to them, "the people" (ὁ λαός) are very favorably disposed to Jesus in the Gospel of Luke except for one episode (23:13-18); certainly that is so in this chapter (20:1, 6, 9, 19, 26, 45). The officials are portrayed — in contrast to the people — as capable of doing a horrible deed, which signifies the crucifixion of Jesus (20:15). The people are horrified that such could happen, a deed that calls forth great wrath on the part of the owner of the vineyard and the entrusting of the vineyard to others.

In Luke's perspective, no less than in Mark's and Matthew's, the leadership of Israel is taken away from the Jerusalem leaders and transferred to others. For Luke, the people of God consists of the repentant of Israel and repentant Gentiles added to them.[79] The leaders of renewed Israel are the apostles and those who come after them.[80]

20:17. Luke adds that Jesus "looked at them" (presumably at his hearers in general), which provides a formal and serious setting for the question to follow. That question differs in form from what is asked in Mark 12:10 and Matthew 21:42. In the latter cases, the opponents are asked whether they have *read* Psalm 118:22-23. Here the question is about the *meaning* of Psalm 118:22 (118:23 is not included). Literally the question is, "What then is this that has been written?" Addressed to the people, the question being raised has the following sense: "If the destruction that I have just foretold is not to come (μὴ γένοιτο), how *then* do you explain this text?"[81] The text quoted from the psalm is exactly that of LXX Psalm 117:22 (as in the other two Gospels).

20:18. The verse has a parallel in some Matthean texts at 21:44, but not in others, and should probably not be included in the Matthean text (see Notes in

77. Rom 3:4, 6, 31; 6:2, 15; 7:7; 9:14; 11:1, 11; 1 Cor 6:15; Gal 2:17; 3:21; 6:14.
78. That it is "the people" who respond is not stated explicitly, but it is implied. Cf. I. H. Marshall, *Luke,* 731; J. Fitzmyer, *Luke,* 1277, 1285.
79. Cf. Jacob Jervell, *Luke and the People of God: A New Look at Luke-Acts* (Minneapolis: Augsburg Publishing House, 1972), 41-74.
80. Cf. E. Schweizer, *Luke,* 304. Contra R. Stein, *Luke,* 490, 493, who suggests that the kingdom is offered to the Gentiles.
81. A. Plummer, *Luke,* 462.

the section on Matthew). If it were firmly attested in Matthew, it could be assigned to Q. But more likely it is a Lukan composition from disparate passages in Isaiah 8:14-15 and Daniel 2:34-35, 44-45. The verse serves to individualize responsibility and judgment.[82] It speaks of both (1) a person's falling upon a stone and (2) a stone's falling upon a person. The stone refers figuratively to Christ. There are those who reject him (stumble over him, since he is an offense to them; cf. 2:34), and there are those whom he shall crush at his coming in glory.

20:19. Luke specifies that it was the "scribes and chief priests" who reacted negatively against Jesus (not the people), and that they sought to "lay hands on him," which is a more hostile act (cf. 21:12; Acts 5:18; 21:27) than simply to "arrest him," as in Mark and Matthew. It signifies "hostile seizure" (cf. also Mark 14:46//Matt 26:50; Luke 21:12; Acts 4:3; 5:18; 21:27).[83] Nevertheless, the opponents refrained from seizing Jesus because they feared "the people." Luke has substituted τὸν λαόν ("the people") for Mark's τὸν ὄχλον ("the crowd"; cf. Matthew's τοὺς ὄχλους, "the crowds"). Luke thus makes use of his favorite term for those who are favorably disposed to Jesus — a term he uses later in Acts for the people of God, both the faithful of Israel (10:2; 21:28; 28:17) and the church (15:14; 18:10).[84]

As in Mark's account, the unit closes with the statement that the opponents of Jesus knew that the parable was spoken against them. In both cases the statement is related not to the words concerning fear of the crowd/the people, but to their reason for seeking to arrest/lay hands upon Jesus. They wanted to seize him because he had offended them by comparing them to the wicked tenants. The arrest of Jesus would come soon enough, however, at 22:54.

Exposition

The Exposition on Mark 12:1-2 is presupposed here. But Luke has some nuances to explore. More than the other two evangelists, Luke emphasizes the patience of God (see the Exegetical Commentary on 20:9). There is a reluctance on God's part even to send the prophets! After all, it is only after a lot of patience that the sending of the slaves is narrated. Furthermore, God here is a deliberating God (20:13), a God who asks, "What shall I do?" and even then wonders whether the Son will be given the respect due him.

Yet, even though God is portrayed in such terms — the so-called Lukan "humanism" — there is a harshness to the conclusion of the parable that is not found in the other accounts (20:18; here we assume that the parallel in some

82. C. Carlston, *Parables*, 80.
83. Friedrich Hauck, "βάλλω," *TDNT* 1:529.
84. Cf. Hans Conzelmann, *The Theology of St. Luke* (New York: Harper & Brothers, 1960), 162-67.

texts of Matthew is secondary). The parable closes with allusions to the offense of the gospel and the coming of the Lord in final judgment. This means that the parable is not so much an exhortation to responsibility on the part of Christian leaders (as in Mark and especially in Matthew), but is now addressed to every reader and hearer. To reject Jesus leads to disaster. Repentance and faith in Jesus lead to life — a common Lukan theme (24:47; Acts 2:38; 3:19; 5:31; 11:18; 17:30-31; 20:21; 26:20).

Select Bibliography

Bammel, Ernst. "Das Gleichnis von den bösen Winzern (Mk. 12,1-9) und das jüdische Erbrecht." *RIDA* 3/6 (1959): 11-17.

Black, Matthew. "The Christological Use of the Old Testament in the New Testament." *NTS* 18 (1971-72): 1-14.

————. "The Parable as Allegory." *BJRL* 42 (1959-60): 273-87.

Brooke, George J. "4Q500 1 and the Use of Scripture in the Parable of the Vineyard." *DSD* 2 (1995): 268-94.

Brown, Raymond E. "Parable and Allegory Reconsidered." *NovT* 5 (1962): 36-45.

Bruce, F. F. "New Wine in Old Wineskins: III. The Corner Stone." *ExpTim* 84 (1972-73): 231-35.

Burkitt, F. C. "The Parable of the Wicked Husbandmen." In *Transactions of the Third International Congress for the History of Religions*, 2:321-28. 2 vols. Ed. P. S. Allen and J. de M. Johnson. Oxford: Clarendon Press, 1908.

Crossan, John Dominic. "The Parable of the Wicked Husbandmen." *JBL* 90 (1971): 451-65.

Derrett, J. Duncan M. "Allegory and the Wicked Vinedressers," *JTS* 25 (1974): 426-32.

————. "Fresh Light on the Wicked Vinedressers." *RIDA* 10 (1963): 11-41. Reprinted as "The Parable of the Wicked Vinedressers," in his *Law in the New Testament*, 286-312. London: Longman and Todd, 1970.

————. "The Stone That the Builders Rejected." *SE* 6 [= TU 102] (1968): 180-86.

Dillon, Richard I. "Towards a Tradition-History of the Parables of the True Israel (Mt 21,33–22,14)." *Bib* 47 (1966): 1-42.

Doran, Robert. "Luke 20:18: A Warrior's Boast?" *CBQ* 45 (1983): 61-67.

Drury, John. "The Sower, the Vineyard and the Place of Allegory in the Interpretation of Mark's Parables." *JTS* 24 (1973): 367-79.

Evans, Craig A. "Jesus' Parable of the Tenant Farmers in Light of Lease Agreements in Antiquity." *JSP* 14 (1996): 25-83.

————. "On the Vineyard Parables of Isaiah 5 and Mark 12." *BZ* 28 (1984): 82-86.

Feldmeier, Reinhard. "Heil im Unheil: Das Bild Gottes nach der Parabel von den bösen Winzern (Mk. 12,1-12 par)," *TBei* 25 (1994): 5-22.

Fridrichsen, Anton. "Till lignelsen om de onde vingartnere: Mk 12:1-12 m. par." *STK* 4 (1928): 355-61.

Gray, Arthur. "The Parable of the Wicked Husbandmen." *HibJ* 19 (1920-21): 42-52.

Hengel, Martin. "Das Gleichnis von den Weingartnern: Mc 12:1-12 im Licht der Zenonpapyri und der rabbinischen Gleichnisse." *ZNW* 59 (1968): 1-39.

Hester, James D. "Socio-rhetorical Criticism and the Parable of the Tenants." *JSNT* 45 (1992): 27-57.

Horne, Edward H. "The Parable of the Tenants as Indictment." *JSNT* 71 (1998): 111-16.

Hubaut, Michel. *La parabole des vignerons homicides.* Paris: Gabalda, 1976.

Huber, Konrad. "Vom 'Weinbergleid' zum 'Winzergleichnis.' Zu einem Beispiel innerbiblischer *relecture.*" *ProtoBib* 5 (1996): 71-94.

Iersel, Bastiaan M. F. van. "Das Gleichnis von den bösen Winzern." In his *"Der Sohn" in den synoptischen Jesusworten,* 124-45. NovTSup 3. Leiden: E. J. Brill, 1964.

Jeremias, Joachim. "Κεφαλὴ γωνίας — Ἀκρογωνιαῖος." *ZNW* 29 (1930): 264-90.

Kim, Seyoon. "Jesus — The Son of God, the Stone, the Son of Man, and the Servant: The Role of Zechariah in the Self-Identification of Jesus." In *Tradition and Interpretation in the New Testament: Essays in Honor of E. Earle Ellis for His 60th Birthday,* 134-48. Ed. Gerald F. Hawthorne and Otto Betz. Grand Rapids: Wm. B. Eerdmans, 1987.

Kingsbury, Jack D. "The Parable of the Wicked Husbandmen and the Secret of Jesus' Divine Sonship in Matthew: Some Literary-Critical Observations." *JBL* 195 (1986): 643-55.

Klauck, Hans-Josef. "Das Gleichnis vom Mord im Weinberg (Mk 12,1-12; Mt 21,33-46; Lk 20,9-19)." *BibLeb* 11 (1970): 118-45.

Kümmel, Werner G. "Das Gleichnis von den bösen Weingärtnern (Mk 12:1-9)." In his *Heilsgeschehen und Geschichte: Gesammelte Aufsätze 1933-64,* 207-17. Ed. Erich Grässer et al. MGT 3. Marburg: N. G. Elwert Verlag, 1965.

Léon-Dufour, Xavier. "The Murderous Vineyard-Workers." *TD* 15 (1967): 30-36.

————. "La parabole des vignerons homicides." *ScEc* 17 (1965): 365-96.

Lohmeyer, Ernst. "Das Gleichnis von den Bösen Weingärtner." *ZST* 18 (1941): 242-59. Reprinted in his *Urchristliche Mystik: Neutestamentliche Studien,* 159-81. 2d ed. Darmstadt: Gentner, 1958.

Lowe, Malcolm. "From the Parable of the Vineyard to a Pre-Synoptic Source." *NTS* 28 (1982): 257-63.

Martens, Allan W. "'Produce Fruit Worthy of Repentance': Parables of Judgment against Jewish Religious Leaders and the Nation (Matt 21:28-22:14, par.; Luke 13:6-9)." In *The Challenge of Jesus' Parables,* 151-76. Ed. Richard N. Longenecker. Grand Rapids: Wm. B. Eerdmans, 2000.

McKelvey, R. J. "Christ the Cornerstone." *NTS* 8 (1961-62): 352-59.

Milavec, Aaron. "A Fresh Analysis of the Parable of the Wicked Husbandmen in the Light of Jewish-Christian Dialogue." In *Parable and Story in Judaism and Christianity*, 81-117. Ed. Clemens Thoma and Michael Wyschogrod. New York: Paulist Press, 1989.

————. "The Identity of 'The Son' and 'The Others': Mark's Parable of the Wicked Husbandmen Reconsidered." *BTB* 20 (1990): 30-37.

————. "Mark's Parable of the Wicked Husbandmen as Reaffirming God's Predilection for Israel." *JES* 26 (1989): 289-312.

Moor, Johannes C. de. "The Targumic Background of Mark 12:1-12: The Parable of the Wicked Tenants." *JSJ* 29 (1998): 63-80.

Morrice, W. G. "The Parable of the Tenants and the Gospel of Thomas." *ExpTim* 98 (1987): 104-7.

Mussner, Franz. "Die bösen Winzer nach Mt 21.33-46." In *Antijudaismus im Neuen Testament? Exegetische und systematische Beiträge*, 129-34. Ed. Willehad P. Eckert et al. Munich: Kaiser Verlag, 1967.

Newell, Jane E., and Raymond R. Newell. "The Parable of the Wicked Tenants." *NovT* 14 (1972): 226-37.

Nolan, Brian M. "The Heir Unapparent: Detecting the Royal Theology in the Parable of the Master's Son (Matthew 21:33-46)." In *Proceedings of the Irish Biblical Association 4*, 84-95. Ed. John Eaton et al. Dublin: Irish Biblical Association, 1980.

Ogawa, Akira. "Paraboles de l'Israël véritable? Reconsidération critique de Mt xxi 28–xxii 14." *NovT* 21 (1979): 121-49.

O'Neill, John C. "The Shocking Prospect of Killing the Messiah (Luke 20:9-19)." In *Jesus and His Parables: Interpreting the Parables of Jesus Today*, ed. V. George Shillington, 165-76. Edinburgh: T. & T. Clark, 1997.

————. "The Source of the Parables of the Bridegroom and the Wicked Husbandmen." *JTS* 39 (1988): 485-89.

Puig I. Tàrrech, Armand. "La paràbola dels vinyaters homicides (Lc 20,9-19) en el context de Lc-Ac." *RCT* 16 (1991): 39-65.

Robinson, John A. T. "The Parable of the Wicked Husbandmen: A Test of Synoptic Relationships." *NTS* 21 (1975): 443-61.

Schmeller, Thomas. "Der Erbe des Weinbergs. Zu den Gerichtsgleichnissen Mk 12,1-12 und Jes 5,1-7." *MTZ* 46 (1995): 183-201.

————. "Das Reich Gottes im Gleichnis. Eine Überprüfung neuer Deutungen der Gleichnisrede und der Reich-Gottes-Verkündigung Jesu." *TLZ* 119 (1994): 599-608.

Schottroff, Willy. "Das Gleichnis von den bösen Weingärtnern (Mk 12,1-9 parr.). Ein Beitrag zur Geschichte der Bodenpacht in Palästina." *ZDPV* 112 (1996): 18-48.

Snodgrass, Klyne R. "The Parable of the Wicked Husbandmen: Is the Gospel of Thomas Version the Original?" *NTS* 21 (1974-75): 142-44.

————. *The Parable of the Wicked Tenants: An Inquiry into Parable Interpretation.* WUNT 27. Tübingen: J. C. B. Mohr (Paul Siebeck), 1983.

————. "Recent Research on the Parable of the Wicked Tenants." *BBR* 8 (1998): 187-215.

Stern, David. "Jesus' Parables from the Perspective of Rabbinic Literature: The Example of the Wicked Husbandmen." In *Parable and Story in Judaism and Christianity,* 42-80. Ed. Clemens Thoma and Michael Wyschogrod. New York: Paulist, 1989.

Trilling, Wolfgang. "Gericht über das falsche Israel (Mt. 21,33-46)." In his *Christusverkündigung in den synoptischen Evangelien: Beispiele gattungsgemässer Auslegung,* 165-90. BiH 4. Munich: Kösel-Verlag, 1969.

Trimaille, Michel. "La parabole des vignerons meurtriers (Mc 12,1-12)." In *Les paraboles évangéliques: perspectives nouvelle,* 247-58. Ed. Jean Delorme. Paris: Cerf, 1989.

Weren, Wim J. C. "The Use of Isaiah 5,1-7 in the Parable of the Tenants (Mark 12,1-12; Matthew 21,33-46)." *Bib* 79 (1998): 1-26.

Young, Brad H. "Prophetic Tension and the Temple: 'The Parable of the Wicked Husbandmen.'" In his *Jesus and His Jewish Parables: Rediscovering the Roots of Jesus' Teaching,* 282-316. New York: Paulist Press, 1989.

CHAPTER 8

Parables of the Kingdom

Several of the parables in the Synoptic Gospels open with a reference to the "kingdom of God" or "kingdom of heaven." They are introduced by a formula, such as "The kingdom of God/heaven is like. . . ." There are eleven such parables:

Two are in Mark:
> Mark 4:26-29, Parable of the Seed Growing Secretly
> Mark 4:30-32//Matthew 13:31-32//Luke 13:18-19, Parable of the Mustard Seed

One is derived from Q:
> Matthew 13:33//Luke 13:20-21, Parable of the Leaven

Eight appear in the Special Matthean Tradition (always using the phrase "kingdom of heaven" rather than "kingdom of God"):
> Matthew 13:24-30, Parable of the Weeds in the Wheat
> Matthew 13:44, Parable of the Treasure in the Field
> Matthew 13:45-46, Parable of the Pearl of Great Price
> Matthew 13:47-50, Parable of the Dragnet
> Matthew 18:23-35, Parable of the Unforgiving Slave
> Matthew 20:1-16, Parable of the Workers in the Vineyard
> Matthew 22:1-14, Parable of the Wedding Feast
> Matthew 25:1-13, Parable of the Ten Maidens

None appears in the Special Lukan Tradition.

In addition to these instances, the term "kingdom of God" or "kingdom of heaven" appears many other times in sayings of Jesus. On the basis of a simple count of the times that one of the two phrases is used (which allows for parallels), there are eighty-three such sayings in the Synoptic Gospels.[1] The kingdom was certainly a main theme, even *the* main theme, of Jesus' message. Virtually all scholars would agree on that point. But what does the term mean? It is impossible to come up with a definition. The Synoptic Gospels do not contain traditions in which Jesus himself defined the term. The Gospels seem to take for granted that anyone should understand the concept; a definition need not be given. Jesus must not have been the first to use the term, nor the last.

Several lengthy studies have been produced concerning the kingdom of God concept. These cannot be reviewed here. Suffice it to say that the term would have been understood in the world of Jesus and the Gospels in light of a long history of Jewish thought. Within the writings of ancient Israel — the Torah, the Prophets, and the Writings — God is portrayed as king over the universe. Some of the most important passages are Psalms 22:28; 47:2, 7-8; 95:1-3 and Isaiah 43:15; 44:6. According to these passages, God has a kingdom, it includes the whole world, and it is an everlasting one. Still other important passages speak of God's dominion over the world, such as Psalm 103:19; others speak of it as everlasting, such as 145:10-13. God's kingship extends over both time and space, history and nature.

But God's kingdom — or kingship, rule, or reign — is not always evident. Israel was often under the rule of various other kings. Especially during times of oppression the evidence of God's rule was lacking. In such times the kingdom of God becomes a *future* hope, an expectation. This becomes apparent in Daniel 7:18, written in the second century B.C. during foreign occupation, and in the Lord's Prayer, in which there is a petition for the coming of God's kingdom (Matt 6:10). The expectation is that then God will rule and vindicate his people.

The frequency of kingdom language in the traditions of Jesus shows how important the theme was in the preaching of Jesus. What is distinctive in his preaching of the kingdom was the claim that the kingdom of God had come into effective operation within his own ministry — his words and his deeds.[2] At the same time, however, he expected the kingdom to come in its fullness yet in the future.

Parables containing kingdom expressions are notoriously awkward. Typically, they say that the kingdom of God is like one who sows, a king who

1. The statistics are: "kingdom of heaven" 32 times in Matthew (and only there); and "kingdom of God" 5 times in Matthew, 14 times in Mark, and 32 times in Luke. The statistics do not include those times in which the solitary word "kingdom" is used to designate the same (e.g., Matt 6:10; 8:12; 9:35, etc.). The total count of the instances of the word "kingdom" is 94 in the Synoptic Gospels.

2. Günther Bornkamm, *Jesus of Nazareth* (New York: Harper & Brothers, 1960), 90-95; Gerd Theissen and Annette Merz, *The Historical Jesus: A Comprehensive Guide* (Minneapolis: Fortress Press, 1998), 240-80; Jürgen Becker, *Jesus of Nazareth* (New York: Walter de Gruyter, 1998), 100-102, 141-86.

gives a marriage feast, ten maidens, and so on. The comparison, however, is not to a person, but to the story that follows.

In these cases the expression cannot simply refer to the reign of God. Something more is meant. Such parables have to do with the following realities:

(1) Some speak of the kingdom of God as growing. These include the Parables of Growth — the Seed Growing Secretly (Mark 4:26-29), the Mustard Seed (4:30-32), and the Leaven (Matt 13:33).

(2) Some speak of the kingdom as a joyful discovery, in which God's reign becomes a wonderful event in one's life — the Treasure (Matt 13:44) and the Pearl of Great Price (13:45-46).

(3) Some speak of the kingdom in the most general way; the parable simply conveys a theological truth, affirming and illumining God's activities as ruler in the present or future — the Weeds among the Wheat (Matt 13:24-30), the Dragnet (13:47-50), the Unforgiving Slave (18:23-35), the Workers in the Vineyard (20:1-16), the Wedding Feast (22:1-14), and the Ten Maidens (25:1-13).

A. PARABLES ON THE GROWTH OF THE KINGDOM

8.34. The Seed Growing Secretly, Mark 4:26-29

Mark 4:26-29

26*And [Jesus] said, "The kingdom of God is as if a man should cast seed upon the ground, 27and should sleep and rise night and day, and the seed should sprout and grow, he knows not how. 28The earth produces of itself, first the stalk, then the head, then the full grain in the head. 29But when the grain is ripe, at once he puts in the sickle, because the harvest has come."*

Notes on the Text and Translation

4:26. There are three other possible readings in place of the reading in the 27th edition of the Nestle-Aland Greek text, ὡς ἄνθρωπος. Two of them, if not original, are attempts at improving the syntax in anticipation of several subjunctive verbs to follow. These are ὡς ἄνθρωπος ὅταν ("as a man whenever . . .") or ὡς (ἐ)ὰν ἄνθρθπος ("as if a man").[1] The third variant is simply ὥσπερ ἄνθρωπος ("just like a man"), which has the same syntactical problem as the reading in the text. In none of these cases, however, is the variant as well attested as the reading in the text.

---

1. BDF 192 (#380, 4).

4:28. In place of the textual reading εἶτα ("then," used twice in the verse), the Westcott-Hort Greek text and the 25th edition of the Nestle-Aland Greek text follow ℵ, B, L, and Δ in adopting εἶτεν. The latter has the same meaning. There is strong evidence for both readings, but the former may have an edge since it is more widely attested. Further, the latter is typically the Hellenistic form,[2] which scribes may have tended to use by habit when copying texts.

Exegetical Commentary

The parable is also called the Parable of the Patient Husbandman (or Farmer),[3] which is also quite fitting, considering its emphasis on patience. In any case, the parable appears only in Mark's Gospel within the NT and is the only one to appear there without having a parallel in one of the others. Instead of this parable, and in its place, the Gospel of Matthew contains the Parable of the Weeds in the Wheat (13:24-30), which is peculiar to that gospel alone. Mark has placed this parable in a series of parables and sayings about parables (4:3-34). It is the second of three "seed parables" (the Sower and the Mustard Seed being first and third). Since the comparison being made is between the kingdom and some timeless and general phenomenon, the unit can be classified as a similitude.[4]

4:26-27. This is the first instance in Mark's Gospel where a parable begins by making a comparison between the kingdom of God and the parabolic imagery to follow (cf. 4:30). As in other cases, the comparison is not exactly between the kingdom and the word following "like," in this case "a man." The comparison is more broadly diffused to encompass the full scope of what is being narrated.[5]

The two verses contain several verbs that are in the subjunctive mood. The first (βάλῃ, "should cast") is an aorist subjunctive; four of them (translated "should sleep," "rise," "sprout," and "grow") are present subjunctives. According to the conventions of classical Greek, one should expect ὡς ἐάν ("as if"), rather than simply ὡς ("as") to introduce the comparative clause, and some Greek witnesses have that (see Notes above). Lacking that, one can still see here that a present general condition is meant. That is to say, life is full of instances where a person sows seeds, and then proceeds with ordinary living. In the meantime the seed sprouts and grows; it happens all the time. The one who sows cannot and need not explain how the growth takes place.

2. BDF 19 (#35, 3)

3. B. Smith, *Parables*, 129; cf. N. Dahl, "Parables of Growth," 157; J. Jeremias, *Parables*, 151.

4. R. Bultmann, *HST* 172-73; E. Linnemann, *Parables*, 9; R. Stein, *Parables*, 19; Robert A. Guelich, *Mark 1–8:26*, WBC 34A (Dallas: Word Books, 1989), 238. On the other hand, A. Jülicher, *Gleichnisreden*, 2:538-46, and C. H. Dodd, *Parables*, 6, consider it a parable proper *(Parabel).*

5. J. Jeremias, *Parables*, 101.

The man goes about ordinary living, rising in the morning and sleeping at night. But the word order "night and day" would be familiar in a Jewish context. There a specific day begins at sundown. So a person experiences night prior to daylight.

4:28. Although the verse may seem initially to restate what 4:27 has already said, and so it has been asserted that the verse is an addition to an earlier parable (4:26-27, 29),[6] it actually redirects the attention of the hearer or reader away from the sower's sense of mystery at the end of 4:27 to the earth, seed, and process of growth, which are so central to the story. The verse therefore belongs to the essential structure of the parable.

The word αὐτομάτη is customarily translated "by itself" (RSV, NIV, NRSV). Unfortunately the phrase "by itself" sounds to the modern ear as though the seed grows "naturally," excluding even divine power or causation. But the phrase can mean simply "without visible cause."[7] Other than here the term appears only at Acts 12:10 in the NT. In the latter case, the term clearly alludes to divine activity, as it does already in the LXX (Josh 6:5). Here, too, divine causation would be taken for granted,[8] even though it is not spoken of as clearly as in the case of other sayings of Jesus (e.g., Matt 6:26, 30//Luke 12:24, 28). But in its present context the primary meaning of the term is that the growth takes place without the farmer's efforts.[9]

The sequence of stalk, head, and grain gives the hearer and reader a vivid and moving picture of the development. The so-called "rule of three" is operative here to good effect.

In 1972 a scholar claimed that a fragment of Mark 2:28 was discovered in Cave 7 at Qumran,[10] a claim that caused considerable sensation. The claim was made that additional fragments in that cave correspond to Mark 6:52-53 and James 1:23-24.[11] If so, these data would show that NT books were at Qumran, and that they originated by the middle of the first century.

The claim has been discounted by a host of scholars.[12] It rests on an insufficient sample of writing. All that appears on the fragment are a few marks and letters in three lines, appearing as follows:

6. J. Crossan, "Seed Parables," 251-52.

7. BAGD 122.

8. R. Stuhlmann, "Beobachtungen," 154-56; H. Weder, Gleichnisse, 118.

9. J. Gnilka, Markus, 1:184; R. Guelich, Mark, 241-42.

10. J. O'Callaghan, "¿Papiros neotestamentarios en la cueva 7 de Qumran?" 97-99 (ET, 10-12).

11. Ibid., 93-97, 99-100 (ET, 4-10, 12-14).

12. M. Baillet, "Les manuscrits," 508-16; P. Benoit, "Note sur les fragments grecs," 321-24; J. Fitzmyer, "A Qumran Fragment of Mark?" 647-50; C. J. Hemer, "New Testament Fragments at Qumran?" 125-28; C. H. Roberts, "On Some Presumed Papyrus Fragments," 446-47.

εıτ..
.λη..

The proposal made was that, when Mark 4:28 is printed with only seventeen to nineteen letters on a line, these represent a dot from a scribe on the first line, εıτ from εῖτεν on the second, and λή from πλήρη on the third. Obviously the fragment could be from any number of Greek texts. To claim that it is from the Gospel of Mark on the basis of the slim evidence provided is going well beyond the bounds of credibility.

4:29. When the fruit matures, harvest time has come. The image of a harvest is the image of judgment. The expression ἀποστέλλει τὸ δρέπανον ("he puts in the sickle") is similar in wording to the command to "put in the sickle, for the harvest is ripe" at Joel 3:13. The wording in Mark is actually closer to the MT and Targum than to the LXX (4:13, ἐξαποστείλατε δρέπανα, "put forth the sickle").[13] In Joel the expression is used for universal judgment (cf. also Rev 14:15).

The essential meaning of the parable is generally agreed upon among interpreters. That is that the kingdom of God, inaugurated by God himself, is inexorably coming into being, even apart from human efforts to bring it about or oppose it. The man's sowing is not the main thing. There is no accent at all upon his working the soil or tending to the plants as they come up. Quite the opposite. He simply sows, then waits.[14] The focus is directed instead on the growth and fruition of the seed that was sown. That process takes place apart from human effort. So the coming of the kingdom of God can be expected as a certainty.[15]

The parable is generally thought to have been spoken by the earthly Jesus.[16] If that is so, to whom was it addressed? It has been suggested that the parable was spoken to counter the views of certain persons within revolutionary movements (including Zealots) who believed that one cannot wait for the kingdom but must bring it about by force.[17] Yet nothing within the parable itself, or

13. R. Stuhlmann, "Beobachtungen," 161-62; J. Gnilka, Markus, 1:183; R. Guelich, Mark, 242.

14. B. Scott, Parable, 367, asserts that the man is not patient but ignorant, perhaps even a sluggard. But the man's not knowing how the plants grow is a sign of wonder at a mystery, not of his ignorance.

15. A. Jülicher, Gleichnisreden, 2:545; J. Jeremias, Parables, 151-52; B. Smith, Parables, 130; E. Schweizer, Mark, 102-3; R. Guelich, Mark, 244-46; H. Weder, Gleichnisse, 118.

16. A. Jülicher, Gleichnisreden, 2:545-46; N. Perrin, Teaching, 159; J. Gnilka, Markus, 1:185-86; Hans-Josef Klauck, Allegorie und Allegorese in synoptischen Gleichnistexten, NTAbh 13 (Münster: Aschendorff, 1978), 224-25; R. Guelich, Mark, 238. In R. Funk, Five Gospels, 58, the font is pink (= Jesus said something like this).

17. N. Dahl, "Parables of Growth," 157; J. Jeremias, Parables, 152; B. Smith, Parables, 130; E. Schweizer, Mark, 103.

even in its setting in Mark, would indicate that the parable was a response to such persons; and the degree of revolutionary movement at the time of Jesus' ministry is less certain today than was assumed in earlier studies.[18] The parable could have been more directly connected to Jesus' own ministry. In that case, it could have been addressed to anyone, including the disciples, who had heard Jesus' preaching about the kingdom and then questioned him about the means and manner of its coming.

Still others have suggested that the parable teaches a "realized eschatology." That is to say, in the preaching of Jesus, the time had already come for the harvest, and so the parable ends with the man's bringing in the sickle for the harvest.[19] Just so, the argument goes, the time of Jesus' ministry was a time of crisis; one could already experience the kingdom with his coming. But that seems to ignore the nuance of patient waiting that is present in the parable and the accent upon God's bringing the kingdom to a triumphant conclusion.

Within the Gospel of Mark the parable has an added meaning. That is that the sowing of the seed upon the earth has been inaugurated already in the ministry of the earthly Jesus. The present is a time of waiting for the harvest, the consummation of the kingdom and the parousia of Jesus. Even in spite of persecution (4:17), the church can continue in confidence that God will bring these realities about. Although no one knows the time of the coming of God's kingdom (13:32), nothing can finally impede the purposes and promises of God for the community of faith.

Exposition

The parable speaks to a perennial concern. In light of the bold affirmations of Scripture and the Christian faith about the coming of the kingdom, or the coming of Christ to gather in his elect (Mark 13:27), why does nothing seem to be happening? Should something be done? The question has been dealt with within the NT itself in a passage that uses imagery related to that in this parable: "Be patient . . . until the coming of the Lord. The farmer waits for the precious crop from the earth, being patient with it until it receives the early and the late rains. You also must be patient" (Jas 5:7-8).

Anyone who has read the narratives of Jesus' teaching and healing ministry in the Gospels has some reliable impressions of what the kingdom will be like. And the Christian will seek to align himself or herself by words and deeds with the kingdom. Since the Christian knows the outcome of history, even if only dimly, he or she will lean into the future that God has in store for the universe.

Nevertheless, there is no way that anyone can force the turning of the

18. David Rhoads, "Zealots," *ABD* 6:1,043-54.
19. C. H. Dodd, *Parables,* 144; V. Taylor, *Mark,* 266.

wheel of history to bring about the kingdom. All such attempts have failed, and some instances have been demonic. Sin affects all attempts at righteousness for the self or for society.

Martin Luther put it well in his *Small Catechism,* when commenting on the petition "your kingdom come" of the Lord's Prayer: "The kingdom of God comes of itself, without our prayer, but we pray in this petition that it may also come to us."[20] (For Luther, that coming to us consisted of the work of the Holy Spirit in our lives, enabling us to believe the Word of God and live a godly life.) There is a modesty in that concerning the self, and a boldness concerning God.

Neither Christians nor anyone else can build the kingdom. At best, persons can align themselves with the future of God as they see it, but knowing that they must not confuse their convictions with the absolute will of God. God will bring about the kingdom. Waiting in patience does not mean being absolutely passive. But it means that we realize that God's purposes are greater than our own.

Select Bibliography

Baillet, Maurice. "Les manuscrits de la Grotte 7 de Qumrân et le Nouveau Testament." *Bib* 53 (1972): 508-16.

Baltensweiler, Heinrich. "Das Gleichnis von der selbstwachsenden Saat (Markus 4,26-29) und die theologische Konzeption des Markusevangelisten." In *Oikonomia: Heilsgeschichte als Thema der Theologie: Festschrift für Oscar Cullmann,* 69-75. Ed. Felix Christ. Hamburg-Bergstedt: Herbert Reich, 1967.

Benoit, Pierre. "Note sur les fragments grecs de la grotte 7 de Qumrân." *RB* 79 (1972): 321-24.

Collins, Raymond F. "The Story of a Seed Growing by Itself: A Parable for Our Times." *Emmanuel* 94 (1998): 446-52.

Crossan, John D. "The Seed Parables of Jesus." *JBL* 92 (1973): 244-66.

Dahl, Nils A. "The Parables of Growth." *ST* 5 (1951): 132-66. Reprinted in *Jesus in the Memory of the Early Church,* 141-66. Minneapolis: Augsburg Publishing House, 1976.

Derrett, J. Duncan M. "Ambivalence: Sowing and Reaping at Mark 4,26-29." *EstBib* 48 (1990): 489-510.

Dupont, Jacques. "La parabole de la semence qui pousse toute seule (Marc 4,26-29)." *RSR* 55 (1979): 367-92.

Eckstein, Richard. "Die von selbst wachsende Saat. Markus 4,26-29." In *Gleichnisse aus Altem und Neuem Testament,* 139-45. Ed. Christine Bourbeck. Stuttgart: Klotz, 1971.

20. Quoted from *The Book of Concord,* ed. Theodore G. Tappert (Philadelphia: Fortress Press, 1959), 346.

Fitzmyer, Joseph A. "A Qumran Fragment of Mark?" *America* 126 (1972): 647-50.

Gottschalk, Ingeborg. "Das Gleichnis vom Samann. Markus 4,26-29." In *Gleichnisse aus Altem und Neuem Testament*, 125-32. Ed. Christine Bourbeck. Stuttgart: Klotz, 1971.

Gourges, Michel. "Faire confiance à la grâce de Dieu: La parabole du blé qui pousse tout seul (Mc 4,25-29)." *NRT* 117 (1995): 364-75.

Harder, Günther. "Das Gleichnis von der selbstwachsenden Saat Mk 4,26-29." *ThViat* 1 (1948-49): 51-70.

Heil, John P. "Reader-Response and the Narrative Context of the Parables about Growing Seed in Mark 4:1-34." *CBQ* 54 (1992): 271-86.

Hemer, Colin J. "New Testament Fragments at Qumran?" *TynB* 23 (1972): 125-28.

Kilpatrick, George D. "Mark IV.29." *JTS* 46 (1945): 191.

Kümmel, Werner G. "Noch einmal: Das Gleichnis von der selbstwachsenden Saat. Bermerkungen zur neuesten Diskussion um die Auslegung der Gleichnisse Jesu." In *Orientierung an Jesus: Zur Theologie der Synoptiker: Für Josef Schmid*, 220-37. Ed. Paul Hoffmann et al. Freiburg: Herder, 1973.

Manson, T. W. "A Note on Mark iv.28f." *JTS* 38 (1937): 399-400.

O'Callaghan, José. "¿Papiros neotestamentarios en la cueva 7 de Qumran?" *Bib* 53 (1972): 91-100. English translation: "New Testament Papyri in Qumran Cave 7." In *Supplement to JBL* 91/2 (1972). Society of Biblical Literature, 1972.

Pavur, Claude N. "The Grain Is Ripe: Parabolic Meaning in Mark 4:26-29." *BTB* 17/1 (1987): 21-23.

Roberts, C. H. "On Some Presumed Papyrus Fragments of the New Testament from Qumran." *JTS* 23 (1972): 446-47.

Sahlin, Harald. "Zum Verständnis von drei Stellen des Markus-Evangeliums." *Bib* 33 (1952): 53-66.

Stuhlmann, Rainer. "Beobachtungen und Überlegungen zu Markus 4:26-29." *NTS* 19 (1973): 153-62.

Theissen, Gerd. "Der Bauer und die von selbst Frucht bringende Erde. Naiver Synergismus in Mk 4,26-29?" *ZNW* 85 (1994): 167-82.

Weder, Hans. "Metapher und Gleichnis. Bemerkungen zur Reichweite des Bildes in religiöser Sprache." *ZTK* 90 (1993): 382-408.

Weiss, Karl. "Mk. 4:26 bis 29: Dennoch die Parabel vom zuversichtlichen Sämann!" *BZ* 18 (1929): 45-68.

———. *Voll Zuversicht! Zur Parabel Jesu vom zuversichtlichen Sämann Mk. 4,26-29*. Münster: Aschendorffsche Verlagsbuchhandlung, 1922.

8.35. The Mustard Seed, Mark 4:30-32//Matthew 13:31-32// Luke 13:18-19; Thomas 20

Mark 4:30-32

30And [Jesus] said, "With what can we compare the kingdom of God, or what parable shall we use for it? 31It is like a grain of mustard seed, which, when sown upon the ground, is the smallest of all the seeds on earth; 32and when it is sown it grows up and becomes the greatest of all shrubs, and puts forth large branches, so that the birds of the air can make nests in its shade."

Matthew 13:31-32

31Another parable [Jesus] put before them, saying, "The kingdom of heaven is like a grain of mustard seed which a man took and sowed in his field; 32it is the smallest of all the seeds, but when it has grown it is the greatest of shrubs and becomes a tree, so that the birds of the air come and make nests in its branches."

Luke 13:18-19

18[Jesus] said therefore, "What is the kingdom of God like? And to what shall I compare it? 19It is like a grain of mustard seed which a man took and cast in his garden; and it grew and became a tree, and the birds of the air made nests in its branches."

Notes on the Texts and Translation

There are few textual problems in the three versions. They can be dealt with together. Only two issues need comment.

Mark 4:32//Matthew 13:32//Luke 13:19. The phrase "birds of the air" is adopted in the translation of each text, as in several modern versions (RSV, NIV, NRSV; cf. KJV, "fowls of the air"), although a literal translation would be "birds of heaven." The problem with the latter is that it could connote birds dwelling in (= within) heaven. Obviously it is the birds flying above that are meant. The NEB has simply "birds."

Luke 13:19. Some important Greek witnesses (including 𝔭45, A, family 13, and the Majority text), plus Latin, Syriac, and Coptic texts, read "a great tree" (δένδρον μέγα) instead of simply "a tree," and that reading is represented in the KJV. But other important Greek witnesses (including 𝔭75, ℵ, B, D), plus other Latin, Syriac, and Coptic texts, do not have the adjective. Although the former reading is possible, it is more likely that it was added in order to heighten the contrast between the mustard seed and the tree (an element existing in Mark 4:31-32//Matt 13:31-32);[1] the shorter reading is to be preferred, as in the 27th edition of the Nestle-Aland Greek text and represented in the RSV, NEB, NIV, and NRSV.

Thomas 20

The disciples said to Jesus, "Tell us what the kingdom of heaven is like."
He said to them, "It is like a mustard seed. It is the smallest of all seeds. But when it falls on tilled soil, it produces a great plant and becomes a shelter for birds of the sky."[2]

General Comments on the Texts

The parable appears in all three Synoptic Gospels, but it is evident that Matthew and Luke — because of certain verbal similarities shared between them, over against Mark — did not make use of Mark's version alone. These include (1) the identical expressions ὃν λαβὼν ἄνθρωποι ("which a man took," Matt 13:31//Luke 13:19); (2) reference to a "tree" (Matt 13:32//Luke 13:19), which is missing in Mark's version; and (3) identical wording against Mark at the end: "the birds of the air made nests in its branches" (a conflation of expressions from the OT, Matt 13:32//Luke 13:19). It is therefore generally thought that, in addition to Mark's version, a Q version existed as well.[3] Most likely that version is represented in Luke's version, and Matthew's is a conflation of his sources, Mark and Q.

The canonical versions are alike and different in the following ways:

Mark: A contrast is made between the smallest of seeds and the greatest of shrubs, which has large branches; birds make nests in its shade.
Luke: A seed grows and becomes a tree; birds make nests in its branches.
Matthew: A contrast is made between the smallest of seeds and the greatest of shrubs, which becomes a tree; birds make nests in its branches.

In each case there is an introductory formula in which a comparison is made. The comparison is not a simple one between the kingdom and the mustard seed. The various expressions mean that it is the case with the kingdom as

1. B. Metzger, *TCGNT* 162.
2. Quoted from *NHLE* 128.
3. Burnett H. Streeter, *The Four Gospels: A Study in Origins* (New York: St. Martin's Press, 1924), 264, 291; R. Bultmann, *HST* 172; T. W. Manson, *Sayings*, 123; A. Polag, *Fragmenta Q,* 25, 66; Rudolf Laufen, *Die Doppelüberlieferungen der Logienquelle und des Markusevangeliums,* BBB 54 (Bonn: Peter Hanstein Verlag, 1980), 174-75; J. Fitzmyer, *Luke,* 1,015; W. D. Davies and D. C. Allison, *Matthew,* 2:416; R. Brown, *Introduction NT,* 119.

it is with the mustard seed and the consequence of its being placed in the soil.[4] All the imagery that follows (especially the accents on small beginnings, great endings) is to be observed.

Since the parable illustrates the kingdom from something typical in a timeless way and lacks a narrative set in past time, it can be classified as a similitude.[5] The fact that the versions in Matthew and Luke (and presumably, therefore, Q) narrate elements of the comparison in past time does not actually outweigh that judgment.[6] Furthermore, as in the case of the Parable of the Leaven from Q (Matt 13:33//Luke 13:20-21) and the Parables of the Treasure and Pearl in Matthew alone (13:44-46), this one has no application at the end in any of its canonical (or its apocryphal) versions.

In the view of some interpreters the version in the *Gospel of Thomas* 20 was derived from a tradition independent of the Synoptics.[7] But others consider it to have been derived from the canonical Gospels and edited by the Gospel's author.[8] The reasons for the latter view are that the *Thomas* version contains phrases and terms reminiscent of the canonical texts — and Mark's version in particular — such as the seed being designated the smallest of all seeds (Mark 4:31//Matt 13:33), the similarity of introducing the subordinate clause by "when" (ὅταν, Mark 4:32//Matt 13:32), and the correspondence be-

4. J. Jeremias, *Parables*, 101, 147.

5. R. Bultmann, *HST* 172; J. Kingsbury, *Matthew 13*, 78; E. Linnemann, *Parables*, 9; R. Stein, *Parables*, 19; J. Lambrecht, *Treasure*, 166. On the other hand, A. Jülicher, *Gleichnisreden*, 2:569-81, and C. H. Dodd, *Parables*, 6, consider it a parable proper (Parabel).

6. H. Hendrickx, *Parables*, 31; U. Luz, *Matthäus*, 2:327; and W. D. Davies and D. C. Allison, *Matthew*, 2:416, maintain that the Q version should be classified as a true parable. Two factors favor that view: (1) the comparison made includes a man who does the sowing, and (2) the man's action is set in past time. But the features of an actual story are missing. The man who does the sowing does not become a character within a story; the focus remains on the seed.

7. Stephen J. Patterson, *The Gospel of Thomas and Jesus* (Sonoma, Calif.: Polebridge Press, 1993), 27-28; Charles W. Hedrick, *Parables as Poetic Fictions: The Creative Voice of Jesus* (Peabody, Mass.: Hendrickson Publishers, 1994), 249-51.

8. Hugh Montefiore, "A Comparison of the Parables of the Gospel according to Thomas and of the Synoptic Gospels," in *Thomas and the Evangelists*, by H. E. W. Turner and H. Montefiore, SBT 35 (Naperville: Alec R. Allenson, 1962), 51; Robert M. Grant and David N. Freedman, *The Secret Sayings of Jesus* (Garden City: Doubleday, 1960), 140; Wolfgang Schrage, *Das Verhältnis des Thomas-Evangeliums zur synoptischen Tradition und zu den koptischen Evangelienübersetzungen: Zugleich ein Beitrag zur gnostischen Synoptikerdeutung*, BZNW 29 (Berlin: Alfred Töpelmann, 1964), 61-66; Jacques-É. Ménard, *L'Évangile selon Thomas*, NHS 5 (Leiden: E. J. Brill, 1975), 109; Christopher Tuckett, "Thomas and the Synoptics," *NovT* 30 (1988), 148-53; Michael Fieger, *Das Thomasevangelium: Einleitung Kommentar Systematik*, NTAbh 22 (Münster: Aschendorff, 1991), 90-91; H. Fleddermann, "The Mustard Seed and the Leaven," 225-29; R. Gundry, *Mark*, 231.

THE MUSTARD SEED

tween "on tilled soil" and "on the ground" (Mark 4:31) over against "in his field" (Matt 13:31) or "in his garden" (Luke 18:19). This evidence is admittedly slim, although it is strengthened if the designation of the mustard seed as the smallest is Markan redaction.[9] Moreover, when one adds to it the high probability that the author of the *Gospel of Thomas* made some use of the canonical Gospels elsewhere,[10] the likelihood of independence from the Synoptic versions in this place diminishes even more.

The *Thomas* version has gnosticizing elements in at least two respects. The mustard seed represents the spark of light, the enlightenment that comes to the Gnostic, and the tilled ground refers to the readiness of the Gnostic to receive it.[11] That means that the parable has been transformed from a parable of the kingdom as an outward, eschatological reality to one in which the kingdom is thought of as an inner, spiritual reality that is available to the individual Gnostic.

Along with three other parables (the Sower, the Seed Growing Secretly, and the Leaven), the Mustard Seed is often called a "parable of growth." These parables are all concerned about the kingdom of God, and they provide pictorial contrasts between tiny beginnings and grand, magnificent endings. They do not portray progress in the sense of a gradual development, but a contrast between small beginnings and big endings.

A "mustard seed" is proverbially known as the smallest of all seeds even in nonbiblical sources — both gentile Hellenistic[12] and rabbinic.[13] That viewpoint is reflected also in another saying in the Gospels (Matt 17:20//Luke 17:6). Here the reference is to the seed of the mustard plant that grows in Galilee (σίναπι in Greek; botanically the *brassica nigra*), an annual herb from which an oil is derived for use as a seasoning.[14] The seed is indeed very small, measuring .075 inches in diameter, but the plant it produces can become six,[15] twelve,[16] or in rare cases even fifteen feet high.[17] In modern times no one would call the mustard plant a "tree" (Matt 13:32//Luke 13:19) but at most a large plant (Mark 4:32), and various interpreters have faulted the Q version of the parable at this

9. As claimed by C. Tuckett, "Thomas and the Synoptics," 149-51.

10. See Chapter 10 on "Parables in the *Gospel of Thomas.*"

11. R. M. Grant and D. N. Freedman, *Secret Sayings,* 140; Bertil Gärtner, *The Theology of the Gospel according to Thomas* (New York: Harper & Brothers, 1961), 232; N. Perrin, *Teaching,* 157; M. Fieger, *Thomasevangelium,* 92.

12. BAGD 751 (with references).

13. *M. Nid.* 5:2; additional references in Str-B 1:699; Claus-Hunno Hunzinger, "σίναπι," *TDNT* 7:288.

14. Irene Jacob and Walter Jacob, "Flora," *ABD* 2:812.

15. Ibid., 2:812.

16. A. Jülicher, *Gleichnisreden,* 2:575; T. W. Manson, *Sayings,* 123.

17. "Mustard," in *The New Encyclopaedia Britannica,* 15th ed., ed. Philip W. Goetz, 32 vols. (Chicago: Encyclopaedia Britannica, 1987), 8:455.

point.[18] Nevertheless, in antiquity the term δένδρον could occasionally refer to tall plants.[19] The term might be due primarily, however, to the process of making allusions to OT imagery.

The coming of the birds to make their nests in the shade of the large plant (Mark 4:32), or to make nests in the branches of a tree (Matt 13:32// Luke 13:19), is generally regarded as an eschatological image of the incorporation of the Gentiles into the people of God. The imagery is based on prior images in OT texts (Judg 9:15; Ezek 17:23; 31:6; Dan 4:12, 21; LXX 103:12) that were interpreted in Jewish traditions to signify the coming of the repentant gentile nations at the end time to worship the God of Israel.[20] In none of the versions of the parable, however, is there a direct quotation from an OT text. Although it has been suggested that the eschatological allusions are due to Christian allegorizing of the parable,[21] that is unlikely for three reasons. First, the imagery belongs to the basic structure and content of the parable. The parable speaks of the tiny seed and its growth to a huge shrub or tree, but that alone is not enough to stop the momentum; in a world of storytellers who make vivid use of imagery, the story cannot end without some statement of the significance of what has come into being.[22] Second, the imagery has double attestation in both the Markan and Q traditions. And, finally, the fact that no actual OT text is quoted, but only a rather elusive symbol derived from a number of texts is alluded to (elusive enough for the writer of the *Gospel of Thomas* to include it, in spite of gnostic antipathy to the OT), speaks in favor of the eschatological ending of the parable as integral to the original parable.

The parable is generally considered to have been uttered by Jesus.[23] The parable would most likely have been told in response to the question, How could the ministry of Jesus and his disciples have anything to do with the kingdom? The glorious kingdom of Israel's expectation has not arrived. The preaching and healing ministry of Jesus hardly seems significant enough as the dawn

---

18. J. Jeremias, *Parables*, 147; J. Kingsbury, *Matthew 13*, 81; B. Scott, *Parable*, 377.

19. LSJ 378 (with references).

20. For references, cf. T. W. Manson, *The Teaching of Jesus: Studies in Its Form and Content* (Cambridge: Cambridge University Press, 1951), 133 (n. 1); J. Jeremias, *Parables*, 147.

21. B. Smith, *Parables*, 121; J. Crossan, "Seed Parables," 255, 258-59.

22. J. Crossan, "Seed Parables," 259, has written that four elements constitute the original parable: "the initial sowing, the growth, the final size, and the shade for the birds." He says this in spite of his claim that the OT allusions are not original.

23. A. Jülicher, *Gleichnisreden*, 2:581; J. Jeremias, *Parables*, 149; N. Perrin, *Teaching*, 157-58; Hans-Josef Klauck, *Allegorie und Allegorese in synoptischen Gleichnistexten*, NTAbh 13 (Münster: Aschendorff, 1978), 216-17; J. Gnilka, *Markus*, 1:188; U. Luz, *Matthäus*, 2:332. According to R. Funk, *Five Gospels*, 59, 194, 346, 484, the Jesus Seminar has concluded that the *Gospel of Thomas* 20 is authentic (red font); the three Synoptic versions are close to what Jesus said, but colored by apocalyptic (therefore pink font).

of a new age. The response to that charge is that one should look to the mustard seed. In spite of its small size, a great plant grows from it.[24] That message could have been addressed to persons who opposed the message of Jesus,[25] but more likely it was addressed to his followers.[26]

The Parable in the Gospel of Mark

Exegetical Commentary

Within the Gospel of Mark the parable is apparently addressed to the crowds (4:33-34) in the presence of the disciples. It appears as the last within a series of three parables in that Gospel (4:1-34), a series that may have constituted a collection prior to the writing of the Gospel of Mark.[27]

Problems of Greek syntax abound. In 4:31 the relative pronoun ὅν ("which") is masculine, and therefore must refer back to the Greek masculine noun κόκκοι ("seed," "grain"; the word translated "mustard," σίναπι, is neuter), which is proper; but the subsequent adjectives μικρότερον ("smallest") and μεῖζον ("greatest") and the participle ὄν (literally, "being") are neuter, corresponding in gender with σίναπι (rather than the masculine κόκκος), which is not proper. Furthermore, the phrase καὶ ὅταν σπαρῇ ("and when it is sown") at the outset of 4:32 is redundant.

In light of the syntactical awkwardness and redundancy of 4:31-32, it is evident that considerable redaction has been supplied by the evangelist, who sought to highlight the contrast between small beginnings and huge endings by adding to his material, but did so in rather cumbersome ways. According to various interpreters, material added by Mark would have included μικρότερον ὄν πάντων τῶν σπερμάτων τῶν ἐπὶ τῇ γῇ (4:31b, "being the smallest of all the seeds on earth"), as various interpreters have held in the past,[28] to which one must also add the redundant καὶ ὅταν σπαρῇ (4:32a, "and when it is sown"), as other interpreters have suggested (in addition to 4:31b),[29] plus καὶ γίνεται μεῖζον πάντων τῶν λαχάνων (4:32b, "and becomes the greatest of all shrubs"),

24. T. W. Manson, *Sayings*, 123; N. Dahl, "The Parables of Growth," 155-56; C. Carlston, *Parables*, 161-62.

25. J. Lambrecht, *Treasure*, 167.

26. B. Smith, *Parables*, 120.

27. Heinz-Wolfgang Kuhn, *Ältere Sammlungen im Markusevangelium*, SUNT 8 (Göttingen: Vandenhoeck & Ruprecht, 1971), 99-146.

28. A. Jülicher, *Gleichnisreden*, 2:580; C. H. Dodd, *Parables*, 153 (n. 1); V. Taylor, *Mark*, 270.

29. H.-W. Kuhn, *Ältere Sammlungen*, 100 (n. 8); J. Crossan, "Seed Parables," 256; Robert A. Guelich, *Mark 1–8:26*, WBC 34A (Dallas: Word Books, 1989), 247, 249; R. Gundry, *Mark*, 229. In the estimation of Kuhn (cf. p. 99), however, the material was added at a redactional stage prior to Mark's own.

as suggested by still others (in addition to 4:31b-32a).[30] Once these materials are removed, the parable is still intact, and in fact it reads better.

4:30. Mark's introductory formula is distinctive. This is the only time he uses the verb ὁμοιόω ("to compare"), which is used eight times in Matthew and three times in Luke. The second half of the verse — also distinctive, not found in either of the other Synoptics — seems repetitious. But it is a beautiful addition that can probably be attributed to Semitic parallelism (cf. Isa 40:18), intended to catch the reader's attention. The entire verse is interrogatory, posing a question twice by different expressions.

4:31-32. The Markan version of the parable (followed by Matthew's) presents a dramatic contrast between the tiny mustard seed and the huge shrub that comes from it. By means of his redactional, parenthetical statements (see above), Mark provides information that is not to be missed: the mustard seed is the "smallest" of all seeds, and the plant is the "greatest" of all shrubs. The contrast is thus underscored.

The adjectives μικρότερον and μεῖζον are comparatives (so "smaller" and "greater"), but they function as superlatives (so "smallest" and "greatest") both here and elsewhere in the NT.[31] But even when they are translated literally as comparatives, the superlative sense comes out by the double use of the plural genitive πάντων ("of all") — "smaller than *all* the seeds" and "greater than *all* the shrubs."

The birds make their nests in the "shade" of the branches rather than "in the branches" themselves, as in the other Gospels (Matt 13:32//Luke 13:19). For the others, the plant becomes a tree, which allows for birds to make nests in the branches. But for Mark the plant is simply a huge shrub. It is more likely that birds will make nests in the shade of the branches of a large shrub than in the branches themselves.

The parable is located within the Galilean ministry of Jesus and among other parables of the kingdom and sayings about parables (4:1-34). The section discloses the certainty of the coming of the kingdom. It is granted that there are at most slight signs of the kingdom's appearance in the teaching and healing ministry of Jesus. But its coming in fulfillment of Israel's expectations can be anticipated, and that will be in an abundance beyond expectations. The Gentiles, too, will be gathered into the people of God. The readers and hearers of the parable in the time of the composition of Mark's Gospel, who have faced — and continue to face — persecution (13:9), are also encouraged to anticipate the coming of the kingdom and the Son of man. As disciples of Jesus — com-

30. H.-W. Kuhn, *Ältere Sammlungen,* 100 (n. 8), but at a pre-Markan stage; J. Crossan, "Seed Parables," 256-57 (by the evangelist Mark); B. Scott, *Parable,* 378.

31. BAGD 521 and 498 (μέγας, 2,b), respectively. Forms of the comparative μείζων are always used for the superlative with the exception of the singular use of μέγιστοι at 2 Peter 1:4.

posing a band of persons that is tiny like the mustard seed — they are given the promise of salvation.

The Parable in the Gospel of Matthew

Exegetical Commentary

The parable is the third of seven within the Parable Discourse (Matt 13:1-50). Within that context it is addressed to the crowds (13:2, 34).

13:31-32. The introductory formula, "another parable he put before them" (13:31a), is typically Matthean, exactly as at 13:24. The expression "the kingdom of heaven is like" is also typical (cf. 13:33, 44, 45, 47).

The man sowed the seed "in his field" rather than upon the ground (Mark) or in his garden (Luke). If the latter were in Q, Matthew may have altered the tradition in light of the prohibition to sow mustard in one's garden.[32] It also corresponds to a man's having sowed good seed "in his field" within an earlier parable (13:24). See further comments on Luke 13:19.

On the use of the comparative adjectives μικρότερον and μεῖζον for superlatives ("smallest" and "greatest"), see comments on Mark 4:31-32.

The use of the aorist indicative ἔσπειρεν ("sowed") at this point indicates that the evangelist sets the action of sowing in past time. It has been suggested that Matthew does so in order to portray the man who has sowed the seed (thereby inaugurating the process of the coming of the kingdom) as Jesus.[33] Actually the use of the aorist is made necessary by what is already in Q (as presented in Luke 13:19), a series of aorists.[34] But there are other indicators that favor the view that, for Matthew, the sowing of the Mustard Seed has indeed been begun by Jesus in the past, and that the present of the Matthean community is a time of expectation. The indicators are the parallels in terminology with the Parable of the Weeds among the Wheat and its Interpretation. The "man" who sows (13:24, 31) is the Son of man (13:37). The "field" (13:24, 31) is the "world" (13:38). Furthermore, Matthew (against Q, as attested in Luke 13:19) has changed the aorist ἐγένετο ("became") into a present, γίνεται ("becomes," "is becoming"), in regard to the growth of the tree. Just so, the kingdom has been inaugurated through the ministry of Jesus. The kingdom and the church are not identical, but they are related, and those who are members of the church think of themselves as living between the ministry of Jesus on earth and his parousia, a time when the kingdom "is becoming," coming into being. In God's

32. M. Kil. 3:2.

33. J. Kingsbury, *Matthew 13*, 80; H. Hendrickx, *Parables*, 42-43; R. Gundry, *Matthew*, 268-69; U. Luz, *Matthäus*, 2:333.

34. That is, an aorist participle (λαβών, "having taken"), then a main verb in the aorist (ἔβαλεν, "he cast") — for which Matthew has replaced his own ἔσπειρεν ("he sowed") — and still another aorist indicative in the next clause (ηὔξησεν, "it grew").

own time, the kingdom will come in its fullness, and the nations will be incorporated into the people of God.

13:32. Matthew follows Mark in reporting that the mustard seed is the smallest of all seeds but that, when it grows, it becomes larger than all the plants. These items are missing in Luke's version. Thus, like Mark, Matthew underscores the great contrast between small beginnings and large outcomes.

As in Luke's version, however, Matthew says that a "tree" results, and the birds rest in its branches. These details are from Q. The expression can be taken as hyperbole in order to emphasize the contrast; it is also fitting insofar as it is an allusion to OT texts.

The meaning of the parable has not been altered significantly by Matthew, even though he conflated his sources (Mark and Q). The reader and hearer of the parable within the Matthean community know well that the kingdom, the reign of God, has not yet triumphed over all, but is apparent at best only in the smallest manner. It is present — and Christ himself is present — even if only two or three are gathered together in his name (18:20), sharing in those things that he has provided, including a designated prayer (6:9-13) and supper (26:26-29), observing what he has commanded (28:20), and serving those in need (25:31-46). Such small, seemingly insignificant beginnings can hardly appear to be signs of the glorious kingdom to come, or indeed even be related foundationally to its coming. But the community is given the certainty by means of this parable that indeed that is so.

The Parable in the Gospel of Luke

Exegetical Commentary

Luke has placed the parable within the Travel Narrative (9:51–19:27). Specifically it follows upon the narration of a miraculous healing on a sabbath within a synagogue (13:10-17), at the close of which Jesus' opponents have been silenced, and the crowd is rejoicing. He goes on to speak, apparently to both his opponents and the crowd within the synagogue.

13:18. The parable is introduced by means of a question. As in Mark, but not dependent upon Mark, the question is asked by means of two clauses, reflecting Semitic parallelism (cf. Isa 40:18).

13:19. The comparison in Luke is the simplest of the three Synoptic versions. Luke (following his source) does not explain that the mustard seed is the smallest of all, and that the plant is the largest of all plants. He says only that when a person plants the seed, it grows and becomes a tree, in the branches of which the birds make nests. The fact that Luke has the seed sown in a "garden" may indicate that he has rewritten the parable for a non-Palestinian, even Hellenistic gentile, setting, as some have suggested.[35] But it is more likely that the

---

35. H. McArthur, "Mustard Seed," 201; I. H. Marshall, *Luke,* 561.

term was in the Q version, which Luke took over, and that Matthew replaced it with "field" in keeping with Jewish law and using the same phrase as he does in 13:24.[36]

The evangelist has placed this parable after a controversy. The power of the kingdom has been manifested in a healing of a crippled woman within a synagogue on the sabbath (13:10-17). But the opponents of Jesus do not recognize the healing in that way. They criticize him for healing on the sabbath. Jesus replies that, since one will release and lead an ox to water on the sabbath, how much more should this woman have release from her bondage on the sabbath? His opponents are thereby put to shame, but the crowd rejoices.

The parable follows, introduced by οὖν ("therefore"), as though it is an immediate addendum to the miracle and the silencing of the opponents. The kingdom, in Luke's perspective, is a present reality in the ministry of Jesus, and it is present among believers in the continuation of history (17:21). But its presence and power are both hidden (12:32; 13:20-21; 17:20) and revealed (11:20). That can be illustrated by means of the Parable of the Mustard Seed.

Exposition

The emphasis in the parable is not on a presumed "growth and development" of the kingdom of God (although there are signs of such thinking in Matthew's version). Instead, by means of the great contrast between the tiny mustard seed, on the one hand, and the tree or huge shrub on the other, the accent is on the certainty and powerful significance of the coming of the kingdom in due course — God's own time — even though its glory may not be visible in the present. As one interpreter has put it: "The Kingdom which [Jesus] preached does not grow — it comes; and its coming does not depend upon its acceptance by the world but upon the will of God."[37]

But the parable does not simply provide information about God, God's kingdom, and its coming. In each of its canonical versions, the parable sets forth a message of encouragement. Christians of every age often wonder whether their efforts of work and witness are of any importance in the world. And what of the church itself, which has relatively little power among the forces that move history?

The parable speaks a word of promise. The seemingly insignificant acts of work and witness by the disciples of Jesus are of ultimate importance.

It is possible to see big results from tiny beginnings within human history.

---

36. Siegfried Schulz, *Q: Die Spruchquelle der Evangelisten* (Zurich: Theologischer Verlag, 1972), 299; H. Weder, *Gleichnisse*, 130. A. Polag, *Fragmenta Q*, 66, favors "field." B. Scott, *Parable*, 376, considers "garden" the original (pre-Lukan) reading since it is the more difficult reading.
37. B. Smith, *Parables*, 120.

The story of the church is a prime example, whether one looks at the church as a whole or at the church in various continents. But one must beware of triumphalism and the measuring of success by secular standards. The church and the kingdom are not identical. God has a greater and more certain reality in store than one can see in the empirical church, which is always under judgment as well as grace. At most the church remains one of several instruments used by God for his reign in nature and history.

The kingdom is certain, and it will be glorious. That is so in spite of the vicissitudes of history. Christian faith rests on the promises of what is seen only from afar (Heb 11:13).

Select Bibliography

Bartsch, Hans-Werner. "Eine bisher übersehene Zitierung der LXX in Mark 4,30." *TZ* 15 (1959): 126-28.

Bowen, Clayton R. "The Kingdom and the Mustard Seed." *AJT* 22 (1918): 562-69.

Casalegno, Alberto. "La parabola del granello di senape (Mc 4,30-32)." *RivB* 26 (1978): 139-61.

Clark, Kenneth W. "The Mustard Plant." *ClW* 37 (1943-44): 81-83.

Cotter, Wendy J. "The Parable of the Mustard Seed and the Leaven: Their Function in the Earliest Stratum of Q." *TJT* 8 (1992): 38-51.

Crossan, John D. "The Seed Parables of Jesus." *JBL* 92 (1973): 244-66.

Dahl, Nils A. "The Parables of Growth." *ST* 5 (1951): 132-66. Reprinted in his *Jesus in the Memory of the Early Church*, 141-66. Minneapolis: Augsburg Publishing House, 1976.

Dupont, Jacques. "Le couple parabolique du sénevé et du levain." In *Jesus Christ in Historie und Theologie: Neutestamentliche Festschrift für Hans Conzelmann zum 60. Geburtstag*, 331-45. Ed. Georg Strecker. Tübingen: J. C. B. Mohr (Paul Siebeck), 1975.

———. "Les paraboles du sénevé et du levain (Mt 13,31-33; Lc 13,18-21)." *NRT* 89 (1967): 897-913.

Fleddermann, Harry. "The Mustard Seed and the Leaven in Q, the Synoptics, and Thomas." In *Society of Biblical Literature 1989 Seminar Papers*, 216-36. Ed. David J. Lull. SBLSP 28. Atlanta: Scholars Press, 1989.

Funk, Robert W. "The Looking-Glass Tree Is for the Birds: Ezekiel 17:22-24; Mark 4:30-32." *Int* 27 (1973): 3-9.

Hertzsch, Klaus-Peter. "Jésus herméneute: Une étude de Marc 4,30-32." In *Reconnaissance à Suzanne de Diétrich: Études et documents recueillis dans le monde à l'occasion de son 80e anniversaire*, 109-16. Ed. Simone Frutiger. CBFVSup. Paris: Foi et Vie, 1971.

Hirth, Volkmar. "Die baumgrosse Senfstaude: Bild der wahren Königsherrschaft." *BibNot* 83 (1996): 15-16.

Hunter, A. M. "The Interpretation of the Parables." *ExpTim* 69 (1957-58): 100-104.

Jehle, Friedrich. "Senfkorn und Sauerteig in der Hl. Schrift." *NKZ* 34 (1923): 713-19.

Kuss, Otto. "Zum Sinngehalt des Gleichnisses vom Senfkorn und Sauerteig." *Bib* 40 (1959): 641-53.

Laufen, Rudolf. "βασιλεία und ἐκκλησία: Eine traditions- und redaktionsgeschichtliche Untersuchung des Gleichnisses vom Senfkorn." In *Begegnung mit dem Wort: Festschrift für Heinrich Zimmermann*, 105-40. Ed. Josef Zmijewski and Ernst Nellessen. BBB 53. Bonn: Peter Hanstein Verlag, 1979.

Mare, W. Harold. "The Smallest Mustard Seed: Matthew 13:32." *GTJ* 9 (1968): 3-9.

Matthews, Albert J. "The Mustard 'Tree.'" *ExpTim* 39 (1927-28): 32-34.

McArthur, Harvey K. "The Parable of the Mustard Seed." *CBQ* 33 (1971): 198-201.

Michaelis, Wilhelm. "Die Gleichnisse vom Senfkorn und vom Sauerteig." *Kirchenfreund* 72 (1938): 118-21, 129-36.

Mussner, Franz. "1QHodajoth und das Gleichnis vom Senfkorn (Mk. 4,30-32 par.)." *BZ* 4 (1960): 128-30.

Pousset, Édouard. "Le sénéve et le levain." *VCh* 174 (1975): 13-16.

Ricoeur, Paul. "Listening to the Parables of Jesus; Text: Matthew 13:31-32 and 45-46." *Criterion* 13 (September 1975): 18-22.

Schultze, Bernard. "Die ekklesiologische Bedeutung des Gleichnisses vom Senfkorn (Matth. 13,31-32; Mk. 4,30-32; Lk. 13,18-10)." *OCP* 27 (1961): 362-86.

Sproule, John A. "The Problem of the Mustard Seed." *GTJ* 1 (1980): 37-42.

Wenham, David. "The Synoptic Problem Revisited: Some New Suggestions about the Composition of Mark 4:1-34." *TynB* 23 (1972): 3-38.

8.36. The Leaven, Matthew 13:33//Luke 13:20-21; *Thomas* 96

Matthew 13:33

33 *[Jesus] told them another parable. "The kingdom of heaven is like leaven that a woman took and hid in three measures of flour, until it was all leavened."*

Luke 13:20-21

20 *And again [Jesus] said, "To what shall I compare the kingdom of God?* 21 *It is like leaven that a woman took and hid in three measures of flour, until it was all leavened."*

Thomas 96

Jesus said, "The kingdom of the father is like [a certain] woman. She took a little leaven, [concealed] it in some dough, and made it into large loaves. Let him who has ears hear."[1]

Exegetical Commentary

Although there are textual variants in both canonical versions, none is superior to the readings provided in the 27th edition of the Nestle-Aland Greek text and represented in the RSV, NIV, and NRSV.

The parable is introduced in Matthew and Luke by clauses that differ (Matt 13:33a//Luke 13:20), but the parable itself is identical in wording between the two Gospels.[2] It is generally thought that both evangelists received the parable from Q, and that the Parables of the Mustard Seed and the Leaven had already been placed together in that source.[3]

The version in the *Gospel of Thomas* 96 differs in two major respects: the subject of the sentence is a woman, not leaven, and the outcome is the yield of large loaves of bread, not the leavening of the flour itself. The effect is that, while the Synoptic versions emphasize the hidden power of the leaven, the *Thomas* version highlights the woman's ability to use the leaven.[4] In addition, the three measures are not mentioned. Although some interpreters regard it as having its source in an independent tradition,[5] others consider it to have been derived from the canonical Gospels but edited by the author of the *Gospel of Thomas*.[6] There is little go on in making a decision. But the similarity of various

---

1. Quoted from *NHLE* 136.
2. The use of brackets for [ἐν]ἔκρυψεν (Luke 13:21) indicates that the editors are not completely convinced of that reading, but consider it preferable to the alternative (ἔκρυψεν).
3. Burnett H. Streeter, *The Four Gospels: A Study of Origins,* rev. ed. (New York: St. Martin's Press, 1930), 264, 291; T. W. Manson, *Sayings,* 123; A. Polag, *Fragmenta Q,* 25, 68; J. Fitzmyer, *Luke,* 1,019; W. Cotter, "Parables of the Mustard Seed and the Leaven," 38-51; W. D. Davies and D. C. Allison, *Matthew,* 2:421; R. Brown, *Introduction to the NT,* 119.
4. H. Fleddermann, "The Mustard Seed and the Leaven," 236.
5. B. Scott, *Parable,* 323; Stephen J. Patterson, *The Gospel of Thomas and Jesus* (Sonoma, Calif.: Polebridge Press, 1993), 66-67; Charles W. Hedrick, *Parables as Poetic Fictions: The Creative Voice of Jesus* (Peabody, Mass.: Hendrickson Publishers, 1994), 249-51.
6. Wolfgang Schrage, *Das Verhältnis des Thomas-Evangeliums zur synoptischen Tradition und zu den koptischen Evangelienübersetzungen: Zugleich ein Beitrag zur gnostischen Synoptikerdeutung,* BZNW 29 (Berlin: Alfred Töpelmann, 1964) 183-85; Jacques-É. Ménard, *L'Évangile selon Thomas,* NHS 5 (Leiden: E. J. Brill, 1975), 196-97; Bruce Chilton, "The Gospel according to Thomas as a Source of Jesus' Teaching," in *The Jesus Tradition outside the Gospels,* ed. David Wenham (Sheffield: JSOT Press, 1984), 158; Michael Fieger, *Das Thomasevangelium: Einleitung Kommentar Systematik,* NTAbh 22 (Münster: Aschen-

elements (leaven, woman, flour, concealing), the introduction and conclusion having similarities to Matthew's,[7] and the likelihood of the author of the *Gospel of Thomas* to have made use of the canonical Gospels[8] all combine to favor dependence in this case. In any case, the parable has a gnostic coloring. The emphasis on the woman's skill and effort — rather than the rising of the dough from the fermenting of the leaven — corresponds to the Gnostic's need to actualize the particle of light within, of which the leaven is itself a symbol.[9] The parable is generally considered to have come from Jesus himself,[10] and the canonical versions are considered superior to that in the *Gospel of Thomas* 96 as a witness to the historical Jesus.[11]

The parable is located in the two canonical Gospels following the Parable of the Mustard Seed (Matt 13:31-32//Mark 4:30-32//Luke 13:18-19), which existed in both Mark and Q. The two parables can be considered twin parables, and they can also be designated "parables of growth." Within the Gospel of Matthew the Parable of the Leaven stands fourth in a series of seven parables of Matthew's Parable Discourse (13:1-50). It is spoken to the crowds, as the three previous ones were. After this parable, however, Jesus speaks to his disciples. In the Gospel of Luke the parable is placed within a series of teachings of Jesus in the Travel Narrative (9:51–19:27). From Luke 13:10 through the parable (13:20-21) the setting appears to be a synagogue, in which Jesus was teaching on a sabbath. It can be classified as a similitude[12] since it illustrates the kingdom from something typical — in a timeless way — and lacks a narrative set it past time. In neither version is there an application appended at the end.

The introductory statements in the two canonical Gospels differ, but they are familiar within their contexts. Matthew's introductory statement contains typically Matthean redactional terminology: ἄλλην παραβολήν ("another para-

dorff, 1991), 245; H. Fleddermann, "The Mustard Seed and the Leaven," 292-30. This would militate against the view of E. Waller, "Parable of the Leaven," 99-109, that the reference would be to the woman, not the leaven, in a version predating both Mark and *Thomas*.

7. H. Fleddermann, "The Mustard Seed and the Leaven," 230. As in Matthew (contra Luke) the parable begins with a statement, not a question; and the closing line (use of the indicative verb rather than the infinitive, as in Mark and Luke) is distinctive of Matthew's usage (13:9, 43).

8. See Chapter 10, "Parables in the *Gospel of Thomas*."

9. Bertil Gärtner, *The Theology of the Gospel according to Thomas* (New York: Harper & Brothers, 1961), 231; N. Perrin, *Teaching*, 158.

10. N. Perrin, *Teaching*, 159; R. Funk, *Five Gospels*, 195, 347; H. Weder, *Gleichnisse*, 131; U. Luz, *Matthäus*, 2:328.

11. R. Funk, *Five Gospels*, 523; W. D. Davies and D. C. Allison, *Matthew*, 2:424.

12. R. Bultmann, *HST* 172; J. Kingsbury, *Matthew 13*, 85, 87; E. Linnemann, *Parables*, 3; R. Stein, *Parables*, 19; J. Lambrecht, *Treasure*, 166. On the other hand, A. Jülicher, *Gleichnisreden*, 2:569-81, and C. H. Dodd, *Parables*, 6, consider it a parable proper (*Parabel*).

ble" (13:24, 31); ἐλάλησεν αὐτοῖς ("he spoke to them," 9:18; 13:3, 10, 13, 34; 14:27; 28:18); and "the kingdom of heaven is like" (13:31, 44, 45, 47; 20:1). Luke's interrogative "To what shall I compare the kingdom of God?" is found elsewhere in Luke's special tradition (13:18) and Q (7:31//Matt 11:16). As interpreters have said, the comparison being made is not between the kingdom and leaven per se. The expression actually means: "it is the case with the kingdom as with leaven."[13]

It has become customary to translate the Greek word ζύμη as "yeast" in modern translations (NEB, NIV, NRSV) in place of the older translation "leaven." The latter is retained in this discussion, however, since the two words are not actual synonyms. While yeast is a leavening agent, not all leaven is yeast in the modern sense, that is, a leavening agent that can be purchased in refrigerated cubes or as a dried substance in a package. In antiquity leaven consisted simply of fermenting dough.

According to the NEB, NIV, and NRSV, the woman "mixed" the leaven into the flour. While that is what a person actually does in making bread, the verb is ἐνέκρυψεν (Matt 13:33//Luke 13:21), and it means that she "hid" (KJV and RSV) the leaven within. The imagery of hiding the leaven should not be lost since it designates the hiddenness of the kingdom.

In the baking of leavened bread, leaven — a one-celled fungus — is combined with other ingredients (including flour, water, and sugar) to make bread dough. When given moisture, warmth, and sugar to feed on, the leaven ferments and generates bubbles of carbon dioxide throughout the dough, causing it to rise.

Elsewhere in the NT leaven is a negative symbol (Matt 16:6//Mark 8:15//Luke 12:1; 1 Cor 5:6-8; Gal 5:9). It has been suggested from that usage that Jesus deliberately used a negative image for the kingdom in order to subvert the hearer's dependency on the rules of the sacred and to "warn that instead the expected evil that corrupts may indeed turn out to be the kingdom."[14] That is pressing details of the parable too far and missing the thrust of the whole. The imagery may indeed have been shocking,[15] but not necessarily, for there are positive uses of the imagery of leaven in Jewish literature as well (although the sources are admittedly rabbinic and post-NT).[16] In any case, the imagery is used here simply to illustrate the inevitable power of the kingdom. Though hidden in the present, the kingdom will transform the whole of creation, just as leaven transforms flour.[17]

The "three measures" (RSV, NRSV) or simply "large amount" (NIV) of flour is immense. The Greek term here for "measure" is σάτον, and each such

13. Cf. J. Jeremias, *Parables*, 147; J. Kingsbury, *Matthew 13*, 85.
14. B. Scott, *Parable*, 328-29.
15. R. Funk, "Beyond Criticism," 161-63; H. Weder, *Gleichnisreden*, 134.
16. Various texts are cited in Str-B 1:728-29.
17. C. H. Dodd, *Parables*, 155.

measure is about a peck and a half.[18] The amount in question, therefore, is roughly 4.5 pecks, 1.125 bushels, or 144 cups. That would weigh about 40 pounds (a 5-pound bag of flour yields about 18 cups). Modern recipes typically call for 3.5 cups of flour to make a good-sized loaf of bread. Using that as a standard, the amount of flour in question would easily make 40 generous-sized loaves of bread — 60 or even 80 small ones.

Whether there is significance in the number of measures of flour used, or in the huge amount of bread produced, is uncertain. The expression ἀλεύρου σάτα τρία ("three measures of flour") is somewhat similar to one at Genesis 18:6, but the latter is different in the LXX (τρία μέτρα σεμιδάλεως, "three measures of semolina"). That such a large amount of bread is used as an illustration may well have significance, for a one-loaf illustration would work just as well (as in the case of one mustard seed) if a contrast is all that has to be made. That hyperbole is being used is evident. It aids the making of a contrast from that which is small and hidden to that which is huge and manifest. Such is the kingdom.

On the essential interpretation of the parable there is widespread agreement. That is that the kingdom of God, though hidden, is an irresistible force inaugurated by God that will have its way and transform all of creation. It may seem hidden, and indeed is, but one can have confidence in God's will and power to bring it about.[19]

In light of his concept of realized eschatology, C. H. Dodd stressed that in the proclamation of Jesus this would have meant that the time of hiddenness was over ("the dough is completely leavened"): "the Kingdom of God, for which the prophets until John made preparations, has now come."[20] Yet it seems better to follow the approach of others concerning all of the parables of growth, and that is that those parables portray the present of Jesus' ministry as a time when the kingdom was not obvious but hidden, and the fullness of its manifestation must be awaited.[21] The hiddenness of the kingdom is emphasized in this parable more than in the Parable of the Mustard Seed through use of the verb "to hide."

Within the two canonical Gospels the parable carries the meaning it had in the traditions (oral and Q) that went before. There is a difference, however, in how the parable functions within the two Gospels. Within the Gospel of Matthew the two parables (Mustard Seed and Leaven) are two of seven in a long discourse. They stand within a didactic context, and the implication is that the

18. BAGD 745, referring to Josephus, *Ant.* 9.85 and Str-B 1:669-70. According to Marvin A. Powell, "Weights and Measures," *ABD* 6:904, the measure would amount to 12 liters. Three would consist of 36 liters or 144 cups of flour.

19. Among interpreters here are N. Dahl, "Parables of Growth," 156-57; N. Perrin, *Teaching,* 158; R. Stein, *Parables,* 94-95; J. Fitzmyer, *Luke,* 1,018-19; J. Lambrecht, *Treasure,* 166-67; D. Hagner, *Matthew,* 389; U. Luz, *Matthäus,* 2:334-35.

20. C. H. Dodd, *Parables,* 154.

21. N. Dahl, "Parables of Growth," 156; J. Jeremias, *Parables,* 149.

followers of Jesus are to persist in spite of seemingly small results. Even now God's rule is being exerted through the mission of the church, and that will conclude only at the consummation of all things. In the Gospel of Luke the same two parables follow upon a sabbath controversy — the healing of a crippled woman. The act of Jesus may be controversial, and the deed may appear inconsequential, but the parables confirm that the kingdom is indeed disruptive and will be astounding in its ultimate effects.

Exposition

The Parable of the Leaven provides, among other things, a message of encouragement. Those committed to following Jesus can legitimately wonder whether their efforts of work and witness are of any importance in the world. By and large all goes on as usual. In spite of a few signs of "success" according to secular standards, which are achieved by some notable personalities, the disciples of Jesus are more likely to find frustration and wonder why there is such little response out there.

The parable affirms that, yes, the work and witness of Jesus' disciples are of ultimate importance. God has a grand outcome in store for the whole creation. The present is a time for realizing it only in part, and seeing through a glass only darkly.

The parable affirms, too, that God is involved in the growth of the kingdom. The disciples of Jesus are involved, but it would be a mistake to say that they are the ones who build the kingdom.

Sometimes one is tempted to look for signs of the kingdom. As the dough rises, one thinks that it is possible to see the effects of the leaven. Surely there must be signs of the kingdom. There may well be, but the parable reminds us that, as the leaven is hidden, so is the kingdom. Events in nature and history are too ambiguous to be faithful and certain signs.

Select Bibliography

Allis, Oswald T. "The Parable of the Leaven." *EvQ* 19 (1947): 254-73.

Campbell, Denis. "The Leaven." *ExpTim* 104 (1993): 307-8.

Cotter, Wendy J. "The Parables of the Mustard Seed and the Leaven: Their Function in the Earliest Stratum of Q." *TJT* 8 (1992): 38-51.

Dahl, Nils A. "The Parables of Growth." *ST* 5 (1951): 132-66. Reprinted in his *Jesus in the Memory of the Early Church*, 141-66. Minneapolis: Augsburg Publishing House, 1976.

Dupont, Jacques. "Le couple parabolique du sénevé et du levain." In *Jesus Christ in Historie und Theologie: Neutestamentliche Festschrift für Hans Conzelmann zum 60. Geburtstag*, 331-45. Ed. Georg Strecker. Tübingen: J. C. B. Mohr (Paul Siebeck), 1975.

————. "Les paraboles du séneve et du levain (Mt 13,31-33; Lc 13,18-21)." *NRT* 89 (1967): 897-913.

Fleddermann, Harry. "The Mustard Seed and the Leaven in Q, the Synoptics, and Thomas." In *Society of Biblical Literature 1989 Seminar Papers*, 216-36. Ed. David J. Lull. SBLSP 28. Atlanta: Scholars Press, 1989.

Funk, Robert W. "Beyond Criticism in Quest of Literacy: The Parable of the Leaven." *Int* 25 (1971): 149-70.

Kuss, Otto. "Zum Sinngehalt des Gleichnisses vom Senfkorn und Sauerteig." *Bib* 40 (1959): 641-53.

Segbroeck, Frans van. "Le scandale de l'incroyance: La signification de Mt 13,35." *ETL* 41 (1965): 344-72.

Waller, Elizabeth. "The Parable of the Leaven: A Sectarian Teaching and the Inclusion of Women." *USQR* 35 (1979-80): 99-109.

B. PARABLES ON THE JOY OF DISCOVERING THE KINGDOM

8.37. The Treasure in the Field, Matthew 13:44; *Thomas* 109

Matthew 13:44

[*Jesus said,*] 44"*The kingdom of heaven is like treasure hidden in a field, which a person found and covered up; and in his joy he goes and sells all that he has and buys that field.*"

Thomas 109

Jesus said, "*The kingdom is like a man who had a [hidden] treasure in his field without knowing it. And [after] he died, he left it to his [son]. The son [did] not know (about the treasure). He inherited the field and sold [it]. And the one who bought it went plowing and [found] the treasure. He began to lend money at interest to whomever he wished.*"[1]

Notes on the Text and Translation

Some Greek witnesses begin the verse with πάλιν ("again," which is reflected in the KJV), but the earliest and most important ones do not. The appearance of the adverb is probably due to assimilation to the beginning of 13:45 and 13:47.

The Greek text actually has ἐν τῷ ἀγρῷ ("in *the* field"), but it is translated

1. Quoted from *NHLE* 137.

here "in *a* field" (as in the KJV, RSV, and NRSV) in order to catch the indefinite generality that is fitting for a parable. The word for "the" (τῷ) is actually lacking in manuscript D, a major Western text, which most likely seeks to aid the reader along these lines at this point.[2]

The word πάντα ("all") is missing in the important majuscule B and is not included in the 25th edition of the Nestle-Aland text. But it is strongly attested in other early and important witnesses, and it is printed in the 26th and 27th editions of the Nestle-Aland text.

Exegetical Commentary

The similitude is found only within the Gospel of Matthew among the Synoptics. Along with two others (the Weeds in the Wheat, 13:24-30, and the Pearl of Great Price, 13:45-46), it is one of three parables distinctive of Matthew that are also in the *Gospel of Thomas* (57, 76, 109). Both versions are devoid of any hortatory comments or applications.

There are similar parables in rabbinic literature,[3] as well as in literatures from various cultures.[4] One of the best known from rabbinic sources is a parable by Simeon ben Yohai (ca. A.D. 140). According to the parable, a man inherited a piece of land and, being too lazy to care for it, sold it. The buyer found a treasure in it, out of which he built a fine palace and had servants. The original owner regretted selling the land, exclaiming, "Alas, what have I thrown away?" The moral drawn from the parable is that the Egyptians cared nothing for Israel, in fact despised Israel, while the latter were in Egypt, but then realized how great Israel was as they made their way to the sea (at the time of the exodus).[5]

The version of the parable in the *Gospel of Thomas* does not appear to be literarily dependent on Matthew's.[6] It differs in various details. In Matthew 13:44 the one who makes the discovery does not first own the field (and its treasure) but finds it in a field that belongs to another and then liquidates all that

2. Cf. BDF 133 (255, 1): the use of the definite article "in 13:44 is incorrect (D and Chr omit) where 'a field' is to be understood."

3. Examples are cited and quoted in Harvey K. McArthur and Robert M. Johnston, *They also Taught in Parables: Rabbinic Parables from the First Centuries of the Christian Era* (Grand Rapids: Zondervan, 1990), 41-42.

4. Comparative work on stories in various literatures involving the discovery of treasures is by J. Crossan, *Finding Is the First Act.*

5. *Cant. Rab.* 4:12:1. The text is in *MidR.* 9:219-20.

6. This is the judgment of others as well, for example, J. Jeremias, *Parables*, 24; Robert McL. Wilson, *Studies in the Gospel of Thomas* (London: A. R. Mowbray, 1960), 54; and H. E. W. Turner and Hugh Montefiore, *Thomas and the Evangelists*, SBT 35 (Naperville: Alec R. Allenson, 1962), 36, 66-67, 72. Dependence on Matthew 13:44 is maintained by Bertil Gärtner, *The Theology of the Gospel according to Thomas* (New York: Harper & Brothers, 1961), 66, 237. That the version at the *Gospel of Thomas* 109 is not from Jesus, but is a gnostic version of a Jewish parable, is held by J. D. Crossan, *Finding Is the First Act*, 105-6.

he has in order to purchase the field. In the *Gospel of Thomas* 109, however, the man who discovered the treasure was already the owner (actually the third owner) and "began to lend money at interest to whomever he wished" (which is in blatant contradiction to the prohibition of lending at interest in logion 95). It would seem that, if there is a point to that parable, it is that there are persons (non-Gnostics) who have riches at hand, but do not know it, that is, the hidden "gnosis," which is within the self.[7] Another (the Gnostic) comes upon that knowledge, however, is enlightened by it, and is able then to share it with others of his own choosing, which results in mutual benefits.

The hiding of valuables in the earth is an age-old method of storing them safely. According to Josephus, in the aftermath of their conquest of Jerusalem (A.D. 70), the Romans discovered gold, silver, and other treasured articles that had been stored underground "in view of the uncertain fortunes of war,"[8] and the *Copper Scroll* from Qumran (3Q15) — which is from the first century A.D. — contains a long list of buried treasures, many items of which are underground.[9] Moreover, in another of Jesus' parables a man is portrayed as hiding money in the ground (Matt 25:18, 25).

In regard to Matthew's version questions inevitably arise concerning the morality and legality of the action carried out by the one who discovered the hidden treasure. After all, he discovered it in a field owned by someone else. What was he doing in the field in the first place? Some interpreters suggest that he must have been a day laborer working the field of a wealthy landowner.[10] Yet that does not seem to fit the case, since he had the means to purchase the field. The picture is simply of a man who walks across a field and discovers what no one else had seen, including (and above all) the owner. And then the most important question arises: No matter who he was, when he came upon the treasure, should he not have notified the owner about it? And when he purchased the field, did ownership of the treasure go with it?

Concerning the last question, that of legality, there is no law in the OT

---

7. Cf. R. McL. Wilson, *Studies in the Gospel of Thomas,* 93; Wolfgang Schrage, *Das Verhältnis des Thomas-Evangeliums zur synoptischen Tradition und zu den koptischen Evangelienübersetzungen: Zugleich ein Beitrag zur gnostischen Synoptikerdeutung,* BZNW 29 (Berlin: Alfred Töpelmann, 1964), 198. For the view that the version in the *Gospel of Thomas* is earlier than that of Matt 13:44, and that it need not be given a gnostic interpretation, cf. Charles W. Hedrick, *Parables as Poetic Fictions: The Creative Voice of Jesus* (Peabody, Mass.: Hendrickson Publishers, 1994), 117-41.

8. Josephus, *J.W.* 7.115; text quoted from *Josephus,* trans. Henry St. John Thackeray et al., LCL, 10 vols. (Cambridge: Harvard University Press, 1961-81), 3:539.

9. For the text of the *Copper Scroll,* cf. Geza Vermes, *The Dead Sea Scrolls in English,* 4th ed. (Sheffield: Sheffield Academic Press, 1995), 374-78. I thank David Noel Freedman for bringing this document to my attention.

10. J. Jeremias, *Parables,* 198; J. Derrett, *Law in the New Testament,* 9-13; B. Scott, *Parable,* 397-98.

that deals with the specific issue at hand. Certain rabbinic texts have some bearing on it.[11] But they do not necessarily settle the matter. For example, according to one *Mishnah* text, everything in a field belongs to its owner under certain conditions of his acquiring it, but not in other cases.[12] According to another *Mishnah* text, "scattered money" that is discovered belongs to its finder,[13] but in the parable the treasure discovered is not necessarily money, and in any case it is apparently not scattered but stored intact. Finally, however, it must be said that the legal question is not at issue,[14] and the moral one is at issue only indirectly. In the oral telling of the story, narrated within a folk culture (as well as the telling of the story in the Matthean situation), the hearer is not likely to worry much about the legal issues but would find delight in the man's getting the best of a landowner. The discovery of a treasure in another's field, and the subsequent overwhelming desire to purchase it, add to the appeal and human interest of the story. The discoverer must do all he can to obtain it. Part of the drama is the acquiring. In matters of the heart, pursuing the object of desire can be as splendid as the acquiring.

Previous parables in chapter 13 of Matthew's Gospel (the Sower, the Weeds in the Wheat, the Mustard Seed, and the Leaven, 13:3-9, 24-33) had been addressed to the crowds. This parable and the next one (the Pearl of Great Price, 13:45-46) are addressed to the disciples (cf. the shift at 13:36). At the outset Matthew uses his customary "kingdom of heaven" rather than the more familiar "kingdom of God." Further, as in some other parables in his Gospel, his version begins with the phrase "the kingdom of heaven is like," followed by a brief account.[15] At this point interpreters have often said that the introductory phrase does not mean that the kingdom is like a hidden treasure, but rather that it is like that which is portrayed in the similitude, meaning "it is the case with the kingdom of heaven as with" that which follows.[16]

But even if that is granted, it is difficult to pin down the actual comparison being made. A literal comparison would mean that the kingdom is likened to a person's discovery of something of great worth, something that must in

11. *Y. B. Mes.* 2:5:8c; *Pesiq. Rab Kah.* 9 (47b); *Lev. Rab.* 27:1; and *m. B. Bat.* 4:8. These are cited by S. Lachs, *Rabbinic Commentary,* 229. Cf. also Str-B 1:674.

12. *M. B. Bat.* 4:9.

13. *M. B. Mes.* 2:1; text in *The Mishnah,* ed. Herbert Danby (Oxford: Oxford University Press, 1933), 348.

14. According to J. Jeremias, *Parables,* 199, the actions of the discoverer were legal, and his morality is not being considered. J. Derrett, *Law in the New Testament,* 6-9, maintains that the actions of the discoverer were both legal and moral. This is contested by J. Crossan, *Finding Is the First Act,* 91.

15. The exact phrase is used five other times (13:31, 33, 45, 47; 20:1); cf. also the use of the verb ὁμοιόω ("to compare") in the expression at 13:24; 18:23; 22:2; 25:1.

16. J. Jeremias, *Parables,* 101-2; E. Linnemann, *Parables,* 98; J. Kingsbury, *Matthew 13,* 111.

turn be grasped on to by the one who discovers it. But that is a very cumbersome comparison. How can God's kingdom be likened to discovery and consequent action? More likely the comparison being made is inexact. The likeness must in fact be reversed: the subject of the thought expressed in the similitude as a whole is not primarily the kingdom itself but the one who makes the discovery and acts upon it. The only proper response of the one who has discovered the kingdom is to relativize all else that one has for the sake of the greater worth of the kingdom.

This means that there is some similarity after all between the kingdom and the treasure; both are discovered. The kingdom is not something that one gains by intention and strategy. It is sheer gift. Further, the term "kingdom of heaven" in this context does not simply denote God's sovereignty, God's rule in creation and history. As elsewhere in Matthew's Gospel, the term refers to the salvation promised to the faithful of Israel and the church (5:20; 7:21; 13:45-46; 22:1-10; 25:1-13, 34),[17] a realm that one enters (5:10, 20; 8:11; 18:3). Therefore the one who discovers it has "joy" and commits himself or herself to it.

Interpreters have been divided concerning the main point of the parable. Is it the overwhelming joy of discovering the kingdom, as some suggest?[18] Is it the exceedingly high value of the kingdom?[19] Is it that a person's response to the kingdom, once the kingdom is discovered or apprehended, must be total?[20] Or could it be a combination of a stress on both the value of the kingdom and the total investment the one who discovers it will have to make?[21]

The note of joy is expressed explicitly in this parable, but it is not mentioned in the twin parable, the Pearl of Great Price (14:45-46), even if it is implicit there. That the kingdom would be of great value for the evangelist goes without saying. But in the final analysis, the parable (like that of its twin) is addressed to the disciples, who, in Matthew's eyes, have found the kingdom already. Moreover, what the twin parables have in common is that the one who makes the discovery liquidates all of his assets in order to acquire the treasure or the pearl. Therefore, it is most likely that the main thrust of the parable is that the disciple of Jesus responds to the kingdom with a commitment that risks all without reserve.[22] As a main thrust, that also allows the other themes (the joy of discovery and the value of the kingdom) a place within the whole, and it coheres with the main thrust of its twin parable as well.

17. Ulrich Luz, "βασιλεία," *EDNT* 1:203-4.

18. J. Jeremias, *Parables*, 200-201; E. Schweizer, *Matthew*, 312.

19. A. Jülicher, *Gleichnisreden*, 2:581-85; W. Allen, *Matthew*, 154.

20. C. H. Dodd, *Parables*, 85-87; B. Smith, *Parables*, 145; E. Linnemann, *Parables*, 101; C. Montefiore, *Synoptic Gospels*, 2:644; W. Oesterley, *Parables*, 82; J. Kingsbury, *Matthew 13*, 115; R. Stein, *Parables*, 103, 105; D. Hare, *Matthew*, 158; D. Hagner, *Matthew*, 397.

21. D. Wenham, *Parables*, 208; W. D. Davies and D. Allison, *Matthew*, 2:435.

22. J. Kingsbury, *Matthew 13*, 115-16.

413

The authenticity of the parable has been challenged on various grounds. It has been suggested, on the one hand, that the parable may have come from Jewish tradition and been ascribed to Jesus within the early church.[23] On the other hand, it has been attributed to the evangelist Matthew. In this case it is claimed that the parable was composed on the basis of Proverbs 2:1-9, which speaks of seeking wisdom as one seeks for "treasures" (2:4; LXX, θησαυρούς), and that such a composition would be characteristic of the evangelist.[24] Yet the one who makes the discovery within the parable was not seeking treasures; he simply stumbled onto one by surprise. And even if there is an allusion to the OT text, it would certainly be possible for Jesus or for some other pre-Matthean person to have made it and to have composed the parable. More serious is the observation that the parable contains typical Matthean expressions.[25] Over against that observation, however, it must be stressed that the parable is exceedingly brief (one verse), and that Matthew has written the present verse with his own expressions at hand. One can expect that that will result in an unusually high proportion of Matthean expressions. There is no compelling reason to exclude Jesus as the originator of the parable. Its teaching concerning the disciple's commitment to the kingdom coheres with other passages derived from those major traditions antecedent to the Synoptic Gospels,[26] and its independent attestation in the *Gospel of Thomas* lends credence to such a possibility.[27]

Exposition

As with any parable, there are aspects of this one that cause one to ask questions. Already the questions of legality and morality of the man who discovered the treasure have been raised in the commentary above. In addition, one commentator has suggested that, not only has the man who discovered the treasure done something illegal (which may actually *not* be the case), but that he dare

---

23. R. Bultmann, *HST* 202-3.

24. R. Gundry, *Matthew*, 275.

25. These include: the use of "the kingdom of heaven is like" five other times (13:31, 33, 45, 47; 20:1), the use of "treasure" eight other times, and the use of the unusual phrase ἀπὸ τῆς χαρᾶς ("with joy") rather than the more common μετὰ χαρᾶς (in classical Greek, the LXX, and the NT); Matthew also uses ἀπό with a genitive to express fear (14:26; 28:4). But the last point does not carry much weight, for the admittedly rare expression ἀπὸ τῆς χαρᾶς ("with joy," Matt 13:44) is also found at Luke 24:41 and Acts 12:14.

26. Cf. Mark 10:23-25 and parallels; Matt 7:21; 13:45-46 (both M); Luke 9:62 (L); and Matt 10:38//Luke 14:27 (Q).

27. C. H. Dodd, *Parables*, 85-87, J. Jeremias, *Parables*, 198-201, R. Stein, *Parables*, 98-104, and J. Crossan, *Finding Is the First Act*, 98-102, discuss the parable as though it is authentic in their judgment. R. Funk, *Five Gospels*, 196, reports that the Jesus Seminar has regarded the parable as having come in some form from Jesus, and it is accordingly printed in pink.

not dig up the treasure "unless he wants to face the rather embarrassing question of whence it came."[28]

Questions and observations such as these arise when an interpreter reflects on this parable for a length of time. They also illustrate how cleverly the parables of Jesus have been crafted. They contain outlandish characters and have surprising twists. But the questions of legality and morality in this particular case would hardly have been germane to the telling of the parable within the oral setting of Jesus (if authentic) or within the community of the evangelist Matthew. Not all questions that a modern interpreter might raise are relevant to the actual interpretation of a parable. The hearers' or readers' attention is directed to the discovery, the joy, and the response that take place in the story, culminating in the response. All else fades in importance.

The discovery of the treasure corresponds to the spiritual experiences of many. Not infrequently people relate experiences they have had of uncanny moments when God comes to them as the Unexpected One, and their lives are transformed, if even for a time. There is a sense of the presence of God in their lives. It calls for response of some kind, even if it is a passing sense of joy.

In the parable, however, the fleeting moment of spirituality is not enough. A claim is made, and it is about the quality and the cost of discipleship. The disciple is addressed who has apprehended the "kingdom of heaven." Here that phrase signifies more than a sense of the presence of God or even the rule of God in a general way. It signifies God's eternal kingdom into which persons are permitted. It has its beginnings on earth, to be sure, but extends into eternity.

To apprehend the kingdom evokes great joy for some, not all. Some may have other priorities (13:19-22), and in the end some may even be shut out from it (7:21; 8:12; 18:3; 25:41). But in the case of those to whom God has disclosed it, and who have received it with joy, the response cannot be halfhearted. Nothing compares to it; all else takes second place (cf. 10:37-39). The man's liquidation of all his assets portrays that. To seek God's kingdom and righteousness is the mark of the true disciple (6:33).

The word "joy" cannot be passed over lightly. Joy is an emotion that cannot be brought on by one's plans, methods, or efforts. It is induced from factors outside the self. Unlike happiness, which people seek, joy can be present in a person's life even in times of pain (Heb 12:2) and in moments when faith is tested severely (Jas 1:2).

The joy of discovering the kingdom is like the joy of finding a hidden treasure. It is due to the grace of God that has shone forth in the person and message of Jesus. Such joy precedes the response of discipleship, just as grace comes prior to good works.

According to this parable, the kingdom is something that one may well stumble upon rather than find by means of a search. Certainly the kingdom was

28. B. Scott, *Parable*, 402.

hidden in the work and words of Jesus, not apparent to ordinary human perception. It was disclosed only to those whom God enlightened in and through the proclamation of Jesus. Here and there it became apparent only as a surprise. The same is true in the case of the post-Easter Jesus. The kingdom is revealed when and where it pleases God, and the risen Jesus calls his disciples into it yet, asking them to follow him with a quality of commitment that compares to no other.

Select Bibliography

Crossan, John D. *Finding Is the First Act: Trove Folktales and Jesus' Treasure Parable.* SemSup 9. Philadelphia: Fortress Press, 1979.

———. "Hidden Treasure Parables in Late Antiquity." In *Society of Biblical Literature 1976 Seminar Papers,* ed. George MacRae, 359-79. SBLSP 10. Missoula: Scholars Press, 1976.

Derrett, J. Duncan M. "Law in the New Testament: The Treasure in the Field (Mt. XIII,44)." *ZNW* 54 (1963): 31-42. Reprinted in his *Law in the New Testament,* 1-16. London: Darton, Longman & Todd, 1970.

Dupont, Jacques. "Les paraboles du trésor et de la perle." *NTS* 14 (1968): 408-18.

Fenton, John C. "Expounding the Parables: IV. The Parables of the Treasure and the Pearl (Mt. 13:44-46)." *ExpTim* 77 (1966): 178-80.

Hedrick, Charles W. "The Treasure Parable in Matthew and Thomas." *FFF* 2/2 (1986): 41-56.

Sider, John W. "Interpreting the Hid Treasure." *CSR* 13 (1984): 360-72.

8.38. The Pearl of Great Price, Matthew 13:45-46; *Thomas* 76

Matthew 13:45-46

[Jesus said,] 45"Again, the kingdom of heaven is like a merchant searching for fine pearls; 46and when he had found one pearl of extraordinary value, he went and sold all that he had and bought it."

Thomas 76

Jesus said, "The kingdom of the father is like a merchant who had a consignment of merchandise and who discovered a pearl. That merchant was shrewd. He sold the merchandise and bought the pearl alone for himself. You too, seek his unfailing and enduring treasure where no moth comes near to devour and no worm destroys."[1]

1. Quoted from *NHLE* 135.

Notes on the Text and Translation

13:45. Various important manuscripts (including ℵ and B) lack the term ἀνθρώπῳ ("man"), and it is omitted in the 25th edition of the Nestle-Aland Greek text. In apposition to ἐμπόρῳ ("merchant") it is superfluous. But it is widely attested in other important Greek witnesses (including C, D, and the third-century Greek writers Origen and Cyprian), and its use in apposition to another noun is characteristic of parables in the Gospel of Matthew (13:28, 52; 18:23; 20:1; 21:33; 22:2).[2] The term has been included, and probably rightly so, in the 26th and 27th editions.

13:46. The term πολύτιμον is translated here as "extraordinary value." In BAGD 690 it is translated "very precious, valuable." Other possibilities would be "a specially valuable pearl,"[3] "an extremely valuable pearl,"[4] or a pearl "of very special value" (NEB). In any case, neither "great price" (KJV) nor "great value" (RSV, NRSV) seems adequate for the contrast between this pearl and the "fine pearls" of 13:45.

Exegetical Commentary

Within the canonical gospels the Parable of the Pearl of Great Price is found only in the Gospel of Matthew. Like the Parable of the Treasure in the Field, it is very brief and does not have an application appended to it. It is one of three parables distinctive to Matthew that appear also in the *Gospel of Thomas;* the other two are the Weeds in the Wheat (13:24-30; *Gos. Thom.* 57) and the Treasure in the Field (13:44; *Gos. Thom.* 109).

The version within the *Gospel of Thomas* is longer and contains an application (the last sentence in the quotation above), as do two other parables in that Gospel (the Burglar, 21; and the Great Supper, 64). Whether it is based on an independent tradition, as some contend, or on Matthew's version is debated.[5] Those who argue that it is based on Matthew's version say that the be-

---

2. The use of ἄνθρωπος in apposition to a noun (and virtually equivalent to the use of the indefinite pronoun τις, "a certain [one]") is designated a Semitism by Matthew Black, *An Aramaic Approach to the Gospels and Acts,* 2d ed. (Oxford: Clarendon Press, 1954), 249-50; cf. also C. F. D. Moule, *The Birth of the New Testament* (New York: Harper & Row, 1962), 218.

3. J. Jeremias, *Parables,* 200; W. D. Davies and D. C. Allison, *Matthew,* 2:439.

4. E. Linnemann, *Parables,* 99.

5. That it is based on an independent tradition is held by J. Jeremias, *Parables,* 24; Hugh Montefiore, "A Comparison of the Parables of the Gospel according to Thomas and of the Synoptic Gospels," in *Thomas and the Evangelists,* by H. E. W. Turner and H. Montefiore, SBT 35 (Naperville: Alec R. Allenson, 1962), 66-67; and Robert McL. Wilson, *Studies in the Gospel of Thomas* (London: A. R. Mowbray, 1960), 54. That it is based on Matt 13:45-56 is maintained by Robert M. Grant and David N. Freedman, *The Secret Sayings of Jesus* (Garden City, N.Y.: Doubleday, 1960), 177; Bertil Gärtner, *The Theology of the*

havior of the merchant — his selling the merchandise to buy the pearl — can be understood only in light of its high value — an item of information provided by Matthew 13:45-46.[6] But since pearls were renowned in antiquity for their great value (see below), that view is not particularly persuasive. In any case, the version of the parable in the *Gospel of Thomas* appears to have a gnostic meaning: the pearl is the divine spark within the self, and once it is found, the Gnostic abandons the material world that worms can devour. It is interesting to note that the main figure of the parable, who is likened to a Gnostic, is a merchant, but in logion 64 Jesus says, "Businessmen and merchants will not enter the places of my Father."[7]

The Parable of the Pearl of Great Price can be considered a twin of the previous one in Matthew's Gospel. But there are some differences. In contrast to that one, in which the single sentence that constitutes it is in the present tense, this one has verbs in past tenses (13:46). Another difference is that, while the Parable of the Treasure begins with a comparison of the kingdom of heaven to a treasure, and the man who discovers it comes in secondarily, here the comparison is to a man, a merchant, and the pearl that is discovered is brought in secondarily. Moreover, the initial comparison in the first of the two parables is plausible (since both the kingdom and a treasure are of great value), but in the second the corresponding initial comparison is less plausible — the comparison of the kingdom with a merchant in search of fine pearls, rather than with a pearl itself. Different Greek verbs are used for going and selling (13:44, 46).[8] The first parable speaks of the joy of discovery, but the second does not. And finally, the first of the two parables portrays the discovery as rather accidental and certainly not as a result of seeking, but in the second the discovery occurs in the course of seeking, even though it is a huge surprise.

13:45. *"The kingdom of heaven is like."* Once again, as with 13:44 and other introductions,[9] interpreters point out that the phrase does not mean that the kingdom is like a merchant searching hidden treasure, but rather that it is like that which is portrayed in the similitude, meaning "it is the case with the kingdom of

---

Gospel according to Thomas (New York: Harper & Brothers, 1961), 38, 66; Wolfgang Schrage, *Das Verhältnis des Thomas-Evangeliums zur synoptischen Tradition und zu den koptischen Evangelienübersetzungen: Zugleich ein beitrag zur gnostischen Synoptikerdeutung*, BZNW 29 (Berlin: Alfred Töpelmann, 1964), 156; and Michael Fieger, *Das Thomasevangelium: Einleitung, Kommentar Systematik*, NTAbh 22 (Münster: Aschendorff, 1991), 211.

6. W. Schrage, *Das Verhältnis*, 156; M. Fieger, *Das Thomasevangelium*, 211.

7. Quoted from *NHLE* 134.

8. Matt 13:44: ὑπάγει ("he goes"), πωλεῖ ("he sells"); Matt 13:46: ἀπελθών ("having gone away"), πέπρακεν ("he sold"). The variation is most likely stylistic, as claimed by A. Jülicher, *Gleichnisreden*, 2:583.

9. The phrase is used five other times (13:31, 33, 44, 47; 20:1); cf. also the use of the verb ὁμοιόω ("to compare") in the expression at 13:24; 18:23; 22:2; 25:1.

heaven as with" that which follows.[10] But the comparison must be considered inexact. As with the Parable of the Treasure, the comparison must be reversed. The subject of the thought being expressed is not primarily the kingdom itself but the one who makes the discovery and responds to the surprising discovery that the person has made. The only proper response is to relativize all else in his possession for the sake of the greater worth of possessing the kingdom.

The parallel to the kingdom is the pearl of extraordinary value. The one who discovers it, though seeking, is totally surprised — not with the discovery of the pearl itself since he is looking for fine pearls, but with the immense value of the one he finds. The kingdom likewise comes to the seeker, to be sure, but it surpasses any expectations one might have. It is the salvation promised to the faithful of Israel and the church (5:20; 7:21; 13:44; 22:1-10; 25:1-13, 34),[11] a realm that one enters (5:10, 20; 8:11; 18:3).

The term translated here as "merchant" (ἔμπορος) is likely to be a wholesale dealer rather than a retail dealer (κάπηλος).[12] The distinction is made by Plato; he speaks of the former as roaming from city to city, and the latter as shopkeepers who remain in the agora.[13] Although some Roman writers looked down upon them as a class,[14] merchants were generally held in high regard among Jews.[15] Yet even in Jewish tradition it could be said that "a merchant [LXX, ἔμπορος] can hardly keep from wrongdoing" (Sir 26:29).

Pearls — taken primarily from the Red Sea, the Persian Gulf, and the Indian Ocean — were considered to be of very high value in ancient India, Mesopotamia, and Persia. They are thought to have been introduced to the Mediterranean world after the conquests of Alexander the Great in the Orient. They are mentioned in neither the literature of ancient Egypt prior to that time nor the OT.[16]

According to Pliny the Elder (first century A.D.) pearls were considered the most valuable of goods, having "the first place" and "topmost rank among all things of price."[17] Within the NT pearls are of great value, classified along

10. J. Jeremias, *Parables*, 101-2; E. Linnemann, *Parables*, 98; J. Kingsbury, *Matthew 13*, 111.

11. Ulrich Luz, "βασιλεία," *EDNT* 1:203-4.

12. BAGD 257; LSJ 546; MM 208. The latter cite *POxy* 1.36 where the term ἔμπορος is used for a man who brings cargo on a ship. Cf. also M. Ernst, "'... verkaufte alles, was er besass," 31-46.

13. Plato, *Republic* 2.371D.

14. Steven E. Sidebotham, "Trade and Commerce: Roman Empire," *ABD* 6:632.

15. Joachim Jeremias, *Jerusalem in the Time of Jesus* (Philadelphia: Fortress Press, 1969), 31, citing various rabbinic sources.

16. Friedrich Hauck, "μαργαρίτης," *TDNT* 4:472-73; Eckhard Plümacher, "μαργαρίτης," *EDNT* 2:385-86. The RSV and NRSV translate the Hebrew word פְּנִינִים as "pearls" at Job 28:18. According to BDB 819, "corals" is to be preferred; cf. NEB, "red coral." The Greek μαργαρίτης is not in the LXX.

17. Pliny, *Natural History* 9.106; quoted from *Pliny: Natural History*, trans. Harris Rackham et al., 10 vols., LCL (Cambridge: Harvard University Press, 1938-63), 3:235.

with gold (1 Tim 2:9) and precious stones (Rev 17:4; 18:12, 16). In some instances pearls were considered more valuable than gold.[18] Seeking after a pearl is a basis for legends. One of the most famous is in the second-century-A.D. (or later) gnostic "Hymn of the Pearl," in which a prince of the East (Parthia) travels to Egypt to rescue a pearl from a dragon, is distracted, but finally returns home with his prize pearl and is met with a glorious homecoming.[19]

The merchant is portrayed in 13:45 as traveling around to various places where pearls can be found. The merchant is a metaphorical model for the disciple of Jesus. The parable itself is addressed to the disciples, as 13:36 makes clear.

13:46. The verbs in this verse are in the past tense (contra the present tense of similar verbs in 13:44).[20] Once he had discovered the pearl of extraordinary value, the merchant went and sold "all that he had." The phrase is inclusive. It does not mean simply "all the [other] pearls that he had" as a result of his search, for then one would expect different Greek terms.[21] As in 13:44 (and also at 18:25), here πάντα ὅσα εἶχεν has to mean "all that he had," that is, all his possessions. The merchant liquidates everything he has — not only any goods that he has acquired and possesses, but even his means of carrying on business (cargo ship, pack animals, wagons, or whatever else) — in order to have enough money to purchase the pearl that he has discovered. In the same way, the disciple of Jesus who has found the kingdom will consider all other things of secondary value.

What will the merchant do with the pearl once he has bought it? He will probably sell it on the retail market and make a good profit. But that detail is not really important for interpreting the parable. What is central to the parable is the merchant's doing all he can to obtain the pearl.

Here we come also upon the essential meaning of the parable. This parable does not, contrary to the Parable of the Treasure in the Field, speak of the man's joy of discovery. As one reads the two parables in sequence, the note of joy in the first spills over into the second. But actually the emotion of joy is not necessary to the parable. In the prior parable it is fitting, since the discovery is by pure accident. In this parable, on the other hand, the merchant is by temper-

---

18. Thus BAGD 491, citing a text from the fourth century B.C., and (second-century A.D.) Arrian, *Indike* 8.13, who says that pearls were triple the value of gold in ancient India. Such statements are general and do not take into account the quantities involved.

19. Cf. Paul A. Mirecki, "Hymn of the Pearl," *ABD* 3:349-50. For an English version, cf. *The Gnostic Scriptures*, ed. Bentley Layton (Garden City, N.Y.: Doubleday, 1987), 371-75.

20. There seems to be no explanation, except stylistic, for Matthew's use of the term πέπρακεν (the perfect of πιπράσκω) for "sold," when the aorist for πωλέω (used in present tense at 13:44) would serve well. The perfect form (πέπρακα) is regularly used for the aorist; cf. BDF 177 (#343, 1); BAGD 659.

21. Cf. A. McNeile, *Matthew*, 203: "πάντα ὅσα, 'all his possessions,' not πάντας ὅσους, 'all the pearls that he had.'"

ament a serious, earnest person seeking what he actually found. And even if his find exceeds his expectations — which we are no doubt to assume — he is not portrayed as a character who is positioned for joy. He is earnest and shrewd. He finds what he seeks. He acts to obtain it in a serious and reasonable way. So, too, with the disciple of Jesus. The disciple has found what is sought, the kingdom of heaven, and the only fitting response for that person is total commitment to it.[22]

Various interpreters have maintained that this parable and the Parable of the Treasure in the Field, although much alike, must have been transmitted to Matthew independently of one another.[23] The reasons have to do with the differences between them (different verbs and tenses; and the quite different manner of comparison — the one to a treasure, the other not to the pearl but to the searcher). It is not likely, in any case, that Matthew has composed the Parable of the Pearl of Great Price as a companion to the other.[24] It can be regarded as pre-Matthean in origin, even though the evangelist has edited it in accord with his own purposes. It could well have been composed by Jesus himself.[25] Its teaching concerning discipleship and commitment to the kingdom coheres with other teachings of Jesus derived from diverse traditions within the Gospel tradition as a whole,[26] and its presence in the *Gospel of Thomas,* if that can be regarded as an independent source in this case, provides further evidence of its great antiquity within the Gospel tradition.

Exposition

It is both difficult and unnecessary to cordon off the Parable of the Pearl of Great Price from the Parable of the Treasure in the Field. The evangelist Matthew certainly did not do so. In fact, he is most likely to have brought them together in contrast to the author of the *Gospel of Thomas,* who either left them apart, as his sources did, or deliberately separated them himself (logia 109 and 76).

Nevertheless, the differences in nuance between the two parables should be respected. They shed light on different kinds of human experience. There are

22. Many have interpreted the parable along these lines: C. H. Dodd, *Parables,* 85-87; B. Smith, *Parables,* 146; E. Linnemann, *Parables,* 101; C. Montefiore, *Synoptic Gospels,* 2:644; W. Oesterley, *Parables,* 84; J. Kingsbury, *Matthew 13,* 115; R. Stein, *Parables,* 103, 105; R. Gundry, *Matthew,* 278; D. Hare, *Matthew,* 158; D. Hagner, *Matthew,* 397.

23. R. Bultmann, *HST* 173; J. Jeremias, *Parables,* 90-91; E. Schweizer, *Matthew,* 312.

24. Contra R. Gundry, *Matthew,* 278.

25. It is treated as an authentic parable by C. H. Dodd, *Parables,* 85-87; J. Jeremias, *Parables,* 198-201; U. Luz, *Matthäus,* 2:350. It is printed in pink (= authenticity probable, modifications possible) in R. Funk, *Five Gospels,* 196.

26. Cf. Mark 10:23-25 and parallels; Matt 7:21; 13:44 (both M); Luke 9:62 (L); and Matt 10:38//Luke 14:27 (Q).

persons who experience epiphanies of the kingdom of heaven "out of the blue," so to speak. They are caught off guard. On the other hand — and here the Parable of the Pearl of Great Price applies — there are persons who are terribly earnest about finding an ultimate meaning for their lives, and they may spend years and substantial resources in their quest. They may (or may not) discover the kingdom; that is not guaranteed. But if they do, the quest has been more than justified. The kingdom of heaven of which Jesus speaks is greater than one could have imagined. The result is detachment from, a kind of disposing of, one's assets and commitment to the kingdom.

The parable is addressed to the disciples in the Gospel of Matthew. In its canonical form, therefore, it addresses disciples as exhortation. It coheres with other sayings of Jesus in which he raises the commitment of the disciple to him and the kingdom above commitment to one's own family (10:37-39; 19:29) and one's possessions (19:21). With its twin, the parable also connects thematically with another twin parable collection in the Gospel of Luke, Building a Tower and the King Going to War (14:28-30, 31-33). In those parables Jesus actually challenges those who would be his disciples to count the cost. The obverse, but not necessarily subordinate, message is that a true disciple makes an immense commitment to the kingdom. As Jesus was committed to the kingdom all the way to the cross, so the disciple of Jesus is exhorted to follow in his pathway without reserve.

As mentioned in the Exegetical Commentary, nothing is said about the merchant's having joy upon discovering the pearl of extraordinary value. It may be implicit, but its absence may also be instructive. In short, joy is not enough. When the disciple of Jesus experiences the kingdom, and thereby also experiences joy, the temptation is to look upon it as a momentary peak experience, an abnormality within the world of ordinary experience. But the parable exhorts the disciple to extraordinary commitment that goes beyond the moment. To dispose of all that one has to buy the pearl is to make a drastic and life-changing act. Even so, the disciple continues to live in the world and for the world, but is not exhausted by its values. The kingdom and its righteousness are the focus of commitment, even while one lives in the midst of that which is perishing.

Select Bibliography

Charles, Robert H. "Two Parables: A Study." *ExpTim* 35 (1923-24): 265-69.

Dupont, Jacques. "Les paraboles du trésor et de la perle." *NTS* 14 (1968): 408-18.

Ernst, M. "'. . . verkaufte alles, was er besass, und kaufte die Perle' (Mt 13,46). Der ἔμπορος im Neuen Testament und in dokumentarischen Papyri." *ProtoBib* 6 (1997): 31-46.

Fenton, John C. "Expounding the Parables: IV. The Parables of the Treasure and the Pearl." *ExpTim* 77 (1966): 178-80.

Glombitza, Otto. "Der Perlenkaufmann: Eine exegetische Studie zur Matth. XIII,45-46." *NTS* 7 (1960-61): 153-61.

Jacobson, Delmar. "An Exposition of Matthew 13:44-52." *Int* 29 (1975): 277-82.

Ricoeur, Paul. "Listening to the Parables of Jesus. Text: Matthew 13:31-32 and 45-46." *Criterion* 13 (September 1974): 18-22.

Schippers, R. "The Mashal-Character of the Parable of the Pearl." *SE* 2 [= TU 87] (1964): 236-41.

CHAPTER 9

The Evangelists as Interpreters
of the Parables of Jesus

In the previous chapters constant attention has been given to exegesis of the parables of Jesus within the contexts of the Gospels in which they appear. Athough questions have frequently been asked concerning the authenticity of the parables under discussion and about their content and significance in their preliterary stages of transmission and development, interest has been directed primarily to the parables as presented within the canonical Gospels.

It is not possible, nor should it even be necessary, at this point to make a comprehensive review of the evangelists as interpreters of the parables. Yet it is fitting to make a few observations about the three Synoptic evangelists as interpreters. The three will be reviewed briefly in the order of Mark, Matthew, and Luke.

Mark as Interpreter of the Parables

The Gospel of Mark contains relatively few parables when compared to the other two. As often remarked, the author of the Gospel of Mark must have been more interested in narrating the story of Jesus, as he understood it, than in providing a rendition of Jesus' teachings. What makes Mark's use of the parables so difficult to track is that early on in his Gospel he sets forth his so-called "theory" of the parables (4:10-12), which is discussed in Appendix 1: "The Purpose of the Parables according to the Evangelists." That discussion need not be repeated here. Apart from the implications of that particular text, three major interests seem to dominate Mark's choice and use of parables:

1. Some of the parables that he uses have to do with the coming of the

kingdom of God through the ministry of the word of Jesus and his disciples (including disciples beyond the time of the earthly Jesus). These are the various "parables of growth" that come early on in the narrative: the Parables of the Sower (4:3-9), the Seed Growing Secretly (4:26-29), and the Mustard Seed (4:30-32). The presence of these parables coheres with the thematic statement at 1:14-15 concerning the ministry of Jesus: "Jesus came into Galilee, preaching the gospel of God, and saying, 'The time is fulfilled, and the kingdom of God is at hand.'" According to the perspective of Mark's Gospel, the kingdom was the primary proclamation and work of Jesus.

2. Another interest that comes to the fore in Mark's selection and use of parables is the parousia of the Son of man. That can be seen in his utilization of the Parable of the Waiting Slaves (13:34-37) within his "little apocalypse" of chapter 13. Moreover, in the same chapter the parabolic saying (but actually called a "parable" by Mark) of the budding fig tree declares that the Son of man is near, that is, he is coming soon (13:28-29). The paucity of parables does not allow one to find more that set forth this theme. But the parable and the parabolic saying cited here cohere with those sayings that speak of the coming of the Son of man (8:38; 13:26; 14:62), a prominent theme in the Gospel of Mark, in which it is said that the Son of man will come "in the glory of his Father with the holy angels" (8:38).

3. One of the parables in Mark's Gospel sets forth salvation history. That is the Parable of the Wicked Tenants (12:1-11). That particular parable is the longest in the Gospel of Mark, and in some ways it is the most impressive of all in terms of craftsmanship. It sums up the history of salvation and is located at a strategic point in the narrative, anticipating the passion narrative, in which the Son of God is rejected, and alluding to his resurrection through the use of Psalm 118. The parable coincides so closely with the theological perspective of the evangelist that one could call it a truly Markan parable (in the sense that it furthers the Markan message), even though it may well be traced back to Jesus himself, as indicated in the treatment of it. In any case, it contributes to the sense that the reader of this Gospel has, that is, that the shadow of the cross falls back upon the ministry of Jesus, particularly in the passion predictions (8:31; 9:31; 10:33-34), but elsewhere as well (3:6; 10:38, 45). What is so fascinating about that parable is that here the most allegorical of all parables is frequently attributed to Jesus. That observation undercuts the old view that Jesus told parables; that allegories are from the early church; and that the two should not be confused.

In all these ways the evangelist Mark undergirds and carries on his major themes and theological emphases: the kingdom, the coming of the Son of man, and the passion and resurrection of Jesus.

Matthew as Interpreter of the Parables

As indicated in Appendix 1, the evangelist Matthew revised the account of the purpose for Jesus' teaching in parables. What Mark's Gospel has at 4:10-12 is recast into a new direction in the Gospel of Matthew (13:10-17). In light of both that passage and the evangelist's use of various parables at least seven items emerge concerning Matthew as interpreter of the parables of Jesus:

1. According to the evangelist Matthew, Jesus told parables for a didactic purpose. He told parables "because" (Greek: ὅτι) people do not see, hear, and understand (13:13). In that respect, some of his parables are addressed explicitly to the crowds as media of revelation (13:34), such as the Father's Good Gifts (7:9-11), the Wise and Foolish Builders (7:24-27), the Children in the Marketplace (11:16-19), the Sower (13:1-9), the Weeds among the Wheat (13:24-30), the Mustard Seed (13:31-32), and the Leaven (13:33).

Other parables are addressed explicitly to the disciples, such as the Treasure in the Field (13:44), the Pearl of Great Price (13:45-46), the Dragnet (13:47-50), the Lost Sheep (18:12-14), the Wedding Feast (22:1-14), the Faithful and Wise Slave (24:45-51), the Ten Maidens (25:1-13), the Talents (25:14-30), and the Final Judgment (25:31-46). But like those addressed to the crowds, these, too, are didactic. The parables of Jesus employed by the evangelist are put to use for teaching the crowds in general or are used to instruct the disciples, and so the leaders of the church after the earthly career of Jesus has ended, in ways to care for the church in the time between the departure and coming again of the risen Christ.

2. The evangelist Matthew uses one of his "formula quotations" to show that Jesus' telling of parables fulfills the Scriptures (13:35, quoting Ps 78:2). That Matthew would use a formula quotation regarding Jesus and his parables shows how important such activity was. His speaking in parables ranks then along with his healing miracles (8:17, quoting Isa 53:4; cf. 12:15-21) and events associated with his birth (1:22; 2:15), his ministry in Galilee (4:14), and the passion (12:17; 21:4; 27:9).

3. The evangelist grants, however, that some of the parables of Jesus need interpretation. He includes allegorical interpretations in three instances: 13:18-23 (on the Sower), 13:36-43 (on the Weeds in the Wheat), and 13:49-50 (on the Dragnet). The first of these is taken from Mark's Gospel, and seems to be addressed to the crowds, but the other two are distinctive to Matthew, and they are addressed to the disciples alone. In addition to these explicit allegorical interpretations, Matthew's Gospel transmits allegorical elements in virtually all of the parables.

4. More than either of the other two evangelists, Matthew includes parables concerning the kingdom. Included here are three so-called "parables of growth" (the Sower, the Mustard Seed, and the Leaven), but several other parables that have the kingdom as their starting point for the comparison that follows, namely, the Treasure in the Field, the Pearl of Great Price, the Dragnet, the

Unforgiving Slave, the Workers in the Vineyard, the Wedding Feast, and the Ten Maidens. The parables are used to speak of the certainty of the kingdom, its extreme value, and the type of human conduct that is fitting for it.

5. As in the case of the Gospel of Mark (and Luke), certain parables in Matthew's Gospel set forth the history of salvation or aspects of it. Included here are the Wicked Tenants taken from Mark's Gospel (Matt 21:33-44//Mark 12:1-11) and two that are distinctive of the Gospel of Matthew: the Parables of the Two Sons (21:28-32) and the Wedding Feast (22:1-14). In each case these parables are addressed to the chief priests. In the first two they are addressed to the elders as well; in the third Jesus speaks to the chief priests and the Pharisees.

6. Various parables are used in the Gospel of Matthew to exhort the followers of Jesus to prepare for the coming of the Son of man and the final judgment. Here, too, the evangelist Matthew has a motif in common with Mark, but there is more of a didactic and ethical accent. The disciples of Jesus are to forgive one another (the Unforgiving Slave, 18:23-35), use their God-given gifts (the Talents, 25:14-30), care for the unfortunate and needy (the Final Judgment, 25:31-46), continue in faith and discipleship even when the parousia seems a long time in coming (the Ten Maidens, 25:1-13); and those in positions of leadership are to care for those for whom they are responsible (the Faithful and Wise Slave, 24:45-51).

7. Noticeable, too, are parables that have to do with the ordering and disciplining of the Christian community. On the one hand, there are parables that call for patience and restraint in the matter of passing judgment on persons within the community (the Weeds in the Wheat and Its Interpretation, 13:24-30, 36-43, and the Dragnet and Its Interpretation, 13:47-50). On the other hand, there are parables that insist upon forgiveness (18:23-35) and the need to exclude one who might be an extreme offender (22:11-14).

In these and other passages a distinct profile of parable interpretation appears within the Gospel of Matthew. As a handbook for preaching, teaching, discipline, and sacramental life, the Gospel of Matthew incorporates parables for theological and ecclesial interests that one has come to associate with that Gospel: catechesis, the fulfillment of the Scriptures in and through the ministry of Jesus, the kingdom, the history of salvation, eschatology, and discipline. To be added to that is the commonsense view that the parables of Jesus need to be interpreted for the life of the Christian community.

Luke as Interpreter of the Parables

It is Luke who customarily gets the credit for transmitting the favorite parables of Jesus. It is Luke after all, and Luke alone, who transmits the Parables of the Good Samaritan and the Prodigal Son, probably the two best-known parables of Jesus.

As indicated in Appendix 1, Luke takes from Mark 4:11-12 the matter of Jesus' speaking in parables (8:9-10), but omits what is said in Mark 4:33-34. Like Matthew, Luke seems to take for granted that the parables are didactic and media for revelation. Most of them are located within the Travel Narrative (9:51–19:27), and the following points can be said about their use in this Gospel:

1. The parables of Jesus are told to teach and to illustrate for specific audiences. The evangelist seems to have had a keen interest in those to whom the parables were addressed, since he is often quite specific about them. To be sure, some are addressed to persons not identified as belonging to any particular group, such as the Parables of the Rich Fool (12:16-21), the Fig Tree (13:6-9), and the Great Banquet (14:16-24). Others, however, are addressed by Jesus either to his opponents or to his disciples; there is no third possibility. Regarding those addressed to opponents, some are addressed specifically to Pharisees who are critical of Jesus and his ways: the Lost Sheep (15:4-7), the Lost Coin (15:8-10), the Prodigal Son (15:11-32), and the Rich Man and Lazarus (16:19-31). Probably the Parable of the Pharisee and the Tax Collector (18:10-14), addressed to those who thought of themselves as righteous, belongs in this group as well. Finally, the Good Samaritan (10:29-37) is addressed to an opponent who is designated as a lawyer who seeks to justify himself.

Other parables, however, are addressed specifically to Jesus' disciples. Some of these have to do with prayer, such as the Friend at Midnight (11:5-8), the Father's Good Gifts (11:11-13), and the Unjust Judge (18:1-8). These cohere with other emphases on prayer in this Gospel (6:12; 9:28; 11:1-4; 21:36; 22:40, 46). Other parables addressed to the disciples have to do with their fidelity at the coming of the Son of man at his parousia, such as the Waiting Slaves (12:35-39), the Faithful and Wise Steward (12:41-46), the Slave at Duty (17:7-10), and the Pounds (19:12-27). In these cases, in Luke's design, the disciples are being prepared for the time between the earthly ministry of Jesus and his coming again.

2. Like Mark and Matthew, Luke exhibits an interest in the history of salvation. He includes one parable that both of the other evangelists included, that is, the Parable of the Wicked Tenants (20:9-18). In addition, he includes the Parable of the Great Banquet (14:16-24), which likewise provides a sketch of this theme.

3. Like the other two evangelists Luke includes parables that exhort the disciples of Jesus to be ready for the coming of the Son of man. Included here are parables already mentioned in connection with teachings addressed to the disciples, such as the Waiting Slaves and the Faithful and Wise Steward.

4. What is striking about Luke's Gospel is the inclusion of parables that have to do with compassion, both human and divine. Among the former are the Parables of the Good Samaritan (10:29-37) and, in an obverse manner, the Rich Man and Lazarus (16:19-31). Among those that set forth the gospel of divine compassion are the parables of Luke 15, the Lost Sheep, the Lost Coin, and the Prodigal Son.

428

5. Finally, it is Luke alone who has parables of exemplary behavior. These are parables that need little in the way of interpretation. They simply provide models for human behavior. They are the Parables of the Good Samaritan, the Rich Fool, the Rich Man and Lazarus, and the Pharisee and the Tax Collector.

Like Matthew, and to some degree Mark, the evangelist Luke made use of parables of Jesus to highlight and carry out various purposes. Several are used to combat a mind-set that is illustrated by the opponents of Jesus (the Pharisees or the righteous). Others are used to instruct the disciples of Jesus for the time of the church, the time between the resurrection and the parousia. Others set forth the need of the church and its leaders to be diligent and faithful in their duties during that time, the time in which salvation history is unfolding. And still others illustrate the divine compassion and instruct the disciples in human compassion.

Concluding Comment

These brief observations show that the three Synoptic evangelists used the parables in furthering their own purposes. They employed and interpreted them in light of goals that they had, which can be detected even apart from their use of the parables. The parables are made to fit into those larger purposes.

On the other hand, the parables themselves must have shaped the outlooks of the three evangelists. It is primarily from the parables that the evangelists learned the essential features and contents of the message of Jesus. Therefore one can argue that the parables were not simply employed by the evangelists to transmit the teachings of Jesus. The parables also shaped and molded the thinking of the evangelists. It would be going too far to say that without the parables there would have been no Gospels. (The Gospel of John, e.g., contains none.) But the evangelists Matthew and Luke, and to a lesser extent Mark, could hardly have produced their Gospels without them.

CHAPTER 10

Parables in the Gospel of Thomas

The Coptic *Gospel of Thomas* contains fourteen units that can clearly be classified as parables.[1] Ten of them have parallels in the Synoptic Gospels. Four are distinctive to the *Gospel of Thomas,* having no parallels. The data are as follows:

Thomas *Parables with Synoptic Parallels*

The Sower, *Thomas* 9//Mark 4:3-8//Matthew 13:3-8//Luke 8:5-8

The Mustard Seed, *Thomas* 20//Mark 4:30-32//Matthew 13:31-32//Luke 13:18-19

The Weeds in the Wheat, *Thomas* 57//Matthew 13:24-30

The Rich Fool, *Thomas* 63//Luke 12:16-21

The Great Banquet, *Thomas* 64//Luke 14:16-24; cf. Matthew 22:1-10 (the Wedding Feast)

The Wicked Tenants, *Thomas* 65//Mark 12:1-12//Matthew 21:33-46// Luke 20:9-19

The Pearl of Great Price, *Thomas* 76//Matthew 13:45-46

The Leaven, *Thomas* 96//Matthew 13:33//Luke 13:20-21

The Lost Sheep, *Thomas* 107//Matthew 18:12-14//Luke 15:4-7

The Treasure in the Field, *Thomas* 109//Matthew 13:44

---

1. The number of parables in the *Gospel of Thomas* differs widely among scholars, depending on what is classified as such. On the one hand, for example, G. Jones, *Art and Truth of the Parables,* 230, says that "about 30" logia can be considered parables; on the other, C. Blomberg, "Tradition and Redaction in the Parables of the Gospel of Thomas," 177, counts 13, as does B. Scott, *Parable,* 33, who omits the Parable of the Disciples as Little Children (*Gos. Thom.* 21). R. McL. Wilson, *Studies in the Gospel of Thomas,* 89-90, enumerates the 14 listed above as parables in the *Gospel of Thomas* Cf. also B. Gärtner, *Theology of the Gospel according to Thomas,* 18.

Thomas *Parables without Synoptic Parallels*

The Wise Fisherman, *Thomas* 8
The Disciples as Little Children, *Thomas* 21
The Woman with a Jar, *Thomas* 97
The Assassin, *Thomas* 98

Where parallels to Synoptic parables exist, three of those in the *Gospel of Thomas* have parallels in all three Synoptic Gospels, beginning with Mark (the Sower, the Mustard Seed, and the Wicked Tenants); two (the Lost Sheep and the Leaven) have parallels in Matthew and Luke alone and are usually considered from Q; three (the Weeds in the Wheat, the Pearl, and the Treasure) have parallels in Matthew's special tradition; and two (the Rich Fool and the Great Banquet) have parallels in Luke's special tradition.[2]

The Parable of the Wise Fisherman (*Gos. Thom.* 8) has much in common with the Parable of the Net in Matthew 13:47-50, but it is also similar to the Pearl in Matthew 13:45 (which has a true parallel in *Gos. Thom.* 76) in that the fisherman finds a "large good fish" and dispenses with the rest. It is possible that the Wise Fisherman is a conflation of these two Matthean parables,[3] or it could be based on an independent tradition.[4] When one does some combining of the data, and includes the Wise Fisherman as a parallel to the Net (Matt 13:47-50), it is of interest that all seven of the parables of Matthew 13 appear in the *Gospel of Thomas* — the Net (8//Matt 13:47-50); the Sower (9//Matt 13:3-8); the Mustard Seed (20//Matt 13:31-32); the Weeds (57//Matt 13:24-30); the Pearl (76//Matt 13:45-56); the Leaven (96//Matt 13:33); and the Treasure (109//Matt 13:44). The sequence, however, is quite different, and their interpretations differ.

Comment has been made in previous chapters on those parables in the *Gospel of Thomas* that have Synoptic parallels. What has been said need not be repeated here. The purpose of this section is to provide a more general discussion of the ways in which the parables have been presented in the *Gospel of Thomas*. But first it is necessary to assess that Gospel.

---

2. The Great Banquet in Luke 14:16-24 and the Wedding Feast in Matthew 22:1-10 are similar in many respects, but finally should be assigned to L and M, respectively. Cf. Burnett H. Streeter, *The Four Gospels: A Study of Origins*, rev. ed. (New York: St. Martin's Press, 1930), 198; W. D. Davies and D. Allison, *Matthew*, 1:123.

3. W. Schrage, *Das Verhältnis*, 37; G. Jones, *Art and Truth of the Parables*, 230; A. Lindemann, "Zur Gleichnisinterpretation im Thomas-Evangelium," 216-18; and M. Fieger, *Thomasevangelium*, 48.

4. R. McL. Wilson, *Studies in the Gospel of Thomas*, 95; and S. Patterson, *Gospel of Thomas*, 239 (n. 83), say that the *Gospel of Thomas* 8 and Matt 13:47 "derive from a common origin," but the former is not dependent on the latter.

The Gospel of Thomas: An Assessment

The oldest complete text of the *Gospel of Thomas*, written in the Coptic language, is preserved at the Cairo Coptic Museum. It was discovered at Nag Hammadi, Egypt, in 1945 and contains 114 sayings attributed to Jesus. The document is usually considered to have been written in the fourth century.[5] In English translation it consists of approximately 5,100 words — about 45 percent of the length of the Gospel of Mark.[6]

In addition to the Coptic text, three Greek fragments of this Gospel — known as *Oxyrhynchus Papyri* 1 (= *Gos. Thom.* 26–30, 77, and 31–33), 654 (= *Gos. Thom.* Prologue and 1–6), and 655 (= *Gos. Thom.* 36–39) — were discovered earlier: *POxy* 1 in 1897 and *POxy* 654 and 655 in 1903.[7] On paleographical grounds these fragments have been judged to be from differing texts, which have been assigned to the years A.D. 200-250.[8] These fragments are kept at the British Library, London (#1), the Bodleian Library at Oxford (#654), and the Harvard Houghton Library in Cambridge, Massachusetts (#655). It is commonly thought that the Gospel was orginally composed in Greek, and that the Coptic version now extant is a translation from an earlier Greek version similar to, but not identical with, the Greek texts in our possession.

The *Gospel of Thomas* is attributed in its Prologue to Didymos Judas Thomas. In Greek "Didymos" means "twin," as does Aramaic "Thomas." The Thomas in mind is Thomas the disciple, who is designated Θωμᾶς ὁ λεγόμενος Δίδυμος ("Thomas, who was called the Twin") three times in the Gospel of John (11:16; 20:24; 21:2). In certain Thomas traditions of Syria this figure is considered to have been the twin brother of Jesus.[9]

For a long time the usual judgment had been that the *Gospel of Thomas* was produced in the middle of the second century A.D., and that view still has

---

5. As attested in many studies; cf. Helmut Koester, "Introduction [to the Gospel of Thomas]," in *Nag Hammadi Codex II,2-7*, ed. Bentley Layton, NHS 20-21, 2 vols. (Leiden: E. J. Brill, 1989), 1:38; B. Blatz, "Coptic Gospel of Thomas," 1:111; and Ron Cameron, "Thomas, Gospel of," *ABD* 6:535.

6. The English version used in this discussion is that of Thomas O. Lambdin in *NHLE* 126-38. According to Robert Morgenthaler, *Statistik des neutestamentlichen Wortschatzes* (Zurich: Gotthelf Verlag, 1958) 164, the Greek text of the Gospel of Mark contains 11,229 words. In English the word count would be somewhat higher.

7. S. Kent Brown, "Sayings of Jesus, Oxyrhynchus," *ABD* 5:999-1,001.

8. Cf. *The Oxyrhynchus Papyri*, ed. Bernard P. Grenfell, Arthur S. Hunt, et al., 31 vols. (London: Egypt Exploration Fund, 1898-1966), 4:1; and Harold W. Attridge, "The Gospel according to Thomas (Greek Fragments)," in *Nag Hammadi Codex II,2-7*, NHS 20, ed. Bentley Layton, 2 vols. (Leiden: E. J. Brill, 1989), 1:96-99. Attridge places *POxy* 1 "shortly after A.D. 200" (p. 97); *POxy* 654 "in the middle of the third century" (p. 97); and *POxy* 655 "between A.D. 200 and 250" (p. 98).

9. In the *Acts of Thomas* 39 Thomas is designated as "Twin of the Messiah." For text, cf. *The Acts of Thomas*, ed. A. F. J. Klijn, 85.

wide support.[10] But some interpreters have claimed that it was produced in the first century or at least by the year A.D. 100.[11]

Assigning a date to this document is both controversial and difficult. In regard to external evidence, the *Gospel of Thomas* is first attested in the writings of Hippolytus (d. ca. A.D. 235) during the first quarter of the third century,[12] and then by Origen about A.D. 233.[13] As indicated above, the Greek fragments are thought to have been written ca. A.D. 200-250. Prior to these items, there is no external or textual evidence for the existence of the *Gospel of Thomas*. On external and textual grounds, therefore, there are good grounds for placing the *Gospel of Thomas* in its final form somewhere in the second century.

In regard to internal evidence, there are four items worth noting. First, the *Gospel of Thomas* contains within itself a veiled reference to the twenty-four books of the OT (logion 52). This reference presupposes the canonization of the OT following the Jewish numerical system.[14] That puts the Gospel somewhere into the second century when the canon had been solidified in Jewish communities.

---

10. Among others, the following can be mentioned: A. Guillaumont et al., *The Gospel according to Thomas,* vi; H.-C. Puech, "Gnostic Gospels and Related Documents," 1:305; O. Cullmann, "Gospel of Thomas," 427; R. McL. Wilson, *Studies in the Gospel of Thomas,* 7-8; B. Gärtner, *Theology of the Gospel according to Thomas,* 271; G. Quispel, "'The Gospel of Thomas' and the 'Gospel of the Hebrews,'" 378; J. Leipoldt, *Das Evangelium nach Thomas,* 17; J.-É. Ménard, *L'Évangile selon Thomas,* 3; K. Snodgrass, "The Gospel of Thomas," 19-38; M. Fieger, *Das Thomasevangelium,* 4, 7; and B. Blatz, "Coptic Gospel of Thomas," 1:113.

11. Helmut Koester, *Introduction to the New Testament,* 2 vols. (Philadelphia: Fortress, 1982), 2:152, has written: "It was probably written during I CE in Palestine or Syria"; cf. idem, *Ancient Christian Gospels,* 83-84. According to R. Funk, *Five Gospels,* 474, "Thomas probably assumed its present form by 100 C.E." Ron Cameron, *The Other Gospels: Non-Canonical Gospel Texts* (Philadelphia: Westminster, 1982), 25, suggests "the second half of the first century" as the time of composition. S. Davies, *Gospel of Thomas,* 3, places the completed work as early as A.D. 50-70. According to S. Patterson, *Gospel of Thomas,* 120, the Gospel was written "in the vicinity of 70-80 C.E." That the Gospel of John was written as a response to the *Gospel of Thomas* (implying the existence of the *Gospel of Thomas* prior to the Fourth Gospel) is asserted by Gregory J. Riley, *Resurrection Reconsidered: Thomas and John in Controversy* (Minneapolis: Fortress, 1995). He thinks that John 2:19 is a Johannine revision of logion 71 in the *Gospel of Thomas.* That is hardly sufficient evidence for his thesis.

12. Hippolytus, *Refutation of All Heresies* 5.2. The reference is according to that in *ANF* 5:50. In other editions, it is found at *Ref.* 5.7.20. Hippolytus died ca. A.D. 235. Hippolytus not only refers to the *Gospel of Thomas* as a document but also cites a variant of logion 4 within it.

13. Origen, *Homily on Luke* 1. This is dated ca. A.D. 233.

14. According to *Gos. Thom.* 52, 24 prophets of Israel spoke of Jesus. The designation 24 "prophets" undoubtedly refers to the 24 books in the Jewish canon. Cf. B. Gärtner, *Theology of the Gospel according to Thomas,* 154.

Second, the fact that the book begins with the claim in its prescript that it is the work of Thomas reflects a time when it was important to appeal to apostolic authorship to establish authority. The canonical Gospels, by contrast, are anonymous. By attributing itself to apostolic authorship, the *Gospel of Thomas* must come from well into the second century when anonymity could no longer stand; an appeal to a specific apostle for the authority of a document is important.[15]

A third point is more complex. A good number of interpreters hold that the *Gospel of Thomas* shows no dependence upon, nor even influences from, the canonical Gospels.[16] On the other hand, there have been, and still are, interpreters who have held the opposite view, saying that the *Gospel of Thomas* shows evidence of dependence in at least some cases where there are parallels.[17] Perhaps the issue cannot be resolved. But it is undeniable that some logia in the *Gospel of Thomas* having parallels to the canonical Gospels bear the marks of specifically Matthean and Lukan redactional work,[18] which speaks against total independence of the text as we have it in its final form in those specific cases. Most impressive are two logia of the *Gospel of Thomas* that appear in Greek in the *Oxyrhynchus Papyri,* and which therefore allow comparisons with their parallels in the canonical Gospels of the Greek NT. The first of these is logion 5 of the *Gospel of Thomas,* a part of which exists in Greek within *Oxyrhynchus Papyrus* 654 (lines 29-30). The portion of that logion that exists in Greek is worded exactly as it is in Luke's Gospel over against its wording in Mark (as well as in Matthew). The similarities are underscored below, supplemented by missing letters and words inserted by editors, who have placed them in brackets. Here it

15. S. Patterson, *Gospel of Thomas,* 116, argues that assigning of apostolic authorship points to the time of the deutero-Pauline epistles (i.e., late first century). This is to overlook the fact that pseudonymous apostolic authorship continues unabated in succeeding centuries, for example, in the case of apocrypha attributed to Peter, Philip, James, Mary, and others, including Thomas (*The Acts of Thomas*).

16. G. Quispel, "Some Remarks," 277; H. Koester, *Introduction to the New Testament,* 2:153; R. Cameron, *Other Gospels,* 24; S. Davies, *Gospel of Thomas,* 5; R. Funk, *Five Gospels,* 474; B. Layton, *The Gnostic Scriptures,* 377; and B. Blatz, "Coptic Gospel of Thomas," 1:113.

17. H. McArthur, "Dependence of the Gospel of Thomas," 286-87; R. M. Grant and D. N. Freedman, *Secret Sayings of Jesus,* 106-16; B. Gärtner, *Theology of the Gospel according to Thomas,* 35-68; O. Cullmann, "Gospel of Thomas," 434; W. Schrage, *Das Verhältnis;* J. Leipoldt, *Evangelium nach Thomas,* 16-18; K. Rudolf, *Gnosis,* 263; C. Tuckett, "Thomas and the Synoptics," 132-57; K. R. Snodgrass, "The Gospel of Thomas," 19-38; M. Fieger, *Das Thomasevangelium,* 6-7; John P. Meier, *A Marginal Jew: Rethinking the Historical Jesus,* 3 vols. projected (New York: Doubleday, 1991–), 1:130-39; and N. T. Wright, *The New Testament and the People of God* (Minneapolis: Fortress, 1992), 442.

18. These passages are surveyed by C. Tuckett, "Thomas and the Synoptics," 145-56. He examines logia 5, 9, 16, 20, and 55 of the *Gospel of Thomas* in relationship to the Synoptic Gospels.

is evident that the *Gospel of Thomas* in its Greek form was dependent on the Gospel of Luke, whose redaction is apparent at this point:[19]

Mark 4:22:
οὐ γάρ ἐστιν κρυπτὸν ἐὰν μὴ
ἵνα φανερωθῇ.

For there is nothing hid, except to be made manifest.

Matthew 10:26:
οὐδὲν γάρ ἐστιν κεκαλυμμένον ὃ οὐκ
ἀποκαλυφθήσεται καὶ κρυπτὸν ὃ οὐ
γνωσθήσεται.

For nothing is covered that will not be revealed and hidden that will not be made known.

Luke 8:17:
οὐ γάρ ἐστιν κρυπτὸν ὃ οὐ
φανερὸν γενήσεται.

For there is nothing hidden that will not be made manifest.

POxy 654.29-30:
[οὐ γάρ ἐσ]τιν κρυπτὸν ὃ οὐ
φανε[ρὸν γενήσεται].

For there is nothing hidden that will not be made manifest.

The second instance is logion 26 of the *Gospel of Thomas,* where the corresponding Greek text appears in *Oxyrhynchus Papyrus* 1 (lines 1-4). It corresponds to the saying of Jesus in Matthew 7:5//Luke 6:42, and every word and form of expression can be found in those Gospels. In the following quotation, words that are found in both Matthew and Luke, as well as in *POxy* 1.1-4 — and in the same sequence — are in bold; one word corresponding to Matthew's wording (but which is also found in Luke in a different sequence, the verb ἐκβαλεῖν, "to cast out") is underscored once, and those corresponding to Luke's are underscored twice:[20]

POxy 1.1-4	Matt 7:5	Luke 6:42
καί τότε διαβλέψεις	καί τότε διαβλέψεις	καί τότε διαβλέψεις
ἐκβαλεῖν τὸ κάρφος	ἐκβαλεῖν τὸ κάρφος	τὸ κάρφος
τὸ ἐν τῷ ὀφθαλμῷ	ἐκ τοῦ ὀφθαλμοῦ	τὸ ἐν τῷ ὀφθαλμῷ
τοῦ ἀδελφοῦ σου.	τοῦ ἀδελφοῦ σου.	τοῦ ἀδελφοῦ σου
		ἐκβαλεῖν.

19. The Greek text of *POxy* 654:29-30 is from the critical text edited by H. W. Attridge, "The Gospel according to Thomas (Greek Fragments)," in *Nag Hammadi Codex II,2-7,* ed. B. Layton, 1:115.

20. The Greek text of *POxy* 1:1-4 is from ibid., 1:118.

Translation (*POxy* 1.1-4): "And then you will see clearly to cast out the speck that is in the eye of your brother."

In this instance the peculiarities of both Matthew and Luke show up in the fragment, and the conclusion to be drawn is that the writer of the papyrus had both texts before him when he wrote his own.

These instances, together with others that can be listed,[21] indicate that the Gospels of both Matthew and Luke were probably available to, and were used by, the author of the *Gospel of Thomas* in its earliest Greek version.

Finally, in logion 13 of the *Gospel of Thomas* there is a scene reminiscent of the Caesarea Philippi event of the Synoptic Gospels in which Peter makes the true confession, and which is elaborated fully in the Gospel of Matthew (16:13-20). In Matthew's account Peter is by all means chief of the apostles. Moreover, the apostle Matthew was obviously important to the community in which the Gospel was produced, and to whom it was attributed subsequently. What is striking in comparing the two accounts is that in the scene within the *Gospel of Thomas* Peter and Matthew are demoted in rank, and Thomas is elevated as the greatest of the apostles. Indeed, Thomas is considered *equal* to Jesus himself — which gnostic teachers held as a possibility for the true disciple[22] — for he has become fully intoxicated with the teachings of Jesus, and he is therefore no longer to speak of Jesus as his "Master." It is my judgment that in this passage the form of Christianity that the Gospel of Matthew represents — Matthean and Petrine in western Syria — is being denigrated by the form of Christianity represented by the *Gospel of Thomas* in eastern Syria.[23] Risking an anachronism, we may say that the Gospel of Matthew reflects catholic and orthodox Christianity. But it is being denigrated by the form of Christianity that is reflected in the *Gospel of Thomas*. The phenomenon of denigration is known elsewhere, particularly among the Valentinian Gnostics, who considered catholic Christianity second-rate.[24] In light of this logion, there can be little doubt but what the *Gospel of Thomas* in its present form comes from a time that is later than the composition of Matthew's Gospel.

Other interpreters have maintained that, in addition to the redactional elements from Matthew and Luke, the *Gospel of Thomas* contains some sayings with parallels that are specific to Mark, and still others with parallels only to

---

21. The clearest of these are as follows: *POxy* 654:12 (= *Gos. Thom.* 3) and Matt 6:26; 654:15-16 (= *Gos. Thom.* 3) and Luke 17:21; 654:25-26 (= *Gos. Thom.* 4) and Mark 10:31// Matt 19:30; and 655:39-46 (= *Gos. Thom.* 39) and Matt 23:13//Luke 11:52. On these and other texts, cf. J. Fitzmyer, "The Oxyrhynchus Logoi of Jesus," 355-433.

22. Cf. Irenaeus, *Against Heresies* 1.25.2, concerning the Carpocratian Gnostics. At *Gospel of Thomas* 108 also the Gnostic is said to be equal to Jesus. According to Hippolytus, *Refutation of All Heresies* 7.22, a similar teaching was held by the Ebionites.

23. On the importance of Thomas, and the insufficiency of the authority of Peter and Matthew in this Gospel, cf. A. F. Walls, "References to Apostles," 268-69.

24. Irenaeus, *Against Heresies* 1.7.5; Epiphanius, *Panarion* 31.7.6–31.7.11; and the (Valentinian) Nag Hammadi text, *The Tripartite Tractate* 118.14-34.

John.[25] All this gives rise to the suspicion that the author had the fourfold collection of Gospels available in his community. That would point to the second half of the second century when such a collection is first attested in the writings of Irenaeus, Clement of Alexandria, and Tertullian. The view that the *Gospel of Thomas* was produced in the middle of the second century at the earliest remains compelling.[26]

But even if the *Gospel of Thomas* in its present form is from a time later than the canonical Gospels, is it possible that an earlier edition existed? The claim keeps being made that indeed an early version — a written text — was composed in the middle of the first century. Such a claim has been made by a number of persons, such as Helmut Koester, Stephen Patterson, Stevan Davies, John Dominic Crossan, and the Fellows of the Jesus Seminar.[27] But how does one establish such a claim? Too often the claim is simply asserted and repeated as though it were an "assured result" of Gospel studies. When one looks for reasons for the claim, there seem to be three.[28] The first has to do with its genre. It is a sayings collection, and since the Q document — a sayings collection — is thought to come from the 50s of the first century, and the two documents have a lot of sayings in common, we can apparently assume that an earlier version of the *Gospel of Thomas* did too.[29] The second claim is that some of the sayings having parallels in the canonical Gospels seem to exhibit an arrested development, lacking the interpretive embellishments found in their canonical parallels; therefore, they can be assigned to an earlier date of composition.[30] Finally, it is argued that the lack of christological titles speaks for the relative antiquity of the document.[31]

---

25. Scholarly discussion is summarized by J. Meier, *A Marginal Jew*, 1:134-37.

26. Cf. n. 10.

27. According to H. Koester and S. Patterson, "Gospel of Thomas," 37, much of the material in the *Gospel of Thomas* may have been written as early as the 30s or 40s of the first century. S. Davies, *Gospel of Thomas*, 3, says, "Thomas should be dated ca. A.D. 50-70." John Dominic Crossan, *The Historical Jesus: The Life of a Mediterranean Jewish Peasant* (San Francisco: HarperCollins, 1991), 428, claims that the first version of the *Gospel of Thomas* was composed by the 50s of the first century. According to R. Funk, *Five Gospels*, 474, "an earlier version [of the *Gospel of Thomas*] may have originated as early as 50-60 C.E."

28. R. Cameron, *The Other Gospels*, 23-25; cf. also H. Koester, *Ancient Christian Gospels*, 85, 95.

29. H. Koester, "Introduction [to the Gospel of Thomas]," in *Nag Hammadi Codex II,2-7*, ed. B. Layton, 1:39; idem, "Introduction [to the Gospel of Thomas]," *NHLE* 125; R. Cameron, *The Other Gospels*, 24; S. Davies, *Gospel of Thomas*, 16-17; and J. Patterson, *Gospel of Thomas*, 117.

30. G. Quispel, "Gospel of Thomas and the New Testament," 205; H. Koester, *Introduction to the New Testament*, 2:154; R. Cameron, *The Other Gospels*, 24; and S. Davies, *The Gospel of Thomas*, 16.

31. H. Koester, "Introduction [to the Gospel of Thomas]," *Nag Hammadi Codex II*, ed. B. Layton, 1:40; idem, *Introduction to the New Testament*, 2:152; and S. Patterson, *Gospel of Thomas*, 118.

The first argument — the analogy to Q — is not convincing. It is not necessary to posit the first edition of a sayings collection in the middle of the first century to account for the preservation of sayings of Jesus. Both Joachim Jeremias and Helmut Koester — scholars very unlike one another — have demonstrated that sayings of Jesus continued to exist in oral circulation well into the second century before they were written down.[32] Jeremias finds some that were written down for the first time by Tertullian and Clement of Alexandria near the end of the second century. Other analogies of sayings collections, such as the discourses of the Fourth Gospel and the sayings of Jesus collected in the *Dialogue of the Savior,* come from times much later than Q in their written form. The *Gospel of Thomas* could actually have been written for the first time in the middle of the second century, based on sayings preserved and collected over time.[33] In any case, the *genre* of a document has little to do with its date.

The second point — that some sayings in the *Gospel of Thomas* appear to be more primitive than their parallels in the canonical Gospels — carries little weight either for at least two reasons.[34] First, it is commonly noticed, by analogy, that the evangelist who produced the Gospel of Matthew abbreviated materials taken over from Mark. The author of the *Gospel of Thomas* could likewise have abbreviated materials taken from the canonical Gospels. Second, the controlling hermeneutic of the *Gospel of Thomas* is, as stated in its prescript, that the sayings are obscure, and their meaning must be acquired. Therefore it is actually fitting that the author of the *Gospel of Thomas* would have stripped any received sayings of their interpretations found in the canonical Gospels.

Finally, the claim that the *Gospel of Thomas* lacks christological titles, and that that would be a reason to give it an early date, does not hold up. Jesus speaks of himself as the Son of man in one saying (86) and of his lordship in another (90). But aside from that, the lack of titles cannot be considered a criterion since the document consists of logia attributed to Jesus himself, and lacks opportunities for christological titles to be used by his disciples. Moreover, one cannot use the amount or range of christological titles in a work as an index of its age (the fewer, the earlier; the more, the later). If that were decisive, one would have to date the Gospel of John earlier than the Synoptics, and the letters of Paul later than the Gospels. The upshot is that the claims being made that an early edition of the *Gospel of Thomas* was composed in the middle of the first century and was therefore prior in composition to the canonical Gospels — claims that give a certain privilege to it — are by no means self-evident.

To be sure, some passages in the *Gospel of Thomas* have parallels in the

---

32. Joachim Jeremias, *Unknown Sayings of Jesus;* Helmut Koester, *Synoptische Überlieferung bei den apostolischen Vätern,* TU 65 (Berlin: Akademie, 1957).

33. Cf. H.-C. Puech, "Gnostic Gospels," 1:305.

34. The two points that follow are taken from J. Meier, *A Marginal Jew,* 1:132-33, who cites still other literature.

Synoptic Gospels and could be based on independent traditions, as some have suggested. The Parables of the Great Banquet and the Wicked Tenants (logia 64–65) are two examples,[35] but it is difficult to know whether they are truly independent. They may well be, but even if they are, that does not mean *a priori* that they provide greater access to the voice of Jesus of Nazareth than their Synoptic parallels do. In addition, there are a few sayings in the *Gospel of Thomas* that have no parallels to those in the canonical Gospels, and some of these could be authentic.[36]

In the current situation there are three major proposals to account for the composition of the *Gospel of Thomas:* (1) It was composed independently of the canonical Gospels.[37] (2) A first edition of the Gospel was composed independently of the canonical Gospels at an early, indeterminate stage but was supplemented and edited at later stages in light of the canonical Gospels.[38] (3) It was composed in the second century by an author who employed and edited sources and traditions distinctive to this gospel and materials from the canonical Gospels.[39] Allowances must also be made in this view for redactional work at both the Greek and Coptic stages of composition. In light of the foregoing discussion — and taking into consideration the textual, external, and internal evidence — either of the latter two views seem to provide a more satisfactory account for the composition of the Gospel than the first. But either would also mean that the *Gospel of Thomas,* as attested in both its Greek and Coptic versions, was dependent upon the canonical Gospels in various places. The view that the *Gospel of Thomas* was composed in stages remains speculative; there is no external evidence that would support such a view, nor can any internal evidence be brought forth for it. When all these factors are considered, there are good reasons to conclude that the third view stated above is the most satisfactory.

The issue whether the *Gospel of Thomas* was of gnostic origin and can be called a gnostic gospel continues to be debated. While the claim has been made that it has neither gnostic origins nor character,[40] major interpreters have considered it to be both gnostic in origin and gnostic in character.[41] Some varia-

---

35. Independence is claimed by, among others, J. Jeremias, *Parables,* 24; and B. Scott, *Parable,* 32-33.

36. Cf., for example, logia 25 and 95, which have the ring of authenticity.

37. Cf. n. 16 above.

38. R. McL. Wilson, *Studies,* 51, 92, 148.

39. Cf. n. 17 above.

40. S. Davies, *Gospel of Thomas,* 18-35.

41. Among others, cf. R. Grant and D. Freedman, *Secret Sayings,* 62-73; R. McL. Wilson, *Studies in the Gospel of Thomas,* 14-44; B. Gärtner, *Theology of the Gospel according to Thomas,* 91-94; W. Schrage, *Das Verhältnis,* 19-27; E. Haenchen, *Die Botschaft,* 34-37; O. Cullmann, "Gospel of Thomas," 425-27, 430; H. Montefiore, "Comparison," 42-44, 52-54; J. Leipoldt, *Evangelium nach Thomas,* 8-11; N. Perrin, *Teaching,* 36; H. Koester, *Ancient*

tions have been suggested. One is that its earliest version may have been of Encratite origin, but that the Gospel was edited by a gnostic redactor.[42] Another is that, whatever its origins, it has a "gnosticizing proclivity."[43] Although the issues continue to be debated, the gnostic character of the Gospel seems fairly well established. In the case of parables, a gnostic interpretation is evident in the case of the Great Banquet and the Lost Sheep (logia 64 and 107), which have Synoptic parallels, and in the four parables distinctive to the *Gospel of Thomas*.

Four Distinctive Parables

As indicated at the outset, there are four parables in the *Gospel of Thomas* that have no parallels, strictly speaking, to parables in the Synoptic Gospels. These are at logia 8, 21, 97, and 98.

The Wise Fisherman, *Gospel of Thomas* 8

And he said, "The man is like a wise fisherman who cast his net into the sea and drew it up from the sea full of small fish. Among them the wise fisherman found a fine large fish. He threw all the small fish back into the sea and chose the large fish without difficulty. Whoever has ears to hear, let him hear."[44]

The parable is a parable of wisdom, but the reader is not told who "the man" is that is being compared to the wise fisherman. Some interpreters have conjectured that the parable, in an earlier form, would have started with "The kingdom [rather than "the man"] is like. . . ."[45] That view has some support from a version of the parable quoted by Clement of Alexandria (ca. A.D. 150-215), who says that it is a parable "in the Gospel" (not saying which one), and it runs as follows:

Christian Gospels, 83-84; M. Fieger, *Thomasevangelium*, 8-11; B. Blatz, "Coptic Gospel of Thomas," 1:114; Craig A. Evans, *Noncanonical Writings and New Testament Interpretation* (Peabody, Mass.: Hendrickson Publishers, 1992), 166; and M. Franzmann, *Jesus in the Nag Hammadi Writings*, 20, 130, 207.

42. H.-C. Puech, "The Gospel of Thomas," 1:305-6; and G. Quispel, "'The Gospel of Thomas' and the 'Gospel of the Hebrews,'" 372, 381 (that the author was an Encratite); idem, "The Gospel of Thomas and the New Testament," 206 (that it was completed by a "gnosticizing editor"); and idem, "Some Remarks," 240 (that it conveys "a gnosticizing interpretation of the Christian message").

43. S. Patterson, *Gospel of Thomas and Jesus*, 155, 157.

44. Text from *NHLE* 127.

45. J. Jeremias, *Parables*, 101-2 (n. 56), 201; idem, *Unknown Sayings*, 88-89; S. Davies, *Gospel of Thomas*, 154; and B. Scott, *Parable*, 314.

The kingdom of heaven is like a man who cast a net into the sea; and out of the multitude of the fishes caught, makes a selection of the better ones.[46]

Yet, in spite of the similarity between the two versions, it is not certain that the parable in the *Gospel of Thomas* is a parable of the kingdom. According to one interpreter, "the man" in the parable is an "enlightened individual who discovers in Jesus' words a personal identity, recognizing therein a religious destiny."[47] Other interpreters have suggested that "the man" is the Gnostic, and that the "fine large fish" is the knowledge (γνῶσις) that is available to him.[48] Another possibility — more likely — is that "the man" is the Gnostic Redeemer, and that the largest fish is the Gnostic, who is selected (indeed, elected) from the mass of humanity.[49] Some interpreters have suggested that either of these interpretations is possible.[50]

In the Parable of the Dragnet in Matthew 13:47-48 the fish that are obtained in the net are both good and bad, and the sorting of them refers to the final judgment. Those features are entirely lacking in logion 8. In the latter the contrast is between the small fish (plural) and the fine large one, and the sorting consists of selecting the latter. The parable in this respect is similar to the Parable of the Lost Sheep in this Gospel, in which the most beloved sheep that went away is the largest (logion 107; cf. also the use of "large" in 20 and 96). In both cases it is probably the Gnostic that is meant in the use of "fine large fish" and "the largest" as the one to be possessed or restored.

The question whether this could be an authentic parable of Jesus has been raised by various interpreters. Its authenticity has been maintained by some,[51] but since it appears to have a gnostic meaning and origin, it should not be attributed to Jesus.[52]

This logion, like four others (logia 21, 63, 65, and 96), has an appended saying similar to one in the Synoptic tradition (Mark 4:9//Matt 13:9//Luke 8:8; Mark 4:23; Matt 11:15; 13:43; Luke 14:35). In logia 63, 65, and 96 the saying is brief ("Let him who has ears, hear"); a similar saying is found within logion 24 ("Whoever has ears, let him hear"). In 8 and 21 the expression is longer ("Who-

46. Clement of Alexandria, *Stromateis* 6.11; quoted from *ANF* 2:502. In some editions this is designated 6.95.3.

47. R. Cameron, "Parable and Interpretation," 30.

48. H. Montefiore, "Comparison," 55, 76 n. 1; B. Gärtner, *Theology of the Gospel according to Thomas,* 233-34; and E. Haenchen, *Die Botschaft,* 48.

49. W. Schrage, *Das Verhältnis,* 41; J. Leipoldt, *Das Evangelium nach Thomas,* 57; J.-É. Ménard, *L'Évangile selon Thomas,* 90; and M. Fieger, *Thomasevangelium,* 49.

50. R. McL. Wilson, *Studies in the Gospel of Thomas,* 40, 94; R. Grant and D. Freedman, *Secret Sayings,* 127.

51. C.-H. Hunzinger, "Unbekannte Gleichnisse," 217-20; J. Jeremias, *Unknown Sayings,* 88-89; N. Perrin, *Teaching,* 89; S. Davies, *Gospel of Thomas,* 9.

52. M. Fieger, *Thomasevangelium,* 47. The parable is printed in black (= not authentic) in R. Funk, *Five Gospels,* 477.

ever has ears *to hear,* let him hear"). The saying serves in these cases to admon-
ish the reader to reflect on the hidden, even esoteric, meaning of the logia,
which was typical of gnostic exegesis of the parables,[53] and in keeping with
logion 1 of the *Gospel of Thomas:* "Whoever finds the interpretation of these
sayings will not experience death."[54] The frequency of the exhortation is greater
in this gospel than in any one of the Synoptics.

The Disciples as Little Children, *Gospel of Thomas* 21

Mary said to Jesus, "Whom are your disciples like?"
He said, "They are like children who have settled in a field which is not
theirs. When the owners of the field come, they will say, 'Let us have back our field.'
They (will) undress in their presence in order to let them have back their field and
to give it back to them."[55]

It has been suggested that behind this parable (as well as logion 37) a baptismal rite may lie,[56] a view that other interpreters have adopted.[57] The objection to that, however, is that the materials used to support the thesis come from
a considerably later time.[58]

On certain occasions the disciples of Jesus are spoken of metaphorically
as children (Mark 10:24; cf. John 1:12) or are compared to children in the canonical Gospels (Mark 10:15//Luke 18:17; Matt 18:3-4). In those instances they
are children because of their open and trusting response to Jesus and his proclamation. In this parable it appears that the true owners of the field are the
powers ruling the present world, the "field" mentioned in the parable. The innocent nakedness of the disciples is found both here and in logion 37, as well as
in other gnostic texts.[59] Most likely it refers here to the gnostic view of stripping
off the body at death. The true disciples of Jesus thus live "in a field which is not

53. Cf. Irenaeus, *Against Heresies* 1.3.1 concerning the Valentinians: "But these
things have not been declared openly (φανερῶς), because not all comprehend the knowledge (τὴν γνῶσιν), but have been revealed mystically by the Savior by means of parable
(διὰ παραβολῷ) to those able to understand." Author's trans. from *PG* 7/1:468. For ET, see
Irenaeus, *Against the Heresies,* trans. Dominic J. Unger, ACW 55 (New York: Paulist Press,
1992), 28.

54. *NHLE* 126.

55. Text from ibid., 129.

56. Jonathan Z. Smith, "The Garments of Shame," *HR* 5 (1965-66): 235-38.

57. S. Davies, *Gospel of Thomas,* 120-21; K. King, "Kingdom in the Gospel of
Thomas," 67-69.

58. S. Patterson, *Gospel of Thomas,* 127-28 (n. 18).

59. Clement of Alexandria, *Stromateis* 3.13.92; Hippolytus, *Refutation* 5.3. Cf. also
the *Acts of Thomas* 14. For texts, respectively, cf. *Alexandrian Christianity,* ed. John E. L.
Oulton and Henry Chadwick, LCC 2 (Philadelphia: Westminster Press, 1954) 83; *ANF*
5:56; and *The Acts of Thomas,* ed. A. F. J. Klijn, 71-72.

theirs," the material world,[60] which they (as Gnostics) reject. The same logion contains the admonition from Jesus to his disciples, "You, then, be on guard against the world" (21:10).[61] The parable is most likely of gnostic origin and not an authentic parable of Jesus.[62]

The Woman with a Jar, *Gospel of Thomas* 97

Jesus said, "The kingdom of the [father] is like a certain woman who was carrying a [jar] full of meal. While she was walking [on the] road, still some distance from home, the handle of the jar broke and the meal emptied out behind her [on] the road. She did not realize it; she had noticed no accident. When she reached her house, she set the jar down and found it empty."[63]

The parable follows — in catchword association — upon the Parable of the Leaven (96), which is also a kingdom parable and about a woman. What is clear about this parable is that the kingdom is compared to a narration that includes loss, indeed "the woman's imperceptible loss of meal from a broken jar."[64] Interpreters have differed concerning the significance of the loss. The parable is at least a warning against false security.[65] Furthermore, one must be attentive, lest the kingdom slip away.[66] It is probable that the parable has a gnostic meaning. According to M. Fieger, the logion can be interpreted in light of logion 113: it stands as a warning against the loss of the knowledge of the kingdom that is "spread out upon the earth," which ordinary (unenlightened, nongnostic) people do not see.[67] It seems better, however, to relate the parable to logion 3. Then it would warn against the loss of the kingdom from within the self. In logion 3 the kingdom is spoken of as both "inside of you" and "outside of you." The kingdom exists inside the self insofar as one knows oneself — one's origin and identity. To possess such knowing is to be known by the Father, to become children of "the living Father"; it is saving knowl-

---

60. Cf. R. Grant and D. Freedman, *Secret Sayings,* 141; E. Haenchen, *Die Botschaft,* 51; J. Leipoldt, *Das Evangelium nach Thomas,* 61; B. Gärtner, *Theology of the Gospel according to Thomas,* 184; H. Montefiore, "Comparison," 70-71; J.-É. Ménard, *L'Évangile selon Thomas,* 111-13; and R. McL. Wilson, *Studies in the Gospel of Thomas,* 36-37.

61. Quoted from *NHLE* 129.

62. M. Fieger, *Thomasevangelium,* 95-96. Cf. R. Funk, *Five Gospels,* 485: the parable "reflects theological concerns that did not originate with Jesus."

63. Text from *NHLE* 136.

64. H. Montefiore, "Comparison," 71.

65. G. Quispel, "The Gospel of Thomas and the New Testament," 204-5; J. Jeremias, *Parables,* 175 (n. 12); E. Haenchen, *Die Botschaft,* 61, n. 86; S. Patterson, *Gospel of Thomas,* 90; and M. Fieger, *Thomasevangelium,* 247.

66. S. Patterson, *Gospel of Thomas,* 90, 210.

67. M. Fieger, *Thomasevangelium,* 247-48.

edge.[68] Loss of the kingdom from within — loss of the knowledge of one's origin and identity — is to lose salvation.

Although some interpreters have concluded that the parable can be, or possibly could be, attributed to Jesus,[69] that is difficult to maintain in light of its gnostic character.[70]

The Assassin, *Gospel of Thomas* 98

Jesus said, "The kingdom of the father is like a certain man who wanted to kill a powerful man. In his own house he drew his sword and stuck it into the wall in order to find out whether his hand could carry through. Then he slew the powerful man."[71]

The Parable of the Assassin (or the Powerful Man) — another kingdom parable — is like the Parables of Building a Tower and the King Going to War (Luke 14:28-30, 31-32) in that the three speak of considering the cost or testing oneself before carrying through what is ultimately being planned. Here the would-be assassin tests his strength before he does the deed; likewise, the hearer should test to see whether he has strength sufficient to carry through.[72] The implication is that whoever seeks the kingdom should count the cost. If he is strong enough, he can slay the "powerful man," which is probably a vivid metaphor for rejecting the material world.[73]

Some interpreters consider the Assassin to be a genuine parable of Jesus.[74] The fact that it has violent imagery is, in their view, an argument in its favor; no early Christian would have invented it and attributed it to Jesus, who is otherwise usually irenic in Gospel traditions.[75] But those who consider it not to have origi-

68. Salvation by knowledge imparted by the Redeemer is commonplace in gnostic systems; cf. Irenaeus, *Against Heresies* 1.23.3; Hippolytus, *Refutation of All Heresies* 7.27.7; and Epiphanius, *Panarion* 31.7.8; 44.2.5.

69. G. Quispel, "The Gospel of Thomas and the New Testament," 204-5; J. Jeremias, *Parables*, 175 (n. 12); H. Montefiore, "Comparison," 70-71; S. Davies, *Gospel of Thomas*, 9; and R. Funk, *Five Gospels*, 523-24 (printed in pink, meaning that Jesus said something like this).

70. R. McL. Wilson, *Studies in the Gospel of Thomas*, 97-99; and M. Fieger, *Thomasevangelium*, 247.

71. Text from *NHLE* 136.

72. J. Jeremias, *Parables*, 197.

73. R. M. Grant and D. N. Freeman, *Secret Sayings of Jesus*, 188; E. Haenchen, *Die Botschaft*, 60; M. Fieger, *Thomasevangelium*, 249.

74. C.-H. Hunzinger, "Unbekannte Gleichnisse," 211-17; H. Montefiore, "Comparison," 70-71; J. Jeremias, *Unknown Sayings*, 13; N. Perrin, *Teaching*, 126-28; S. Davies, *Gospel of Thomas*, 9; R. Funk, *Five Gospels*, 524-25 (printed in pink on the basis of the third ballot, preceded by gray results on two earlier occasions).

75. N. Perrin, *Teaching*, 127; and R. Funk, *Five Gospels*, 524.

nated with Jesus are probably correct.[76] Its forceful rejection of the material world by means of imagery of an assassination points to a gnostic origin, since Gnostics regularly looked upon the material world with contempt,[77] and one of their writers could even claim that "the world came about through a mistake."[78]

Parables of the Kingdom

As in the Synoptic Gospels, several parables in the *Gospel of Thomas* are parables of the kingdom. Five are parables of the kingdom in both traditions, as the following chart shows (where the parable is absent in a particular Gospel an ellipsis is used):

Parables of the Kingdom?

	Matthew	Mark	Luke	*Thomas*
Mustard Seed	Yes	Yes	Yes	Yes
Weeds in the Wheat	Yes	—	—	Yes
Leaven	Yes	—	—	Yes
Treasure	Yes	—	—	Yes
Pearl	Yes	—	—	Yes

Differences exist among four others. These can be illustrated by the following chart:

Parables of the Kingdom?

	Matthew	Mark	Luke	*Thomas*
Wedding Feast/ Great Banquet	Yes	—	Yes	No
Lost Sheep	No	No	No	Yes
Woman with a Jar	—	—	—	Yes
Assassin	—	—	—	Yes

The net result is that there are eight parables of the kingdom in the *Gospel of Thomas*. Five are parables of the kingdom in common with the Synoptics.

76. R. McL. Wilson, *Studies in the Gospel of Thomas*, 97; and M. Fieger, *Thomasevangelium*, 249.

77. Irenaeus, *Against Heresies* 1.24.4; 1.25.3; cf. Hans Jonas, *The Gnostic Religion: The Message of the Alien God and the Beginnings of Christianity*, 2d ed. (Boston: Beacon Press, 1963), 51-54; and idem, "Delimitation of the Gnostic Phenomenon — Typological and Historical," in *Le Origini dello Gnosticismo*, ed. Ugo Bianchi, SHR 12 (Leiden: E. J. Brill, 1967), 100.

78. *The Gospel of Philip* 75:2-3; quoted from *NHLE* 154.

One (the Lost Sheep) is now a kingdom parable that was not such in the Synoptics. In addition, two other kingdom parables have no synoptic parallels (the Woman with a Jar and the Assassin). On the other hand, there is one major loss. The Parable of the Great Banquet, a kingdom parable in the Synoptic parallels, is not such in the *Gospel of Thomas.*

One of the striking things about the kingdom parables in the *Gospel of Thomas* is the specific language that introduces them. One (logion 20, the Mustard Seed) is introduced as a parable of "the kingdom of heaven," as in the Gospel of Matthew (13:31; but "kingdom of God" at Mark 4:30 and Luke 13:18). Five are introduced by the phrase distinctive to the *Gospel of Thomas,* namely, "the kingdom of the Father." These are the Parables of the Weeds, the Pearl, and the Leaven (logia 57, 76, and 96), which are introduced as parables of the "kingdom of heaven" at Matthew 13:24, 44, 45; and the two Parables of the Woman with the Jar and the Assassin (logia 97, 98), which have no Synoptic parallels. Two parables are introduced simply as parables of "the kingdom." These are the Lost Sheep (logion 107) — which is not a kingdom parable in the Synoptics — and the Treasure (109), which is a parable of "the kingdom of heaven" at Matthew 13:44.

An examination of kingdom expressions shows similarities and differences from Synoptic usage. The phrase "the kingdom of heaven" — used some 32 times in the Gospel of Matthew — appears three times in the *Gospel of Thomas* (logia 20, 54, 114). But what is striking are three major differences: (1) The expression "the kingdom of the Father" appears seven times in the *Gospel of Thomas* (logia 57, 76, 96, 97, 98, 99, 113).[79] Among the Synoptics, Matthew alone uses something similar, and then only twice (13:43, "the kingdom of their father"; 26:29, "my father's kingdom"). (2) The simple term "the kingdom" appears twelve times in the *Gospel of Thomas* (logia 3 [twice], 22 [three times], 27, 46, 49, 82, 107, 109, 113),[80] introducing parables on two occasions (107, 109). It is used only a few times in special cases in Matthew (4:23; 6:33; 9:35; 13:19, 38, 41; 24:14; 25:43) and Luke (12:31, 32), and never does it introduce parables in the Synoptics. (3) The phrase "the kingdom of God" — so frequent in the Synoptics (4 times in Matthew, 14 in Mark, and 32 in Luke) — does not appear in the Coptic *Gospel of Thomas* at all.[81]

Closely allied with kingdom expressions are those that speak of God. The actual term "God" is used in only one logion in the *Gospel of Thomas* (100, "give God what belongs to God," parallel to Mark 12:17//Matt 22:21//Luke 20:25).

---

79. In logion 99 the actual wording is "the kingdom of my Father."

80. The term appears three times in logion 22 in current editions. The third occurrence, however, is in brackets, indicating the restoration of an apparent lacuna.

81. The term does, however, appear in the Greek text of the *Oxyrhynchus Papyrus* 1 (lines 7-8), but not in the corresponding Coptic text, *Gospel of Thomas* 27 (which has simply "the kingdom").

More typically the expression for God is "the Father" or "my Father" (logia 27, 40, 44, 50, 69, 79, 83, 99).

Several kingdom sayings in the *Gospel of Thomas* have syntactical and theological similarities to those in the Synoptics. One "enters" the kingdom (logia 22, 99, 114); the true disciple is "not far" from it (82); it can be discovered (27, 49); and the poor possess it (54). But there is also a distinctive element. Although the kingdom is "spread out upon the earth," ordinary people do not recognize or find it (27, 113). It is only "the elect" who discover it, which comes by discovering their true origin (49, 111). For them, the kingdom is "inside" themselves, for they know themselves (3) and are superior to the world (111). This distinctive view of the kingdom has been summarized by Hugh Montefiore:

> According to gnostic thought, the Kingdom of Heaven is not a future eschatological event involving the community, but a state of being which is achieved when the individual is enlightened with true knowledge. It is a present reality rather than a future event. This difference in outlook influences some of Thomas's parables and similitudes.[82]

Furthermore, the view that the kingdom of God is the present reign of God in history has been supplanted by the view that it is an inner spiritual reality obtained by knowledge; "in the Thomas gospel the Kingdom is located neither in time nor in space, but in experience."[83] To experience self-knowledge is to experience the kingdom. To expect God's reign as an external reality is rejected explicitly (113). Those Synoptic sayings concerning the kingdom as being realized in the historical minstry of Jesus (e.g., Luke 11:20//Matt 12:28) and as a future expectation beyond history (e.g., Matt 8:11; 25:34; Mark 14:25//Matt 26:29//Luke 22:18) have no place in the thought-world of the *Gospel of Thomas*. Salvation in this Gospel, according to Bentley Layton, "is not the future reign of God on earth, to be ushered in by a messiah, but rather the recognition of one's true nature and acquaintance with oneself, leading to immediate repose and rendering 'death' (i.e. the realm of human affairs) trivial."[84]

Features of the Parables and Their Use in the Gospel of Thomas

The features of the parables and their use in the *Gospel of Thomas* can be surveyed by making the following points:

82. H. Montefiore, "Comparison," 60. On the noneschatological character of the kingdom in this gospel, cf. also K. King, "Kingdom in the Gospel of Thomas," 50-52.

83. B. Miller, "A Study of the Theme of 'Kingdom,'" 52. Cf. the comment of B. Blatz, "Coptic Gospel of Thomas," 1:114, citing Philipp Vielhauer: "the 'kingdom' is a concept interchangeable with the divine self of the disciple (= the gnostic)."

84. B. Layton, *The Gnostic Scriptures*, 376.

1. The parables in the *Gospel of Thomas* differ in one important respect from certain Synoptic parables. They are totally free of appended allegorical interpretations, as opposed to two in the Synoptic tradition (e.g., the Sower and the Weeds in the Wheat). They are not, however, devoid of allegorical elements. The Parable of the Wicked Tenants (logion 65), for example, contains allegorical elements within itself comparable to its Synoptic parallels.

2. Some parables in this Gospel contain hortatory comments and applications, not unlike their Synoptic parallels. Several contain the exhortation to "hear" what is being said (logia 8, 21, 63, 65, 96), which implies that there is an interpretation and application to be drawn from them. Two contain direct applications — the Great Banquet (64, "Businessmen and merchants will not enter the Places of my Father") and the Pearl (76, "You, too, seek [the Father's] unfailing and enduring treasure where no moth comes near to devour and no worm destroys"). At 21:10, although not immediately after the Parable of the Disciples as Little Children, there is an admonition to "be on . . . guard against the world."

3. In the Synoptic tradition, especially in Luke, parables are often spoken by Jesus in response to questions or comments. Of the fourteen parables in the *Gospel of Thomas* only two (logia 20 and 21) are given in response to questions. The other 12 have no frameworks; they are simply uttered as words from Jesus. They are freestanding parables given for the apparent purpose of instruction of the reader.

4. Within the Synoptic tradition, four parables — all in Luke — have been classified by form critics as Exemplary Narratives *(Beispielerzählungen)*. These are the Good Samaritan (10:25-37), the Rich Fool (12:16-21), the Rich Man and Lazarus (16:19-31), and the Pharisee and the Publican (18:9-14). The *Gospel of Thomas* contains one, the Rich Fool (63). Thereby a matter of conduct is illustrated for the reader.

5. The parables are often given a gnostic interpretation in the *Gospel of Thomas.*[85] Gnostic interpretations — where they exist — have been highlighted in previous chapters concerning those parables that have Synoptic parallels, such as the Great Banquet and the Lost Sheep. Furthermore, all four of the parables distinctive to Thomas have a gnostic significance from the point of their composition.

6. The parables in the *Gospel of Thomas* are scattered throughout the Gospel. There are some, however, that are placed together in small collections. These include the parables in logia 8–9, 20–21, 63–65, and 96–98. The location of the parables appears to be arbitrary. However, there are catchword connec-

---

85. Cf. W. Schrage, *Das Verhältnis,* passim; W. R. Schoedel, "Parables in the Gospel of Thomas," 548-60; A. Lindemann, "Zur Gleichnisinterpretation im Thomas-Evangelium," 214-43; and M. Fieger, *Thomasevangelium,* passim. This view is opposed by R. Cameron, "Parable and Interpretation," 3-39.

tions between some of them. Logion 20 opens with a question from the disciples, and 21 is about them. Logia 63–65 narrate actions of wealthy men, and logia 96 and 97 relate the actions of women.

Select Bibliography

The Acts of Thomas: Introduction–Text–Commentary. Ed. A. F. J. Klijn. NovTSup 5. Leiden: E. J. Brill, 1962.

Baker, Aelred. "The Gospel of Thomas and the Diatessaron." *JTS* 16 (1965): 449-54.

Blatz, Beate, "The Coptic Gospel of Thomas." In *New Testament Apocrypha,* 1:110-33. Ed. Wilhelm Schneemelcher. Rev. ed. 2 vols. Louisville: Westminster/John Knox, 1991-92.

Blomberg, Craig. "Tradition and Redaction in the Parables of the Gospel of Thomas." In *The Jesus Tradition outside the Gospels,* 177-205. Ed. David Wenham. Sheffield: JSOT Press, 1984.

Broek, Roelof van den, *Studies in Gnosticism and Alexandrian Christianity,* NHMS 39 (New York: E. J. Brill, 1996).

Cameron, Ron. "Parable and Interpretation in the Gospel of Thomas." *FFF* 2/2 (1986): 3-39.

Chilton, Bruce. "The Gospel according to Thomas as a Source of Jesus' Teaching." In *The Jesus Tradition outside the Gospels,* 155-75. Ed. David Wenham. Sheffield: JSOT Press, 1984.

Cullmann, Oscar. "The Gospel of Thomas and the Problem of the Age of the Tradition Contained Therein." *Int* 16 (1962): 418-38.

Dahl, Nils. "The Parables of Growth." *ST* 5 (1951): 132-66. Reprinted in his *Jesus in the Memory of the Early Church,* 141-166. Minneapolis: Augsburg Publishing House, 1976.

Davies, Stevan. *The Gospel of Thomas and Christian Wisdom.* New York: Seabury Press, 1983.

Dehandschutter, Boudewijn. "La parabole de la perle (Mt 13,45-46) et l'Évangile selon Thomas." *ETL* 55 (1979): 243-65.

—————. "La parabole des vignerons homicides (Mc. XII,1-12) et l'Évangile selon Thomas." In *L'Évangile selon Marc,* 203-19. Ed. M. Sabbe. BETL 34. Leuven: Peeters, 1974.

—————. "Les paraboles de l'évangile selon Thomas: La parole du trésor caché (log. 109)." *ETL* 47 (1971): 199-219.

Ehlers, Barbara. "Kann das Thomasevangelium aus Edessa Stammen? Ein Beitrag zur Frühgeschichte des Christentums in Edessa." *NovT* 12 (1970): 284-317.

Fieger, Michael. *Das Thomasevangelium: Einleitung Kommentar Systematik.* NTAbh 22. Münster: Aschendorff, 1991.

Fitzmyer, Joseph A. "The Oxyrhynchus Logoi of Jesus and the Coptic Gospel according to Thomas." In his *Essays on the Semitic Background of the New Testament*, 355-433. SBLSBS 5. Missoula, Mont.: Scholars Press, 1974.

Franzmann, Majella. *Jesus in the Nag Hammadi Writings*. Edinburgh: T. & T. Clark, 1996.

Frenschkowski, Marco. "The Enigma of the Three Words of Jesus in the Gospel of Thomas Logion 13." *JHC* 1 (1994): 73-84.

Gärtner, Bertil. *The Theology of the Gospel according to Thomas*. New York: Harper & Brothers, 1961.

Grant, Robert M., and David N. Freedman, *The Secret Sayings of Jesus*. Garden City, N.Y.: Doubleday, 1960.

Grenfell, Bernard P., and Arthur S. Hunt, eds. *The Oxyrynchus Papyri*. Vol. 4. London: Egypt Exploration Fund, 1904.

Guillaumont, Antoine, et al., *The Gospel according to Thomas*. New York: Harper & Brothers, 1959.

Haenchen, Ernst. *Die Botschaft des Thomas-Evangeliums*. TBT 6; Berlin: Alfred Töpelmann, 1961.

———. "Literatur zur Thomasevangelium." *ThR* 27 (1961): 147-78.

Hedrick, Charles W. "Thomas and the Synoptics: Aiming at a Consensus." In his *Parables as Poetic Fictions: The Creative Voice of Jesus*, 236-51. Peabody, Mass.: Hendrickson Publishers, 1994.

———. "The Treasure Parable in Matthew and Thomas." *FFF* 2/2 (1986): 41-56.

Horman, J. "The Source of the Version of the Parable of the Sower in the Gospel of Thomas." *NovT* 21 (1979): 326-43.

Hultgren, Arland J. "Jesus and Gnosis: The Saying on Hindering Others in Luke 11:52 and Its Parallels." *FFF* 7/3-4 (1991): 165-82.

Hunzinger, Claus-Hunno, "Aussersynoptisches Traditionsgut im Thomasevangelium." *TLZ* 85 (1960): 843-46.

———. "Unbekannte Gleichnisse Jesu aus dem Thomas-Evangelium." *Judentum Urchristentum Kirche: Festschrift für Joachim Jeremias*, 209-20. Ed. Walther Eltester. BZNW 26. Berlin: Verlag Alfred Töpelmann, 1960.

Jeremias, Joachim. *Unknown Sayings of Jesus*, 2d ed. London: S.P.C.K., 1964.

Jones, Geraint Vaughan. "The Parables of the Gospel of Thomas." In his *The Art and the Truth of the Parables: A Study in Their Literary Form and Modern Interpretation*, 230-40. London: SPCK, 1964.

King, Karen. "Kingdom in the Gospel of Thomas." *FFF* 3/1 (1987): 48-97.

Koester, Helmut. *Ancient Christian Gospels: Their History and Development*. Philadelphia: Trinity Press International, 1990.

Koester, Helmut, and Stephen J. Patterson. "The Gospel of Thomas: Does It Contain Authentic Sayings of Jesus?" *BiRe* 6/2 (April 1990): 28-39.

Koester, Helmut. "Three Thomas Parables." In *The New Testament and Gnosis: Essays in Honor of Robert McL. Wilson*, 195-203. Ed. A. H. B. Logan and A. J. M. Wedderburn. Edinburgh: T. & T. Clark, 1983.

Layton, Bentley. *The Gnostic Scriptures: A New Translation with Annotations and Introductions.* Garden City, N.Y.: Doubleday, 1987.

———. "Prolegomena to the Study of Ancient Gnosticism." In *The Social World of the First Christians: Essays in Honor of Wayne A. Meeks,* 334-50. Ed. L. Michael White and O. Larry Yarbrough. Minneapolis: Fortress Press, 1995.

Leipoldt, Johannes. *Das Evangelium nach Thomas: Koptisch und Deutsch.* TU 101. Berlin: Akademie, 1967.

Lindemann, Andreas. "Zur Gleichnisinterpretation im Thomas-Evangelium." *ZNW* 71 (1980): 214-43.

McArthur, Harvey K. "The Dependence of the Gospel of Thomas on the Synoptics." *ExpTim* 71 (1959-60): 286-87.

Ménard, Jacques-É. *L'Évangile selon Thomas.* NHS 5. Leiden: E. J. Brill, 1975.

Meyer, Marvin. *The Gospel of Thomas: The Hidden Sayings of Jesus: New Translation, with Introduction and Notes.* San Francisco: HarperSanFrancisco, 1992.

Miller, Betsey F. "A Study of the Theme of 'Kingdom': The Gospel according to Thomas: Logion 18." *NovT* 9 (1967): 52-60.

Montefiore, Hugh W. "A Comparison of the Parables of the Gospel according to Thomas and of the Synoptic Gospels." *NTS* 7 (1960/61): 220-48. Reprinted in *Thomas and the Evangelists,* 40-78. By H. E. W. Turner and H. Montefiore. SBT 35. Naperville: Alec R. Allenson, 1962.

Morrice, W. G. "The Parable of the Dragnet and the Gospel of Thomas." *ExpTim* 95 (1984): 269-73.

Patterson, Stephen J. *The Gospel of Thomas and Jesus.* Sonoma, Calif.: Polebridge Press, 1992.

Peterson, W. L. "The Parable of the Lost Sheep in the Gospel of Thomas and the Synoptics." *NovT* 23 (1981): 128-47.

Puech, Henri-Charles. "Gnostic Gospels and Related Documents." In *New Testament Apocrypha,* 1:231-62. Ed. Edgar Hennecke and Wilhelm Schneemelcher. 2 vols. Philadelphia: Westminster Press, 1963-65.

Quispel, Gilles. "The Gospel of Thomas and the New Testament." *VC* 11 (1957): 189-207.

———. "Some Remarks on the Gospel of Thomas." *NTS* 5 (1958-59): 276-90.

———. "'The Gospel of Thomas' and the 'Gospel of the Hebrews.'" *NTS* 12 (1965-66): 371-82.

———. "The Gospel of Thomas Revisited." In *Colloque international sur les Testes de Nag Hammadi,* 218-66. Ed. Bernard Barc. Quebec: Les presses de l'Universite Laval, 1981.

Robinson, James M. "LOGOI SOPHON: On the Gattung of Q." In *Trajectories through Early Christianity,* 71-113. By James M. Robinson and Helmut Koester. Philadelphia: Fortress Press, 1971.

Rudolph, Kurt. *Gnosis: The Nature and History of Gnosticism.* San Francisco: HarperSanFrancisco, 1987.

Schoedel, William R. "Parables in the Gospel of Thomas: Oral Tradition or Gnostic Exegesis?" *CTM* 43 (1972): 548-60.

Scholer, David M. *Nag Hammadi Bibliography 1948-1969.* Leiden: E. J. Brill, 1971. (Since 1971 this bibliography has been updated annually in *NovT.*)

Schrage, Wolfgang. *Das Verhältnis des Thomas-Evangeliums zur synoptischen Tradition und zu den koptischen Evangelienübersetzungen: Zugleich ein Beitrag zur gnostischen Synoptikerdeutung.* BZNW 29. Berlin: Alfred Töpelmann, 1964.

Sieber, John H. "A Redactional Analysis of the Synoptic Gospels with regard to the Question of the Sources of the Gospel according to Thomas." Ph.D. diss., Claremont Graduate School, 1965.

Snodgrass, Klyne R. "The Gospel of Thomas: A Second Century Gospel." *SC* 7 (1989-90): 19-38.

Tuckett, Christopher, *Nag Hammadi and the Gospel Tradition.* Edinburgh: T. & T. Clark, 1986.

Tuckett, Christopher. "Thomas and the Synoptics." *NovT* 30 (1988): 132-57.

Turner, H. E. W. "The Gospel of Thomas: Its History, Transmission and Sources." In *Thomas and the Evangelists.* By H. Turner and Hugh Montefiore, 11-39. SBT 35. Naperville: Alec R. Allenson, 1962.

———. "The Theology of the Gospel of Thomas." In *Thomas and the Evangelists,* by H. Turner and Hugh Montefiore, 79-116. SBT 35. Naperville: Alec R. Allenson, 1962.

Unnik, Willem C. van. *Newly Discovered Gnostic Writings: A Preliminary Survey of the Nag-Hammadi Find.* SBT 30. Naperville, Ill.: Alec R. Allenson, 1960.

Walls, A. F. "The References to Apostles in the Gospel of Thomas." *NTS* 7 (1960-61): 266-70.

Wilson, Robert McL. *Studies in the Gospel of Thomas.* London: A. R. Mowbray, 1960.

———. "'Thomas' and the Growth of the Gospels." *HTR* 53 (1960): 231-50.

———. "Thomas and the Synoptic Gospels." *ExpT* 72 (1960): 36-39.

APPENDIX 1

The Purpose of Parables according to the Evangelists

Mark's Enigmatic Text

Within the Synoptic Gospels there is an account in which Jesus is asked about the purpose of his parables (Mark 4:10-12//Matt 13:10-17//Luke 8:9-10). The text from Mark — the most enigmatic of the three — is quoted here:

> 10*And when he was alone, those who were around him with the twelve were asking him about the parables.* 11*And he said to them, "To you has been given the secret of the kingdom of God, but to those outside all is in parables;* 12*in order that*
>
> > *they may indeed see but not perceive,*
> > *and may indeed hear but not understand;*
>
> *lest they should turn again, and it be forgiven them."*

Later in the same chapter of Mark (4:33-34) and Matthew (13:34-35), but not in Luke, there is another passage that relates to the first. The text from Mark is quoted here:

> 33*And by many such parables he spoke the word to them, as they were able to hear [it];* 34*he did not speak to them without a parable, but privately he explained everything to his own disciples.*

The question to Jesus concerning parables is asked by persons "around him with the twelve." The circle of questioners is thus more than the Twelve (cf. such a comparable circle of persons at 3:32, 34). They ask concerning "the para-

453

bles" (plural), even though, strictly speaking, only one has been given so far in the narrative (the Sower, 4:1-9). Yet there have been the parabolic sayings of 3:23-27 (called "parables" at Mark 3:23) and the reference to other "parables" taught by Jesus that have not been recorded (4:2). Jesus responds to the questioners as though they are "insiders" in contrast to "those outside" mentioned later (4:11b). In Mark's view, the "insiders" consist of (1) those who followed Jesus during his earthly ministry and (2) those who make up the community of believers in his day.[1] At the Markan level of the Gospel tradition, the latter would be the primary audience of the sayings in this unit.

A contrast is made between what is given to the insiders and outsiders, respectively. The insiders receive "the μυστήριον ("secret," "mystery") of the kingdom of God." But "to those outside" all things are ἐν παραβολαῖς ("in parables").

If the "insiders" have been identified correctly, the "outsiders" would consist of their opposite. They would include (1) those who are outside the circle of disciples in the Gospel of Mark and (2) those who stand outside that circle in Mark's community,[2] as similar expressions in Josephus and NT letters confirm regarding persons "outside" of a religious group.[3] The contrast between what is given to the "insiders" and "outsiders," respectively, can be seen in the following way:[4]

Mark 4:11a	Mark 4:11b
A. The mystery of the kingdom	A'. All things
B. is granted	B'. are
C. to you (disciples)	C'. to those outside
D. [by Jesus' direct explanation].	D'. in parables.

The authorization for item D is 4:34b, "but privately he explained everything to his disciples."

The term μυστήριον appears only here in the Gospels (Matt 13:11//Mark 4:11//Luke 8:10). In its background stand apocalyptic texts, in which the term "mystery" signifies those hidden, eschatological secrets that can be revealed by God alone (LXX, Dan 2:18-19, 28-30, 47; 2 Esdr 14.5; 1 Enoch 63:3; 103:2). The secrets will be revealed to all at the end of time (1 Enoch 38:3), but they have al-

---

1. Cf. J. Marcus, *Mystery*, 92.

2. W. Marxsen, "Redaktionsgeschichtliche Erklärung," 23-25; A. Ambrozic, *Hidden Kingdom*, 53-72, 105; J. Marcus, *Mystery*, 95.

3. 1 Cor 5:12; Col 4:5; 1 Thess 5:12; Josephus, *J.W.* 2.133: "To persons outside (τοῖς ἔξωθεν) the silence of [the Essenes] appears like some awful mystery (μυστήριον)"; quoted from *Josephus*, trans. Henry St. John Thackeray et al., LCL, 10 vols. (Cambridge: Cambridge University Press, 1961-81), 2:373.

4. Based on Raymond E. Brown, *The Semitic Background of the Term 'Mystery' in the New Testament*, FBBS 21 (Philadelphia: Fortress Press, 1968), 34, who is indebted to J. A. Baird, "A Pragmatic Approach," 202.

ready been disclosed to certain chosen ones, who are to disclose them, in turn, to the wise (2 Esdr 12:36-39; 14:5-6; *1 Enoch* 51:3) or to any others destined to receive them (Rom 16:25-26; Eph 3:3-6).[5] The "mystery" or "secret" that is spoken about in our present context is the secret of the kingdom of God. Thus Jesus is saying that there is some inner, hidden knowledge of the kingdom that is being disclosed to certain "insiders," and which is not shared with "those outside." He goes on to provide for the "insiders" an explanation of the Parable of the Sower (which had been taught to the public) in 4:13-20. Regarding the "outsiders," Jesus quotes Isaiah 6:9-10, introduced by a purpose clause, "in order that (ἵνα)" they may neither perceive nor understand, lest they repent and be forgiven. As pointed out long ago, the quotation differs from both the standard Hebrew text and the Septuagint reading, but corresponds exactly in form to the Aramaic Targum, including its use of third person plural (rather than second, as in the MT and LXX) and its use of the phrase "it be forgiven them" (rather than "and I heal them," MT and LXX).[6]

The sequence of sayings prompts the question: Is Mark 4:11-12 a programmatic statement that provides a pattern regarding the telling and explaining of parables in the Gospel of Mark? The following chart helps to provide an answer (a negative response):

Parable	Audience	Explanation
3:23-27, Parabolic Sayings	Jerusalem scribes (3:22)	None
4:3-9, Sower	The crowd (4:1)	To disciples (4:10)
4:26-29, Seed Growing Secretly	The crowd (4:33, 36)	None
4:30-32, Mustard Seed	The crowd (4:33, 36)	None
7:14-15, On Defilement	The crowd (7:14)	To disciples (7:17)
12:1-11, Wicked Tenants	Opponents (11:27; 12:1)	None; the opponents understand (12:12)
13:28, Fig Tree	Peter, James, John, and Andrew privately (13:3)	To Peter, James, John, and Andrew (13:29)
13:34, Man on a Journey	Peter, James, John, and Andrew privately (13:3)	To Peter, James, John, and Andrew (13:35-37)

5. Günther Bornkamm, "μυστήριον," *TDNT* 4:802-28; Helmut Krämer, "μυστήριον," *EDNT* 2:447.

6. T. W. Manson, *The Teaching of Jesus: Studies of Its Form and Content,* 2d ed. (Cambridge: Cambridge University Press, 1935), 77.

Although the chart is helpful in answering our question in the negative, there are some ambiguities. Are the two parables at 4:26-29, 30-32 actually spoken to the crowd, as suggested above? From 4:10 on, Jesus is speaking to his disciples (the Twelve and others), so these two parables may also be addressed to them alone. To say that they are addressed to the crowd requires a transition at 4:21, but there is none in the text. On the other hand, 4:33, 36 require the reader to assume that the two parables were spoken to the crowd. In any case, despite the ambiguity here, it is clear that the passage (4:10-12) does not provide a pattern for the telling of parables and explanations in the Gospel of Mark.

Rather than being a basis for a pattern, 4:11-12 can be taken as a passage that sets forth what was commonly held in certain Jewish, Christian, and gnostic traditions of antiquity. That is that parables are by nature enigmatic and require explanations. In the Septuagint the term παραβολή can signify figures of speech whose meanings are not readily obvious. For example, at Psalm 78:2 (LXX 77:2) the term "parables" (παραβολαί) and "dark sayings" (προβλήματα, "problems," "riddles") are placed in synonymous parallelism, signifying equivalence. In the wisdom literature the term refers to sayings that require skill in understanding (Prov 1:5-6), sayings that a wise man will ponder (Sir 3:29), and sayings that contain subtleties and obscurities that must be brought out by the wise (Sir 39:2-3). Parables need interpretation (2 Esdr 4:47; Sir 47:15-17).

Within the NT and other early Christian literature several passages speak of the obscurity of parables and other figures of speech. In the Gospel of John, Jesus is said to have spoken figuratively in such a way that his disciples do not understand him (10:6), and he announces that the hour is coming when he will no longer speak in figures but will tell them "plainly" (παρρησία) of the Father (16:25, 29). The designation of parables as obscure is found in the writings of Justin and Irenaeus of the second century,[7] as well as among gnostic writers of the second and third centuries.[8] According to the gnostic *Apocryphon of James* of the second century, it was necessary for Jesus to spend eighteen days explaining his parables to his disciples after his resurrection (8:1-10), and Irenaeus says that certain Valentinian Gnostics of his day claimed that Jesus conversed with his disciples for eighteen months after his resurrection in order to clarify his teachings.[9]

Already within the New Testament there are references to persons and movements that were considered to have false interpretations of the teachings of Jesus and of the apostles (Mark 13:22//Matt 24:24; Acts 20:29-30; 2 Cor 11:13-15; 2 Peter 2:1-3). According to Irenaeus, the Valentinian Gnostics of the second century sought to "derive proofs for their opinions by perverse inter-

---

7. Justin, *Dialogue with Trypho* 52.1; 68.6; Irenaeus, *Against Heresies* 1.3.6.

8. *Ap. Jas.* 7.1-6; 7.35–8.11; *Pistis Sophia* 1–6; cf. Irenaeus, *Against Heresies* 1.3.1; 1.3.6; 1.8.1.

9. Irenaeus, *Against Heresies* 1.3.2.

pretations and deceitful expositions" from the Gospels,[10] and they adapted Jesus' parables to conform to their own teachings.[11] It is not unusual, therefore, that the claim would be made in the Gospel of Mark that Jesus had provided private explanations of his teachings to his disciples in order that they might understand Jesus' message and ministry at a deeper level of insight than most who were associated with him in some way. The consequence would be that, for the evangelist and his community, there is a tradition of instruction from Jesus that is to be passed on by the disciples to the post-Easter church,[12] of which the Gospel of Mark is itself an authoritative source.

By way of summary, it appears that behind Mark's Gospel, and in Mark's own awareness, there are at least four things that inform 4:10-12: (1) Jesus taught publicly in parables; (2) parables were considered obscure and in need of interpretation; (3) Jesus, as in Jewish apocalyptic, provided special revelation to those "inside"; and (4) others, the "outsiders," were considered capable of a basic understanding of Jesus' parables but, due to hardness of heart, do not perceive the true import of his ministry.

The Gospel of Mark became the authoritative account of the Gospel story (1:1) for the Markan community. At a literary level, Mark goes on from 4:10-12 to have Jesus give special explanations to his disciples (4:13-20, 34; 7:17-23). Especially important, because of its immediate proximity, is the Interpretation of the Sower, which is about his own ministry of proclaiming the word (4:14; cf. 4:33). To be sure, as the narrative unfolds, the disciples turn out to be persons who do not hear and understand the full meaning of Jesus' mission prior to Easter. Jesus must continue to explain himself and his mission to his disciples, which they refuse to, or cannot, comprehend (cf. 4:35-41; 6:45-52; 8:17-21). Finally, at 8:32 Mark indicates that when Jesus told of his coming death and resurrection, he did so "plainly" (παρρησίᾳ), the opposite of speaking "in parables" or speaking by means of a "figure of speech" (παροιμία).[13] The apostle Peter will not hear of it, however. It is only after Jesus' death and resurrection — after the story has been concluded — that his disciples will understand and take the message to heart.

Whether the "secret of the kingdom of God" (4:11) is related explicitly to the "messianic secret" within the Gospel of Mark or not will have to be taken up later. At a minimum, however, it can be said at this point that the "secret" is that specific understanding which has been disclosed to certain persons (the disciples) by God alone through Jesus, namely, the understand-

10. Ibid., 1.3.6; quoted from *St. Irenaeus of Lyons against the Heresies*, trans. Dominic J. Unger, ACW 55 (New York: Paulist Press, 1992), 29.

11. Ibid., 1.8.1.

12. S. Brown, "'The Secret,'" 74; H. Räisänen, *Parabeltheorie*, 122.

13. The contrast between speaking "in parables" and "plainly" is made in *Ap. Jas.* 7.1-6; Irenaeus, *Against Heresies* 1.3.1; and *Pistis Sophia* 1-6; the contrast between "in figures" and "plainly" is at John 16:25, 29.

ing that God's kingdom is breaking in and operative through Jesus' words and deeds.[14] Although that understanding is fully comprehended by Jesus' disciples only after his resurrection, the saying of Jesus in 4:11a can be understood by the post-Easter community of Mark's Gospel as already having some force during his earthly ministry, as in the "already" of an "already/not yet" dialectic. The earthly Jesus did have followers, the disciples, and they were schooled in regard to the kingdom.

To those persons on the "outside," however, "all things" are, and remain, "in parables." Here the term "parable" cannot have the narrow signification it has in modern form-criticism but must refer to and include all that is figurative in the teaching of Jesus.

The larger problem of 4:12 is the use of the introductory conjunction ἵνα, which can be translated "in order that." That particular (although regular) translation causes problems for interpretation,[15] since it implies that the purpose of telling parables would be to *prevent* insight, understanding, repentance, and forgiveness. Concerning such an implication, T. W. Manson has written: "This is simply absurd. If parables had this object or result, that in itself would be the strongest possible argument against making use of them, and would make it impossible to imagine why Jesus should have employed such a way of delivering his teaching."[16] Not surprisingly, therefore, at least five other possibilities of rendering the conjunction have been proposed.[17] But the plainest meaning of the term (that of introducing a purpose clause) is required, since it is complemented by the μήποτε ("lest") clause in the same sentence, which expresses purpose in a negative sense.[18] Moreover, the plainest sense works well. Those outside — those whom God has not chosen to be recipients of the secret of the kingdom — are given a glimpse of the kingdom through the words and deeds of Jesus; they do indeed see and hear "all" that Jesus has to teach and do, but they do not perceive and understand. Whatever the verbs may mean elsewhere in Greek literature, it is clear that in this verse the verbs about seeing (βλέπω) and hearing (ἀκούω) carry with them the connotation of sense perception, while those of perceiving (ὁράω) and understanding (συνίημι) connote spiritual discernment.[19] If those outside did in fact perceive and understand, they would turn and be forgiven. But that is not the divine purpose in the pres-

---

14. Cf. H. Krämer, "μυστήριον," *EDNT* 2:447.

15. The Greek term ἵνα is translated "in order that," denoting a purpose clause, at Mark 4:12 in the NRSV, but as "so that," denoting a consecutive clause, in the RSV, NEB, and NIV. All four versions translate the term as "so that" at Luke 8:10b.

16. T. W. Manson, *Teaching of Jesus*, 76.

17. Peter Lampe, "ἵνα," *EDNT* 2:189.

18. Archibald T. Robertson, "The Causal Use of Ἵνα," in *Studies in Early Christianity,* ed. Shirley J. Case (New York: Century Company, 1928), 57; C. F. D. Moule, *An Idiom-Book of New Testament Greek,* 2d ed. (Cambridge: Cambridge University Press, 1960), 142-43.

19. A useful discussion of the distinction is made by J. Marcus, *Mystery,* 104-5.

ent moment of Jesus' ministry.[20] It is in the post-Easter situation, and not until then, that "the gospel" — which sets forth the meaning of Jesus' ministry of proclaiming the kingdom, as well as his death and resurrection — will be preached to the nations of the world (13:10), and it is only then that what is hidden will be made manifest (4:22). It is only then, too, that repentance and forgiveness will take place for any who are reached with the gospel, receive it, and become believers. But the fact remains that there will be the many who see and hear what is proclaimed, but not perceive and understand; that is to say, they will reject the gospel. And that is due to the working out of the dark side of the divine purpose in election.

A number of issues have been raised concerning this unit. Five of them are listed here and dealt with briefly:

1. The christological question: Does the unit relate in some way to the so-called "messianic secret" of Mark's Gospel? Some have made the claim that it does,[21] but others deny a direct connection. Reasons for the denial are that (1) while the messianic secret is explicitly christological in intent, this passage is not;[22] (2) whereas the messianic secret has to do with the disciples' own lack of understanding of Jesus' identity, this passage reflects the church's experience of the negative attitude to the preaching of the gospel in its mission, particularly within Israel;[23] and (3) while the messianic secret is kerygmatic, the secret in this case has to do with instruction that the disciples of Jesus are to pass on to the church in the post-Easter situation.[24] All of these are valid points. The "connection with the messianic secret is at best a loose one."[25]

2. The source question: From whence was Mark 4:10-12 derived? Here there are several possibilities. According to some, it is essentially a composition of the evangelist Mark.[26] According to others, it existed in a pre-Markan collection of parables.[27] For still others, it was a traditional unit that Mark inserted

20. Attempts have been made to render the μήποτε of 4:12 as "unless" instead of "lest" by J. Jeremias, *Parables*, 17, and E. Schweizer, *Mark*, 93, but they have not been convincing. See negative responses by C. Carlston, *Parables*, 107, and B. Scott, *Parable*, 23.

21. William Wrede, *The Messianic Secret* (London: James Clark, 1971), 56-60; T. Burkill, *Mysterious Revelation*, 100; J. Gnilka, *Markus*, 1:170-72.

22. J. Lambrecht, *Astonished*, 105-6; M. Boucher, *Mysterious Parable*, 80-81; Robert A. Guelich, *Mark 1–8:26*, WBC 34A (Dallas: Word Books, 1989), 206; P. Perkins, *NIB (Mark)*, 8:572.

23. Heikki Räisänen, *The "Messianic Secret" in Mark* (Edinburgh: T. & T. Clark, 1990), 130-37, 143, 242-43.

24. S. Brown, "'The Secret,'" 60-74; J. Lambrecht, *Astonished*, 106; R. Pesch, *Markus*, 240.

25. H. Räisänen, *The "Messianic Secret,"* 143.

26. R. Bultmann, *HST* 325 (n. 1); J. Lambrecht, *Astonished*, 93-94, 140-41; B. Scott, *Parable*, 24.

27. E. Schweizer, "The Question of the Messianic Secret in Mark," 69; R. Guelich, *Mark*, 200; H. Räisänen, *Parabeltheorie*, 46. In *The "Messianic Secret,"* 130-36, Räisänen is

between the Parable of the Sower and its Interpretation.[28] Some claim that, whatever Mark's immediate source for the saying, the material in 4:11-12 is an authentic logion of Jesus.[29]

If the verses express a theology that is pre-Markan, rather than one distinctive to the evangelist himself, it is likely that the passage was composed prior to the writing of Mark's Gospel. This likelihood becomes more certain on other grounds — mainly two. First, the passage contains terms and expressions that are not characteristic of the Gospel of Mark.[30] Even more important, while the quotation of Isaiah 6:9-10 varies from both the Septuagint and the standard Hebrew text, it corresponds to that of the Aramaic Targum. That fact, in turn, suggests a pre-Markan origin within an Aramaic-speaking community. Since the passage does not give expression to Mark's own theology, it is likely that it existed within a pre-Markan collection of parables. It is difficult to see why Mark would have inserted it himself. Finally, since the saying appears to presuppose considerable reflection on the question of why so many refused the Christian message, it is not likely to have been an authentic saying of Jesus.

3. The literary question: Does the unit truly "fit" into the Gospel of Mark? A strong case has been made that it does.[31] Certainly the unit must fit in in some way; the question is how. There are elements within the Gospel of Mark that cohere with this passage (such as private and public teaching, healing the deaf and blind, and hardness of heart).[32] The unit therefore anticipates things to come later in the narrative. But having said that, it would be going too far to claim that the passage has a determinative function in how the parables of Jesus are regarded in the Gospel of Mark beyond 4:33-34.

4. The theological question: It has been said that the passage is "theologically outrageous."[33] On the other hand, it can be maintained that the unit has deep and positive theological significance. The teachings of Jesus — whether parables or other forms of discourse — are clear, but they are not grasped, perceived, or understood in a life-changing way except through faith. The parables

---

less explicit; he concludes that the material existed in the tradition, and Mark modified it, but he does not speak of it as having been within a preformed parable collection.

28. T. Burkill, *Mysterious Revelation*, 99; V. Taylor, *Mark*, 254-55; J. Jeremias, *Parables*, 18; E. Linnemann, *Parables*, 180; C. Carlston, *Parables*, 105; R. Pesch, *Markus*, 1:237-38; A. Ambrozic, *Hidden Kingdom*, 47-53; J. Marcus, *Mystery*, 29, 80-87; P. Perkins, *NIB (Mark)*, 8:571-72.

29. T. W. Manson, *Teaching of Jesus*, 77; J. Jeremias, *Parables*, 15; J. R. Kirkland, "Earliest Understanding," 21.

30. These are itemized by J. Jeremias, *Parables*, 15 (n. 12): "μυστήριον, δέδοται as a circumlocution of the divine action," and so on.

31. M. Beavis, *Mark's Audience*.

32. Illustrated in ibid., 157-66.

33. John C. Meagher, *Clumsy Construction in Mark's Gospel: A Critique of Form- and Redaktionsgeschichte*, TST 3 (Toronto: Edwin Mellen, 1979), 121.

do not themselves generate faith. Faith is a gift of God. The parables reveal by means of human discourse, but revelation is actually a miraculous event that takes place in a person's life by divine decision, election. For Mark the evangelist, then, the parables of Jesus present to "those outside" some hints of God's kingdom, but not the deeper and life-transforming meaning that they can also bring. In all this, however, what is gained theologically on the positive side is not matched on the negative side. One cannot help but sense that descriptive facets and experiential factors in the mission of the early church have become theological necessities.

5. The hermeneutical question: Does the unit have significance for parable interpretation? In the modern era few have found it to have significance for actual interpretation. The parables of Jesus are often enigmatic, to be sure. But to say that they were given to the public as riddles that cannot be understood, and that the disciples were in fact given private explanations, is impossible to maintain. The statement of Joachim Jeremias seems to hold up well: "the passage affords no criterion for the interpretation of the parables, nor any warrant for seeking to find in them by means of an allegorical interpretation some secret meaning hidden from the outsiders."[34] Moreover, it is widely held that any actual explanations given to the parables of Jesus that appear in our Gospels (such as those given to the Sower at Mark 4:14-20 and parallels or the Weeds in the Wheat at Matt 13:36-42) are not actually from Jesus himself, but from early Christian interpreters, perhaps the evangelists themselves. These matters are taken up in the chapters where those parables are discussed.

Matthew's Alterations

Matthew's account (13:10-17, 34-35) is based on that of Mark, but it is modified in several ways,[35] resulting in some radical changes. The most important

---

34. J. Jeremias, *Parables*, 18.

35. Major changes include the following: (1) the questioners are simply "the disciples," not persons along with the Twelve; (2) the question of 13:10 is put in direct discourse, and it differs from that in Mark by being more general: "Why do you speak to them in parables?" (instead of Mark's "[They] were asking him about the parables"); (3) At 13:11a the statement of Jesus differs in three respects: "to you has been given *to know* (γνῶναι) the *secrets* (μυστήρια) of the kingdom of *heaven* (τῶν οὐρανῶν)" over against Mark's words (no verb corresponding to γνῶναι, singular *secret*, kingdom of *God*); (4) at 13:11b it is no longer said (contra Mark 4:11b) that parables are for those outside; it is simply said that the secrets of the kingdom are not given to them; (5) at 13:12 a saying of Jesus from Mark 4:25 is added; (6) at 13:13a an additional saying of Jesus is inserted ("for this reason I speak to them in parables") to indicate the reason, which will be from Isaiah; (7) at 13:13b Matthew has substituted the word ὅτι ("because") for Mark's ἵνα ("in order that"), and he has abbreviated the words of Mark 4:12; (8) at 13:14a Matthew has constructed a saying of Jesus that introduces the following passage from Isaiah, making it a

are (1) the revision of the question to, and answer of, Jesus at the outset; (2) the textual change at 13:13; and (3) the use of Isaiah 6:9-10.

The question raised by the disciples is no longer ambiguous, as it is in Mark. In the latter Gospel the question could be either about the meaning of any parables Jesus has taught up to that point or about the nature of parables in general. In the Gospel of Matthew, however, neither of these is a possibility; the question is strictly one of pedagogy. Why does Jesus speak to the crowds in parables? Jesus responds in a manner that still divides people into two categories: those to whom the ability to know the secrets of the kingdom has been given, and those to whom it has not. But over against what Mark has, the parables in Mark are not given to the crowds to conceal anything from them, but rather to reveal. At 13:13 Matthew has replaced the ἵνα ("in order that") of Mark 4:12, which introduces a purpose clause in that gospel, with ὅτι ("because"), a causal conjunction that inaugurates a clause telling why Jesus speaks in parables. Jesus speaks in parables *because* the people do not see, hear, and understand. The parables are media of revelation (cf. 13:34-35), not of concealment. Nevertheless, that does not mean that they will be understood by all who hear them. There are many who do not perceive, listen, and understand. The emphasis is now placed more squarely on human responsibility for rejecting Jesus and his message than it was in Mark's Gospel.[36] Since those who do not respond are obdurate, God's revelation through the parables of Jesus comes to them in speech that they cannot understand.[37]

The use of Isaiah 6:9-10 differs in that Matthew has Jesus quote the entire passage in 13:14b-15 as an oracle that is being fulfilled in his own ministry. Although it is somewhat redundant after 13:13, and although it is not customary for Matthew to have Jesus speak of the fulfillment of the Scriptures,[38] here the Matthean Jesus speaks in a descriptive way of those in his own day who do not hear, see, and understand. The oracle of Isaiah is being fulfilled: the crowds are incapable of comprehending, and the reason is that their hearts have become dull, their ears hard of hearing, and their eyes closed. The outcome is lack of understanding. The oracle of Isaiah — a word of judgment in the days of the

---

passage that is being fulfilled in the time of Jesus; (9) all of 13:14b-17 is identical to Isa 6:9-10 in the LXX, except for the omission at 13:15 of one word (αὐτῶν, "their," after "ears") in the LXX; (10) additional material has been inserted by Matthew at 13:16-17, which has been derived from Q (//Luke 10:23-24); and (11) the section 13:34-35 is quite different; while 13:34 is based on Mark 4:33, but abbreviated, 13:35 is totally new as a fulfillment of Ps 78:2 (the first line is exactly like the reading of the LXX, Ps 77:2, but the second line differs a great deal from it).

36. W. D. Davies and D. C. Allison, *Matthew*, 2:392.

37. Cf. J. Kingsbury, *Matthew 13*, 51.

38. The "formula quotations" within the Gospel of Matthew (1:22; 2:15, 17, 23; 4:14; 8:17; 12:17; 13:14, 35; 21:4; 27:9; cf. 2:5) are otherwise in redactional comments made by the evangelist between sections of narrative.

prophet himself — is now a word of judgment fitting for those who do not accept the message of Jesus. As for the disciples, they are persons who "understand" Jesus and his teaching (13:23, 51; 16:12; 17:13); they see and hear what "many prophets and righteous people" longed to see, but did not see it, and to hear but did not hear it, that is, the messianic ministry of Jesus and his proclamation of the kingdom. They are persons to whom revelation has been given, and who have received it with understanding, which is not simply cognitive comprehension but a matter of faith and being a disciple.[39] They are the ones to whom "it has been given to know the secrets of the kingdom" (13:11). As one interpreter has put it in regard to the disciples and those who have refused to understand: "the understanding of the disciple is due to the grace of God; the failure to understand of the non-disciple is due to that person's rejection of the message."[40]

Matthew moves gingerly in the direction of "rehabilitating" the parables of Jesus as media of instruction. In fact, later on at 13:34-35, the evangelist says that Jesus spoke to the crowds by means of parables, in order to fulfill another passage of Scripture (Ps 78:2), a passage that speaks of Jesus' proclaiming things hidden from the foundation of the world. It would seem, then, that the parables are altogether revelatory. That may indeed have been the case in history, and Matthew may have thought that that was the case, but he knows also that not all who hear the parables actually see, hear, and understand, and that is because of the hardness of their hearts. The history and circumstances of the Matthean community are no doubt in view.

Luke's Alterations

If Matthew clarifies the rather ambiguous question of the disciples to Jesus in Mark's Gospel one way, Luke does so in another (8:9-10). Here the question — stated in indirect discourse, as in Mark — is simply a request for an explanation of the Parable of the Sower (8:5-8). The response of Jesus is based on Mark 4:11-12, but there is no parallel to Mark 4:33-34. As in the case of Matthew, Luke has "mysteries" (μυστήρια) rather than Mark's "mystery," and the verb "to know" (γνῶναι); in fact, the similarities between portions of Matthew 13:11 and Luke 8:10 are so great that these verses are counted among the "minor agreements" between the two against Mark.[41] In any case, there is a more positive emphasis on the gift as knowledge of the secrets of the kingdom than in

39. The meaning of συνίημι is explored in detail by Heinz J. Held, "Matthew's Understanding of the Law," in *Tradition and Interpretation in Matthew*, by Günther Bornkamm, Gerhard Barth, and H. J. Held (Philadelphia: Westminster Press, 1963), 105-12.

40. D. Hagner, *Matthew*, 375.

41. Burnett H. Streeter, *The Four Gospels: A Study of Origins*, rev. ed. (New York: St. Martin's Press, 1930), 313.

Mark's version.[42] Over against both Mark and Matthew, however, there are no clear "outsiders" or "those" to whom Jesus speaks parables. Instead Jesus speaks "to the rest" (τοῖς δὲ λοιποῖς) in parables. The distinction is simply between "his disciples" and "the rest."

Luke, unlike Matthew however, takes over Mark's ἵνα ("in order that"), thereby introducing a purpose clause, and he abbreviates the passage in Mark from Isaiah 6:9, omitting Mark's "lest they should turn again, and it be forgiven them." The net effect of Luke's alterations is to soften Mark's reading. It is no longer that "all things" are in parables to "those outside" (Mark), but that Jesus speaks "parables" to "others."

It is possible that Luke did not fully comprehend the consequence of what Mark had. Yet his alterations could have been deliberate and fitting within his theological perspective. For him, Jesus' teaching ministry consisted of (1) revelation to his disciples, who would become apostles in the post-Easter era, and (2) teaching in parables to "others" who would not catch the full significance of his message (but only in part) in accord with the divine plan. That is spelled out when Luke quotes the Isaiah passage in full at Acts 28:26-27 to illustrate the blindness of the unfaithful of Israel and to justify the apostolic mission to the Gentiles (28:28). What came to be in the later, post-Easter situation thus had its roots in the ministry of Jesus.[43]

Select Bibliography

Ambrozic, Aloysius M. *The Hidden Kingdom: A Redaction Critical Study of the References to the Kingdom in Mark's Gospel.* CBQMS 2. Washington: Catholic Biblical Association, 1972.

———. "Mark's Concept of Parable: Mk 4:11f. in the Context of the Second Gospel." *CBQ* 29 (1967): 220-27.

Baird, J. Arthur. "A Pragmatic Approach to Parable Exegesis: Some New Evidence on Mark 4:11, 33-34." *JBL* 76 (1957): 201-7.

Beavis, Mary Ann. *Mark's Audience: The Literary and Social Setting of Mark 4.11-12.* JSNTSup 33. Sheffield: Sheffield Academic Press, 1989.

Best, Ernest. "Mark's Use of the Twelve." *ZNW* 69 (1978): 11-35.

Bishop, Jonathan. "*Parabole* and *Parrhesia* in Mark." *Int* 40 (1986): 39-52.

Böhlig, Alexander. *Mysterion und Wahrheit.* AGSJU 6. Leiden: E. J. Brill, 1968.

Boobyer, G. H. "The Secrecy Motif in St. Mark's Gospel." *NTS* 6 (1959-60): 225-35.

Bornkamm, Günther. "μυστήριον," *TDNT* 4:802-28.

Boucher, Madeleine. *The Mysterious Parable: A Literary Study.* CBQMS 6. Washington: Catholic Biblical Association, 1977.

---

42. I. H. Marshall, *Luke*, 322; J. Fitzmyer, *Luke*, 707.
43. Cf. C. Carlston, *Parables*, 57.

Bowker, J. W. "Mystery and Parable: Mark IV.1-20." *JTS* 25 (1974): 300-317.

Brown, Schuyler. "'The Secret of the Kingdom of God' (Mark 4:11)." *JBL* 92 (1973): 60-74.

Burkill, T. A. *Mysterious Revelation: An Examination of the Philosophy of St. Mark's Gospel.* Ithaca: Cornell University Press, 1963.

Cerfaux, Lucien. "La connaissance des secrets du royaume d'après Matt XIII.11 et parallèles." *NTS* 2 (1955-56): 238-49.

Coutts, John. "'Those Outside' (Mark 4,10-12)." *SE* 2 (= TU 87 [1964]): 155-57.

Daube, David. "Public Pronouncement and Private Explanation in the Gospels." *ExpTim* 57 (1946): 175-77. Reprinted in his *The New Testament and Rabbinic Judaism* (London: Athlone, 1956), 141-50.

Eakin, Frank E., Jr. "Spiritual Obduracy and Parable Purpose." In *The Use of the Old Testament in the New and Other Essays: Studies in Honor of William Franklin Stinespring,* ed. James M. Efird, 87-109. Durham: Duke University Press, 1972.

Elderen, Bastiaan van. "The Purpose of the Parables according to Matthew 13:10-17." In *New Dimensions in New Testament Study,* 180-90. Ed. Merrill C. Tenney and Richard E. Longenecker. Grand Rapids: Zondervan, 1974.

Evans, Craig A. "A Note on the Function of Isaiah vi,9-10 in Mark iv." *RB* 88 (1981): 234-35.

———. "The Function of Isaiah 6:9-10 in Mark and John." *NovT* 24 (1982): 124-28.

———. *To See and Not Perceive: Isaiah 6.9-10 in Early Jewish and Christian Interpretation.* JSOTSup 64. Sheffield: JSOT Press, 1989.

Falusi, Gabriel K. "Jesus' Use of Parables in Mark with Special Reference to Mark 4:10-12." *IJT* 31 (1982): 35-46.

Gnilka, Joachim. *Die Verstockung Israels: Isaias 6,9-10 in der Theologie der Synoptiker.* SANT 3. Munich: Kösel Verlag, 1961.

———. "Das Verstockungsproblem nach Matthäus 13,13-15." In *Antijudaismus im Neuen Testament?* 119-28. Ed. Willehad P. Eckert et al. Munich: Kaiser Verlag, 1967.

Goulder, Michael. "Those Outside (Mark 4:10-12)." *NovT* 33 (1991): 289-302.

Haacker, Klaus. "Erwägungen zu Mc IV 11." *NovT* 14 (1977): 219-25.

Haufe, Günter. "Erwägungen zum Ursprung der sogenannten Parabeltheorie Markus 4,11-12." *EvT* 32 (1972): 413-21.

Hooker, Morna D. "Mark's Parables of the Kingdom (Mark 4:1-34)." In *The Challenge of Jesus' Parables,* 79-101. Ed. Richard N. Longenecker. Grand Rapids: Wm. B. Eerdmans, 2000.

Hubaut, Michel. "Le 'mystère' révélé dans les paraboles." *RTL* 5 (1974): 454-61.

Igarashi, Peter H. "Mystery of the Kingdom of God (Mark 4:10-12)." *JBR* 24 (1956): 83-89.

Jones, Geraint Vaughan. "Mark 4.10-12." In his *The Art and Truth of the Parables: A Study in Their Literary Form and Modern Interpretation*, 225-30. London: SPCK, 1964.

Kirkland, J. R. "The Earliest Understanding of Jesus' Use of Parables: Mark IV 10-12 in Context." *NovT* 19 (1977): 1-21.

Lampe, Peter. "Die markinische Deutung des Gleichnisses vom Sämann Markus 4:10-12." *ZNW* 65 (1974): 140-50.

Link, Wilhelm. "Die Geheimnisse des Himmelreiches: Eine Erklärung von Matth. 13.10-13." *EvT* 2 (1935): 115-27.

Manson, William. "The Purpose of the Parables: A Re-Examination of St Mark iv.10-12." *ExpTim* 68 (1956-57): 132-35.

Marcus, Joel. "Mark 4:10-12 and Marcan Epistemology." *JBL* 103 (1984): 557-74.

———. *The Mystery of the Kingdom of God*. SBLDS 90. Atlanta: Scholars Press, 1986.

Marion, D. "Simples et mystérieuses paraboles. X. La parabole-mystère Marc 4,1-34." *EeV* 106/37-38 (1996): 273-82.

Marxsen, Willi. "Redaktionsgeschichtliche Erklärung der sogenannten Parabeltheorie des Markus." *ZTK* 52 (1955): 255-372.

Mearns, Chris L. "Parables, Secrecy and Eschatology in Mark's Gospel." *SJT* 44 (1991): 423-42.

Meye, Robert P. "Mark 4.10: 'Those about Him with the Twelve.'" *SE* 2 (= TU 87 [1964]): 211-18.

Moore, Carey A. "Mark 4.12: More Like the Irony of Micaiah than Isaiah." In *A Light unto My Path: Old Testament Studies in Honor of Jacob M. Myers*, 335-44. Ed. Howard N. Bream et al. Philadelphia: Temple University Press, 1974.

Nock, Arthur D. "Mysterion." *HSCP* 60 (1951): 201-4.

Patten, Priscilla. "The Form and Function of Parables in Select Apocalyptic Literature and Their Significance for Parables in the Gospel of Mark." *NTS* 29 (1983): 246-58.

Peisker, Carl H. "Konsekutives ἵνα in Markus IV,12." *ZNW* 59 (1968): 126-27.

Piper, Otto A. "The Mystery of the Kingdom of God: Critical Scholarship and Christian Doctrine." *Int* 1 (1947): 183-200.

Pryor, J. W. "Marcan Parable Theology: An Inquiry into Mark's Principles of Redaction." *ExpTim* 83 (1972): 242-45.

Räisänen, Heikki. *Die Parabeltheorie im Markusevangelium*. SFEG 26. Helsinki: Finnish Exegetical Society, 1973.

Schelkle, Karl H. "Der Zweck der Gleichnisreden (Mk 4,10-12)." In *Neues Testament und Kirche: Festschrift für Rudolf Schnackenburg*, 71-75. Ed. Joachim Gnilka. Freiburg: Herder, 1974.

Schenke, Hans-Martin. "The Mystery of the Gospel of Mark." *SC* 4 (1984): 65-82.

Schweizer, Eduard. "The Question of the Messianic Secret in Mark." In *The Messianic Secret*, 65-74. Ed. Christopher Tuckett. IRT 1. Philadelphia: Fortress Press, 1983.

Siegman, Edward F. "Teaching in Parables (Mk 4,10-12; Lk 8,9-10; Mt 13,10-15)." *CBQ* 23 (1961): 61-81.

Trocmé, Étienne. "Why Parables? A Study of Mark IV." *BJRL* 59 (1977): 458-71.

Via, Dan O. "Matthew on the Understandability of the Parables." *JBL* 84 (1965): 430-32.

Windisch, Hans. "Die Verstockungsidee in Mc 4,12 und das kausale ῞Ινα der späteren Koine." *ZNW* 26 (1927): 203-9.

Yarbro Collins, Adela. "Mysteries in the Gospel of Mark." In *Mighty Minorities? Minorities in Early Christianity — Positions and Strategies: Essays in Honour of Jacob Jervell on His 70th Birthday 21 May 1995*, 11-23. Ed. David Hellholm, Halvor Moxnes, and Turid Karlsen Seim. Oslo: Scandinavian University Press, 1995.

The Three Parables of Luke 15

Three parables are located in Luke 15:3-32 — the Lost Sheep (15:4-7), the Lost Coin (15:8-10), and the Prodigal Son (15:11-32). These three are among a total of fifteen that are spoken by Jesus within the Travel Narrative of the Gospel of Luke (9:51–19:27).

The Travel Narrative opens with the notice that "the days drew near for [Jesus] to be taken up" (through death, resurrection, and ascension), and so "he set his face to go to Jerusalem" (9:51). Jesus therefore leaves Galilee for his appointed destiny in Jerusalem, which is repeatedly stated to be his goal (9:51, 53; 13:22, 33-34; 17:11; 18:31; 19:11). As interpreters have often pointed out, in spite of geographical references within the section (9:52; 10:38; 13:22; 17:11-12; 18:35; 19:1, 28-29, 41), Luke does not actually provide here an "itinerary" that can be followed; at 17:11, for example, Jesus is no closer to Jerusalem than at the outset. What is clear, however, is that the section is thematic.[1] Within the narrative Jesus provides instruction for his disciples as forerunners of the new community within Israel (hence, consolidation) and disputation with his opponents (division). The consolidation and division occur through Luke's incorporation of parables, conflict stories, and a host of isolated sayings.

It is typical of Luke to provide parables with settings as a framework for interpreting them. Such settings — all important for the interpretations of the parables that follow — are at 12:13-16 (for the Rich Fool), 12:41 (for the Faithful and Wise Servant), 14:15 (for the Great Banquet), 16:14-15 (for the Rich

---

1. For various perspectives, cf. B. Reicke, "Instruction and Discussion in the Travel Narrative," 1.206-16; J. Resseguie, "Point of View in the Central Section of Luke," 41-47; J. A. Fitzmyer, *Luke,* 823-27; D. Moessner, *Lord of the Banquet;* F. Matera, "Jesus' Journey to Jerusalem," 57-77; and A. Denaux, "Old Testament Models for the Lukan Travel Narrative," 271-305.

Man and Lazarus), 18:1 (for the Unjust Judge), 18:9 (for the Pharisee and the Publican), and 19:11 (for the Pounds).

The immediate context of the three parables of Luke 15 is set forth in the opening verses (15:1-3, in language reminiscent of 5:30):

> 1 *"All the tax collectors and sinners were drawing near to [Jesus] to hear him. 2And the Pharisees and the scribes were grumbling, saying, 'This man welcomes sinners and eats with them.' 3So he told them this parable, saying. . . ."*

With hyperbole Luke speaks of those present with Jesus as "*all* the tax collectors and sinners." Such persons are stock-in-trade for the despised. Yet that Jesus had table fellowship with persons so designated is deeply rooted in the tradition, as in another scene of table fellowship with them (Matt 9:10-11// Mark 2:15-16//Luke 5:29-30) and in the epithet contained in a saying of Jesus himself in Q (Matt 11:19//Luke 7:34), "Behold, a glutton and a drunkard, a friend of tax collectors and sinners!" The likelihood is that the historical Jesus himself associated with such persons, who are linked together. The linkage was clearly based on the view that they belong in the same category. The "sinners" consisted of all who, in the eyes of their critics, had abandoned the law and for all practical purposes had denied God's covenant with Israel.[2] The identity of the tax collectors has been debated. According to one view, they were primarily toll collectors at transport and commercial centers.[3] According to another view, however, the term τελώνης ("tax collector") probably referred to more than that. The tax collectors were well-to-do persons, including Jews, who paid for the privilege to collect tolls, market duties, and all kinds of local taxes (sales, income, property, and inheritance).[4] They made their own income by overcharging people, as Zacchaeus admits (Luke 19:8), thereby preying upon them. Scorn for them is attested not only in the NT but also in rabbinic writings and secular literature of antiquity.[5]

The criticism of the Pharisees and scribes against Jesus — that he has table fellowship with sinners — rests largely upon the view in ancient Judaism, as well as the wider Greco-Roman society, that such an event creates a special tie

---

2. E. P. Sanders, "Jesus and the Sinners," *JSNT* 19 (1983): 5-36.

3. John R. Donahue, "Tax Collectors and Sinners: An Attempt at Identification," *CBQ* 33 (1971): 39-61.

4. Fritz Herrenbrück, "Wer waren die 'Zöllner'?" *ZNW* 72 (1981): 178-94; idem, *Jesus und die Zöllner: Historische und neutestamentlich-exegetische Untersuchungen*, WUNT 41 (Tübingen: J. C. B. Mohr [Paul Siebeck], 1990); Helmut Merkel, "τελώνης," *EDNT* 3:349.

5. Rabbinic references are cited by Joachim Jeremias, *Jerusalem in the Time of Jesus: An Investigation into Economic and Social Conditions during the New Testament Period* (Philadelphia: Fortress Press, 1969), 310-11; secular sources in John R. Donahue, "Tax Collector," *ABD* 6:337.

among the diners, a social bonding. Eating together, or excluding people from the table, functioned as a means to define boundaries between those present and the rest of the world.[6] All this is familiar to Luke the evangelist.[7] The Pharisees themselves (as well as other Jewish groups) shared common meals as a major component of their group identity.[8] All the more reason there was, then, to criticize Jesus for his action, which implied the creation of a social bond between him and his fellow table companions. His selection of table companions was "no mere lapse of regard for the customs of his day but a formal strategy" by which he signaled that "God extends an inclusive invitation to nonobservant and sinful outsiders for covenant membership and for status as forgiven persons."[9]

The three parables have a thematic unity, which is punctuated by linguistic commonalities. In each of them, as well as in the introduction (15:1-2), the noun "sinner" (ἁμαρτωλός or plural forms) or the verb "to sin" (ἁμαρτάνω) appears: the noun in 15:1-2, 7, 10; the verb in 15:18, 21. In each of the parables also the verbs "to lose" (ἀπόλλυμι, ἀπόλλυμαι) and "to find" (εὑρίσκω, εὑρίσκομαι) appear: "to lose" at 15:4, 6, 8, 9, 24, 32, and "to find" at 15:4, 5, 6, 8, 9, 24, 32. The one who has lost and found rejoices (χαίρω, 15:5, 6, 32) and then either invites others to "rejoice with" him or her (συγχαίρω, 15:6, 9) or declares that it is necessary for him and others to "make merry" (εὐφραίνω, 15:32; cf. 15:24). Finally, the verbs of rejoicing are echoed also in the appended sayings to the first two parables concerning the "joy" (χαρά) in heaven (15:7) or before the angels (15:10) as a consequence of a sinner's repentance.

The way that the parables close is in some ways surprising. The Parable of the Prodigal Son closes without an appended application at all. One interpreter has suggested that, since the parable is great art, no further word or application is required, for its meaning is self-evident.[10] That is true, however, only when the larger context in which Luke has placed it is considered (see commentary). The other two parables end with an interpretive saying or application concerning the divine joy over repentance (15:7, 10). But a lost sheep or lost coin that has been found is hardly "found" on the basis of "repentance." The sayings actually apply more directly to the prodigal son who has returned home. On the other hand, the father's sayings about that which has been "lost and found" at 15:24 and 32 apply more directly to the situation of the sheep and coin that had been "found" (15:5, 6, 9). Most likely, the sayings of the father in 15:24 and 32 are integral to the Parable of the Prodigal Son as Luke received it from the tradi-

6. D. Smith, "Table Fellowship," 6.302-4.
7. Cf. J. Neyrey, "Ceremonies in Luke-Acts," 361-87.
8. J. Neusner, *From Politics to Piety*, 67-96.
9. J. Neyrey, "Ceremonies in Luke-Acts," 378.
10. Geraint V. Jones, *The Art and Truth of the Parables: A Study in Their Literary Form and Modern Interpretation* (London: SPCK, 1964), 168.

tion. The interpretive sayings at the conclusions of the other two parables (15:7, 10) may be due to Luke's redactional work. That issue has been taken up in the commentaries on those parables.

Select Bibliography

Agnew, Francis H. "The Parables of Divine Compassion." *BiTod* 27 (1989): 35-40.

Barton, Stephen C. "Parables on God's Love and Forgiveness (Luke 15:1-7//Matthew 18:12-14; Luke 15:8-32)." In *The Challenge of Jesus' Parables*, 199-216. Ed. Richard N. Longenecker. Grand Rapids: Wm. B. Eerdmans, 2000.

Denaux, Adelbert. "Old Testament Models for the Lukan Travel Narrative: A Critical Survey." In *The Scriptures in the Gospels*, 271-305. Ed. Christopher M. Tuckett. BETL 131. Leuven: Leuven University Press, 1997.

Giblin, Charles H. "Structural and Theological Considerations on Luke 15." *CBQ* 24 (1962): 15-31.

Kozar, Joseph V. "Absent Joy: An Investigation of the Narrative Pattern of Repetition and Variation of the Parables of Luke 15." *TJT* 8 (1992): 85-94.

Matera, Frank J. "Jesus' Journey to Jerusalem (Luke 9.51–19.46): A Conflict with Israel." *JSNT* 51 (1993): 57-77.

Moessner, David P. *Lord of the Banquet: The Literary and Theological Significance of Luke's Travel Narrative.* Minneapolis: Fortress Press, 1989.

Moxnes, Halvor. "Meals and the New Community in Luke." *SEÅ* 51 (1986): 158-67.

Neusner, Jacob, *From Politics to Piety: The Emergence of Pharisaic Judaism,* 2d ed. New York: Ktav Publishing House, 1979.

———. "Two Pictures of the Pharisees: Philosophical Circle or Eating Club." *ATR* 64 (1982): 525-38.

Neyrey, Jerome H. "Ceremonies in Luke-Acts: The Case of Meals and Table Fellowship." In *The Social World of Luke-Acts: Models for Interpretation,* 361-87. Ed. Jerome H. Neyrey. Peabody, Mass.: Hendrickson Publishers, 1991.

Ramsey, George W. "Plots, Gaps, Repetitions, and Ambiguity in Luke 15." *PRS* 17 (1990): 33-42.

Reicke, Bo, "Instruction and Discussion in the Travel Narrative." *SE* 1:206-16. Ed. Kurt Aland. TU 73 (Berlin: Akademie Verlag, 1959).

Resseguie, James L. "Point of View in the Central Section of Luke (9:51–19:44)." *JETS* 25 (1982): 41-47.

Smith, Dennis E. "The Historical Jesus at Table." In *Society of Biblical Literature 1989 Seminar Papers,* 468-86. Ed. David J. Lull. SBLSP 28. Atlanta: Scholars Press, 1989.

———. "Table Fellowship." *ABD* 6:302-4.

———. "Table Fellowship as a Literary Motif in the Gospel of Luke." *JBL* 106 (1987): 613-38.

Stevens, Gerald L. "Luke 15: Parables of God's Search for Sinners." *ThEd* 56 (1997): 67-76.

Wendland, Ernest. "Finding Some Lost Aspects of Meaning in Christ's Parables of the Lost — and Found (Luke 15)." *TJ* 17 (1996): 19-65.

Doulos — *Servant or Slave?*

The Greek term δοῦλος ("servant" or "slave") appears in singular or plural forms within the following parables of Jesus:

> The Wicked Tenants: Mark 12:2//Matthew 21:34//Luke 20:10-11
> A Man on a Journey: Mark 13:34//Luke 12:37
> The Weeds among the Wheat: Matthew 13:27-28
> The Unforgiving Servant: Matthew 18:23, 26-28, 32
> The Wedding Feast: Matthew 22:3-4, 6, 8, 10
> The Faithful and Wise Servant: Matthew 24:45-46, 48, 50//Luke 12:43,
>   45-47
> The Talents: Matthew 25:14, 19, 21, 23, 26, 30
> The Great Banquet: Luke 14:17, 21-23
> The Prodigal Son: Luke 15:22
> The Servant at Duty: Luke 17:7, 9-10
> The Pounds: Luke 19:13, 15, 17, 22

Wherever the Greek term occurs, it has usually been translated in modern English versions by "servant" (KJV, RSV, NEB, JB, TEV, NIV). But the NRSV departs from that tradition by translating it as "slave."

There are problems with both translations. In the history of the English language the word "servant" designates a person who is actually employed, not owned, by a master. The servant is free, even if living and working in a difficult situation. He or she is usually a domestic employee working as a butler, housekeeper, caregiver for a child or incapacitated member of a household, or perhaps a groundskeeper.

The term "slave" is a problem too, particularly in the context of North America, where slavery was an institution for several centuries. Slavery in the

Greco-Roman world differed in several respects from the American type. Although it is difficult to define slavery in that world, it was defined in the *Institutes* (1.3.2) of Justinian (ca. A.D. 533) — drawing on an earlier definition by the second-century-A.D. jurist, Florentinus — in the following way:

> Slavery is an institution of the law of nations *(ius gentium)* by which, contrary to nature, a person is subjected to the dominion of another.[1]

The differences from the early American institution of slavery are several: it was not based on race; slaves could become citizens after emancipation, and citizens could sell themselves into slavery; they could own property; they were regarded as persons (not simply as property or subhuman); they could be educated — and some were better educated than their owners; and they could be, and were, involved in many tasks and professions as business managers and agents, craftsmen, bankers, physicians, farm tenants, government bureaucrats, teachers and tutors, artists, accountants, actors, domestic and farm laborers, gladiators, and even sea captains.[2] What distinguished the slave from a free person was that he or she was owned by another.[3]

In spite of the risks of using the term "slave" as a translation for the Greek term in a North American context, it is, in the end, preferable to the term "servant" in the case of the parables. It is clear that the persons referred to are the possession of a master in each case, and it can be assumed that they, like their masters, are Jews.[4]

The slaves portrayed in the parables are stock figures who carry on a number of activities. They work the fields and tend sheep for their masters (Matt 13:27-28; Luke 17:7), serve them meals (Luke 17:8), collect produce from tenants on behalf of their masters (Mark 12:2//Matt 21:34//Luke 20:10-11), make loans to fellow servants (Matt 18:28), carry messages for their masters (Matt 22:3-10; Luke 14:17-23), and care for their masters' wardrobe (Luke 15:22). Moreover, they are authorized by their masters to take charge of households during their masters' absence (Mark 13:34//Luke 12:37; Matt 24:45-51//Luke 12:42-48), and they are entrusted by their masters with property to make investments (Matt 25:14-30; Luke 19:12-25).

Given such relatively free rein, slaves in the parables have opportunities to misbehave. They are capable of mistreating fellow servants (Matt 18:28-30; 24:48-51//Luke 12:45-46) and even of defrauding their masters (Luke 16:1-8).

---

1. Text quoted from A. Watson, *Roman Slave Law*, 7.

2. Ibid., 3; W. W. Buckland, *The Roman Law of Slavery*, 1-9; K. Hopkins, *Conquerors and Slaves*, 123.

3. W. W. Buckland, *The Roman Law of Slavery*, 10.

4. On slavery among Jews in Palestine of the first century A.D., cf. Joachim Jeremias, *Jerusalem in the Time of Jesus: An Investigation into Economic and Social Conditions during the New Testament Period* (Philadelphia: Fortress Press, 1969), 110-11, 312-16.

But if caught, they can suffer severe beatings (Matt 24:51//Luke 12:47-48) and even be handed over to torture (Matt 18:34). It is possible also for a slave who is heavily indebted to his master to be thrown into prison along with his wife and children (Matt 18:25). The degree to which the latter was legally possible is beside the point.[5] The telling of a parable of a wealthy king and his servant knows no bounds of hyperbole, whether that be in regard to release from debts (10,000 talents!) or punishment.

Select Bibliography

Bartchy, S. Scott. "Slavery: New Testament." *ABD* 6:65-73.

Bradley, K. R. *Slaves and Masters in the Roman Empire: A Study in Social Control.* New York: Oxford University Press, 1987.

Brandt, Wilhelm. *Dienst und Dienen im Neuen Testament,* NTF 2/5. Gütersloh: C. Bertelsmann, 1931.

Buckland, W. W. *The Roman Law of Slavery: The Condition of the Slave in Private Law from Augustus to Justinian.* Cambridge: Cambridge University Press, 1908. Reprinted, New York: AMS Press, 1969.

Finley, Moses I. *Ancient Slavery and Modern Ideology.* New York: Viking Press, 1980.

Hopkins, Keith. *Conquerors and Slaves.* SSRH 1. Cambridge: Cambridge University Press, 1978.

Jeremias, Joachim. *Jerusalem in the Time of Jesus: An Investigation into Economic and Social Conditions during the New Testament Period.* Philadelphia: Fortress Press, 1969.

MacMullen, Ramsay. *Roman Social Relations 50 b.c. to a.d. 284.* New Haven: Yale University Press, 1974.

Mendelsohn, Isaac. "Slavery in the OT." *IDB* 4:383-91.

Rengstorf, Karl H. "δοῦλος." *TDNT* 2:261-80.

Rollins, Wayne G. "Slavery in the NT." *IDBSup* 830-32.

Vogt, Joseph. *Ancient Slavery and the Ideal of Man.* Cambridge: Harvard University Press, 1975.

Watson, Alan. *Roman Slave Law.* Baltimore: Johns Hopkins University Press, 1987.

Weiser, Alfons. "δουλεία." *EDNT* 1:349-52.

————. *Die Knechtsgleichnisse der synoptischen Evangelien.* SANT 29. Munich: Kösel Verlag, 1971.

5. That it was not likely is the view of S. Lachs, *Rabbinic Commentary,* 273. Lachs points out that there are biblical passages allowing for the selling of children for their father's insolvency (2 Kings 4:1; Neh 5:5; Isa 50:1) but denies that even this would have been done during the time of Jesus.

Wiedemann, Thomas. *Greek and Roman Slavery.* Baltimore: Johns Hopkins University Press, 1981.
Wolf, C. Umhau. "Servant." *IDB* 4:291-92.

Bibliography on the Parables of Jesus

Ambrozic, Aloysius M. "Mark's Concept of the Parable: Mark 4:11f. in the Context of the Second Gospel." *CBQ* 29 (1976): 220-27.

Baasland, Ernst. "Zum Beispiel der Beispielerzählungen: Zur Formenlehre der Gleichnisse und zum Methodik der Gleichnisauslegung." *NovT* (1986): 193-219.

Bailey, Kenneth E. *Finding the Lost: Cultural Keys to Luke 15.* St. Louis: Concordia Publishing House, 1992.

———. *Poet and Peasant: A Literary Cultural Approach to the Parables in Luke.* Grand Rapids: Wm. B. Eerdmans, 1976.

———. *Through Peasant Eyes: More Lucan Parables, Their Culture and Style.* Grand Rapids: Wm. B. Eerdmans, 1980.

Barnard, Leslie W. "To Allegorize or Not to Allegorize." *StPat* 36 (1982): 1-10.

Baudler, Georg. *Jesus im Spiegel seiner Gleichnisse: Das erzählerische Lebenswerk Jesu — ein Zugang zum Glauben,* 2d ed. Stuttgart: Calwer Verlag, 1988.

Beardslee, William A. "Listening to the Parables of Jesus: An Exploration of the Uses of Process Theology in Biblical Interpretation." In *Texts and Testaments: Critical Essays on the Bible and Early Church Fathers,* 201-18. Ed. W. Eugene March. San Antonio: Trinity University Press, 1980.

Bishop, Jonathan. "*Parabole* and *Parrhesia* in Mark." *Int* 49 (1986): 39-52.

Black, Matthew. "The Parables as Allegory." *BJRL* 42 (1959-60): 273-87.

Blomberg, Craig L. *Interpreting the Parables.* Downers Grove, Ill.: InterVarsity Press, 1990.

———. "Interpreting the Parables of Jesus: Where Are We and Where Do We Go from Here?" *CBQ* 53 (1991): 50-78.

———. "Parable." *ISBE* 3:655-59.

———. "The Parables of Jesus: Current Trends and Needs in Research." In

Studying the Historical Jesus: Evaluations of the State of Current Research, 231-54. Ed. Bruce Chilton and Craig A. Evans. Leiden: E. J. Brill, 1994.

Borsch, Frederick H. *Many Things in Parables: Extravagant Stories of New Community.* Philadelphia: Fortress Press, 1988.

Boucher, Madeleine I. *The Mysterious Parable: A Literary Study.* CBQMS, 6. Washington, D.C.: Catholic Biblical Association of America, 1977.

―――. *The Parables.* Rev. ed. Wilmington, Del.: Michael Glazier, 1983.

Breech, James. *The Silence of Jesus: The Authentic Voice of the Historical Man.* Philadelphia: Fortress Press, 1983.

Brown, Raymond E. "Parable and Allegory Reconsidered." *NovT* 5 (1962): 36-45. Reprinted in his *New Testament Essays,* 321-33. Milwaukee: Bruce Publishing Company, 1965.

Browne, Laurence E. *The Parables of the Gospels in the Light of Modern Criticism.* Cambridge: Cambridge University Press, 1913.

Bruce, Alexander B. *The Parabolic Teaching of Christ: A Systematic and Critical Study of the Parables of Our Lord.* 4th ed. New York: Hodder & Stoughton, 1914.

Bugge, Christian A. *Die Haupt-Parabeln Jesu: Mit einer Einleitung über die Methode der Parabel-Auslegung.* 2 vols. Giessen: Ricker'sche (Alfred Töpelmann), 1903.

Buttrick, George A. *The Parables of Jesus.* New York: Harper & Brothers, 1928.

Cadoux, A. T. *The Parables of Jesus: Their Art and Use.* New York: Macmillan, 1931.

Capon, Robert F. *The Parables of Grace.* Grand Rapids: Wm. B. Eerdmans, 1988.

―――. *The Parables of Judgment.* Grand Rapids: Wm. B. Eerdmans, 1989.

―――. *The Parables of the Kingdom.* Grand Rapids: Wm. B. Eerdmans, 1985.

Carlston, Charles E. "Parable and Allegory Revisited: An Interpretive Review." *CBQ* 43 (1981): 228-42.

―――. *The Parables of the Triple Tradition.* Philadelphia: Fortress Press, 1975.

Carson, D. A. "The OMOIOS Word-Group as Introduction to Some Matthean Parables." *NTS* 31 (1985): 277-82.

Carter, Warren. "Challenging by Confirming, Renewing by Repeating: The Parables of 'the Reign of the Heavens' in Matthew 13 as Embedded Narratives." In *Society of Biblical Literature 1995 Seminar Papers,* 399-424. Ed. Eugene H. Lovering, Jr. SBLSP 34. Atlanta: Scholars Press, 1995.

Carter, Warren, and John P. Heil. *Matthew's Parables: Audience-Oriented Perspectives.* CBQMS 30. Washington: The Catholic Biblical Association of America, 1998.

Cave, C. H. "The Parables and the Scriptures." *NTS* 11 (1964/65): 374-87.

The Challenge of Jesus' Parables. Ed. Richard N. Longenecker. Grand Rapids: Wm. B. Eerdmans, 2000.

Crossan, John Dominic. "Aphorism in Discourse and Narrative." *Semeia* 43 (1988): 121-40.

————. *Cliffs of Fall: Paradox and Polyvalence in the Parables of Jesus*. New York: Seabury, 1980.

————. *Finding Is the First Act: Trove Folktales and Jesus' Treasure Parables*. Philadelphia: Fortress Press, 1979.

————. *In Fragments: The Aphorisms of Jesus*. San Francisco: Harper & Row, 1983.

————. *In Parables: The Challenge of the Historical Jesus*. 2d ed. Sonoma, Calif.: Polebridge Press, 1992.

————. "Parable." *ABD* 5:146-52.

————. "Parable and Example in the Teaching of Jesus." In *Semeia 1: A Structuralist Approach to the Parables*, 63-104. Ed. Robert W. Funk. Missoula, Mont.: Scholars Press, 1974.

————. "Parable as Religious and Poetic Experience." *JR* 53 (1973): 330-58.

————. "The Seed Parables of Jesus." *JBL* 92 (1973): 244-66.

————. "The Servant Parables of Jesus." In *Semeia 1: A Structuralist Approach to the Parables*, 17-62. Ed. Robert W. Funk. Missoula, Mont.: Scholars Press, 1974.

Culbertson, Philip L. *A Word Fitly Spoken: Context, Transmission, and Adoption of the Parables of Jesus*. Albany: State University of New York Press, 1995.

Dahl, Nils. "The Parables of Growth." *ST* 5 (1951): 132-66. Reprinted in N. A. Dahl, *Jesus in the Memory of the Early Church*, 141-66. Minneapolis: Augsburg Publishing House, 1976.

Dodd, C. H. *The Parables of the Kingdom*. Rev. ed. New York: Charles Scribner's Sons, 1961.

Dods, Marcus. *The Parables of Our Lord*. 2 vols. London: Hodder & Stoughton, 1905.

Donahue, John R. *The Gospel in Parable: Metaphor, Narrative, and Theology in the Synoptic Gospels*. Philadelphia: Fortress Press, 1988.

Drury, John. *The Parables in the Gospels: History and Allegory*. New York: Crossroad, 1985.

Dschulnigg, Peter. "Positionen des Gleichverständnisses im 20. Jahrhundert: Kurze Darstellung von fünf wichtigen Positionen der Gleichnistheorie." *TZ* 45 (1989): 335-51.

————. *Rabbinische Gleichnisse und das Neue Testament: Die Gleichnisse der PesK im Vergleich mit den Gleichnissen Jesu und dem Neuen Testament*. JC 12. Bern: Peter Lang, 1988.

Eichholz, Georg. *Einführung in die Gleichnisse*. Neukirchen-Vluyn: Neukirchener Verlag, 1963.

————. *Gleichnisse der Evangelien: Form, Überlieferung, Auslegung*. Neukirchen-Vluyn: Neukirchener Verlag, 1971.

Etchells, Ruth. *A Reading of the Parables of Jesus*. London: Darton, Longman, and Todd, 1998.

Feldman, Asher. *The Parables and Similes of the Rabbis.* Cambridge: Cambridge University Press, 1927.

Fiebig, Paul W. J. *Altjüdische Gleichnisse und die Gleichnisse Jesu.* Tübingen: J. C. B. Mohr (Paul Siebeck), 1904.

————. *Die Gleichnisreden Jesu im Lichte der rabbinischen Gleichnisse des neutestamentlichen Zeitalters.* Tübingen: J. C. B. Mohr (Paul Siebeck), 1912.

Findlay, James Alexander. *Jesus and His Parables.* London: Epworth Press, 1950.

Fisher, Neal F. *The Parables of Jesus: Glimpses of God's Reign.* New York: Crossroad, 1990.

Ford, Richard Q. *The Parables of Jesus: Recovering the Art of Listening.* Minneapolis: Fortress Press, 1997.

Fridrichsen, Anton. "The Parables in Recent Research." In his *Exegetical Writings: A Selection,* 58-70. Trans. and ed. Chrys C. Caragounis and Tord Fornberg. WUNT 76. Tübingen: J. C. B. Mohr (Paul Siebeck), 1994. Original in Norwegian: "Den nyere tids parabelforskning." *STK* 5 (1929): 34-48.

Fuchs, Ernst. "Bermerkungen zur Gleichnisauslegung." In *Zur Frage nach dem historischen Jesus,* 136-42. Tübingen: J. C. B. Mohr (Paul Siebeck), 1960.

Funk, Robert W. "The Parable as Metaphor." In his *Language, Hermeneutic, and the Word of God: The Problem of Language in New Testament and Contemporary Theology,* 133-62. New York: Harper & Row, 1966.

————. *Parables and Presence: Forms of the New Testament Tradition.* Philadelphia: Fortress Press, 1982.

Funk, Robert W., Bernard B. Scott, and James R. Butts. *The Parables of Jesus: Red Letter Edition, A Report of the Jesus Seminar.* Sonoma, Calif.: Polebridge Press, 1988.

Gerhardsson, Birger. "If We Do Not Cut the Parables Out of Their Frames." *NTS* 37 (1991): 321-35.

————. "Illuminating the Kingdom: Narrative Meshalim in the Synoptic Gospels." In *Jesus and the Oral Gospel Tradition,* 266-309. Ed. Henry Wansbrough. Sheffield: Sheffield Academic Press, 1991.

————. "The Narrative Meshalim in the Synoptic Gospels: A Comparison with the Narrative Meshalim in the Old Testament." *NTS* 34 (1988): 339-63.

————. "The Seven Parables in Matthew XIII." *NTS* 19 (1972-73): 16-37.

Glen, John Stanley. *The Parables of Conflict in Luke.* Philadelphia: Westminster Press, 1962.

Goebel, Siegfried A. *The Parables of Jesus: A Methodical Exposition.* Edinburgh: T. & T. Clark, 1894.

Goulder, Michael D. "Characteristics of the Parables in the Several Gospels." *JTS* 19 (1968): 51-69.

Granskou, David. *Preaching on the Parables.* Philadelphia: Fortress Press, 1972.

Guthrie, Thomas. *The Parables.* New York: Alexander Strahan, 1866.

Güttgemanns, Erhardt. "Narrative Analyse Synoptischer Textes." *LingBibl* 25 (1973): 50-73.

Harnisch, Wolfgang. *Die Gleichniserzählungen Jesu: Eine hermeneutische Einführung.* 3d ed. Göttingen: Vandenhoeck & Ruprecht, 1995.

Harrington, Daniel J. "Polemical Parables in Matthew 24 and 25." *USQR* 44 (1991): 287-98.

Harrington, Wilfrid J. "The Parables in Recent Study (1960-1971)." *BTB* 2 (1972): 219-41.

Hauck, Friedrich. "παραβολή." *TDNT* 5:744-61.

Hedrick, Charles W. *Parables as Poetic Fictions: The Creative Voice of Jesus.* Peabody, Mass.: Hendrickson Publishers, 1994.

Heininger, Bernhard. *Metaphorik, Erzählstruktur und szenisch-dramatische Gestaltung in den Sondergutgleichnissen bei Lukas.* NTAbh 24. Münster: Aschendorff, 1991.

Hendrickx, Herman. *The Parables of Jesus.* San Francisco: Harper & Row, 1986.

Hermaniuk, Maxime. *La parabole évangélique: Enquête exégétique et critique.* Paris: Desclée, 1947.

Herzog, William R., II. *Parables as Subversive Speech: Jesus as Pedagogue of the Oppressed.* Louisville: Westminster/John Knox, 1994.

Huffman, Norman A. "Atypical Features in the Parables of Jesus." *JBL* 97 (1978): 207-20.

Hughes, Robert G. "Preaching the Parables." In *The Promise and Practice of Biblical Theology,* 157-70. Ed. John Reumann. Minneapolis: Fortress Press, 1991.

Hunter, Archibald M. *Interpreting the Parables.* Philadelphia: Westminster Press, 1960.

———. *The Parables for Today.* London: SCM Press, 1983.

Jeremias, Joachim. *The Parables of Jesus.* 2d rev. ed. Upper Saddle River, N.J.: Prentice Hall, 1972.

Jesus and His Parables: Interpreting the Parables of Jesus Today. Ed. V. George Shillington. Edinburgh: T. & T. Clark, 1997.

Jones, Geraint V. *The Art and Truth of the Parables: A Study in Their Literary Form and Modern Interpretation.* London: SPCK, 1964.

Jones, Ivor H. *The Matthean Parables: A Literary and Historical Commentary.* NovTSup 80. Leiden: E. J. Brill, 1995.

Jones, Peter R. *The Teaching of the Parables.* Nashville: Broadman Press, 1982.

Jordan, G. J. "The Classification of the Parables." *ExpTim* 45 (1933-34): 264-51.

Jülicher, Adolf. *Die Gleichnisreden Jesu,* 2d ed. 2 vols. Tübingen: J. C. B. Mohr (Paul Siebeck), 1899. Reprinted, Darmstadt: Wissenschaftliche Buchgesellschaft, 1963.

Kähler, Christoph. *Jesu Gleichnisse als Poesie und Therapie: Versuch eines integrativen Zugangs zum kommunikativen Aspekt von Gleichnissen Jesu.* WUNT 78. Tübingen: J. C. B. Mohr (Paul Siebeck), 1995.

Keach, Benjamin. *Exposition of the Parables in the Bible*. Grand Rapids: Kregel Publications, 1974.

Kennedy, Gerald. *The Parables: Sermons on the Stories Jesus Told*. New York: Harper & Brothers, 1960.

Kermode, Frank. *The Genesis of Secrecy: On the Interpretation of Narrative*. Cambridge: Harvard University Press, 1979.

Kingsbury, Jack D. "Major Trends in Parable Interpretation." *CTM* 42 (1971): 579-96.

―――. "The Parables of Jesus in Current Research." *Dialog* 11 (1972): 101-7.

―――. *The Parables of Jesus in Matthew 13: A Study in Redaction Criticism*. Richmond: John Knox Press, 1969.

Kissinger, Warren S. *The Parables of Jesus: A History of Interpretation and Bibliography*. Metuchen, N.J.: Scarecrow Press, 1979.

Kistemaker, Simon. *The Parables of Jesus*. Grand Rapids: Baker Book House, 1980.

Klauck, Hans-Joseph. *Allegorie und Allegorese in synoptischen Gleichnistexten*. NTAb 13. Münster: Aschendorff, 1978.

Ladd, George E. "The Life-setting of the Parables of the Kingdom." *JBR* 31 (1963): 193-99.

Lambrecht, Jan. *Once More Astonished: The Parables of Jesus*. New York: Crossroad, 1981.

―――. *Out of the Treasure: The Parables in the Gospel of Matthew*. Grand Rapids: Wm. B. Eerdmans, 1992.

Levison, Nahum. *The Parables: Their Background and Local Setting*. Edinburgh: T. & T. Clark, 1926.

Linnemann, Eta. *Parables of Jesus: Introduction and Exposition*. London: SPCK, 1966.

Little, James C. "Parable Research in the Twentieth Century." *ExpTim* 87-88 (1976): 356-60, 40-44, 71-75.

Lohmeyer, Ernst. "Vom Sinn der Gleichnisse Jesu." *ZST* 15 (1938): 319-46.

McArthur, Harvey K., and Robert M. Johnston. *They Also Taught in Parables: Rabbinic Parables from the First Centuries of the Christian Era*. Grand Rapids: Zondervan Publishing House, 1990.

McFadyen, Joseph M. *The Message of the Parables*. London: J. Clark, 1933.

McFague Teselle, Sallie. *Speaking in Parables: A Study in Metaphor and Theology*. Philadelphia: Fortress Press, 1975.

Marshall, I. Howard. *Eschatology and Parables*. London: Tyndale Press, 1963.

Maturin, Basil W. *Practical Studies of the Parables of Our Lord*. New York: Longmans, Green, 1899.

Michaelis, Wilhelm. *Die Gleichnisse Jesu: Eine Einführung*. 3d ed. UCB 32. Hamburg: Furche-Verlag, 1956.

Michaels, J. Ramsey. *Servant and Son: Jesus in Parable and Gospel*. Atlanta: John Knox Press, 1981.

Miller, J. Hillis. "Parable and Performative in the Gospels and in Modern Literature." In *Humanizing America's Iconic Book,* 57-71. Ed. Gene M. Tucker and Douglas A. Knight. Chico, Calif.: Scholars Press, 1982.

Miller, John W. *Step by Step through the Parables.* New York: Paulist Press, 1981.

Montefiore, Hugh W. "A Comparison of the Parables of the Gospel according to Thomas and of the Synoptic Gospels." *NTS* 7 (1960/61): 220-48. Reprinted in *Thomas and the Evangelists,* by H. E. W. Turner and H. Montefiore. SBT 35. Naperville, Ill.: Alec R. Allenson, 1962.

Mowry, M. Lucetta. "Parable." *IDB* 3:649-54.

Nouwen, Henri J. *The Return of the Prodigal Son: A Meditation on Fathers, Brothers, and Sons.* New York: Doubleday, 1992.

Oesterley, W. O. E. *The Gospel Parables in Light of Their Jewish Background.* London: SPCK, 1936.

Overman, J. Andrew. "Matthew's Parables and Roman Politics: The Imperial Setting of Matthew's Narrative with Special Reference to His Parables." In *Society of Biblical Literature 1995 Seminar Papers,* 425-39. Ed. Eugene H. Lovering, Jr. Atlanta: Scholars Press, 1995.

Parable Interpretation in America: The Shift to Language. Ed. Bernard B. Scott. Sonoma, Calif.: Polebridge Press, 1988.

Les paraboles évangéliques: perspectives nouvelles. Ed. Jean Delorme. Paris: Cerf, 1989.

Parker, Andrew. *Painfully Clear: The Parables of Jesus.* The Biblical Seminar 37. Sheffield: Sheffield Academic Press, 1997.

Parsons, Mikeal C. "'Allegorizing Allegory': Narrative Analysis and Parable Interpretation." *PRS* 15 (1988): 147-64.

Patte, Daniel, ed. *Semiology and Parables: Exploration of the Possibilities Offered by Structuralism for Exegesis.* Pittsburgh: Pickwick Press, 1976.

Perkins, Pheme. *Hearing the Parables of Jesus.* New York: Paulist Press, 1981.

Perrin, Norman. "Historical Criticism, Literary Criticism, and Hermeneutics: The Interpretation of the Parables of Jesus and the Gospel of Mark Today." *JR* 52 (1972): 361-75.

———. *Jesus and the Language of the Kingdom.* Philadelphia: Fortress Press, 1976.

———. "The Modern Interpretation of the Parables of Jesus and the Problem of Hermeneutics." *Int* 25 (1971): 131-48.

———. "The Parables of Jesus as Parables, as Metaphors, and as Aesthetic Objects: A Review Article." *JR* 47 (1967): 340-47.

Rabinowitz, Louis I. "Parable: In the Talmud and Midrash." *EncJud* 13:73-76.

Ricoeur, Paul. "Listening to the Parables of Jesus." *Criterion* 13/3 (Spring 1974): 18-22.

Riesenfeld, Harald. "The Parables in the Synoptic and Johannine Traditions." *SEÅ* 25 (1960): 37-61.

Robinson, D. W. B. "The Use of the Parables in the Synoptic Gospels." *EvQ* 21 (1949): 93-108.

Royster, Dmitri. *The Parables: Biblical, Patristic and Liturgical Interpretation.* Crestwood: St. Vladimir's Seminary Press, 1996.

Sabourin, Leopold. "Parables of the Kingdom." *BTB* 6 (1976): 115-60.

Scharlemann, Martin. *Proclaiming the Parables.* St. Louis: Concordia Publishing House, 1963.

Schmithals, Walter. "The Parabolic Teachings in the Synoptic Tradition." *JHC* 4/2 (1997): 3-32.

Schneider, Gerhard. *Parusiegleichnisse im Lukasevangelium.* SBS 74. Stuttgart: Katholisches Bibelwerk, 1975.

Scott, Bernard Brandon. "Essaying the Rock: The Authenticity of the Jesus Parable Tradition." *FFF* 2/1 (1986): 4.

———. *Hear Then the Parable: A Commentary on the Parables of Jesus.* Philadelphia: Fortress Press, 1989.

Sellew, Philip, "Interior Monologue as a Narrative Device in the Parables of Jesus," *JBL* 111 (1992): 239-53.

Sider, John W. *Interpreting the Parables: A Hermeneutical Guide to Their Meaning.* Grand Rapids: Zondervan Publishing House, 1995.

Siegmann, Edward. F. "Teaching in Parables (Mk iv,10-12; Lk viii,9-10, Mt xiii,10-15)." *CBQ* 23 (1961): 161-81.

Sleed, Nicola. "Parables and Women's Experience." *Modern Churchman* 26/2 (1984): 20-31.

Smith, B. T. D. *The Parables of the Synoptic Gospels.* Cambridge: Cambridge University Press, 1937.

Smith, Charles W. F. *The Jesus of the Parables.* Rev. ed. Philadelphia: United Church Press, 1975.

Stein, Robert H. *An Introduction to the Parables of Jesus.* Philadelphia: Westminster Press, 1981.

———. "The Parables of Jesus in Recent Study." *WW* 5 (1985): 248-57.

A Structuralist Approach to the Parables. Ed. Robert W. Funk. *Semeia 1.* Missoula, Mont.: Scholars Press, 1974.

Swete, Henry B. *Parables of the Kingdom: A Course of Lectures.* London: Macmillan, 1920.

Thielicke, Helmut. *The Waiting Father.* New York: Harper, 1959.

Thiselton, Anthony C. "The Parables as Language Event." *SJT* 23 (1970): 437-68.

Thomson, Clarence. *Parables and the Enneagram.* New York: Crossword Publishing Company, 1996.

Tolbert, Mary A. *Perspectives on the Parables: An Approach to Multiple Interpretations.* Philadelphia: Fortress Press, 1979.

Tucker, Jeffrey T. *Example Stories: Perspectives on Four Parables in the Gospel of Luke.* JSNTSup 162. Sheffield: Sheffield Academic Press, 1998.

Via, Dan O. *The Parables: Their Literary and Existential Dimensions.* Philadelphia: Fortress Press, 1967.

————. "Parable and Example Story: A Literary-Structuralist Approach." In *Semeia 1: A Structuralist Approach to the Parables,* ed. Robert W. Funk, 105-33. Missoula, Mont.: Scholars Press, 1974.

Wailes, Stephen L. *Medieval Allegories of Jesus' Parables.* Berkeley: University of California Press, 1987.

Weaver, Walter P. "Jesus as Parable." In *Earthing Christologies: From Jesus' Parables to Jesus the Parable,* ed. Walter P. Weaver and James H. Charlesworth, 19-45. Valley Forge, Penn.: Trinity Press International, 1995.

Weder, Hans. *Die Gleichnisse Jesu als Metaphern: Traditions- und redaktionsgeschichtliche Analysen und Interpretationen.* FRLANT 120. Göttingen: Vandenhoeck & Ruprecht, 1978.

Weiser, Alfons. *Die Knechtgleichnisse der synoptischen Evangelien.* SANT 29. Munich: Kösel-Verlag, 1971.

Wenham, David. *The Parables of Jesus.* Downers Grove, Ill.: InterVarsity Press, 1989.

Wilder, Amos N. *Jesus' Parables and the War of Myths: Essays on Imagination in Scripture.* Philadelphia: Fortress Press, 1982.

————. "The Parable." In his *The Language of the Gospel: Early Christian Rhetoric,* 79-96. New York: Harper & Row, 1964.

Wiles, M. F. "Early Exegesis of the Parables." *SJT* 11 (1968): 287-301.

Winterhalter, Robert. *Jesus' Parables: Finding Our God Within.* New York: Paulist Press, 1993.

Witherington, Ben. *Jesus the Sage: The Pilgrimage of Wisdom.* Minneapolis: Fortress Press, 1994.

Young, Brad H. *Jesus and His Jewish Parables: Rediscovering the Roots of Jesus' Teaching.* New York: Paulist Press, 1989.

————. *The Parables: Jewish Tradition and Christian Interpretation.* Peabody, Mass.: Hendrickson Publishers, 1999.

Index of Scripture References

487

Index of Other Ancient Sources

Index of Modern Authors

Bruce, Alexander B., 478

Bruce, F. F., 127, 379

Büchler, Adolf, 178

Buckland, W. W., 474, 475

Buckley, Thomas W., 32

Bühner, Jan-Adolf, 222

Bultmann, Rudolf, 14, 15, 38, 39, 44, 49,
  60, 64, 65, 68, 84-85, 92, 94, 100, 106,
  107, 114, 120, 125, 127, 138, 148, 151,
  159, 165, 176, 199, 204, 213, 223, 249,
  250, 257, 264, 277, 284, 288, 308, 318,
  321, 324, 327, 328, 338, 340, 347, 360,
  363, 364, 386, 393, 394

Burkill, T. A., 459, 460, 465

Burkitt, F. C., 178, 379

Burnett, Fred W., 168, 208

Burney, Charles F., 328

Bussby, Frederick, 53, 62

Busse, Ulrich, 44

Buttrick, George A., 131, 478

Butts, James R., 480

Cadbury, Henry J., 44, 117

Cadoux, Arthur T., 15, 18, 60, 107, 108,
  115, 131, 151, 152, 190, 204, 216, 219,
  230, 236, 237, 250, 287, 312, 318, 325,
  328, 331, 346, 348, 356, 361, 368, 478

Caemmerer, Richard R., 155

Cameron, Ron, 223, 225, 432, 433, 434,
  437, 441, 448, 449

Campbell, Denis, 408

Candlish, Robert, 280, 290

Candor, Claude R., 133, 134

Capon, Robert F., 478

Capps, Donald, 39

Caragounis, Chrys C., 479

Carey, W. Gregory, 340

Carlston, Charles E., 3, 83, 88, 194, 190,
  200, 331, 354, 356, 359, 361, 363, 364,
  373, 375, 378, 397, 459, 460, 464, 478

Carson, D. A., 23, 172, 295, 343, 478

Carter, Warren, 346, 478

Casalegno, Alberto, 402

Case, Shirley J., 458

Casper, Bernhard, 89

Catchpole, David R., 227, 233, 257, 260,
  300, 303, 312, 318, 321, 322, 324, 328

Cave, C. H., 117, 477

Cerfaux, Lucien, 465

Cevallos, Juan C., 101

Chadwick, Henry, 442

Charles, Robert H., 242, 422

Charlesworth, James H., 155, 364, 485

Charpentier, Étienne, 127

Chilton, Bruce, 12, 49, 404, 449, 477

Christ, Felix, 208, 390

Christian, Paul, 312, 328

Clark, Kenneth W., 402

Clarke, A. K., 168

Clavier, Henri, 155

Clines, David J. A., 157

Cohn, Haim H., 28

Colella, Pasquale, 155

Collie, N. E. W., 168

Collins, R. L., 155

Collins, Raymond F., 111, 390

Combrink, H. J. B., 155

Comiskey, John P., 155

Compston, H. F. B., 155

Condor, Claude R., 371

Conzelmann, Hans, 167, 208, 284, 334,
  378

Cope, Lamar, 319, 325, 328, 373

Corlett, Tom, 82, 88

Corswant, Willy, 297

Cotter, Wendy J., 204, 206, 212, 402, 404,
  408

Court, John M., 312, 328

Coutts, John, 148, 155, 465

Craddock, Fred B., 82

Cranfield, C. E. B., 32, 101, 189, 200, 260,
  312, 318, 328

Crawford, Robert G., 88

Creed, John M., 71, 76, 81, 99, 111, 113,
  114, 147, 163, 210, 216, 228, 238, 251,
  257, 263, 268, 284, 287, 288, 289, 337

Crenshaw, James I., 341

Crespy, Georges, 101

Cripps, K. R. J., 350

Cross, Frank L., 88

Crossan, John Dominic, 16, 39, 90, 91, 94,
  95, 101, 105, 148, 149, 185, 187, 189,
  190, 200, 230, 232, 236, 248, 250, 264,
  273, 284, 287, 295, 303, 346, 359, 360,
  361, 365, 367, 379, 387, 390, 396, 397,
  398, 402, 410, 412, 414, 416, 437, 478